ISBN 978-1-332-53697-9
PIBN 10014914

FB &c Ltd, Dalton House, 60 Windsor Avenue, London, SW19 2RR.
Company number 08720141. Registered in England and Wales.

For support please visit www.forgottenbooks.com

OUTLINES OF EUROPEAN HISTORY

PART II

FROM THE SEVENTEENTH CENTURY
TO THE PRESENT TIME

BY

JAMES HARVEY ROBINSON

AND

CHARLES A. BEARD

REVISED TO INCLUDE
THE GREAT WAR, 1914-1918

1919

GINN AND COMPANY
BOSTON · NEW YORK · CHICAGO · LONDON
ATLANTA · DALLAS · COLUMBUS · SAN FRANCISCO

321.1

The Athenæum Press
GINN AND COMPANY · PRO-
PRIETORS · BOSTON · U.S.A.

PREFACE

This volume is the second part of a two-year course covering the history of European civilization from the earliest times of which we have any knowledge to the outbreak of the war of 1914. It is based on the authors' larger work, *The Development of Modern Europe*; the narrative has, however, been much simplified as well as shortened by the sedulous omission of all details that could be spared. The illustrations are so numerous and so fully explained as to form a sort of parallel pictorial narrative which amplifies and reënforces the text and adds a sense of reality extremely difficult to give in a highly condensed review.

This second part of the *Outlines* is devoted mainly to the eighteenth and nineteenth centuries, for it is the avowed purpose of the writers not to deal with history for its own sake, but ever and always with a view of making plain the world of to-day, which can be understood only in the light of the past. In order to enable us to catch up with our own times it is essential that the vast changes of the last two centuries be studied with special care. In short, Part I is the essential introduction to Part II, and Part II is arranged to bear directly on the conditions and problems which we confront to-day and upon which all intelligent persons should feel called to form some opinion.

The introductory chapter will serve to recall and place in proper historical perspective the essentials of the period of transition from the Middle Ages to modern times — the Renaissance and the Protestant revolt, the chief political events of the sixteenth century, and the conflicts which were brought to a close by the Peace of Westphalia.

The authors wish to express their great indebtedness to their friend and colleague Professor James T. Shotwell for his most cordial coöperation in the preparation of this revised edition of their volume. He has furnished the introductory review, and the revision and readjustment of the text owes much to his scholarship and critical insight. The authors are also under obligations to Miss Isabel McKenzie, of the History Department of Barnard College, for suggestions and assistance in the matter of illustration and for the preparation of the questions at the close of each chapter and the Index.

In preparing the new edition of this volume the story of Europe has not only been brought down to the close of the war but a number of changes have been made, especially in the sections dealing with modern Germany. It is no longer possible to view that country and its government in the same light in which it appeared before the Great War. The recent world conflict, with all its incalculable loss and suffering, was largely attributable to the plots of the German war party and to the nature of German militarism, against which a great part of the peoples of the world arrayed themselves in mortal combat.

J. H. R.
C. A. B.

New York City

CONTENTS

LIST OF COLORED PLATES

LIST OF COLORED MAPS

OUTLINES OF EUROPEAN HISTORY

INTRODUCTION

The theme of this volume is modern times

In a companion volume[1] the history of European civilization has been traced from the dim, prehistoric ages, when men lived in caves and used stone weapons and tools, through the civilizations of Egypt, Babylon, Greece, and Rome and of the Middle Ages, to the new era which we call modern times. This modern era is the theme of the present volume.

What is meant by modern times

Just what is meant by "modern times," however, is rather difficult to define. The term is an old one; Cicero, the Roman statesman, talked in antiquity of "these modern times of ours," and so did the Greeks before him; and so, no doubt, did every people in every age that had any idea of time at all. But although we often use the term in this somewhat vague sense to mean the period in which our own lives are passed, historians have come to apply it to a somewhat definite era, namely, that stretch of three or four centuries, from the sixteenth or seventeenth to the twentieth, during which time the ways of thinking and living have been, upon the whole, more like what they are now than what they had been during the preceding centuries. In politics, literature, philosophy, in business methods, in ideas of progress and of national organization, the men of these centuries have had, more or less, a modern outlook.

But what is meant by the modern outlook? This is a puzzling question, for there are so many fields of thought and action covered by it. Life is so varied in the modern world. Still this

[1] Robinson and Breasted, *Outlines of European History*, Part I.

The variety and scope of the modern outlook

same variety furnishes us with a clue to part of the answer; for the modern world differs from the medieval in just this regard: the outlook is wider, more people are interested in more different things. During the Middle Ages, when farming was the main useful industry, the mass of the population was ignorant of all but village gossip. Even the cities were jealous of each other and each was absorbed in its own separate interests. Although traveling merchants, wandering knights, and educated churchmen widened the horizon somewhat with their information of the great world outside, still the routine of daily life kept on with little change and relatively little variety. In contrast with this, the world we live in is constantly changing, and even those who lack the wealth or leisure to travel or study are constantly affected by new discoveries and enterprises, and so acquire an interest in things far beyond their own lives. The villein on a medieval feudal estate was aware of little outside his manor. The modern farmer lives in touch with the whole world. Modern times, therefore, have brought a great extension of the scope of people's interest and a great variety in their ideas and in their work. This, in turn, is based upon a continual progress which is more and more rapidly changing the conditions of living.

When did modern times begin?

There is naturally no one date when modern times in this sense began. Indeed, the transition from medieval to modern conditions came at different times in different fields. In some it was gradual, in others rapid. For instance, the introduction of Roman law, which was almost a necessity for modern business and politics, took place back in the heart of the Middle Ages, in the twelfth and thirteen centuries. In the thirteenth century too came the first parliaments and the organization of that most definitely modern political institution, the national state. But it was not until the seventeenth and eighteenth centuries — in some cases later — that these states got rid of their distinctly medieval parliaments or "estates" dominated by kings or nobles, while the representatives of the middle classes hardly dared do more than present petitions. The English middle class, after a century of struggle, finally achieved control of the government by a revolution in 1688, the French by a revolution in 1789. In the history of politics this advent of the middle classes to power marks a new epoch, that of the self-government of nations, and the first chapter of this book begins with the story of how it was accomplished in England — the first nation to establish representative government effectively. It is interesting to note, also, that the rise of modern science comes at the same time as this advent of the middle class, in the seventeenth and eighteenth centuries.

Significant achievements since the seventeenth century

But if one may choose the seventeenth century as a starting point for both modern political history and the history of science, in other fields, such as culture, religion, and business, the new era began rather in the sixteenth century. Indeed, so important a change took place then in the general outlook of Europe that many historians prefer to date modern times from that period. It was the time of what is called the Renaissance, or "new birth" in art and literature; of the Protestant Reformation, or revolt from the Medieval Church in religion; and of geographical discovery and the beginnings of over-sea trade in the realm of business. Although the story of this period of transition has been told in the earlier volume, it forms a natural introduction to the narrative which follows, and we shall therefore hurriedly review the main facts.

The sixteenth century as a transitional period

The Renaissance in Art and Literature

In the first place there was the Renaissance, which had its main home in Italy. This was a twofold movement — in art and in literature. In the history of art there is no more splendid age than the fifteenth and sixteenth centuries, in which such masters lived and worked as Leonardo da Vinci, scientist as well as painter; Michael Angelo, painter, sculptor, architect, and poet; and Raphael, the perfect painter, revealing new ideals

The Renaissance in art

of loveliness. These and the other Italian artists of the period created a new era in the history of sculpture and painting, for, not content with the stilted or grotesque decorative figures which ornamented medieval cathedrals,[1] they reproduced the forms of natural beauty in a real world.

Slight influence of art upon most people

The heritage which these masters left was of the greatest value, but it made, and still makes, only a limited appeal. Relatively few people can see the originals, and of these fewer still learn to appreciate them. Historians have sometimes so overestimated the influence of these artists in such a busy world as this as to have seen in their creations the real beginning of the modern era. As a matter of fact the art of the Italian Renaissance was only one part — though a glorious one — of the general change.

Humanism

The literary and scholarly phase of this movement is called humanism, from the Latin word *humanitas*, which means "literary culture." This movement was of more general significance. What we read often determines what we think. During the Middle Ages those who were able to read were mainly churchmen or lawyers, and neither cared much for pure literature. There had been some literary people, but their influence was relatively slight. It was, therefore, an important event when, early in the fifteenth century, humanists began to recover the works of the old pagan writers and to admire them to such an extent that they became critical of the traditional and, as they thought, narrow views of the medieval theologians. Moreover, they applied this criticism to spurious texts long accepted as genuine, and so helped to reconstruct the current ideas of history. To be sure, these humanists, being scholars rather than men of genius, did not add many new ideas of their own. But in the texts they edited and in the new critical attitude they contributed, they prepared the way for further change in the outlook of the cultured world.

The influence of the work of these scholars, like that of the artists, has probably been overestimated by historians,

[1] See *Outlines*, Part I, pp. 514–515

who, being scholars themselves, have been somewhat unduly interested in these forerunners of theirs. But their books were more widely read than any others had ever been, because there was placed at their disposal one of the greatest inventions in the history of civilization, that of printing by movable type. The earliest book of any considerable size to be printed was a Bible, published at Mayence in Germany in 1456,[1] but by the opening of the next century there were at least forty presses busily at work, which had already, so it is estimated, printed about eight millions of volumes.

Invention of printing

Although most of these books were still in Latin, the universal language of the cultured world, the literatures which ultimately profited most by the printing press were those in the languages of the modern nations, which now attained the dignity of being preserved in the same way as theology or the classics.[2]

Rise of the vernacular literatures

Geographical Discovery and the Effect upon Europe

A greater factor in widening ideas and stimulating enterprise than art or scholarship was the geographical exploration and discovery, which reached its climax during this period. The discovery of America by Columbus in 1492 was but a single incident in the great story of adventure. In 1498 Vasco da Gama, the Portuguese navigator, reached India — the land Columbus supposed he had reached — by sailing around Africa. There he gathered in rich cargoes of spices and brought them to Lisbon; so that after his third voyage, in 1502, the merchants of Venice, who had relied upon the overland caravan trade from India across western Asia to fill their ships at Alexandria in Egypt or Beirut in Syria, found their supply cut off, while the wharves of Lisbon were so full that the price went down.

Exploration and the opening of world trade

Effect upon the Mediterranean cities

1 On the invention of printing see *Outlines*, Part I, pp. 556 ff.

2 The use of the mother tongues in writing books was hindered rather than helped by the humanists. Their ideal was to reproduce the style of Cicero in purest Latin. The vernacular literatures are a normal result of the growth of national life, and began in the heart of the Middle Ages. The general stimulation of the sixteenth and seventeenth centuries, through the growth of wealth, did as much as anything else to further the production of vernacular literature.

As Venice and Genoa and other Mediterranean ports had relied largely upon this oriental trade, they were henceforth ruined. The Mediterranean ceased to be the center of the world, for with the opening of ocean commerce those countries which were situated nearest to the Atlantic began to gather in the wealth of the new world-trade.

Venice

At the opening of the sixteenth century Venice had been to the Mediterranean countries what England has been to modern Europe.[1] The Venetian republic ruled over about as large a population as that of England at that time. Its fleet was supreme on the sea; its bankers handled most of the precious metals of Europe that went to pay for the goods of the Orient. It had a system of merchant ambassadors or agents, much like our consular service, reporting from cities of importance in Europe the habits and customs of the people, the likelihood of markets, and the political conditions which might interest their great trading republic. The taking of Constantinople by the Turks in 1453 did not injure its prosperity; on the contrary, Constantinople, which had generally favored Genoa, was a rival which had now suffered an eclipse. In any case the proudest days of Venice were during the last half of the fifteenth century — just before its fall. Its great enemy was not the Turk, but the sailors who opened the sea routes. For there is no way of carrying goods so cheaply as to put them in the hold of a ship and let it sail away until it reaches home. Ocean freight has

Advantages of sea freight

[1] There is no more impressive object lesson in the influence of economic factors upon history than in the fate of Venice. It retains most of its medieval splendor untouched by modern changes, as the frontispiece shows. The cathedral, modeled after one in Constantinople, was planned before the First Crusade, and is adorned with richly colored columns and brilliant mosaics. Seldom has architecture produced such a poem in color. The doge's palace, with its beautiful Gothic façade, stands along the main water front. In front of both, the tall campanile, recently restored, watches, as of old, over the Adriatic. (Its base is shown to the right of the picture.) But no ships with cargoes from the Orient anchor now off the wharf by the doge's palace, and the other palaces along the canals are no longer inhabited by rich merchants who trade at Syrian bazaars. The city is a sort of museum of its own history. In contrast with it, northern seaports like Antwerp, Hamburg, London, and Liverpool have now the world's trade, and the reason for the change is the cheapness of sea freight.

no caravans to hire and feed, no horsemen for protection from savage tribes, no bazaars along the route at which the haggling merchants raise the price. To these advantages over land trade, upon which the medieval countries had so largely to rely, the sea route added another still more important. The hold of a ship might carry more goods than many caravans. Therefore the age of exploration did more than discover the new world and the Far East; it also changed the geography of Europe.[1]

Portugal and Spain were the first to grow rich from the over-sea trade — the one from oriental spices and the slave traffic, the other from the gold and silver of America. Both countries were badly governed, however, especially when united under the Spanish king, Philip II,[2] in 1580, for the next sixty years. Then the Dutch and the English, who had formerly been good customers of the Portuguese, entered on a bitter war with Philip, attacked the Portuguese, and established themselves in the Far East instead. Portugal kept Brazil, but lost all but a few trading posts in the Orient. Portugal

As for Spain, it had followed up the expeditions of Columbus with the conquest of Mexico by Cortez in 1519 and that of Peru by Pizarro a few years later. The gold and silver which these countries furnished filled many a Spanish treasure ship, and although the English seamen lay in wait for them and captured some, the ports of Spain saw priceless cargoes unloaded on their wharves. But Spain was unable to make good use of these vast treasures, for in the effort to preserve its religion true to the Catholic faith, it had destroyed the most thrifty portions of its population. The Jews, who were bankers and traders, and the Moors, who were industrious and clever workers, were expelled, while the heretics who suffered in the Inquisition were often the most independent members of the middle class. So Spain did not apply its imported wealth to set industry and commerce going; and it was not long before the money slipped out of its grasp to the more thrifty nations north of it. It also Spain's rise and fall

[1] See map in *Outlines*, Part I, p. 527. [2] See below, p. 29.

suffered defeat in war; Holland gained its independence, and England overcame the great Armada which Spain sent against it in 1587. But the decline of Spain, which immediately set in, was due less to these disasters than to the failure to organize business in the modern way, such as Holland, England, France, and, later, Germany learned to do.

Maritime trade of northern Europe

The advantages of Holland and England for ocean commerce are clear from a study of the map of Europe. They have good harbors, placed just where the merchandise can best be distributed through the country. It was almost inevitable, therefore, that they should become great sea powers and ultimately rivals. Neither of them had been very important in the commerce of the Middle Ages. Then the trade of the North Sea, and indeed most of the maritime trade of northern Europe, had been in the hands of a league of German cities known as the Hansa.[1] This league, which at one time or another included some seventy cities, purchased and controlled settlements in London — the so-called Steelyard near London Bridge — and others on the Baltic and even in Russia.

The Hansa

The Netherlands

The medieval trade of the Netherlands was largely in the hands of the Hansa, which, until the fifteenth century,[2] exported English wool to the cities of Belgium (then called Flanders), where the industrious citizens of Bruges, Ghent, Ypres, and other towns spun and wove the best cloth of the day. The people of the northern Netherlands — now Holland — were more given to fishing than weaving, though they were also good farmers; to the fishing they added a coasting trade and, when the sixteenth century came, had developed considerable commerce. Then events happened by which this little seagoing people became a free and independent nation. In order to understand this we must now sketch the political history of western Europe in general through this period.

[1] See *Outlines*, Part I, p. 508.

[2] In the fifteenth century England began to manufacture cloth itself, and laid the basis of its great textile industries, in which it still leads the world.

England and France in the Middle Ages

Throughout the Middle Ages the national states of England and France were taking shape, mainly through the efforts of their kings to establish their control over the whole country and to put down the opposition of feudal nobles. In this the English kings had the easier task, since the country was thoroughly conquered by the Norman William I (1066), who knew how to keep his Norman nobles in check. Under weak or bad kings these nobles showed their power, however, as when in 1215 they forced King John to sign the Great Charter, or *Magna Carta*, which guaranteed the liberties of Englishmen, secured the assurance that they should not be tried or imprisoned without the lawful judgment of their equals, and forbade the king to levy new forms of taxes without the consent of a great council of the realm. Formation of the national state: England

Such checks upon royalty were in the interest of the whole nation, as was also the calling of the first English parliament in 1265 by the barons, led by Simon de Montfort, when in rebellion against the king. Thirty years later, however, King Edward I summoned a "Model Parliament," to which representatives of the common people were invited as well as the great nobles, and in the course of the next century, while Edward III was fighting the Hundred Years' War for the throne of France, need of money made Parliament indispensable to the monarch, who passed no new law without adding "by and with the consent of the lords spiritual [the bishops] and temporal and of the commons." Parliament

After the Hundred Years' War, which lasted, with various interruptions, from about 1340 to 1450, a series of civil wars arose between rival claimants for the throne — the Wars of the Roses, named from the emblem of the white rose for the adherents of the duke of York, the red rose for the adherents of the House of Lancaster. These were mainly wars between noble factions, in which the common people were but little involved. The most important result was that many of the Strength of the Tudor kings old nobles were killed off; so that when the wars were ended by a Lancastrian claimant — Henry Tudor, founder of the Tudor line — defeating the Yorkist king, Richard III, and marrying a Yorkist princess, this new king, Henry VII, (1485–1509), found himself powerful enough to rule much as he wanted to. He proved to be a good king, and, as England in his day was rapidly developing manufactures and commerce, he was able to amass a large treasure. This was speedily spent, however, by his extravagant and willful son and successor, Henry VIII, of whom we shall learn more shortly.

Formation of the national state: France

The history of France prior to the sixteenth century was somewhat similar. The kings of the Capetian line[1] had harder work than the English kings in establishing their authority over the feudal nobles, but during the thirteenth century they had succeeded in doing this. In the middle of that century they developed a central law court, the *Parlement* of Paris, which was housed in the royal palace and which helped administer the business of the realm. At the opening of the next century (1302), seven years after the English "Model Parliament," an assembly similar to it was called together in France, known as the Estates General, which means that the three "estates" or classes — clergy, nobles, and commons — were represented from the whole realm. At the opening of the fourteenth century, therefore, France was being organized, like England, for representative and constitutional government. Then came the Hundred Years' War, caused by the English king, Edward III, and his successors claiming the throne of France. This devastating war was an immeasurable calamity for France. The Estates General attempted once to assert some independence during the height of the war, in the middle of the fourteenth century, but its great leader, Étienne Marcel, a citizen of Paris, was murdered and the hope of a parliamentary system of government for France died with him. For in wartime the institutions of popular government suffer.

[1] Descendants of Hugh Capet, who was chosen king in 987.

O C E A N
SHETLAND IS.
ORKNEY IS.
HEBRIDES IS.
Bergen
Aberdeen
Glasgow
Edinburgh
N O R T H
S E A
IRELAND
Dublin
Waterford
Cork
Gloucester
Severn
Oxford
KM. OF ENGLAND
London
JUTLAND
KM. OF DENMARK
Copenhagen
SCHLESWIG
RUGEN
Hamburg
Bremen
Elbe
Berlin
Stet
Magdeburg
Wittenberg
Leipzig
Prague
ENGLISH CHANNEL
Calais
Ghent
NETHERLANDS
Cologne
Aix-la-Chapelle
Cherbourg
Brest
BRETAGNE
NORMANDY
Seine
Paris
Orleans
Loire
Nantes
KM. OF FRANCE
G E R M A N
E M P I R E
Spires
Frankfort
Strasburg
KM. OF BOHEMIA
DUCHY OF BURGUNDY
FRANCHE COMTE
SWISS CONFEDERATION
Augsburg
Salzburg
TYROL
STYRIA
CARINTHIA
CARNIOLA
BAY OF BISCAY
Bordeaux
S. Jago
Oviedo
Leon
Burgos
Braganza
PORTUGAL
Douro
NAVARRE
Toulouse
LANGUEDOC
Rhone
Lyons
SAVOY
Milan
Verona
VENICE
Venice
DAUPHINE
Turin
Avignon
PROVENCE
Nice
Genoa
Florence
Toulon
Ravenna
STATES OF THE CHURCH
Siena
Ancona
ADRIATIC
Saragossa
Ebro
KM. OF
Toledo
Madrid
Tagus
Alcantara
ARAGON
Tortosa
Barcelona
CASTILE
SPAIN
Valencia
Cordova
Palos
Seville
Granada
GRANADA
Malaga
Gibraltar
Ceuta
MAJORCA
MINORCA
IVIZA
BALEARIC IS.
CORSICA
(To Genoa)
KM. OF SARDINIA
(To Aragon)
Cagliari
Rome
KM. OF NAPLES
(To Aragon)
Naples
M E D I T E R R A N
Oran
Algiers
Tunis
Palermo
KM. OF SICILY
Messina
Syracuse
MALTA
FEZ

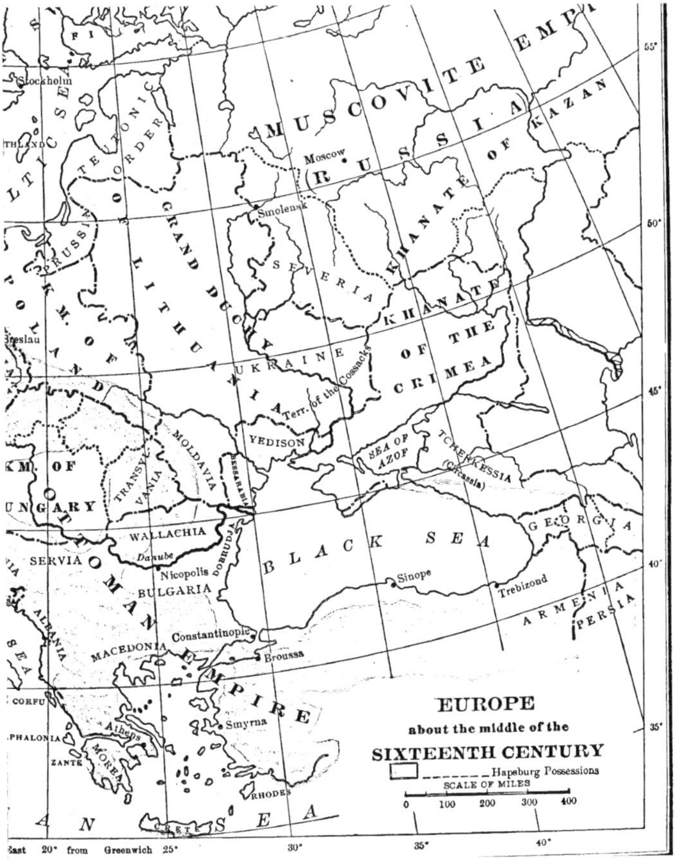

EUROPE
about the middle of the
SIXTEENTH CENTURY

After the danger from the English was over, civil war continued and bandit soldiery plundered the whole land. A meeting of the Estates therefore voted the king a royal *taille*, or land tax, to police the realm, and his lawyers took advantage of the occasion to claim that it had been allowed the king for all time to come. The result was that he did not need, like the king of England, to call a parliament (or Estates General) every little while to raise money. The king of France therefore had much less check upon his actions; and as there had never been a French *Magna Carta*, the right of the king to imprison without trial remained in force up to the French Revolution of 1789. The one constitutional check upon the absolutism of the French king was the court of law, the *Parlement* of Paris, which still claimed that only those edicts of the king which it had registered were law. But it could not refuse to register any edict which the king in person ordered it to register. Since most of these arrangements lasted until the Revolution, they are described in detail in Chapter VII, below.

Strength of the French monarchy

The Medieval Empire

The history of Germany and of Italy during the Middle Ages was quite different from that of England or France. The Holy Roman Empire, begun by the coronation of Charlemagne in 800 and renewed by the German king Otto I in 967, made vast claims to sovereignty over all Europe, as the successor to the world dominion of the Cæsars; but in reality the emperors were seldom able to secure obedience within the boundaries of their own realm, which included practically all central Europe, down to Rome. The great barrier of the Alps made it impossible to unite the realms of the German emperors into a single strong state, such as took shape in England and France. When an emperor took up his residence in Italy his German nobles soon grew unruly and rebellious, and Italy acknowledged his sway only while he and his German armies were in sight.

Germany and Italy in the Middle Ages

The independent states of northern Italy

The towns of northern Italy had won practical independence at the close of the twelfth century, when the Hohenstaufen Emperor, Frederick Barbarossa, was defeated by their Lombard League. Most of them then fell under the sway of petty tyrants, sprung from their hired soldiery, under whom they prospered in spite of local wars. The most notable of these lines of rulers was the Sforza family, which seized the duchy of Milan. Two famous republics developed — Florence and Venice; but Venice was ruled by a small group of oligarchs, while Florence came to accept the "boss" rule of the Medici. It was in these cities, grown rich by trade and manufactures, that the Renaissance blossomed forth.

Central and southern Italy: the papacy and the Two Sicilies

Across central Italy lay the States of the Church, or, more properly, of the papacy, over which the Pope claimed temporal sovereignty. In the south was the kingdom of Naples, which, from the time it and Sicily had been conquered from the Eastern Empire by the Norman Robert Guiscard, in the middle of the eleventh century, had had a checkered history, passing by inheritance to the Hohenstaufen Frederick II in the thirteenth century, then by conquest to Charles of Anjou, brother of St. Louis of France, who established the Angevin dynasty. In 1282 Sicily had rebelled and had fallen to the House of Aragon, which in 1435–1438 drove the French out of Naples too, and reunited the two in what was called the Kingdom of the Two Sicilies.

Invasion by Charles VIII

Such was the condition of Italy when, in 1494–1495, two years after the discovery of America, Charles VIII, a young and injudicious king of France, invaded the peninsula to reëstablish the French in Naples. At first his invasion was like a triumphal progress. State after state yielded before him. Naples, too, speedily fell into his hands and his success seemed marvelous. But he and his troops were demoralized by the wines and other pleasures of the south, and meanwhile his enemies at last began to form a combination against him. Ferdinand of Aragon was fearful lest he might lose Sicily, and

Emperor Maximilian objected to having the French control Italy. Charles's situation became so dangerous that he may well have thought himself fortunate, at the close of 1495, to escape, with the loss of only a single battle, from the country he had hoped to conquer. His successor, Louis XII, sold his claim to Naples to Ferdinand of Aragon in 1503. It was to remain in Spanish hands for the next two centuries.

Results of Charles's expedition

The results of Charles VIII's expedition appear at first sight trivial; in reality they were momentous. In the first place, it was now clear to Europe that the Italians had no real national feeling, however much they might despise the "barbarians" who lived north of the Alps. From this time down to the latter half of the nineteenth century Italy was dominated by foreign nations, especially Spain and Austria. In the second place, the French learned to admire the art and culture of Italy. The nobles began to change their feudal castles, which since the invention of gunpowder were no longer impregnable, into luxurious palaces and country houses.[1] The new scholarship of Italy also took root and flourished not only in France but in England and Germany as well, and Greek began to be studied outside of Italy. Consequently, just as Italy was becoming, politically, the victim of foreign aggressions, it was also losing that intellectual leadership which it had enjoyed since the revival of interest in Latin and Greek literature.

French absorbed in a struggle for Milan

Moreover, although Louis XII gave up southern Italy, he laid claims to the duchy of Milan, for which his successor, Francis I (1515–1547), fought with varying success for many years, but which he finally surrendered to his rival, Charles V.

"The Germanies" of the sixteenth century

Germany at the opening of the sixteenth century was no such powerful and well-organized state as it is to-day. It was rather what the French called "the Germanies"; that is, two or three hundred states, which differed greatly from one another in size and character. This one had a duke, that a count, at its head, while others were ruled over by archbishops, bishops, or

[1] See *Outlines*, Part I, p. 572.

abbots. There were many single cities, like Nuremberg, Frankfort, and Cologne, which were just as independent as the great duchies of Bavaria, Würtemberg, and Saxony. Lastly there were the knights, whose possessions might consist of no more than a single strong castle with a wretched village lying at its foot.

Weakness of the Emperor

As for the Emperor, he no longer had any power to control his vassals. He could boast of unlimited pretensions and great traditions, but he had neither money nor soldiers. At the time of Luther's birth (1483) the poverty-stricken Frederick III (Maximilian's father) might have been seen picking up a free meal at a monastery or riding behind a slow but economical ox team. The real power in Germany lay in the hands of the more important vassals.

The electors

First among these were the seven *electors*, so called because, since the thirteenth century, they had enjoyed the right to elect the Emperor. Three of them were archbishops — kings in all but name of considerable territories on the Rhine, namely, the electorates of Mayence, Treves, and Cologne. Near them, to the south, was the region ruled over by the elector of the Palatinate; to the northeast were the territories of the electors of Brandenburg and of Saxony; the king of Bohemia made the seventh of the group.

Other princes

Besides these states, there were other rulers scarcely less important. Würtemberg, Bavaria, Hesse, and Baden are familiar to us to-day as members of the present German Empire, but all of them were smaller then, having grown since by incorporating the little states that formerly lay within and about them.

The towns

The towns, which had grown up since the thirteenth century, were centers of culture in the north of Europe, just as those of Italy were in the south. Some of them were immediate vassals of the Emperor and were consequently independent of the particular prince within whose territory they were situated. These were called *free*, or *imperial*, cities and must be reckoned among the states of Germany.

The knights

The knights, who ruled over the smallest of the German territories, had earlier formed a very important class, but the introduction of gunpowder and new methods of fighting put them at a disadvantage; for they clung to their medieval traditions. Their tiny realms were often too small to support them, and they frequently turned to robbery for a living and proved a great nuisance to the merchants and townspeople.

No central power to maintain order

It is clear that these states, little and big, all tangled up with one another, would be sure to have disputes among themselves which would have to be settled in some way. The Emperor was not powerful enough to keep order, and the result was that each ruler had to defend himself if attacked.

Neighborhood war

Neighborhood war was permitted by law if only some courteous preliminaries were observed. For instance, a prince or town was required to give warning three days in advance before attacking another member of the Empire.

The diet

Germany had a national assembly, called the *diet*, which met at irregular intervals, now in one town and now in another, for Germany had no capital city. The towns were not permitted to send delegates until 1487, long after the townspeople were represented in France and England. The knights and other minor nobles were not represented at all, and consequently did not always consider the decisions of the diet binding upon them.

Reasons why the German kings failed to establish a strong state

One of the main reasons why the German kings had failed to create a strong kingdom such as those of France and of England was that their office was not strictly hereditary. Although the emperors were often succeeded by their sons, each new emperor had to be elected, and those great vassals who controlled the election naturally took care to bind the candidate by solemn promises not to interfere with their privileges and independence. The result was that, from the downfall of the Hohenstaufens in the thirteenth century, the emperors saw that it was more to their advantage to increase their own family estates and dominions than to spend their energies for the service of the country as a whole. This was especially the policy of the Hapsburgs, whose founder, Rudolf, had been chosen Emperor in 1273.[1] Rudolf established his family in Austria and Styria, which became, under his successors, the center of the wide Austrian possessions. Finally, from the middle of the fifteenth century, the electors regularly chose a Hapsburg as Emperor.

Royal marriages of Hapsburg, Burgundy, and Spain

At the opening of the sixteenth century the Emperor was Maximilian I. While still a very young man he had married Mary of Burgundy, the heiress to the Netherlands and to much of that middle strip of territory which lies between France and Germany west of the Rhine. Mary died shortly, and her lands fell to her infant son. He, in his turn, was later to marry the richest heiress in Europe, Joanna of Spain, daughter of that Ferdinand of Aragon and Isabella of Castile, whose marriage, together with the expulsion of the Moors from Granada in 1492, had for the first time made possible a united Spanish kingdom. This, along with the exploitation of America, which the good queen had enabled Columbus to discover, made the possessions of the Spanish princess the greatest dowry to be found for any prince in Europe.

Charles V

The son of Maximilian who made such a fortunate marriage died young, leaving a six-year-old boy, Charles — born in 1500 at the Flemish city of Ghent — to succeed to all the glorious titles of Spain and Austria as soon as his grandfathers, Ferdinand and Maximilian, should pass away. Ferdinand died in 1516 and Maximilian in 1519. Then the young boy was in his own right king of Castile, Aragon, and Naples, and of the vast Spanish possessions in America, archduke of Austria, count of Tyrol, and (in the Netherlands) duke of Brabant, margrave of Antwerp, count of Holland — to mention a few of his more important titles. Finally, in 1519, he was chosen by the electors to be Emperor, and is known in history as Charles V.

[1] See Part I, p. 458. The original seat of the Hapsburgs was in northern Switzerland, where the vestiges of their original castle may still be seen.

Charles visited Germany for the first time in 1520, and held a diet at Worms, where the most important business of the assembly proved to be the consideration of the case of a university professor, Martin Luther, who was accused of writing heretical books and who had in reality begun the first successful revolt against the Medieval Church. Charles at the diet at Worms

The Protestant Revolt in Germany

The greatest and the most efficiently organized institution of the Middle Ages had been neither empire nor national state, but the Church, presided over by the Pope at Rome. The structure of this wonderful organization has been described in the previous volume; but the main principles upon which it rested may be stated in a word. They were, in the first place, that there was no salvation outside the Church; in the second place, that within the Church God bestowed his grace through the sacraments, which the priest (and bishops) alone had the power to dispense. Of these sacraments baptism and the Eucharist, or Lord's Supper, were the two most important; but one could not partake of the Eucharist unless he had confessed to a priest and received absolution of his sins. This double rite of confession and absolution was called the sacrament of penance, since absolution was not supposed to be granted unless one were *penitent* enough to make amends for one's sin by doing *penance* (see p. 19). The Medieval Church

The sole authority to dispense the sacraments which were the means of salvation naturally gave the clergy great power. At the same time it made necessary a great organization composed of priests and bishops (in Latin *episcopi*, which means "overseers"), graded into a hierarchy under the sway of the bishop of Rome — the Pope. In spite of such arrangements it was natural that the government of so vast a system should sometimes be managed in such a way as to awaken protests of earnest men, and, indeed, various reforming movements took The government of the Church

Protests against "misgovernment"

place during the Middle Ages. These protests — which must be carefully distinguished from the opposition of kings and emperors to what they regarded as the clergy's interference in politics — were particularly strong in the opening of the fifteenth century, when there were rival popes, splitting the Church into factions and misgoverning generally.

The conciliar movement

The result was that a series of general — or ecumenical — councils were called, representing the Church as a whole, which was like introducing a church parliament in the papal monarchy. The greatest of these met in Constance, in Switzerland, in 1414; but its extensive program of reform was not carried out, and in the course of the next fifty years the popes managed to discredit this attempt to limit their sovereign powers. Parliamentary government in the Church had failed.

The papacy at the close of the fifteenth century

Meanwhile, however, the papacy had shown few signs of reform. On the contrary, at the close of the fifteenth century, the popes were apparently so much absorbed in Italian politics — trying to enlarge their temporal possessions in central Italy — as to give the impression to many earnest people that what they were mainly after was the splendor of a worldly sovereign. To this end they needed money, and since their main income came from Germany — which had no strong king to prohibit the heavy drainage of money to Rome, as the kings of England and France had done — we need not be surprised to find that when the German monk, Martin Luther, protested against some of these practices, there was an almost national response.

Satires of Erasmus

Already, in Luther's youth, the greatest scholar of the day, Erasmus, had written biting satires on the ignorance and lack of high ideals in the clergy, which had, in his eyes, grown worldly. But Erasmus and the group of earnest scholars with whom he worked, both on the Continent and in England, were merely anxious for reform *within* the Church. They did not want to bring about a revolution. For that matter, Luther, too, had no idea at first that his protest would bring about a split in the Church.

Martin Luther was a monk who had become a professor in Wittenberg, in Saxony. Through his study of the Bible and of the writings of St. Augustine he had come to believe that the only hope for salvation lay in *faith*, that is, in a personal relationship between man and God, without which, "good works," such as going to church or on pilgrimages, or visiting the relics of the saints, could do nothing for the sinner. On the other hand, if one were "justified by faith," he might properly go about his daily duties, for they would be pleasing to God without what the Church was accustomed to regard as "good works." Luther and "justification by faith"

These views would probably not have attracted much attention if they had not led Luther in 1517 to attack the distribution of *indulgences* in Germany, by means of which contributions were collected to aid in the rebuilding of St. Peter's in Rome. Indulgences in Germany in 1517

The granting of indulgences was a practice which had grown up in connection with the sacrament of penance, to which reference has been made. The Church taught that God would forgive the sinner who was penitent and confessed his sin, but that he must still do penance; that is, accept some kind of punishment, such as fasting, saying certain prayers, going on a pilgrimage, or doing some other "good work." Even if one died with sins forgiven, there still remained this satisfaction to be rendered, by suffering in purgatory. Now an indulgence, which was issued usually by the Pope himself, freed the person to whom it was granted from some penances in this life or from some or all of his suffering in purgatory. It was not a pardon of sin, therefore, but a commutation of the penance.[1] Doctrine of indulgences

The contribution to the Church, remission of which at times might form a part of the indulgence, varied greatly; the rich were asked to give a considerable sum, while the very poor were to receive these pardons gratis. Those in charge of these particular indulgences, however, seem to have been anxious to collect all the money possible, and they made claims for the indulgences to which thoughtful churchmen might well object. Method of distribution

1 For a fuller discussion see *Outlines*, Part I, pp. 584 f.

Luther's theses on indulgences

In October, 1517, Tetzel, a Dominican monk, began preaching indulgences in the neighborhood of Wittenberg, and making claims for them which appeared to Luther wholly irreconcilable with the deepest truths of Christianity as he understood and taught them. Therefore, in accordance with the custom of the time, he wrote out a series of ninety-five statements in regard to indulgences. These *theses*, as they were called, he posted on the church door and invited any one interested in the matter to enter into a discussion with him on the subject, which he believed was very ill understood.

Contents of Luther's theses

In posting these theses Luther did not intend to attack the Church and had no expectation of creating a sensation. The theses were in Latin and addressed, therefore, only to learned men. But they were promptly translated into German, printed, and scattered abroad throughout the land. In these *Ninety-five Theses* Luther declared that the indulgence was very unimportant and that the poor man might better spend his money for the needs of his household. *Faith* in God, not the procuring of pardons, brings forgiveness, and every Christian who feels true sorrow for his sins will receive full remission of the punishment as well as of the guilt.

Luther becomes suspicious of the papacy

Luther now began to read church history, and reached the conclusion that the influence of the popes had not been very great until the time of Gregory VII, in the eleventh century, and therefore that they had not enjoyed their supremacy over the Church for more than four hundred years before his own birth. Historical criticism of papal claims has been constantly urged by Protestants ever since, although they do not go as far as Luther did. They assert that the power of the Medieval Church and of the papacy developed gradually, and that the apostles knew nothing of masses, indulgences, pilgrimages, purgatory, or the headship of the bishop of Rome.

Luther's *Address to the German Nobility*

Meanwhile Luther was studying and writing with prodigious energy. He had a powerful style and a fine command of his native tongue, and in the year 1520 published some pamphlets which finally marked the outbreak of revolt. Of these the most stirring was his *Address to the German Nobility*, in which he called upon the rulers of Germany to reform the abuses themselves, since he believed that it was vain to wait for the Church to do so. He began by denying that there was anything especially sacred about clergymen except the duties which they had been designated to perform. They should be completely subject, therefore, to the civil government. Monks should be free to leave their monasteries, of which there were nine times too many. The clergy should be allowed to marry. The Germans should resent the action of Italian prelates, who took so much German money over the Alps. These denunciations of the clergy resounded like a trumpet call in the ears of Luther's countrymen.

Luther advocates social as well as religious reforms

Naturally, the Pope excommunicated such a pronounced heretic; but Luther boldly burned the papal bull of excommunication. Such was the condition of affairs when Charles V came to the Diet of Worms in 1520 and called Luther to appear before him. This Luther did; but he refused to recant, and the Emperor, while allowing him a safe conduct home, declared him an outlaw and worthy of a heretic's fate.

Luther burns the papal bull. Cited to Worms

Charles, however, immediately left Germany and for nearly ten years was too busily occupied with troubles in Spain and wars with Francis I of France to bother over the case of this German monk. On the other hand, Luther's own prince, the elector Frederick of Saxony, saw fit to protect the popular professor of his university at Wittenberg. So Luther was kidnaped by friends while on his way home from Worms, and hidden for two years in the elector's castle of the Wartburg. There he continued to write and, above all, to work on a new German translation of the Bible.

Luther hidden at the Wartburg

Meanwhile the revolt against the papacy had taken a new form, that of a great social revolution. In the first place, there was a movement of some of the knights, or lesser nobility, against certain prince bishops, who, it must be remembered, ruled large territories in Germany. These knights were defeated,

Revolution by the lesser nobility

but the civil war was responsible for much damage, and Luther and his teachings were naturally blamed for the uprising.

The "Peasants' Revolt"

Much more serious was the "Peasants' Revolt," which burst out in 1525. The serfs rose, in the name of "God's justice," to avenge their wrongs. Some of their demands were perfectly reasonable. The most popular statement of them was in the dignified "Twelve Articles."[1] In these they claimed that the Bible did not sanction any of the dues which the lords demanded of them, and that, since they were Christians like their lords, they should no longer be held as serfs. They were willing to pay all the old and well-established dues, but they asked to be properly paid for extra services. They thought, too, that each community should have the right freely to choose its own pastor and to dismiss him if he proved negligent or inefficient.

Luther urges the government to suppress the revolt

There were, however, leaders who were more violent and who proposed to kill the "godless" priests and nobles. Hundreds of castles and monasteries were destroyed by the frantic peasantry, and some of the nobility were murdered with shocking cruelty. Luther tried to induce the peasants, with whom, as the son of a peasant, he was at first inclined to sympathize, to remain quiet; but when his warnings proved vain, he turned against them and urged the government to put down the insurrection without pity.

The peasant revolt put down with great cruelty

Luther's advice was followed with terrible literalness by the German rulers, and the nobility took fearful revenge on the peasants. In the summer of 1525 their chief leader was defeated and killed, and it is estimated that ten thousand peasants were put to death, many with the utmost cruelty. The old exactions of the lords of the manors were in no way lightened, and the situation of the serfs for centuries following the great revolt was worse rather than better.

The "protest" at Speyer

In 1529 the Emperor, Charles V, again turned his attention to the situation in Germany and ordered the diet which met that year in Speyer to enforce the edict of the Diet of Worms against

[1] See Robinson, *Readings in European History*, Vol. II, chap. xxvi.

the heretics. Several princes and cities had, however, in the interval since 1520 gone ahead in their own realms to introduce the Lutheran form of worship and also to carry out Luther's ideas about monasteries and Church property.[1] As these princes formed only a minority in the diet, all they could do was to draw up a *protest*, in which they fell back upon the decision of a former diet of Speyer, held in 1526, in which each ruler was left free to adjust such things in his own realm as he saw fit. These *Protestants* — for this is how the name originated — therefore appealed to the Emperor and to a future general council of the Church against the tyranny of a majority in the diet.

The *Augsburg Confession*

The next year, 1530, Charles V came to Germany himself, and held a brilliant diet at Augsburg, in the hope of settling the religious problem, which he understood very imperfectly. For this diet the Protestants drew up a statement of what they believed. This *Augsburg Confession* is still the creed of the Lutheran Church. Charles V, however, commanded the Protestants to accept the statement which the Catholics drew up, to give back all Church property which they had seized, and cease troubling Catholics. But again he was called away from Germany, for the next ten years, and again the movement was left to the princes and cities of Germany to be settled as each saw fit. The result was a steady growth of Protestantism.

Peace of Augsburg

Finally, Charles V, after a serious attempt to suppress the Protestant princes, was obliged, in 1555, to accept the religious Peace of Augsburg. Its provisions are memorable. Each German prince and each town and knight immediately under the Emperor was to be at liberty to make a choice between the beliefs of the Catholic Church and those embodied in the Augsburg Confession. If, however, an ecclesiastical prince — an archbishop, bishop, or abbot — declared himself a Protestant, he must surrender his possessions to the Church. Every German was either to conform to the religious practices of his

1 Upon the whole, southern Germany remained Catholic, while the northern princes — finally, practically all — became Protestant.

particular state or emigrate from it. Every one was supposed to be either a Catholic or a Lutheran, and no provision was made for any other belief. There was no freedom of conscience, except for the rulers.

The Huguenots in France

John Calvin

Meanwhile the Protestant movement had spread to other countries. France produced, in John Calvin, a leader who ranks with Luther in energy and above him in intellectual power. He was forced to flee to Switzerland, however, to escape persecution, first to Basel and then to Geneva, which he made his home from about 1540. The Genevans intrusted him with the task of reforming the town, which had secured its independence of the duke of Savoy. He drew up a constitution and established an extraordinary government in which the Church and the civil government were as closely associated as they had ever been in any Catholic country. Calvin intrusted the management of church affairs to the ministers and the elders, or *presbyters*; hence the name "Presbyterian." The Protestantism which found its way into France was that of Calvin, not that of Luther, and the same may be said of Scotland.[1]

Calvin's reformation in Geneva

The Huguenots in France

The Protestants in France were much persecuted by Francis I and his son Henry II (1547–1559). Nevertheless the *Huguenots*, as they were called, continued to increase, especially among the middle classes and the nobility, and formed a *political* as well as a *religious* party, which was able, in the second half of the century, to defend itself by arms. Henry II's eldest son, Francis II, reigned but a year; his second son, Charles IX (1560–1574), was but ten years old at his accession, and his mother, Catherine de' Medici, ruled for him.

[1] Calvin's great work is *The Institute of Christianity*. It rejected the infallibility of Church and Pope but accepted that of the Bible. Calvin's most distinctive doctrine was that of "predestination," that is, that God had already, from before the beginning of the world, arranged the fate of all. For the other Swiss reformer, Zwingli, see *Outlines*, Part I, pp. 605 ff. The Scottish reformer was John Knox, a student of Calvin.

Catherine at first tried to conciliate both Catholics and Protestants; but the duke of Guise, head of a fanatical Catholic party, precipitated civil war by massacring a number of Protestants whom he and his troop found worshiping in a barn at Vassy. For a generation France was filled with burnings, pillage, and every form of barbarity, mainly in the name of religion. In 1570 a brief truce was made, and the Huguenot leader, Coligny, won the confidence of the queen mother and Charles by his patriotic efforts to unite Catholics and Protestants against Spain. The jealous party of the Guises frustrated this plan by a fearful expedient. They easily induced Catherine to believe that Coligny was deceiving her, and an assassin was hired to murder him, but only wounded his victim. Fearful that the young king, who was faithful to Coligny, might discover her guilt, Catherine invented a story of a great Huguenot conspiracy. The credulous king was deceived, and the Catholic leaders at Paris arranged that at a given signal on St. Bartholomew's Eve, 1572, not only Coligny should be killed but also all the Huguenots, who had gathered in great numbers in the city for the marriage of the king's sister Margaret to the Protestant Henry, king of the little realm of Navarre, in the Pyrenees, and a member of the Bourbon branch of the royal house of France. The massacre was only too successful. About two thousand were murdered in Paris and ten thousand outside it. (Catherine de' Medici and St. Bartholomew)

Civil war followed. Charles's brother and successor, Henry III (1574–1589), finally found himself at war with both Henry of Navarre — who had become the Huguenot leader — and Henry, duke of Guise, leader of the extreme Catholics. He secured the assassination of Guise, but was himself assassinated in turn by Guise's followers. So Henry of Navarre became King Henry IV of France — the first of the Bourbon line. He accepted the religion of the majority of his subjects (1593), on the ground that, as he remarked, "Paris was worth a mass." In 1598, by the famous Edict of Nantes, he granted toleration to the Huguenots. His reign is gratefully (War of the three Henrys, 1585–1589) (Henry IV, 1589–1610) (Edict of Nantes) remembered by the French as a time of peace and new prosperity, due to his wise encouragement of agriculture and commerce. He was murdered in 1610 and left the throne to his young son, Louis XIII (1610–1643). Louis's reign was rather that of his great minister, Cardinal Richelieu, who ruled France with an iron hand from 1624 to 1642. He crushed the political independence of the Huguenots and made royalty supreme over all France.

Cardinal Richelieu

The Church of England

Henry VIII

Henry VIII (1509–1547) of England had succeeded to all his father's power. The nobility had been weakened by the Wars of the Roses, and the middle classes had not yet become strong enough to check the monarch. His chief adviser at first was Cardinal Wolsey, who managed to keep Henry from mixing in continental wars. Henry had no sympathy with Luther and even wrote a book against him; but split first with Wolsey, and then with the Pope, because they would not secure for him a divorce from his queen, Catherine of Aragon, aunt of Charles V. The first break with Rome, therefore, came over a question of Church government rather than any difference of religious belief. In 1534 Parliament passed the Act of Supremacy, which declared the king to be "the only supreme head on earth of the Church of England," with power to appoint all prelates and enjoy the income which formerly went to Rome. This legislation was enforced by a vicious persecution. It must be carefully observed that Henry VIII still believed himself a good Catholic. He persecuted those who had forsaken the old beliefs. He claimed merely that he, in place of the Pope, should control and manage a national branch of the Church. This did not prevent his dissolving the English monasteries, however, and appropriating their great wealth for himself and his favorites. A thorough despot, he acted from unworthy motives, but the general trend of his actions fitted in with a certain national feeling of independence of the papacy, which had shown itself in England at various times in the past.

Under Henry's young son, Edward VI, who died in 1553, aged sixteen, the revolt became definitely doctrinal; and a prayer book in English and forty-two articles of faith were drawn up. These articles, revised later, in Elizabeth's time, and reduced to thirty-nine, became the creed of the Church of England. The formation of the Church of England

Mary (1553–1558), the daughter of the divorced Queen Catherine, next succeeded — an ardent Catholic. Married to Philip II of Spain, she adopted his policy of persecution; but the heroism of the Protestant victims won more friends for their cause. Upon the accession of Mary's Protestant half sister, Elizabeth (1558–1603), the work begun under Edward VI was again taken up, and the Church of England still remains in much the same form as then established. Mary's futile persecutions Elizabeth

The Roman Catholic Church and its Champions

Meanwhile the Catholic Church had not been idle. A general council, which met at Trent at various times during the eighteen years from 1545 to 1563, drew up statements of what it declared to be the orthodox belief, which is still the accepted creed of that large portion of the Christian Church which remained faithful to the papacy and which is commonly known as the Roman Catholic Church.[1] The work of the council of Trent

The most powerful Catholic organization of the period was the new Society of Jesus, or Jesuits, founded by the Spaniard Ignatius Loyola, and sanctioned by the Pope in 1540. The Jesuits were noted for the absolute obedience which they rendered to their officers and to the Pope. They were teachers The Jesuits

[1] The council naturally condemned the distinctively Protestant beliefs, accepted the Pope as head of the Church, and declared accursed those who, like Luther, believed that man could be saved by faith in God's promises alone. It reaffirmed all the seven sacraments, several of which the Protestants had rejected. The ancient Latin translation of the Bible — the Vulgate — was proclaimed the standard of belief, and no one was to publish any views, interpreting the Bible, differing from those approved by the Church.

as well as priests, and their schools were so successful that through their influence many children grew up as stanch Catholics who otherwise might have become Protestant. Their missionary efforts extended over the whole world, but Protestants were especially suspicious of them as confessors of kings.

Philip II of Spain

The chief ally of the Pope and the Jesuits in their efforts to check Protestantism was the son of Charles V, Philip II (1556–1598), who succeeded to the kingdom of Spain and its colonies, Milan, the Two Sicilies, and the Netherlands.[1] Philip was a fanatic, who was willing to sacrifice even his kingdom to put down heretics. The Inquisition was used to effect this, as it had been by his father, and Spain was kept orthodox. To the Netherlands Philip sent the remorseless duke of Alva (1567–1573) with his cruel Spanish soldiery to quiet any opposition. Thousands of Flemish weavers fled to England to escape the Council of Blood, as Alva's tribunal was popularly called, but the northern provinces, of which Holland was the chief, found a leader in William, Prince of Orange.[2]

The Dutch war of independence

The Dutch had become Protestant, while most of the people of the southern Netherlands remained Catholic. Alva's reign of terror, however, had alienated the south as well as the north, and after his recall his unpaid soldiers sacked the rich city of Antwerp, in what is called "the Spanish fury" (1576). So for the next three years the whole country united against their king. But the union was dissolved when Philip sent a wiser and more moderate governor. Then only the seven northern provinces held together, in what was called the Union of Utrecht (1579), and these united provinces declared themselves independent of Spain in 1581. The soul of their revolt was William "the Silent," Prince of Orange, whose great

[1] Charles V abdicated in 1555–1556. The Austrian realms went to his brother Ferdinand (d. 1564), who married the heiress to the kingdoms of Bohemia and Hungary, and whose son, Maximilian II (d. 1576), thus inherited these "Austrian" dominions.

[2] The title comes from the little town of Orange on the east side of the Rhone, in what is now southern France but was once part of the Empire.

courage nerved the people to resist. Philip had him assassinated in 1584; but the Dutch independence was already won.

Philip's other foe was England, which, under Elizabeth, was becoming definitely Protestant. Besides the religious issue, however, there was a more practical one; for English seamen had been capturing Spanish merchant ships, and there was continual war between the two countries. To end all this Philip prepared a great fleet, the famous Spanish Armada — perhaps the greatest fleet the world had ever seen. But the swift English ships, aided by a great gale, in which the huge Spanish ships became unmanageable, brought about its utter destruction. The Spanish Armada against England

Philip had exhausted Spain and met with failure — perhaps the most colossal failure in modern history; for Spain has never recovered its former power.

The Thirty Years' War in Germany

In Germany the Peace of Augsburg had permitted a steady growth of Protestantism, and for the next sixty years the country adjusted itself on the whole peacefully to this change. But when, in 1618, Bohemia, which had become strongly Protestant, rebelled from its Hapsburg ruler, a war broke out which, with varying intensity, devastated Germany for the next thirty years. The first phase of this war, that over Bohemia, ended in the complete victory of the Catholic princes, who rallied to the Hapsburg cause. The Protestant princes were divided and incapable. The king of Denmark came to their aid, but he was beaten in 1629 by the Emperor's able general, Wallenstein, who swept all before him. This second phase of the war was closed by an Edict of Restitution, in which the Protestants were ordered to restore all the Church property they had seized since the Peace of Augsburg. That meant giving up vast possessions, and the war broke out anew, this time with the Swedish king, Gustavus Adolphus, as the Protestant champion. He proved to be a great general and, after

The first phase of the war

Second phase

Third phase

severe fighting, drove the imperial forces out of the north. But he was killed at the moment of victory in the battle of Lützen, 1632. Just at this moment Richelieu, though a cardinal, decided that it was to the interest of France to help the Protestants in Germany, in order to humble the Emperor. Hired soldiery — on both sides — laid waste the land, and the war wore on until 1648, when peace was made at two towns in Westphalia. Peace, however, could not bring back prosperity, and Germany was crushed for more than a generation by the awful suffering of this war.

Fourth phase

The Treaty of Westphalia, 1648

By the Treaty of Westphalia the Protestant princes were to retain the lands they had taken prior to 1624 and were still to determine the religion of their own states. They were to be free to make treaties among themselves and with foreign powers, which was equivalent to recognizing their practical independence and the dissolution of the Empire — which, however, lasted in name until the day of Napoleon. Sweden was given territory on the Baltic; and the Emperor ceded to France the three towns of Metz, Toul, and Verdun, and his rights in Alsace, except Strassburg. The independence of Holland and Switzerland was also acknowledged.

Thus the "wars of religion" came to an end about the middle of the seventeenth century. It is evident from the narrative, however, that they were not waged merely for religion, but also for political and economic ends. The era of the national states had at last fully dawned, and the first chapter of this book here takes up the theme.

CHAPTER I

THE STRUGGLE IN ENGLAND BETWEEN KING AND PARLIAMENT

This volume deals with the last three hundred years of European history. Compared with the long period of more than five thousand years which lies between Menes I — the first ruler whose name we know — and James I of England, this seems a very short time. In many ways, however, it has seen far more astonishing changes than those which took place in all the preceding centuries. Scope of this volume

Could James I now see the England he once ruled, how startling the revolution in politics and industry would seem to him! The railroads, the steel steamships, the great towns with well-lighted, smoothly paved, and carefully drained streets; the innumerable newspapers and the beautifully illustrated periodicals, the government schools, the popular elections, and a parliament ruling with little attention to its king; the vast factories full of machinery, working with a precision and rapidity far surpassing those of an army of skilled workmen; and, most astonishing of all, the mysterious and manifold applications of electricity which he knew only in the form of lightning playing among the storm clouds — all these marvels would combine to convince him that he died on the eve of the greatest revolution in industry, government, and science that the world has ever seen. Great changes of the last three centuries

It is the aim of this volume, after describing the conditions in Europe during the seventeenth and eighteenth centuries, to show as clearly as possible the changes which have made the world what we find it to-day. To do this, we must begin with England, which led other states by many years in permitting the nation's representatives to control the government. Aim of this volume

Section 1. James I and the Divine Right of Kings

England and her Parliament

The English people were more fortunately placed than other European peoples in living upon an island which was seldom troubled by war. While the rest of Europe was so often swept by pillaging hordes, England prospered in the arts of peace. Its great achievement during the Middle Ages had been the development of parliamentary government. This had been established in the thirteenth century,[1] but was often of little importance during the later Middle Ages. In the early sixteenth century, for instance, Henry VIII either defied Parliament or used it as a tool.[2]

Parliament resents Elizabeth's attempts to control it

But when his daughter Elizabeth, at the end of the century, tried to assert her will over it, she found that Parliament, backed by the nation, had grown strong enough to refuse to submit. For, during her reign, the new wealth from world trade, the general spread of knowledge, and the strong sense of common interests awakened by the war with Spain, had called into being a new spirit in the nation — one which insisted on "the rights of Englishmen" as against any despotically inclined monarch. Unfortunately the next monarchs — the Stuarts — who ascended the throne were inclined to claim great powers for themselves. The result was civil war and disorder during most of the seventeenth century. Finally Parliament definitely won the mastery, and the kings of England ceased to contest its power.

Accession of James I as king of Great Britain, 1603

On the death of Elizabeth in 1603, King James VI of Scotland ascended the throne of England as James I, the first king of *Great Britain*, as the united realms of England, Scotland, and Wales were termed. Through his mother, the ill-fated Mary Queen of Scots,[3] he was a descendant of Henry VII, the first of the Tudors, and this was the reason why the Scottish House of Stuart came to rule in England.[4]

[1] See Part I, p. 421. [2] See Part I, p. 611. [3] See Part I, pp. 641–644.

[4] Although the crowns were united, the two countries kept their separate parliaments and constitutions for another century.

James I soon showed that his ideas were much like those of his English relatives, the Tudors; for he was determined to rule without regard to Parliament. Moreover, instead of attempting to control Parliament in quiet ways, as Elizabeth had done, he boldly stated his claims in the most irritating manner. He was King James's views of kingship

FIG. 1. JAMES I

a learned man and fond of writing books. He published a work on monarchs, in which he claimed that the king could make any law he pleased without consulting Parliament; that he was the master of every one of his subjects and might put to death whom he pleased. A good king would act according to law, but is not bound to do so and has the power to change the law to suit himself. "It is atheism and blasphemy," he declared, "to dispute what God can do; . . . so it is presumption and high contempt in a subject to dispute what a king can do, or say that a king cannot do this or that."

The "divine right of kings"

These theories seem strange and very unreasonable to us, but James was only trying to justify the powers which the Tudor monarchs had actually exercised and which the kings of France enjoyed down to the French Revolution of 1789. According to the theory of "the divine right of kings" it had pleased God to appoint the monarch the father of his people. People must obey him as they would God and ask no questions. The king was responsible to God alone, to whom he owed his powers, not to Parliament or the nation (see below, p. 59).

It is unnecessary to follow the troubles between James I and Parliament, for his reign only forms the preliminary to the fatal experiences of his son Charles I, who came to the throne in 1625.

Great writers of James's reign — Shakespeare

The writers of James's reign constituted its chief glory. They outshone those of any other European country. Shakespeare is generally admitted to be the greatest dramatist that the world has produced. While he wrote many of his plays before the death of Elizabeth, some of his finest — *Othello*, *King Lear*, and *The Tempest*, for example — belong to the time of James I. During the same period Francis Bacon (see Part I, p. 656) was writing his *Advancement of Learning*, which he dedicated to James I in 1605, and in which he urged that men should cease to rely upon the old textbooks, like Aristotle, and turn to a careful examination of animals, plants, and chemicals, with a view of learning about them and using the knowledge thus gained to improve the condition of mankind. Bacon's ability to write English is equal to that of Shakespeare, but he chose to write prose, not verse. It was in James's reign that the authorized English translation of the Bible was made, which is still used in all countries where English is spoken.

Francis Bacon

King James version of the Bible

William Harvey

An English physician of this period, William Harvey, examined the workings of the human body more carefully than any previous investigator, and made the great discovery of the manner in which the blood circulates from the heart through the arteries and capillaries and back through the veins — a matter which had previously been entirely misunderstood.

Section 2. How Charles I got along without Parliament

Charles I, James I's son and successor, was somewhat more dignified than his father, but he was quite as obstinately set upon having his own way, and showed no more skill in winning the confidence of his subjects. He did nothing to remove the disagreeable impressions of his father's reign and began immediately to quarrel with Parliament. When that body refused to grant him any money, mainly because they thought that it was likely to be wasted by his favorite, the Duke of Buckingham, Charles formed the plan of winning their favor by a great military victory.

Charles I, 1625–1649

He hoped to gain popularity by prosecuting a war against Spain, whose king was energetically supporting the Catholic League in the Thirty Years' War. Accordingly, in spite of Parliament's refusal to grant him the necessary funds, he embarked in war. With only the money which he could raise by irregular means, Charles arranged an expedition to capture the Spanish treasure ships which arrived in Cadiz once a year from America, laden with gold and silver; but this expedition failed.

Charles's exactions and arbitrary acts

In his attempts to raise money without a regular grant from Parliament, Charles resorted to vexatious exactions. The law prohibited him from asking for *gifts* from his people, but it did not forbid his asking them to *lend* him money, however little prospect there might be of his ever repaying it. Five gentlemen who refused to pay such a forced loan were imprisoned by the mere order of the king. This raised the question of whether the king had the right to send to prison those whom he disliked, without any legal reasons for their arrest.

The *Petition of Right*

This and other attacks upon the rights of his subjects aroused Parliament. In 1628 that body drew up the celebrated *Petition of Right*, which is one of the most important documents in the history of the English Constitution. In it Parliament called the king's attention to his unlawful exactions, and to the acts of his agents who had in sundry ways molested and disquieted the people of the realm. Parliament therefore "humbly prayed" the king that no man need thereafter "make or yield any gift, loan, benevolence, tax, or such like charge" without consent of Parliament; that no free man should be imprisoned or suffer any punishment except according to the laws and statutes of the realm as presented in the Great Charter; and that soldiers should not be quartered upon the people on any pretext whatever. Very reluctantly Charles consented to this restatement of the limitations which the English had always, in theory at least, placed upon the arbitrary power of their king.

FIG. 2. CHARLES I OF ENGLAND

This portrait is by one of the greatest painters of the time, Anthony Van Dyck, 1599–1641 (see below, Fig. 4)

The disagreement between Charles and Parliament was rendered much more serious by religious differences. The king had married a French Catholic princess, and the Catholic cause seemed to be gaining on the Continent. The king of Denmark had just been defeated by Wallenstein and Tilly (see Part I, p. 647), and Richelieu had succeeded in depriving the Huguenots of their cities of refuge. Both James I and Charles I had shown their readiness to enter into agreements with France and Spain to protect Catholics in England,

and there was evidently a growing inclination in England to revert to the older ceremonies of the Church, which shocked the more strongly Protestant members of the House of Commons. The communion table was again placed by many clergymen at the eastern end of the church and became fixed there as an altar, and portions of the service were once more chanted.

Charles dissolves Parliament (1629) and determines to rule by himself

These practices, with which Charles was supposed to sympathize, served to widen the breach between him and the Commons, which had been caused by the king's attempt to raise taxes on his own account. The Parliament of 1629, after a stormy session, was dissolved by the king, who determined to rule thereafter by himself. For eleven years no new Parliament was summoned.

Charles's financial exactions

Charles was not well fitted by nature to run the government of England by himself. He had not the necessary tireless energy. Moreover, the methods resorted to by his ministers to raise money without recourse to Parliament rendered the king more and more unpopular and prepared the way for the triumphant return of Parliament. For example, Charles applied to his subjects for "ship money." He was anxious to equip a fleet, but instead of requiring the various ports to furnish ships, as was the ancient custom, he permitted them to buy themselves off by contributing money to the fitting out of large ships owned by himself. Even those living inland were asked for ship money. The king maintained that this was not a tax but simply a payment by which his subjects freed themselves from the duty of defending their country.

John Hampden

John Hampden, a squire of Buckinghamshire, made a bold stand against this illegal demand by refusing to pay twenty shillings of ship money which was levied upon him. The case was tried before the king's judges, and he was convicted, but by a bare majority. The trial made it tolerably clear that the country would not put up long with the king's despotic policy.

In 1633 Charles made William Laud Archbishop of Canterbury. Laud believed that the English Church would strengthen

William Laud made Archbishop of Canterbury

both itself and the government by following a middle course, which should lie between that of the Church of Rome and that of Calvinistic Geneva. He declared that it was the part of good citizenship to conform outwardly to the services of the

FIG. 3. JOHN HAMPDEN

state church, but that the State should not undertake to oppress the individual conscience, and that every one should be at liberty to make up his own mind in regard to the interpretation to be given to the Bible and to the church fathers. As soon as he became archbishop he began a series of visitations through his province. Every clergyman who refused to conform to the prayer book, or opposed the placing of the communion table at the east end of the church, or declined to bow at the name of Jesus, was, if obstinate, to be brought before the king's special Court of High Commission to be tried and, if convicted, to be deprived of his position.

The different sects of Protestants—High Church and Low Church

Laud's conduct was no doubt gratifying to the High Church party among the Protestants, that is, those who still clung to some of the ancient practices of the Roman Church, although they rejected the doctrine of the Mass and refused to regard the Pope as their head. The Low Church party, or *Puritans*, on the contrary, regarded Laud and his policy with aversion. While, unlike the Presbyterians, they did not urge the abolition of the bishops, they disliked all "superstitious usages," as they called the wearing of the surplice by the clergy, the use of the sign of the cross at baptism, the kneeling posture in partaking of the communion, and so forth. The Presbyterians, who are often confused with the Puritans, agreed with them in many respects, but went farther and demanded the introduction of Calvin's system of church government.

The Independents

Lastly, there was an ever-increasing number of Separatists, or Independents. These rejected both the organization of the Church of England and that of the Presbyterians, and desired that each religious community should organize itself independently. The government had forbidden these Separatists to hold their little meetings, which they called *conventicles*, and about 1600 some of them fled to Holland. The community of them which established itself at Leyden dispatched the *Mayflower*, in 1620, with colonists — since known as the Pilgrim Fathers — to the New World across the sea.[1] It was these colonists who laid the foundations of a *New England* which has proved a worthy offspring of the mother country. The form of worship which they established in their new home is still known as Congregational.

The Pilgrim Fathers

[1] The name "Puritan," it should be noted, was applied loosely to the English Protestants, whether Low Churchmen, Presbyterians, or Independents, who aroused the antagonism of their neighbors by advocating a godly life and opposing popular pastimes, especially on Sunday.

Section 3. How Charles I lost his Head

Charles I's quarrel with the Scotch Presbyterians

In 1640 Charles found himself forced to summon Parliament, for he was involved in a war with Scotland, which he could not carry on without money. There the Presbyterian system had been pretty generally introduced by John Knox in Elizabeth's time (see Part I, p. 640). An attempt on the part of Charles to force the Scots to accept a modified form of the English prayer book led to the signing of the National Covenant in 1638. This pledged those who attached their names to it to reëstablish the purity and liberty of the Gospel, which, to most of the covenanters, meant Presbyterianism.

The National Covenant, 1638

Charles summons the Long Parliament, 1640

Charles thereupon undertook to coerce the Scots. Having no money, he bought on credit a large cargo of pepper, which had just arrived in the ships of the East India Company, and sold it cheap for ready cash. The soldiers, however, whom he got together showed little inclination to fight the Scots, with whom they were in tolerable agreement on religious matters. Charles was therefore at last obliged to summon a Parliament, which, owing to the length of time it remained in session, is known as the Long Parliament.

The measures of the Long Parliament against the king's tyranny

The Long Parliament began by imprisoning Archbishop Laud in the Tower of London. They declared him guilty of treason, and he was executed in 1645, in spite of Charles's efforts to save him. Parliament also tried to strengthen its position by passing the Triennial Bill, which provided that it should meet at least once in three years, even if not summoned by the king. In fact, Charles's whole system of government was abrogated. Parliament drew up a "Grand Remonstrance" in which all of Charles's errors were enumerated and a demand was made that the king's ministers should thereafter be responsible to Parliament. This document Parliament ordered to be printed and circulated throughout the country.

Exasperated at the conduct of the Commons, Charles attempted to intimidate the opposition by undertaking to arrest five of its most active leaders, whom he declared to be traitors. But when he entered the House of Commons and looked around for his enemies, he found that they had taken shelter in London, whose citizens later brought them back in triumph to Westminster, where Parliament held its meetings (see p. 102). Charles's attempts to arrest five members of the House of Commons

FIG. 4. CHILDREN OF CHARLES I

This very interesting picture, by the Flemish artist Van Dyck, was painted in 1637. The boy with his hand on the dog's head was destined to become Charles II of England. Next on the left is the prince who was later James II. The girl to the extreme left, the Princess Mary, married the governor of the United Netherlands, and her son became William III of England in 1688 (see below, p. 52). The two princesses on the right died in childhood

Both Charles and Parliament now began to gather troops for the inevitable conflict, and England was plunged into civil war. Those who supported Charles were called *Cavaliers.* They included not only most of the aristocracy and the Catholic party, but also a number of members of the House of Commons who were fearful lest the Presbyterians should succeed in The beginning of civil war, 1642 — *Cavaliers* and *Roundheads* doing away with the English Church. The parliamentary party was popularly known as the *Roundheads*, since some of them cropped their hair close because of their dislike for the long locks of their more aristocratic and worldly opponents.

Oliver Cromwell

The Roundheads soon found a distinguished leader in Oliver Cromwell (b. 1599), a country gentleman and member of Parliament, who was later to become the most powerful ruler of his time. Cromwell organized a compact army of God-fearing men, who were not permitted to indulge in profane words or light talk, as is the wont of soldiers, but advanced upon their enemies singing psalms. The king enjoyed the support of northern England, and also looked for help from Ireland, where the royal and Catholic causes were popular.

Battles of Marston Moor and Naseby

The war continued for several years, and a number of battles were fought which, after the first year, went in general against the Cavaliers. The most important of these were the battle of Marston Moor in 1644, and that of Naseby the next year, in which Charles was disastrously defeated. The enemy came into possession of his correspondence, which showed them how their king had been endeavoring to bring armies from France and Ireland into England. This encouraged Parliament to prosecute the war with more energy than ever. The king, defeated on every hand, put himself in the hands of the Scotch army which had come to the aid of Parliament (1646), and the Scotch soon turned him over to Parliament. During the next two years Charles was held in captivity.

The losing cause of the king

Pride's Purge

There were, however, many in the House of Commons who still sided with the king, and in December, 1648, that body declared for a reconciliation with the monarch, whom they had safely imprisoned in the Isle of Wight. The next day Colonel Pride, representing the army, — which constituted a party in itself and was opposed to all negotiations between the king and the Commons, — stood at the door of the House with a body of soldiers and excluded all the members who took the side of the king. This outrageous act is known in history as "Pride's Purge."

In this way the House of Commons was brought completely under the control of those most bitterly hostile to the king, whom they immediately proposed to bring to trial. They declared that the House of Commons, since it was chosen by the people, was supreme in England and the source of all just power, and that consequently neither king nor House of Lords was necessary. The mutilated House of Commons appointed a special High Court of Justice made up of Charles's sternest opponents, who alone would consent to sit in judgment on him. They passed sentence upon him, and on January 30, 1649, Charles was beheaded in front of his palace of Whitehall, London. It must be clear from the above account that it was not the nation at large which demanded Charles's death, but a very small group of extremists who claimed to be the representatives of the nation. **Execution of Charles, 1649**

Section 4. Oliver Cromwell: England a Commonwealth

The "Rump Parliament," as the remnant of the House of Commons was contemptuously called, proclaimed England to be thereafter a "commonwealth," that is, a republic, without a king or House of Lords. But Cromwell, the head of the army, was nevertheless the real ruler of England. He derived his main support from the Independents; and it is very surprising that he was able to maintain himself so long, considering what a small portion of the English people was in sympathy with the religious ideas of that sect and with the abolition of kingship. Even the Presbyterians were on the side of Charles I's son, Charles II, the legal heir to the throne. Cromwell was a vigorous and skillful administrator and had a well-organized army of fifty thousand men at his command, otherwise the republic could scarcely have lasted more than a few months. **England becomes a commonwealth, or republic. Cromwell at the head of the government**

Cromwell found himself confronted by every variety of difficulty. The three kingdoms had fallen apart. The nobles and

Ireland and Scotland subdued

Catholics in Ireland proclaimed Charles II as king, and Ormond, a Protestant leader, formed an army of Irish Catholics and English royalist Protestants with a view of overthrowing the Commonwealth. Cromwell accordingly set out for Ireland, where, after taking Drogheda, he mercilessly slaughtered two thousand

FIG. 5. OLIVER CROMWELL

This portrait is by Peter Lely and was painted in 1653

of the "barbarous wretches," as he called them. Town after town surrendered to Cromwell's army, and in 1652, after much cruelty, the island was once more conquered. A large part of it was confiscated for the benefit of the English, and the Catholic landowners were driven into the mountains. In the meantime (1650) Charles II, who had taken refuge in France, had landed in Scotland, and upon his agreeing to be a Presbyterian king, the whole Scotch nation was ready to support him. But Scotland was subdued by Cromwell even more promptly than Ireland had been. So completely was the Scottish army destroyed that Cromwell found no need to draw the sword again in the British Isles.

FIG. 6. GREAT SEAL OF ENGLAND UNDER THE COMMONWEALTH, 1651

This seal is reduced considerably in the reproduction. It gives us an idea of the appearance of a session of the House of Commons when England was for a short period a republic. Members to-day still commonly sit with their hats on, except when making a speech or when wishing to indicate respect for the speaker by uncovering

Although it would seem that Cromwell had enough to keep him busy at home, he had already engaged in a victorious foreign war against the Dutch, who had become dangerous The Navigation Act, 1651 commercial rivals of England. The ships which went out from Amsterdam and Rotterdam were the best merchant vessels in the world and had got control of the carrying trade between Europe and the colonies. In order to put an end to this, the English Parliament passed the Navigation Act (1651), which permitted only English vessels to bring goods to England, unless the goods came in vessels belonging to the country which had produced them. This led to a commercial war between Holland and England, and a series of battles was fought between the English and Dutch fleets, in which sometimes one and sometimes the other gained the upper hand. This war is notable as the first example of the commercial struggles which were thereafter to take the place of the religious conflicts of the preceding period.

Commercial war between Holland and England

Cromwell dissolves the Long Parliament (1653) and is made Lord Protector by his own Parliament

Cromwell failed to get along with Parliament any better than Charles I had done. The Rump Parliament had become very unpopular, for its members, in spite of their boasted piety, accepted bribes and were zealous in the promotion of their relatives in the public service. At last Cromwell upbraided them angrily for their injustice and self-interest, which were injuring the public cause. On being interrupted by a member, he cried out, "Come, come, we have had enough of this! I'll put an end to this. It's not fit that you should sit here any longer," and calling in his soldiers he turned the members out of the House and sent them home. Having thus made an end of the Long Parliament (April, 1653), he summoned a Parliament of his own, made up of "God-fearing" men whom he and the officers of his army chose. This extraordinary body is known as Barebone's Parliament, from a distinguished member, a London merchant, with the characteristically Puritan name of Praisegod Barebone. Many of these godly men were unpractical and hard to deal with. A minority of the more sensible ones got up early one winter morning (December, 1653) and, before their opponents had a chance to protest, declared Parliament dissolved and placed the supreme authority in the hands of Cromwell.

The Protector's foreign policy

For nearly five years Cromwell was, as Lord Protector, — a title equivalent to that of Regent, — practically king of England, although he refused actually to be crowned. He did not succeed in permanently organizing the government at home, but showed remarkable ability in his foreign negotiations. He formed an alliance with France, and English troops aided the French in winning a great victory over Spain. England gained thereby Dunkirk, and the West Indian island of Jamaica. The French king, Louis XIV, at first hesitated to address Cromwell, in the usual courteous way of monarchs, as "my cousin," but soon admitted that he would have even to call Cromwell "father" should he wish it, as the Protector was undoubtedly the most powerful person in Europe. Indeed, he found himself forced to play the part of a monarch, and it seemed to many persons that he was quite as despotic as James I and Charles I.

FIG. 7. A SHIP OF THE HANSEATIC LEAGUE

There had been a great increase in the size of merchant ships and war vessels since the days of the Hanseatic League (see Part I, p. 508). This illustration is taken from a picture at Cologne, painted in 1409. It, as well as other pictures of the time, makes it clear that the Hanseatic ships were tiny compared with those used two hundred and fifty years later, when Cromwell fought the Dutch (see Fig. 8)

In May, 1658, Cromwell fell ill, and as a great storm passed over England at that time, the Cavaliers asserted that the devil had come to fetch home the soul of the usurper. Cromwell was dying, it is true, but he was no instrument of the devil.

He closed a life of honest effort for his fellow beings with a last touching prayer to God, whom he had consistently sought to serve: "Thou hast made me, though very unworthy, a mean instrument to do Thy people some good and Thee service: and many of them have set too high a value upon me, though

FIG. 8. DUTCH WAR VESSEL IN CROMWELL'S TIME

This should be compared with Fig. 7 to realize the change that had taken place in navigation since the palmy days of the Hanseatic League

others wish and would be glad of my death. Pardon such as desire to trample upon the dust of a poor worm, for they are Thy people too; and pardon the folly of this short prayer, even for Jesus Christ's sake, and give us a good night, if it be Thy pleasure. Amen."

SECTION 5. THE RESTORATION

After Cromwell's death his son Richard, who succeeded him, found himself unable to carry on the government. He soon abdicated, and the remnants of the Long Parliament met once more. But the power was really in the hands of the soldiers. In 1660 George Monk, who was in command of the forces in Scotland, came to London with a view of putting an end to the anarchy. He soon concluded that no one cared to support the Rump, and that body peacefully disbanded of its own accord. Resistance would have been vain in any case with the army against it. The nation was glad to acknowledge Charles II, whom every one preferred to a government by soldiers. A new Parliament, composed of both houses, was assembled, which welcomed a messenger from the king and solemnly resolved that, "according to the ancient and fundamental laws of this kingdom, the government is, and ought to be, by king, lords, and commons." Thus the Puritan revolution and the short-lived republic was followed by the *Restoration* of the Stuarts.

The Restoration

Charles II welcomed back as king, 1660

Charles II was quite as fond as his father of having his own way, but he was a man of more ability. He disliked to be ruled by Parliament, but, unlike his father, he was too wise to arouse the nation against him. He did not propose to let anything happen which would send him on his travels again. He and his courtiers were fond of pleasure of a light-minded kind. The immoral dramas of the Restoration seem to indicate that those who had been forced by the Puritans to give up their legitimate pleasures now welcomed the opportunity to indulge in reckless gayety without regard to the bounds imposed by custom and decency.

Character of Charles II

Charles's first Parliament was a moderate body, but his second was made up almost wholly of Cavaliers, and it got along, on the whole, so well with the king that he did not dissolve it for eighteen years. It did not take up the old question, which was still unsettled, as to whether Parliament or the king

Religious measures adopted by Parliament

was really supreme. It showed its hostility, however, to the Puritans by a series of intolerant acts, which are very important in English history. It ordered that no one should hold a town office who had not received the communion according to the rites of the Church of England. This was aimed at both the Presbyterians and the Independents. By the Act of Uniformity (1662) every clergyman who refused to accept everything contained in the Book of Common Prayer was to be excluded from holding his benefice. Two thousand clergymen thereupon resigned their positions for conscience' sake.

The Act of Uniformity

The *Dissenters*

These laws tended to throw all those Protestants who refused to conform to the Church of England into a single class, still known to-day as *Dissenters*. It included the Independents, the Presbyterians, and the newer bodies of the Baptists and the Society of Friends, commonly known as Quakers. These sects abandoned any idea of controlling the religion or politics of the country, and asked only that they might be permitted to worship in their own way outside of the English Church.

Toleration favored by the king

Toleration found an unexpected ally in the king, who, in spite of his dissolute habits, had interest enough in religion to have secret leanings toward Catholicism. He asked Parliament to permit him to moderate the rigor of the Act of Uniformity by making some exceptions. He even issued a declaration in the interest of toleration, with a view of bettering the position of the Catholics and Dissenters. Suspicion was, however, aroused lest this toleration might lead to the restoration of Catholic beliefs and ceremonies, so Parliament passed the harsh Conventicle Act (1664).

The Conventicle Act

Any adult attending a conventicle — that is to say, any religious meeting not held in accordance with the practice of the English Church — was liable to penalties which might culminate in transportation to some distant colony. Samuel Pepys, who saw some of the victims of this law upon their way to a terrible exile, notes in his famous diary: "They go like lambs without any resistance. I would to God that they would conform, or be

PLATE II. A FIGHT IN THE BRITISH CHANNEL BETWEEN THE ENGLISH AND THE DUTCH

(See pp. 46 and 51)

more wise and not be catched." A few years later Charles II issued a declaration giving complete religious liberty to Roman Catholics as well as to Dissenters. Parliament not only forced him to withdraw this enlightened measure but passed the Test Act, which excluded every one from public office who did not accept the views of the English Church.[1]

The Test Act

Importance of the *Habeas Corpus* Act, 1679

The most important act of Parliament of this reign was that of *Habeas Corpus*, of 1679, which provided that any one who was arrested should be informed of the reason and should be speedily tried by a regular tribunal and dealt with according to the law of the land. This principle is still one of the chief safeguards of our personal liberty. In France, for instance, down until the Revolution of 1789 the king could arrest his subjects and imprison them without assigning any reason (see below, p. 183). To-day the principles of the Habeas Corpus Act are recognized in all free countries.

War with Holland

The old war with Holland, begun by Cromwell, was renewed under Charles II, who was earnestly desirous to increase English commerce and to found new colonies. The two nations were very evenly matched on the sea, but in 1664 the English seized some of the West Indian Islands from the Dutch and also their colony on Manhattan Island, which was re-named New York in honor of the king's brother, the Duke of York. In 1667 a treaty was signed by England and Holland which confirmed these conquests.

Section 6. The Revolution of 1688

James II, 1685–1688

Upon Charles II's death he was succeeded by his brother, James II, who was an avowed Catholic and had married, as his second wife, Mary of Modena, who was also a Catholic. He

[1] A bill of toleration was finally passed by Parliament in 1689, which freed Dissenters from all penalties for failing to attend services in Anglican churches and allowed them to have their own meetings. Even Catholics, while not included in the act of toleration, were permitted to hold services undisturbed by the government (see p. 137, below).

was ready to reëstablish Catholicism in England regardless of what it might cost him. Mary, James's daughter by his first wife, had married her cousin, William III, Prince of Orange, the head of the United Netherlands.[1] The nation might have tolerated James so long as they could look forward to the accession of his Protestant daughter. But when a son was born to his Catholic second wife, and James showed unmistakably his purpose of favoring the Catholics, messengers were dispatched by a group of Protestants to William of Orange, asking him to come and rule over them.

The revolution of 1688 and the accession of William III, 1688–1702

William landed in November, 1688, and marched upon London, where he received general support from all the English Protestants, regardless of party. James II started to oppose William, but his army refused to fight and his courtiers deserted him. William was glad to forward James's flight to France, as he would hardly have known what to do with him had James insisted on remaining in the country. A convention, made up of members of Parliament and some prominent citizens, declared

[1] English monarchs from James I to George III:

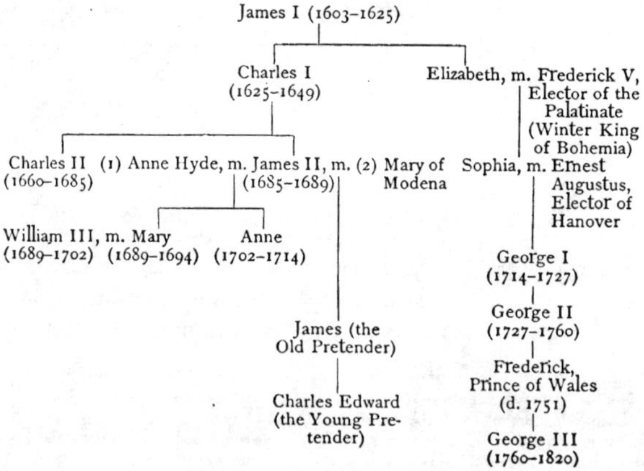

the throne vacant, on the ground that King James II, "by the advice of the Jesuits and other wicked persons, having violated the fundamental laws and withdrawn himself out of the kingdom, had abdicated the government."

This parliamentary convention then drew up a Declaration of Rights, which the next Parliament formally passed and made the law of the land. It is known as the Bill of Rights and is one of the most important documents in the whole history of

The Bill of Rights

FIG. 9. WILLIAM III

England. It forbade the king to suspend or violate the laws of the realm, to lay taxes or keep a standing army without the consent of Parliament, to interfere in any way with the freedom of speech in Parliament, to deny trial by jury to any one, to impose excessive fines or inflict cruel or unusual punishments, or to prevent his subjects from respectfully petitioning the throne. Then it went on to declare William and Mary, who accepted these conditions, king and queen of England. Should they have no children Mary's sister Anne was to succeed them.

Results of "the Glorious Revolution"

Thus "the Glorious Revolution" of 1688 was completed by an act in which it was freely admitted by the English king that his powers were strictly limited by Parliament and by certain ancient principles of government which protected the rights and liberty of Englishmen. Although the monarchs of England might still claim to be kings "by the grace of God," it was now perfectly clear that Parliament could replace one king by another if the nation so wished. Parliament, not the king, was unmistakably the supreme power in the land.

The Act of Settlement

The House of Hanover

This was illustrated a few years later when Parliament passed the Act of Settlement, according to the terms of which after Anne's death her cousin, Sophia of Hanover, or Sophia's heirs should succeed to the throne of Great Britain. This was to prevent any possibility of the return of James II or his sons.[1] Sophia's son ascended the English throne on Queen Anne's death, in 1714, as George I, and the Hanoverian line, which still reigns over Great Britain and her vast colonies, owe their kingdom to an act of Parliament.

The English freed from the fear of royal interference

The Act of Settlement was more than the mere adjustment of the question who should be England's sovereign. Like the Bill of Rights it contained a number of clauses further limiting the powers of the monarch and safeguarding "the liberties of Englishmen." The most important of these restrictions was, that judges should hold office for life, or during good behavior, and might only be removed by Parliament.[2] Thus the kings of England were forbidden to interfere, even indirectly, with the administration of justice.

[1] James II's son, "the Old Pretender," attempted to gain the English throne by means of an uprising in 1715. This was unsuccessful. His son, Prince Charles, known to his Scottish admirers as "Bonnie Prince Charlie," ventured to invade England by way of Scotland in 1745. He was completely defeated at Culloden Moor.

[2] This is one of the most important differences between the English and American constitutions. In the United States judges are usually elected for a term of years, not appointed for life. Those of the Supreme Court form an exception. There is a feeling among certain reformers in the United States that the English principle should be introduced, and that it would increase the independence of the judges.

Section 7. Nature of the English Constitution

The English constitution an unwritten one

It was through the passing by Parliament of acts such as those mentioned in the preceding section that the English constitution was gradually given the shape which it still retains. Unlike modern written constitutions, such as most civilized countries have to-day, the English constitution is unwritten. Its provisions have never been brought together in any one solemn document, such as the Constitution of the United States. It is made up of the various principles of government stated in the Bill of Rights, the Act of Settlement, and other important acts of Parliament, together with the various practices and customs that have grown up. Some of these practices reach back to the Middle Ages, for the English people do not change them so long as they can be made to work. This is due to a great respect for precedent — that is to say, for what has been done in the past; and it serves to give a certain quaintness to the English government, as seen, for instance, in the gray wigs still worn by the judges. But when the methods of the past finally become too clumsy, or stand in the way of important reform, they will be given up and a new precedent will be established for the guidance of future generations.

Love of precedent

The Mutiny Act and the annual Army Bill

Some important changes in the English constitution have come about almost incidentally. For instance, early in the reign of William and Mary there was a mutiny in the army. Parliament did not wish to give the new king unlimited control over the troops in putting down the mutiny lest he might perhaps put himself at the head of a standing army and renew a danger that had shown itself under the Stuarts. So Parliament gave the king control over the army for the following six months only. Later, Parliament got in the habit of extending the king's control over the army for a year at a time; each year it must still be renewed, by passing a new law called the Army Bill.

The civil list and budget

The source of Parliament's power lay, as we have seen, in its right to hold the purse string. The principle of "no taxation without consent of Parliament" was reasserted in the Bill of Rights. In carrying out this principle, Parliament divided the expenses of the State into two parts. The regular expenses of running the government (with the exception of the army and navy) and of maintaining the royal household were drawn up in a so-called "civil list." The amounts to be paid were fixed and Parliament did not reconsider them every year, unless there was some special cause for altering them. On the other hand, the extraordinary expenses had to be met annually by appropriations granted for the purpose by Parliament. These expenses were based upon a careful estimate called the *budget*. This businesslike way of voting money, foreshadowed under the Stuarts, was perfected under William III. A very important result of this method of extending the king's command over the army for no more than a year and of making appropriations annually was that the king was of course forced to summon Parliament each year to pass the necessary measures to keep the government going.[1]

Annual meetings of Parliament

Slight powers left the king

In ways such as this Parliament had become England's real ruler. Having gained power over the imposing of taxes and the spending of the money so raised, and having never let the army escape its control, it left the king little more than the ornaments of royalty and the right to advise, warn, and expostulate. Even the monarch's former right of vetoing bills passed by Parliament fell into disuse and was exercised for the last time by Queen Anne in 1707. Moreover, William III found out that since Parliament was the real ruler, he had to choose for his ministers men in whom the majority of the members of Parliament had confidence, otherwise they might refuse the necessary appropriations. The king was forced to select a ministry from the party which happened to be in power at the time. The

The cabinet

[1] As for the frequency with which there must be a new general election of the members of the House of Commons, it was provided by the Triennial Act of 1694 that the country should be permitted to reëlect the members every three years at least. This term was changed by the Septennial Act in 1716 and made seven years. Not until 1911 was this reduced by act of Parliament to five years.

old Cavalier party, now known as the Tories, had been much weakened by its sympathy with the unpopular cause of the Stuarts. Accordingly William selected his ministers from among the Whig party, as the old Roundheads were now called. The ministry, a group of a half dozen or so advisers, came to be called the *cabinet*. This cabinet was destined finally to become the directing force in the English government. How this came about and just what "cabinet government" means we shall see later (see below, p. 503). Tories and Whigs

QUESTIONS

SECTION 1. What was the great issue during the period of the Stuarts? What were the views of kingship held by James I? Mention some of the books of his time.

SECTION 2. What policy did Charles I adopt in regard to Parliament? What was the Petition of Right? What were the chief religious parties in England in the time of Charles I? Who was John Hampden? Mention some of the religious sects dating from that time which still exist in the United States.

SECTION 3. What measures did the Long Parliament take against the king? Describe the civil war. What led to the execution of Charles I?

SECTION 4. What were the chief events during Cromwell's administration? What are your impressions of Cromwell?

SECTION 5. What led to the restoration of the Stuarts? What was the attitude of Charles II toward the religious difficulties? Who were the Dissenters? What is *Habeas Corpus?* Why was it important?

SECTION 6. Why was James II unpopular? Give an account of the revolution which put William and Mary on the English throne. Give the provisions of the Bill of Rights. What is the claim of the Hanoverian line to the throne of England?

SECTION 7. What change did the Act of Settlement make in the administration of English judges? Compare the advantages of an appointed with those of an elective judiciary. How does Parliament exercise its control of the purse? What are the civil list and the budget? How did the cabinet arise? Describe its connection with party government.

CHAPTER II

FRANCE UNDER LOUIS XIV

Section 8. Position and Character of Louis XIV

France in the first half of the seventeenth century

After the wars of religion were over, the royal authority in France had been reëstablished by the wise conduct of Henry IV. Henry IV's son, Louis XIII, allowed his great minister, Richelieu, to rule, and Richelieu solidified the monarchy by depriving the Huguenots of the exceptional privileges granted to them for their protection by Henry IV; he also destroyed the fortified castles of the nobles, whose power had greatly increased during the turmoil of the Huguenot wars. Louis XIII died in 1643, leaving the throne to a mere child, Louis XIV. Richelieu, however, had been succeeded by a clever minister, Cardinal Mazarin, who was able to put down a last rising of the discontented nobility.

Louis XIV, 1643-1715

What Richelieu and Mazarin had done for the French monarchy

When Mazarin died, in 1661, he left the young monarch with a kingdom such as no previous French king had enjoyed. The nobles, who for centuries had disputed the power with the king, were no longer feudal lords but only courtiers. The Huguenots, whose claim to a place in the State beside the Catholics had led to the terrible civil wars of the sixteenth century, were reduced in numbers and no longer held fortified towns from which they could defy the king's officers. Richelieu and Mazarin had successfully taken a hand in the Thirty Years' War, and France had come out of it with enlarged territory and increased importance in European affairs.

The government of Louis XIV

Louis XIV carried the work of these great ministers still farther. He gave that form to the French monarchy which it retained until the French Revolution. He made himself the very mirror of kingship. His marvelous court at Versailles became the model and the despair of other less opulent and powerful princes, who accepted his theory of the absolute power of kings but could not afford to imitate his luxury. By his incessant wars he kept Europe in turmoil for over half a century. The distinguished generals who led his newly organized troops, and the

FIG. 10. LOUIS XIV

wily diplomats who arranged his alliances and negotiated his treaties, made France feared and respected by even the most powerful of the other European states.

Louis XIV had the same idea of kingship that James I had tried in vain to induce the English people to accept. God had given kings to men, and it was His will that monarchs should be regarded as His lieutenants and that all those subject to them should obey them absolutely, without asking any questions or making any criticisms; for in submitting to their

The theory of the "divine right of kings" in France

prince they were really submitting to God Himself. If the king were good and wise, his subjects should thank the Lord; if he proved foolish, cruel, or perverse, they must accept their evil ruler as a punishment which God had sent them for their sins. But in no case might they limit his power or rise against him.[1]

Different attitude of the English and French nations toward absolute monarchy

Louis XIV had two great advantages over James I. In the first place, the English nation has always shown itself far more reluctant than France to place absolute power in the hands of its rulers. By its Parliament, its courts, and its various declarations of the nation's rights, it had built up traditions which made it impossible for the Stuarts to establish their claim to be absolute rulers. In France, on the other hand, there was no Great Charter or Bill of Rights; the Estates General did not hold the purse strings, and the king was permitted to raise money without asking their permission or previously redressing the grievances which they chose to point out. They were therefore only summoned at irregular intervals. When Louis XIV took charge of the government, forty-seven years had passed without a meeting of the Estates General, and a century and a quarter was still to elapse before another call to the representatives of the nation was issued in 1789.

Moreover, the French people placed far more reliance upon a powerful king than the English, perhaps because they were not protected by the sea from their neighbors, as England was. On every side France had enemies ready to take advantage of any weakness or hesitation which might arise from dissension between a parliament and the king. So the French felt it best, on the whole, to leave all in the king's hands, even if they suffered at times from his tyranny.

Personal characteristics of Louis XIV

Louis had another great advantage over James. He was a handsome man, of elegant and courtly mien and the most exquisite perfection of manner; even when playing billiards

[1] Louis XIV does not appear to have himself used the famous expression "*I am the State*," usually attributed to him, but it exactly corresponds to his idea of the relation of the king and the State.

he is said to have retained an air of world mastery. The first of the Stuarts, on the contrary, was a very awkward man, whose slouching gait, intolerable manners, and pedantic conversation were utterly at variance with his lofty pretensions. Louis added, moreover, to his graceful exterior a sound judgment and quick apprehension. He said neither too much nor too little. He was, for a king, a hard worker and spent several hours each morning attending to the business of government.

FIG. 11. FAÇADE OF THE PALACE OF VERSAILLES

The strenuous life of a despotic ruler

It requires, in fact, a great deal of energy and application to be a real despot. In order thoroughly to understand and to solve the problems which constantly face the ruler of a great state, a monarch must, like Frederick the Great or Napoleon, rise early and toil late. Louis XIV was greatly aided by the able ministers who sat in his council, but he always retained for himself the place of first minister. He would never have consented to be dominated by an adviser as his father had been by Richelieu. "The profession of the king," he declared, "is great, noble, and delightful if one but feels equal to performing the duties which it involves" — and he never harbored a doubt that he himself was born for the business.

Section 9. How Louis encouraged Art and Literature

The king's palace at Versailles

Louis XIV was careful that his surroundings should suit the grandeur of his office. His court was magnificent beyond anything that had been dreamed of in the West. He had an enormous palace constructed at Versailles, just outside of Paris, with interminable halls and apartments and a vast garden

Fig. 12. One of the Vast Halls of Versailles

stretching away behind it. About this a town was laid out, where those who were privileged to be near his majesty or supply the wants of the royal court lived. This palace and its outlying buildings, including two or three less gorgeous residences for the king when he occasionally tired of the ceremony of Versailles, probably cost the nation about a hundred million dollars, in spite of the fact that thousands of peasants and soldiers were forced to turn to and work without pay. The furnishings and decorations were as rich and costly as the palace was splendid and still fill the visitor with wonder. For over a century Versailles continued to be the home of the French kings and the seat of their government.

This splendor and luxury helped to attract the nobility, who no longer lived on their estates in well-fortified castles, planning how they might escape the royal control. They now dwelt in the effulgence of the king's countenance. They saw him to bed at night and in stately procession they greeted him in the

Life at Louis XIV's court

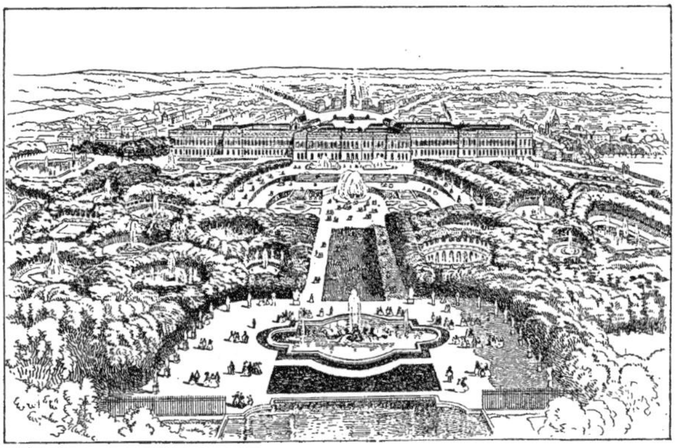

FIG. 13. FAÇADE OF THE PALACE OF VERSAILLES TOWARD THE GARDENS

morning. It was deemed a high honor to hand him his shirt as he was being dressed or, at dinner, to provide him with a fresh napkin. Only by living close to the king could the courtiers hope to gain favors, pensions, and lucrative offices for themselves and their friends, and perhaps occasionally to exercise some little influence upon the policy of the government. For they were now entirely dependent upon the good will of their monarch.

The reforms of Colbert

The reforms which Louis XIV carried out in the earlier part of his reign were largely the work of the great financier Colbert, to whom France still looks back with gratitude. He early discovered that the king's officials were stealing and wasting vast sums. The offenders were arrested and forced to disgorge, and a new system of bookkeeping was introduced, similar to that employed by business men. He then turned his attention to increasing the manufactures of France by establishing new industries and seeing that the older ones kept to a high standard, which would make French goods sell readily in foreign markets. He argued justly that if foreigners could be induced to buy French goods, these sales would bring gold and silver into the country and so enrich it. He made rigid rules as to the width and quality of cloths which the manufacturers might produce and the dyes which they might use. He even reorganized the old medieval guilds; for through them the government could keep its eye on all the manufacturing that was done; this would have been far more difficult if every one had been free to carry on any trade which he might choose.

Art and literature in the reign of Louis XIV

It was, however, as a patron of art and literature that Louis XIV gained much of his celebrity. Molière, who was at once a playwright and an actor, delighted the court with comedies in which he delicately satirized the foibles of his time. Corneille, who had gained renown by the great tragedy of *The Cid* in Richelieu's time, found a worthy successor in Racine, the most distinguished, perhaps, of French tragic poets. The charming letters of Madame de Sévigné are models of prose style and serve at the same time to give us a glimpse into the more refined life of the court circle. In the famous memoirs of Saint-Simon, the weaknesses of the king, as well as the numberless intrigues of the courtiers, are freely exposed with inimitable skill and wit.

The government fosters the development of the French language and literature

Men of letters were generously aided by the king with pensions. Colbert encouraged the French Academy, which had been created by Richelieu. This body gave special attention to making the French tongue more eloquent and expressive by determining what words should be used. It is now the greatest honor that a Frenchman can obtain to be made one of the forty members of this association. A magazine which still exists, the *Journal des Savants*, was founded for the promotion of science at this time. Colbert had an astronomical observatory built at Paris; and the Royal Library, which only possessed about sixteen thousand volumes, began to grow into that great collection of two and a half million volumes — by far the largest in existence — which to-day attracts scholars to Paris from all parts of the world. In short, Louis XIV and his ministers believed one of the chief objects of any government to be the promotion of art, literature, and science, and the example they set has been followed by almost every modern state.

Section 10. Louis XIV attacks his Neighbors

Louis XIV's warlike enterprises

Unfortunately for France, the king's ambitions were by no means exclusively peaceful. Indeed, he regarded his wars as his chief glory. He employed a carefully reorganized army and the skill of his generals in a series of inexcusable attacks on his neighbors, in which he finally squandered all that Colbert's economies had accumulated and led France to the edge of financial ruin.

He aims to restore the "natural boundaries" of France

Louis XIV's predecessors had had, on the whole, little time to think of conquest. They had first to consolidate their realms and gain the mastery of their feudal dependents, who shared the power with them; then the claims of the English Edwards and Henrys had to be met, and the French provinces freed from their clutches; lastly, the great religious dispute was only settled after many years of disintegrating civil war. But Louis XIV was now at liberty to look about him and consider how he might best realize the dream of his ancestors and perhaps reëstablish the ancient boundaries which Cæsar reported that the Gauls had occupied. The "natural limits" of France appeared to be the Rhine on the north and east, the Jura Mountains and the Alps on the southeast, and to the south the Mediterranean and the Pyrenees. Richelieu had believed that it was the chief end of his ministry to restore to France the boundaries determined for it by nature. Mazarin had labored hard to win Savoy on the east and Nice on the Mediterranean coast and to reach the Rhine on the north. Before his death France at least gained Alsace and reached the Pyrenees, "which," as the treaty with Spain says (1659), "formerly divided the Gauls from Spain."

Louis XIV lays claim to the Spanish Netherlands

Louis XIV first turned his attention to the conquest of the Spanish Netherlands, to which he laid claim through his wife, the elder sister of the Spanish king, Charles II (1665–1700). In 1667 he surprised Europe by publishing a little treatise in which he set forth his claims not only to the Spanish Netherlands, but even to the whole Spanish monarchy. By confounding the kingdom of France with the old empire of the Franks he could maintain that the people of the Netherlands were his subjects.

The invasion of the Netherlands, 1667

Louis placed himself at the head of the army which he had re-formed and reorganized, and announced that he was to undertake a "journey," as if his invasion was only an expedition into another part of his undisputed realms. He easily took a number of towns on the border of the Netherlands and then turned south and completely conquered Franche-Comté. This was an outlying province of Spain, isolated from her other lands, and a most tempting morsel for the hungry king of France.[1]

These conquests alarmed Europe, and especially Holland, which could not afford to have the barrier between it and France removed, for Louis XIV would be an uncomfortable neighbor. A Triple Alliance, composed of Holland, England, and Sweden, was accordingly organized to induce France to make peace with Spain. Louis contented himself for the moment with the dozen border towns that he had taken and which Spain ceded to him on condition that he would return Franche-Comté.

[1] See Part I, pp. 573 and 649.

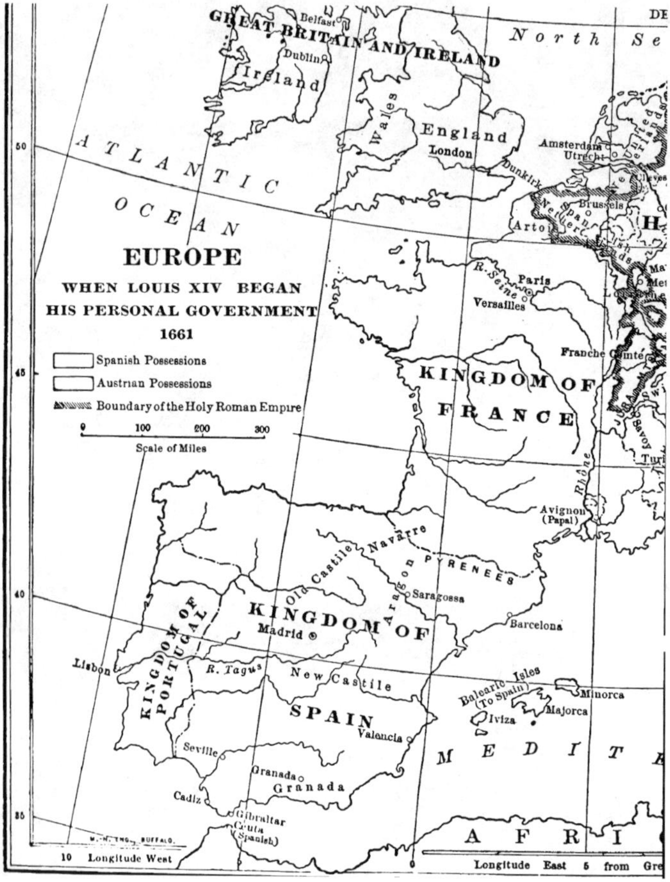
EUROPE
WHEN LOUIS XIV BEGAN
HIS PERSONAL GOVERNMENT
1661
Spanish Possessions
Austrian Possessions
Boundary of the Holy Roman Empire
0 100 200 300
Scale of Miles
GREAT BRITAIN AND IRELAND
Belfast
Dublin
Ireland
Wales
England
London
North Se
ATLANTIC
OCEAN
Amsterdam
Utrecht
Dunkirk
Brussels
Artois
Paris
R. Seine
Versailles
Franche Comté
KINGDOM OF FRANCE
Rhône
Avignon (Papal)
Navarre
PYRENEES
Old Castile
Aragon
Saragossa
Barcelona
KINGDOM OF
Madrid
KINGDOM OF PORTUGAL
Lisbon
R. Tagus
New Castile
SPAIN
Valencia
Balearic Isles (To Spain)
Minorca
Majorca
Iviza
Seville
Granada
Granada
Cadiz
Gibraltar
Ceuta (Spanish)
MEDIT
AFRI
10 Longitude West
Longitude East 5 from Gre

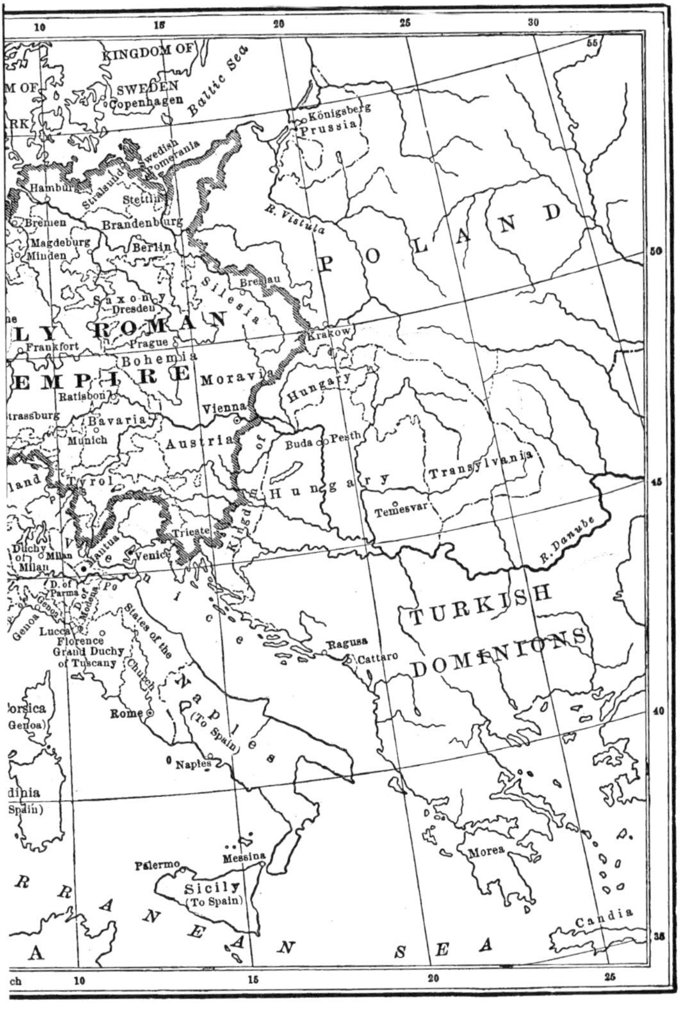
KINGDOM OF
SWEDEN
M OF
RK
Copenhagen
Baltic Sea
Königsberg
Prussia
Stralsund
Swedish Pomerania
Hamburg
Stettin
Bremen
Brandenburg
Magdeburg
Minden
Berlin
R. Vistula
POLAND
Breslau
Silesia
Saxony
Dresden
LY ROMAN
EMPIRE
Frankfort
Prague
Bohemia
Krakow
Moravia
Hungary
Ratisbon
Vienna
trassburg
Bavaria
Munich
Austria
Kingd. of
Buda
Pesth
Tyrol
Hungary
Transylvania
Temesvar
Trieste
R. Danube
Duchy of Milan
Milan
Mantua
Venice
Venice
D. of Parma
Po
D. of Modena
Genoa
States of the Church
Lucca
Florence
Grand Duchy of Tuscany
TURKISH
DOMINIONS
Ragusa
Cattaro
Rome
Naples
(To Spain)
Naples
orsica
Genoa)
dinia
Spain)
Palermo
Messina
Sicily
(To Spain)
Morea
Candia
R R A N E A N SEA
A
10
15
20
25
30
55
50
45
40
35
ch

The success with which Holland had held her own against the navy of England and brought the proud king of France to a halt produced an elation on the part of that tiny country which was very aggravating to Louis XIV. He was thoroughly vexed that he should have been blocked by so trifling an obstacle as Dutch intervention. He consequently conceived a strong dislike for the United Provinces, which was increased by the protection that they afforded to writers who annoyed him with their attacks. He broke up the Triple Alliance by inducing Charles II of England to conclude a treaty which pledged England to help France in a new war against the Dutch.

Louis XIV breaks up the Triple Alliance and allies himself with Charles II of England

Louis XIV then startled Europe again by seizing the duchy of Lorraine, which brought him to the border of Holland. At the head of a hundred thousand men he crossed the Rhine (1672) and easily conquered southern Holland. For the moment the Dutch cause appeared to be lost. But William of Orange showed the spirit of his great ancestor William the Silent; the sluices in the dikes were opened and the country flooded, so the French army was checked before it could take Amsterdam and advance into the north. The Emperor sent an army against Louis, and England deserted him and made peace with Holland.

Louis XIV's invasion of Holland, 1672

When a general peace was concluded at the end of six years, the chief provisions were that Holland should be left intact, and that France should this time retain Franche-Comté, which had been conquered by Louis XIV in person. This bit of the Burgundian heritage thus became at last a part of France, after France and Spain had quarreled over it for a century and a half. For the ten years following there was no open war, but Louis seized the important free city of Strassburg and made many other less conspicuous but equally unwarranted additions to his territory. The Emperor was unable to do more than protest against these outrageous encroachments, for he was fully occupied with the Turks, who had just laid siege to Vienna.

Peace of Nimwegen, 1678

Louis XIV seizes Strassburg

Section ii. Louis XIV and his Protestant Subjects

Situation of the Huguenots at the beginning of Louis XIV's reign

Louis XIV exhibited as woeful a want of statesmanship in the treatment of his Protestant subjects as in the prosecution of disastrous wars. The Huguenots, deprived of their former military and political power, had turned to manufacture, trade, and banking; "as rich as a Huguenot" had become a proverb in France. There were perhaps a million of them among fifteen million Frenchmen, and they undoubtedly formed by far the most thrifty and enterprising part of the nation. The Catholic clergy, however, did not cease to urge the complete suppression of heresy.

Louis's policy of suppression

Louis XIV had scarcely taken the reins of government into his own hands before the perpetual nagging and injustice to which the Protestants had been subjected at all times took a more serious form. Upon one pretense or another their churches were demolished. Children were authorized to renounce Protestantism when they reached the age of seven. Rough dragoons were quartered upon the Huguenots with the hope that the insulting behavior of the soldiers might frighten the heretics into accepting the religion of the king.

Revocation of the Edict of Nantes and its results

At last Louis XIV was led by his officials to believe that practically all the Huguenots had been converted by these harsh measures. In 1685, therefore, he revoked the Edict of Nantes, and the Protestants thereby became outlaws and their ministers subject to the death penalty. Even liberal-minded Catholics, like the kindly writer of fables, La Fontaine, and the charming letter writer, Madame de Sévigné, hailed this reëstablishment of "religious unity" with delight. They believed that only an insignificant and seditious remnant still clung to the beliefs of Calvin. But there could have been no more serious mistake. Thousands of the Huguenots succeeded in eluding the vigilance of the royal officials and fled, some to England, some to Prussia, some to America, carrying with them their skill and industry to strengthen France's rivals. This was the last great and terrible example in western Europe of that fierce religious intolerance which had produced the Albigensian Crusade, the Spanish Inquisition, and the Massacre of St. Bartholomew.

Louis XIV now set his heart upon conquering the Palatinate, a Protestant land, to which he easily discovered that he had a claim. The rumor of his intention and the indignation occasioned in Protestant countries by the revocation of the Edict of Nantes resulted in an alliance against the French king headed by William of Orange. Louis speedily justified the suspicions of Europe by a frightful devastation of the Palatinate, burning whole towns and destroying many castles, including the exceptionally beautiful one of the elector at Heidelberg. Ten years later, however, Louis agreed to a peace which put things back as they were before the struggle began. He was preparing for the final and most ambitious undertaking of his life, which precipitated the longest and bloodiest war of all his warlike reign. Louis's operations in the Rhenish Palatinate

Section 12. War of the Spanish Succession

The king of Spain, Charles II, was childless and brotherless, and Europe had long been discussing what would become of his vast realms when his sickly existence should come to an end. Louis XIV had married one of his sisters, and the Emperor, Leopold I, another, and these two ambitious rulers had been considering for some time how they might divide the Spanish possessions between the Bourbons and the Hapsburgs. But when Charles II died, in 1700, it was discovered that he had left a will in which he made Louis's younger grandson, Philip, the heir to his twenty-two crowns, but on the condition that France and Spain should never be united. The question of the Spanish succession

It was a weighty question whether Louis XIV should permit his grandson to accept this hazardous honor. Should Philip become king of Spain, Louis and his family would control all of southwestern Europe from Holland to Sicily, as well as a great Louis's grandson, Philip, becomes king of Spain part of North and South America. This would mean the establishment of an empire more powerful than that of Charles V. It was clear that the disinherited Emperor and the ever-watchful William of Orange, who had now become king of England, would never permit this unprecedented extension of French influence. They had already shown themselves ready to make great sacrifices in order to check far less serious aggressions on the part of the French king. Nevertheless, family pride and personal ambition led Louis criminally to risk the welfare of his country. He accepted the will and informed the Spanish ambassador at the French court that he might salute Philip V as his new king. The leading French newspaper of the time boldly proclaimed that the Pyrenees were no more.

The War of the Spanish Succession

King William soon succeeded in forming a new Grand Alliance (1701) in which Louis's old enemies, England, Holland, and the Emperor, were the most important members. William himself died just as hostilities were beginning, but the long War of the Spanish Succession was carried on vigorously by the great English general, the Duke of Marlborough, and the Austrian commander, Eugene of Savoy. The conflict was more general than the Thirty Years' War; even in America there was fighting between French and English colonists, which passes in American histories under the name of Queen Anne's War. All the more important battles went against the French, and after ten years of war, which was rapidly ruining the country by the destruction of its people and its wealth, Louis XIV was willing to consider some compromise, and after long discussion a peace was arranged in 1713.

The Treaty of Utrecht, 1713

The Treaty of Utrecht changed the map of Europe as no previous treaty had done, not even that of Westphalia. Each of the chief combatants got his share of the Spanish booty over which they had been fighting. The Bourbon Philip V was permitted to retain Spain and its colonies on condition that the Spanish and French crowns should never rest on the same head. To Austria fell the Spanish Netherlands, hereafter called the Austrian Netherlands, which continued to form a barrier between Holland and France. Holland received certain fortresses to make its position still more secure. The Spanish possessions in Italy, that is, Naples and Milan, were also given to Austria, and in this way Austria got the hold on Italy which it retained until 1866. From France, England acquired Nova Scotia, Newfoundland, and the Hudson Bay region, and so began the expulsion of the French from North America. Besides these American provinces she received the rock and fortress of Gibraltar, which still gives her command of the narrow entrance to the Mediterranean.

The development of international law

The period of Louis XIV is remarkable for the development of international law. The incessant wars and great alliances embracing several powers made increasingly clear the need of well-defined rules governing states in their relations with one another both in peace and in war. It was of the utmost importance to determine, for instance, the rights of ambassadors and of the vessels of neutral powers not engaged in the war, and what should be considered fair conduct in warfare and in the treatment of prisoners.

Grotius's *War and Peace*

The first great systematic treatise on international law was published by Grotius in 1625, when the horrors of the Thirty Years' War were impressing men's minds with the necessity of finding some means other than war of settling disputes between nations. While the rules laid down by Grotius and later writers have, as we must sadly admit, by no means put an end to war, they have prevented many conflicts by increasing the ways in which nations may come to an understanding with one another through their ambassadors without recourse to arms.

Louis XIV outlived his son and his grandson and left a sadly demoralized kingdom to his five-year-old great-grandson, Louis XV (1715–1774). The national treasury was depleted, the people were reduced in numbers and were in a miserable state, and the army, once the finest in Europe, was in no condition to gain further victories.

QUESTIONS

SECTION 8. What did Richelieu accomplish in strengthening the French monarchy? What were Louis XIV's ideas of kingship? Why did the French view the "divine right of kings" differently from the English? Contrast Louis XIV with James I.

SECTION 9. Describe the palace of Versailles. What were the chief reforms of Colbert? Mention some of the great writers of Louis XIV's time. How did the government aid scholarship and science?

SECTION 10. What led Louis XIV to attack his neighbors? What are the "natural" boundaries of France? What country did Louis first attack? What additions did he make to French territory?

SECTION 11. What was the policy of Louis XIV toward the Huguenots? Who were Louis XIV's chief enemies?

SECTION 12. What were the causes of the War of the Spanish Succession? What were the chief changes provided for in the Treaty of Utrecht?

CHAPTER III

THE RISE OF RUSSIA AND PRUSSIA; AUSTRIA

SECTION 13. PETER THE GREAT PLANS TO MAKE RUSSIA A EUROPEAN POWER

While much was said in the previous volume of France, England, Spain, the Netherlands, the Holy Roman Empire, and the Italian states, it was not necessary hitherto to speak of Russia and Prussia. In the eighteenth and nineteenth centuries these states, however, played a great part in European affairs, and in order to understand how they grew up, we must turn from the Rhine and the Pyrenees to the shores of the Baltic and the vast plains of eastern Europe. While the long War of the Spanish Succession had been in progress, due to Louis XIV's anxiety to add Spain to the possessions of his family, another conflict was raging in the north, and changes were taking place there comparable in importance to those which were ratified by the Peace of Utrecht. Russia, which had hitherto faced eastward, was turning toward the west, upon which she was destined to exert an ever-increasing influence. In the newly founded kingdom of Prussia Frederick the Great was gathering those forces which under his leadership became a menace to the peace of Europe.

The Slavic peoples of Europe and the extent of Russia

There has been no occasion in dealing with the situation in western Europe to speak heretofore of the Slavic peoples, to which the Russians, as well as the Poles, Bohemians, Bulgarians, and other nations of eastern Europe belong, although together they constitute the most numerous race in Europe. Not until the opening of the eighteenth century did Russia begin to take an active part in western affairs. Now she is one of the most important factors in the politics of the world. Of the realms of the Tsar, that portion which lies in Europe exceeded in extent the territories of all the other rulers of the Continent put together, and yet European Russia comprised scarcely a quarter of the Tsar's whole dominion, which embraced northern and central Asia, extended to the Pacific Ocean, and formed all together an empire covering about three times the area of the United States.

Beginnings of Russia

The beginnings of the Russian state fall in the ninth century; some of the Northmen invaded the districts to the east of the Baltic, while their relatives were causing grievous trouble in France and England. It is generally supposed that one of their leaders, Rurik, was the first to consolidate the Slavic tribes about Novgorod into a sort of state in 862. Rurik's successor extended the bounds of the new empire so as to include the important town of Kiev on the Dnieper. The word "Russia" is probably derived from *Rous*, the name given by the neighboring Finns to the Norman adventurers. Before the end of the tenth century the Greek form of Christianity was introduced and the Russian ruler was baptized. The frequent intercourse with Constantinople might have led to rapid advance in civilization had it not been for a great disaster which put Russia back for centuries.

The Tartar invasion in the thirteenth century

Russia is geographically nothing more than an extension of the vast plain of northern Asia, which the Russians were destined finally to conquer. It was therefore exposed to the great invasion of the Tartars, or Mongols, who swept in from the East in the thirteenth century. The powerful Tartar ruler, Genghis Khan (1162–1227), conquered northern China and central Asia, and the mounted hordes of his successors crossed into Europe and overran Russia, which had fallen apart into numerous principalities. The Russian princes became the dependents of the Great Khan, and had frequently to seek his far-distant court, some three thousand miles away, where he freely disposed of both their crowns and their heads. The

NORTHEASTERN EUROPE In the time of PETER THE GREAT
0 50 100 200 300 400
SCALE OF MILES
Territory added to Russia by Peter the Great
NOTE: The boundaries of the various powers are of the year of accession of Peter the Great
KINGDOM OF NORWAY
KINGDOM OF SWEDEN
FINLAND
KARELIA
INGRIA
ESTHONIA
LIVONIA
Courland
KINGDOM OF DENMARK
KINGDOM OF SCOTLAND
KINGDOM OF ENGLAND
NORTH SEA
BALTIC SEA
White Sea
Gulf of Bothnia
Gulf of Finland
Lake Onega
Lake Ladoga
Peipus L.
RUSSIA
Archangel
Dvina
Volga
Vyatka
Perm
Nizhni Novgorod
Kasan
Moscow
Tver
Novgorod
St. Petersburg
Narva
Viborg
Pskov
Dorpat
Riga
Reval
Helsingfors
Abo
Nystadt
ÅLAND IS.
DAGO
OESEL
GOTLAND
ÖLAND
BORNHOLM
Stockholm
Upsala
Fredrickshald
Christiania
Trondhjem
Bergen
Kalmar
Halland
Skane
Lund
Copenhagen
Holstein
Hamburg
Bremen
Stralsund
Wismar
Pomerania
Stettin
Danzig
Königsberg
Prussia
Memel
Düna
Vilna
Grodno
Mohilev
Smolensk
Ryazan
Voronesh
Saratov
Uralsk (Yaik)
Ural
KINGDOM OF POLAND
Lithuania
Thorn
Posen
Pultusk
Brest Litovsk
Warsaw
Lublin
Klissow
Breslau
Silesia
Oder
Elbe
BRANDENBURG
Berlin
Saxony
Prague
Bohemia
HOLY ROMAN EMPIRE
Frankfort
Rhine
Strassburg
Munich
Danube
Austria
Vienna
AUSTRIAN POSSESSIONS
HUNGARY
Austrian 1699
Budapest
Krakow
Lemberg
Podolia
Dniester
Bessarabia
Moldavia
Pruth
Transylvania
Banat
Belgrade
Wallachia
Bucharest
TURKISH DOMINIONS
Bender
Bug
Dnieper
Kiev
Chernigov
Pultowa
Don
Cherkask
Azov
Crimea
BLACK SEA
Stavropol
Astrakhan
CASPIAN SEA
NETHERLANDS
Brussels
Paris
KINGDOM OF FRANCE
Lyon
Marseille
SWITZERLAND
Milan
Venice
Longitude 10° East from 15° Greenwich 20°
THE MATTHEWS-NORTHRUP WORKS.

Tartars exacted tribute of the Russians, but left them undisturbed in their laws and religion.

Influence of the Tartar occupation on manners and customs

Of the Russian princes who went to prostrate themselves at the foot of the Great Khan's throne, none made a more favorable impression upon him than did the prince of Moscow, in whose favor the Khan was wont to decide all cases of dispute between the prince and his rivals. When the Mongol power had begun to decline in strength and the princes of Moscow had grown stronger, they ventured, in 1480, to kill the Mongol ambassadors sent to demand tribute, and thus freed themselves from the Mongol yoke. In 1547 Ivan the Terrible assumed the imposing title of "Tsar."[1] But the Tartar occupation had left its mark, for the princes of Moscow imitated the Khans rather than the western rulers, of whom, in fact, they knew nothing. The costumes and etiquette of the court were Asiatic. The Russian armor suggested that of the Chinese, and their head-dress was a turban.

Ivan the Terrible assumes the title of "Tsar"

Peter the Great (1672–1725)

At the time of Peter's accession, Russia, which had grown greatly under Ivan the Terrible and other enterprising rulers, still had no outlet to the sea. In manners and customs the kingdom was still Asiatic, and its government that of a Tartar prince. Peter had no quarrel with the despotic power which fell to him and which all the Russian monarchs exercised. But he knew that Russia was very much behind the rest of Europe, and that his crudely equipped soldiers could never make head against the well-armed and disciplined troops of the West. He had no seaport and no ships, without which Russia could never hope to take part in the world's affairs. His two great tasks were, therefore, to introduce western habits and to "make a window," as he expressed it, through which Russia might look abroad.[2]

1 The word "Tsar" or "Czar" is derived from "Cæsar" (German, *Kaiser*), that is, emperor, but was used in Slavic books for the title of the kings of antiquity as well as for Roman emperors. The Tsar was also called "Autocrat of all the Russias."

2 See Robinson and Beard, *Readings in Modern European History*, Vol. I, pp. 57 ff. In all subsequent notes this is the source book referred to as *Readings*.

Peter's travels in Europe

In the year 1697–1698, Peter himself visited Germany, Holland, and England, with a view to investigating every art and science of the West, as well as the most approved methods of manufacture, from the making of a man-of-war to the etching of an engraving. Nothing escaped the keen eyes of this rude, half-savage northern giant. For a week he put on the wide

FIG. 14. PETER THE GREAT

Peter was a tall, strong man, impulsive in action, sometimes vulgarly familiar, but always retaining an air of command. When he visited Louis XV of France in 1717, he astonished the court by taking the seven-year-old king under the arms and hoisting him up in the air to kiss him. The courtiers were much shocked at his conduct

breeches of a Dutch laborer and worked in the shipyard at Saardam near Amsterdam. In England, Holland, and Germany he engaged artisans, scientific men, architects, ship captains, and those versed in artillery and the training of troops, all of whom he took back with him to aid in the reform and development of Russia so that it should be able to take its place in European history.

He was called home by the revolt of the royal guard, who had allied themselves with the very large party of nobles and churchmen who were horrified at Peter's desertion of the habits and customs of his forefathers. They hated what they called "German ideas," such as short coats, tobacco smoking, and beardless faces. The clergy even suggested that Peter was perhaps Antichrist. Peter took a fearful revenge upon the rebels, and is said to have himself cut off the heads of many of them.

Suppression of revolt against foreign ideas

Peter's reforms extended through his whole reign. He made his people give up their cherished oriental beards and long flowing garments. He forced the women of the better class, who had been kept in a sort of oriental harem, to come out and meet the men in social assemblies, such as were common in the West. He invited foreigners to settle in Russia, and insured them protection, privileges, and the free exercise of their religion. He sent young Russians abroad to study. He reorganized the government officials on the model of a western kingdom, and made over his army in the same way.[1]

Peter's reform measures

Finding that the old capital of Moscow clung persistently to its ancient habits, he prepared to build a new capital for his new Russia. He selected for this purpose a bit of territory on the Baltic which he had conquered from Sweden, — very marshy, it is true, — where he hoped to construct Russia's first real port. Here he built St. Petersburg at enormous expense and colonized it with Russians and foreigners.

Founding of a new capital, St. Petersburg

In his ambition to get to the sea, Peter naturally collided with Sweden, to which the provinces between Russia and the Baltic belonged. Never had Sweden, or any other country, had a more warlike king than the one with whom Peter had to contend — the youthful prodigy, Charles XII. When Charles came to the throne in 1697 he was only fifteen years old, and it seemed to the natural enemies of Sweden an auspicious time to profit by the supposed weakness of the boy ruler. So a union was formed between Denmark, Poland, and Russia, with

The military prowess of Charles XII of Sweden

[1] See *Readings*, Vol. I, pp. 61 ff.

the object of increasing their territories at Sweden's expense. But Charles turned out to be a second Alexander the Great in military prowess. He astonished Europe by promptly besieging Copenhagen and forcing the king of Denmark to sign a treaty of peace. He then turned like lightning against Peter, who was industriously besieging Narva, and with eight thousand Swedes

FIG. 15. CHARLES XII OF SWEDEN

wiped out an army of fifty thousand Russians (1700). Lastly he thoroughly defeated the king of Poland.

Defeat and death of Charles XII

Though Charles was a remarkable military leader, he was a foolish ruler. He undertook to wrest Poland from its king, to whom he attributed the formation of the league against him. He had a new king crowned at Warsaw, whom he at last succeeded in getting recognized. He then turned his attention to Peter, who had meanwhile been conquering the Baltic provinces. This time fortune turned against the Swedes. The long march through Russia proved as fatal to them as to

Napoleon a century later, Charles XII being totally defeated in the battle of Pultowa (1709). He fled to Turkey, where he spent some years in vainly urging the Sultan to attack Peter. Returning at last to his own kingdom, which he had utterly neglected for years, he was killed in 1718 while besieging a town.

Russia acquires the Baltic provinces and attempts to get a footing on the Black Sea

Soon after Charles's death a treaty was concluded between Sweden and Russia by which Russia gained Livonia, Esthonia, and the other Swedish provinces at the eastern end of the Baltic. Peter had made less successful attempts to get a footing on the Black Sea. He had first taken Azof (which he soon lost during the war with Sweden), and then captured several towns on the Caspian. It had become evident that if the Turks should be driven out of Europe, Russia would be a mighty rival of the western powers in the division of the spoils.

For a generation after the death of Peter the Great, Russia fell into the hands of incompetent rulers. It appears again as a European state when the great Catherine II, of whose reforms we shall read further on,[1] came to the throne in 1762. From that time on, the western powers had always to consider the vast Slavic empire in all their great struggles. They had also to consider a new kingdom in northern Germany, Prussia, which was destined in time to become a menace to the whole world.

Section 14. Rise of Prussia

The House of Hohenzollern

The electorate of Brandenburg had figured on the map of Europe for centuries, and there was no particular reason to suppose that it was one day to become the dominant state in Germany. Early in the fifteenth century the old line of electors had died out, and the impecunious Emperor Sigismund had sold the electorate to a hitherto inconspicuous house, the Hohenzollerns, who are known to us now through such names as those of Frederick the Great, William I, the first German emperor, and his grandson, William II. It has always been the

[1] See below, p. 163.

boast of the Hohenzollern family that practically every one of its reigning members added something to what his ancestors handed down to him. The first great extension took place in 1614, when the elector of Brandenburg inherited Cleves and Mark, and thus got his first hold on the Rhine district.

FIG. 16. THE OLD ROYAL CASTLE AT KÖNIGSBERG

This imposing castle at the old capital of Prussia dates from the days of the warring knights. It was reconstructed in the sixteenth and eighteenth centuries

What was quite as important, he won, four years later, far to the east, the duchy of Prussia, which was separated from Brandenburg by Polish territory. Prussia was originally the name of a region on the Baltic inhabited by heathen Slavs. These had been conquered in the thirteenth century by one of the orders of crusading knights, who, when the conquest of the Holy Land was abandoned, looked about for other occupations. The territory of this Teutonic Order, as it was called, was largely settled with German colonists, but the warlike kings of Poland had conquered the western portion of it (West Prussia) in the early fifteenth century and forced the knights to acknowledge Polish sovereignty over the rest of it. In Luther's day (1525) the knights, headed by the Grand Master, a Hohenzollern, accepted Protestantism and dissolved their order. They then formed their lands into the duchy of Prussia, and their Grand Master, a relative of the elector of Brandenburg, became the first duke, under the suzerainty of the king of Poland. About a hundred years later (1618) this branch of the Hohenzollerns died out, and the duchy then fell to the elector of Brandenburg.

The territories of the Great Elector (1640–1688)

Notwithstanding this substantial territorial gain, there was little promise that the hitherto obscure electorate would ever become a dangerous power when, in 1640, Frederick William, known as the Great Elector, came to his inheritance. His territories were scattered from the Rhine to the Vistula, his army was of small account, and his authority disputed by powerful nobles and local assemblies. The center of his domain was Brandenburg. Far to the west was Mark, bordering on the Rhine valley, and Cleves, lying on both banks of that river. Far to the east, beyond the Vistula, was the duchy of Prussia, outside the borders of the Empire and subject to the overlordship of the king of Poland.

Character of the Great Elector

Frederick William was, however, well fitted for the task of welding these domains into a powerful state. He was coarse by nature, heartless in destroying opponents, treacherous in his diplomatic negotiations, and entirely devoid of the culture which distinguished Louis XIV and his court. He set resolutely to work to build up a great army, destroy the local assemblies in his provinces, place all government in the hands of his officials, and add new territories to his patrimony.

The Great Elector makes important gains in territory

In all of these undertakings he was largely successful. By shrewd tactics during the closing days of the Thirty Years' War he managed to secure, by the Treaty of Westphalia, the territories of the bishoprics of Minden and Halberstadt and the duchy of Farther Pomerania, which gave him a good shore line on the Baltic. He also forced Poland to surrender her overlordship of the duchy of Prussia and thus made himself a duke independent of the Empire.

Reforms of the Great Elector

Knowing that the interests of his house depended on military strength, he organized, in spite of the protests of the taxpayers, an army out of all proportion to the size and wealth of his dominions. He reformed the system of administration and succeeded in creating an absolute monarchy on the model furnished by his contemporary, Louis XIV. He joined England and Holland in their alliances against Louis, and the army of Brandenburg began to be known and feared.

In short, Elector Frederick William of Brandenburg laid the foundations for that autocratic, militaristic Prussia which did not

Territories of the Great Elector of Brandenburg

Militaristic Prussia founded by the Great Elector

fully exhibit its hateful ideas of merciless aggression and heartless ambition until the Great War of 1914. Through many vicissitudes under its Hohenzollern rulers, some of them warlike and ruthless, some of them feeble and timid, Prussia gradually added to its territory by seizing that of its neighbors until it brought all of Germany under its domination. Then its ruling class began, as we shall see, to dream of nothing less than a Middle European Empire which Germany should control in her own interests.

Brandenburg becomes the kingdom of Prussia, 1701

It was accordingly a dangerous legacy which the Great Elector left in 1688 to his son, Frederick III, and although the career of the latter was by no means as brilliant as that of his father, he was able by a bold stroke to transform his electorate into a kingdom. The opportunity for this achievement was offered by the need of the powers for his assistance against the designs of Louis XIV. When the Emperor called upon Frederick III in 1700 to assist him in securing a division of the Spanish dominions (see above, p. 69), the elector exacted as the price of his help the recognition of his right to take the title of king.

The title "King in Prussia"[1] was deemed preferable to the more natural "King of Brandenburg" because Prussia lay wholly

FIG. 17. VIEW OF BERLIN IN 1717

Berlin was only a small town until the days of the Great Elector. It increased from about eight thousand inhabitants in 1650 to about twenty thousand in 1688. It is therefore not a really ancient city, like Paris or London. Most of its great growth has taken place in the nineteenth and twentieth centuries

without the bounds of the Empire and consequently its ruler was not in any sense subject to the Emperor but was entirely independent. So the *elector* Frederick III became *King* Frederick I and was crowned with great state at the Prussian capital, Königsberg.

Frederick III, elector of Brandenburg, becomes King Frederick I of Prussia

The second ruler of the new kingdom, Frederick William I, the father of Frederick the Great, is known to history as the rough and boorish barrack king who devoted himself entirely to governing his realm, collecting tall soldiers, drilling his battalions,

Government of Frederick William I (1713-1740)

[1] Since West Prussia still belonged to Poland in 1701, the new king satisfied himself with the title King *in* Prussia. It was changed by Frederick the Great to King *of* Prussia.

hunting wild game, and smoking strong tobacco. He ruled his family and his country with an iron hand, declaring to those who remonstrated, "Salvation belongs to the Lord; everything else is my business."[1]

Frederick William and his soldiers

Frederick William was passionately fond of military life from his childhood. He took special pride in stalwart soldiers and collected them at great expense from all parts of Europe. He raised the army, which numbered twenty-seven thousand in the days of the Great Elector, to eighty-four thousand, making it almost equal to that maintained by France or Austria. He reserved to himself the right to appoint subordinates as well as high officials in the service, and based promotion on ability and efficiency rather than on family connections. He was constantly drilling and reviewing his men, of whom he was extravagantly proud.

His statesmanship

Frederick William, however, combined with this extravagant militarism unusual statesmanship. He made Prussia a well-governed state, although he insisted on running everything himself. Moreover, by wise management and miserly thrift, he treasured up a huge sum of money. He discharged a large number of court servants, sold at auction many of the royal jewels, and had a great portion of the family plate coined into money. Consequently he was able to leave to his son, Frederick II, not only a strong army but an ample supply of gold. Indeed, it was his toil and economy that made possible the achievements of his far better known son.

Miserly economy in finances

Section 15. The Wars of Frederick the Great

Accession of Frederick II of Prussia, called "the Great" (1740–1786)

Frederick II came to the throne in the spring of 1740. In his early years he had grieved and disgusted his boorish old father by his dislike for military life and his interest in books and music. He was a particular admirer of the French

[1] For Frederick William's instructions for the education of his son, see *Readings*, Vol. I, p. 65.

and preferred their language to his own. No sooner had he become king, however, than he suddenly developed great energy and ruthlessness in warlike enterprises. Chance favored his designs. The Emperor Charles VI, the last representative of the direct male line of the Hapsburgs died in 1740, just a few

FIG. 18. MILITARY PUNISHMENT

The armies of the old régime were mostly made up of hired soldiers or serfs, and the officers maintained discipline by cruel punishments. In this picture of a Prussian regiment one soldier is being flogged while half suspended by his wrists; another is forced to walk between two files of soldiers who must beat his bared back with heavy rods. It has been said that these soldiers found war a relief from the terrors of peace, since in war time the punishments were lessened

months before Frederick ascended the throne, leaving only a daughter, Maria Theresa, to inherit his vast and miscellaneous dominions. He had induced the other European powers to promise to accept the "pragmatic sanction" or solemn will in which he left everything to the young Maria Theresa; but she had no sooner begun to reign than her greedy neighbors

Maria Theresa and the pragmatic sanction

prepared to seize her lands. Her greatest enemy was the newly crowned king of Prussia, who at first pretended friendship for her. Frederick determined to seize Silesia, a strip of Hapsburg territory lying to the southeast of Brandenburg. In true Prussian

FIG. 19. FREDERICK II OF PRUSSIA, COMMONLY CALLED "THE GREAT"

fashion he marched his army into the coveted district, and occupied the important city of Breslau without declaring war or offering any excuse except a vague claim to a portion of the land.[1]

The War of the Austrian Succession

Within a short time France had joined with Bavaria in the attack upon Maria Theresa. It seemed for a time as if her struggle to maintain the integrity of her realm would be vain, but the loyalty of all the various peoples under her scepter

[1] As no woman had ever been elected Empress, the Duke of Bavaria managed to secure the Holy Roman Empire, as Emperor Charles VII. Upon his death, however, in 1745, Maria Theresa's husband, Francis, Duke of Lorraine, was chosen Emperor. Their son, Joseph II, succeeded his father in 1765, and upon his death in 1790 his brother Leopold II was elected. When he died, in 1792, the Empire fell to his son Francis II, who was the last of the "Roman" emperors and assumed the new title "Emperor of Austria." See below, p. 286.

was roused by her extraordinary courage and energy. The French were driven back, but Maria Theresa was forced to grant Silesia to Frederick in order to induce him to retire from the war. Finally, England and Holland joined in an alliance for maintaining the balance of power, for they had no desire to see France annex the Austrian Netherlands. A few years later (1748)[1] all the powers, tired of the war, laid down their arms and agreed to what is called in diplomacy the *status quo ante bellum*, which simply means that things were to be restored to the condition in which they had been before the opening of hostilities.

Frederick promotes the material development of Prussia

Frederick, however, managed to retain Silesia, which increased his dominions by about one third of their former extent. He now turned his attention to making his subjects happier and more prosperous, by draining the swamps, promoting industry, and drawing up a new code of laws. He found time, also, to gratify his interest in men of letters, and invited the great French writer, Voltaire,[2] to make his home at Berlin.

The Seven Years' War

Maria Theresa was by no means reconciled to the loss of Silesia, and she began to lay her plans for expelling the perfidious Frederick and regaining her lost territory. This led to one of the most important wars in modern history, in which not only almost every European power joined, but which involved the whole world, from the Indian rajahs of Hindustan to the colonists of Virginia and New England. This Seven Years' War (1756–1763) will be considered in its broader aspects in the next chapter. We note here only the part played in it by the king of Prussia.

The alliance against Prussia

Maria Theresa's ambassador at Paris was so skillful in his negotiations with the French court that in 1756 he induced it, in spite of its two hundred years of hostility to the House of Hapsburg, to enter into an alliance with Austria against Prussia. Russia, Sweden, and Saxony also agreed to join in a concerted attack on Prussia. Their armies, coming as they did

[1] By the Peace of Aix-la-Chapelle. [2] See below, pp. 140 ff.

PRUSSIA
at the Accession of
FREDERICK THE GREAT
(with dates of acquisition)

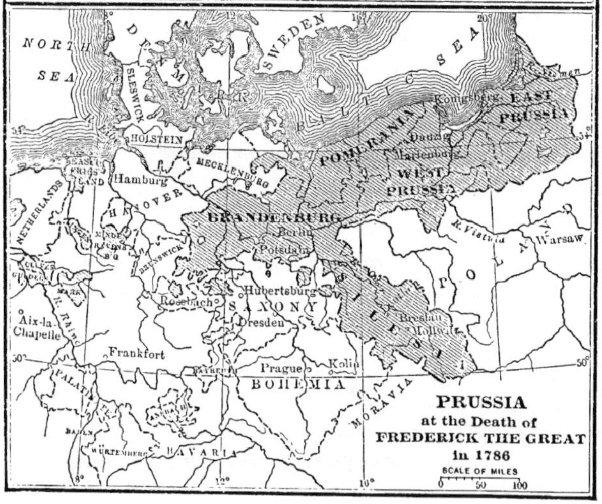

PRUSSIA
at the Death of
FREDERICK THE GREAT
in 1786

from every point of the compass, threatened the complete annihilation of Austria's rival.. It seemed as if the new kingdom of Prussia might disappear altogether from the map of Europe.

Frederick's victorious defense

However, it was in this war that Frederick earned his title of "the Great" and because of his successes he has often been classed with the ablest generals the world has seen. Learning the object of the allies, he did not wait for them to declare war against him, but occupied Saxony at once and then moved on into Bohemia, where he nearly succeeded in taking the capital, Prague. Here he was forced to retire, but in 1757 he defeated the French and his German enemies in the most famous, perhaps, of his battles, at Rossbach. A month later he routed the Austrians at Leuthen,[1] not far from Breslau. Thereupon the Swedes and the Russians retired from the field and left Frederick for the moment master of the situation.

Frederick finally triumphs over Austria

England now engaged the French and left Frederick at liberty to deal with his other enemies. While he exhibited great military skill, he was by no means able to gain all the battles in which he engaged. For a time, indeed, it looked as if he might, after all, be vanquished. But the accession of a new Tsar, who was an ardent admirer of Frederick, led Russia to conclude peace with Prussia, whereupon Maria Theresa reluctantly agreed to give up once more her struggle with her inveterate enemy. Shortly afterwards England and France came to terms, and a general settlement was made at Paris in 1763.[2]

Section 16. Three Partitions of Poland, 1772, 1793, and 1795

Frederick's success in seizing and holding one of Austria's finest provinces did not satisfy him. The central portions of his kingdom — Brandenburg, Silesia, and Pomerania — were completely cut off from East Prussia by a considerable tract known

[1] For Frederick's address to his officers before the battle of Leuthen, see *Readings*, Vol. I, p. 80.

[2] See below, p. 111.

as West Prussia, which belonged to the kingdom of Poland. The map will show how great must have been Frederick's temptation to fill this gap, especially as Poland was in no condition to defend its possessions.

With the exception of Russia, Poland was the largest kingdom in Europe. It covered an immense plain with no natural

FIG. 20. THE ELECTION OF A POLISH KING IN THE EIGHTEENTH CENTURY

This is an eighteenth-century engraving of a Polish diet, meeting in the open country outside of Warsaw, whose churches are just visible, in order to elect a king. In the center of the picture a ditch surrounds the meeting place of the senators, who are holding a solemn public session out in front of their little house. On the plain there are processions of nobles and various indications of a celebration

Mixed population and discordant religions in Poland

boundaries, and the population, which was very thinly scattered, belonged to several races. Besides the Poles themselves, there were Germans in the cities of West Prussia, and the Lithuanians and Russians in Lithuania. The Jews were very numerous everywhere, forming half of the population in some of the towns. The Poles were usually Catholics, while the Germans were Protestants, and the Russians adhered to the Greek Church. These differences in religion, added to those of race, created endless difficulties and dissensions.

The government of Poland was the worst imaginable. Instead of having developed a strong monarchy, as her neighbors — Prussia, Russia, and Austria — had done, she remained in a state of feudal anarchy which the nobles had taken the greatest pains to perpetuate by binding their kings in such a way that they had no power either to maintain order or to defend the country from attack. The king could not declare war, make peace, impose taxes, or pass any law without the consent of the diet. As the diet was composed of representatives of the nobility, any one of whom could freely veto any measure, — for no measure could pass that had even one vote against it, — most of the diets broke up without accomplishing anything.

The defective system of government

The *liberum veto*

The kingship was not hereditary in Poland, but whenever the ruler died, the nobles assembled and chose a new one, commonly a foreigner. These elections were tumultuous, and the various European powers regularly interfered, by force or bribery, to secure the election of a candidate who they believed would favor their interests.

The elective kingship

The nobles in Poland were numerous. There were perhaps a million and a half of them, mostly very poor, owning only a trifling bit of land. There was a jocular saying that the poor noble's dog, even if he sat in the middle of the estate, was sure to have his tail upon a neighbor's land. It was the few rich and powerful families that really controlled such government as might be said to have existed in Poland. There was no middle class except in the few German towns. In the Polish and Lithuanian towns such industry and commerce as existed were in the hands of the Jews, who were not recognized as citizens and who both oppressed and were oppressed. The peasants were miserable indeed. They had sunk from serfs to slaves over whom their lords had the right of life and death.

The Polish nobles and peasants

It required no great insight to foresee that Poland was in danger of falling a prey to her greedy and powerful neighbors, Russia, Prussia, and Austria, who clamped in the unfortunate kingdom on all sides. They had long shamelessly interfered in

Catherine II and Frederick II agree on Polish matters, 1764

its affairs and had actually taken active measures to oppose all reforms of the constitution in order that they might profit by the existing anarchy. When Augustus III died in 1763, just as the Seven Years' War had been brought to a close, Frederick immediately arranged with the new Russian ruler, the famous Catherine II, to put upon the vacant Polish throne her favorite, Poniatowski, who took the title of Stanislas II.

FIG. 21. THE CATHEDRAL OF CRACOW

In this picturesque old cathedral many Polish kings were crowned and many lie buried. The chapels are beautiful, partly of the best Renaissance style

Catherine was soon disappointed in Stanislas Poniatowski, who showed himself favorable to reform. He even proposed to do away with the *liberum veto* — the sacred right of any member of the diet to block a measure no matter how salutary. Russia, however, supported by Prussia, intervened to demand that the *liberum veto*, which insured continued anarchy, should be maintained. Then came several years of civil war between the several factions, a war in which the Russians freely intervened.

Austria agrees to the partition of Poland

Austria was a neighbor of Poland and deeply interested in her affairs. She consequently approached her old enemy, Frederick, and between them they decided that Russia should be allowed to take a portion of Poland if Catherine would consent to give up most of the conquests her armies had just made in Turkey; then Austria, in order to maintain the balance of power, should be given a slice of Poland, and Frederick should take the longed-for West Prussia.

First partition of Poland, 1772

Accordingly in 1772 Poland's three neighbors arranged to take each a portion of the distracted kingdom. Austria was assigned a strip inhabited by almost three million Poles and Russians, and thus added two new kinds of people and two new languages to her already varied collection of races and tongues. Prussia was given a smaller piece, but it was the coveted West Prussia which she needed to fill out her boundaries, and its inhabitants were to a considerable extent Germans and Protestants. Russia's strip on the east was inhabited entirely by Russians. The Polish diet was forced, by the advance of Russian troops to Warsaw, to approve the partition.[1]

Revival of Poland, 1772–1791

Poland seemed at first, however, to have learned a great lesson from the disaster. During the twenty years following its first dismemberment there was an extraordinary revival in education, art, and literature; the old universities at Vilna and Cracow were reorganized and many new schools established. King Stanislas Poniatowski summoned French and Italian artists and entered into correspondence with the French philosophers and reformers. Historians and poets sprang up to give distinction to the last days of Polish independence. The old intolerance and bigotry decreased, and, above all, the constitution which had made Poland the laughingstock and the victim of its neighbors was abolished and an entirely new one worked out.

The new Polish constitution of 1791

The new Polish constitution, approved on May 3, 1791, did away with the *liberum veto*, made the crown hereditary, established a parliament something like that of England — in short, gave to the king power enough to conduct the government efficiently and yet made him and his ministers dependent upon the representatives of the nation.

[1] Catherine's announcement of the first partition of Poland is in the *Readings*, Vol. I, p. 82.

Catherine frustrates the reform

There was a party, however, which regretted the changes and feared that they might result in time in doing away with the absolute control of the nobles over the peasants. These opponents of reform appealed to Catherine for aid. She, mindful as always of her own interests, denounced all changes in a

FIG. 22. A CARTOON OF THE PARTITION OF POLAND

Catherine II, Joseph II, and Frederick II are pointing out on the map the part of Poland they each propose to take. The king of Poland is trying to hold his crown from falling off his head. The map should be turned upside down to see what is left of Poland

government "under which the Polish republic had flourished for so many centuries," and declared that the reformers were no better than the abhorred French Jacobins, who were busy destroying the power of their king.[1] She sent her soldiers and her wild Cossacks into Poland, and the enemies of the new constitution were able with her help to undo all that had been done and to reëstablish the *liberum veto*.

[1] See below, pp. 217 ff.

Not satisfied with plunging Poland into her former anarchy, Russia and Prussia determined to rob her of still more territory. Frederick the Great's successor, Frederick William II, ordered his forces across his eastern boundary on the ground that Danzig was sending grain to the French revolutionists, that Poland was infested with Jacobins, and that, in general, she threatened the tranquillity of her neighbors. Prussia cut deep into Poland, added a million and a half of Poles to her subjects, and acquired the towns of Thorn, Danzig, and Posen.[1] Russia's gains were three millions of people, who at least belonged to her own race. On this occasion Austria was put off with the promises of her confederates, Russia and Prussia, that they would use their good offices to secure Bavaria for her in exchange for the Austrian Netherlands.

Second partition of Poland, 1793

At this juncture the Poles found a national leader in the brave Kosciusko, who had fought under Washington for American liberty. With the utmost care and secrecy he organized an insurrection in the spring of 1794 and summoned the Polish people to join his standard of national independence. The Poles who had been incorporated into the Prussian monarchy thereupon rose and forced Frederick William to withdraw his forces.

Revolt of Poles under Kosciusko, 1794

Catherine was ready, however, to crush the patriots. Kosciusko was wounded and captured in battle, and by the end of the year Russia was in control of Warsaw. The Polish king was compelled to abdicate, and the remnants of the dismembered kingdom were divided, after much bitter contention, among Austria, Russia, and Prussia. In the three partitions which blotted out the kingdom of Poland from the map of Europe, Russia received nearly all of the old grand duchy of Lithuania, or nearly twice the combined shares of Austria and Prussia.

Third and final partition, 1795

But the Poles have never lost their strong national feeling, and have steadily resisted the efforts of the governments of Russia or Germany[2] to absorb them or crush their patriotism.

[1] For Frederick William II's proclamation to the Poles, see *Readings*, Vol. I, p. 85.

[2] Austria has granted them favored terms in Galicia.

Section 17. The Austrian Realms: Maria Theresa and Joseph II

The Hapsburgs in Austria

While the Hohenzollerns of Prussia from their capital at Berlin had been extending their power over northern Germany, the rival House of Hapsburg, established in the southeastern corner of Germany, with its capital at Vienna, had been grouping together, by conquest or inheritance, the vast realm over which they desired to rule. It will be remembered that Charles V, shortly after his accession, ceded to his brother, Ferdinand I, the German or Austrian possessions of the House of Hapsburg,[1] while he himself retained the Spanish, Burgundian, and Italian dominions. Ferdinand, by a fortunate marriage with the heiress of the kingdoms of Bohemia and Hungary, greatly augmented his territory. Hungary was, however, almost completely conquered by the Turks at that time, and till the end of the seventeenth century the energies of the Austrian rulers were largely absorbed in a long struggle against the Mohammedans.

Conquests of the Turks in Europe

A Turkish tribe from Western Asia had, at the opening of the fourteenth century, established themselves in western Asia Minor under their leader Othman (d. 1326). It was from him that they derived their name of Ottoman Turks, to distinguish them from the Seljuk Turks, with whom the crusaders had come into contact. The leaders of the Ottoman Turks showed great energy. They not only extended their Asiatic territory far toward the east, and later into Africa, but they gained a footing in Europe as early as 1353. They gradually conquered the Slavic peoples in Macedonia and occupied the territory about Constantinople, although it was a hundred years before they succeeded in capturing the ancient capital of the Eastern Empire.

This advance of the Turks naturally aroused grave fears in the states of western Europe lest they too might be deprived of

[1] For the origin of the Austrian dominions, see Part I, pp. 562 ff.

their independence. The brunt of the defense against the common foe devolved upon Venice and the German Hapsburgs, who carried on an almost continuous war with the Turks for nearly two centuries. As late as 1683 the Mohammedans collected a large force and besieged Vienna, which might very well have fallen into their hands had it not been for the timely assistance which the city received from the king of Poland. From this time on, the power of the Turks in Europe rapidly decreased, and the Hapsburgs were able to regain the whole territory of Hungary and Transylvania, their right to which was formally recognized by the Sultan in 1699.

The defense of Europe against the Turks

The conquest of Silesia by Frederick the Great was more than a severe blow to the pride of Maria Theresa; for, since it was inhabited by Germans, its loss lessened the Hapsburg power inside the Empire. In extent of territory the Hapsburgs more than made up for it by the partitions of Poland, but since the Poles were an alien race, they added one more difficulty to the very difficult problem of ruling so many different peoples, each of whom had a different language and different customs and institutions. The Hapsburg possessions were inhabited by Germans in Austria proper, a Slav people (the Czechs) mixed with Germans in Bohemia and Moravia, Poles in Galicia, Hungarians or Magyars along with Roumanians and smaller groups of other peoples in Hungary, Croats and Slovenes (both Slavs) in the south, Italians in Milan and Tuscany, Flemish and Walloons in the Netherlands.

Maria Theresa ruled these races with energy and skill. She patiently attended to all the tiresome matters of State, read long documents and reports, and conferred with the ambassadors of foreign powers. After her long reign of forty years her son Joseph, who had already been elected Emperor as Joseph II, tried in the ten years of his rule (1780–1790) to modernize his backward states of southeastern Europe by a series of sweeping reforms. These reforms, which are described below,[1]

[1] See p. 166.

were bitterly opposed, however, and the Hapsburg realms were not unified into a strong modern state. Poles, Italians, Magyars, and Germans could never be united by such common interests as Englishmen or Frenchmen have felt so keenly in the last two centuries. Instead of fusing together to form a nation, the peoples ruled over by the Hapsburgs were on such bad terms with each other that it often seemed as if they would

FIG. 23. MARIA THERESA

split apart, forming separate nations. Moreover, since some of these peoples, especially the Slavs, Poles, and Roumanians, lived in neighboring states as well, the Hapsburg monarchy was much concerned with what happened outside its borders. The immediate cause of the terrible European war which began in 1914 was trouble between Austria and her neighbor Serbia. So if one hopes to understand the great questions of our own time, he must follow carefully the complicated history of Austria and her ever-changing realms.

QUESTIONS

SECTION 13. What part did the Northmen play in the history of Russia? What is the significance of the introduction of the Greek form of Christianity into Russia? What new people entered Russia in the thirteenth century? What was the result of this invasion? Who first bore the title of Tsar? When did Peter the Great reign? What two tasks did he set himself? Describe the reforms of Peter the Great.

How did Peter the Great come into conflict with Charles XII of Sweden? When and where did Charles XII meet defeat? Draw a map and on it show the permanent territorial gains which Peter made as a result of his war with Charles XII. What territory was lost and gained by Russia during the reign of Peter the Great?

SECTION 14. Who are the Hohenzollerns? How did the electorate of Brandenburg come into the possession of the Hohenzollerns? What territory was gained by the elector of Brandenburg in 1614? in 1618? Give the history of Prussia down to 1618. Describe the character and work of the Great Elector. Draw a map and on it show (*a*) the territory belonging to the Great Elector at the time of his accession, (*b*) the territory gained during his lifetime.

What was the importance of the Great Elector from the standpoint of to-day? In what way and where did Frederick I add to the power of the House of Hohenzollern? Account for the choice of "King of Prussia" rather than "King of Brandenburg," as well as for the royal title in its earlier form, "King in Prussia." Describe the character and the government of Frederick William I.

SECTION 15. Describe the circumstances under which Maria Theresa came to the throne of Austria. What problems faced Maria Theresa from the first? In what way did Frederick the Great take advantage of Maria Theresa? What war resulted from this act of aggression? Between what nations and during what years was it fought? What was the outcome? To what second war did the loss of Silesia lead? Between what countries, where, and when was it fought? Give the terms of the treaty which ended this war.

SECTION 16. Make an outline map of the territory ruled over by Frederick the Great previous to 1772. What country separated the eastern and western portions of the Hohenzollern dominions? Describe the races which made up the population of Poland. Give an account of the government of Poland. Into what classes were the people divided? Describe the relations between Poland and the countries which surrounded her. What part did Frederick the Great and Catherine II of Russia play in the history of Poland in the years closely following the end of the Seven Years' War?

What proposal did Maria Theresa make to Frederick the Great and Catherine II prior to 1772? What was the result of the agreement made between these three monarchs? Compare the gains made by the parties to this agreement as a result of the first partition of Poland, in 1772. What was the result of this partition in Poland between the years 1772 and 1791? Describe the Polish constitution of 1791. Were the Poles unanimous in their approval of the change in government? What measures were taken to prevent the reforms of the new constitution from being carried out? What excuse was offered for the second partition of Poland, in 1793? What was the outcome of this partition?

SECTION 17. Explain the relations of Austria and the Turks. What was the extent of the Hapsburg dominions when Maria Theresa came to the throne? Compare the nations ruled by Joseph II with those under Peter the Great and Frederick II. Why is Austria specially interesting to us to-day?

CHAPTER IV

THE STRUGGLE BETWEEN FRANCE AND ENGLAND IN INDIA AND NORTH AMERICA

SECTION 18. HOW EUROPE BEGAN TO EXTEND ITS COMMERCE OVER THE WHOLE WORLD

The long and disastrous wars of the eighteenth century which we have been reviewing seem, from the standpoint of the changes they produced in Europe, to have been scarcely worth our attention. It was not a vital question in the world's history whether a member of the House of Bourbon or of the House of Hapsburg sat on the throne of Spain, whether Silesia belonged to Frederick or Maria Theresa, or even whether Poland continued to exist or not. But in addition to these contentions among the various dynasties and these shiftings of territory were other interests far beyond the confines of Europe, and to these we must now turn.[1]

The history of Europe only to be explained by the history of Europe's colonies

Constant wars have been waged during the past two centuries by the European nations in their efforts to extend and defend their distant possessions. The War of the Spanish Succession concerned the trade as well as the throne of Spain. The internal affairs of each country have been constantly influenced by the demands of its merchants and the achievements of its sailors and soldiers, fighting rival nations or alien peoples thousands of miles from London, Paris, or Vienna. The great manufacturing towns of England — Leeds, Manchester, and Birmingham — owe their prosperity to India, China, and Australia. Liverpool, Amsterdam, and Hamburg, with their long

[1] For a more detailed account of the contest between France and England in India and North America, see Robinson and Beard, *Development of Modern Europe*, Vol. I, chaps. vi and vii.

FIG. 24. LONDON IN THE EIGHTEENTH CENTURY

London was almost destroyed by a great fire in 1666. The old city had been a picturesque mass of timbered houses; the new one was built of brick and stone. In the center rose the new St. Paul's Cathedral, whose dome, 370 feet high, is still higher than any other building in the city. Its architect, Sir Christopher Wren, also built most of the churches whose spires are visible here, the eighteenth-century artist having drawn them, indeed, somewhat out of proportion in order to attract attention to them. The column with a gallery around it is "The Monument," erected to commemorate the great fire. At the lower right-hand side is the Tower. Note the houses on London Bridge. The two towers farthest up the river are those of Westminster Abbey, and the roof of the old Parliament buildings can be just made out below them, beside the bridge

ENGLAND
FRANCE AND SPAIN
IN AMERICA
1750

lines of docks and warehouses and their fleets of merchant vessels, would dwindle away if their trade were confined to the demands of their European neighbors.

Europe includes scarcely a twelfth of the land upon the globe, and yet over three fifths of the world is to-day either occupied by peoples of European origin or ruled by European states. The possessions of France in Asia and Africa exceed the entire area of Europe; even the little kingdom of the Netherlands administers a colonial dominion more than three times the size of France. The British empire, of which the island of Great Britain constitutes but a hundredth part, includes one fifth of the world's dry land. Moreover, European peoples have populated the United States, which is nearly as large as all of Europe, and they rule all of Mexico and South America. Vast extent of the European colonial dominion

In this chapter the origin of European colonization will be briefly explained, as well as the manner in which England succeeded in extending her sway over the teeming millions of India. We shall also review England's victory over France in the western hemisphere. In this way the real meaning of the Seven Years' War will become clear.

The widening of the field of European history is one of the most striking features of modern times. Though the Greeks and Romans carried on a large trade in silks, spices, and precious stones with India and China, they really knew little of the world beyond southern Europe, northern Africa, and western Asia, and much that they knew was forgotten during the Middle Ages. Slowly, however, the interest in the East revived and travelers began to add to the scanty knowledge handed down from antiquity. Narrow limits of the ancient and medieval world

The voyages which had brought America and India within the ken of Europe during the fifteenth and early sixteenth centuries were, as we know, mainly undertaken by the Portuguese and Spaniards. Portugal was the first to realize the advantage of extending her commerce by establishing stations in India after Vasco da Gama rounded the Cape of Good Hope in Colonial policy of Portugal, Spain, and Holland in the sixteenth and seventeenth centuries

1498;[1] and later by founding posts on the Brazilian coast of South America; then Spain laid claim to Mexico, the West Indies, and a great part of South America. These two powers found formidable rivals in the Dutch; for when Philip II was

FIG. 25. A NAVAL BATTLE BETWEEN SAILING SHIPS

This is the way the rival navies of Holland, France, and England fought in the seventeenth and eighteenth centuries. Note how the ships sail right up to the foe and fire broadsides at close range. The large ship in front has rammed an enemy ship; this was often done, not with the idea of sinking it, since the heavily timbered wooden ships did not sink so easily as ironclads do, but in order that a boarding party could clamber over on to its decks. Thus naval warfare still resembled somewhat the method of fighting of the Greeks and Romans

able to add Portugal to the realms of the Spanish monarchs for a few decades (1580–1640), he immediately closed the port of Lisbon to the Dutch ships. Thereupon the United Provinces, whose merchants could no longer procure the spices which the Portuguese brought from the East, resolved to take possession

[1] See *Readings*, Vol. I, p. 92.

of the source of supplies. They accordingly expelled the Portuguese from a number of their settlements in India and the Spice Islands, and brought Java, Sumatra, and other tropical regions under Dutch control.

Settlements of the French and English in North America

In North America the chief rivals were England and France, both of which succeeded in establishing colonies in the early part of the seventeenth century. Englishmen successively settled at Jamestown in Virginia (1607), then in New England, Maryland, Pennsylvania, and elsewhere. The colonies owed their growth in part to the influx of refugees, — Puritans, Catholics, and Quakers, — who exiled themselves in the hope of gaining the right freely to enjoy their particular forms of religion.[1] On the other hand, many came to better their fortunes in the New World, and thousands of bond servants and slaves were brought over as laborers.

Section 19. The Contest between France and England for Colonial Empire

Just as Jamestown was being founded by the English the French were making their first successful settlement in Nova Scotia and at Quebec. Although England made no attempt to oppose the French occupation of Canada, it progressed very slowly. In 1673 Marquette, a Jesuit missionary, and Joliet, a merchant, explored a part of the Mississippi River.[2] La Salle sailed down the great stream and named the new country which he entered Louisiana, after his king. The city of New Orleans was founded near the mouth of the river in 1718, and the French established a chain of forts between it and Montreal.

England was able, however, by the Treaty of Utrecht, to establish herself in the northern regions, for France thereby ceded to her Newfoundland, Nova Scotia, and the borders of

[1] For the settlement of the English and French in North America, see *Readings*, Vol. I, pp. 121 ff. For a fuller narrative, see Muzzey, *American History*

[2] For Marquette's account of his journey, see *Readings*, Vol. I, p. 116.

Hudson Bay. While the number of English in North America at the beginning of the Seven Years' War is reckoned to have been over a million, the French did not reach a hundred thousand. Yet careful observers at the time were by no means sure that France, seemingly the most powerful state in Europe, was not destined to dominate the new country rather than England.

Extent of India

The rivalry of England and France was not confined to the wildernesses of North America, occupied by half a million of savage red men. At the opening of the eighteenth century both countries had gained a firm foothold on the borders of the vast Indian empire, inhabited by two hundred millions of people and the seat of an ancient and highly developed civilization. One may gain some idea of the extent of India by laying the map of Hindustan upon that of the United States. If the southernmost point, Cape Comorin, be placed over New Orleans, Calcutta will lie nearly over New York City, and Bombay in the neighborhood of Des Moines, Iowa.

The Mongolian emperors of Hindustan

A generation after Vasco da Gama rounded the Cape, a Mongolian conqueror, Baber,[1] had established his empire in India. The dynasty of Mongolian rulers which he founded was able to keep the whole country under its control for toward two centuries; then after the death of the Great Mogul Aurangzeb in 1707, their empire began to fall apart in much the same way as that of Charlemagne had done. Like the counts and dukes of the Carolingian period, the emperor's officials, the subahdars and nawabs (nabobs), and the rajahs — that is, Hindu princes temporarily subjugated by the Mongols — had gradually got the power in their respective districts into their own hands. Although the emperor, or Great Mogul, as the English called him, continued to maintain himself in his capital of Delhi, he could no longer be said to rule the country at the opening of

[1] Baber claimed to be descended from an earlier invader, the famous Timur (or Tamerlane), who died in 1405. The so-called Mongol (or Mogul) emperors were really Turkish rather than Mongolian in origin.

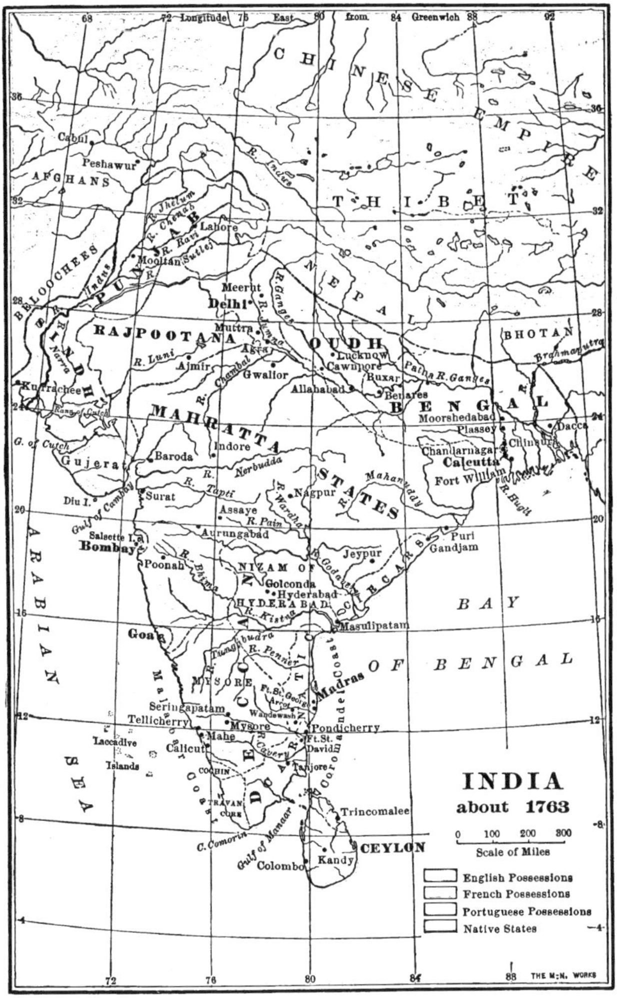
INDIA
about 1763
Scale of Miles
0 100 200 300
English Possessions
French Possessions
Portuguese Possessions
Native States
Longitude East from Greenwich
CHINESE EMPIRE
THIBET
NEPAL
BHOTAN
AFGHANS
BELOOCHEES
PUNJAB
SINDH
RAJPOOTANA
OUDH
BENGAL
MAHRATTA STATES
NIZAM OF HYDERABAD
CARNATIC
DECCAN
MYSORE
CIRCARS
ARABIAN SEA
BAY OF BENGAL
CEYLON
Cabul
Peshawur
Lahore
Mooltan
Delhi
Meerut
Muttra
Agra
Ajmir
Gwalior
Lucknow
Cawnpore
Allahabad
Buxar
Benares
Patna
Moorshedabad
Plassey
Dacca
Chinsura
Chandarnagar
Calcutta
Fort William
Kurrachee
Rann of Cutch
G. of Cutch
Gujerat
Baroda
Indore
Surat
Diu I.
Gulf of Cambay
Assaye
Nagpur
Aurungabad
Salsette I.
Bombay
Poonah
Golconda
Hyderabad
Jeypur
Puri
Gandjam
Masulipatam
Goa
Malabar Coast
Coromandel Coast
Seringapatam
Tellicherry
Mysore
Mahe
Calicut
Cochin
Travancore
Madras
Ft.St.George
Arcot
Wandewash
Pondicherry
Ft.St.David
Tanjore
Laccadive Islands
C. Comorin
Gulf of Manaar
Colombo
Kandy
Trincomalee
R. Indus
R. Jhelum
R. Chenab
R. Ravi
R. Sutlej
R. Ganges
R. Jumna
R. Luni
R. Chambal
Narra
R. Nerbudda
R. Tapti
R. Wardha
R. Pain
R. Mahanuddy
R. Brahmaputra
R. Hugli
R. Bhima
R. Godavery
R. Kistna
R. Tungabudra
R. Penner
R. Cavery
THE M.N. WORKS

the eighteenth century when the French and English were beginning to turn their attention seriously to his coasts.[1]

At the opening of the seventeenth century an English East India Company had been formed to develop the trade with India. This important company was destined to acquire and

English and French settlements in India

FIG 26. THE TAJ MAHAL

This mausoleum of an emperor was built at Agra, India, in 1632. It has been described as "the most splendidly poetic building in the world . . . a dream in marble, which justifies the saying that the Moguls designed like Titans but finished like jewelers." The entire building is of white marble, inlaid with precious stones. Although this is regarded as its most perfect building, India has many others of great magnificence, witnesses of the power and wealth of her princes

govern an empire and to control the greater part of the oriental trade of England. In the time of Charles I (1639), it had purchased a village on the southeastern coast of Hindustan, which grew into the important English station of Madras. About the same time posts were established in the district of

[1] For accounts of the Moguls, see *Readings*, Vol. I, pp. 101 ff.

Bengal, and later Calcutta was fortified. Bombay was already an English station. The Mongolian emperor of India at first scarcely deigned to notice the presence of a few foreigners on the fringe of his vast realms. But before the end of the seventeenth century hostilities began between the English East India Company and the native rulers, which made it plain that the foreigners would be forced to defend themselves.

The English had not only to face the opposition of the natives, but of a European power as well. France also had an East India Company, and Pondicherry, at the opening of the eighteenth century, was its chief center, with a population of sixty thousand, of which two hundred only were Europeans. It soon became apparent that there was little danger from the Great Mogul; moreover the Portuguese and Dutch were out of the race, so the native princes and the French and English were left to fight among themselves for the supremacy.

England victorious in the struggle for supremacy in America

Just before the clash of European rulers, known as the Seven Years' War, came in 1756, the French and English had begun their struggle for control in both America and India. In America the so-called French and Indian War began in 1754 between the English and French colonists. General Braddock was sent from England to capture Fort Duquesne, which the French had established to keep their rivals out of the Ohio valley. Braddock knew nothing of border warfare, and he was killed and his troops routed.[1] Fortunately for England, France, as the ally of Austria, was soon engaged in a war with Prussia that prevented her from giving proper attention to her American possessions. A famous statesman, William Pitt,[2] was now at the head of the English ministry. He was able not only to succor the hard-pressed king of Prussia with money and men, but also to support the militia of the thirteen American colonies. The French forts at Ticonderoga and Niagara were taken in 1758–1759. Quebec was won in Wolfe's heroic attack, and

[1] For an account of Braddock's defeat (1755), see *Readings*, Vol. I, p. 126.

[2] Called the elder Pitt to distinguish him from his son; see below, p. 171.

the next year all Canada submitted to the English.[1] England's supremacy on the sea was demonstrated by three admirals, each of whom destroyed a French fleet in the same year that Quebec was lost to France.

In India conflicts between the French and the English had occurred during the War of the Austrian Succession. The governor of the French station of Pondicherry was Dupleix, a **Dupleix and Clive in India**

FIG. 27. QUEBEC

Wolfe's army climbed the cliff (over 300 feet high) to the west of the city (left of the picture) and fought there on the plain known as the Heights of Abraham

soldier of great energy, who proposed to drive out the English and firmly establish the power of France over Hindustan. His chances of success were greatly increased by the quarrels among the native rulers, some of whom belonged to the earlier Hindu inhabitants and some to the Mohammedan Mongolians who had conquered India in 1526. Dupleix had very few French soldiers, but he began the enlistment of the natives, a custom eagerly adopted by the English. These native soldiers,

[1] The battle of Quebec (1759) is described in the *Readings*, Vol. I, p. 128.

whom the English called sepoys, were taught to fight in the manner of Europeans.

Clive defeats Dupleix

But the English colonists, in spite of the fact that they were mainly traders, discovered among the clerks in Madras a leader equal in military skill and energy to Dupleix himself. Robert

FIG. 28. WILLIAM PITT

Pitt, more than any other one man, was responsible for the victories of England in the Seven Years' War. A great orator, as well as a shrewd statesman, he inspired his country with his own great ideals. He boldly upheld in Parliament the cause of the American colonists, but died before he could check the policy of the king. He was known as "the great Commoner" from his influence in the House of Commons, but late in life became Earl of Chatham

Clive, who was but twenty-five years old at this time, organized a large force of sepoys and gained a remarkable ascendancy over them by his astonishing bravery. Dupleix paid no attention to the fact that peace had been declared in Europe at Aix-la-Chapelle, but continued to carry on his operations against the English. But Clive proved more than his equal, and in two years had very nearly established English supremacy in the southeastern part of India.

At the moment that the Seven Years' War was beginning, bad news reached Clive from the English settlement of Calcutta, about a thousand miles to the northeast of Madras. The nawab of Bengal had seized the property of some English merchants and imprisoned one hundred and forty-five Englishmen in a little room, where most of them died of suffocation before morning.[1] Clive hastened to Bengal, and with a little army of nine hundred Europeans and fifteen hundred sepoys he gained a great victory at Plassey in 1757 over the nawab's army of fifty thousand men. Clive then replaced the nawab of Bengal by a man whom he believed to be friendly to the English. Before the Seven Years' War was over the English had won Pondicherry and deprived the French of all their former influence in the region of Madras.

Clive renders English influence supreme in India

When the Seven Years' War was brought to an end in 1763 by the Treaty of Paris, it was clear that England had gained far more than any other power. She was to retain her two forts commanding the Mediterranean, Gibraltar, and Port Mahon on the island of Minorca; in America, France ceded to her the vast region of Canada and Nova Scotia, as well as several of the islands in the West Indies. The region beyond the Mississippi was ceded to Spain by France, who thus gave up all her claims to North America. In India, France, it is true, received back the towns which the English had taken from her, but she had permanently lost her influence over the native rulers, for Clive had made the English name greatly feared among them.

England's gains in the Seven Years' War

The erection of this world empire of Great Britain was the main fact of British history during the eighteenth century, as the overthrow of absolute monarchy had been that of the seventeenth. At the same time, a great change, known as the Industrial Revolution, was taking place in England, as machinery and steam engines were invented, supplying her with the wealth which made her more powerful still in the nineteenth century.[2]

The world empire of Britain and the Industrial Revolution

[1] See *Readings*, Vol. I, p. 107.

[2] See below, p. 357.

Section 20. Revolt of the American Colonies from England

England had, however, no sooner added Canada to her possessions and driven the French from the broad region which lay between her dominions and the Mississippi than she lost the better part of her American empire by the revolt of the irritated colonists, who refused to submit to her interference in their government and commerce.

For a long period England left her colonies very free

The English settlers had been left alone, for the most part, by the home government and had enjoyed far greater freedom in the management of their affairs than had the French and Spanish colonies. Virginia established its own assembly in 1619 and Massachusetts became almost an independent commonwealth. Regular constitutions developed, which were later used as the basis for those of the several states when the colonies gained their independence. England had been busied during the seventeenth century with a great struggle at home and with the wars stirred up by Louis XIV. After the Peace of Utrecht Walpole for twenty years prudently refused to interfere with the colonies. The result was that by the end of the Seven Years' War the colonists numbered over two millions. Their rapidly increasing wealth and strength, their free life in a new land, and the confidence they had gained in their successful conflict with the French — all combined to render the renewed interference of the home government intolerable to them.

England taxes the colonies

During the war with the French England began to realize for the first time that the colonies had money, and so Parliament decided that they should be required to pay part of the expenses of the recent conflict and support a small standing army of English soldiers. The Stamp Act was therefore passed, which taxed the colonists by requiring them to pay the English government for stamps which had to be used upon leases, deeds, and other legal documents in order to make them binding. But the indignant colonists declared that they had already borne the

Stamp Act of 1765

brunt of the war and that in any case Parliament, in which they were not represented, had no right to tax them. Representatives of the colonies met in New York in 1765 and denounced the Stamp Act as indicating "a manifest tendency to subvert the rights and liberties of the colonists."

Navigation laws

More irritating than the attempts of Great Britain to tax the colonists were the vexatious navigation and trade laws by which she tried to keep all the benefits of colonial trade and industry to herself. The early navigation laws passed under Cromwell and Charles II were specially directed against the enterprising Dutch traders. They provided that all products grown or manufactured in Asia, Africa, or America should be imported into England or her colonies only in English ships. Thus if a Dutch merchant vessel laden with cloves, cinnamon, teas, and silks from the Far East anchored in the harbor of New York, the inhabitants could not lawfully buy of the ship's master, no matter how much lower his prices were than those offered by English shippers. Furthermore, another act provided that no commodity of European production or manufacture should be imported into any of the colonies without being shipped through England and carried in ships built in England or the colonies. So if a colonial merchant wished to buy French wines or Dutch watches, he would have to order through English merchants. Again, if a colonist desired to sell to a European merchant such products as the law permitted him to sell to foreigners, he had to export them in English ships and even send them by way of England.

Trade laws

What was still worse for the colonists, certain articles in which they were most interested, such as sugar, tobacco, cotton, and indigo, could be sold only in England. Other things they were forbidden to export at all, or even to produce. For instance, though they possessed the finest furs in abundance, they could not export any caps or hats to England or to any foreign country. They had iron ore in inexhaustible quantities at their disposal, but by a law of 1750 they were forbidden to erect any rolling mill or furnace for making steel, in order that English steel manufacturers might enjoy a monopoly of that trade. The colonists had built up a lucrative lumber and provision trade with the French West Indies, from which they imported large quantities of rum, sugar, and molasses, but in order to keep this trade within British dominions, the importation of these commodities was forbidden.

The colonists evade the English restrictions

The colonists naturally evaded these laws as far as possible; they carried on a flourishing smuggling trade and built up industries in spite of them. Tobacco, sugar, hemp, flax, and cotton were grown and cloth was manufactured. Furnaces, foundries, nail and wire mills supplied pig and bar iron, chains, anchors, and other hardware. It is clear that where so many people were interested in both manufacturing and commerce a loud protest was sure to be raised against the continued attempts of England to restrict the business of the colonists in favor of her own merchants.

Taxes withdrawn except that on tea

The unpopular stamp tax was repealed, in spite of the bitter opposition of King George, who thought the colonists ought to be punished rather than conciliated. His high-handed policy was put into force the following year. New duties on glass, paper, and tea were imposed, and a board was established to secure a firm observance of the navigation laws and other restrictions. But the protests of the colonists finally moved Parliament to remove all the duties except that on tea, which was retained to prove England's right to tax the colonists.

Opposition to "taxation without representation"

The effort to make the Americans pay a very moderate import duty on tea and to force upon Boston markets the company's tea at a low price produced trouble in 1773. The young men of Boston seditiously boarded a tea ship in the harbor and threw the cargo into the water.[1] This fanned the slumbering embers of discord between the colonies and the mother country.

[1] A contemporary account of the "tea party" is given in the *Readings*, Vol. I, pp. 130 ff. The revenue from the tax on tea was to pay government officials in America.

Burke, perhaps the most able member of the House of Commons, urged the ministry to leave the Americans to tax themselves, but George III, and Parliament as a whole, could not forgive the colonists for their opposition. They believed that the trouble was largely confined to New England and could easily be overcome. In 1774 acts were passed prohibiting the landing and shipping of goods at Boston; and the colony of Massachusetts was deprived of its former right to choose its judges and the members of the upper house of its legislature, who were thereafter to be selected by the king.

These measures, instead of bringing Massachusetts to terms, so roused the apprehension of the rest of the colonists that a congress of representatives from all the colonies was held at Philadelphia in 1774 to see what could be done. This congress decided that all trade with Great Britain should cease until the grievances of the colonies had been redressed. The following year the Americans attacked the British troops at Lexington and made a brave stand against them in the battle of Bunker Hill. The second congress decided to prepare for war, and raised an army which was put under the command of George Washington, a Virginia planter who had gained some distinction in the late French and Indian War. Up to this time the colonies had not intended to secede from the mother country, but the proposed compromises came to nothing, and in July, 1776, Congress declared that "these United States are, and of right ought to be, free and independent."

The Continental Congress

Declaration of Independence, July 4, 1776

This occurrence naturally excited great interest in France. The outcome of the Seven Years' War had been most lamentable for that country, and any trouble which came to her old enemy, England, could not but be a source of congratulation to the French. The United States therefore regarded France as their natural ally and immediately sent Benjamin Franklin to Versailles in the hope of obtaining the aid of the new French king, Louis XVI. The king's ministers were uncertain whether the colonies could long maintain their resistance against the

The United States seeks and receives aid from France

overwhelming strength of the mother country. It was only after the Americans had defeated Burgoyne at Saratoga that France, in 1778, concluded a treaty with the United States in which the independence of the new republic was recognized. This was equivalent to declaring war upon England. The enthusiasm for the Americans was so great in France that a number of the younger nobles, the most conspicuous of whom was the Marquis of Lafayette, crossed the Atlantic to fight as volunteers in the American army.

FIG. 29. STATUE OF LAFAYETTE

A gift to France from the school children of the United States, July 4, 1900. This statue stands in the gardens of the Louvre palace, Paris

In spite of the skill and heroic self-sacrifice of Washington, the Americans lost more battles than they gained. It is extremely doubtful whether they would have succeeded in bringing the war to a favorable close, by forcing the English general, Cornwallis, to capitulate at Yorktown (1781), had it not been for the aid of the French fleet.[1] The chief result of the war was the recognition by England of the independence of the United States, whose territory was to extend to the Mississippi River. To the west of the Mississippi the vast territory of Louisiana still remained in the hands of Spain, as well as Florida, which England had held since 1763 but now gave back.

[1] Cornwallis's account of his surrender is given in the *Readings*, Vol. I, p. 135.

Spain and Portugal were able to hold their American possessions a generation longer than the English, but in the end practically all of the Western Hemisphere, with the exception of Canada, completely freed itself from the domination of the European powers. Cuba, one of the very last vestiges of Spanish rule in the West, gained its independence with the aid of the United States in 1898.

Revolt of the English colonies the beginning of the emancipation of the Western Hemisphere

The results of the European wars during the seventy years which elapsed between the Treaty of Utrecht and the French Revolution may be summarized as follows. In the northeast two new powers, Russia and Prussia, had come into the European family of nations. Prussia had greatly extended her territory by gaining Silesia and West Poland. She and Austria were, in the nineteenth century, to engage in a struggle for supremacy in Germany, which was to result in substituting the German Empire under the headship of the Hohenzollerns for the Holy Roman Empire, of which the House of Hapsburg had so long been the nominal chief.

Results in Europe of the wars between the Treaty of Utrecht and the Peace of Paris

The power of the Sultan of Turkey was declining so rapidly that Austria and Russia were already considering the seizure of his European possessions. This presented a new problem to the European powers, which came to be known in the nineteenth century as the "eastern question." Were Austria and Russia permitted to aggrandize themselves by adding the Turkish territory to their possessions, it would gravely disturb the balance of power which England had so much at heart. So it came about that, from this time on, Turkey was admitted in a way to the family of western European nations, for it soon appeared that some of the states of western Europe were willing to form alliances with the Sultan, and even aid him directly in defending himself against his neighbors.[1]

Origin of the "eastern question"

England had lost her American colonies, and by her perverse policy had led to the creation of a sister state speaking her own language and destined to occupy the central part of the

England's colonial possessions

[1] See below, p. 574.

North American continent from the Atlantic to the Pacific. She still retained Canada, however, and in the nineteenth century added a new continent in the southern hemisphere, Australia, to her vast colonial empire. In India she had no further rivals among European nations, and gradually extended her influence over the whole region south of the Himalayas.

France under Louis XV, 1715–1774

As for France, she had played a rather pitiful rôle during the long reign of Louis XIV's great-grandson, Louis XV (1715–1774). She had, however, been able to increase her territory by the addition of Lorraine (1766) and, in 1768, of the island of Corsica. A year later a child was born in the Corsican town of Ajaccio, who one day, by his genius, was to make France the center for a time of an empire rivaling that of Charlemagne in extent. When the nineteenth century opened France was no longer a monarchy, but a republic; and her armies were to occupy in turn every European capital, from Madrid to Moscow. In order to understand the marvelous transformations produced by the French Revolution and the wars of Napoleon, we must consider somewhat carefully the conditions in France which led to a great reform of her institutions in 1789, and to the founding of a republic four years later.

QUESTIONS

SECTION 18. What is the explanation of the wars of the sixteenth and seventeenth centuries? What countries in the fifteenth and sixteenth centuries were responsible for bringing Europe into contact with the East and the West? What parts of the world did they discover and settle?

SECTION 19. Mention the names of three French explorers in North America during the last quarter of the seventeenth century. What did they accomplish? In what way did the Treaty of Utrecht affect the North American possessions of England? In what other part of the world were the French and the English rivals? How was India governed from the sixteenth to the eighteenth century? What effect did the death in 1707 of the Great Mogul Aurangzeb have upon the government of India? Draw a map of India showing the principal rivers and mountains. Indicate the location of the trading posts belonging to the English in the seventeenth century. What was the center of the French possessions in India at the same period? Locate the place on the map just drawn.

Describe the struggle between the French and the English which took place in North America between 1754 and 1763. What prevented France from giving sufficient attention to her North American colonies during the French and Indian War? What name was given to the war as waged in Europe and in India? Describe the part taken by William Pitt in the Seven Years' War. Tell of the work done by Clive and by Dupleix in the conflict between the English and the French in India during the War of the Austrian Succession. What led to the outbreak of the Seven Years' War in India? Mention the territorial gains which England made as a result of the Treaty of Paris, 1763.

SECTION 20. What was the attitude of England toward the American colonies down to the close of the French and Indian War? What was the purpose for which the Stamp Act of 1765 was passed? How did the American colonists view the act? What were the Navigation Acts, and when were the first passed? Describe the trade laws and tell of the attitude of the American colonists toward them. How did the English meet the colonial opposition to the Stamp Act of 1765? What caused the Boston Tea Party of 1773? Was Burke's advice followed by King George III and Parliament? What was the First Continental Congress? Where and when was it held?

What decision did it come to? Describe the work of the Second Continental Congress in 1775. What had taken place between the meeting of the First and Second Continental congresses? Describe the attitude of the Second Continental Congress. On what mission was Benjamin Franklin sent to the court of Louis XVI? What was the result of this visit? What was the extent of the United States in 1783? To what nation did the rest of what is now the United States belong? What is meant by the "eastern question"? Name the colonial possessions of Great Britain after 1783. What was the British colonial policy? Who succeeded Louis XIV on the throne of France? Mention, with dates, two important events of his reign.

Section 21. Life in the Country — Serfdom

If a peasant who had lived on a manor in the time of the Crusades had been permitted to return to earth and travel about Europe at the opening of the eighteenth century, he would have found much to remind him of the conditions under which, seven centuries earlier, he had extracted a scanty living from the soil. It is true that the gradual extinction of serfdom in western Europe appears to have begun as early as the twelfth century, but it proceeded at very different rates in different countries. In France the old type of serf had largely disappeared by the fourteenth century, and in England a hundred years later. In Prussia, Austria, Poland, Russia, Italy, and Spain, on the contrary, the great mass of the country people were still bound to the soil in the eighteenth century.

Survivals of the manorial system in France in the eighteenth century

Even in France there were still many annoying traces of the old system.[1] The peasant was, it is true, no longer bound to a particular manor; he could buy or sell his land at will, could marry without consulting the lord, and could go and come as he pleased. Many bought their land outright, while others disposed of their holdings and settled in town. But the lord might still require all those on his manor to grind their grain at his mill, bake their bread in his oven, and press their grapes in his wine press. The peasant might have to pay a toll to cross a bridge or ferry which was under the lord's control, or a certain sum for driving his flock past the lord's mansion. Many of the old arrangements still forced the peasant occupying a particular

[1] For a list of feudal dues, see *Readings*, Vol. I, p. 139.

plot of land to turn over to the lord a certain portion of his crops, and, if he sold his land, to pay the lord a part of the money he received for it.

Survivals in England of the manorial system

In England in the eighteenth century the prominent features of serfdom had disappeared more completely than in France. The services in labor due to the lord had long been commuted

FIG. 30. THE OVEN OF THE MANOR

The oven at which those on the manor had to bake their bread was sometimes a large stone structure in the open air. The one in the picture has fallen into ruins since now the country people bake at home and so avoid paying the owner of the oven a part of the flour or bread for its use

into money payments, and the peasant was thus transformed into a renter or owner of his holding. He still took off his hat to the squire of his village, and was liable to be severely punished by his lord, who was commonly a justice of the peace, if he was caught shooting a hare on the game preserves.

In central, southern, and eastern Europe the medieval system still prevailed; the peasant lived and died upon the same manor, and worked for his lord in the same way that his ancestors had

Condition of the serfs in a great part of Europe in the eighteenth century

worked a thousand years before. Everywhere the same crude agricultural instruments were still used, and most of the implements and tools were rudely made in the village itself. The wooden plows commonly found even on English farms were constructed on the model of the old Roman plow; wheat was

FIG. 31. INTERIOR OF A PEASANT'S HUT

The house consists of one room. Milk jugs, kettles, and pails stand around the fireplace, where the cooking is done. In the corner stands the bed, curtained off from the room to secure privacy. Notice the heavy beam supporting the ceiling

cut with a sickle, grass with an unwieldy scythe, and the rickety cart wheels were supplied only with wooden rims.

Wretched houses of the peasants

The houses occupied by the country people differed greatly from Sicily to Pomerania, and from Ireland to Poland; but, in general, they were small, with little light or ventilation, and often they were nothing but wretched hovels with dirt floors and neglected thatch roofs. The pigs and the cows were frequently better housed than the people, with whom they associated upon

FIG. 32. A MERCHANT IN HIS SHOP IN THE OLD RÉGIME

Most of the shops of the eighteenth century were just rooms of private houses fitted up for business. The merchant, dozing behind the counter, has had to hang his goods from the ceiling and arrange them on shelves over the doorway, although he has only a few articles to sell. Outside, a richly painted sign, giving pictures of his wares, informed those who could not read, what the merchant had for sale

FIG. 33. INTERIOR OF A HOUSE IN THE OLD RÉGIME

This is a room in the house of a well-to-do Norman sailor, as shown in the municipal museum of Honfleur. The flax wheel was kept busy beside the open fire; cupboards and shelves show how crowded the little house was, and the trim headdresses and well-arranged chairs indicate that the women's work was neatly done, and that the sailor did well to take off his muddy boots very familiar terms, since the barn and the house were commonly in the same building. The drinking water was bad, and there was no attempt to secure proper drainage. Fortunately every one was out of doors a great deal of the time, for the women as well as the men usually worked in the fields, cultivating the soil and helping to gather in the crops.[1]

Unattractive character of country life

Country life in the eighteenth century was obviously very arduous and unattractive for the most part. The peasant had no newspapers to tell him of the world outside his manor, nor could he have read them if he had them. Even in England not one farmer in five thousand, it is said, could read at all; and in France the local tax collectors were too uneducated to make out their own reports. Farther east conditions must have been still more cheerless, for a Hungarian peasant complains that he owed four days of his labor to his lord, spent the fifth and sixth hunting and fishing for him, while the seventh belonged to God.

Section 22. The Towns and the Guilds

Towns still medieval in the eighteenth century

Even in the towns there was much to remind one of the Middle Ages. The narrow, crooked streets, darkened by the overhanging buildings and scarcely lighted at all by night, the rough cobblestones, the disgusting odors even in the best quarters—all offered a marked contrast to the European cities of to-day, which have grown tremendously in the last hundred years in size, beauty, and comfort.

London

In 1760 London had half a million inhabitants, or about a tenth of its present population. There were of course no street cars or omnibuses, to say nothing of the thousands of automobiles which now thread their way in and out through the press of traffic. A few hundred hackney coaches and sedan chairs served to carry those who had not private conveyances and could not, or would not, walk. The ill-lighted streets were

[1] The picture facing this page shows the interior of a town house belonging to the owner of a fishing boat, who is better off than the peasantry.

guarded at night by watchmen who went about with lanterns, but afforded so little protection against the roughs and robbers that gentlemen were compelled to carry arms when passing through the streets after nightfall.

FIG. 34. STREET OF A TOWN IN THE EIGHTEENTH CENTURY

The streets were still narrow, though wider than in medieval cities, for there were no longer walls to inclose them. But the houses often had projecting gables with heavy beams like those in this quaint French town of Honfleur

Paris was somewhat larger than London and had outgrown its medieval walls.[1] The police were more efficient there, and the highway robberies which disgraced London and its suburbs were almost unknown. The great park, the "Elysian fields," and many boulevards which now form so distinguished a feature of Paris were already laid out; but, in general, the streets were still narrow, and there were none of the fine broad avenues which now radiate from a hundred centers. There were few sewers to carry off the water which, when it rained, flowed through the middle of the streets. The filth of former times still remained, and the people relied upon easily polluted wells or the dirty River Seine for their water supply.

[1] For a description of the streets of Paris in 1787, see *Readings*, Vol. I, p. 141. Wide streets were laid out along the line of the earlier walls, known as "boulevards" from the "bulwarks" which they superseded.

In Germany very few of the towns had spread beyond their medieval walls. They had, for the most part, lost their former prosperity, which was still attested by the fine houses of the merchants and of the once flourishing guilds. Berlin had a population of only about two hundred thousand. Vienna, in Austria, was slightly larger. This city then employed from thirty to a hundred street cleaners and boasted that the street lamps were lighted every night, while many towns contented themselves with dirty streets and with light during the winter months, and then only when the moon was not scheduled to shine.

German towns

Even the famous cities of Italy, — Milan, Genoa, Florence, Rome, — notwithstanding their beautiful palaces and public buildings, were, with the exception of water-bound Venice, crowded into the narrow compass of the town wall, and their streets were narrow and crooked.

Italian cities

Another contrast between the towns of the eighteenth century and those of to-day lay in the absence of the great wholesale warehouses, the vast factories with their tall chimneys, and the attractive department stores which may now be found in every city from Dublin to Budapest. Commerce and industry were in general conducted upon a very small scale, except at the great ports like London, Antwerp, or Amsterdam, where goods coming from and going to the colonies were brought together.

Trade and industry conducted on a small scale

The growth of industry under the influence of the various machines which were being invented during the latter part of the eighteenth century will form the subject of a later chapter. It is clear, however, that before the introduction of railroads, steamships, and machine-equipped factories, all business operations must have been carried on in what would seem to us a slow and primitive fashion.

A great part of the manufacturing still took place in little shops where the articles when completed were offered for sale. Generally those who owned the various shops carrying on a

The trades organized into guilds

particular trade, such as tailoring, shoemaking, baking, tanning, bookbinding, hair cutting, or the making of candles, knives, hats, artificial flowers, swords, or wigs, were organized into a guild — a union — the main object of which was to prevent all other citizens from making or selling the articles in which the members of the guild dealt. The number of master workmen who might open a shop of their own was often limited by the guild, as well as the number of apprentices each master could train. The period of apprenticeship was long, sometimes seven or even nine years, on the ground that it took years to learn the trade properly, but really because the guild wished to maintain its monopoly by keeping down the number who could become masters. When the apprenticeship was over, the workman became a journeyman, but, unless he had influential friends, he might never perhaps become a master workman and open a shop of his own.

FIG. 35. PUBLIC LETTER WRITER

Since most common people could not read or write, they had to employ letter writers, who often had stalls like this along the street

Guilds in England

This guild system had originated in the Middle Ages and was consequently hundreds of years old. In England the term of seven years was required for apprenticeship in all the staple trades, although the rule was by no means universally enforced. In Sheffield no master cutler could have more than one apprentice at a time; the master weavers of Norfolk and Norwich were limited to two apprentices each, and no master hatter in England could have more than two.[1]

Guilds in France and Germany

In France the guilds were more powerful than in England, since they had been supported and encouraged by Colbert, who believed that they kept up the standard of French products. In Germany the organization was much stricter and more widespread than either in England or in France. Old regulations concerning apprenticeship and the conduct of the various trades were still enforced. As a general rule, no master could have more than one apprentice, manage more than one workshop, or sell goods that he had not himself produced.

Strife among the guilds

Everywhere a workman had to stick to his trade; if a cobbler should venture to make a pair of new boots, or a baker should roast a piece of meat in his oven, he might be expelled from the guild unless he made amends. In Paris a hatter, who had greatly increased his trade by making hats of wool mixed with silk, had his stock destroyed by the guild authorities on the ground that the rules permitted hats to be made only of wool and said nothing of silk. The trimming makers had an edict passed forbidding any one to make buttons that were cast or turned or made of horn.

The guilds not only protected themselves against workmen who opened shops without their permission, but each particular trade was in more or less constant disagreement with the other trades as to what each might make. The goldsmiths were the natural enemies of all who used gold in their respective operations, such as the clockmakers and watchmakers, the money changers, and those who set precious stones. Those who dealt in natural flowers were not allowed to encroach upon those who made artificial ones. One who baked bread must not make pies or cakes. The tailor who mended clothes must not make new garments. Such regulations were naturally too strict to be rigorously enforced, but they hampered industry.

[1] Adam Smith's account of the guilds of his day is printed in the *Readings*, Vol. I, p. 142.

Three important differences between the guilds and the modern trade-unions

The guilds differed from the modern trade-unions in several important respects. In the first place, it was only the master workmen, who owned the shops, tools, or machines, who belonged to them. The apprentices and journeymen, that is, the ordinary workmen, were excluded and had no influence whatever upon the policy of the organization. In the second place, the government enforced the decisions of the guilds. For example, in Paris, if it was learned that a journeyman goldbeater was working for himself, a representative of the guild went to the offender's house, accompanied by a town officer, and seized his tools and materials, after which the unfortunate man might be sent to the galleys for three years or perhaps get off with a heavy fine, imprisonment, and the loss of every chance of ever becoming a master. Lastly, the guilds were confined to the old-established industries which were still carried on, as during the Middle Ages, on a small scale in the master's house.

Decline of the guilds

In spite, however, of the seeming strength of the guilds, they were really giving way before the entirely new conditions which had arisen. Thoughtful persons disapproved of them on the ground that they hampered industry and prevented progress by their outworn restrictions. In many towns the regulations were evaded or had broken down altogether, so that enterprising workmen and dealers carried on their business as they pleased. Then, as we have said, it was only the old industries that were included in the guild system. The newer manufactures, of silk and cotton goods, porcelain, fine glassware, etc., which had been introduced into Europe, were under the control of individuals or companies who were independent of the old guilds and relied upon monopolies and privileges granted by the rulers, who, in France at least, were glad to foster new industries.

Meanwhile, as we shall see later,[1] the progress of invention was preparing the new age of machinery and factories, which was to change the whole nature of industry, and bring the modern problems of employer and workman, or capital and labor.

[1] See below, pp. 143 ff.

Section 23. The Nobility and the Monarchy

Not only had the medieval manor and the medieval guilds maintained themselves down into the eighteenth century, but the successors of the feudal lords continued to exist as a conspicuous and powerful class. They enjoyed various privileges and distinctions denied to the ordinary citizen, although they were, of course, shorn of the great power that the more important dukes and counts had enjoyed in the Middle Ages, when they ruled over vast tracts, could summon their vassals to assist them in their constant wars with their neighbors, and dared defy even the authority of the king himself.

The former independence of the feudal nobles lost by the eighteenth century

It is impossible to recount here how the English, French, and Spanish kings gradually subjugated the turbulent barons and brought the great fiefs directly under royal control. Suffice it to say that the monarchs met with such success that in the eighteenth century the nobles no longer held aloof but eagerly sought the king's court. Those whose predecessors had once been veritable sovereigns within their own domains, had declared war even against the king, coined money, made laws for their subjects, and meted out justice in their castle halls, had, by the eighteenth century, deserted their war horses and laid aside their long swords; in their velvet coats and high-heeled shoes they were contented with the privilege of helping the king to dress in the morning and attending him at dinner. The battlemented castle, once the stronghold of independent chieftains, was transformed into a tasteful country residence where, if the king honored the owner with a visit, the host was no longer tempted, as his ancestors had been, to shower arrows and stones upon the royal intruder.

The French nobility

The French noble, unlike the English, was not fond of the country, but lived with the court at Versailles whenever he could afford to do so, and often when he could not. He liked the excitement of the court, and it was there that he could best advance his own and his friends' interests by obtaining lucrative offices in the army or Church or in the king's palace. By their prolonged absence from their estates the nobles lost the esteem of their tenants, while their stewards roused the hatred of the peasants by strictly collecting all the ancient manorial dues in order that the lord might enjoy the gayeties at Versailles.

The unpopularity of the French nobility was further increased by their exemptions from some of the heavy taxes, on the

FIG. 36. FRENCH CASTLE TRANSFORMED INTO A COUNTRY RESIDENCE

The round towers, covered with ivy, date from the Middle Ages. The rest has been rebuilt with pleasant sunny windows in place of loopholes in the walls. The terrace and lawn lying between the old drawbridge towers and the house once formed the castle courtyard [1]

The French nobility a privileged class

ground that they were still supposed to shed their blood in fighting for their king instead of paying him money like the unsoldierly burghers and peasants. They enjoyed, moreover, the preference when the king had desirable positions to grant. They also claimed a certain social superiority, since they were excluded by their traditions of birth from engaging in any ordinary trade or industry, although they might enter some

[1] This was the residence of the French historian de Tocqueville, near Cherbourg.

FIG. 37. A NOBLE FAMILY OF THE OLD RÉGIME

Extravagance in dress, of which the men were as guilty as the women, was largely due to the influence of court life, where so many nobles were rivaling each other in display. This brought hardship to the people on their estates in the country, since they had to support their masters' expenses

professions, such as medicine, law, the Church, or the army, or even participate in maritime trade without derogating from their rank. In short, the French nobility, including, it is estimated, a hundred and thirty thousand or forty thousand persons, constituted a privileged class, although they no longer performed any of the high functions which had been exercised by their predecessors.

The ennobled

To make matters worse, very few of the nobles really belonged to old feudal families. For the most part they had been ennobled by the king for some supposed service, or had bought an office, or a judgeship in the higher courts, to which noble rank was attached. Naturally this circumstance served to rob them of much of the respect that their hereditary dignity and titles might otherwise have gained for them.

Peculiar position of the English peerage

In England the feudal castles had disappeared earlier even than in France, and the English law did not grant to any one, however long and distinguished his lineage, special rights or privileges not enjoyed by every freeman. Nevertheless there was a distinct noble class in England.[1] The monarch had formerly been accustomed to summon his earls and some of his barons to take council with him, and in this way the *peerage* developed; this included those whose title permitted them to sit in the House of Lords and to transmit this honorable prerogative to their eldest sons. But the peers paid the same taxes as every other subject and were punished in the same manner if they were convicted of an offense. Moreover only the eldest surviving son of a noble father inherited his rank, while on the Continent all the children became nobles. In this way the number of the English nobility was greatly restricted, and their social distinction roused little antagonism.

The German knights still resembled medieval lords

In Germany, however, the nobles continued to occupy very much the same position which their ancestors held in the Middle Ages. There had been no king to do for all Germany what the French kings had done for France; no mighty man had risen strong enough to batter down castle walls and bend all barons, great and small, to his will. The result was that there were in Germany in the eighteenth century hundreds of nobles dwelling in strong old castles and ruling with a high hand domains which were sometimes no larger than a big American farm. They

[1] For Voltaire's account of the English nobility, see *Readings*, Vol. I, p. 146.

levied taxes, held courts, coined money, and maintained standing armies of perhaps only a handful of soldiers.

In all the countries of Europe the chief noble was of course the monarch himself, to whose favor almost all the lesser nobles owed their titles and rank. He was, except in a few cases, always despotic, permitting the people no share in the management of the government and often rendering them miserable by needless wars and ill-advised and oppressive taxes. He commonly maintained a very expensive court and gave away to unworthy courtiers much of the money which he had wrung from his people. He was permitted to imprison his subjects upon the slightest grounds and in the most unjust manner; nevertheless he usually enjoyed their loyalty and respect, since they were generally ready to attribute his bad acts to evil councilors.

The chief noble was the king

His arbitrary powers

On the whole, the king merited the respect paid him. He it was who had destroyed the power of innumerable lesser despots and created something like a nation. He had put a stop to the private warfare and feudal brigandage which had disgraced the Middle Ages. His officers maintained order throughout the country so that merchants and travelers could go to and fro with little danger. He opened highroads for them and established a general system of coinage, which greatly facilitated business operations. He interested himself more and more in commerce and industry and often encouraged learning. Finally, by consolidating his realms and establishing a regular system of government, he prepared the way for the European State of to-day in which the people either secured control over lawmaking and national finances, or, as in the case of France, the monarch has been discarded altogether as no longer needful. Democracy and political equality would, in fact, have been impossible if monarchs had not leveled down the proud and mighty nobles who aspired to be petty kings in their domains. But still the monarchs preferred to associate with nobles at their courts, rather than with the great middle class which formed the mass of the nation.

The services performed by even despotic kings

Section 24. The Catholic Church

Importance of the medieval Church in explaining modern problems

The eighteenth century had inherited from the Middle Ages the nobility with their peculiar privileges. At the same time the clergy, especially in Catholic countries, still possessed privileges which set them off from the nation at large. They were far more powerful and better organized than the nobility and exercised a potent influence in the State. The clergy owed their authority to the Church, which for many centuries had been the great central institution of Europe.

It must be remembered that every one in the Middle Ages had been required to belong to the Church, somewhat in the same way that we to-day all belong as a matter of course to the State. Before the Protestant Revolt all the states of western Europe had formed a single religious association from which it was a crime to revolt. To refuse allegiance to the Church or to question its authority or teachings was reputed treason against God, the most terrible of all crimes.

The Church did not rely for its support, as churches must to-day, upon the voluntary contributions of its members, but enjoyed the revenue from vast domains which kings, nobles, and other landholders had from time to time given to the churches and monasteries. In addition to the income from its lands, the Church had the right, like the State, to impose a regular tax, which was called the tithe. All who were subject to this were forced to pay it, whether they cared anything about religion or not, just as we are all compelled to pay taxes imposed by the government under which we live.

Great powers still retained by the Catholic Church in the eighteenth century

In spite of the changes which had overtaken the Church since the Middle Ages, it still retained its ancient external appearance in the eighteenth century — its gorgeous ceremonial, its wealth, its influence over the lives of men, its intolerance of those who ventured to differ from the conceptions of Christianity which it held. The Church could fine and imprison those whom it convicted of blasphemy, contempt of religion, or heresy. The clergy managed the schools in which, of course, the children were brought up in the orthodox faith. Hospitals and other charitable institutions were under their control. They registered all births and deaths, and only the marriages which they sanctified were regarded by the State as legal. The monasteries still existed in great numbers and owned vast tracts of land. A map of Paris made in 1789 shows no less than sixty-eight monasteries and seventy-three nunneries within the walls. The tithe was still paid as in the Middle Ages; and the clergy still enjoyed exemption from the direct taxes.

Intolerance of both Catholics and Protestants

Judged by the standards of the twentieth century, both the Catholic and the Protestant churches were very intolerant, and in this were usually supported by the government, which was ready to punish or persecute those who refused to conform to the State religion, whatever it might be, or ventured to speak or write against its doctrines. There was none of that freedom which is so general now, and which permits a man to worship or not as he pleases, to reject and even to denounce religion in any or all of its forms without danger of imprisonment, loss of citizenship, or death.

Position of the Protestants in France

In France, after the revocation of the Edict of Nantes in 1685, Protestants had lost all civil rights. According to a decree of 1724, those who assembled for any form of worship other than the Roman Catholic were condemned to lose their property; the men were to be sent to the galleys and the women imprisoned for life. The preachers who convoked such assemblies or performed Protestant ceremonies were punishable with death; but only a few executions took place, for happily the old enthusiasm for persecution was abating. None the less, all who did not accept the Catholic teachings were practically outlawed, for the priests would neither recognize the marriages nor register the births and deaths over which they were not called to preside. This made it impossible for Protestants to marry legally and have legitimate children, or to inherit or bequeath property.

Censorship of the press

Books and pamphlets were carefully examined in order to see whether they contained any attacks upon the orthodox Catholic beliefs or might in any way serve to undermine the authority of the Church or of the king. The Pope had long maintained a commission (which still exists) to examine new books, and to publish from time to time a list, called the Index, of all those which the Church condemned and forbade the faithful to read. The king of France, as late as 1757, issued a declaration establishing the death penalty for those who wrote, printed, or distributed any work which appeared to be an attack upon religion. The teachings of the professors in the university were watched. A clergyman who ventured to compare the healing of the sick by Christ to the cures ascribed to Æsculapius was arrested (about 1750) by order of the king's judges at Paris and forced to leave the country. A considerable number of the books issued in France in the eighteenth century, which ventured to criticize the government or the Church, were condemned either by the clergy or the king's courts, and were burned by the common hangman or suppressed. Not infrequently the authors, if they could be discovered, were imprisoned.

Censorship ineffective

Nevertheless books attacking the old ideas and suggesting reforms in Church and State constantly appeared and were freely circulated.[1] The writers took care not to place their names or those of the publishers upon the title-pages, and many such books were printed at Geneva or in Holland, where great freedom prevailed. Many others which purported to be printed abroad were actually printed secretly at home.

Strength of the Church in Spain, Austria, and Italy

In Spain, Austria, and Italy, however, and especially in the Papal States, the clergy, particularly the Jesuits, were more powerful and enjoyed more privileges than in France. In Spain the censorship of the press and the Inquisition constituted a double bulwark against change until the latter half of the eighteenth century.

[1] See following chapter.

In Germany the position of the Church varied greatly. The southern states were Catholic, while Prussia and the north had embraced Protestantism. Many bishops and abbots ruled as princes over their own lands. Their estates covered almost a third of the map of western and southern Germany, and were, of course, quite distinct from the spiritual provinces or dioceses. Peculiar situation of the great German prelates

SECTION 25. THE ENGLISH ESTABLISHED CHURCH AND THE PROTESTANT SECTS

In England Henry VIII had thrown off his allegiance to the Pope and declared himself the head of the English Church. Under his daughter, Queen Elizabeth (1558–1603), Parliament had established the Church of England. It abolished the mass and sanctioned the Book of Common Prayer, which has since remained the official guide to the services in the Anglican Church. The beliefs of the Church were brought together in the Thirty-Nine Articles, from which no one was to vary or depart. The system of government of the Roman Catholic Church, with its archbishops, bishops, and priests, was retained, but the appointment of bishops was put in the hands of the monarch or his ministers. All clergymen were required to subscribe solemnly to the Thirty-Nine Articles. All public religious services were to be conducted according to the Prayer Book, and those who failed to attend services on Sunday and holydays were to be fined. The Anglican Church as established under Queen Elizabeth (1558–1603)

Those who persisted in adhering to the Roman Catholic faith fared badly, although happily there were no such general massacres as overwhelmed the Protestants in France. Under the influence of the Jesuits some of the English Catholics became involved in plots against the Protestant queen, Elizabeth, who had been deposed by the Pope. These alleged "traitors" were in some instances executed for treason. Indeed, any one who brought a papal bull to England, who embraced Catholicism, or converted a Protestant was declared a traitor. Persecution of the Catholics in England

Fines and imprisonment were inflicted upon those who dared to say or to hear a mass.[1]

The Puritans

But, as we have seen,[2] there were many Protestants who did not approve of the Anglican Church as established by law. These "Dissenters" developed gradually into several sects with differing views. By far the most numerous of the Dissenters were the Baptists. They spread to America, and were the first Protestant sect to undertake foreign missions on a large scale, having founded a society for that purpose as early as 1792.[3]

The Friends, or Quakers

Another English sect which was destined also to be conspicuous in America was the Society of Friends, or Quakers, as they are commonly called. This group owes its origin to George Fox, who began his preaching in 1647. The Friends were distinguished by their simplicity of life and dress, their abhorrence of war, and their rejection of all ceremonial, including even the Lord's Supper. Their chief stronghold in America has always been Pennsylvania, more particularly Philadelphia and its neighborhood, where they settled under the leadership of William Penn.

The Quakers were the first religious sect to denounce war ever and always, and they should have the credit of beginning the movement against war which had gained much headway before the outbreak of the war in 1914.

John Wesley and the Methodists

The last of the great Protestant sects to appear was that of the Methodists. Their founder, John Wesley, when at Oxford had established a religious society among his fellow students. Their piety and the regularity of their habits gained for them the

[1] It may be noted here that the Catholics found a refuge in America from their Protestant persecutors, as did the Huguenots who fled from the oppression of the Catholic government in France. The colony of Maryland was founded by Lord Baltimore in 1634 and named after the French wife of Charles I. In the nineteenth century the number of Catholics in the United States was vastly increased by immigration from Ireland, Italy, and other countries, so that there are over thirteen millions to-day who have been baptized into the Roman Catholic Church.

[2] See above, pp. 39 and 50.

[3] For the legal position of the Catholics and Dissenters, see Blackstone's description in the *Readings*, Vol. I, p. 162.

nickname of "Methodists." After leaving Oxford, Wesley spent some time in the colony of Georgia. On his return to England in 1738 he came to believe in the sudden and complete forgiveness of sins known as "conversion," which he later made the basis of his teaching. He began a series of great revival meetings in London and other large towns. He journeyed up and

FIG. 38. JOHN WESLEY

down the land, aided in his preaching by his brother Charles and by the impassioned Whitefield.[1]

Only gradually did the Methodists separate themselves from the Church of England, of which they at first considered themselves members. In 1784 the numerous American Methodists were formally organized into the Methodist Episcopal Church, and early in the nineteenth century the English Methodists became an independent organization. At the time of Wesley's

[1] For extracts from Wesley's famous Journal, see *Readings*, Vol. I, p. 168.

death his followers numbered over fifty thousand, and there are now in the United States over six millions, including the various branches of the Church.

Decline of the persecution of Dissenters

We have seen[1] how little of the spirit of toleration there was in England in the seventeenth century, during the Stuart period and the Commonwealth. With the reign of William and Mary, however, the spirit of persecution died down. To be sure, England had its State Church, and even if, by the Act of Toleration of 1689, the Dissenters were permitted to hold services in their own way, they were excluded from government offices unless they violated their own faith, nor could they obtain a degree at the universities. Only the members of the Anglican Church could hold a benefice. Its bishops had seats in the House of Lords and its priests enjoyed a social preëminence denied to the dissenting ministers.

The privileges of the Anglican clergy

Existence of Catholics not recognized in England

Towards Roman Catholics the law remained as harsh as ever. Those who clung to the Roman Catholic faith, to the Pope and the mass, were forbidden to enter England. The celebration of the mass was strictly prohibited. All public offices were closed to Catholics and of course they could not sit in Parliament. Indeed, legally, they had no right whatever to be in England at all. But as in the case of the Dissenters, the laws were enforced less and less as time went on.

Freedom of the press in England

The Church courts still existed in England and could punish laymen for not attending church, for heresy, and for certain immoral acts. But their powers were little exercised compared with the situation on the Continent. Moreover one who published a book or pamphlet did not have to obtain the permission of the government as in France. Indeed, nowhere was there such unrestrained discussion of scientific and religious matters at this period as in England. As we shall see in the following chapter, England, in the early eighteenth century, was the center of progressive thought from which the French philosophers and reformers drew their inspiration.

[1] See above, pp. 50 f

As a matter of fact there were too many different sects in England for any one church to crush the others. Blackstone, writing at the opening of the reign of George III, summed up the legal view in the following manner: "Certainly our ancestors were mistaken in their plans of compulsion and intolerance. The sin of schism, as such, is by no means the object of temporal coercion and punishment. If through weakness of intellect, through misdirected piety, through perverseness and acerbity of temper, or (which is often the case) through a prospect of secular advantage in herding with a party, men quarrel with the ecclesiastical establishment, the civil magistrate has nothing to do with it, unless their tenets and practice are such as threaten ruin or disturbance to the State. He is bound indeed to protect the Established Church, and if this can be better effected by admitting none but its genuine members to offices of trust and emolument, he is certainly at liberty to do so, the disposal of offices being matter of favor and discretion. But, this point being once secured, all persecution for diversity of opinions, however ridiculous or absurd they may be, is contrary to every principle of sound policy and civil freedom."

QUESTIONS

SECTION 21. Who were the serfs? In what parts of Europe were they to be found in the eighteenth century? Describe the life of the peasants on a French estate.

SECTION 22. Contrast the towns of the eighteenth century with those of to-day. Describe the guild system. What were the advantages, and the disadvantages, of the system? In what respects are the modern trade-unions unlike the guilds?

SECTION 23. What privileges did a French noble enjoy in the old régime? How did one become a noble? Contrast the English nobility with the French. In what respects did the noble of Germany differ from his equals in France or in England? What justification, if any, is there for the despotic rule of the kings of the old régime?

SECTION 24. In what ways did the Church of the Middle Ages differ from the Church, Catholic or Protestant, of modern times? How many of its medieval powers did the Roman Catholic Church retain in the seventeenth century? What was the Index? What examples are there of religious intolerance in France and England during the period just named?

SECTION 25. What Church replaced the Roman Catholic Church in England after the Protestant Revolt? Describe its system of government. Where may a statement of its beliefs be found? Mention the different religious sects (Dissenters) which appeared in England after the break with Rome. Who founded them? Do these religious sects exist to-day? If so, has their influence been felt beyond England? Describe the attitude of Parliament toward Dissenters during the reign of Charles II. Contrast it with that of the reign of William and Mary.

CHAPTER VI

THE SPIRIT OF REFORM

SECTION 26. THE DEVELOPMENT OF MODERN SCIENCE

The spirit of reform

A thoughtful observer in the eighteenth century would, as we have seen, have discovered many medieval institutions which had persisted in spite of the considerable changes which had taken place in conditions and ideas during the previous five hundred years. Serfdom, the guilds, the feudal dues, the nobility and clergy with their peculiar privileges, the declining monastic orders, the confused and cruel laws — these were a part of the heritage which Europe had received from what was coming to be regarded as a dark and barbarous period. People began to be keenly alive to the deficiencies of the past and to look to the future for better things, even to dream of progress beyond the happiest times of which they had any record. They came to feel that the chief obstacles to progress were the outworn institutions, the ignorance and prejudices of their forefathers, and that if they could only be freed from this burden, they would find it easy to create new and enlightened laws and institutions to suit their needs.

Veneration for the past: "the good old days"

This attitude of mind seems natural enough in our progressive age, but two centuries ago it was distinctly new. Mankind has in general shown an unreasoning respect and veneration for the past. Until the opening of the eighteenth century the former times were commonly held to have been better than the present; for the evils of the past were little known, while those of the present were, as always, only too apparent. Men looked backward rather than forward. They aspired to fight as well, or be as saintly, or write as good books, or paint as beautiful pictures, as the great men of old. That they might excel the achievements of their predecessors did not occur to them. Knowledge was sought not by studying the world about them but in some ancient authority. In Aristotle's vast range of works on various branches of science, the Middle Ages felt that they had a mass of authentic information which it should be the main business of the universities to explain and impart rather than to increase or correct by new investigations. Men's ideals centered in the past, and improvement seemed to them to consist in reviving, so far as possible, "the good old days."

How the scientists have created the spirit of progress and reform

It was mainly to the patient men of science that the western world owed its first hopes of future improvement. It is they who have shown that the ancient writers were mistaken about many serious matters and that they had at best a very crude and imperfect notion of the world. They have gradually robbed men of their old blind respect for the past, and by their discoveries have pointed the way to indefinite advance, so that now we expect constant change and improvement and are scarcely astonished at the most marvelous inventions.

In the Middle Ages the scholars and learned men had been but little interested in the world about them. They devoted far more attention to philosophy and theology than to what we should call the natural sciences. They were satisfied in the main to get their knowledge of nature from reading the works of the ancients — above all, those of Aristotle.

Their modern scientific methods of discovering truth

As early as the thirteenth century, however, a very extraordinary Franciscan friar, Roger Bacon, showed his insight by protesting against the exaggerated veneration for books. Bacon advocated three methods of reaching truth which are now

* Contrast this alchemist's laboratory with one of a modern chemist. Although the alchemist was as intelligent and earnest as the modern scientist, he worked on such futile tasks as trying to change base metals to gold. For he still held with the Greeks that there were four elements — earth, air, fire, and water. In the last part of the eighteenth century Boyle, Priestly, and Lavoisier broke up air and water into their component gases, and chemistry began to show what the world was really made of.

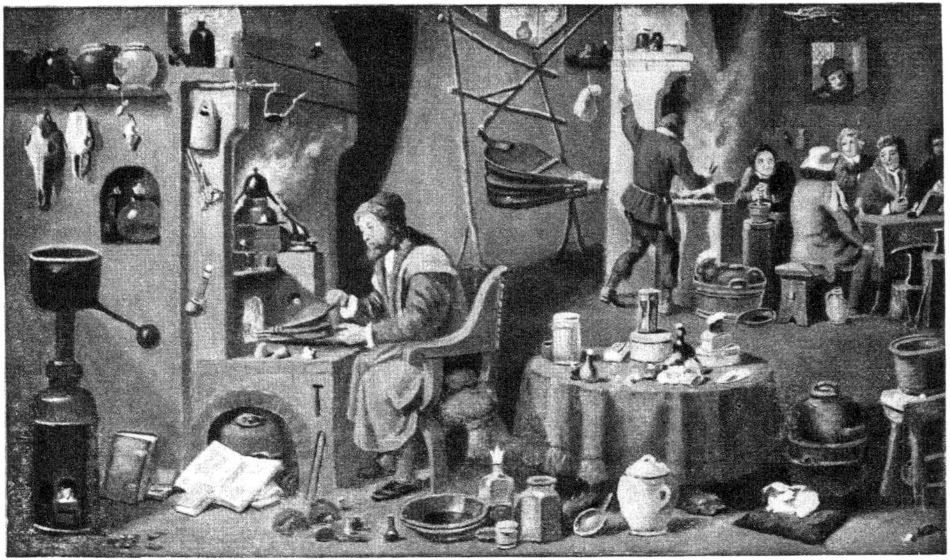

Plate III. Alchemist's Laboratory *

followed by all scientific men.[1] In the first place, he proposed that natural objects and changes should be examined with great care, in order that the observer might determine exactly what happened in any given case. This has led in modern times to incredibly refined measurement and analysis. The chemist, for example, can now determine the exact nature and amount of every substance in a cup of impure water, which may appear perfectly limpid to the casual observer. Then, secondly, Bacon advocated experimentation. He was not contented with mere observation of what actually happened, but tried new and artificial combinations and processes. Nowadays experimentation is, of course, constantly used by scientific investigators, and by means of it they ascertain many things which the most careful observation would never reveal. Thirdly, in order to carry on investigation and make careful measurements and experiments, apparatus designed for this special purpose was found to be necessary. Already in the thirteenth century it was discovered, for example, that a convex crystal or bit of glass would magnify objects, although several centuries elapsed before the microscope and telescope were devised.

1. Exact observation of the phenomena themselves

2. Experimentation

3. Scientific apparatus

Francis Bacon (1561–1626)

The first scholar to draw up a great scheme of all the known sciences and work out a method of research which, if conscientiously followed, promised wonderful discoveries, was Francis Bacon, a versatile English statesman and author who wrote in the time of James I.[2] It seemed to him (as it had seemed to his namesake, Roger Bacon, three centuries earlier) that the discoveries which had hitherto been made were as nothing compared with what could be done if men would but study and experiment with things themselves, abandon their confidence in vague words like "moist" and "dry," "matter" and "form," and repudiate altogether "the thorny philosophy" of Aristotle which was taught in the universities. "No one," he declares,

[1] See Part I, p. 549.

[2] See Part I, p. 656. For extracts from Bacon's works, see *Readings*, Vol. I, p. 174.

"has yet been found so firm of mind and purpose as resolutely to compel himself to sweep away all theories and common notions, and to apply the understanding, thus made fair and even, to a fresh examination of details. Thus it comes about that human knowledge is as yet a mere medley and ill-digested mass, made up of much credulity and much accident, and also of childish notions which we early have imbibed."

Discovery of natural laws

The observation and experimentation of which we have been speaking were carried on by many earnest workers and soon began to influence deeply men's conceptions of the earth and of the universe at large. Of the many scientific discoveries, by far the most fundamental was the conviction that all things about us follow certain natural and immutable laws; and it is the determination of these laws and the seeking out of their applications to which the modern scientific investigator devotes his efforts, whether he be calculating the distance of a star or noting the effect of a drop of acid upon a frog's foot. He has given up all hope of reading man's fate in the stars, or of producing any results by magical processes. He is convinced that the natural laws work regularly. Moreover, his study of the regular processes of nature has enabled him, as Roger Bacon foresaw, to work wonders far more marvelous than any attributed to the medieval magician.

Opposition to scientific discoveries

The path of the scientific investigator has not always been without its thorns. Mankind has changed its notions with reluctance. The churchmen and the professors in the universities were wedded to the conceptions of the world which the medieval theologians and philosophers had worked out, mainly from the Bible and Aristotle. They clung to the textbooks which they and their predecessors had long used in teaching, and had no desire to work in laboratories or keep up with the ideas of the scientists.

Hostile attitude of theologians

Many theologians looked with grave suspicion upon some of the scientific discoveries, on the ground that they did not harmonize with the teachings of the Bible as commonly accepted. It was naturally a great shock to them, and also to the public at large, to have it suggested that man's dwelling place, instead of being God's greatest work, around which the whole starry firmament revolved, was after all but a tiny speck in comparison with the whole universe, and its sun but one of an innumerable host of similar glowing bodies of stupendous size, each of which might have its particular family of planets revolving about it.

FIG. 39. BALLOON ASCENSION, 1783

The crowds along paths of the garden of the Tuileries palace in Paris, on December 1, 1783, saw for the first time two men ascend 2000 feet in a balloon

The bolder thinkers were consequently sometimes made to suffer for their ideas, and their books prohibited or burned. Galileo was forced to say that he did not really believe that the earth revolved about the sun; and he was kept in partial confinement for a time and ordered to recite certain psalms every day for three years for having ventured to question the received views in a book which he wrote in Italian, instead of Latin, so that the public at large might read it.[1]

[1] But even the scientists themselves did not always readily accept new discoveries. Francis Bacon, who lived some seventy years after Copernicus, still clung to the old idea of the revolution of the sun about the earth and still believed in many quite preposterous illusions, as, for example, that "it hath been observed by the ancients that where a rainbow seemeth to hang over or to touch, there breatheth forth a sweet smell"; and that "since the ape is a merry and a bold beast, its heart worn near the heart of a man comforteth the heart and increaseth audacity." In the latter half of the eighteenth century Lavoisier was burned in effigy in Berlin because his discovery of oxygen threatened the accepted explanation of combustion.

Section 27. How the Scientific Discoveries produced a Spirit of Reform

Effects of scientific discoveries on religious belief

Those who accepted the traditional views of the world and of religion, and opposed change, were quite justified in suspecting that scientific investigation would sooner or later make them trouble. It taught men to distrust, and even to scorn, the past which furnished so many instances of ignorance and gross superstition. Instead of accepting the teachings of the theologians, both Catholic and Protestant, that mankind through Adam's fall was rendered utterly vile, and incapable (except through God's special grace) of good thoughts or deeds, certain thinkers began to urge that man was by nature good; that he should freely use his own God-given reason; that he was capable of becoming increasingly wise by a study of nature's laws, and that he could indefinitely better his own condition and that of his fellows if he would but free himself from the shackles of error and superstition. Those who had broadened their views of mankind and of the universe came to believe that God had revealed himself not only to the Jewish people but also, in greater or less degree, to all his creatures in all ages and in all parts of a boundless universe where everything was controlled by his immutable laws. This is illustrated in the famous "Universal Prayer" of Alexander Pope, written about 1737:

> Father of all! in ev'ry age,
>   In ev'ry clime adored,
> By saint, by savage, and by sage,
>   Jehova, Jove, or Lord!
>
> . . . .
>
> Yet not to earth's contracted span
>   Thy goodness let me bound,
> Or think Thee Lord alone of man,
>   When thousand worlds are 'round.

The deists

Such ideas of God's providence had in them nothing essentially unchristian, for they are to be found in writings of early church fathers. But those who advanced them now were often "free thinkers," who attacked the Christian religion in no doubtful terms, and whose books were eagerly read and discussed. These "deists" maintained that their conception of God was far worthier than that of the Christian believer, who, they declared, accused the deity of violating his own laws by miracles and of condemning a great part of his children to eternal torment.

How Voltaire came to England, 1726

In the year 1726 there landed in England a young and gifted Frenchman, who was to become the great prophet of deism in all lands. Voltaire, who was then thirty-two years old, had already deserted the older religious beliefs and was consequently ready to follow enthusiastically the more radical of the English thinkers, who discussed matters with an openness which filled him with astonishment. He became an ardent admirer of the teachings of Newton, whose stately funeral he attended shortly after his arrival. He regarded the discoverer of universal gravitation as greater than an Alexander or a Cæsar, and did all he could to popularize Newton's work in France. "It is to him who masters our minds by the force of truth, not to those who enslave men by violence; it is to him who understands the universe, not to those who disfigure it, that we owe our reverence."

Voltaire charmed by the English freedom of speech

Voltaire was deeply impressed by the Quakers — their simple life and their hatred of war. He was delighted with the English philosophers, especially with John Locke[1] (died in 1704); he

[1] Locke rejected the notion that man was born with certain divinely implanted ideas, and maintained that we owe all that we know to the sensations and impressions which come to us from without. Locke was a man of extraordinary modesty, good sense, and caution, and he and his gifted successor, Bishop Berkeley, did much to found modern psychology. Berkeley's *New Theory of Vision* is a clear account of the gradual way in which we learn to see. He shows that a blind man, if suddenly restored to sight, would make little or nothing of the confused colors and shapes which would first strike his eye. He would learn only from prolonged experience that one set of colors and contours meant a man and another a horse or a table, no matter how readily he might recognize the several objects by touch.

thought Pope's "An Essay on Man" the finest moral poem ever composed; he admired the English liberty of speech and writing; he respected the general esteem for the merchant class. "In France," he said, "the merchant so constantly hears his business spoken of with disdain that he is fool enough to blush for it; yet I am not sure that the merchant who enriches his country, gives orders from his countinghouse at Surat or Cairo, and contributes to the happiness of the globe is not more useful to a state than the thickly bepowdered lord who knows exactly what time the king rises and what time he goes to bed, and gives himself mighty airs of greatness while he plays the part of a slave in the minister's anteroom."

Voltaire's *Letters on the English*

Voltaire proceeded to enlighten his countrymen by a volume of essays in which he set forth his impressions of England; but the high court of justice (the *parlement*) of Paris condemned these *Letters on the English* to be publicly burned, as scandalous and lacking in the respect due to kings and governments. Voltaire was to become, during the remainder of a long life, the chief advocate throughout Europe of unremitting reliance upon reason and of confidence in enlightenment and progress.

Voltaire's wide influence and popularity

His keen eye was continually discovering some new absurdity in the existing order, which, with incomparable wit and literary skill, he would expose to his eager readers. He was interested in almost everything; he wrote histories, dramas, philosophic treatises, romances, epics, and innumerable letters to his innumerable admirers. The vast range of his writings enabled him to bring his bold questionings to the attention of all sorts and conditions of men — not only to the general reader, but even to the careless playgoer.[1]

Voltaire's attack upon the Church

While Voltaire was successfully inculcating free criticism in general, he led a relentless attack upon the most venerable, probably the most powerful, institution in Europe, the Roman Catholic Church. The absolute power of the king did not trouble him, but the Church, with what appeared to him to be

[1] For extracts from Voltaire's writings, see *Readings*, Vol. I, pp. 179 ff.

its deep-seated opposition to a free exercise of reason and its hostility to reform, seemed fatally to block all human progress. The Church, as it fully realized, had never encountered a more deadly enemy.[1]

Weakness of Voltaire

Were there space at command, a great many good things, as well as plenty of bad ones, might be told of this extraordinary man. He was often superficial in his judgments, and sometimes jumped to unwarranted conclusions. He saw only evil in the Church and seemed incapable of understanding all that it had done for mankind during the bygone ages. He maliciously attributed to evil motives teachings which were accepted by the best and loftiest of men. He bitterly ridiculed cherished religious ideas, along with the censorship of the press and the quarrels of the theologians.

Real greatness of Voltaire

He could, and did, however, fight bravely against wrong and oppression. The abuses which he attacked were in large part abolished by the Revolution. It is unfair to notice only Voltaire's mistakes and exaggerations, as many writers, both Catholic and Protestant, have done; for he certainly did much to prepare the way for great and permanent reforms of the Church, as a political and social institution, which every one would now approve.

Diderot's *Encyclopædia*

Voltaire had many admirers and powerful allies. Among these none were more important than Denis Diderot and the scholars whom Diderot induced to coöperate with him in preparing articles for a new *Encyclopædia*, which was designed to spread among a wide range of intelligent readers a knowledge of scientific advance and rouse enthusiasm for reform and progress.[2] An encyclopedia was by no means a new thing.

1 Voltaire repudiated the beliefs of the Protestant churches as well as of the Roman Church. He was, however, no atheist. He believed in God, and at his country home, near Geneva, he dedicated a temple to him. Like many of his contemporaries, he was a deist, and held that God had revealed himself in nature and in our own hearts, not in Bible or Church.

2 See *Readings*, Vol. I, p. 185, for an extract from Diderot's preface to the last installment of the *Encyclopædia*.

Diderot's plan had been suggested by a proposal to publish a French translation of Chambers's *Cyclopædia*. Before his first volume appeared, a vast *Universal Dictionary* had been completed in Germany in sixty-four volumes. But few people outside of that country could read German in those days, whereas the well-written and popular articles of Diderot and his helpers, ranging from "abacus," "abbey," and "abdication" to "Zoroaster," "Zurich," and "zymology," were in a language that many people all over Europe could understand.

The *Encyclopædia* rouses the hostility of the theologians

Diderot and his fellow editors endeavored to rouse as little opposition as possible. They respected current prejudices and gave space to ideas and opinions with which they were not personally in sympathy. They furnished material, however, for refuting what they believed to be mistaken notions, and Diderot declared that "time will enable people to distinguish what we have thought from what we have said." But no sooner did the first two volumes appear in 1752 than the king's ministers, to please the clergy, suppressed them, as containing principles hostile to royal authority and religion, although they did not forbid the continuation of the work.

Diderot, nevertheless, completes the *Encyclopædia*

As volume after volume appeared, the subscribers increased; but so did the opposition. The Encyclopedists were declared to be a band bent upon the destruction of religion and the undermining of society; the government again interfered, withdrew the license to publish the work, and prohibited the sale of the seven volumes that were already out. Nevertheless seven years later Diderot was able to deliver the remaining ten volumes to the subscribers in spite of the government's prohibition.

Value of the *Encyclopædia*

The *Encyclopædia* attacked temperately, but effectively, religious intolerance, the bad taxes, the slave trade, and the atrocities of the criminal law; it encouraged men to turn their minds to natural science with all its beneficent possibilities, and this helped to discourage the old interest in theology and barren metaphysics. The article "Legislator," written by Diderot, says: "All the men of all lands have become necessary to one

FIG. 40. LEADERS OF THE REVOLUTION IN THOUGHT

another for the exchange of the fruits of industry and the products of the soil. Commerce is a new bond among men. In these days every nation has an interest in the preservation by every other nation of its wealth, its industry, its banks, its luxury, its agriculture. The ruin of Leipzig, of Lisbon, of Lima, has led to bankruptcies on all the exchanges of Europe and has affected the fortunes of many millions of persons." The English statesman, John Morley, is doubtless right when he says, in his enthusiastic account of Diderot and his companions, that "it was this band of writers, organized by a harassed man of letters, and not the nobles swarming around Louis XV, nor the churchmen, who first grasped the great principle of modern society, the honor that is owed to productive industry. They were vehement for the glories of peace and passionate against the brazen glories of war."

Montesquieu (1689–1755) and his *Spirit of Laws*

Neither Voltaire nor Diderot had attacked the kings and their despotic system of government. Montesquieu, however, while expressing great loyalty to French institutions, opened the eyes of his fellow citizens to the disadvantages and abuses of their government by his enthusiastic eulogy of the limited monarchy of England. In his celebrated work, *The Spirit of Laws, or the Relation which Laws should bear to the Constitution of Each Country, its Customs, Climate, Religion, Commerce,* etc., he proves from history that governments are not arbitrary arrangements, but that they are the natural products of special conditions and should meet the needs of a particular people at a particular period. England, he thought, had developed an especially happy system.

Rousseau (1712–1778) attacks civilization

Next to Voltaire, the writer who did most to cultivate discontent with existing conditions was Jean Jacques Rousseau[1] (1712–1778). Unlike Voltaire and Diderot, Rousseau believed that people thought too much, not too little; that we should trust to our hearts rather than to our heads, and may safely rely upon our natural feelings and sentiments to guide us. He

[1] Extracts from his writings are to be found in the *Readings*, Vol. I, pp. 187 ff.

declared that Europe was overcivilized, and summoned men to return to nature and simplicity. His first work was a prize essay written in 1750, in which he sought to prove that the development of the arts and sciences had demoralized mankind, inasmuch as they had produced luxury, insincerity, and arrogance.

FIG. 41. JEAN JACQUES ROUSSEAU

He extolled the rude vigor of Sparta and denounced the refined and degenerate life of the Athenians.

Rousseau's *Émile* deals with education

Later Rousseau wrote a book on education, called *Émile*, which is still famous. In this he protests against the efforts made by teachers to improve upon nature, for, he maintains, "All things are good as their Author made them, but everything degenerates in the hands of man. . . . To form this rare creature, man, what have we to do? Much doubtless, but chiefly to prevent anything from being done. . . . All our wisdom consists in servile prejudices; all our customs are but anxiety and restraint. Civilized man is born, lives, dies in a state of slavery. At his birth he is sewed in swaddling clothes; at his death he is nailed in a coffin; as long as he preserves the human form he is fettered by our institutions."

The Social Contract

Rousseau's plea for the simple life went to the heart of many a person who was weary of complications and artificiality. Others were attracted by his firm belief in the natural equality of mankind and the right of every man to have a voice in the government. In his celebrated little treatise, *The Social Contract*, he takes up the question, By what right does one man rule over others? The book opens with the words: "Man is born free and yet is now everywhere in chains. One man believes himself the master of others and yet is after all more of a slave than they. How did this change come about? I do not know. What can render it legitimate? I believe that I can answer that question." It is, Rousseau declares, the will of the people that renders government legitimate. The real sovereign is the people. Although they may appoint a single person, such as a king, to manage the government for them, they should make the laws, since it is they who must obey them. We shall find that the first French constitution accepted Rousseau's doctrine and defined law as "the expression of the general will" — not the will of a king reigning by the grace of god.

Popular sovereignty

Beccaria (1738-1794) and his book, *On Crimes and Punishments*

Among all the books advocating urgent reforms which appeared in the eighteenth century none accomplished more than a little volume by the Italian economist and jurist, Beccaria, which exposed with great clearness and vigor the atrocities of the criminal law. The trials in all countries were scandalously unfair and the punishments incredibly cruel. The accused was not ordinarily allowed any counsel and was required to give evidence against himself. Indeed, it was common enough to use torture to force a confession from him. Witnesses were examined secretly and separately and their evidence recorded before they faced the accused. Informers were rewarded, and the flimsiest evidence was considered sufficient in the case of atrocious crimes. After a criminal had been convicted he might

Unfairness of criminal trials

be tortured by the rack, thumbscrews, applying fire to different parts of his body, or in other ways, to induce him to reveal the names of his accomplices. The death penalty was established for a great variety of offenses besides murder — for example, heresy, counterfeiting, highway robbery, even sacrilege. In England there were, according to the great jurist Blackstone, a hundred and sixty offenses punishable with death, including cutting down trees in an orchard, and stealing a sum over five shillings in a shop, or more than twelve pence from a person's pocket. Yet in spite of the long list of capital offenses, the trials in England were far more reasonable than on the Continent, for they were public and conducted before a jury, and torture was not used. Moreover, owing to *Habeas Corpus* no one could be imprisoned long before the trial would take place.

Cruelty of the punishments

Beccaria advocated public trials in which the accused should be confronted by those who gave evidence against him. Secret accusations should no longer be considered. Like Voltaire, Montesquieu, and many others, he denounced the practice of torturing a suspected person with a view of compelling him by bodily anguish to confess himself guilty of crimes of which he might be quite innocent. As for punishments, he advocated the entire abolition of the death penalty, on the ground that it did not deter the evil doer as life imprisonment at hard labor would, and that in its various hideous forms — beheading, hanging, mutilation, breaking on the wheel — it was a source of demoralization to the spectators. Punishments should be less harsh but more certain and more carefully proportioned to the danger of the offense to society. Nobles and magistrates convicted of crime should be treated exactly like offenders of the lowest class. Confiscation of property should be abolished, since it brought suffering to the innocent members of the criminal's family. It was better, he urged, to prevent crimes than to punish them, and this could be done by making the laws very clear and the punishments for their violation very certain, but, above all, by spreading enlightenment through better education.

Beccaria advocates public trials and milder, but certain, punishments

The science of political economy develops in the eighteenth century

About the middle of the eighteenth century a new social science was born, namely, political economy. Scholars began to investigate the sources of a nation's wealth, the manner in which commodities were produced and distributed, the laws determining demand and supply, the function of money and credit, and their influence upon industry and commerce. Previous to the eighteenth century these matters had seemed unworthy of scientific discussion. Few suspected that there were any great laws underlying the varying amount of wheat that could be bought for a shilling, or the rate of interest that a bank could charge. The ancient philosophers of Greece and Rome had despised the tiller of the soil, the shopkeeper, and the artisan, for these indispensable members of society at that period were commonly slaves. The contempt of manual labor had decreased in the Middle Ages, but the learned men who studied theology, or pondered over Aristotle's teachings in regard to "form" and "essence," never thought of considering the effect of the growth of population upon serfdom, or of an export duty upon commerce, any more than they tried to determine why the housewife's milk soured more readily in warm weather than in cold, or why a field left fallow regained its fertility.[1]

Tendency of the governments to regulate commerce and industry

Although ignorant of economic laws, the governments had come gradually to regulate more and more both commerce and industry. We have seen how each country tried to keep all the trade for its own merchants by issuing elaborate regulations and restrictions, and how the king's officers enforced the monopoly of the guilds. Indeed, the French government, under Colbert's influence, fell into the habit of regulating well-nigh everything. In order that the goods which were produced in France might find a ready sale abroad, the government fixed the quality and width of the cloth which might be manufactured and the

[1] The medieval philosophers and theologians discussed, it is true, the question whether it was right or not to charge interest for money loaned, and what might be a "just price." But both matters were considered as ethical or theological problems rather than in their economic aspects. See Ashley, *English Economic History*, Vol. I, chap. iii; Vol. II, chap. vi.

character of the dyes which should be used. The king's ministers kept a constant eye upon the dealers in grain and breadstuffs, forbidding the storing up of these products or their sale outside a market. In this way they had hoped to prevent speculators from accumulating grain in order to sell it at a high rate in times of scarcity.

Doctrines of the "mercantilists"

In short, at the opening of the eighteenth century statesmen, merchants, and such scholars as gave any attention to the subject believed that the wealth of a country could be greatly increased by government regulation and encouragement, just as in the United States to-day it is held by the majority of citizens that the government can increase prosperity and improve the conditions of the wage-earners by imposing high duties upon imported articles. It was also commonly believed that a country, to be really prosperous, must export more than it imported, so that foreign nations would each year owe it a cash balance, which would have to be paid in gold or silver and in this way increase its stock of precious metals. Those who advocated using the powers of government to encourage and protect shipping, to develop colonies, and to regulate manufactures are known as "mercantilists."

Origin of the "free-trade" school of economists

About the year 1700, however, certain writers in France and England reached the conclusion that the government did no good by interfering with natural economic laws which it did not understand and whose workings it did not reckon with. They argued that the government restrictions often produced the worst possible results; that industry would advance far more rapidly if manufacturers were free to adopt new inventions instead of being confined by the government's restrictions to old and discredited methods; that, in France, the government's frantic efforts to prevent famines by making all sorts of rules in regard to selling grain only increased the distress, since even the most powerful king could not violate with impunity an economic law. So the new economists rejected the formerly popular mercantile policy. They accused the mercantilists of identifying gold and silver with wealth, and maintained that a country might be prosperous without a favorable cash balance. In short, the new school advocated "free trade." A French economist urged his king to adopt the motto, *Laissez faire* (Let things alone), if he would see his realms prosper.

Adam Smith's *Wealth of Nations* (1776)

The first great systematic work upon political economy was published by a Scotch philosopher, Adam Smith, in 1776. His *Inquiry into the Nature and Causes of the Wealth of Nations* became the basis of all further progress in the science. He attacked the doctrines of the mercantilists and the various expedients which they had favored, — import duties, bounties, restrictions upon exporting grain, etc., — all of which he believed "retard instead of accelerating the progress of society toward real wealth and greatness; and diminish instead of increasing the real value of the annual produce of its labor and land." In general he held that the State should content itself with protecting traders and business men and seeing that justice was done; but he sympathized with the English navigation laws, although they obviously hampered commerce, and was not as thoroughgoing a free trader as many of the later English economists.

The economists attack existing abuses

While the economists in France and England by no means agreed in details, they were at one in believing that it was useless and harmful to interfere with what they held to be the economic laws. They brought the light of reason to bear, for example, upon the various bungling and iniquitous old methods of taxation then in vogue, and many of them advocated a single tax which should fall directly upon the landowner. They wrote treatises on practical questions, scattered pamphlets broadcast, and even conducted a magazine or two in the hope of bringing home to the people at large the existing economic evils.

It is clear from what has been said that the eighteenth century was a period of unexampled advance in general enlightenment. New knowledge spread abroad by the Encyclopedists, the economists, and writers on government — Adam Smith,

Montesquieu, Rousseau, Beccaria, and many others of lesser fame — led people to see the vices of the existing system and gave them at the same time new hope of bettering themselves by abandoning the mistaken beliefs and imperfect methods of their predecessors. The spirit of reform penetrated even into kings' palaces, and we must now turn to the actual attempts to better affairs made by the more enlightened rulers of Europe.

The eighteenth century a period of rapidly increasing enlightenment

Section 28. Reforms of Frederick II, Catherine II, and Joseph II

The "enlightened despots"

It happened in the eighteenth century that there were several remarkably intelligent monarchs — Frederick II of Prussia, Catherine the Great of Russia, Maria Theresa of Austria, Emperor Joseph II, and Charles III of Spain. These rulers read the works of the reformers, and planned all sorts of ways in which they might better the conditions in their realms by removing old restrictions which hampered the farmer and merchant, by making new and clearer laws, by depriving the clergy of wealth and power which seemed to them excessive, and by encouraging manufactures and promoting commerce.

These monarchs are commonly known as the "enlightened" or "benevolent" despots. They were no doubt more "enlightened" than the older kings; at least they all read books and associated with learned men. But they were not more "benevolent" than Charlemagne, or Canute, or St. Louis, or many other monarchs of earlier centuries, who had believed it their duty to do all they could for the welfare of their people. On the other hand, the monarchs of the eighteenth century were certainly despots in the full sense of the word. They held that all the powers of the State were vested in them, and had no idea of permitting their subjects any share in the government. Moreover they waged war upon one another as their predecessors had done, and were constantly trying to add to their own territories by robbing their neighbors, as we have seen above.

Frederick the Great of Prussia (1740–1786)

One of the most striking and practical of the reforming rulers was Frederick the Great of Prussia. As a youth he had grieved and disgusted his father by his fondness for books and his passion for writing verses and playing the flute. A French tutor had instilled in him a love for the polished language of France and an enthusiasm for her literature and for her philosophers who were busy attacking the traditional religious ideas to which Frederick's father stoutly clung. When eighteen years old Frederick had tried to run away in order to escape the harsh military discipline to which he was subjected. He was captured and brought before the king, who was in such a rage that he seemed upon the point of killing his renegade son with his sword. He contented himself, however, with imprisoning Frederick in the citadel of Küstrin, with no books except a Bible, and forced him to witness the execution of one of his companions, who had aided his flight.

Frederick's boyhood

The apprenticeship of a king

After this Frederick consented to give some contemptuous attention to public affairs. He inspected the royal domains near Küstrin and began, for the first time, to study the peasants, their farms, and their cattle. He even agreed to marry a princess whom his father had selected for him, and settled down to a scholarly life, studying literature, philosophy, history, and mathematics, and carrying on a correspondence with learned men of all nations, especially with Voltaire, whom he greatly admired. He was very fond indeed of writing and seized every spare moment of a busy life to push forward his works upon history, politics, and military matters. No less than twenty-four volumes of his writings, all in French, were published shortly after his death, and these did not include everything that he had managed to write.[1]

The business of a king

When he became king, Frederick devoted himself less to music and philosophy and more to the practical problems of government. He allowed the people no part in the government, it is true, but he worked very hard himself. He rose

[1] For Frederick's description of a king's duties, see *Readings*, Vol. I, p. 202.

Fig. 42. Charles III of Spain

FIG. 43. PETER THE GREAT WATCHING THE PROCEDURE OF THE HOUSE OF LORDS IN ENGLAND

He was taken to the roof one night where he could get a clear view of the House early and was busy all day. He was his own prime minister and the real head of all branches of the government, watching over the army and leading it in battle, attending to foreign affairs, guarding the finances, overseeing the courts, journeying up and down the land investigating the conduct of his officials and examining into the condition of his people.

Religious toleration in Prussia

In religious matters Frederick was extremely tolerant; he held that his subjects should be allowed to worship God in any way they pleased. He was himself a "deist."[1] Although his kingdom had long been Protestant, there were large numbers of Catholics in scattered parts of it. He welcomed Huguenots and Jesuits into his kingdom with equal cordiality and admitted Catholics as well as Protestants to his service. "I stand neutral between Rome and Geneva," he once said; "he who wrongs his brother of a different faith shall be punished; were I to declare for one or the other creed I should excite party spirit and persecution; my aim, on the contrary, is to show the adherents of the different churches that they are all fellow citizens."

Catherine II, empress of Russia (1762–1796)

In Russia, Peter the Great had been a genuine "benevolent despot," although the benevolence was more apparent to later generations than to his own half-Asiatic subjects.[2] But in the days of Voltaire and Rousseau, the ruler of all the Russias was a German woman, Catherine II, who is one of the most picturesque and interesting figures in history. She was the daughter of one of Frederick the Great's officers and had been selected by him in 1743, at the request of the Tsarina

1 See above, p. 148.

2 Peter's visit to England included an investigation of Parliament. But he did not imitate this western institution upon his return to Russia. On the recent attempts to establish a parliament in Russia, see Chapter XXIII, below.

Peter was succeeded in 1725 by his widow Catherine, who ruled ably for two years. His son Alexis had been tortured to death in prison for rebellion, and Alexis' son Peter II, who followed Catherine, was reactionary. Under Anne (1730–1740), niece of Peter I, German influence triumphed. Then came Elizabeth (1741–1762), Peter's younger daughter, referred to in the text. She hated Frederick II for his personal remarks about her and aided Maria Theresa against him.

Elizabeth, Peter's younger daughter, as a suitable wife for her nephew, the heir to the throne. At the age of fourteen this inexperienced girl found herself in the midst of the intrigues of the court at St. Petersburg; she joined the Greek Church, exchanged her name of Sophia for that of Catherine, and, by zealous study of both books and men, prepared to make her

FIG. 44. CATHERINE II

new name famous. Her husband, who ruled for six months as Peter III, proved to be a worthless fellow, who early began to neglect and maltreat her. Catherine won over the imperial guard and had herself proclaimed empress. Peter was forced to abdicate and was carried off by some of Catherine's supporters, who put him to death, probably with her tacit consent.

Catherine's character

In the spirit of Peter the Great, Catherine determined to carry on the Europeanizing of Russia and extend her empire.[1] She was thoroughly unscrupulous and hypocritical, but she was

[1] See above, pp. 73 ff.

shrewd in the choice and management of her ministers and was herself a hard worker. She rose at six o'clock in the morning, hurried through her toilet, prepared her own light breakfast, and turned to the exacting and dull business of government, carefully considering the reports laid before her relating to the army, the navy, finances, and foreign affairs.

Catherine's interest in French culture

Catherine II showed herself almost as interested in the philosophers and reformers as did Frederick.[1] She invited Diderot to spend a month with her and was disappointed that d'Alembert, the great French mathematician, would not consent to become the tutor of the grand duke Paul, the heir to the throne. She subscribed for the Encyclopedia, and bought Diderot's library when he got into trouble, permitting him to continue to use the books as long as he wished. In her frequent letters to Voltaire she explained to him her various plans for reform.

Catherine maintains serfdom but secularizes the Church lands

There was some talk of abolishing serfdom in Russia, but Catherine rather increased than decreased the number of serfs, and she made their lot harder than it had been before by forbidding them to complain of the treatment they received at the hands of their masters. She appropriated the vast property of the churches and monasteries, using the revenue to support the clergy and monks, and such surplus as remained she devoted to schools and hospitals.

Rash reforms of Joseph II of Austria (emperor, 1765–1790)

It is clear that while Frederick and Catherine expressed great admiration for the reformers, they did not attempt to make any sweeping changes in the laws or the social order. Emperor Joseph II, who, after the death of his mother, Maria Theresa, in 1780, became ruler of the Austrian dominions, had, however, the courage of his convictions.[2] He proposed to transform the scattered and heterogeneous territories over which he ruled into a well-organized state in which disorder, confusion, prejudice, fanaticism, and intellectual bondage should disappear

[1] For an account of Catherine by a contemporary, see *Readings*, Vol. I, p. 210.

[2] See above, p. 97. For Joseph's statement of his views, see *Readings*, Vol. I, p. 213.

and all his subjects be put in possession of their "natural" rights. Germans, Hungarians, Italians, Poles, Bohemians, and Belgians were all to use the German language in official communications. The old irregular territorial divisions were abolished and his realms divided up into thirteen new provinces. All the ancient privileges enjoyed by the towns and the local assemblies were

FIG. 45. JOSEPH II

done away with and replaced by a uniform system of government in which his own officials enjoyed the control.

Joseph II attacks the Church

Joseph visited France and was personally acquainted with Rousseau and Turgot. In harmony with their teachings, he attacked the Church, which was so powerful in his realms. He was heartily opposed to the monks. "The principles of monasticism," he declared, "are in flat contradiction to human reason." He particularly objected to those orders whose members devoted themselves to religious contemplation; he consequently abolished some six hundred of their monasteries and used their property for charitable purposes and to establish schools. He appointed the bishops without consulting the Pope and forbade money to be sent to Rome. Marriage was declared to be merely a civil contract and so was taken out of the control of the priests. Lutherans, Calvinists, and other heretics were allowed to worship in their own way.

Joseph attacks the survivals of feudalism and encourages manufactures

Joseph II sought to complete his work by attacking the surviving features of feudalism and encouraging the development of manufactures. He freed the serfs in Bohemia, Moravia, Galicia, and Hungary, transforming the peasants into tenants; elsewhere he reduced the services due from them to the lord. He taxed nobles and clergy without regard to their claims to exemption, and supplanted the confused and uncertain laws by a uniform system which remained the basis of Austrian law. He introduced a protective tariff and caused a large number of factories to be built. He showed his preference for home industries by giving away to the hospitals all the foreign wines in his cellars, and his spirit of economy, by forbidding the use of gold and silver for candlesticks, and prohibiting the burial of the dead in coffins for the reason that this was a waste of wood which might be better employed.

Opposition to Joseph's reforms

Naturally Joseph met opposition on every hand. The clergy abhorred him as an oppressor, and all who were forced to sacrifice their old privileges did what they could to block his reforms, however salutary they might be. The Netherlands, which he proposed to transform into an Austrian province, finally followed the example of the American colonies and declared themselves independent in 1790. The same year Joseph died, a sadly disappointed man, having been forced to undo almost all that he had hoped to accomplish.

Revolt of the Austrian Netherlands (1790)

Summary of the activities of the benevolent despots

It has become clear, as we have reviewed the activities of these benevolent despots, that all of them were chiefly intent upon increasing their own power; they were more despotic than they were benevolent. They opposed the power of the Pope and brought the clergy under their own control. In some cases they took a portion of the property of the churches and monasteries. They tried to improve the laws and do away with the existing contradictions and obscurities. They endeavored to "centralize" the administration and to place all the power in the hands of their own officials instead of leaving it with the nobles or the old local assemblies. They encouraged agriculture, commerce, and industries in various ways. All these measures were undertaken primarily with a view to strengthening the autocratic power of the ruler and increasing the revenue and the military strength of his government, for none of these energetic monarchs showed any willingness to admit the people to a share in the government, and only Joseph II ventured to attempt to free the serfs.

Section 29. The English Limited Monarchy in the Eighteenth Century and George III

The limited monarchy of England

In striking contrast to the absolute rule of these "despots" on the Continent, the island of Britain was, as we have seen,[1] governed by its Parliament. There the king, from the Revolution of 1688 on, had owed his crown to Parliament and admitted that he was limited by the constitution, which he had to obey. This did not prevent at least one English king from trying to have his own way in spite of the restrictions placed upon him, as we shall see.

Whig supremacy in the early eighteenth century

It will be recalled that there were two great political parties in England, the Whigs, successors of the Roundheads, who advocated the supremacy of Parliament and championed toleration for the Dissenters, and the Tories, who, like the earlier Cavaliers, upheld the divine right of kings and the supremacy of the Anglican, or Established, Church. After the death of Anne many of the Tories favored calling to the throne the son of James II (popularly called "the old Pretender"), whereupon the Whigs succeeded in discrediting their rivals by denouncing

[1] See above, p. 55.

them as Jacobites[1] and traitors. They made the new Hanoverian king, George I, believe that he owed everything to the Whigs, and for a period of nearly fifty years, under George I and George II, they were able to control Parliament.

Robert Walpole, prime minister (1721-1742)

George I himself spoke no English, was ignorant of English politics, and was much more interested in Hanover than in his new kingdom. He did not attend the meetings of his ministers, as his predecessors had done, and turned over the management of affairs to the Whig leaders. They found a skillful "boss" and a judicious statesman in Sir Robert Walpole, who maintained his own power and that of his party by avoiding war and preventing religious dissensions at home. He used the king's funds to buy the votes necessary to maintain the Whig majority in the House of Commons and to get his measures through that body. He was England's first "prime minister."

Development of the cabinet and the office of prime minister

The existence of two well-defined political parties standing for widely different policies forced the king, as we have seen,[2] to choose all his ministers from either one or the other. The more prominent among his advisers came gradually to form a little group who resigned together if Parliament refused to accept the measures they advocated. In this way the "cabinet government," begun under William III, developed, with a prime minister, or premier, at its head. Under weak monarchs the prime minister would naturally be the real ruler of the kingdom.

The position of the king

It was still possible, to be sure, for the king to profit by the jealousies of rival statesmen and by favoring first one, then another, to keep the upper hand. This was especially the case after the Tories gave up hope of restoring the Stuarts, upon the failure of Prince Charles in 1745,[3] so that the Hanoverian kings no longer needed to rely upon the Whigs as the one loyal party.

[1] This name, applied to the supporters of James, is derived from the Latin form of his name, *Jacobus*. [2] See above, p. 56. [3] See above, p. 54, note 1.

George III rules despotically by bribing Parliament

Finally, George III, who came to the throne in 1760, succeeded in getting a party of his own, known as the King's Friends, and with their aid, and a liberal use of what would now be regarded as bribery and graft, ran the government much as he wanted to. His mother, a German princess, had taught him that he ought to be a king like those on the Continent; and, in spite of the restrictions of Parliament, he did rule in

FIG. 46. AN ELECTION IN THE EIGHTEENTH CENTURY. (DRAWN BY HOGARTH)

a high-handed and headstrong way. During the war with the American colonies he was practically his own prime minister.

Growing demand for reform

The really weak spot in the English constitution, however, was less the occasional high-handedness of the king than the fact that Parliament did not represent the nation as a whole. Already in the eighteenth century there was no little discontent with the monopoly which the landed gentry and the rich enjoyed in Parliament. There was an increasing number of writers to point out to the people the defects in the English system. They urged that every man should have the right to participate in the government by casting his vote, and that the unwritten constitution of England should be written down and so made clear and unmistakable. Political clubs were founded, which entered into correspondence with political societies in France; newspapers and pamphlets poured from the press in enormous quantities, and political reform found champions in the House of Commons.

The younger Pitt

This demand for reform finally induced the younger Pitt, son of the Earl of Chatham, who was prime minister from 1783 to 1801, to introduce bills into the House of Commons for remedying some inequalities in representation. But the violence and disorder which accompanied the French Revolution involved England in a long and tedious war, and discredited reform with Englishmen who had formerly favored change, to say nothing of the Tories, who regarded with horror any proposal looking toward an extension of popular government.

England had already the elements of a modern free government, but the political system was not democratic

It is clear that England possessed the elements of a modern free government, for her king was master of neither the persons nor the purses of his subjects, nor could he issue arbitrary laws. Political affairs were discussed in newspapers and pamphlets, so that weighty matters of government could not be decided secretly in the king's closet without the knowledge of his subjects. Nevertheless it would be far from correct to regard the English system as democratic.

An hereditary House of Lords could block any measure introduced in the House of Commons; and the House of Commons itself represented not the nation but a small minority of landowners and traders. Government offices were monopolized by members of the Established Church, and the poor were oppressed by cruel criminal laws administered by officials chosen by the king. Workingmen were prohibited from forming associations to promote their interests. It was more than a century after the accession of George III before the English peasant could go to the ballot box and vote for members of Parliament.

QUESTIONS

SECTION 26. Contrast the spirit of reform with that of conservatism. What justifications are there for each? What is meant by "progress"? What class of men is responsible for changing the intellectual viewpoint of the eighteenth century? Name some pioneers of the new methods of discovering truth. Describe these methods. Why was the discovery of natural law the most important of all scientific discoveries? Why were conservative theologians opposed to the new view of the world?

SECTION 27. What things in England most interested Voltaire? What were Voltaire's chief claims to greatness? What were his weaknesses? How did Diderot's encyclopedia influence public opinion in France? In what way did the work of Montesquieu influence the making of constitutions?

How did Rousseau's doctrines lead to a criticism of despotism in France? Describe the evils of criminal law in the eighteenth century. What is political economy? Why was it not studied in the Middle Ages? Who were the Mercantilists? What is meant by *Laissez faire*? Discuss the doctrines of Adam Smith.

SECTION 28. What is meant by the term "benevolent despot"? Name the four great benevolent despots of the eighteenth century. Give an account of the youth of Frederick the Great of Prussia. Describe the life of Frederick the Great after he came to the throne. What were his views on the subject of religion?

Sketch the early life of Catherine II of Russia. Compare her work as a ruler with that of Frederick the Great. Describe the reforms of Joseph II of Austria. In what general way does his work differ from that of the monarch just named? What points of agreement or of difference are there between his policy and that of Frederick the Great? between his policy and that of Catherine II?

SECTION 29. Contrast the limited monarchy of England with the benevolent despotism of the Continent. Discuss the two great political parties of England. Who was Sir Robert Walpole? Describe the origin of the cabinet. Explain the position of the king during the eighteenth century. What was the great cause of dissatisfaction with parliamentary government in England in the eighteenth century?

CHAPTER VII

THE EVE OF THE FRENCH REVOLUTION

SECTION 30. THE OLD RÉGIME IN FRANCE

How the French people accomplished reforms which had foiled the benevolent despots

It was France that first carried out the great reforms that did away with most of the old institutions and confusion that had come down from the Middle Ages. It is true that some of the monarchs of the time ("benevolent despots," as they are called), especially Frederick the Great, and Catherine II of Russia, and the Emperor Joseph II, introduced some reforms, largely in their own interests, but even in England little was done in the eighteenth century to remedy the great abuses of which the reformers complained. But in 1789 the king of France asked his people to submit their grievances to him and to send representatives to Versailles to confer with him upon the state of the realm and the ways in which the government might be improved so as to increase the general happiness and the prosperity of the kingdom. And then the miracle happened! The French National Assembly swept away the old abuses with an ease and thoroughness which put the petty reforms of the benevolent despots to shame. It accomplished more in a few months than the reforming kings had done in a century; for the kings had never dreamed of calling in their people to aid them. Instead of availing themselves of the great forces of the nation, they had tried to do everything alone by royal decrees, and so had failed.

The unique greatness of the reformation accomplished by the French Assembly is, however, often obscured by the disorder which accompanied it. When one meets the words "French Revolution," he is pretty sure to call up before his

The real French Revolution not to be confused with the Reign of Terror

mind's eye the guillotine and its hundreds of victims, and the Paris mob shouting the hymn of the Marseillaise as they paraded the streets with the heads of unfortunate "aristocrats" on their pikes. Every one has heard of this terrible episode in French history even if he knows practically nothing of the permanent good which was accomplished at the time. Indeed, it has made so deep an impression on posterity that the Reign of Terror is often mistaken for the real Revolution. It was, however, only a sequel to it, an unhappy accident which will seem less and less important as the years go on, while the achievements of the Revolution itself will loom larger and larger. The Reign of Terror will be explained and described in good time, but it is a matter of far greater importance to understand clearly how the fundamental and permanent reforms were wrought out, and how France won the proud distinction of being the first nation to do away with the absurd and vexatious institutions which weighed upon Europe in the eighteenth century.

Meaning of the term "the old régime"

We have already examined these institutions which were common to most of the European countries, — despotic kings, arbitrary imprisonment, unfair taxation, censorship of the press, serfdom, feudal dues, friction between Church and State, — all of which the reformers had been busy denouncing as contrary to reason and humanity, and some of which the benevolent despots and their ministers had, in a half-hearted way, attempted to remedy. The various relics of bygone times and of outlived conditions which the Revolution abolished forever are commonly called in France the old régime.[1] In order to see why France took the lead of other European countries in modernizing itself, it is necessary to examine somewhat carefully the particular causes of discontent there. We shall then see how almost every one, from the king to the peasant, came to realize that the old system was bad and consequently resolved to do away with it and substitute a more rational plan of government for the long-standing disorder.

[1] From the French *ancien régime*, the old or former system.

Of the evils which the Revolution abolished, none was more important than the confusion in France due to the fact that it was not in the eighteenth century a well-organized, homogeneous state whose citizens all enjoyed the same rights and privileges. A long line of kings had patched it together, adding bit

France not a well-organized state in the eighteenth century

THE PROVINCES OF FRANCE IN THE EIGHTEENTH CENTURY, SHOWING INTERIOR CUSTOMS LINES

by bit as they could. By conquest and bargain, by marrying heiresses, and through the extinction of the feudal dynasties, the original restricted domains of Hugh Capet about Paris and Orleans had been gradually increased by his descendants. We have seen how Louis XIV gained Alsace and Strassburg and some towns on the borders of the Spanish Netherlands,

Louis XV added Lorraine in 1766. Two years later the island of Corsica was ceded to France by Genoa. So when Louis XVI came to the throne in 1774 he found himself ruler of practically the whole territory which makes up France to-day. But these different parts had different institutions.

The old provinces

Some of the districts which the kings of France brought under their sway, like Languedoc, Provence, Brittany, and Dauphiny, were considerable states in themselves, each with its own laws, customs, and system of government. When these provinces had come, at different times, into the possession of the king of France, he had not changed their laws so as to make them correspond with those of his other domains. He was satisfied if a new province paid its due share of the taxes and treated his officials with respect. In some cases the provinces retained their local assemblies and controlled, to a certain extent, their own affairs. The provinces into which France was divided before the Revolution were not, therefore, merely artificial divisions created for the purposes of convenience, like the modern French *départements*,[1] but represented real historical differences. Their inhabitants generally spoke different dialects, or, as in Brittany and parts of Provence, different languages.

THE SALT TAX

Showing the different amounts paid in the various parts of France in the eighteenth century for a given amount of salt

[1] See below, p. 207.

Various systems of law

While in a considerable portion of southern France the Roman law still prevailed, in the central parts and in the west and north there were no less than two hundred and eighty-five different local codes of law in force; so that one who moved from his own to a neighboring town might find a wholly unfamiliar legal system.

One of the heaviest taxes was that on salt. This varied so greatly in different parts of France that the government had to go to great expense to guard the boundary lines between the various districts, for there was every inducement to smugglers to carry salt from those parts of the country where it was cheap into the regions where it sold for a high price on account of the tax. (See map on opposite page.)

The privileged classes

Besides these unfortunate local differences, there were class differences which caused great discontent. All Frenchmen did not enjoy the same rights as citizens. Two small but very important classes, the nobility and the clergy, were treated differently by the State from the rest of the people. They did not have to pay one of the heaviest of the taxes, the notorious *taille*; and on one ground or another they escaped other burdens which the rest of the citizens bore. For instance, they were not required to serve in the militia or help build the roads.

The Church

We have seen how great and powerful the Medieval Church was. In France, as in other Catholic countries of Europe, it still retained in the eighteenth century a considerable part of the power that it had possessed in the thirteenth, and it still performed important public functions. It took charge of education and of the relief of the sick and the poor. It was very wealthy and is supposed to have owned one fifth of all the land in France. The clergy claimed that their property, being dedicated to God, was not subject to taxation. They consented, however, to help the king from time to time by a "free gift," as they called it. The Church still collected the tithes from the people, and its vast possessions made it very independent.

The clergy

A great part of the enormous income of the Church went to the higher clergy — the bishops, archbishops, and abbots. Since these were appointed by the king, often from among his courtiers, they tended to neglect their duties as officers of the Church and to become little more than "great lords with a hundred thousand francs income." But while they were spending their time at Versailles the real work was performed — and well performed — by the lower clergy, who often received scarcely enough to keep soul and body together. This explains why, when the Revolution began, the parish priests sided with the people instead of with their ecclesiastical superiors.

The privileges of the nobility

The privileges of the nobles, like those of the clergy, had originated in the medieval conditions described in an earlier chapter. A detailed study of their rights would reveal many survivals of the institutions which prevailed in the eleventh and twelfth centuries, when the great majority of the people were serfs living upon the manors. While serfdom had largely disappeared in France long before the eighteenth century, and the peasants were generally free men who owned or rented their land, it was still the theory of the French law that there was "no land without its lord." Consequently the lords still enjoyed the right to collect a variety of time-honored dues from the inhabitants living within the limits of the former manors.

The feudal dues

The privileges and dues enjoyed by the nobles varied greatly in different parts of France. It was quite common for the noble landowner to have a right to a certain portion of the peasant's crops; occasionally he could still collect a toll on sheep and cattle driven past his house. In some cases the lord maintained, as he had done in the Middle Ages, the only mill, wine press, or oven within a certain district, and could require every one to make use of these and pay him a share of the product. Even when a peasant owned his land, the neighboring lord usually had the right to exact one fifth of its value every time it was sold.

The hunting rights

The nobles, too, enjoyed the exclusive privilege of hunting, which was deemed an aristocratic pastime. The game which they preserved for their amusement often did great damage to the crops of the peasants, who were forbidden to interfere with hares and deer. Many of the manors had great pigeon houses, built in the form of a tower, in which there were one or two thousand nests. No wonder the peasants detested these, for they were not permitted to protect themselves against the innumerable pigeons and their progeny, which spread over the fields

FIG. 47. A CHÂTEAU AND PIGEON HOUSE

The round tower at the right hand in front is a pigeon house. The wall inside is honeycombed with nests, and the pigeons fly in and out at the side of the roof

devouring newly sown seed. These dovecotes constituted, in fact, one of the chief grievances of the peasants.

Offices at court and in the Church and army reserved for the nobles

The higher offices in the army were reserved for the nobles, as well as the easiest and most lucrative places in the Church and about the king's person. All these privileges were vestiges of the powers which the nobles had enjoyed when they ruled their estates as feudal lords. Louis XIV had, as we know, induced them to leave their domains and gather round him at Versailles, where all who could afford it lived for at least a part of the year.

Only a small part of the nobles belonged to old families

Only relatively few of the nobility in the eighteenth century were, however, descendants of the ancient and illustrious feudal families of France. The greater part of them had been ennobled in recent times by the king, or had purchased or

FIG. 48. COURT SCENE AT VERSAILLES

The king is surrounded by princes of the royal family and the greatest nobles of France while he is dressed and shaved upon rising in the morning (the *levée*). Similar ceremonies were performed when the king went to bed at night (the *couchée*). The bed, hung with rich tapestries, is behind the railing. The door at the left leads into a small room — called the Bull's Eye Room (*Salon de l'Œil de Bœuf*) from the round window above the door — where the ambassadors and other dignitaries waited to be admitted, and while waiting often planned and plotted how to win the king's favor. Louis XIV's bedroom at Versailles is still preserved, in much of its old-time splendor;[1] for the palace is now a museum and is open to the public

inherited a government office or judgeship which carried the privileges of nobility with it. This fact rendered the rights and exemptions claimed by the nobility even more odious to the people at large than they would otherwise have been.

[1] Its windows are shown in Fig. 11, on the second floor, at the end of the courtyard, under the flag.

The third estate

Everybody who did not belong to either the clergy or the nobility was regarded as being of the *third estate*. The third estate was therefore really the nation at large, which was made up in 1789 of about twenty-five million souls. The privileged classes can scarcely have counted altogether more than two hundred or two hundred and fifty thousand individuals. A great part of the third estate lived in the country and tilled the soil. Most historians have been inclined to make out their condition as very wretched. They were certainly oppressed by an abominable system of taxation and were irritated by the dues which they had to pay to the lords. They also suffered frequently from local famines. Yet there is no doubt that the evils of their situation have been greatly exaggerated. When Thomas Jefferson traveled through France in 1787 he reports that the country people appeared to be comfortable and that they had plenty to eat. Arthur Young, a famous English traveler who has left us an admirable account of his journeys in France during the years 1787 and 1789, found much prosperity and contentment, although he gives, too, some forlorn pictures of destitution.

Favorable situation of the peasant in France compared with other countries

The latter have often been unduly emphasized by historical writers; for it has commonly been thought that the Revolution was to be explained by the misery and despair of the people, who could bear their burdens no longer. If, however, instead of comparing the situation of the French peasant under the old régime with that of an English or American farmer to-day, we contrast his position with that of his fellow peasant in Prussia, Russia, Austria, Italy, or Spain, in the eighteenth century, it will be clear that in France the agricultural classes were really much better off than elsewhere on the Continent. In almost all the other European countries, except England, the peasants were still serfs: they had to work certain days in each week for their lord; they could not marry or dispose of their land without his permission. Moreover, the fact that the population of France had steadily increased from seventeen

Rapid increase of population in the eighteenth century

millions after the close of the wars of Louis XIV to about twenty-five millions at the opening of the Revolution indicates that the general condition of the people was improving rather than growing worse.

Popular discontent, not the exceptionally miserable condition of the French people, accounts for the Revolution

The real reason why France was the first among the European countries to carry out a great reform and do away with the irritating survivals of feudalism was not that the nation was miserable and oppressed above all others, but that it was sufficiently free and enlightened to realize the evils and absurdities of the old régime. Mere oppression and misery does not account for a revolution; there must also be active *discontent*; and of that there was a great abundance in France, as we shall see. The French peasant no longer looked up to his lord as his ruler and protector, but viewed him as a sort of legalized robber who demanded a share of his precious harvest, whose officers awaited the farmer at the crossing of the river to claim a toll, who would not let him sell his produce when he wished, or permit him to protect his fields from the ravages of the pigeons which it pleased his lord to keep.

France still a despotism in the eighteenth century

In the eighteenth century France was still the despotism that Louis XIV had made it. Louis XVI once described it very well in the following words: "The sovereign authority resides exclusively in my person. To me solely belongs the power of making the laws, and without dependence or coöperation. The entire public order emanates from me, and I am its supreme protector. My people are one with me. The rights and interests of the nation are necessarily identical with mine and rest solely in my hands." In short, the king still ruled "by the grace of God," as Louis XIV had done. He needed to render account to no man for his governmental acts; he was responsible to God alone. The following illustrations will make clear the dangerous extent of the king's power.

The king's control of the government funds

In the first place, it was he who levied each year the heaviest of the taxes, the hated *taille*, from which the privileged classes were exempted. This tax brought in about one sixth of the whole revenue of the State. The amount collected was kept secret, and no report was made to the nation of what was done with it or, for that matter, with any other part of the king's income. Indeed, no distinction was made between the king's private funds and the State treasury, whereas in England the monarch was given a stated allowance. The king of France could issue as many drafts payable to bearer as he wished; the royal officials must pay all such orders and ask no questions. Louis XV is said to have spent no less than seventy million dollars in this irresponsible fashion in a single year.

Lettres de cachet

But the king not only controlled his subjects' purses; he had a terrible authority over their persons as well. He could issue orders for the arrest and arbitrary imprisonment of any one he pleased. Without trial or formality of any sort a person might be cast into a dungeon for an indefinite period, until the king happened to remember him again or was reminded of him by the poor man's friends. These notorious orders of arrest were called *lettres de cachet*, that is, sealed letters. They were not difficult to obtain for any one who had influence with the king or his favorites, and they furnished a particularly easy and efficacious way of disposing of an enemy. These arbitrary orders lead one to appreciate the importance of the provision of Magna Carta, which runs: "No freeman shall be taken or imprisoned except by the lawful judgment of his peers and in accordance with the law of the land." Some of the most eminent men of the time were shut up by the king's order, often on account of books or pamphlets written by them which displeased the king or those about him. The distinguished statesman, Mirabeau, when a young man, was imprisoned several times through *lettres de cachet* obtained by his father as a means of checking his reckless dissipation.

Limitations on the power of the French king

Yet, notwithstanding the seemingly unlimited powers of the French king, and in spite of the fact that France had no written constitution and no legislative body to which the nation sent representatives, the monarch was by no means absolutely free to do just as he pleased. In the first place, the high courts of law, the so-called *parlements*, could often hamper the king.

The *parlements* and their protests

These resembled the English Parliament in almost nothing but name. The French *parlements* — of which the most important one was at Paris and a dozen more were scattered about the provinces — did not, however, confine themselves solely to

FIG. 49. A ROYAL SESSION OF *PARLEMENT*, AT VERSAILLES, 1776

The name *lit de justice* (bed of justice) is supposed to come from the fact that the king once reclined on a couch, but here he is seated on a throne. The members of the *parlement*, with long gowns and caps, can be distinguished from the nobles and princes in their richer court dress. Each person had his exact place assigned him, in order of rank

the business of trying lawsuits. They claimed, and quite properly, that when the king decided to make a new law he must send it to them to be registered, for how, otherwise, could they adjust their decisions to it? Now although they acknowledged that the right to make the laws belonged to the monarch, they nevertheless often sent a "protest" to the king instead of registering an edict which they disapproved. They would urge that the ministers had abused his Majesty's confidence. They would also take pains to have their protest printed and sold on the streets at a penny or two a copy, so that people should get the idea that the *parlement* was defending the nation against the oppressive measures of the king's ministers.

When the king received one of these protests two alternatives were open to him. He might recall the distasteful decree altogether, or modify it so as to suit the court; or he could summon the *parlement* before him and in a solemn session (called a *lit de justice*) command it with his own mouth to register the law in its records. The *parlement* would then reluctantly obey; but as the Revolution approached, it began to claim that a decree registered against its will was not valid.

The *parlements* help to prepare the way for the Revolution

Struggles between the *parlements* and the king's ministers were very frequent in the eighteenth century. They prepared the way for the Revolution, first, by bringing important questions to the attention of the people; for there were no newspapers, and no parliamentary or congressional debates, to enable the public to understand the policy of the government. Secondly, the *parlements* not only frankly criticized the proposed measures of the king and his ministers, but they familiarized the nation with the idea that the king was not really at liberty to alter what they called "the fundamental laws" of the State. By this they meant that there was an unwritten constitution, which limited the king's power and of which they were the guardians. In this way they promoted the growing discontent with a government which was carried on in secret and which left the nation at the mercy of the men in whom the king might for the moment repose confidence.

Public opinion

In addition to the *parlements* public opinion often exercised a powerful check upon the king, even under the autocratic old régime. It was, as one of Louis XVI's ministers declared, "an invisible power which, without treasury, guards, or an army, ruled Paris and the court, — yes, the very palace of the king." The latter half of the eighteenth century was a period of outspoken and acrid criticism of the whole existing social and governmental system. Reformers, among whom many of the king's ministers were counted, loudly and eloquently discussed the numerous abuses and the vicious character of the government, which gradually came to seem just as bad to the intelligent people of that day as it does to us now.

Attempts to check the discussion of public questions

Although there were no daily newspapers to discuss public questions, large numbers of pamphlets were written and circulated by individuals whenever there was an important crisis, and they answered much the same purpose as the editorials in a modern newspaper. We have already seen how French philosophers and reformers, like Voltaire and Diderot, had been encouraged by the freedom of speech which prevailed in England, and how industriously they had sown the seeds of discontent in their own country. We have seen how in popular works, in poems and stories and plays, and above all in the *Encyclopædia*, they explained the new scientific discoveries, attacked the old beliefs and misapprehensions, and encouraged progress.

Section 31. How Louis XVI tried to play the Benevolent Despot

Death of Louis XV and the accession of Louis XVI (1774)

In 1774 Louis XV[1] died, after a disgraceful reign of which it has not seemed necessary to say much. His unsuccessful wars, which had ended with the loss of all his American possessions and the victory of his enemies in India, had brought France to the verge of bankruptcy; indeed in his last years his ministers repudiated a portion of the government's debts. The taxes were already so oppressive as to arouse universal discontent, and yet the government was running behind seventy millions of dollars a year. The king's personal conduct was scandalous, and he allowed his mistresses and courtiers to meddle in public affairs and plunder the royal treasury for

[1] He came to the throne in 1715 as a boy of five, on the death of Louis XIV, his great-grandfather.

themselves and their favorites. When at last he was carried off by smallpox every one hailed, with hopes of better times, the accession of his grandson and successor, Louis XVI.

The new king was but twenty years old, ill educated, indolent, unsociable, and very fond of hunting and of pottering about Character of Louis XVI

FIG. 50. LOUIS XVI

Louis was a well-meaning man, but not clever. He enjoyed working with tools like a locksmith or going hunting, but did not understand the needs of France. His clever, strong-willed queen, Marie Antoinette, was responsible for most of the few things he did to try to stop the Revolution, and she was too headstrong to listen to wise advice

in a workshop, where he spent his happiest hours. He was a well-meaning young man, with none of his grandfather's vices, who tried now and then to attend to the disagreeable business of government, and would gladly have made his people happy if that had not required more energy than he possessed. He had none of the restless interest in public affairs that we found in Peter the Great, Catherine II, or his brother-in-law,

Joseph II; he was never tempted to rise at five o'clock in the morning in order to read State papers.

Marie Antoinette

His wife was the beautiful Marie Antoinette, daughter of Maria Theresa. The marriage had been arranged in 1770 with a view of maintaining the alliance which had been concluded

FIG. 51. MARIE ANTOINETTE

The tragic fate of the queen has obscured the fact that she was not a good sovereign. She was always influencing her husband the wrong way. She prevented reform, and when the people rose in revolt they thought of her as an Austrian princess who had no care for the well-being of France

between France and Austria in 1756.[1] The queen was only nineteen years old when she came to the throne, light-hearted and on pleasure bent. She disliked the formal etiquette of the court at Versailles and shocked people by her thoughtless pranks. She rather despised her heavy husband, who did not care to share in the amusements which pleased her best. She did not hesitate

[1] See above, p. 87.

to interfere in the government when she wished to help one of her favorites or to make trouble for some one she disliked.

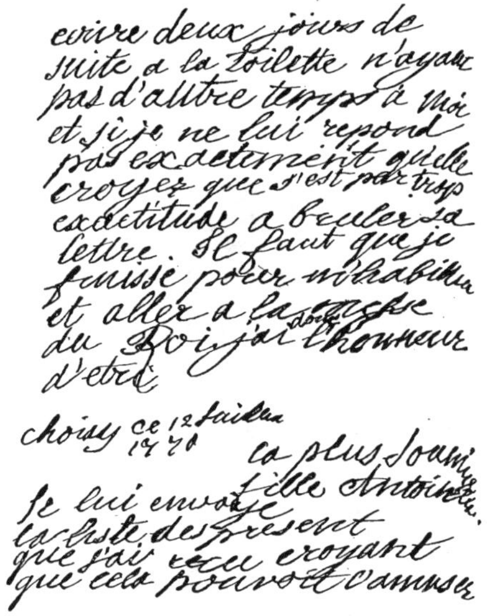
ecrire deux jours de
suite a la toilette n'ayant
pas d'autre temps a moi
et si je ne lui repond
pas exactement quelle
croyez que c'est par trop
exactitude a bruler sa
lettre. Il faut que je
finisse pour m'habiller
et aller a la messe
du Roi j'ai l'honneur
d'etre

choisy ce 12 juillet
1770 la plus soumise
fille Antoinette.
je lui envoye
la liste des present
que j'ai recu croyant
que cela pourroit l'amuser

FIG. 52. A LETTER OF MARIE ANTOINETTE

A page of a letter written July 12, 1770, to her mother, Maria Theresa. The handwriting, mistakes in spelling, and general carelessness show what an undeveloped girl she was when she came to the gay court of Versailles. She says in the letter that she has no other time to write than while she is dressing and cannot reply exactly to the last letter because she has burned it. Now she must stop in order to dress and go to the king's mass. She adds in postscript that she is sending a list of the wedding presents, thinking that that will entertain (*amuser*) her mother

At first Louis XVI took his duties very seriously. It seemed for a time that he might find a place among the benevolent despots who were then ruling in Europe. He almost immediately placed the ablest of all the French economists, Turgot,

Turgot, controller general (1774-1776)

in the most important of the government offices, that of controller general. Turgot was an experienced government official as well as a scholar.

Turgot advocates economy

The first and most natural measure was economy, for only in that way could the government be saved from bankruptcy and the burden of taxation be lightened. Turgot felt that the

FIG. 53. TURGOT

Turgot was the one great enlightened statesman of the time who might have saved France from a revolution. His frankness displeased the king, however, for he lectured him like a schoolmaster. The queen and the gay courtiers of Versailles brought about his fall

vast amount spent in maintaining the luxury of the royal court at Versailles should be reduced. The establishments of the king, the queen, and the princes of the blood royal cost the State annually about twelve million dollars. Then the French king had long been accustomed to grant "pensions" in a reckless manner to his favorites, and this required nearly twelve million dollars more.

Any attempt, however, to reduce this amount would arouse the immediate opposition of the courtiers, and it was the courtiers who really governed France. They had every opportunity to influence the king's mind against a man whose economies they disliked. They were constantly about the monarch from the moment when he awoke in the morning until he went to bed at night; therefore they had an obvious advantage over Turgot, who only saw him in business hours.[1]

How the courtiers governed France

An Italian economist, when he heard of Turgot's appointment, wrote to a friend in France as follows: "So Turgot is controller general! He will not remain in office long enough to carry out his plans. He will punish some scoundrels; he will bluster about and lose his temper; he will be anxious to do good, but will run against obstacles and rogues at every turn. Public credit will fall; he will be detested; it will be said that he is not fitted for his task. Enthusiasm will cool; he will retire or be sent off, and we shall have a new proof of the mistake of filling a position like his in a monarchy like yours with an upright man and a philosopher."

Turgot's position

The Italian could not have made a more accurate statement of the case had he waited until after the dismissal of Turgot, which took place in May, 1776, much to the satisfaction of the court. Although the privileged classes so stoutly opposed Turgot's reforms that he did not succeed in abolishing the abuses himself,[2] he did a great deal to forward their destruction not many years after his retirement.

Turgot dismissed, May, 1776

Necker, who after a brief interval succeeded Turgot, contributed to the progress of the coming revolution in two ways. He borrowed vast sums of money in order to carry on the war which France, as the ally of the United States, had undertaken against England. This greatly embarrassed the treasury later

Necker succeeds Turgot

Necker's financial report

1 See Turgot's outspoken letter to the king, August, 1774, in *Readings*, Vol. I, pp. 237 ff.

2 Turgot succeeded in inducing the king to abolish the guilds and the forced labor on the roads, but the decrees were revoked after Turgot's dismissal.

and helped to produce the financial crisis which was the immediate cause of the Revolution. Secondly, he gave the nation its first opportunity of learning what was done with the public funds, by presenting to the king (February, 1781) a *report* on the financial condition of the kingdom; this was publicly printed and eagerly read. There the people could see for the first time how much the *taille* and the salt tax actually took from them, and how much the king spent on himself and his favorites.

Calonne, controller general, 1783–1787

Necker was soon followed by Calonne, who may be said to have precipitated the French Revolution. He was very popular at first with king and courtiers, for he spent the public funds far more recklessly than his predecessors. But, naturally, he soon found himself in a position where he could obtain no more money. The *parlements* would consent to no more loans in a period of peace, and the taxes were as high as it was deemed possible to make them. At last Calonne, finding himself desperately put to it, informed the astonished king that the State was on the verge of bankruptcy, and that in order to save it a radical reformation of the whole public order was necessary. This report of Calonne's may be taken as the beginning of the French Revolution, for it was the first of the series of events that led to the calling of a representative assembly which abolished the old régime and gave France a written constitution.

Calonne informs the king that France is on the verge of bankruptcy, August, 1786

QUESTIONS

SECTION 30. How should the French Revolution be distinguished from the Reign of Terror? What is the meaning of "ancient régime"? Why was France so ill organized in the eighteenth century? Give some examples of the differences which existed between the various provinces. Who were the privileged classes, and what were their privileges? Give examples of the feudal dues.

In what respects was the French peasant more happily situated than his fellows in other parts of Europe? What were the chief powers of the French monarch? What were *lettres de cachet*?

What limitations were placed upon the king's power? What did the *parlements* do to forward the coming revolution? What is meant by public opinion, and what chances does it have to express itself to-day that it did not have in France before the Revolution?

SECTION 31. Who was Louis XVI? Tell something of his wife. Why did Turgot fail to remedy any of the abuses? What happened under Necker to forward the Revolution? Why was Calonne forced to admit that he could not carry on the government unless reforms were introduced?

CHAPTER VIII

THE FRENCH REVOLUTION

SECTION 32. HOW THE ESTATES WERE SUMMONED IN 1789

Reforms proposed by Calonne

It was necessary, in order to avoid ruin, Calonne claimed, "to reform everything vicious in the state." He proposed, therefore, to reduce the *taille*, reform the salt tax, do away with the interior customs lines, correct the abuses of the guilds, etc. But the chief reform, and by far the most difficult one, was to force the privileged classes to surrender their important exemptions from taxation. He hoped, however, that if certain concessions were made to them they might be brought to consent to a land tax to be paid by all alike. So he proposed to the king that he should summon an assembly of persons prominent in Church and State, called *Notables*, to ratify certain changes which would increase the prosperity of the country and give the treasury money enough to meet the necessary expenses.

Summoning of the Notables, 1786

The summoning of the Notables in 1786 was really a revolution in itself. It was a confession on the part of the king that he found himself in a predicament from which he could not escape without the aid of his people. The Notables whom he selected — bishops, archbishops, dukes, judges, high government officials — were practically all members of the privileged classes; but they still represented the nation, after a fashion, as distinguished from the king's immediate circle of courtiers. At any rate it proved an easy step from calling the Notables to summoning the ancient Estates General, and that, in its turn, speedily became a modern representative body.

Calonne denounces the abuses

In his opening address Calonne gave the Notables an idea of the sad financial condition of the country. The government was running behind some forty million dollars a year. He could not continue to borrow, and economy, however strict, would not suffice to cover the deficit. "What, then," he asked, "remains to fill this frightful void and enable us to raise the revenue to the desired level? *The Abuses!* Yes, gentlemen, the abuses offer a source of wealth which the state should appropriate, and which should serve to reëstablish order in the finances. . . . The abuses which must now be destroyed for the welfare of the people are the most important and the best guarded of all, the very ones which have the deepest roots and the most spreading branches. For example, those which weigh on the laboring classes, the privileges, exceptions to the law which should be common to all, and many an unjust exemption which can only relieve certain taxpayers by embittering the condition of others; the general want of uniformity in the assessment of the taxes and the enormous difference which exists between the contributions of different provinces and of the subjects of the same sovereign;" — all these evils, which public-spirited citizens had long criticized, Calonne proposed to do away with forthwith.

Calonne and the Notables dismissed

The Notables, however, had no confidence in Calonne, and refused to ratify his program of reform. The king then dismissed him, and soon sent them home too (May, 1787). Louis XVI then attempted to carry through some of the more pressing financial reforms in the usual way by sending them to the *parlements* to be registered.

The *parlement* of Paris refuses to register new taxes and calls for the Estates General

The *parlement* of Paris resolved, as usual, to make the king's ministry trouble and gain popularity for itself. This time it resorted to a truly extraordinary measure. It not only refused to register two new taxes which the king desired but asserted that "*Only the nation assembled in the Estates General can give the consent necessary to the establishment of a permanent tax.*" "Only the nation," the *parlement* continued, "after it has

The Estates General summoned

learned the true state of the finances can destroy the great abuses and open up important resources." This declaration was followed in a few days by the humble request that the king assemble the Estates General of his kingdom. The *parlements* not only refused to register taxes but continued during the following months to do everything that they could to embarrass the king's ministers. There seemed no other resort except to call the representatives of the people together. The Estates General were accordingly summoned to meet on May 1, 1789.

General ignorance in regard to the Estates General

It was now discovered that no one knew much about this body of which every one was talking, for it had not met since 1614. The king accordingly issued a general invitation to scholars to find out all they could about the customs observed in the former meetings of the Estates. The public naturally became very much interested in a matter which touched them so closely, and there were plenty of readers for the pamphlets which now began to appear in great numbers. The old Estates General had been organized in a way appropriate enough to the feudal conditions under which they originated.[1] All three of the estates of the realm — clergy, nobility, and third estate — were accustomed to send an *equal* number of representatives, who were expected to consider not the interests of the nation but the special interests of the particular social class to which they respectively belonged. Accordingly, the deputies of the three estates did not sit together, or vote as a single body. The members of each group first came to an agreement among themselves, and then a single vote was cast for the whole order.

The old system of voting by classes in the Estates General

Objections to this system

It was natural that this system should seem preposterous to the average Frenchman in 1788. If the Estates should be convoked according to the ancient forms, the two privileged classes would be entitled to twice the number of representatives allotted to the nation at large. What was much worse, it seemed impossible that any important reforms could be adopted in an assembly where those who had every selfish reason for opposing

[1] See Part I, pp. 427 ff.

the most necessary changes were given two votes out of three. Necker, whom the king had recalled in the hope that he might succeed in adjusting the finances, agreed that the third estate might have as many deputies as both the other orders put together, namely six hundred, but he would not consent to having the three orders sit and vote together like a modern representative body.

The *cahiers*

Besides the great question as to whether the deputies should vote *by head* or *by order*, the pamphlets discussed what reforms the Estates should undertake. We have, however, a still more interesting and important expression of public opinion in France at this time, in the *cahiers*,[1] or lists of grievances and suggestions for reform which, in pursuance of an old custom, the king asked the nation to prepare. Each village and town throughout France had an opportunity to tell quite frankly exactly what it suffered from the existing system, and what reforms it wished that the Estates General might bring about. These *cahiers* were the "last will and testament" of the old régime, and they constitute a unique historical document, of unparalleled completeness and authenticity. No one can read the *cahiers* without seeing that the whole nation was ready for the great transformation which within a year was to destroy a great part of the social and political system under which the French had lived for centuries.

Desire of the nation for a constitutional, instead of an absolute, monarchy

Almost all the *cahiers* agreed that the prevailing disorder and the vast and ill-defined powers of the king and his ministers were perhaps the fundamental evils. One of the *cahiers* says: "Since arbitrary power has been the source of all the evils which afflict the state, our first desire is the establishment of a really national constitution, which shall define the rights of all and provide the laws to maintain them." No one dreamed at this time of displacing the king or of taking the government out of his hands. The people only wished to change an absolute monarchy into a limited, or constitutional, one. All that

[1] Pronounced kă-yā′.

Fig. 54. The Opening of the Estates General, May 5, 1789*

was necessary was that the things which the government might *not* do should be solemnly and irrevocably determined and put upon record, and that the Estates General should meet periodically to grant the taxes, give the king advice in national crises, and expostulate, if necessary, against any violations of the proposed charter of liberties.

The Estates General meet May 5, 1789

With these ideas in mind, the Estates assembled in Versailles and held their first session on May 5, 1789. The king had ordered the deputies to wear the same costumes that had been worn at the last meeting of the Estates in 1614; but no royal edict could call back the spirit of earlier centuries. In spite of the king's commands the representatives of the third estate refused to organize themselves in the old way as a separate order. They sent invitation after invitation to the deputies of the clergy and nobility, requesting them to join the people's representatives and deliberate in common on the great interests of the nation. Some of the more liberal of the nobles — Lafayette, for example — and a large minority of the clergy wished to meet with the deputies of the third estate. But they were outvoted, and the deputies of the third estate, losing patience, finally, on June 17, declared themselves a "National Assembly." They argued that, since they represented at least ninety-six per cent of the nation, the deputies of the privileged orders might be neglected altogether. This usurpation of power on the part of the third estate transformed the old feudal Estates, voting by orders, into the first modern national representative assembly on the continent of Europe.

The representatives of the third estate declare themselves a "National Assembly"

The "Tennis Court" oath

Under the influence of his courtiers the king tried to restore the old system by arranging a solemn joint session of the three orders, at which he presided in person. He presented a long

* The clergy, as the first estate of the realm, are seated on the right of the king; the nobles, or second estate, on the left; the representatives of the third estate, clad in sober black, are given what places remain. The princes of the blood are on the platform. Necker, the minister, is making his speech by the table below the throne

program of excellent reforms, and then bade the Estates sit apart, according to the old custom. But it was like bidding water to run uphill. Three days before, when the commons had found themselves excluded from their regular place of meeting on account of the preparations for the royal session, they had betaken

FIG. 55. MIRABEAU

Count Mirabeau was the greatest statesman and orator of the French Revolution. He tried to establish a limited monarchy like that of England. But he had led a scandalous life as a young man, and people were suspicious of his designs and ambition. He died early in 1791 without accomplishing his plans

themselves to a neighboring building called the "Tennis Court." Here, on June 20, they took the famous "Tennis Court" oath, "to come together wherever circumstances may dictate, until the constitution of the kingdom shall be established."

Consequently, when the king finished his address and commanded the three orders to disperse immediately in order to resume their separate sessions, most of the bishops, some of the parish priests, and a great part of the nobility obeyed; the rest sat still, uncertain what they should do. When the master of ceremonies ordered them to comply with the king's commands, Mirabeau, the most distinguished statesman among the deputies, told him bluntly that they would not leave their places except at the point of the bayonet. The weak king almost immediately gave in and a few days later ordered all the deputies of the privileged orders who had not already done so to join the commons.

The nobility and clergy forced to join the third estate

This was a momentous victory for the nation. The representatives of the privileged classes had been forced to unite with the third estate, to deliberate with them, and to vote "by head." Moreover the National Assembly had pledged itself never to separate until it had regenerated the kingdom and given France a constitution. It was no longer simply to vote taxes and help the king's treasury out of its continual difficulties.

First momentous victory of the nation

Section 33. First Reforms of the National Assembly, July–October, 1789

The National Assembly now began in earnest the great task of preparing a constitution for France. The work was, however, soon interrupted. The little group of noblemen and prelates who spent much of their time in the king's palace formed what was known as the court party. They were not numerous but could influence the king as no other group in the nation could do. They naturally opposed reform; they neither wished to give up their own privileges nor to have the king come under the control of the National Assembly, for that would mean that he would no longer be able to give them the pensions and lucrative positions which they now readily obtained. This court "ring" enjoyed the hearty support of the queen, Marie Antoinette, and of the king's younger brother, the count of Artois, both of whom regarded the deputies of the third estate as insolent and dangerous agitators who proposed to rob the monarch of the powers which had been conferred upon him by God himself. The queen

The court party determines to disperse the National Assembly

Fig. 56. The Taking of the Bastille*

and her friends had got rid of Turgot and Calonne, who had endeavored to change the old order; why should they not disperse the Estates General, which was escaping from the control of the clergy and nobility?

Troops sent to Paris; Necker's dismissal, July, 1789

The king agreed to the court party's plans. He summoned the Swiss and German troops in the employ of France and sent a company of them into Paris in order that they might suppress any violence on the part of the townspeople, should he decide to send the arrogant deputies home. He was also induced to dismiss Necker, who enjoyed a popularity that he had, in reality, done little to merit. When the people of Paris saw the troops gathering and heard of the dismissal of Necker they became excited. Camille Desmoulins, a brilliant young journalist, rushed into the garden of the Palais Royal, where crowds of people were discussing the situation, and, leaping upon a table, announced that the Swiss and German soldiers would soon be slaughtering all the "patriots." He urged the people to arm and defend both themselves and the National Assembly from the attacks of the court party, which wished to betray the nation. All night the mob surged about the streets, seeking arms in the shops of the gunsmiths and breaking into bakeries and taverns to satisfy their hunger and thirst.

Camille Desmoulins excites the Parisians, July 12, 1789

Attack on the Bastille, July 14, 1789

This was but the prelude to the great day of July 14, when crowds of people assembled to renew the search for arms, and to perform, mayhap, some deed of patriotism. One of the lawless bands made its way to the ancient fortress of the Bastille, which stood in the poorer quarter of the city. Here the mob expected to find arms, but the governor of the fortress, de Launay, naturally refused to supply the crowd with weapons. He had, moreover, mounted cannon on the parapets, which

* This picture is from a print by an artist of the time. It shows the few little cannon the besiegers possessed. They would have been relatively harmless if the garrison had fought bravely, but, instead, it was in a panic and the drawbridges were left improperly guarded, so the attacking party assailed the central towers with little loss.

made the inhabitants of the region very nervous. The people hated the castle, which they imagined to be full of dark dungeons and instruments of torture. It appeared to them a symbol of tyranny, for it had long been used as a place of confinement for those whom the king imprisoned by his arbitrary orders, the *lettres de cachet*. While there seemed no hope of taking the fortress, whose walls, ten feet thick, towered high above them, the attempt was made. Negotiations with the governor were opened and, during these, a part of the crowd pressed across a drawbridge into the court. Here, for some reason that has never been explained, the troops in the castle fired upon the people and killed nearly a hundred of them. Meanwhile the mob on the outside continued an ineffectual but desperate attack until de Launay was forced by the garrison to surrender on condition that it should be allowed to retire unmolested. The drawbridge was then let down and the crowd rushed into the gloomy pile. They found only seven prisoners, whom they freed with great enthusiasm. But the better element in the crowd was unable to restrain the violent and cruel class, represented in every mob, who proposed to avenge the slaughter of their companions in the courtyard of the Bastille. Consequently the Swiss soldiers, who formed the garrison, were killed, and their heads, with that of de Launay, were paraded about the streets on pikes.

Significance of the fall of the Bastille

The fall of the Bastille is one of the most impressive, striking, and dramatic events in modern history, and its anniversary is still celebrated in France as the chief national holiday. On that day the people of Paris rose to protect themselves against the plots of the courtiers, who wished to maintain the old despotic system. They attacked an ancient monument of despotism, forced the king's officer in charge of it to capitulate, and then destroyed the walls of the fortress so that nothing now remains except a line of white stones to mark its former site. The events of the 14th of July, 1789, have been "disfigured and transfigured by legends," but none the less

Beginning of the emigration of the nobles

they opened a new era of freedom inasmuch as they put an end to the danger of a return to the *Ancien Régime*. It is true that the court party continued to make trouble, but its opposition served to hasten rather than to impede reform. Some of the leaders of the group, among them the king's younger brother, the count of Artois (who was destined to become king as Charles X), left France immediately after the fall of the Bastille and began actively urging foreign monarchs to intervene to protect Louis XVI from the reformers.

The national guard

It had become clear that the king could not maintain order in Paris. The shopkeepers and other respectable citizens were compelled to protect themselves against the wild crowds made up of the criminal and disorderly class of the capital and reënforced by half-starving men who had drifted to Paris on account of the famine which prevailed in the provinces. In order to prevent attacks on individuals and the sacking of shops, a "national guard" was organized, made up of volunteers from the well-to-do citizens. General Lafayette, one of the most liberal-minded of the nobles, was put in command. This deprived the king of every excuse for calling in his regular troops to insure order in Paris, and put the military power into the hands of the *bourgeoisie*, as the French call the class made up of the more prosperous business men.

Establishment of *communes* in Paris and other cities

The government of Paris was reorganized, and a mayor, chosen from among the members of the National Assembly, was put at the head of the new *commune*, as the municipal government was called. The other cities of France also began with one accord, after the dismissal of Necker and the fall of the Bastille, to promote the Revolution by displacing or supplementing their former governments by committees of their citizens. These improvised communes, or city governments, established national guards, as Paris had done, and thus maintained order. The news that the king had approved the changes at Paris confirmed the citizens of other cities in the conviction that they had done right in taking the control into their own hands. We shall hear a good deal of the commune, or municipal government, of Paris later, as it played a very important rôle in the Reign of Terror.

Disorder in the country districts

By the end of the month of July the commotion reached the country districts. A curious panic swept over the land, which the peasants long remembered as "the great fear." A mysterious rumor arose that the "brigands" were coming! The terrified people did what they could to prepare for the danger, although they had no clear idea of what it was; neighboring communities combined with one another for mutual protection. When the panic was over and people saw that there were no brigands after all, they turned their attention to an enemy by no means imaginary, that is, the old régime. The peasants assembled on the village common, or in the parish church, and voted to pay the feudal dues no longer. The next step was to burn the *châteaux*, or castles of the nobles, in order to destroy the records of the peasants' obligations to their feudal lords.

Night of August 4–5

About the first of August news reached the National Assembly of the burning of *châteaux* in various parts of the kingdom, and of the obstinate refusal of the country people to pay the tithes, taxes, rents, and feudal dues. It seemed absolutely necessary to pacify and encourage the people by announcing sweeping reforms. Consequently during the celebrated night session of August 4–5, amid great excitement, the members of the privileged orders, led by the Viscount of Noailles, a relative of Lafayette who had fought with him in America, vied with one another in surrendering their ancient privileges.[1]

[1] Of course the nobles and clergy had very little prospect of retaining their privileges even if they did not give them up voluntarily. This was bitterly emphasized by Marat in his newspaper, *The Friend of the People*. "Let us not be duped! If these sacrifices of privileges were due to benevolence, it must be confessed that the voice of benevolence has been raised rather late in the day. When the lurid flames of their burning *châteaux* have illuminated France, these people have been good enough to give up the privilege of keeping in fetters men who had already gained their liberty by force of arms. When they see the punishment that awaits robbers, extortioners, and tyrants like themselves they generously abandon the feudal dues and agree to stop bleeding the wretched people who can barely keep body and soul together."

The exclusive right of the nobility to hunt and to maintain their huge pigeon houses was abolished, and the peasant was permitted to kill game which he found on his land. The tithes of the Church were done away with. Exemptions from the payment of taxes were abolished forever. It was decreed that "taxes shall be collected from all citizens and from all property in the same manner and in the same form," and that "all citizens, without distinction of birth, are eligible to any office or dignity." Moreover, inasmuch as a national constitution would be of more advantage to the provinces than the privileges which some of these enjoyed, and — so the decree continues — "inasmuch as the surrender of such privileges is essential to the intimate union of all parts of the realm, it is decreed that all the exceptional privileges, pecuniary or otherwise, of the provinces, principalities, districts, cantons, cities, and communes, are once for all abolished and are absorbed into the law common to all Frenchmen."[1]

Decree abolishing the feudal dues, hunting rights, and other privileges

This decree thus proclaimed the equality and uniformity for which the French people had so long sighed. The injustice of the former system of taxation could never be reintroduced. All France was to have the same laws, and its citizens were henceforth to be treated in the same way by the State, whether they lived in Brittany or Dauphiny, in the Pyrenees or on the Rhine. A few months later the Assembly went a step farther in consolidating and unifying France. It wiped out the old provinces altogether by dividing the whole country into districts of convenient size, called *départements*. These were much more numerous than the ancient divisions, and were named after rivers and mountains. This obliterated from the map all reminiscences of the feudal disunion.

Unification of France through the abolition of the ancient provinces and the creation of the present *départements*

Many of the *cahiers* had suggested that the Estates should draw up a clear statement of the rights of the individual citizen. It was urged that the recurrence of abuses and the insidious

The Declaration of the Rights of Man

[1] This edict is given in the *Readings*, section 35. The nobles were to be indemnified for some of the important but less offensive of the feudal dues

encroachments of despotism might in this way be forever prevented. The National Assembly consequently determined to prepare such a declaration in order to gratify and reassure the people and to form a basis for the new constitution.

This Declaration of the Rights of Man (completed August 26) is one of the most notable documents in the history of Europe. It not only aroused general enthusiasm when it was first published, but it appeared over and over again, in a modified form, in the succeeding French constitutions down to 1848, and has been the model for similar declarations in many of the other continental states. It was a dignified repudiation of the abuses described in the preceding chapter. Behind each article there was some crying evil of long standing against which the people wished to be forever protected — *lettres de cachet*, religious persecution, censorship of the press, and despotism in general.

Contents of the Declaration

The Declaration sets forth that "Men are born and remain equal in rights. Social distinctions can only be founded upon the general good." "Law is the expression of the general will. Every citizen has a right to participate, personally or through his representative, in its formation. It must be the same for all." "No person shall be accused, arrested, or imprisoned except in the cases and according to the forms prescribed by law." "No one shall be disquieted on account of his opinions, including his religious views, provided that their manifestation does not disturb the public order established by law." "The free communication of ideas and opinions is one of the most precious of the rights of man. Every citizen may, accordingly, speak, write, and print with freedom, being responsible, however, for such abuses of this freedom as shall be defined by law." "All citizens have a right to decide, either personally or by their representative, as to the necessity of the contribution to the public treasury, to grant this freely, to know to what uses it is put, and to fix the proportion, the mode of assessment and of collection, and the duration of the taxes." "Society has the right to require of every public agent an account of his administration." Well might the Assembly claim, in its address to the people, that "the rights of man had been misconceived and insulted for centuries," and boast that they were "reëstablished for all humanity in this declaration, which shall serve as an everlasting war cry against oppressors."

Section 34. The National Assembly in Paris, October, 1789, to September, 1791

The king hesitated to ratify the Declaration of the Rights of Man, and about the first of October rumors became current that, under the influence of the courtiers, he was calling together troops and preparing for another attempt to put an end to the Revolution, similar to that which the attack on the Bastille had frustrated. A regiment arrived from Flanders and was entertained at a banquet given by the king's guard at Versailles. The queen was present, and it was reported in Paris that the officers, in their enthusiasm for her, had trampled under foot the new national colors, — the red, white, and blue, — which had been adopted after the fall of the Bastille. These things, along with the scarcity of food due to the poor crops of the year, aroused the excitable Paris populace to fever heat.

The court party once more plans a counter-revolution

On October 5 several thousand women and a number of armed men marched out to Versailles to ask bread of the king, in whom they had great confidence personally, however suspicious they might be of his friends and advisers. Lafayette marched after the crowd with the national guard, but did not prevent some of the people from invading the king's palace the next morning and nearly murdering the queen, who had become very unpopular. She was believed to be still an Austrian at heart and to be in league with the counter-revolutionary party.

A Paris mob invades the king's palace and carries him off to Paris

The people declared that the king must accompany them to Paris, and he was obliged to consent. Far from being disloyal, they assumed that the presence of the royal family would insure plenty and prosperity. So they gayly escorted the "baker and the baker's wife and the baker's boy," as they jocularly termed the king and queen and the little dauphin, to the Palace of the Tuileries, where the king took up his residence, practically a prisoner, as it proved. The National Assembly soon followed him and resumed its sittings in a riding school near the Tuileries.

Disastrous results of transferring the king and the Assembly to Paris

This transfer of the king and the Assembly to the capital was the first great misfortune of the Revolution. The work of reform was by no means completed, and now the disorderly element of Paris could at any time invade the galleries and interrupt those deputies who proposed measures that did not meet with their approval. Marat's newspaper, *The Friend of the People*, assured the poor of the city that they were the real "patriots." Before long they came to hate the well-to-do middle class (the *bourgeoisie*) almost as heartily as they hated the nobles, and were ready to follow any leader who talked to them about "liberty" and vaguely denounced "traitors." Under these circumstances the populace might at any time get control of Paris, and Paris of the National Assembly. And so it fell out, as we shall see.

The new constitution

But for some time there was no considerable disorder. The deputies worked away on the constitution, and on February 4, 1790, the king visited the National Assembly and solemnly pledged himself and the queen to accept the new form of government. This provided that the sovereign should rule both by the grace of God and by the constitutional law of the State, but the nation was to be superior to the law and the law to the king.

The Legislative Assembly established by the new constitution

The constitution naturally provided that the laws should be made and the taxes granted by a representative body that should meet regularly. This was to consist, like the National Assembly, of one house, instead of two like the English Parliament. Many had favored the system of two houses, but the nobility and clergy, who would have composed the upper house

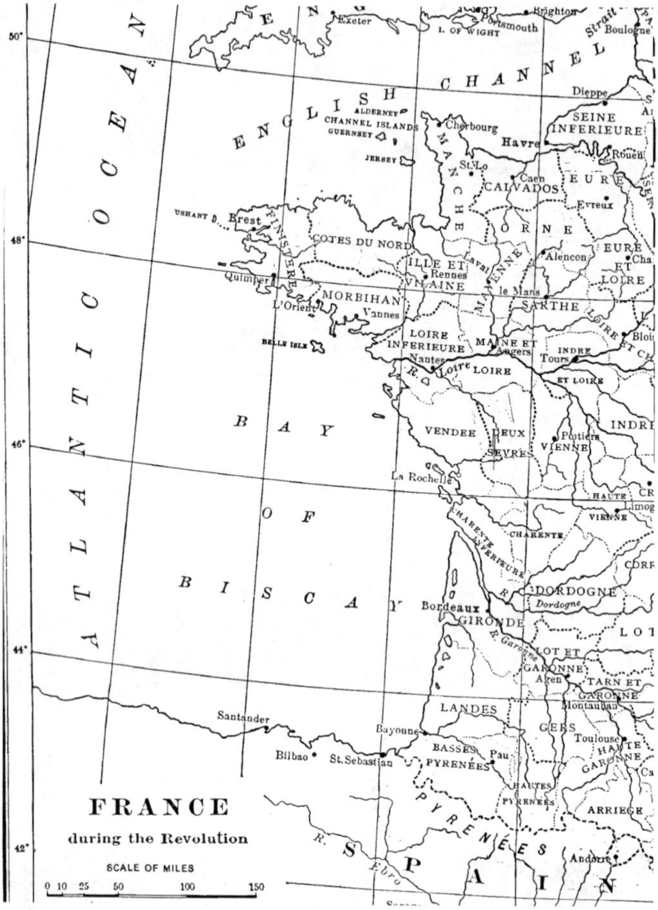
FRANCE
during the Revolution
SCALE OF MILES
0 10 25 50 100 150
ATLANTIC OCEAN
ENGLISH CHANNEL
BAY OF BISCAY
SPAIN
50°
48°
46°
44°
42°
Exeter
I. OF WIGHT
Portsmouth
Brighton
Strait
Boulogne
Dieppe
ALDERNEY
CHANNEL ISLANDS
GUERNSEY
JERSEY
Cherbourg
MANCHE
SEINE INFERIEURE
Havre
Rouen
St. Lo
Caen
CALVADOS
EURE
Evreux
USHANT
Brest
FINISTERE
COTES DU NORD
ORNE
Alencon
EURE ET LOIRE
ILLE ET VILAINE
Rennes
Laval
MAYENNE
Quimper
MORBIHAN
L'Orient
Vannes
le Mans
SARTHE
LOIRE ET CHER
Blois
BELLE ISLE
LOIRE INFERIEURE
MAINE ET LOIRE
Angers
INDRE ET LOIRE
Tours
Nantes
R. Loire
VENDEE
DEUX SEVRES
VIENNE
Poitiers
INDRE
La Rochelle
HAUTE VIENNE
Limog
CHARENTE INFERIEURE
CHARENTE
CORR
DORDOGNE
Dordogne
Bordeaux
GIRONDE
R. Garonne
LOT
LOT ET GARONNE
Agen
TARN ET GARONNE
Montauban
LANDES
GERS
Toulouse
HAUTE GARONNE
Santander
Bayonne
BASSES PYRENÉES
Pau
Bilbao
St. Sebastian
HAUTES PYRENÉES
ARRIEGE
PYRENÉES
Andorre
R. Ebro

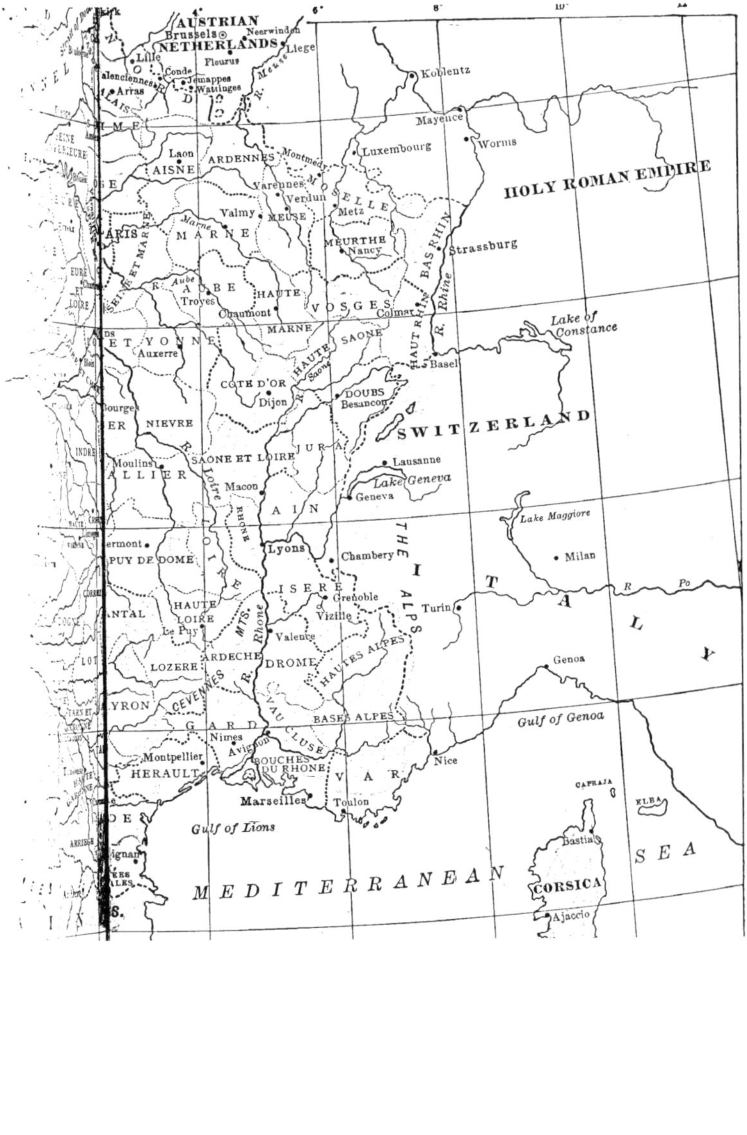

AUSTRIAN NETHERLANDS
Brussels
Neerwinden
Liege
Lille
Fleurus
Conde
Jemappes
Wattignes
Arras
R. Meuse
Koblentz
Mayence
Worms
Luxembourg
HOLY ROMAN EMPIRE
Laon
AISNE
ARDENNES
Montmedy
Varennes
Verdun
MOSELLE
Metz
Valmy
MEUSE
MARNE
PARIS
SEINE ET MARNE
MEURTHE
Nancy
BAS RHIN
Strassburg
R. Aube
AUBE
Troyes
HAUTE MARNE
Chaumont
VOSGES
Colmar
R. Rhine
HAUT RHIN
Lake of Constance
Basel
YONNE
Auxerre
HAUTE SAONE
R. Saone
COTE D'OR
Dijon
DOUBS
Besancon
SWITZERLAND
NIEVRE
SAONE ET LOIRE
JURA
Lausanne
Moulins
ALLIER
R. Loire
Macon
Lake Geneva
Geneva
RHONE
AIN
Lake Maggiore
LOIRE
Lyons
Chambery
THE ALPS
Milan
PUY DE DOME
ISERE
Grenoble
Vizille
ITALY
R. Po
Turin
HAUTE LOIRE
Le Puy
MTS.
R. Rhone
Valence
ARDECHE
DROME
HAUTES ALPES
LOZERE
Genoa
CEVENNES
VAUCLUSE
BASES ALPES
GARD
Nimes
Avignon
Gulf of Genoa
Montpellier
HERAULT
BOUCHES DU RHONE
VAR
Nice
Marseilles
Toulon
CAPRAJA
ELBA
Gulf of Lions
Bastia
SEA
MEDITERRANEAN
CORSICA
Ajaccio

on the English analogy, were still viewed with suspicion as likely to wish to restore the privileges of which they had just been deprived. Only those citizens who paid a tax equal to three days' labor were permitted to vote for deputies to the Legislative Assembly. The poorer people had, consequently, no voice in the government in spite of the Declaration of the Rights of Man, which assured equal rights to all. This and other restrictions tended to keep the power in the hands of the middle class.

The Assembly reforms the Church

Of the other reforms of the National Assembly, the most important related to the Church, which, as has been explained, continued up to the time of the Revolution to be very rich and powerful, and to retain many of its medieval prerogatives and privileges. Its higher officials, the bishops and abbots, received very large revenues and often one prelate held a number of rich benefices, the duties of which he utterly neglected. The parish priests, on the other hand, who really performed the manifold and important functions of the Church, were scarcely able to live on their incomes. This unjust apportionment of the vast revenue of the Church naturally suggested the idea that, if the State confiscated the ecclesiastical possessions, it could see that those who did the work were properly paid for it, and might, at the same time, secure a handsome sum which would help the government out of its financial troubles. Those who sympathized with Voltaire's views were naturally delighted to see their old enemy deprived of its independence and made subservient to the State, and even many good Catholics hoped that the new system would be an improvement upon the old.

Unjust division of the revenue of the Church

The National Assembly declares the property of the Church to be at the disposal of the nation

The tithes had been abolished in August along with the feudal dues. This deprived the Church of perhaps thirty million dollars a year. On November 2, 1789, a decree was passed providing that "All the ecclesiastical possessions are at the disposal of the nation on condition that it provides properly for the expenses of maintaining religious services, for the support of those who conduct them, and for the succor of the poor." This decree deprived the bishops and priests of their benefices and made them dependent on salaries paid by the State. The monasteries and convents were also, when called upon, to give up their property to meet the needs of the State.[1]

The *assignats*, or paper currency

The National Assembly a little later ordered inventories to be made of the lands and buildings and various sources of revenue which the bishops, priests, and monks had so long enjoyed, and then the Church property was offered for sale. Meanwhile, in order to supply an empty treasury, the Assembly determined to issue a paper currency for which the newly acquired lands would serve as security. Of these *assignats*, as this paper money was called, we hear a great deal during the revolutionary period. They soon began to depreciate, and ultimately a great part of the forty billions of francs issued during the next seven years was repudiated.

After depriving the Church of its property, the Assembly deemed it necessary completely to reorganize it, and drew up the so-called Civil Constitution of the Clergy. The one hundred

[1] The medieval monastic orders, feeble and often degenerate, still continued to exist in France at the opening of the Revolution — Benedictines, Carthusians, Cistercians, Franciscans, Dominicans. The State still recognized the solemn vows of poverty taken by the monks and viewed them as incapable of holding any property or receiving any bequests. It also regarded it as its duty to arrest a runaway monk and restore him to his monastery. The National Assembly, shortly after declaring the property of the monasteries at the disposal of the nation, refused (February 13, 1790) longer legally to recognize perpetual monastic vows, and abolished all the orders which required them. The monks and nuns were to be free to leave their monasteries and were, in that case, to receive a pension from the government of from seven hundred to twelve hundred francs. Those, however, who preferred to remain were to be grouped in such houses as the government assigned them. In a year or so a good many of the monks appear to have deserted their old life, but very few of the nuns. Those who remained were naturally the most conservative of all; they opposed the Revolution and sided with the nonjuring clergy. This made them very unpopular with the Legislative Assembly, which in August, 1792, ordered all the monasteries to be vacated and turned over to the government for its use. At the same time it abolished all the other religious communities and associations, like the Oratorians and the Sisters of Charity, who, without requiring any solemn vows, had devoted themselves to teaching or charitable works. Many of these religious *congregations*, as the French call them, were revived in the nineteenth century and have been the cause of a good deal of agitation. See below, section 78.

and thirty-four ancient bishoprics, some of which dated back to the Roman Empire, were reduced to eighty-three, so as to correspond with the new "departments" into which France had just been divided. Each of these became the diocese of a bishop, who was no longer to be appointed by the king and confirmed by the Pope[1] but was looked upon as a government official, to be elected, like other government officials, by the people, and paid a regular salary. The priests, too, were to be

The Civil Constitution of the Clergy completed, July, 1790

FIG. 57. ASSIGNAT

This piece of paper money, which resembled the bank note of to-day, was of the face value of 10 *livres*; but before the Revolution was over it was almost worthless. So many were printed, however, that one can still find specimens in old curiosity shops, costing only a few cents

chosen by the people instead, as formerly, by the bishop or lord of the manor; and their salaries were to be substantially increased. In Paris they were to have six thousand francs, in smaller places less, but never an amount below twelve hundred francs; even in the smallest villages they received over twice the minimum paid under the old régime. Lastly, it was

[1] The decrees abolishing the feudal system (August 11, 1789) had already prohibited all payments to the Pope. The bishoprics were grouped into ten districts, each presided over by a "metropolitan," who corresponded to the former archbishop

provided that clergymen, upon accepting office, must all take an oath, like other government officials, to be faithful to the nation, the law, and the king, and to "maintain with all their might the constitution decreed by the Assembly."[1]

Opposition aroused by the Civil Constitution

The Civil Constitution of the Clergy proved a serious mistake. While the half-feudalized Church had sadly needed reform, the worst abuses might have been remedied without overturning the whole system, which was hallowed in the minds of most of the French people by age and religious veneration. The arbitrary suppression of fifty-one bishoprics, the election of the bishops by the ordinary voters, who included Protestants, Jews, and unbelievers, the neglect of the Pope's rights — all shocked and alienated thousands of those who had hitherto enthusiastically applauded the reforms which the Assembly had effected. The king gave his assent to the Civil Constitution, but with the fearful apprehension that he might be losing his soul by so doing. From that time on he became an enemy of the Revolution on religious grounds.

Oath to the Constitution required of the clergy

The bishops, with very few exceptions, opposed the changes and did all they could to prevent the reforms from being carried out. Accordingly (November 27, 1790) the irritated Assembly ordered all the bishops and priests to take the oath to the Constitution (which, of course, included the new laws in regard to the Church) within a week. Those who refused were to be regarded as having resigned; and if any of them still continued to perform their functions they were to be treated as "disturbers of the peace."

The "non-juring" clergy become the enemies of the Revolution

Only four of the bishops consented to take the required oath and but a third of the lower clergy, although they were much better off under the new system. Forty-six thousand parish priests refused to sacrifice their religious scruples. Before long the Pope condemned the Civil Constitution and forbade the clergy to take the oath. As time went on the

[1] For the text of the Civil Constitution of the Clergy, see the *Readings*, section 36.

"nonjuring" clergy were dealt with more and more harshly by the government, and the way was prepared for the horrors of the Reign of Terror. The Revolution ceased to stand for liberty, order, and the abolition of ancient abuses, and came to mean — in the minds of many besides those who had lost their former privileges — irreligion, violence, and a new kind of oppression more cruel than the old.

Celebration of the fall of the Bastille

A year after the fall of the Bastille a great festival was held in Paris to celebrate the glorious anniversary, which has been commemorated on the 14th of July ever since. Delegates were sent to Paris from all parts of France to express the sympathy of the country at large. This occasion made a deep impression upon all, as well it might. It was more than a year later, however, before the National Assembly at last finished its work and dissolved, to give place to the Legislative Assembly for which the constitution provided.

The extraordinary achievements of the National Assembly

It was little more than two years that the National Assembly had been engaged upon its tremendous task of modernizing France. No body of men has ever accomplished so much in so short a period. The English Parliament, during an existence of five hundred years, had done far less to reform England; and no monarch, with the possible exception of the unhappy Joseph II, has ever even attempted to make such deep and far-reaching changes as were permanently accomplished by the first French Assembly.

The hostility aroused by the policy of the Assembly

Despite the marvelous success of the Assembly, as measured by the multiplicity and the decisiveness of its reforms, it had made many and dangerous enemies. The king and queen and the courtiers were in correspondence with the king of Prussia and the Emperor, with a hope of inducing them to intervene to check the Revolution. The runaway nobles were ready to call in foreign forces to restore the old system, and many of the clergy now regarded the Revolution as hostile to religion. Moreover the populace in Paris and in other large towns had been aroused against the Assembly by their radical leaders, their newspapers, and the political clubs. They felt that the deputies had worked only for the prosperous classes and had done little for the poor people, who should have been supplied with bread and allowed to vote. They were irritated also by the national guard commanded by that ex-noble, the marquis of Lafayette, who looked altogether too fine on his white horse. The members of the guard, too, were well dressed and only too ready to fire on the "patriots" if they dared to make a demonstration. Altogether it is easy to see that there was trouble ahead. The Revolution had gone much too far for some and not far enough for others.

QUESTIONS

SECTION 32. What were the reforms proposed by Calonne? What was the significance of the summoning of the Notables in 1786? What was the result? Tell of the work of the *parlement* of Paris in the year 1787–1788. Describe the organization and the methods of voting of the Estates General.

What were the objections to the system of voting, and what measures were taken to overcome them? What were the *cahiers*? On what points did they agree? What matter occupied the attention of the Estates General from May 5 to June 17, 1789? What was the "Tennis Court" oath?

SECTION 33. Describe the events of July 12 and July 14, 1789. What was the cause of forming the "national guard"? Who was chosen to command it? What were the communes? What took place in the National Assembly at the night session of August 4–5? By what means did the National Assembly still further consolidate France? When and why did the National Assembly draw up the Declaration of the Rights of Man? Give the terms of this Declaration.

SECTION 34. What was the effect of transferring the king and the Assembly to Paris? Mention the terms of the French constitution to which the king and the queen pledged themselves on February 4, 1790. What kind of government did it promise France? What was the decree of November 2, 1789? What were the assignats? Describe the Civil Constitution of the Clergy. Discuss the work of the National Assembly.

CHAPTER IX

THE FIRST FRENCH REPUBLIC

SECTION 35. THE LIMITED MONARCHY, 1791–1792

We have now studied the progress and nature of the revolution which destroyed the old régime and created modern France. Through it the unjust privileges, the perplexing irregularities, and the local differences were abolished, and the people admitted to a share in the government. This vast reform had been accomplished without serious disturbance and, with the exception of some of the changes in the Church, it had been welcomed with enthusiasm by the French nation.

The second revolution

This permanent, peaceful revolution, or reformation, was followed by a second, violent revolution, which for a time destroyed the French monarchy. It also introduced a series of further changes, many of which were fantastic and unnecessary and could not endure, since they were approved by only a few fanatical leaders. France, moreover, became involved in a war with most of the powers of western Europe. The weakness of her government, which permitted the forces of disorder and fanaticism to prevail, combined with the imminent danger of an invasion by the united powers of Europe, produced the Reign of Terror. After a period of national excitement and partial anarchy, France gladly accepted the rule of one of her military commanders, who was to prove himself far more despotic than her former kings had been. This general, Napoleon Bonaparte, did not, however, undo the great work of 1789; his colossal ambition was, on the contrary, the means of extending, directly or indirectly, many of the benefits of the Revolution to other parts of western Europe. When, after Napoleon's fall, the elder brother of Louis XVI came to the throne, the first thing that he did was solemnly to assure the people that all the great gains of the first revolution should be maintained.

The emigration of the nobles

While practically the whole of the nation heartily rejoiced in the earlier reforms introduced by the National Assembly, and celebrated the general satisfaction and harmony by that great national festival held in Paris on the first anniversary of the fall of the Bastille, of which mention has been made,[1] some of the higher nobility refused to remain in France. The count of Artois (the king's younger brother), Calonne, the prince of Condé, and others, set the example by leaving the country just after the events of July 14, 1789. They were followed by others who were terrified or disgusted by the burning of the *châteaux*, the loss of their privileges, and the injudicious abolition of hereditary nobility by the National Assembly in June, 1790. Before long these emigrant nobles (*émigrés*), among whom were many military officers, organized a little army across the Rhine, and the count of Artois began to plan an invasion of France. He was ready to ally himself with Austria, Prussia, or any other foreign government which he could induce to help undo the Revolution and give back to the French king his former absolute power, and to the nobles their old privileges.

The conduct of the emigrant nobles discredits the king and queen

The threats and insolence of the emigrant nobles and their shameful negotiations with foreign powers discredited the members of their class who still remained in France. The people suspected that the plans of the runaways met with the secret approval of the king, and more especially of the queen, whose brother, Leopold II, was now Emperor, and ruler of the Austrian dominions. This, added to the opposition of the nonjuring clergy, produced a bitter hostility between the so-called "patriots" and those who, on the other hand, were supposed to be secretly hoping for a counter-revolution which would reëstablish the old régime.

[1] See above, p. 215.

Mirabeau fails to strengthen the monarchy

Had the king been willing to follow the advice of Mirabeau, the tragedy of the approaching Reign of Terror might probably have been avoided. Mirabeau saw that France needed a strong king who would adjust himself to the new constitution, guide the Assembly, maintain order, and, above all, avoid any suspicion of wishing for a restoration of the old régime. His advice, however, was not heeded any more by the king or queen than by the Assembly. He died April 2, 1791, at the age of forty-three, worn out by a life of dissipation, and the king was thus left with no one to hold him back from destruction.

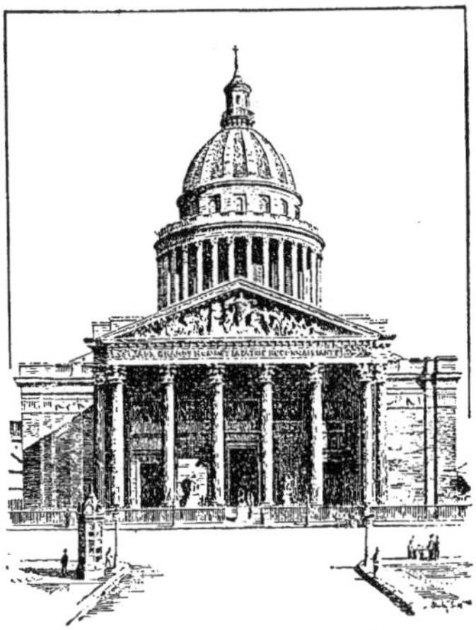

FIG. 58. THE PANTHEON, PARIS

At the death of Mirabeau a magnificent new church, just building on the site of one that dated back to Clovis, the first Frankish king, was made over to be a monumental sepulcher for the great men of France. Mirabeau's body was later taken from it when it was discovered that he had been in the pay of Louis XVI, but many great men are buried in its vaults. The impressive inscription can just be read, in the picture, "To great men, from their grateful country"

The worst fears of the people seemed to be justified by the secret flight of the royal family from Paris, in June, 1791. Ever since the king had reluctantly signed the Civil Constitution of the Clergy, flight had seemed to him his only resource. A body of regular troops was collected on the northeastern boundary ready to receive and protect him. If he could escape and join them he hoped that, aided by a demonstration on the part of the queen's brother, Leopold II, Emperor of Germany, he might march back and check the further progress of the revolutionary movement. He and the queen were, however, arrested at Varennes, when within twenty-five miles of their destination, and speedily brought back to Paris.

Effect of the king's flight

The desertion of the king appears to have terrified rather than angered the nation. The consternation of the people at the thought of losing, and their relief at regaining, a poor weak ruler like Louis XVI clearly shows that France was still profoundly royalist in its sympathies. The National Assembly pretended that the king had not fled but had been carried off. This gratified France at large; in Paris, however, there were some who advocated the deposition of the king, on the ground that he was clearly a traitor. Indeed, for the first time a *republican* party appeared, though it was still small.

The leaders of the new republican party

Of those who had lost confidence in the king and in the monarchy, the most prominent was Dr. Marat, a physician and scholar, who before the Revolution had published several scientific works, but was now conducting the very violent newspaper already quoted, *The Friend of the People*. In this he denounced in the most extravagant language both the "aristocrats" and the "bourgeoisie"—for by "the people" he meant the great mass of workingmen in the towns and the peasants in the fields. Then there was the gentle and witty Camille Desmoulins, who had made the famous address in the Palais Royal on the 12th of July, 1789, which roused the populace to defend themselves against the plots of the courtiers. He too edited a newspaper and was a leader in the radical club called the *Cordeliers*.[1] Lastly Desmoulins's good friend Danton, with his coarse, strong face, his big voice, and his fiery eloquence, was becoming a sort of Mirabeau of the masses. He had much good sense and was not so virulent in his language as Marat,

[1] So named after the monastery where the club held its meetings. The monks had belonged to the order of St. Francis and were called *Cordeliers* on account of the heavy "cord," a rope with three knots, which they wore instead of a girdle

but his superabundant vitality led him to condone violence and cruelty in carrying on the Revolution and destroying its enemies.

It was in the following September that the National Assembly at last put the finishing touches on the constitution which had

FIG. 59. DANTON

Danton was in favor of a policy of terror only so long as France was really in peril. He thought that the Terror was necessary in order to suppress rebellion and conspiracies; but when he tried to stop it, Robespierre's party claimed that he had himself turned traitor to the Jacobin ideal, since that was not yet attained

The National Assembly gives way to the Legislative Assembly (September, 1791)

occupied them for more than two years. The king swore to obey it faithfully, and a general amnesty was proclaimed so that all the discord and suspicion of the past few months might be forgotten. The Assembly had completed its great task, and now gave way to the regular Legislative Assembly, provided for in the constitution. This held its first meeting October 1, 1791.

Sources of danger at the opening of the Legislative Assembly, October, 1791

In spite of the great achievements of the National Assembly it left France in a critical situation. Besides the emigrant nobles abroad there were the nonjuring clergy at home, and a king who was treacherously corresponding with foreign powers in the hope of securing their aid. When the news of the capture of the king and queen at Varennes reached the ears of Marie Antoinette's brother, Leopold II, he declared that the violent arrest of the king sealed with unlawfulness all that had been done in France and "compromised directly the honor of all the sovereigns and the security of every government." He therefore proposed to the rulers of Russia, England, Prussia, Spain, Naples, and Sardinia that they should come to some understanding between themselves as to how they might "re-establish the liberty and honor of the most Christian king and his family, and place a check upon the dangerous excesses of the French Revolution, the fatal example of which it behooves every government to repress."

The Declaration of Pillnitz, August 27, 1791

On August 27 Leopold, in conjunction with the king of Prussia, had issued the famous Declaration of Pillnitz. In this the two sovereigns state that, in accordance with the wishes of the king's brothers (the leaders of the emigrant nobles), they are ready to join the other European rulers in an attempt to place the king of France in a position to establish a form of government "that shall be once more in harmony with the rights of sovereigns and shall promote the welfare of the French nation." They agreed in the meantime to prepare their troops for active service.

Effect of the Declaration

The Declaration was little more than an empty threat; but it seemed to the French people a sufficient proof that the monarchs were ready to help the seditious French nobles to reëstablish the old régime against the wishes of the nation and at the cost of infinite bloodshed. The idea of foreign rulers intermeddling with their internal affairs would in itself have been intolerable to a proud people like the French, even if the new reforms had not been endangered. Had it been the object of the allied monarchs to hasten instead of to prevent the deposition of Louis XVI, they could hardly have chosen a more efficient means than the Declaration of Pillnitz.

The newspapers

Political excitement and enthusiasm for the Revolution were kept up by the newspapers which had been established, especially in Paris, since the convening of the Estates General. Except in England there had been no daily newspapers before the French Revolution, and those journals that were issued weekly or at longer intervals had little to say of politics — commonly a dangerous subject on the Continent. But after 1789 the public did not need longer to rely upon an occasional pamphlet, as was the case earlier. Many journals of the most divergent kinds and representing the most various opinions were published. Some, like the notorious *Friend of the People*, were no more than a periodical editorial written by one man. Others, like the famous *Moniteur*, were much like our papers of to-day and contained news, both foreign and domestic, reports of the debates in the assembly and the text of its decrees, announcements of theaters, etc. The royalists had their organ called *The Acts of the Apostles*, witty and irreverent as the court party itself. Some of the papers were illustrated, and the representations of contemporaneous events, especially the numerous caricatures, are highly diverting, as the accompanying illustration shows.[1]

FIG. 60. CARICATURE: LOUIS XVI AS CONSTITUTIONAL MONARCH[1]

[1] In the caricature reproduced here the formerly despotic king is represented as safely confined by the National Assembly in a huge parrot cage. When asked by his brother-in-law, Leopold II, what he is about, Louis XVI replies, "I am signing my name" — that is, he had nothing to do except meekly to ratify the measures which the Assembly chose to pass.

The Jacobins

Of the numerous political clubs, by far the most famous was that of the *Jacobins*. When the Assembly moved into Paris some of the provincial representatives of the third estate rented a large room in the monastery of the Jacobin monks, not far from the building where the National Assembly itself met. A hundred deputies perhaps were present at the first meeting. The next day the number had doubled. The aim of this society was to discuss questions which were about to come before the National Assembly. The club decided at its meetings what should be the policy of its members and how they should vote; and in this way they successfully combined to counteract the schemes of the aristocratic party in the Assembly. The club rapidly grew, and soon admitted to its sessions some who were not deputies. In October, 1791, it decided to permit the public to attend its discussions.

Gradually similar societies were formed in the provinces.[1] These affiliated themselves with the "mother" society at Paris and kept in constant communication with it. In this way the Jacobins of Paris stimulated and controlled public opinion throughout France and kept the opponents of the old régime alert. When the Legislative Assembly met, the Jacobins had not as yet become republicans but they believed that the king should have hardly more power than the president of a republic. They were even ready to promote his deposition if he failed to stand by the Revolution.

Parties in the Legislative Assembly

The new Legislative Assembly was not well qualified to cope with the many difficulties which faced it. It was made up almost entirely of young and inexperienced men, for the National Assembly, on motion of the virtuous Robespierre, had passed a self-denying ordinance excluding all its members from election to the new body. The Jacobin clubs in the provinces had succeeded in securing the election of a good many of their candidates, sometimes by resorting to violence in order to

[1] By June, 1791, there were 406 of these affiliated Jacobin clubs. See *Readings*, section 37.

defeat the more conservative candidates. Consequently the most active and powerful party in the Legislative Assembly was, on the whole, hostile to the king.

The Girondists

Many young and ardent lawyers had been elected, among whom the most prominent were from the department of the Gironde, in which the important city of Bordeaux was situated. They and their followers were called Girondists. They had much to say in their brilliant speeches of the glories of Sparta and of the Roman Republic; they too longed for a republic and inveighed against "tyrants." They applauded the eloquence of their chief orator, Vergniaud, and frequently assembled at the house of the ardent and fascinating Madame Roland to consider the regeneration of their beloved country. But in spite of their enthusiasm they were not statesmen and showed no skill in meeting the troublesome problems that kept arising.

The emigrant nobles declared traitors

The Assembly, not unnaturally, promptly turned its attention to the emigrant nobles. These had been joined by the king's elder brother, the count of Provence, who had managed to escape at the time that the royal family had been arrested at Varennes. Having succeeded in inducing the Emperor and the king of Prussia to issue the Declaration of Pillnitz, they continued to collect troops on the Rhine. The Assembly declared that "the Frenchmen assembled on the frontier" were under suspicion of conspiring against their country. The count of Provence was ordered to return within two months or forfeit any possible claim to the throne.[1] Should the other *émigrés* fail to return to France by January 1, 1792, they were to be regarded as convicted traitors, and punished, if caught, with death; their property was to be confiscated.

Harsh measures of the Assembly toward nonjuring clergy

The harsh treatment of the emigrant nobles was perhaps justified by their desertion and treasonable intrigues; but the conduct of the Assembly toward the clergy was impolitic as well as cruel. Those who had refused to pledge themselves to support a system which was in conflict with their religious

[1] See *Readings*, section 37, for the count of Provence's saucy reply.

convictions and which had been condemned by the Pope were commanded to take the prescribed oath within a week, on penalty of losing their income from the State and being put under surveillance as "suspects." As this failed to bring the clergy to terms, the Assembly later (May, 1792) ordered the deportation from the country of those who steadily persisted in their refusal to accept the Civil Constitution of the Clergy. In this way the Assembly aroused the active hostility of a great part of the most conscientious among the lower clergy, who had loyally supported the commons in their fight against the privileged orders. It also lost the confidence of the great mass of faithful Catholics, — merchants, artisans, and peasants, — who had gladly accepted the abolition of the old abuses, but who would not consent to desert their priests at the bidding of the Assembly.

The Legislative Assembly precipitates a war with Europe

By far the most important act of the Legislative Assembly during the one year of its existence was its precipitation of a war between France and Austria.[1] To many in the Assembly, including the Girondists, it seemed that the existing conditions were intolerable. The emigrant nobles were forming little armies on the boundaries of France and had induced Austria and Prussia to consider interfering in French affairs. The Assembly suspected — what was quite true [2] — that Louis was negotiating with foreign rulers and would be glad to have them intervene and reëstablish him in his old despotic power. The Girondist deputies argued, therefore, that a war against the hated Austria would unite the sympathies of the nation and force the king to show his true character; for he would be obliged either to become the nation's leader or to show himself the traitor they believed him to be.

[1] See *Readings*, section 37, for reasons assigned by the French for going to war.

[2] See *Readings*, section 37, for a letter of Louis XVI, to the king of Prussia, suggesting the intervention of the foreign powers in French affairs.

Section 36. The Founding of the First French Republic

France declares war on Austria (April 20, 1792)

It was with a heavy heart that Louis XVI, urged on by the clamors of the Girondists, declared war upon Austria on April 20, 1792. Little did the ardent young lawyers of the Assembly surmise that this was the beginning of the most terrific and momentous series of wars that, up to that time, had ever swept over Europe, involving, during twenty-three years of almost continuous conflict, every country and people from Ireland to Turkey, and from Norway to Naples. Moreover, although they later became wars of conquest and empire, these wars brought the principles of the French Revolution home to all the European peoples, everywhere slowly but surely destroyed the old régime, and gave to the people liberty and the control of the government.

The French fail in their first attack on the Austrian Netherlands

The French army was in no condition for war. The officers, who, according to the law, were all nobles, had many of them deserted and joined the *émigrés*. The regular troops were consequently demoralized, and the new national guard had not yet been employed except to maintain order in the towns. It was not unnatural, therefore, that the first troops dispatched to the frontier ran away as soon as they caught sight of Austrian cavalry. The emigrant nobles rejoiced, and Europe concluded that the "patriots" were made of poor stuff.

The king vetoes two measures of the Legislative Assembly and dismisses his Girondist ministers (May–June, 1792)

Meanwhile matters were going badly for the king of France. The Assembly had passed two bills, one ordering those priests who refused to take the oath to the constitution to leave the country within a month; the other directing the formation, just without the walls of Paris, of a camp of twenty thousand volunteers from various parts of France as a protection to the capital. The king resolved, for very good reasons, to veto both of these measures and to dismiss his Girondist ministry.

Rising of June 20, 1792

All this served to make the king far more unpopular than ever. The "Austrian woman," or "Madame Veto," as the queen was called, was rightly believed to be actively betraying France, and it is now known that she did send to Austria the plan of campaign which had been adopted before the war began. In June some of the lesser leaders of the Paris populace arranged a "demonstration" to influence the Assembly and the king. A crowd of "patriots" invaded the palace of the Tuileries. They wandered through the beautiful apartments shouting, "Down with Monsieur Veto!" The king might have been killed by some ruffian had he not consented to drink to the health of the "nation" — whose representatives were roughly crowding him into the recess of a window — and put on a red "liberty cap," the badge of the "citizen patriots."

Invasion of the Tuileries

Approach of the Prussian army

This invasion of the Tuileries seemed to the European rulers a new and conclusive proof that the Revolution meant anarchy. Prussia had immediately joined Austria when France declared war against the latter in April, and now the army which Frederick the Great had led to victory was moving, under his old general, the duke of Brunswick, toward the French boundary with a view of restoring Louis XVI to his former independent position.

The country declared in danger (July 11, 1792)

The Assembly now declared the country in danger. Every citizen, whether in town or country, was to report, under penalty of imprisonment, what arms or munitions he possessed. Every citizen was ordered to wear the tricolored cockade — the red, white, and blue of the Revolution. In this way the peasants, who had been accustomed to regard war as a matter of purely personal interest to kings, were given to understand that they were not now called upon to risk their lives, as formerly, because the Polish king had lost his throne, or because Maria Theresa had a grudge against Frederick the Great. Now, if they shed their blood, it would be to keep out of France two "tyrants" who proposed to force them to surrender the precious reforms of the past three years and restore to the hated runaway nobles their former privileges.

The proclamation of the duke of Brunswick (July 25, 1792)

As the allies approached the French frontier it became clearer and clearer that the king was utterly incapable of defending the country, even if he were willing to oppose the armies which claimed to be coming to his rescue and with which he was believed to be in league. France seemed almost compelled under the circumstances to rid herself of her traitorous and utterly incompetent ruler. The duke of Brunswick, who was in command of the Prussian army, sealed the king's fate by issuing a manifesto in the name of both the Emperor and the king of Prussia, in which he declared that the allies proposed to put an end to anarchy in France and restore the king to his rightful powers; that the inhabitants of France who dared to oppose the Austrian and Prussian troops "shall be punished immediately according to the most stringent laws of war, and their houses shall be burned." If Paris offered the least violence to king or queen, or again permitted the Tuileries to be invaded, the allies promised to "inflict an ever-to-be-remembered vengeance by delivering over the city of Paris to military execution and complete destruction."

The volunteers of Marseilles and their war song

The leaders in Paris now determined to force the Assembly to depose the king. Five hundred members of the national guard of Marseilles were summoned to their aid. This little troop of "patriots" came marching up through France singing that most stirring of all national hymns, the "Marseillaise," which has ever since borne their name.[1]

1 This famous song was not meant originally as a republican chant. It had been composed a few months before by Rouget de Lisle at Strassburg. War had just been declared, and it was designed to give heart to the French army on the Rhine. The "tyrants" it refers to were the foreign kings Frederick William II of Prussia and the Emperor, who were attacking France, not Louis XVI. The "Marseillaise" begins as follows:

Allons, enfants de la patrie,
Le jour de gloire est arrivé;
Contre nous de la tyrannie
L'étendard sanglant est levé. (repeat)
Entendez-vous, dans les campagnes,
Mugir ces féroces soldats?
Ils viennent jusque dans vos bras

The Tuileries again attacked (August 10, 1792)

Danton and other leaders of the insurrection had set their hearts on doing away with the king altogether and establishing a republic. After careful preparations, which were scarcely concealed, the various sections into which Paris was divided arranged to attack the Tuileries on August 10. The men from Marseilles led in this attack. The king, who had been warned, retired from the palace with the queen and the dauphin to the neighboring Riding School, where they were respectfully received by the Assembly and assigned a safe place in the newspaper reporters' gallery. The king's Swiss guards fired upon the insurgents, but were overpowered and almost all of them slain. Then the ruffianly element in the mob ransacked the palace and killed the servants. Napoleon Bonaparte, an unknown lieutenant who was watching affairs from across the river, declared that the palace could easily have been defended had not the commander of the guards been brutally murdered before hostilities opened.

The revolutionary Commune of Paris

Meanwhile the representatives of the various quarters of Paris had taken possession of the City Hall. They pushed the members of the municipal council off their seats and took their places. In this way a new revolutionary Commune was formed, which seized the government of the capital and then sent messengers to demand that the Assembly dethrone the king.

The Assembly agreed with the Commune. If, as was proposed, France was henceforth to do without a king, it was

Égorger vos fils, vos compagnes!
Aux armes, citoyens! formez vos bataillons!
Marchons, qu'un sang impur abreuve nos sillons.

Que veut cette horde d'esclaves,
De traîtres, de rois conjurés?
Pour qui ces ignobles entraves,
Ces fers dès longtemps préparés? (repeat)
Français, pour nous, ah! quel outrage!
Quels transports il doit exciter!
C'est nous qu'on ose méditer
De rendre à l'antique esclavage!
Aux armes, citoyens! formez vos bataillons!
Marchons, qu'un sang impur abreuve nos sillons.

obviously necessary that the monarchical constitution so recently completed should be replaced by a republican one. Consequently, the Assembly arranged that the people should elect delegates to a constitutional *Convention*.

The Legislative Assembly calls the Convention

The task of this Convention was truly appalling since it had not only to draft a new constitution to suit both monarchists and republicans, but to conduct the government, repel invading armies, keep down the Paris mob — in a word, see France through the Reign of Terror.

Appalling task of the Convention

SECTION 37. THE REVOLUTIONARY WAR

The Convention met on the twenty-first of September, and its first act was to abolish the ancient monarchy and proclaim France a republic. It seemed to the enthusiasts of the time that a new era of liberty had dawned, now that the long oppression by "despots" was ended forever. The twenty-second day of September, 1792, was reckoned as the first day of the Year One of French Liberty.[1]

France proclaimed a republic (September 22, 1792)

Meanwhile the usurping Paris Commune had taken matters into its own hands and had brought discredit upon the cause of liberty by one of the most atrocious acts in history. On the pretext that Paris was full of traitors who sympathized with the Austrians and the emigrant nobles, they had filled the prisons with three thousand citizens, including many of the priests who had refused to take the oath required by the Constitution. On September 2 and 3, hundreds of these were executed with scarcely a pretense of a trial. The excuse offered was: "How can we go away to the war and leave behind us three thousand prisoners who may break out and destroy our wives and our children!" The members of the Commune who perpetrated

The September massacres (1792)

[1] A committee of the Convention was appointed to draw up a new republican calendar. The year was divided into twelve months of thirty days each. The five days preceding September 22, at the end of the year, were holidays. Each month was divided into three *décades*, and each "tenth day" (*décadi*) was a holiday. The days were no longer dedicated to saints, but to agricultural implements, vegetables, domestic animals, etc.

this deed probably hoped to terrify those who might still dream of returning to the old system of government.

The Prussian army checked at Valmy

Late in August the Prussians crossed the French boundary and on September 2 took the fortress of Verdun. It now seemed as if there was nothing to prevent their marching upon Paris. The French general, Dumouriez, blocked the advance of the Prussian army, however, at Valmy, scarcely a hundred miles from the capital, and forced the enemy to retreat without fighting a pitched battle. Notwithstanding the fears of the French, King Frederick William II of Prussia (who had succeeded his uncle, Frederick the Great, six years before) had but little interest in the war. As for the Austrian troops, they were lagging far behind, for both powers were far more absorbed in dividing Poland, than in the fate of the French king.

The French occupy Savoy, the Rhine valley, and the Netherlands

The French were able, therefore, in spite of their disorganization, not only to expel the Prussians but to carry the Revolution beyond the bounds of France. They invaded Germany and took several important towns on the Rhine, including Mayence, which gladly opened its gates to them. They also occupied Savoy on the southeast. Then Dumouriez led his barefooted, ill-equipped volunteers into the Austrian Netherlands. This time they did not run away, but, shouting the "Marseillaise," they defeated the Austrians at Jemappes (November 6) and were soon in possession of the whole country.

How the Convention proposed to spread the Revolution abroad (December 15, 1792)

The Convention now proposed to use its armies to revolutionize Europe. It issued a proclamation addressed to the peoples of the countries that France was occupying: "We have driven out your tyrants. Show yourselves freemen and we will protect you from their vengeance." Feudal dues, unjust taxes, and all the burdens which had been devised by the "tyrants" were forthwith abolished, and the French nation declared that it would treat as enemies every people who, "refusing liberty and equality, or renouncing them, may wish to maintain or recall its prince or the privileged classes."[1]

[1] This decree may be found in the *Readings*, section 38.

Trial and execution of the king (January, 1793)

Meanwhile the Convention was puzzled to determine what would best be done with the king. A considerable party felt that he was guilty of treason in secretly encouraging the foreign powers to come to his aid. He was therefore brought to trial, and when it came to a final vote he was, by a small majority, condemned to death. He mounted the scaffold on January 21, 1793, with the fortitude of a martyr. Nevertheless it cannot be denied that, through his earlier weakness and indecision, he brought untold misery upon his own kingdom and upon Europe at large. The French people had not dreamed of a republic until his absolute incompetence forced them, in self-defense, to abolish the monarchy in the hope of securing a more efficient government.

FIG. 61. LOUIS XVI ON THE ROOF OF HIS PRISON

The prison to which the royal family was taken on August 13 was known as the Temple, because it had been part of the building of the Knights Templars in Paris. It was a gloomy tower with massive walls. It was torn down in 1811

The execution of Louis XVI had immediate and unhappy effects. The Convention had thrown down the head of their king as a challenge to the "despots" of Europe; the monarchs accepted the challenge, and the French Republic soon found all the powers of Europe ranged against it. Nowhere did the tragic event of January 21 produce more momentous results than in England. George III went into mourning and ordered the French envoy to be expelled from the kingdom. The prime minister, Pitt, forgetting the work of Cromwell and the Puritan revolutionists, declared the killing of the French king to be the most awful and atrocious crime in all recorded history. All England's old fears of French aggression were aroused. It was clear that the Republic was bent upon carrying out the plans of Louis XIV for annexing the Austrian Netherlands and Holland and thereby extending her frontiers to the Rhine. Indeed there was no telling where the excited nation, in its fanatical hatred of kings, would stop. On February 1 Pitt urged, in the House of Commons, that the Revolution was incompatible with the peace of Europe, and England must in honor join the allies and save Europe from falling under the yoke of France.[1]

Pitt declares that England must oppose the Revolution

France declares war on England (February 1, 1793) and gives her reasons

On the same day that Pitt made this speech, the French Convention boldly declared war upon England and Holland. No one could have foreseen that England, the last of the European powers to join the coalition against France, was to prove her most persistent enemy. For over twenty years the struggle was to continue, until an English ship carried Napoleon Bonaparte to his island prison.

Second partition of Poland (1793)

The war now began to go against the French. Prussia and Austria had been hitherto suspicious of one another, and especially afraid that Russia would take advantage of their preoccupation with France to seize more than her share of Poland. The second partition was made in January, 1793,[2] and the allies then turned with new energy against France.

French driven from the Netherlands; desertion of Dumouriez

The war of the Revolution now took on a wholly new aspect. When, in March, 1793, Spain and the Holy Roman Empire joined the coalition, France was at war with all her neighbors. The Austrians defeated Dumouriez at Neerwinden, March 18, and drove the French out of the Netherlands. Thereupon

[1] Many Englishmen sympathized with the Revolution. Against Pitt's arguments some of the Whigs, especially Fox, urged in vain the bloody manifesto of the duke of Brunswick which had maddened the French, and the atrocious conduct of the allies in the partition of Poland upon which they were just then engaged.

[2] See above, p. 95.

Dumouriez, disgusted by the failure of the Convention to support him and by their execution of the king, deserted to the enemy with a few hundred soldiers who consented to follow him.

Encouraged by this success, the allies began to consider partitioning France as they had Poland. Austria might take the northern regions for herself and then assign Alsace and Lorraine to Bavaria in exchange for the Bavarian territory on her boundaries, which Austria had long wished to annex. England could have Dunkirk and what remained of the French colonies. A Russian diplomat suggested that Spain and the king of Sardinia should also help themselves. "This done, let us all work in concert to give what remains of France a stable and permanent monarchical government. She will in this way become a second-rate power which will harm no one, and we shall get rid of this democratic firebrand which threatens to set Europe aflame."

The allies consider a possible partition of France

Section 38. The Reign of Terror

The loss of the Netherlands and the treason of their best general made a deep impression upon the members of the Convention. If the new French Republic was to defend itself against the "tyrants" without and its many enemies within, it could not wait for the Convention to draw up an elaborate, permanent constitution. An efficient government must be devised immediately to maintain the loyalty of the nation to the Republic, and to raise and equip armies and direct their commanders. The Convention accordingly put the government into the hands of a small committee, consisting originally of nine, later of twelve, of its members. This famous Committee of Public Safety was given practically unlimited powers. "We must," one of the leaders exclaimed, "establish the despotism of liberty in order to crush the despotism of kings."

The French government put in the hands of the Committee of Public Safety, April, 1793

Within the Convention itself there was dissension, especially between two groups of active men who came into bitter

The Girondists

conflict over the policy to be pursued. There was, first, the party of the Girondists, led by Vergniaud, Brissot, and others. They were enthusiastic republicans and counted among their numbers some speakers of remarkable eloquence. The Girondists had enjoyed the control of the Legislative Assembly in 1792 and had been active in bringing on the war with Austria and Prussia. They hoped in that way to complete the Revolution by exposing the bad faith of the king and his sympathy with the emigrant nobles. They were not, however, men of sufficient decision to direct affairs in the terrible difficulties in which France found herself after the execution of the king. They consequently lost their influence, and a new party, called the "Mountain" from the high seats that they occupied in the Convention, gained the ascendency.

The extreme republicans, called the "Mountain"

This was composed of the most vigorous and uncompromising republicans, like Danton, Robespierre, and Saint-Just, who had obtained control of the Jacobin clubs and were supported by the Commune of Paris. They believed that the French people had been depraved by the slavery to which their kings had subjected them. Everything, they argued, which suggested the former rule of kings must be wiped out. A new France should be created, in which liberty, equality, and fraternity should take the place of the tyranny of princes, the insolence of nobles, and the impostures of the priests. The leaders of the Mountain held that the mass of the people were by nature good and upright, but that there were a number of adherents of the old system who would, if they could, undo the great work of the Revolution and lead the people back to slavery under king and Church. All who were suspected by the Mountain of having the least sympathy with the nobles or the persecuted priests were branded as "counter-revolutionary." The Mountain was willing to resort to any measures, however shocking, to rid the nation of those suspected of counter-revolutionary tendencies, and its leaders relied upon the populace of Paris to aid them in carrying out their designs.

Girondist leaders expelled from the Convention, June 2, 1793

The Girondists, on the other hand, abhorred the restless populace of Paris and the fanatics who composed the Commune of the capital. They argued that Paris was not France, and that it had no right to assume a despotic rule over the nation. They proposed that the Commune should be dissolved and that

FIG. 62. MAXIMILIEN ROBESPIERRE

Robespierre was an honest though narrow-minded man. It was his intense love of liberty and equality that made him a dangerous fanatic. He sanctioned using terror to force upon France an ideal democracy, with the sad results that for a long time to come, Jacobinism and democracy in France suffered from the memory of his acts

the Convention should remove to another town where they would not be subject to the intimidation of the Paris mob. The Mountain thereupon accused the Girondists of an attempt to break up the Republic, "one and indivisible," by questioning the supremacy of Paris and the duty of the provinces to follow the lead of the capital. The mob, thus encouraged, rose against the Girondists. On June 2 it surrounded the meeting place of the Convention, and deputies of the Commune demanded the expulsion from the Convention of the Girondist leaders, who were placed under arrest.

France threatened with civil war

The conduct of the Mountain and its ally, the Paris Commune, now began to arouse opposition in various parts of France, and the country was threatened with civil war at a time when it was absolutely necessary that all Frenchmen should combine in the loyal defense of their country against the invaders who were again approaching its boundaries.

The revolt of the peasants of Brittany against the Convention

The first and most serious opposition came from the peasants of Brittany, especially in the department of La Vendée. There the people still loved the monarchy and their priests, and even the nobles; they refused to send their sons to fight for a republic which had killed their king and was persecuting those clergymen who declined to take an oath which their conscience forbade.

Revolt of the cities against the Convention

The cities of Marseilles and Bordeaux were indignant at the treatment to which the Girondist deputies were subjected in Paris, and they also organized a revolt against the Convention. In the manufacturing city of Lyons the merchants hated the Jacobins and their republic, since the demand for silk and other luxuries produced at Lyons had come from the nobility and clergy, who were now no longer in a position to buy. The prosperous classes were therefore exasperated when the commissioners of the Convention demanded money and troops. The citizens gathered an army of ten thousand men, placed it under a royalist leader, and prepared to bid defiance to the Jacobins who controlled the Convention.

French fortresses fall into the hands of Austria and England (July, 1793)

Meanwhile France's enemies were again advancing against her. The Austrians laid siege to the border fortress of Condé, which they captured on July 10, 1793, and two weeks later the English took Valenciennes. In this way the allies gained a foothold in France itself. Once more they were hardly more than a hundred miles away from the capital, and there appeared to be no reason why they should not immediately march upon

Paris and wreak the vengeance which the duke of Brunswick had threatened in his proclamation of the previous year. The Prussians had driven the French garrison out of Mayence and were ready to advance into Alsace. Toulon, the great naval station of southern France, now revolted against the Convention. It proclaimed the little dauphin as king, under the title of Louis XVII, and welcomed the English fleet as an ally.

Carnot organizes the French armies

The French Republic seemed to be lost; but never did a body of men exhibit such marvelous energy as the Committee of Public Safety. Carnot, who was to earn the title of Organizer of Victory, became a member of the Committee in August. He immediately called for a general levy of troops and soon had no less than seven hundred and fifty thousand men. These he divided into thirteen armies which he dispatched against the allies. Each general was accompanied by two "deputies on mission" who were always on the watch lest the commanders desert, as Lafayette had done after August 10, 1792, and Dumouriez a few months later. These Jacobin deputies not only roused the patriotism of the raw recruits, but they let it be known that for a general to lose a battle meant death.

The French easily repulse the allies

Fortunately for the Convention the allies did not march on Paris, but Austria began occupying the border towns and the English moved westward to seize the seaport, Dunkirk. The French were able to drive off the English and Hanoverians who were besieging Dunkirk, and in October General Jourdan defeated the Austrians at Wattignies. Since Frederick William continued to give his attention mainly to Poland, there was little to fear from the duke of Brunswick and his army, so that by the close of 1793 all danger from foreign invasion was over for the time being.

The revolt of the cities suppressed by the Committee of Public Safety

As for the revolt of the cities and of the Vendean peasants, the Committee of Public Safety showed itself able to cope with that danger too. It first turned its attention to Lyons. Some of the troops from the armies on the frontiers were recalled and the city was bombarded and captured. Then Collot d'Herbois, one of the stanchest believers in terrorism, was sent down to demonstrate to the conquered city what a fearful thing it was to rise against the Mountain. Nearly two thousand persons were executed, or rather massacred, as traitors, within five months. Indeed the Convention declared its intention to annihilate the great and flourishing city and rename its site Freedville (*Commune affranchie*). Happily a close friend of Robespierre, who was sent to execute this decree, contented himself with destroying forty houses.

Bonaparte at Toulon

Frightened by the awful fate of Lyons, the cities of Bordeaux and Marseilles judged it useless to oppose the Convention and admitted its representatives, who executed three or four hundred "traitors" in each place. Toulon held out until an artillery officer hitherto entirely unknown, a young Corsican by the name of Napoleon Bonaparte, suggested occupying a certain promontory in the harbor, from which he was able to train his cannon on the British fleet which was supporting the city. It sailed away with some refugees, leaving the town to the vengeance of the Convention, December 19, 1793.

Defeat of the peasants of the Vendée

Although the Vendean peasants fought bravely and defeated several corps of the national guard sent against them, their insurrection was also put down in the autumn — at least for a time — with atrocious cruelty. A representative of the Convention at Nantes had perhaps two thousand Vendean insurgents shot or drowned in the Loire. This was probably the most horrible episode of the Revolution, and was not approved by the Convention, which recalled its bloodthirsty agent, who was finally sent to the scaffold for his crimes.

The Reign of Terror

In spite of the extraordinary success with which the Committee of Public Safety had crushed its opponents at home and repelled the armies of the monarchs who proposed to dismember France, it was clear that the task of rendering the Revolution complete and permanent was by no means accomplished. The revolt of the Vendée and of the cities had shown that there were thousands of Frenchmen who hated the Jacobins.

All such were viewed by the Convention as guilty of holding counter-revolutionary sentiments and therefore "suspect." It was argued that any one who was not an ardent *sans-culotte* might at any time become a traitor to the Republic. In order

FIG. 63. THE PALACE OF JUSTICE (LAW COURTS) IN PARIS

In the thirteenth century part of the royal palace on the island in the Seine was made over to the lawyers of the court, and it has remained ever since the seat of the chief law courts of France. The square clock tower at the corner, the round towers, and the chapel (Sainte-Chapelle, just visible at the left), all date from the old palace — also the lower floor and cellar facing the river, made over into the prison of the Conciergerie. In it Marie Antoinette and many other illustrious prisoners were kept when tried by the Revolutionary Tribunal.

to prevent this the Convention decided that they must be terrorized by observing the fearful vengeance which the Republic wrought upon traitors. The Reign of Terror was only a systematic attempt to secure the success of the Revolution by summarily punishing or intimidating its enemies. While it had no definite beginning or end, it lasted, in its more acute stages, for about ten months — from September, 1793, to July, 1794.

The Revolutionary Tribunal

Even before the fall of the Girondists a special court had been established in Paris, known as the Revolutionary Tribunal. Its function was to try all those who were suspected of treasonable acts. At first the cases were very carefully considered and few persons were condemned. In September, after the revolt of the cities, two new men who had been implicated in the September massacres were added to the Committee of Public Safety. They were selected with the particular purpose of intimidating the counter-revolutionary party by bringing all the disaffected to the guillotine.[1] A terrible law was passed, declaring all those to be suspects who by their conduct or remarks had shown themselves enemies of liberty. The former nobles, including the wives, fathers, mothers, and children of the "emigrants," unless they had constantly manifested their attachment to the Revolution, were ordered to be imprisoned.

Execution of Marie Antoinette (October, 1793)

In October Marie Antoinette, after a trial in which false and atrocious charges were urged against her in addition to the treasonable acts of which she had been guilty, was executed in Paris. A number of high-minded and distinguished persons, including Madame Roland and a group of Girondists, suffered a like fate. But the most horrible acts of the Reign of Terror were, as has been noted, perpetrated in the provinces, especially at Lyons and Nantes.

Schism in the party of the Mountain

It was not long before the members of the radical party who were conducting the government began to disagree among themselves. Danton, a man of fiery zeal for the Republic, who had hitherto enjoyed great popularity with the Jacobins, became tired of bloodshed and convinced that the system ot terror was no longer necessary. On the other hand, the radical leader of the Paris Commune, Hébert, called on the people to complete

[1] In former times it had been customary to inflict capital punishment by decapitating the victim with a sword. At the opening of the Revolution a certain Dr. Guillotin recommended a new device, which consisted of a heavy knife sliding downward between two uprights. This instrument, called after him the guillotine, which has until very recently been used in France, was more speedy and certain in its action than the sword in the hands of the executioner.

Hébert and the ultra-radicals

the Revolution. He proposed that the worship of Reason should be substituted for that of God and arranged a service in the cathedral of Notre Dame where Reason, in the person of a handsome actress, took her place on the altar.

Robespierre and Saint-Just

Robespierre, who was a member of the Committee of Public Safety, sympathized neither with the moderates nor with Hébert and his Goddess of Reason. He himself enjoyed a great reputation for high ideals, republican virtue, and incorruptibility. He and Saint-Just had read their Rousseau with prayerful attention and dreamed of a glorious republic in which there should be neither rich nor poor; in which men and women should live in independence and rear healthy and robust children. These should be turned over to the republic at five years of age to be educated in Spartan fashion by the nation; they were to eat together and to live on roots, fruit, vegetables, milk, cheese, bread, and water. The Eternal was to be worshiped in temples, and in these temples at certain times every man should be required publicly to state who were his friends. Any man who said he had no friends, or was convicted of ingratitude, was to be banished.[1]

Robespierre has the leaders of both the moderates and extremists executed (March and April, 1794)

Robespierre, in his fanatical attempt to establish his ideal republic, now viewed the moderation of Danton and his friends as treason, and coldly advocated the execution of his former associates for attempting to betray the Republic and frustrate the Revolution. On the other hand, as a deist, he believed that Hébert and his followers were discrediting the Revolution by their atheism. Accordingly, through his influence, the leaders of both the moderate and the extreme parties were arrested and sent to the guillotine (March and April, 1794).

Robespierre now enjoyed a brief dictatorship. But it was impossible for him to maintain his power long. When he had the Revolutionary Tribunal divided into four sections in order to work more rapidly, and a law passed by which it could

[1] See *Readings*, section 38, for extracts from Saint-Just's book on *Republican Institutions*.

Fall of Robespierre on the 9th Thermidor (July 27, 1794)

condemn any suspected "enemy of the people" on almost any evidence, many of his colleagues in the Convention began to fear that they might at any moment follow Danton and Hébert to the guillotine. A conspiracy was formed against him and the Convention was induced to order his arrest. When, on July 27,—the 9th Thermidor of the new republican calendar,—he appeared in the Convention and attempted to speak he was silenced by cries of "Down with the tyrant!" In his consternation he could not at first recover his voice, whereupon one of the deputies shouted, "The blood of Danton chokes him!" Finally he called upon the Commune of Paris to defend him, but the Convention was able to maintain its authority and to send Robespierre and Saint-Just, his fellow idealist, to the guillotine. It is sad enough that two of the most sincere and upright of all the revolutionists should, in their misguided and over-earnest efforts to better the condition of their fellow men, have become objects of execration to posterity.

Reaction after the overthrow of Robespierre

In successfully overthrowing Robespierre the Convention and Committee of Public Safety had rid the country of the only man who, owing to his popularity and his reputation for uprightness, could have prolonged the Reign of Terror. There was almost an immediate reaction after his death, for the country was weary of executions. The Revolutionary Tribunal henceforth convicted very few indeed of those who were brought before it. It made an exception, however, of those who had themselves been the leaders in the worst atrocities, as, for example, the public prosecutor, who had brought hundreds of victims to the guillotine in Paris, and the terrorists who had ordered the massacres at Nantes and Lyons. Within a few months the Jacobin Club at Paris was closed by the Convention and the Commune of Paris abolished.

Review of the Reign of Terror

The importance and nature of the Reign of Terror are so commonly misunderstood that it is worth our while to stop a moment to reconsider it as a whole. When the Estates General met, the people of France were loyal to their king but wished to establish a more orderly government; they wanted to vote the taxes, have some share in making the laws, and abolish the old feudal abuses, including the unreasonable privileges of the nobility and the clergy. The nobility were frightened and began to run away. The king and queen urged foreign powers First stage

FIG. 64. THE CLOSING OF THE JACOBIN CLUB

The hall of the Jacobins had been the scene of debates almost as important as those in the Convention, during the attempt to found a democratic republic. When it was closed and the Commune of Paris abolished, the wealthier classes resumed their rule

to intervene and even tried to escape to join the traitorous emigrant nobles. Austrian and Prussian troops reached the frontier and the Prussian commander threatened to destroy Paris unless the royal family were given complete liberty. Paris, aided by the men of Marseilles, retaliated by deposing the king, and the Convention decided by a narrow majority to execute Louis XVI for treason, of which he was manifestly guilty. In the summer, just as Austria and England were taking the French border fortresses of Condé and Valenciennes, the cities of Lyons, Marseilles, and Toulon and the peasants of the Vendée revolted. The necessity of making head against invasion and putting down the insurrection at home led to harsh measures on the part of the Convention and its Committee of Public Safety.

Second stage

When the immediate danger was dispelled Robespierre, Saint-Just, and others sought to exterminate the enemies of that utopian republic of which they dreamed and in which every man was to have a fair chance in life. This led to the second, and perhaps less excusable, phase of the Reign of Terror. To the executions sanctioned by the government must be added the massacres and lynchings perpetrated by mobs or by irresponsible agents of the Convention. Yet Camille Desmoulins was right when he claimed that the blood that had flowed "for the eternal emancipation of a nation of twenty-five millions" was as nothing to that shed by the Roman emperors (and it may be added, by bishops and kings), often in less worthy causes.

A great part of the French people unaffected by the Reign of Terror

Then it should be remembered that a great part of the French people were nearly or quite unaffected by the Reign of Terror. In Paris very few of the citizens stood in any fear of the guillotine. The city was not the gloomy place that it has been pictured by Dickens and other story-tellers. Business went on as usual. Theaters and restaurants were crowded. The mass of the people were little affected by the execution of "aristocrats."

Sound reforms introduced by the Convention

Moreover the Convention had by no means confined its attention during the months of the Reign of Terror to hunting down "suspects" and executing traitors. Its committees had raised a million troops, organized and equipped them with arms, and sent them forth to victory. The reforms sketched out by the National Assembly had been developed and carried on. The Convention had worked out a great system of elementary education which should form the basis of the new

Republic and which became a model for later reform. It had drafted a new code of laws which should replace the confusion of the *ancien régime*, although it was left for Napoleon to order its revision and gain the credit of the enterprise. The republican calendar was not destined to survive, but the rational system of weights and measures known as the metric system, which the Convention introduced, has been adopted by most of the nations of Continental Europe and is used by men of science in England and America.

The metric system

In its anxiety to obliterate every suggestion of the old order of things, the Convention went to excess. The old terms of address, Monsieur and Madame, seemed to smack of the *ancien régime* and so were replaced by "citizen" and "citizeness." The days were no longer dedicated to St. Peter, St. James, St. Bridget, or St. Catherine, but to the cow, the horse, celery, the turnip, the harrow, the pitchfork, or other useful creature or utensil. The Place Louis XV became Place de la Révolution. Throne Square was rechristened Place of the Overturned Throne. The Convention endeavored to better the condition of the poor man and deprive the rich of their superfluity. The land which had been taken from the Church and the runaway nobles was sold in small parcels, and the number of small landholders was thus greatly increased. In May, 1793, the Convention tried to keep down the price of grain by passing the Law of the Maximum, which forbade the selling of grain and flour at a higher price than that fixed by each commune. This was later extended to other forms of food and worked quite as badly as the grain laws which Turgot had abolished.

Anxiety of the Convention to blot out all suggestions of the past

The Convention's efforts to improve the condition of the poorer classes

The reckless increase of the paper currency, or *assignats*, and the efforts to prevent their depreciation by a law which made it a capital offense to refuse to accept them at par caused infinite confusion. There were about forty billions of francs of these *assignats* in circulation at the opening of the year 1796. At that time it required nearly three hundred francs in paper to procure one in specie.

Trouble with depreciated paper money

Constitution of the Year III

At last the Convention turned its attention once more to the special work for which it had been summoned in September, 1792, and drew up a constitution for the Republic. This was preceded by a "Declaration of the Rights and Duties of Man and the Citizen," which summed up, as the first Declaration of Rights had done, the great principles of the Revolution. The lawmaking power is vested by the Constitution of the Year III in a Legislative Body to be composed of two chambers, the Council of Five Hundred and the Council of the Elders. Members of the latter were to be at least forty years old and either married or widowers. To take the place of a king, a Directory composed of five members chosen by the Legislative Body was invested with the executive power.

The Directory

Opposition to the Convention

Before the Convention completed the constitution its enemies had become very strong. The richer classes had once more got the upper hand; they abhorred the Convention which had killed their king and oppressed them, and they favored the reëstablishment of the monarchy without the abuses of the *ancien régime.* The Convention, fearing for itself and the Republic, decreed that in the approaching election, at least two thirds of the new Legislative Body were to be chosen from the existing members of the Convention. Believing that it could rely upon the armies, it ordered that the constitution should be submitted to the soldiers for ratification and that bodies of troops should be collected near Paris to maintain order during the elections. These decrees roused the anger of the wealthier districts of Paris, which did not hesitate to organize a revolt and prepare to attack the Convention.

The 13th Vendémiaire (October 5, 1795)

The latter, however, chose for its defender that same Napoleon Bonaparte who, after helping to take Toulon, had resigned his commission rather than leave the artillery and join the infantry as he had been ordered to do, and was earning a bare subsistence as a clerk in a government office. Bonaparte stationed the regulars around the building in which the Convention sat and then loaded his cannon with grapeshot. When the bourgeois national guard attacked him, he gave the order to fire and easily swept them from the streets.[1] The royalists were defeated. The day had been saved for the Convention by the army and by a military genius who was destined soon not only to make himself master of France but to build up an empire comprising a great part of western Europe.

QUESTIONS

SECTION 35. Account for the failure of Mirabeau to strengthen the monarchy. What was the effect of the king's flight to Varennes, June, 1791? Name the leaders of the new republican party and give an account of their work. What legislative body replaced the National Assembly, October 1, 1791? What problems were before it from the beginning?

Describe the effect of the Declaration of Pillnitz on the French. Who were the Jacobins? What parties were to be found in the Legislative Assembly? Name the leaders of the Girondists. Give the reasons which prompted the Assembly to declare war against Austria.

SECTION 36. What caused the uprising of June 20, 1792? Give the terms of the manifesto of the duke of Brunswick. What was its effect upon the leaders of Paris? What problems did the Legislative Assembly leave to be solved by the Convention?

SECTION 37. What was the first act of the Convention? Trace the course of the war. What effect did the death of the French king have upon the relations of England and France? Account for the success of the French in the Austrian Netherlands during the autumn of 1792. What change took place in the following spring?

SECTION 38. Name the leading parties in the Convention and tell about their quarrel. What was the Reign of Terror? Describe the work of the Revolutionary Tribunal. In what way did Robespierre differ from the other factions of the Mountain? What means did he take to secure his ends? What was the effect of his death upon the Reign of Terror? Describe the Constitution of the Year III. How was opposition to the Convention overcome?

[1] More people were killed on the 13th Vendémiaire than on August 10, 1792, when the monarchy was overthrown.

CHAPTER X

NAPOLEON BONAPARTE

SECTION 39. BONAPARTE'S FIRST ITALIAN CAMPAIGN

How the Revolution transformed and democratized the army

The French army had undergone a complete transformation during the Revolution. The rules of the *ancien régime* had required all officers to be nobles, and many of these had left France after the fall of the Bastille. Others, like Lafayette and Dumouriez, who had at first favored the Revolution, deserted soon after the opening of the war which began in 1792. Still others, like Custine and Beauharnais (the Empress Josephine's first husband), were executed because the "deputies on mission" believed that they were responsible for the defeats that the armies of the French Republic had suffered.

The former rigid discipline disappeared, and the hundreds of thousands of volunteers who pressed forward to defend and extend the boundaries of the Republic found new leaders, who rose from the ranks, and who hit upon novel and quite unconventional ways of beating the enemy. Any one might now become a general if he could prove his ability to lead troops to victory. Moreau was a lawyer from Brittany, Murat had been a waiter, Jourdan before the Revolution had been selling cloth in Limoges. In short, the army, like the State, had become democratic.

The Napoleonic Period

Among the commanders who by means of their talents rose to take the places of the "aristocrats" was one who was to dominate the history of Europe as no man before him had ever done. For fifteen years his biography and the political history of Europe are so nearly identical that the period we are now entering upon may properly be called after him, the Napoleonic Period.

Napoleon Bonaparte was hardly a Frenchman by birth. It is true that the island of Corsica where he was born, August 15, 1769, had at that time belonged to France for a year,[1] but Napoleon's native language was Italian, and he was descended from Italian ancestors who had come to the island in the sixteenth century. His father, Carlo Buonaparte, although he claimed to be of noble extraction, busied himself with the profession of the law in the town of Ajaccio, where Napoleon was born. He was poor and found it hard to support his eight boys and girls, all of whom were one day to become kings and queens, or at worst, princes and princesses. Accordingly he took his two eldest sons, Joseph and Napoleon, to France, where Joseph was to be educated for the priesthood and Napoleon, who was but ten years old, after learning a little French was to prepare for the army in the military academy at Brienne.

Napoleon Bonaparte (b. 1769), a Corsican by birth, an Italian by descent

FIG. 65. NAPOLEON'S BIRTHPLACE

Here the boy led an unhappy life for five or six years. He soon came to hate the young French nobles with whom he was associated. He wrote to his father, "I am tired of exposing my poverty and seeing these shameless boys laughing over it, for they are superior to me only in wealth, and infinitely beneath

Bonaparte at the military school (1779-1784)

[1] It is possible that Bonaparte was born in the previous year, when Corsica still belonged to the republic of Genoa.

me in noble sentiments." Gradually the ambition to free his little island country from French control developed in him.

His political intrigues in Corsica

On completing his course in the military school he was made second lieutenant. Poor and without influence, he had little hope of any considerable advance in the French army, and he was drawn to his own country both by a desire to play a political rôle there and to help his family, which had been left in straitened circumstances by his father's death. He therefore absented himself from his command as often and as long as he could, and engaged in a series of intrigues in Corsica. When the Revolution came, he tried to turn it to his own advantage on the island, but he and his family were banished in 1793, and fled to France.

The Bonapartes banished from Corsica (1793)

How Bonaparte won the confidence of Barras and the Directory

The next three years were for Bonaparte a period of great uncertainty. Soon after his return his knowledge of artillery enabled him, as we have seen, to suggest the way to capture Toulon. This brought him some recognition; but he refused a chance to fight the rebels of La Vendée and remained in Paris, waiting for something to turn up. His opportunity came two years later, when his friend Barras selected him to defend the Convention on the 13th Vendémiaire. This was the beginning of his career, for Barras, now one of the Directors, introduced him into the gay and reckless social circle to which he belonged. Here he met and fell in love with the charming widow of General Beauharnais, who had lost his head just before Thermidor. Madame Beauharnais agreed to marry the pale, nervous little republican officer in spite of his awkward manners and ill-fitting uniform. Nine years later he was able to place an imperial crown upon her brow.

Napoleon marries Josephine Beauharnais

Bonaparte made commander in chief of the army of Italy (1796)

In the spring of 1796 Bonaparte was selected by the Directory to command one of the three armies which it was sending against Austria. This important appointment at the age of twenty-seven forms the opening of an astonishing military career which can be compared only with that of Alexander the Great.

How Prussia and Austria neglected the war with France in 1794

France, as has been pointed out, found herself in 1793 at war with Austria, Prussia, England, Holland, Spain, the Holy Roman Empire, Sardinia, the kingdom of Naples (that is, of the Two Sicilies), and Tuscany. This formidable alliance, however, only succeeded in taking a few border fortresses which the French easily regained. Prussia and Austria were far more interested in Poland, where the third and last partition was pending, than in fighting the Revolution and keeping the French out of the Austrian Netherlands. The Polish patriot, Kosciusko, had led a revolt of the Poles against their oppressors, and the Russian garrison which Catherine had placed in Warsaw was cut down by the Polish rebels in April, 1794. Catherine then appealed to Frederick William for assistance. He therefore turned his whole attention to Poland,[1] and Pitt had to pay him handsomely to induce him to leave sixty thousand Prussian troops to protect the Netherlands from the French invaders. But England's money was wasted, for the Prussians refused to take active measures, and even Austria, after one or two reverses, decided to evacuate the Netherlands, in the summer of 1794, in order to center all her energies upon Polish affairs and prevent Russia and Prussia from excluding her, as they had done the last time, when it came to a division of the booty.

England unable to check the French, who occupy Holland and the Rhine region

England was naturally disgusted. She had joined the war in order to aid Austria and Prussia to maintain the balance of power and defend the Netherlands, which formed a protective barrier between Holland and France. Lord Malmesbury, one of the English diplomats, declared that in his dealings with the allies he encountered only "shabby art and cunning, ill will, jealousy and every sort of dirty passion." By October, 1794, the Austrians had disappeared beyond the Rhine; the English were forced to give up Holland and to retreat forlornly into Hanover before the French under General Pichegru, who captured the Dutch fleet imprisoned in the ice near Texel. The

[1] See above, p. 95.

Dutch towns contained some enthusiastic republicans who received the French cordially. The office of hereditary stadholder, which was really that of a king except in name, was abolished, and the United Netherlands became the Batavian Republic under French control.

The French Republic concludes the Treaties of Basel with Prussia and Spain (April and July, 1795)

Instead of being crushed by the overwhelming forces of the allies, the armies of the French Republic had, in the three years since the opening of the war, conquered the Austrian Netherlands, Savoy, and Nice; they had changed Holland into a friendly sister republic, and had occupied western Germany as far as the Rhine. The Convention was now ready to conclude its first treaties of peace. Prussia signed the Treaty of Basel with the new republic (April, 1795), in which she secretly agreed not to oppose the permanent acquisition by France of the left bank of the Rhine provided Prussia were indemnified for the territory which she would in that case lose. Three months later Spain also made peace with France. Early in 1796 the Directory decided, in accordance with General Bonaparte's advice, to undertake a triple movement upon Vienna, the capital of its chief remaining enemy. Jourdan was to take a northerly route along the river Main; Moreau was to lead an army through the Black Forest and down the Danube, while Bonaparte invaded Lombardy, which was, since the French had occupied the Netherlands, the nearest of the Austrian possessions.

Divisions of Italy

Italy was still in the same condition in which it had been left some fifty years before at the Peace of Aix-la-Chapelle, when the Austrian Hapsburgs and the Spanish Bourbons had come to a final agreement as to what each was to have for the younger members of the two families.[1] In the kingdom of Naples[2] the feeble Ferdinand IV[3] reigned with Caroline his

[1] See *Development of Modern Europe*, Vol. I, pp. 44–46.

[2] We shall use this name hereafter instead of the more cumbersome title, Kingdom of the Two Sicilies.

[3] The successor of Don Carlos, who had become Charles III, king of Spain, in 1759.

wife, the sister of Marie Antoinette. To the north, stretching across the peninsula, lay the Papal States. Tuscany enjoyed the mild and enlightened rule of the successors of Joseph of Lorraine. Parma's duke was related to the Spanish house and Modena's to the Austrian, but the only part of Italy actually under foreign rule was Lombardy and its capital, Milan, which had fallen to Austria after the War of the Spanish Succession. The once flourishing republics of Venice and Genoa still existed, but had long since ceased to play a rôle in European affairs. The only vigorous and promising state in Italy that was not more or less under the influence of either Austria or Spain was the kingdom of Sardinia, composed of Piedmont, Savoy, Nice, and the island of Sardinia.

Bonaparte forces Sardinia to conclude peace and enters Milan (May, 1796)

General Bonaparte had to face the combined forces of Austria and Sardinia, which had joined the enemies of France in 1793. By marching north from Savona he skillfully separated his two enemies. He forced the Sardinian troops back toward Turin and compelled the king to conclude a treaty by which Savoy and Nice were ceded to France. Bonaparte was now free to advance into Lombardy. He marched down the Po, and the Austrians, fearing that he might cut them off, hastened eastward, leaving Milan to be occupied by the French. Here Bonaparte made a triumphal entry on May 15, 1796, scarcely more than a month after the campaign opened.

The French begin to plunder Italy

As he descended the mountains into the plains of Lombardy, Bonaparte had announced that the French army came to break the chains of the tyrants, for the French people was the friend of all peoples. Nevertheless the Directory expected him to force those that he "freed" to support the French armies. Their directions to Bonaparte were sufficiently explicit: "Leave nothing in Italy which will be useful to us and which the political situation will permit you to remove." Accordingly Milan was not only required to pay its deliverers twenty million francs but also to give up some of the finest old masterpieces in its churches and galleries. The dukes of Parma and Modena made similar "contributions" on condition that Bonaparte would grant them an armistice.

The campaign about Mantua (May, 1796–February, 1797)

Bonaparte soon moved east and defeated the Austrian army, a part of which took refuge in the impregnable fortress of Mantua, to which the French promptly laid siege. There is no more fascinating chapter in the history of warfare than the story of the audacious maneuvers by which Bonaparte successfully repulsed the Austrian armies sent to relieve Mantua. Toward the end of July an Austrian army nearly twice the size of Bonaparte's descended in three divisions from Tyrol. The situation of the French was critical, but Bonaparte managed to defeat each of the three divisions before they had an opportunity to join forces. In five days the Austrians retired, leaving fifteen thousand prisoners in the hands of the French. Bonaparte now determined to advance up the river Adige into Germany. He again routed the Austrians and took possession of Trent. Wurmser, the Austrian commander, tried to cut him off from Italy but was himself shut up in Mantua with the remains of his army.

Bonaparte defeats the Austrians at Arcole (November 15–17, 1796) and at Rivoli (January 14–15, 1797)

In November two more Austrian armies were sent down to relieve Mantua, one approaching by the Adige and the other descending the Piave. Bonaparte met and defeated the Piave army in a three days' battle at Arcole, after which the other Austrian division retreated. The last effort to relieve the fortress was frustrated by Bonaparte at Rivoli (January 14–15, 1797) and resulted in the surrender of Mantua, which gave the French complete control of northern Italy.

Fall of Mantua

Truce at Leoben (April, 1797)

All danger of an attack in the rear was now removed, and the victorious French general could lead his army through the mountains to Vienna. He forced back the Austrians, who attempted to block the road, and when, on April 7, he was within eighty miles of the capital, the Austrian commander requested a truce, which Bonaparte was not unwilling to grant, since he was now far from home, and both the other armies which the Directory had sent out, under Moreau and Jourdan, had been routed and forced back over the Rhine. A preliminary peace was accordingly arranged, which was followed by the definitive Treaty of Campo Formio (October, 1797).

CENTRAL EUROPE TO ILLUSTRATE NAPOLEON'S CAMPAIGNS, 1796–1801

The provisions of the Treaty of Campo Formio illustrate the unscrupulous manner in which Bonaparte and Austria disposed of the helpless lesser states. It inaugurated the bewilderingly rapid territorial redistribution of Europe which was so characteristic of the Napoleonic Period. Austria ceded to France the Austrian Netherlands and secretly agreed to use its good offices to secure for France a great part of the left bank of the Rhine.

Provisions of the Treaty of Campo Formio (October, 1797)

Creation of the Cisalpine Republic

Austria also recognized the Cisalpine Republic, which Bonaparte had created out of the smaller states of northern Italy, and which was under the "protection" of France. This new state included Lombardy, which Bonaparte had conquered, the duchy of Modena, some of the papal dominions, and, lastly, a part of the possessions of the venerable and renowned but now defenseless republic of Venice, which Napoleon had ruthlessly destroyed. Austria received as an indemnity for the Netherlands and Lombardy the rest of the possessions of the Venetian republic, including Venice itself.

General Bonaparte establishes a court

While the negotiations were going on, the young general had established a brilliant court at a villa near Milan. "His salons," an observer informs us, "were filled with a throng of generals, officials, and purveyors, as well as the highest nobility and the most distinguished men of Italy, who came to solicit the favor of a glance or a moment's conversation." It would appear, from the report of a most extraordinary conversation which occurred at this time, that he had already conceived the rôle that he was to play later.

Bonaparte's analysis of the French character and of his own aims

"What I have done so far," he declared, "is nothing. I am but at the opening of the career that I am to run. Do you suppose that I have gained my victories in Italy in order to advance the lawyers of the Directory, — the Carnots and the Barrases? Do you think either that my object is to establish a republic? What a notion! . . . Let the Directory attempt to deprive me of my command and they will see who is the master. The nation must have a head, a head who is rendered illustrious by glory and not by theories of government, fine phrases, or the talk of idealists."

There is no doubt whom General Bonaparte had in mind when he spoke of the needed head of the French nation who should be "rendered illustrious by glory." This son of a poor Corsican lawyer, but yesterday a mere unlucky adventurer, had arranged his program; two years and a half later, at the age of thirty, he was the master of the French Republic.

Bonaparte was a little man, less than five feet four inches in height. At this time he was extremely thin, but his striking features, quick, searching eye, abrupt, animated gestures, and rapid speech, incorrect as it was, made a deep impression upon those who came in contact with him. He possessed in a supreme degree two qualities that are ordinarily considered incompatible. He was a dreamer and, at the same time, a man whose practical skill and mastery of detail amounted to genius. He once told a friend that he was wont, when a poor lieutenant, to allow his imagination full play and fancy things just as he would have them. Then he would coolly consider the exact steps to be taken if he were to try to make his dream come true. Personal characteristics

In order to explain Bonaparte's success it must be remembered that he was not hampered or held back by the fear of doing wrong. He was utterly unscrupulous, whether dealing with an individual or a nation, and appears to have been absolutely without any sense of moral responsibility. Neither did affection for his friends and relatives ever stand in the way of his personal aggrandizement. To these traits must be added unrivaled military genius and the power of intense and almost uninterrupted work. Sources of power in Napoleon's character

But even Bonaparte, unexampled as were his abilities, could never have extended his power over all of western Europe, had it not been for the peculiar political weakness of most of the states with which he had to deal. There was no strong German Empire in his day, no united Italy. The French Republic was surrounded by petty, independent, or practically independent, principalities, which were defenseless against an unscrupulous invader. Moreover the larger powers were inclined to be jealous of each other and did not support each other properly. Prussia, much smaller than it is now, offered no efficient opposition to the extension of French control, while Austria had been forced to capitulate, after a short campaign, by an enemy far from its source of supplies and led by a young and inexperienced general. The political conditions which rendered Napoleon's wonderful successes possible

Section 40. How Bonaparte made himself Master of France

Bonaparte conceives the plan of an expedition to Egypt

After arranging the Peace of Campo Formio, General Bonaparte returned to Paris. He at once perceived that France, in spite of her enthusiasm over his victories, was not yet ready to accept him as her ruler. The pear was not yet ripe, as he observed. He saw, too, that he would soon sacrifice his prestige if he lived quietly in Paris like an ordinary person. His active mind promptly conceived a plan which would forward his interests. France was still at war with England, its most persevering enemy during this period. Bonaparte convinced the Directory that England could best be ruined in the long run by occupying Egypt and so threatening her commerce in the Mediterranean, and perhaps ultimately her dominion in the East. Fascinated by the career of Alexander the Great, Bonaparte pictured himself riding to India on the back of an elephant and dispossessing England of her most precious colonial dependencies.[1] He had, however, still another and a characteristic reason for undertaking the expedition. France was on the eve of a new war with the European powers. Bonaparte foresaw that, if he could withdraw with him some of France's best officers, the Directory might soon find itself so embarrassed that he could return as a national savior. And even so it fell out.

Accordingly General Bonaparte, under authority of the Directory, collected forty thousand of the best troops and fitted out

[1] The expedition to Egypt did not establish a new empire, but it led to the revelation of thousands of years of ancient history. A band of French scholars accompanied the army and started collecting the remains of monuments and tombs.

The tombs were covered with hieroglyphs which no one could read; but in the spoil collected — and captured by Nelson so that it is now in the British Museum — was a stone with both Greek text and hieroglyphs in parallel columns, which a French scholar, Champollion, used, a few years later, as a key to unlock the literature of ancient Egypt. So it turned out that the few scientists, whom the soldiers on the expedition heartily despised, accomplished most. See Part I, chap. ii.

a strong fleet, which should serve to give France the control of the Mediterranean. He did not forget to add to the expedition a hundred and twenty scientists and engineers, who were to study the country and prepare the way for French colonists to be sent out later.

The campaign in Egypt (1798-1799)

The French fleet left Toulon, May 19, 1798. It was so fortunate as to escape the English squadron under Nelson, which sailed by it in the night. Bonaparte arrived at Alexandria, July 1, and easily defeated the Turkish troops in the famous battle of the Pyramids. Meanwhile Nelson, who did not know the destination of the enemy's fleet, had returned from the Syrian coast, where he had looked for the French in vain. He discovered Bonaparte's ships in the harbor of Alexandria and completely annihilated them in the first battle of the Nile (August 1, 1798). The French troops were now completely cut off from Europe.

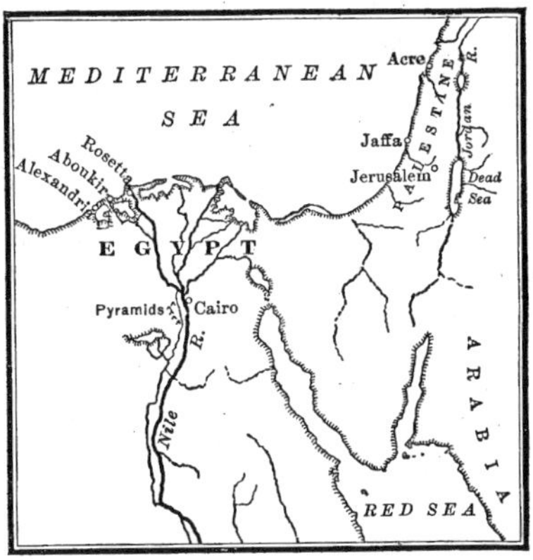

EGYPTIAN CAMPAIGN

Nelson destroys the French fleet

Syrian campaign

The Porte (that is, the Turkish government) having declared war against France, Bonaparte resolved to attack Turkey by land. He accordingly marched into Syria in the spring of 1799, but was repulsed at Acre, where the Turkish forces were aided by the English fleet. Pursued by pestilence, the army regained Cairo in June, after terrible suffering and loss. It was still strong enough to annihilate a Turkish army that landed at Alexandria, but news now reached Bonaparte from Europe

Bonaparte deserts the army in Egypt and returns to Paris

which convinced him that the time had come for him to hasten back. The powers had formed a new coalition against France. Northern Italy, which he had won, was lost; the allies were about to invade France itself, and the Directory was hopelessly demoralized. Bonaparte accordingly secretly deserted his army and managed, by a series of happy accidents, to reach France by October 9, 1799.

The *coup d'état* of the 18th Brumaire (November 9, 1799)

The Directory, one of the most corrupt and inefficient governmental bodies that the world has ever seen, had completely disgraced itself, and Bonaparte readily found others to join with him in a conspiracy to overthrow it. A plan was formed for abruptly destroying the old government and replacing it by a new one without observing any constitutional forms. This is a procedure so familiar in France during the past century that it is known even in English as a *coup d'état* (literally translated, a "stroke of state"). The conspirators had a good many friends in the two assemblies, especially among the "Elders." Nevertheless Bonaparte had to order his soldiers to invade the hall in which the Assembly of the Five Hundred was in session and scatter his opponents before he could accomplish his purpose. A chosen few were then reassembled under the presidency of Lucien Bonaparte, one of Napoleon's brothers, who was a member of the Assembly. They voted to put the government in the hands of three men, — General Bonaparte and two others, — to be called "Consuls." These were to proceed, with the aid of a commission and of the Elders, to draw up a new constitution.

Bonaparte made First Consul

The constitution of the Year VIII

The new constitution was a very cumbrous and elaborate one. It provided for no less than four assemblies, one to propose the laws, one to consider them, one to vote upon them, and one to decide on their constitutionality. But Bonaparte saw to it that as First Consul he himself had practically all the power in his own hands. The Council of State, to which he called talented men from all parties and over which he presided, was the most important of the governmental bodies.

The Council of State

FIG. 66. BONAPARTE'S *COUP D'ÉTAT* OF THE 18TH BRUMAIRE

Bonaparte's invasion of the hall of the Assembly with his soldiers, to "restore liberty," was a military conspiracy against the existing government. The legislators accused him of treason, and he almost lost his nerve at the critical moment. His brother, however, harangued the soldiers outside, telling them their general's life was in danger, and they drove everyone from the hall. Thus Bonaparte got control of France

Bonaparte's chief aim was to *centralize* the government. Nothing was left to local assemblies, for he proposed to control everything from Paris. Accordingly, in each *département* he put an officer called a *prefect*; in each subdivision of the *département* a *subprefect*. These, together with the mayors and

The centralized administrative system established by Bonaparte police commissioners of the towns, were all appointed by the First Consul. The prefects — "little First Consuls," as Bonaparte called them — resembled the former intendants, the king's officers under the old régime. Indeed, the new government suggested in several important respects that of Louis XIV. This administrative system which Bonaparte perfected has endured, with a few changes, down to the present day. It has rendered the French government very stable in spite of the startling changes in the constitution which have occurred. There is no surer proof of Napoleon's genius than that, with no previous experience, he could conceive a plan of government that should serve a great state like France through all its vicissitudes for a century.

The new government accepted by a plebiscite

The new ruler objected as decidedly as Louis XIV had done to the idea of being controlled by the people, who, he believed, knew nothing of public affairs. It was enough, he thought, if they were allowed to say whether they wished a certain form of government or not. He therefore introduced what he called a *plébiscite*.[1] The new constitution when completed was submitted to the nation at large, and all were allowed to vote "yes" or "no" on the question of its adoption. Over three million voted in favor of it, and only fifteen hundred and sixty-two against it. This did not necessarily mean, however, that practically the whole nation wished to have General Bonaparte as its ruler. A great many may have preferred what seemed to them an objectionable form of government to the risk of rejecting it. Herein lies the injustice of the plebiscite; there are many questions that cannot be answered by a simple "yes" or "no."

Bonaparte generally acceptable to France as First Consul

Yet the accession to power of the popular young general was undoubtedly grateful to the majority of citizens, who longed above all for a stable government. The Swedish envoy wrote, just after the *coup d'état*: "A legitimate monarch has perhaps never found a people more ready to do his

[1] The *plebiscitum* of the Romans, from which the French derived their term *plébiscite*, was originally a law voted in the Assembly of the *plebs*, or people.

bidding than Bonaparte, and it would be inexcusable if this talented general did not take advantage of this to introduce a better form of government upon a firmer basis. It is literally true that France will perform impossibilities in order to aid him in this. The people (with the exception of a despicable horde of anarchists) are so sick and weary of revolutionary horrors and folly that they believe that any change cannot fail to be for the better. . . . Even the royalists, whatever their views may be, are sincerely devoted to Bonaparte, for they attribute to him the intention of gradually restoring the old order of things. The indifferent element cling to him as the one most likely to give France peace. The enlightened republicans, although they tremble for their form of government, prefer to see a single man of talent possess himself of the power than a club of intriguers."

Section 41. The Second Coalition against France

The Second Coalition

Upon becoming First Consul, General Bonaparte found France at war with England, Russia, Austria, Turkey, and Naples — a somewhat strange coalition which must be explained. After the treaties of Basel and Campo Formio, England had been left to fight the Revolution single-handed. But in 1798 Pitt, the English prime minister, found an unexpected ally in the Tsar Paul.[1] Like his mother, Catherine II, whom he succeeded in 1796, he hated the Revolution; but, unlike her, he consented to send troops to fight against France, for which Pitt agreed to help pay. Austria was willing to take up the war again since she saw no prospect of getting all the territory that Bonaparte had half promised her in the Treaty

Russia enters the war as England's ally

[1] Paul was an ill-balanced person whose chief grievance against the French was that Bonaparte, on the way to Egypt, had captured the island of Malta. Malta had for centuries been held by the Order of the Knights of Malta, which had originated during the Crusades. Now the knights had chosen Paul as their "Protector," an honor which enchanted his simple soul and led him to dream of annexing Malta to his empire. Bonaparte's seizure of the island interfered with his plans and served to rouse a desire for vengeance.

The Sultan

of Campo Formio. As for the Sultan, Bonaparte's Egyptian expedition brought the French to his very doors and led him to join his ancient enemy, Russia, in a common cause.

France republicanizes her neighbors

It certainly appeared to be high time to check the restless new Republic which was busily engaged in spreading "liberty" in her own interest. Holland had first been *republicanized*; then Bonaparte had established the Cisalpine Republic in northern Italy; and the French had stirred up a revolution in Genoa, which led to the abolition of the old aristocratic government and the founding of a new Ligurian Republic which was to be the friend and ally of France.

The Roman Republic proclaimed (February, 1798)

Next, with the encouragement of Joseph Bonaparte, Napoleon's brother, who was the French ambassador in Rome, the few republicans in the Pope's capital proclaimed a republic. In the disturbance which ensued a French general was killed, a fact which gave the Directory an excuse for declaring war and occupying Rome. On February 15, 1798, the republicans assembled in the ancient forum and declared that the Roman Republic was once more restored. The brutal French commissioner insulted the Pope, snatched his staff and ring from his hand, and ordered him out of town. The French seized the pictures and statues in the Vatican and sent them to Paris and managed to rob the new republic of some sixty million francs besides.

The Directory revolutionizes and plunders Switzerland (1798)

More scandalous still was the conduct of the Directory and its commissioners in dealing with Switzerland. In that little country, certain of the *cantons*, or provinces, had long been subject to others which possessed superior rights. A few persons in the canton of Vaud were readily induced by the French agitators to petition the Directory to free their canton from the overlordship of Berne. In January, 1798, a French army entered Switzerland and easily overpowered the troops of Berne and occupied the city (in March), where they seized the treasure — some four millions of dollars — which had been gradually brought together through a long period by the thrifty government of the confederation. A new Helvetic Republic, "one and indivisible," was proclaimed, in which all the cantons should be equal and all the old feudal customs and inequalities should be abolished. The mountaineers of the conservative cantons about the lake of Lucerne rose in vain against the intruders, but the French party mercilessly massacred those who dared to oppose the changes which they chose to introduce.

The Helvetic Republic

The new outbreak of war against France was due to Naples, where Marie Antoinette's sister, Caroline, watched with horror the occupation of Rome by the French troops. Nelson, after destroying Bonaparte's fleet in the battle of the Nile, had returned to Naples and there arranged a plan for driving the French from the Papal States. But everything went badly; the French easily defeated the Bourbon armies and the members of the royal family of Naples were glad to embark on the British ships and make their way to Palermo. Thereupon the French republicanized Naples (renaming it the Parthenopean Republic), seized millions of francs as usual, and carried off to Paris the best works of art.

Naples reopens the war against France (November, 1798)

Naples turned into the Parthenopean Republic (January, 1799)

At the same time Piedmont was occupied by the French, and the king was forced to abdicate. He retired to Sardinia, where he remained until Napoleon's downfall fifteen years later.

Piedmont occupied by the French

Early in the year 1799 the French Republic seemed everywhere victorious. It had at last reached its "natural boundaries" by adding to the Austrian Netherlands those portions of the Holy Roman Empire which lay on the left bank[1] of the Rhine, and, to the south, the duchy of Savoy. It had reorganized its neighbors, the Batavian Republic, the Helvetic Republic, the Ligurian Republic, the Cisalpine Republic, the Roman Republic, and the Parthenopean Republic — all of which were to accept its counsel and aid it with money, troops, and supplies. Bonaparte had occupied Egypt and was on his way to Syria with gorgeous visions of subjugating the whole Orient.

France reaches its "natural boundaries" in 1799

[1] That is to say, the bank which would lie to the left of one traveling down the river, in this case the west bank.

Suvaroff and the Austrians force the French out of Italy (April–August, 1799)

Within a few months, however, the situation was completely changed. The Austrians defeated the French in southern Germany, and they retreated to the Rhine. In Italy the brave Russian general, Suvaroff, with the small but valiant army which the Tsar had sent to the west, forced the French out of northern Italy and, with the aid of the Austrians, repeatedly defeated their armies and shut up the remains of their forces in Genoa, to which the Austrians laid siege. Suvaroff then turned north through the Swiss mountains, across which he forced his way in spite of incredible difficulties, only to find that a second Russian army, which he had expected would join him, had been defeated by the French. Thereupon the Tsar, attributing the reverses of his armies to the intrigues of Austria, broke off all relations with her and recalled his generals (October, 1799).[1]

Russia withdraws from the war (October, 1799)

The First Consul writes to George III and Francis II in the interests of peace

In November, 1799, the corrupt and inefficient Directory was, as we have seen, thrust aside by a victorious general to whom France now looked for peace and order. The First Consul sought to make a happy impression upon France by writing personal letters on Christmas Day to both George III and Emperor Francis II, in which he deplored a continuation of war among the most enlightened nations of Europe. Why should they "sacrifice to ideas of empty greatness the blessings of commerce, internal prosperity, and domestic happiness? Should they not recognize that peace was at once their first need and their chief glory?"

His advances not well received

The English returned a gruff reply in which Pitt declared that France had been entirely at fault and had precipitated war by her aggressions in Holland, Switzerland, and Egypt. England must continue the struggle until France offered pledges of peace, and the best security would be the recall of the Bourbon

[1] Naturally the republics which had been formed in Italy under French influence collapsed. Ferdinand returned to Naples and instituted a royalist reign of terror, in which Nelson took part. His general's conduct met with hearty disapproval in England.

dynasty.[1] The Austrians also refused, though somewhat more graciously, to come to terms, and Bonaparte began secretly collecting troops which he could direct against the Austrian army that was besieging the French in Genoa.

Bonaparte crosses the St. Bernard Pass (May, 1800)

Bonaparte now proceeded to devise one of the boldest and most brilliant of campaigns. Instead of following one of the usual roads into Italy, either along the coast to Genoa or across the Alps of Savoy, he resolved to take the enemy in the rear. In order to do this he concentrated his forces in Switzerland and, emulating Hannibal, he led them over the difficult Alpine pass of the Great St. Bernard. There was no carriage road then as there is now, and the cannons had to be dragged over in trunks of trees which had been hollowed out for the purpose. Bonaparte arrived safely in Milan on June 2, 1800, to the utter astonishment of the Austrians, who had received no definite news of his line of approach. He immediately restored the Cisalpine Republic, wrote to Paris that he had delivered the Lombards from the "Austrian rod," and then moved westward to find and crush the enemy.

The battle of Marengo (June 14, 1800)

In his uncertainty as to the exact whereabouts of the Austrians, Bonaparte divided his forces when near the village of Marengo (June 14) and sent a contingent under Desaix southward to head off the enemy in that direction. In the meantime the whole Austrian army bore down upon the part of the French army which Bonaparte commanded and would have utterly defeated it if Desaix had not heard the firing and hurried back to charge the Austrians on the flank. The brave Desaix, who had really saved the day, was killed; Bonaparte simply said nothing of his own temporary defeat, and added one more to the list of his great military triumphs. A truce was signed next day, and the Austrians retreated behind the Mincio River, leaving Bonaparte to restore French influence in Lombardy. The districts that he had "freed" were obliged to

[1] This suggestion irritated the French and convinced them that England was their implacable enemy.

support his army, and the reëstablished Cisalpine Republic was forced to pay a monthly tax of two million francs.

Moreau defeats the Austrian army in the forest of Hohenlinden (December, 1800)

While Bonaparte had been making his last preparations to cross the St. Bernard, a French army under Moreau, a very able commander, had invaded southern Germany and prevented the Austrian forces there from taking the road to Italy. Some months later, in the early winter, when the truce concluded after Marengo had expired, he was ordered to march on Vienna. On December 3 he met the Austrian army in the snowy roads of the forest of Hohenlinden and overwhelmingly defeated it. This brought Austria to terms and she agreed to a treaty of peace at Lunéville, February, 1801.

Provisions of the Treaty of Lunéville (February, 1801)

In this, the arrangements made at Campo Formio were in general reaffirmed. France was to retain the Austrian Netherlands and the left bank of the Rhine. The Batavian, Helvetic, Ligurian, and Cisalpine republics were to be recognized and included in the peace. Austria was to keep Venice.[1]

General peace of 1801

Austria's retirement from the war was the signal for a general peace. Even England, who had not laid down her arms since hostilities first opened in 1793, saw no advantage in continuing the struggle. After defeating the French army which Bonaparte had left in Egypt, she suspended hostilities and made a treaty of peace at Amiens.

Two most important results of the treaties of 1801

(*a*) Bonaparte sells Louisiana to the United States (1803)

Among many merely transitory results of these treaties, there were two provisions of momentous import. The first of these, Spain's cession of Louisiana to France in exchange for certain advantages in Italy, does not concern us here directly. But when war again broke out Bonaparte sold the district to the United States, and among the many transfers of territory that he made during his reign, none was more important than this. We must, however, treat with some detail the second of the great changes, which led to the complete reorganization of Germany and ultimately rendered possible the establishment of the later German Empire.

[1] The text of this treaty may be found in the *Readings*, section 42.

In the Treaty of Lunéville, the Emperor had agreed on his own part, as the ruler of Austria, and on the part of the Holy Roman Empire, that the French Republic should thereafter possess in full sovereignty the territories of the Empire which lay on the left bank of the Rhine, and that thereafter the Rhine should form the boundary of France from the point where it left the Helvetic Republic to the point where it entered the Batavian Republic. As a natural consequence of this cession, numerous German rulers and towns — nearly a hundred in number — found themselves dispossessed wholly or in part of their lands. The territories involved included, besides Prussia's duchy of Cleves and Bavaria's possessions (the Palatinate and the duchy of Jülich), the lands of prince-bishops like those of Treves and Cologne, the ancient free cities of Worms, Speyer, and Cologne, and the tiny realms of dozens of counts and abbots.

(*b*) Effects of the cession of the left bank of the Rhine to France

The Empire bound itself by the treaty to furnish the *hereditary* princes who had been forced to give up their territories to France "an indemnity within the Empire." Those who did not belong to the class of hereditary rulers were of course the bishops and abbots and the free cities. The ecclesiastical princes were to be indemnified by pensions for life. As for the towns, once so prosperous and important, they now seemed to the more powerful rulers of Germany scarcely worth considering.

Only the hereditary princes to be indemnified

There was, however, no unoccupied land within the Empire with which to indemnify even the hereditary princes, — like the elector of Bavaria, the margrave of Baden, the king of Prussia, or the Emperor himself, — who had seen their possessions on the left bank of the Rhine divided up into French *départements*. So the ecclesiastical rulers and the free towns throughout the Empire were obliged to surrender their lands for the benefit of the dispossessed secular princes. This *secularization* of the church lands — as the process of transferring them to lay rulers was called — and the annexation of the free towns implied a veritable revolution in the old Holy Roman Empire, for the possessions of the ecclesiastical princes were vast in

The ecclesiastical states and the free towns to be used to indemnify the hereditary rulers extent and were widely scattered, thus contributing largely to the disunion of Germany.

The work of the Imperial Commission in reconstructing Germany

A commission of German princes was appointed to undertake the reconstruction of the map; and the final distribution was preceded by an undignified scramble among the hereditary rulers for bits of territory. All turned to Paris for favors, since it was really the First Consul and his minister, Talleyrand, who determined the distribution. Needy princelings are said to have caressed Talleyrand's poodle and played "drop the handkerchief" with his niece in the hope of adding a monastery or a shabby village to their share. At last the Imperial Commission, with France's help, finished its intricate task, and the *Reichsdeputationshauptschluss*, as the outcome of their labors was officially called, was ratified by the diet in 1803.

Destruction of the ecclesiastical states and free towns

All the ecclesiastical states, except Mayence were turned over to lay rulers, while of the forty-eight imperial cities only six were left. Three of these — Hamburg, Bremen, and Lübeck — continued to be members of the German Empire. No map could make clear all the shiftings of territory which the Imperial Commission sanctioned. A few examples will serve to illustrate the complexity of their procedure and the strange microscopic divisions of the Empire.[1]

Examples of indemnification

Prussia received in return for Cleves and other small territories the bishoprics of Hildesheim and Paderborn, a part of the bishopric of Münster, various districts of the elector of Mayence, and the free towns of Mühlhausen, Nordhausen, and Goslar — over four times the area that she had lost. The elector of Bavaria, for more considerable sacrifices on the left bank, was rewarded with the bishoprics of Würzburg, Bamberg, Freising, Augsburg, and Passau, besides the lands of twelve abbots and of seventeen free towns; which materially extended his boundaries. Austria got the bishoprics of Brixen and Trent;

[1] It has not been deemed feasible to give a map here to illustrate the innumerable changes effected by the *Reichsdeputationshauptschluss*. See map in Shepherd's *Historical Atlas*.

the duke of Würtemberg and the margrave of Baden also rounded out their dominions. A host of princes and counts received little allotments of land or an income of a few thousand gulden to solace their woes,[1] but the more important rulers carried off the lion's share of the spoils. Bonaparte wished to add Parma as well as Piedmont to France, so the duke of Parma was given Tuscany, and the grand duke of Tuscany was indemnified with the archbishopric of Salzburg.[2]

Over two hundred independent states extinguished

These bewildering details are only given here to make clear the hopelessly minute subdivision of the old Holy Roman Empire and the importance of the partial amalgamation which took place in 1803. One hundred and twelve sovereign and independent states lying to the east of the Rhine were wiped out by being annexed to larger states, such as Prussia, Austria, Bavaria, Würtemberg, Baden, Hesse, etc., while nearly a hundred more had disappeared when the left bank of the Rhine was converted into *départements* by the French.

Bonaparte's purpose to gain allies in southern Germany

Although Germany had never sunk to a lower degree of national degradation than at this period, this consolidation marked the beginning of her political regeneration. Bonaparte, it is true, hoped to weaken rather than to strengthen the Empire, for by increasing the territory of the southern states — Bavaria, Würtemberg, Hesse, and Baden — he expected to gain the friendship of their rulers and so create a "third Germany" which he could play off against Austria and Prussia. He succeeded for a time in this design, but the consolidation of 1803 paved the way, as we shall see, for the creation sixty-seven years later of the German Empire.

[1] For example, the prince of Bretzenheim, for the loss of the villages of Bretzenheim and Winzenheim, was given a "princely" nunnery on the lake of Constance; the poor princess of Isenburg, countess of Parkstein, who lost a part of the tiny Reipoltskirchen, received an annuity of twenty-three thousand gulden and a share in the tolls paid by boats on the Rhine, and so on.

[2] As for the knights, who were the least among the German rulers, those who had lost their few acres on the left bank were not indemnified, and those on the right bank were quietly deprived of their political rights within the next two or three years by the princes within whose territories they happened to lie.

QUESTIONS

SECTION 39. Outline the life of Napoleon Bonaparte to the year 1796. What did France gain by the Treaty of Basel? Describe the political condition of Italy at the end of the eighteenth century. Trace on a map Bonaparte's Italian campaign of 1796–1797. State the terms of the Treaty of Campo Formio.

SECTION 40. Describe the political situation which made possible the career of Napoleon Bonaparte. Why did Bonaparte undertake the Egyptian expedition? What was the *Coup d'État* of the 18th Brumaire? Outline the constitution of the Year VIII.

SECTION 41. What means did the Directory take to injure England? Name the countries republicanized by France. Draw a map showing the boundaries of France early in 1797. Indicate the change which took place before the close of the year. Trace on a map Bonaparte's Italian campaign of 1800.

State the terms of the Treaty of Lunéville. Mention the two most important results of the treaties of 1801. Explain fully the problems involved in the cession of the left bank of the Rhine. How was this difficulty settled? What was Bonaparte's reason for insisting upon the cession of German territory?

CHAPTER XI

EUROPE AND NAPOLEON

SECTION 42. BONAPARTE RESTORES ORDER AND PROSPERITY IN FRANCE

General disorder in France under the Directory

Bonaparte was by no means merely a military genius; he was a distinguished statesman as well. He found France in a sad plight after ten years of rapid and radical change, incompetent government, and general disorder. The turmoil of the Reign of Terror had been followed by the mismanagement and corruption of the Directory. There had been no opportunity to perfect the elaborate and thoroughgoing reforms introduced by the first National Assembly, and the work of the Revolution remained but half done. Bonaparte's officials reported to him that the highways were infested with murderous bands of robbers, that the roads and bridges were dilapidated and the harbors filled with sand. The manufacturers and business men were discouraged and industry was demoralized.

The paper money

The financial situation was intolerable. The disorder had reached such a pitch that scarcely any taxes were paid in the year 1800. The *assignats* had depreciated so as to be almost worthless, and the Directory had become almost bankrupt.[1]

Bonaparte's financial measures

The First Consul and his able ministers began at once to devise measures to remedy the difficulties, and his officials, scattered throughout France, saw to it that the new laws were

[1] In March, 1796, three hundred francs in *assignats* were required to procure one in gold. Thereupon the Directory had withdrawn them at one thirtieth of their value and substituted another kind of paper money which rapidly declined in value in the same way that the *assignats* had done. The hard-beset government had issued all sorts of government securities which were at a hopeless discount, and had repudiated a considerable part of the public debt.

enforced. The police was everywhere reorganized and the robbers were brought to summary justice. The tax rate was fixed and the taxes were regularly collected. A fund was established designed gradually to extinguish the public debt; this served to raise the credit of the State. New government securities replaced the old ones, and a Bank of France was founded to stimulate business. The Directory had so grossly mismanaged the disposal of the lands of the clergy and emigrant nobles that they had brought in very little to the government. Bonaparte saw to it that future buyers paid higher prices.

The Convention had separated Church and State (February, 1795), but the Directory continued to persecute the clergy

In no respect had the revolutionary governments been less successful than in dealing with the Church. We have seen how those priests who refused to swear to support the Civil Constitution of the Clergy had been persecuted. After Hébert's attempt to replace Christianity by the worship of Reason, and that of Robespierre to establish a new deistic worship of the Supreme Being, the Catholic churches began early in 1795 to be opened once more, and the Convention declared (February 21, 1795) that the government would no longer concern itself with religion; it would not in the future pay salaries to any clergyman, but every one should be free to worship in any way he pleased.[1] Thereupon the clergy began actively to reorganize their churches. But while thousands of priests managed to perform their duties, the Convention, and later the Directory, continued to persecute those who did not take a new oath to submit to the laws of the Republic, and many suspected of hostility to the government were exiled or imprisoned.

[1] This first law separating Church and State is interesting in view of the efforts at the opening of the twentieth century to effect the same result (see below, sect. 78). The Convention's decree read as follows: "No form of worship shall be interfered with. The Republic will subsidize none of them. It will furnish no buildings for religious exercises nor any dwellings for clergymen. The ceremonies of all religions are forbidden outside of the confines of the place chosen for their performance. The law recognizes no minister of religion and no one is to appear in public with costumes or ornaments used in religious ceremonies." The Convention gruffly added other limitations on religious freedom. It required, for example, that all services be conducted in a semi-private manner, with none of the old gorgeous display or public ceremonials and processions.

General Bonaparte, although himself a deist, nevertheless fully appreciated the importance of gaining the support of the Church and the Pope, and consequently, immediately upon becoming First Consul, he set to work to settle the religious difficulties. He freed the imprisoned priests upon their promising not to oppose the constitution, while those who had been exiled began to return in considerable numbers after the 18th

Bonaparte hopes to gain the support of the Church

FIG. 67. NAPOLEON I

Brumaire. Sunday, which had been abolished by the republican calendar, was once more generally observed, and all the revolutionary holidays, except July 14, the anniversary of the fall of the Bastille, and September 22, the first day of the republican year, were done away with.

The *Concordat* of 1801

A formal treaty with the Pope, known as the *Concordat*, was concluded in September, 1801, which was destined to remain in force for over a hundred years. It declared that the Roman Catholic religion was that of the great majority of the French citizens and that its rites might be freely observed; that the

Pope and the French government should arrange a new division of the country into bishoprics; that the bishops should be appointed by the First Consul and confirmed by the Pope, and the priests should be chosen by the bishops. Both bishops and priests were to receive a suitable remuneration from the government, but were to be required to swear to support the constitution of the Republic. The churches which had not been sold should be put at the disposition of the bishops, but the Pope agreed never to disturb in any way those who had acquired the former property of the clergy.

Bonaparte brings the Church under the control of the State

It is to be observed that Bonaparte showed no inclination to separate Church and State, but carefully brought the Church under the control of the State by vesting the appointment of the bishops in the head of the government, — the First Consul.[1] The Pope's confirmation was likely to be a mere form. The bishops were to choose no priests who were not agreeable to the government, nor was any papal bull or decree to be published in France without its permission.

How the Revolution had changed the Church

In some ways the arrangements of the Concordat of 1801 resembled those which prevailed under the *ancien régime*, but the Revolution had swept away the whole medieval substructure of the Church, its lands and feudal rights, the tithes, the monks and nuns with their irrevocable vows enforced by law, the Church courts, the monopoly of religion, and the right to persecute heretics, — all of these had disappeared and General Bonaparte saw no reason for restoring any of them.

The emigrant nobles permitted to return

As for the emigrant nobles, Bonaparte decreed that no more names should be added to the lists. The striking of names from the lists, and the return of confiscated lands that had not already been sold, he made favors to be granted by him self. Parents and relatives of emigrants were no longer to be

[1] The appointment of bishops by the French government, instead of by the Pope or by election of their own clergy, was not an innovation in France. In the old régime the upper clergy were appointed by the king, and this was one of the evils which the Revolution sought to get rid of; for it had led to intrigues at Versailles and appointments of unworthy men.

regarded as incapable of holding public offices. In April, 1802, a general amnesty was issued, and no less than forty thousand families returned to France.

Old habits resumed

Many of the innovations of the Reign of Terror were gradually given up. The old titles of address, Monsieur and Madame, again came into use instead of the revolutionary "Citizen." Streets which had been rebaptized with republican names resumed their former ones. Old titles of nobility were revived, and something very like a royal court began to develop at the Palace of the Tuileries; for Bonaparte, in all but his title, was already a king, and his wife, Josephine, a queen.

The grateful reliance of the nation on Bonaparte

It had been clear for some years that the nation was weary of political agitation. How great a blessing, after the anarchy of the past, to put all responsibility upon one who showed himself capable of concluding a long war with unprecedented glory for France and of reëstablishing order and the security of person and property, the necessary conditions for renewed prosperity! How natural that the French should welcome a despotism to which they had been accustomed for centuries, after suffering as they had under nominally republican institutions!

The *Code Napoléon*

One of the greatest and most permanent of Bonaparte's achievements still remains to be noted. The heterogeneous laws of the old régime had been much modified by the legislation of the successive assemblies. All this needed a final revision and Bonaparte appointed a commission to undertake this task. Their draft of the new code was discussed in the Council of State, and the First Consul had many suggestions to make. The resulting codification of the civil law — the *Code Napoléon* — is still used to-day, not only in France but also, with some modifications, in Rhenish Prussia, Bavaria, Baden, Holland, Belgium, Italy, and even in the state of Louisiana. The criminal and commercial law was also codified. These codes carried with them into foreign lands the principles of equality upon which they were based, and thus diffused the benefits of the Revolution beyond the borders of France.

General Bonaparte becomes Napoleon I, emperor of the French (1804)

Bonaparte had always shown the instincts of a despotic ruler, and France really ceased to be a republic except in name after the 18th Brumaire. The First Consul was able to bring about changes, one by one, in the constitution, which rendered his own power more and more absolute. In 1802 he was appointed Consul for life with the right to choose his successor. But this did not satisfy his insatiable ambition. He longed to be a monarch in name as well as in fact. He believed heartily in kingship and was not averse to its traditional splendor, its palaces, ermine robes, and gay courtiers. A royalist plot gave him an excuse for secretly urging that he be made emperor. Bonaparte used it to advantage.[1] The Senate was induced to ask him (May, 1804) to accept the title of Emperor of the French, which he was to hand down to his children or adopted heirs.[2]

A new royal court established in the Tuileries

December 2, 1804, General Bonaparte was crowned, in the Cathedral of Notre Dame, as Napoleon I, emperor of the French. The Pope consented to grace the occasion, but the new monarch seized the golden laurel chaplet before the Pope could take it up, and placed it on his own head, since he wished the world to understand that he owed the crown not to the head of the Church but to his own sagacity and military genius. A royal court was reëstablished in the Tuileries, and Ségur, an emigrant noble, and Madame de Campan — one of Marie Antoinette's ladies-in-waiting, who had been earning an honest livelihood by conducting a girls' school — were called in to show the new courtiers how to conduct themselves according to the rules of etiquette which had prevailed before the red cap of liberty had come into fashion. A new nobility was established to take the place of that abolished by the first National Assembly in 1790: Bonaparte's uncle was made Grand Almoner; Talleyrand, Lord High Chamberlain; General Duroc, High Constable; and fourteen of the most important generals were

[1] See *Readings*, section 42, for Napoleon's report of recent events submitted at the close of the year 1804.

[2] Josephine had borne him no children.

FIG. 68. THE CORONATION OF NAPOLEON AND JOSEPHINE

The coronation took place in Notre Dame, the cathedral of Paris, with pomp and ceremony copied after that observed in the Holy Roman Empire. Napoleon placed the diadem on his own head and then crowned Josephine. The Pope is seated at the extreme left of the picture, and in the background Napoleon's mother is seen looking on

Fig. 69. The Palace of the Tuileries

exalted to the rank of Marshals of France. The stanch republicans, who had believed that the court pageantry of the old régime had gone to stay, were either disgusted or amused by these proceedings, according to their temperaments. But Emperor Napoleon would brook no strictures or sarcastic comment.

Napoleon's censorship of the press

From this time on he became increasingly tyrannical and hostile to criticism. At the very beginning of his administration he had suppressed a great part of the numerous political newspapers and forbidden the establishment of new ones. As emperor he showed himself still more exacting. His police furnished the news to the papers, and carefully omitted all that might offend their suspicious master. He ordered the editors to "put in quarantine all news that might be disadvantageous or disagreeable to France."[1] He would have liked to suppress all newspapers but one, which should be used for official purposes.

Section 43. Napoleon destroys the Holy Roman Empire and reorganizes Germany

Napoleon on the necessity of war for France

A great majority of the French undoubtedly longed for peace, but Napoleon's position made war a personal necessity for him. No one saw this more clearly than he. "If," he said to his Council of State in the summer of 1802, "the European states intend ever to renew the war, the sooner it comes the better. Every day the remembrance of their defeats grows dimmer and at the same time the prestige of our victories

* The Palace of the Tuileries is one of the beauty spots of Paris, and dates from about 1565. It has served as a royal residence and as offices for a republican government. The Communards of 1871 attempted to destroy it by fire, but during the years 1875–1878 it was reconstructed. The Gardens of the Tuileries are now a popular playground for the children of the city.

1 When the French fleet was annihilated by Nelson at Trafalgar in 1805, the event was not mentioned in the *Moniteur*, the official newspaper.

pales. . . . France needs glorious deeds, and hence war. . . . I shall put up with peace as long as our neighbors can maintain it, but I shall regard it as an advantage if they force me to take up my arms again before they rust. . . . In our position I shall look on each conclusion of peace as simply a short armistice, and I regard myself as destined during my term of office to fight almost without intermission."

Napoleon dreams of becoming emperor of Europe

On another occasion, in 1804, Napoleon said, "There will be no rest in Europe until it is under a single chief — an emperor who shall have kings for officers, who shall distribute kingdoms to his lieutenants, and shall make one man king of Italy, another of Bavaria; one ruler of Switzerland, another governor of Holland, each having an office of honor in the imperial household." This was the ideal that he now found himself in a position to carry out with marvelous exactness.

Reasons for England's persistent opposition to Napoleon

There were many reasons why the peace with England (concluded at Amiens in March, 1802) should be speedily broken. Napoleon obviously intended to conquer as much of Europe as he could, and to place high duties on English goods in those territories that he controlled. This filled commercial and industrial England with apprehension. The English people longed for peace, but peace appeared only to offer an opportunity to Napoleon to develop French commerce at their expense. This was the secret of England's perseverance. All the other European powers concluded treaties with Napoleon at some time during his reign. England alone did not lay down her arms a second time until the emperor of the French was a prisoner.

War between France and England renewed in 1803. Napoleon institutes a coast blockade

War was renewed between England and France, May, 1803. Bonaparte promptly occupied Hanover, of which it will be remembered that the English king was elector, and declared the coast blockaded from Hanover to Otranto. Holland, Spain, and the Ligurian Republic — formerly the republic of Genoa — were, by hook or by crook, induced to agree to furnish their contingents of men or money to the French army and to exclude English ships from their ports.

To cap the climax, England was alarmed by the appearance of a French army at Boulogne, just across the Channel. A great number of flatboats were collected and troops trained to embark and disembark. Apparently Napoleon harbored the firm purpose of invading the British Isles. Yet the transportation of a large body of troops across the English channel, trifling as is the distance, would have been very hazardous, and by many it was deemed downright impossible.[1] No one knows whether Napoleon really intended to make the trial. It is quite possible that his main purpose in collecting an army at Boulogne was to have it in readiness for the continental war which he saw immediately ahead of him. He succeeded, at any rate, in terrifying England, who prepared to defend herself.

Napoleon threatens to invade England

The new Tsar, Alexander I,[2] had submitted a plan for the reconciliation of France and England in August, 1803; the rejection of this, the aggressions of Napoleon during the next year, and above all, his shocking execution of the duke of Enghien, a Bourbon prince whom he had arrested on the ground that he was plotting against the First Consul, roused the Tsar's indignation and led him to conclude an alliance with England, the objects of which were the expulsion of the French from Holland, Switzerland, Italy, and Hanover, and the settlement of European affairs upon a sound and permanent basis by a great international congress.

Alexander I joins England, April, 1805

Russia and England were immediately joined by Austria, who found Napoleon intent upon developing in northern Italy a strong power which would threaten her borders. He had been crowned king of Italy in May, 1805, and had annexed the Ligurian Republic to France. There were rumors, too, that he was planning to seize the Venetian territories which had been assigned to Austria at Campo Formio. The timid

Austria joins the coalition of 1805, but Prussia remains neutral

1 The waves and currents caused by winds and tides make the Channel very uncertain for all except steam navigation. Robert Fulton offered to put his newly invented steamboat at Napoleon's disposal, but his offer was declined.

2 Alexander had succeeded his father, Paul, when the latter was assassinated in a palace plot, March, 1801.

king of Prussia, Frederick William III, could not be induced to join the alliance, nor would he ally himself with Napoleon, although he was offered the electorate of Hanover, a very substantial inducement. He persisted in maintaining a neutrality which was to cost him dear.

Napoleon fails to get control of the sea and turns his attention to Austria

Napoleon had been endeavoring to get the advantage of the English on the sea, for there was no possibility of ferrying his armies across to England so long as English men-of-war were guarding the Channel. But the English fleets blockaded the French in port, and kept England safe from invasion. Consequently, August 27, 1805, four days after the declaration of war with Austria, Napoleon suddenly turned his well-trained Boulogne army eastward to meet an Austrian army advancing through southern Germany.

Napoleon captures Mack's army at Ulm (October 20, 1805) and then occupies Vienna

He misled Austria by massing troops about Strassburg, and the Austrian general, Mack, came on as far as Ulm to meet him. Napoleon was, however, really taking his armies around to the north through Mayence and Coblenz, so that he occupied Munich, October 14, and, getting in behind the Austrians, cut them off from Vienna. Six days later General Mack, finding himself surrounded and shut up in Ulm, was forced to capitulate, and Napoleon made prisoners of a whole Austrian army, sixty thousand strong, without losing more than a few hundred of his own men. The French could now safely march down the Danube to Vienna, which they reached, October 31.

Battle of Austerlitz (December 2, 1805)

Emperor Francis II had retired before the approaching enemy and was joined by the Russian army a short distance north of Vienna. The allies determined to risk a battle with the French and occupied a favorable position on a hill near the village of Austerlitz, which was to be made forever famous by the terrible winter battle which occurred there, December 2. The Russians having descended the hill to attack the weaker wing of Napoleon's army, the French occupied the heights which the Russians had deserted, and poured a deadly fire upon the enemy's rear. The allies were routed and reports of the battle tell how thousands of their troops were drowned as they sought to escape across the thin ice of a little lake which lay at the foot of the hill. The Tsar withdrew the remnants of his forces, while the Emperor in despair agreed to submit to a humiliating peace, the Treaty of Pressburg.

The Treaty of Pressburg (December 26, 1805)

By this treaty Austria recognized all Napoleon's changes in Italy, and ceded to his kingdom of Italy that portion of the Venetian territory which she had received at Campo Formio. Moreover, she ceded Tyrol to Bavaria, which was friendly to Napoleon, and other of her possessions to Würtemberg and Baden, also friends of the French emperor. As head of the Holy Roman Empire, Francis II also agreed that the rulers of Bavaria and Würtemberg should be raised to the rank of kings, and that they and the grand duke of Baden should enjoy "the plenitude of sovereignty" and all rights derived therefrom, precisely as did the rulers of Austria and Prussia.

Napoleon forms a new dependency, — the Confederation of the Rhine (1806)

These provisions of the Treaty of Pressburg are of vital importance in the history of Germany. By explicitly declaring several of the larger of the German states altogether independent of the German Emperor, Napoleon prepared the way for the formation in Germany of another dependency which, like Holland and the kingdom of Italy, should support France in future wars. In the summer of 1806 Bavaria, Würtemberg, Baden, and thirteen lesser German states united into a league known as the Confederation of the Rhine. This union was to be under the "protection" of the French emperor and to furnish him with sixty-three thousand soldiers, who were to be organized by French officers and to be at his disposal when he needed them.

Napoleon refuses longer to recognize the existence of the Holy Roman Empire

On August 1 Napoleon announced to the diet of the Holy Roman Empire at Ratisbon that he had, "in the dearest interests of his people and of his neighbors," accepted the title of Protector of the Confederation of the Rhine, and that he could therefore no longer recognize the existence of the Holy Roman Empire, which had long been merely a shadow of its former self. A considerable number of its members had become sovereign powers and its continuation could only be a source of dissension and confusion.

Francis II of the Holy Roman Empire becomes Francis I of Austria (1804)

The Emperor, Francis II, like his predecessors for several hundred years, was the ruler of the various Austrian dominions. He was officially known as King of Hungary, Bohemia, Dalmatia, Croatia, Galicia, and Laodomeria, Duke of Lorraine,

FIG. 70. FRANCIS I OF AUSTRIA

Venice, Salzburg, etc., etc. When, however, the First Consul received as ruler of France the title of Emperor of the French, Francis had determined to substitute for his long array of individual titles the brief and dignified formula, Hereditary Emperor of Austria and King of Hungary.

Francis abdicates as Emperor (August 6, 1806) and the Holy Roman Empire is dissolved

After the Treaty of Pressburg and the formation of the Confederation of the Rhine, he became convinced of the utter impossibility of longer fulfilling the duties of his office as head of the Holy Roman Empire and accordingly abdicated on August 6, 1806. In this way he formally put an end to a line of rulers who had, for well-nigh eighteen centuries, proudly maintained that they were the successors of Augustus Cæsar, the first Roman Emperor.

Napoleon assigns Naples to Joseph Bonaparte and Holland to Louis

Napoleon went on steadily developing what he called "the real French Empire," namely, the dependent states under his control which lay outside the bounds of France itself. Immediately after the battle of Austerlitz, he had proclaimed that Ferdinand IV, the Bourbon king of Naples, had ceased to reign. He ordered one of his generals to proceed to southern Italy and "hurl from the throne that guilty woman," Queen Caroline, who had favored the English and entertained Lord Nelson. In March he appointed his elder brother, Joseph, king of Naples and Sicily, and a younger brother, Louis, king of Holland.

Prussia forced into war with France

One of the most important of the continental states, it will have been noticed, had taken no part as yet in the opposition to the extension of Napoleon's influence. Prussia, the first power to conclude peace with the new French Republic in 1795, had since that time maintained a strict neutrality. Had it yielded to Tsar Alexander's persuasions and joined the coalition in 1805, it might have turned the tide at Austerlitz, or at any rate have encouraged further resistance to the conqueror. The hesitation of Frederick William III at that juncture proved a grave mistake, for Napoleon now forced him into war at a time when he could look for no efficient assistance from Russia or the other powers.

The question of Hanover

The immediate cause of the declaration of war was the disposal of Hanover. This electorate Frederick William had consented to hold provisionally, pending its possible transfer to him should the English king give his assent. Prussia was anxious to get possession of Hanover because it lay just between her older possessions and the territory which she had gained in the redistribution of 1803.

Napoleon, as usual, did not fail either to see or to use his advantage. His conduct toward Prussia was most insolent.

Napoleon's insolent behavior toward Prussia

After setting her at enmity with England and promising that she should have Hanover, he unblushingly offered to restore the electorate to George III. His actions now began to arouse a national spirit in Prussia, and the reluctant Frederick William was forced by the party in favor of war, which included his beautiful queen, Louise, and the statesman Stein, to break with Napoleon.

Decisive defeat of the Prussian army at Jena, 1806

The Prussian army was, however, as has been well said, "only that of Frederick the Great grown twenty years older"; one of Frederick's generals, the aged duke of Brunswick, who had issued the famous manifesto in 1792, was its leader. A double defeat near Jena (October 14, 1806) put Prussia entirely in the hands of her enemy. This one disaster produced complete demoralization throughout the country. Fortresses were surrendered without resistance and the king fled to the uttermost parts of his realm on the Russian boundary.

The campaign in Poland (November–June, 1806–1807)

After crushing Prussia, Napoleon led his army into what had once been the kingdom of Poland. Here he spent a winter of great hardships and dangers in operations against the Russians and their feeble allies, the Prussians. He closed a difficult campaign far from France by the signal victory of Friedland (not far from Königsberg), and then arranged for an interview with the Tsar. The two rulers met on a raft in the river Niemen (June 25, 1807), and there privately arranged the provisions of the Treaty of Tilsit between France, Russia, and Prussia. The Tsar, Alexander I, was completely won over by Napoleon's skillful diplomacy. He shamefully deserted his helpless ally, Frederick William III of Prussia, and turned against England, whose subsidies he had been accepting.

Napoleon dismembers Prussia to create the grand duchy of Warsaw and the kingdom of Westphalia

Napoleon had no mercy upon Prussia, which he ruthlessly dismembered by depriving it of all its possessions west of the Elbe River, and all that it had gained in the second and third partitions of Poland. From the lands which he forced Frederick William to cede to him at Tilsit, Napoleon established two new French dependencies by forming the Polish territories into the grand duchy of Warsaw, of which his friend, the king of Saxony, was made ruler; and creating from the western territory (to which he later added Hanover) the kingdom of Westphalia for his brother Jerome.

Terms of the secret alliance of Tilsit between Napoleon and the Tsar

Russia, on the other hand, he treated with marked consideration, and proposed that he and the Tsar should form an alliance which would enable him to have his way in western Europe and Alexander in the east. The Tsar consented to the dismemberment of Prussia and agreed to recognize all the sweeping changes which Napoleon had made during previous years. He secretly promised, if George III refused to conclude peace, to join France against England, and to force Denmark and Portugal to exclude English ships from their ports. In this way England would be cut off from all of western Europe, since Napoleon would have the whole coast practically under his control. In return for these promises, Napoleon engaged to aid the Tsar in seizing Finland from Sweden and annexing the so-called Danubian provinces, — Moldavia and Wallachia, — which belonged to the Sultan of Turkey.[1]

Section 44. The Continental Blockade

Napoleon's plan of bringing England to terms by ruining her commerce

In arranging the Treaty of Tilsit, it is evident that Napoleon had constantly in mind his most persistent and inaccessible enemy, England. However marvelous his successes by land might be, he had no luck on the sea. He had beheld his Egyptian fleet sink under Nelson's attack in 1798. When he was making preparations to transport his army across the Channel in 1805, he was humiliated to discover that the English were keeping his main squadron penned up in the harbors of Brest and Cadiz. The day after he captured General Mack's whole army with such ease at Ulm, Nelson had annihilated off Cape Trafalgar the French squadron which had ventured out from Cadiz. After Tilsit, Napoleon set himself more earnestly than

[1] They now form the kingdom of Roumania.

FIG. 71. NELSON'S COLUMN, TRAFALGAR SQUARE, LONDON

The English regard Nelson as the man who safeguarded their liberty by the victories of the fleet. Nelson was killed at Trafalgar and buried with great ceremony in the crypt of St. Paul's, under the very center of the dome. Some years later "Trafalgar Square" was laid out at the point where the street leading to the Parliament buildings joins a chief business street — the Strand — and a gigantic column to Nelson erected, surmounted by a statue of the admiral. In the distance one can see the towers of the Parliament buildings

ever to bring England to terms by ruining her commerce and industry, since he had no hope of subduing her by arms. He proposed to make "that race of shopkeepers" cry for peace by absolutely cutting them off from trade with the continent of Europe and so drying up their sources of prosperity.

In May, 1806, England had declared the coast from the mouth of the Elbe to Brest to be "blockaded," that is to say, she gave warning that her war vessels and privateers would capture any vessel that attempted to enter or leave any of the ports between these two points. After he had won the battle of Jena, Napoleon replied to this by his Berlin Decree (November, 1806), in which he proclaimed that England had "disregarded all ideas of justice and

PLATE IV. CHARGE OF THE FRENCH CAVALRY, FRIEDLAND

(See p. 288)

every high sentiment which civilization should bring to mankind"; that it was a monstrous abuse on her part to declare great stretches of coast in a state of blockade which her whole fleet would be unable to enforce. Nevertheless he believed it a natural right to use the same measures against her that she employed against him. He therefore retaliated by declaring the British Isles in a state of blockade and forbidding all commerce with them. Letters or packages addressed to England or to an Englishman, or even written in the English language, were not to be permitted to pass through the mails in the countries he controlled. All trade in English goods was prohibited. Any British subject discovered in the countries occupied by French troops, or in the territories of Napoleon's allies, was to be regarded as a prisoner of war and his property as a lawful prize. This was, of course, only a "paper" blockade, since France and her allies could do little more than capture, now and then, some unfortunate vessel which was supposed to be coming from, or bound to, an English port.

England prepared to grant licenses to neutral ships. Napoleon's Milan Decree (December 7 1807)

A year later England established a similar paper blockade of the ports of the French Empire and its allies, but hit upon the happy idea of permitting the ships of neutral powers to proceed, provided that they touched at an English port, secured a license from the English government, and paid a heavy export duty. Napoleon was ready with a still more outrageous measure. In a decree issued from "our royal palace at Milan" (December, 1807), he ordered that all vessels, of whatever nationality, which submitted to the humiliating regulations of England, should be regarded as lawful prizes by the French privateers.

Sad plight of the vessels of the United States

The ships of the United States were at this time the most numerous and important of the neutral vessels carrying on the world's trade, and a very hard time they had between the Scylla of the English orders and the Charybdis of Napoleon's Berlin and Milan decrees.[1] The Baltimore *Evening Post* in

[1] For the text of the Berlin and Milan decrees, see *Readings*, section 44.

September, 1808, calculated that if an American ship bound for Holland with four hundred hogsheads of tobacco should decide to meet England's requirements and touch at London on the way, its owners would pay one and a half pence per pound on the tobacco, and twelve shillings for each ton of the ship. With a hundred dollars for England's license to proceed on her way, and sundry other dues, the total would come to about thirteen thousand dollars. On the way home, if the neutral vessel wished to avoid the chance of capture by an English cruiser, she might pay, perhaps, sixteen thousand five hundred dollars more to England for the privilege of returning to Baltimore with a cargo of Holland gin. This would make the total contributions paid to Great Britain for a single voyage, about thirty thousand dollars.

The United States tries to defend its shipping interests by an embargo

Alarmed and exasperated at the conduct of England and France, the Congress of the United States, at the suggestion of President Jefferson, passed an embargo act (December, 1807), which forbade all vessels to leave port. It was hoped that this would prevent the further loss of American ships and at the same time so interfere with the trade of England and France that they would make some concessions. But the only obvious result was the destruction of the previously flourishing commerce of the Atlantic coast towns, especially in New England. Early in 1809 Congress was induced to permit trade once more with the European nations, excepting France and England, whose vessels were still to be strictly excluded from all the ports of the United States.

Napoleon proposes to render Europe independent of colonial products

Napoleon expressed the utmost confidence in his plan of ruining England by cutting her off from the Continent. He was cheered to observe that a pound sterling was no longer worth twenty-five francs, but only seventeen, and that the discouraged English merchants were beginning to urge Parliament to conclude peace. In order to cripple England permanently, he proposed to wean Europe from the use of those colonial products with which it had been supplied by English ships.

He therefore encouraged the substitution of chicory for coffee, the cultivation of the sugar beet, and the discovery of new dyes to replace those — such as indigo and cochineal — which came from the tropics. This "Continental System," as it was called, caused a great deal of distress and discontent and contributed to Napoleon's downfall, inasmuch as he had to resort to despotic measures to break up the old system of trade. Then he was led to make continual additions to his already unwieldy empire in order to get control of the whole coast line of western Europe, from the boundaries of Prussia around to those of the Turkish Empire.

Section 45. Napoleon at the Zenith of his Power (1808–1812)

Napoleon's policy in France

France owed much to Napoleon, for he had restored order and guaranteed many of the beneficent achievements of the Revolution of 1789. His boundless ambition was, it is true, sapping her strength by forcing younger and younger men into his armies in order to build up the vast international federation which he planned. But his victories and the commanding position to which he had raised France could not but fill the nation with pride.

Public works

He sought to gain popular approval by great public improvements. He built magnificent roads along the Rhine and the Mediterranean and across the Alps, which still fill the traveler with admiration. He beautified Paris by opening up wide streets and quays and constructing bridges and triumphal arches that kept fresh in the people's minds the recollection of his victories. By these means he gradually converted a medieval town into the most beautiful of modern capitals.

The "university" established by Napoleon in 1806

In order to be sure that the young people were brought up to venerate his name and support his government, Napoleon completely reorganized the schools and colleges of France. These he consolidated into a single "university," which comprised all the instruction from the most elementary to the most advanced. A "grand master" was put at its head, and a university council of thirty members drew up regulations for all the schools, prepared the textbooks, and controlled the teachers, high and low, throughout France. The university had its own large endowment, and its instructors were to be suitably prepared in a normal school established for the purpose.

FIG. 72. ARCH OF TRIUMPH

Begun by Napoleon in 1806, this largest arch of triumph in the world was not completed until 1836. It is 160 feet high and stands on a slight hill, with streets radiating from all sides, so that it is known as the Arch of Triumph of the Star. It is therefore visible from all over the western part of the city. The monument recalls the days of the Roman Empire, upon which so many of the institutions and ideas of Republican and Napoleonic France were based

The government could at any time interfere if it disapproved of the teaching; the prefect was to visit the schools in his department and report on their condition to the minister of the interior. The first schoolbook to be drawn up was the *Imperial Catechism*; in this the children were taught to say: "Christians owe to the princes who govern them, and we in particular owe to Napoleon I, our emperor, love, respect, obedience, fidelity, military service, and the taxes levied for the preservation and defense of the empire and of his throne. We also owe him fervent prayers for his safety and for the spiritual and temporal prosperity of the State."

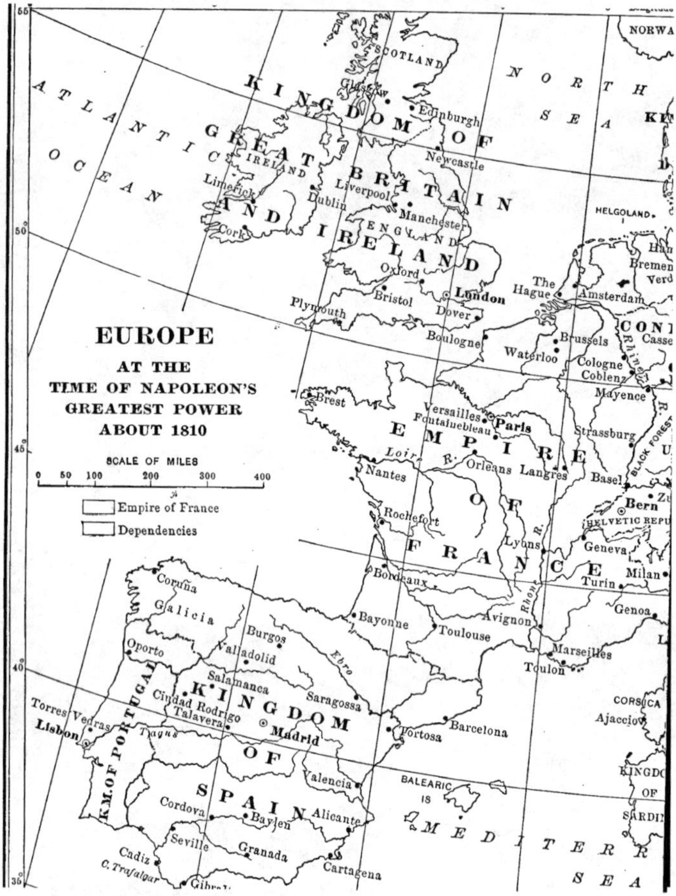
EUROPE
AT THE
TIME OF NAPOLEON'S
GREATEST POWER
ABOUT 1810
SCALE OF MILES
0 50 100 200 300 400
Empire of France
Dependencies
ATLANTIC OCEAN
NORTH SEA
NORWA
KINGDOM OF GREAT BRITAIN AND IRELAND
SCOTLAND
IRELAND
ENGLAND
Glasgow
Edinburgh
Newcastle
Limerick
Dublin
Liverpool
Manchester
Cork
Oxford
Bristol
London
Plymouth
Dover
HELGOLAND
The Hague
Amsterdam
Bremen
Boulogne
Brussels
Waterloo
Cologne
Coblenz
Rhine
Mayence
Brest
Versailles
Fontainebleau
Paris
EMPIRE OF FRANCE
Loire R.
Orleans
Langres
Strassburg
Basel
BLACK FOREST
Nantes
Bern
HELVETIC REPU
Rochefort
Lyons
Geneva
Bordeaux
Milan
Turin
Rhone
Genoa
Bayonne
Toulouse
Avignon
Marseilles
Toulon
CORSICA
Ajaccio
Coruña
Galicia
Burgos
Oporto
Valladolid
Ebro
Salamanca
KINGDOM OF SPAIN
Ciudad Rodrigo
Saragossa
Torres Vedras
Talavera
Madrid
Tortosa
Barcelona
Lisbon
Tagus
KM. OF PORTUGAL
Valencia
BALEARIC IS
KINGDO OF SARDI
Cordova
Baylen
Alicante
MEDITERR SEA
Seville
Granada
Cadiz
C. Trafalgar
Cartagena
55
50
45
40
35

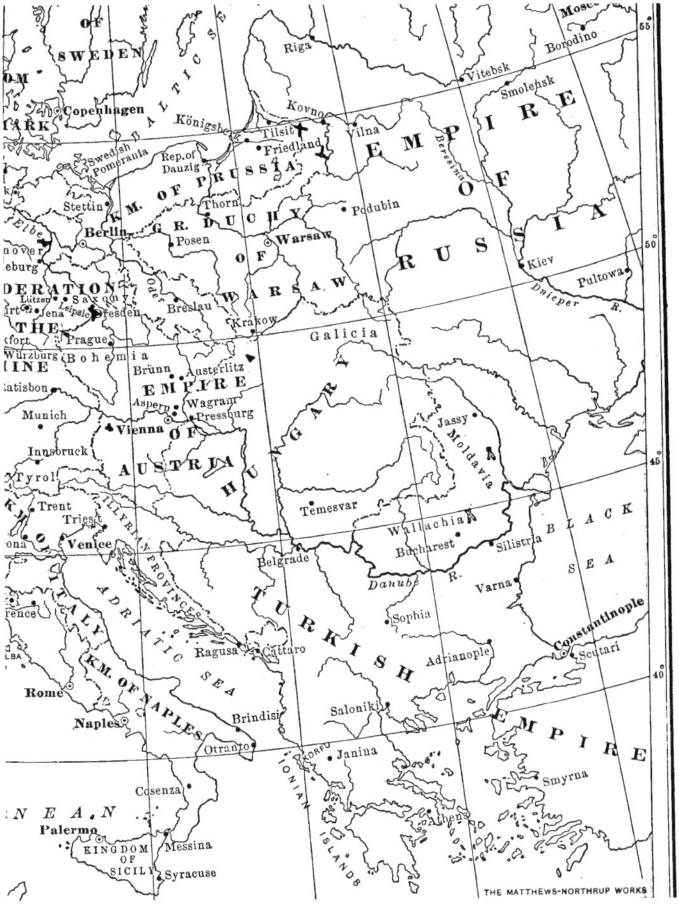

SWEDEN
Copenhagen
BALTIC SEA
Königsberg
Swedish Pomerania
Rep. of Dauzig
Riga
Kovno
Tilsit
Friedland
Vilna
Vitebsk
Smolensk
Borodino
EMPIRE OF RUSSIA
Beresina
KM. OF PRUSSIA
Stettin
Berlin
Elbe
Thorn
Posen
GR. DUCHY OF WARSAW
Warsaw
Podubin
Kiev
Pultowa
Dnieper R.
Saxony
Lützen
Jena
Leipsic
Dresden
Oder
Breslau
Krakow
Prague
Galicia
Würzburg
Bohemia
Brünn
Austerlitz
EMPIRE OF AUSTRIA
Aspern
Wagram
Pressburg
Vienna
Munich
Innsbruck
Tyrol
HUNGARY
Jassy
Moldavia
Trent
Triest
ILLYRIAN PROVINCES
Temesvar
Wallachia
Bucharest
Silistria
BLACK SEA
Venice
Belgrade
Danube R.
Varna
ITALY
ADRIATIC SEA
TURKISH EMPIRE
Sophia
Constantinople
Scutari
Ragusa
Cattaro
Adrianople
Rome
KM. OF NAPLES
Naples
Brindisi
Saloniki
Otranto
Korfu
Janina
IONIAN ISLANDS
Smyrna
Cosenza
Athens
Palermo
KINGDOM OF SICILY
Messina
Syracuse
55
50
45
40
THE MATTHEWS-NORTHRUP WORKS

Napoleon not only created a new nobility but he endeavored to assure the support of distinguished individuals by making them members of the Legion of Honor which he founded. The "princes," whom he nominated, received an annual income of two hundred thousand francs. The ministers of state, senators, members of his Council of State, and the archbishops received the title of Count and a revenue of thirty thousand francs, and so on. The army was not forgotten, for Napoleon felt that to be his chief support. The incomes of his marshals were enormous, and brave actions among the soldiers were rewarded with the decoration of the Legion of Honor.[1]

The new nobility and the Legion of Honor

As time went on Napoleon's despotism grew more and more oppressive. No less than thirty-five hundred prisoners of state were arrested at his command, one because he hated Napoleon, another because in his letters he expressed sentiments adverse to the government. No grievance was too petty to attract the attention of the emperor's jealous eye. He ordered the title of *A History of Bonaparte* to be changed to *The History of the Campaigns of Napoleon the Great.* He forbade the performance of certain of Schiller's and Goethe's plays in German towns, as tending to arouse the patriotic discontent of the people with his rule.

Napoleon's despotism in France

Up to this time Napoleon had had only the opposition of the several European courts to overcome in the extension of his power. The people of the various states which he had conquered showed an extraordinary indifference toward the political changes. It was clear, however, that as soon as the national

Napoleon's European power threatened by the growth of national opposition to him

1 Napoleon was, however, never content with his achievements or his glory. On the day of his coronation he complained to his minister, Decrès, that he had been born too late, that there was nothing great to be done any more. On his minister's remonstrating, he added: "I admit that my career has been brilliant and that I have made a good record. But what a difference is there if we compare ours with ancient times. Take Alexander the Great, for example. When he announced himself the son of Jupiter, the whole East, except his mother, Aristotle, and a few Athenian pedants, believed this to be true. But now, should I declare myself the son of the Eternal Father, there is n't a fishwife who would n't hiss me. No, the nations are too sophisticated, nothing great is any longer possible."

spirit was once awakened, the highly artificial system created by the French emperor would collapse. His first serious reverse came from the people, and from an unexpected quarter.

A French army occupies Portugal (November, 1807)

After concluding the Treaty of Tilsit, Napoleon turned his attention to the Spanish peninsula. He was on friendly terms with the court of Spain, but little Portugal continued to admit English ships to her harbors. In October he ordered the Portuguese government to declare war on England and to confiscate all English property. Upon its refusal to obey the second part of the order, he commanded General Junot to invade Portugal and take charge of the government. Thereupon the royal family resolved to take refuge in their vast Brazilian empire, and when Junot reached Lisbon they were receiving the salutes of the English squadron as they moved down the Tagus on the way to their new home across the Atlantic. Easy and simple as was the subsequent occupation of Portugal, it proved one of Napoleon's serious mistakes.

Napoleon makes his brother Joseph king of Spain (1808)

Owing to quarrels in the Spanish royal family, Spain also seemed to Napoleon an easy prey and he determined to add it to his subject kingdoms. In the spring of 1808 he induced both Charles IV of Spain and the Crown Prince Ferdinand to meet him at Bayonne. Here he was able to persuade or force both of them to surrender their rights to the throne,[1] and on June 6 he appointed his brother Joseph king of Spain. Murat, one of Napoleon's ablest generals, who had married his sister, succeeded Joseph on the throne of Naples.

Joseph entered Madrid in July, armed with excellent intentions and a new constitution. The general rebellion in favor of the Crown Prince Ferdinand, which immediately broke out,

[1] Charles IV resigned all his rights to the crown of Spain and the Indies "to the emperor of the French as the only person who, in the existing state of affairs, can reëstablish order." He and his disreputable queen retired to Rome, while Napoleon kept Ferdinand under guard in Talleyrand's country estate Here this despicable prince lived for six years, occasionally writing a cringing letter to Napoleon. In 1814 he was restored to the Spanish throne as Ferdinand VII, and, as we shall see later, showed himself the consistent enemy of reform. See below, section 53.

had an element of religious enthusiasm in it; for the monks stirred up the people against Napoleon, on the ground that he was an enemy of the Pope and an oppressor of the Church. One French army was captured at Bailén, and another capitulated to the English forces which had landed in Portugal. Before the end of July Joseph and the French troops had been compelled to retreat behind the Ebro River.

Revolt in Spain against the foreign ruler (1808)

In November the French emperor himself led into Spain a magnificent army, two hundred thousand strong, in the best of condition and commanded by his ablest marshals. The Spanish troops, perhaps one hundred thousand in number, were ill clad and inadequately equipped; what was worse, they were overconfident in view of their late victory. They were, of course defeated, and Madrid surrendered on December 4.[1]

Spain subdued by arms (December, 1808)

Decrees were immediately issued in which Napoleon abolished all vestiges of the feudal system, and declared that it should be free to every one who conformed to the laws to carry on any industry that he pleased. The tribunal of the Inquisition, for which Spain had been noted for hundreds of years, was abolished and its property seized. The monasteries and convents were to be reduced to one third of their number, and no one, for the time being, was to be permitted to take any monastic vows. The customs lines which separated the Spanish provinces and hampered trade were obliterated and the customhouses transferred to the frontiers of the kingdom. These measures illustrate the way in which Napoleon spread the principles of the French Revolution by arms in those states which, in spite of their benevolent despots, still clung to their half-medieval institutions.

Napoleon begins radical reform in Spain

[1] Napoleon thereupon issued a proclamation to the Spanish people in which he said: "It depends upon you alone whether this moderate constitution that I offer you shall henceforth be your law. Should all my efforts prove vain, and should you refuse to justify my confidence, then nothing will remain for me but to treat you as a conquered province and find a new throne for my brother. In that case I shall myself assume the crown of Spain and teach the ill-disposed to respect that crown, for God has given me the power and the will to overcome all obstacles."

Spain continues to require the presence of French troops

The next month Napoleon was back in Paris, as he saw that he had another war with Austria on his hands. He left Joseph on a very insecure throne, and, in spite of the arrogant confidence of his proclamation to the Spaniards, he was soon to discover that they could maintain a guerilla warfare against which his best troops and most distinguished generals were powerless. His ultimate downfall was in no small measure due to the persistent hostility of the Spanish people.

Austria takes the field against Napoleon (April, 1809)

Austria was fearful, since Napoleon had gained Russia's friendship, that he might be tempted, should he succeed in putting down the stubborn resistance of the Spaniards, still further to increase his empire at her expense. She had been reorganizing and increasing her army, and decided that it was best to strike while some two hundred thousand of Napoleon's troops were busy in Spain.

Battles of Aspern and Wagram (May and July, 1809)

Napoleon hurried eastward, easily defeated the Archduke Charles in Bavaria, and marched on to Vienna. But he did not succeed in crushing the Austrian forces as easily and promptly as he had done at Austerlitz in 1805. Indeed he was actually defeated at the battle of Aspern (May 21–22), but finally gained a rather doubtful victory in the fearful battle of Wagram, near Vienna (July 5–6). Austria was disheartened and again consented to conclude a peace quite as humiliating as that of Pressburg.

The Treaty of Vienna (October, 1809)

She had announced that her object in going to war once more was the destruction of Napoleon's system of dependent states and had proposed "to restore to their rightful possessors all those lands belonging to them respectively before the Napoleonic usurpation." The battle of Wagram put an end to these dreams and the emperor of Austria was forced to surrender to the victor and his friends extensive territories, together with four million Austrian subjects. A strip of land, including Salzburg, was given to the king of Bavaria; on the north, Galicia (which Austria had received in the first partition of Poland) was ceded to Napoleon's ally, the grand duke of

Warsaw; and finally, along the Adriatic, Napoleon exacted a district which he added to his own empire under the name of the Illyrian Provinces. This last cession served to cut Austria entirely off from the sea.

The new Austrian minister, Metternich, was anxious to establish a permanent alliance with the seemingly invincible

FIG. 73. MUSIC ROOM IN THE PALACE OF COMPIÈGNE

Napoleon used the various palaces erected by the previous rulers of France. That at Compiègne, fifty miles from Paris, was built by Louis XV. The smaller harp was made, it is said, for Napoleon's heir, "the King of Rome," as his father called him. The boy was but three years old, however, when Napoleon abdicated in 1814, and was carried off to Austria by his Austrian mother, Maria Louisa. He was known by the Bonapartists as Napoleon II, but never ruled over France

Napoleon marries the Archduchess Maria Louisa (April, 1810)

emperor of the French and did all he could to heal the breach between Austria and France by a royal marriage. Napoleon ardently desired an heir to whom he could transmit his vast dominions. As Josephine had borne him no children, he decided to divorce her, and, after considering and rejecting a Russian princess, he married (April, 1810) the Archduchess Maria Louisa, the daughter of the Austrian emperor and a grand-niece of Marie Antoinette. In this way the former Corsican adventurer gained admission to one of the oldest and proudest of reigning families, the Hapsburgs. His second wife soon bore him a son, who was styled "King of Rome."

Napoleon "reunites" the Papal States to France (1809)

While Napoleon was in the midst of the war with Austria, he had issued a proclamation "reuniting" the Papal States to the French Empire. He argued that it was Charlemagne, emperor of the French, his august predecessor, who had given the lands to the Popes and that now the tranquillity and welfare of his people required that the territory be reunited to France.

Annexation of Holland and the Hanseatic towns (1810)

Holland, it will be remembered, had been formed into a kingdom under the rule of Napoleon's brother Louis. The brothers had never agreed,[1] and in 1810 Holland was annexed to France, as well as the German territory to the north, including the great ports of Bremen, Hamburg, and Lübeck.

Maximum extent of Napoleon's power

Napoleon had now reached the zenith of his power. All of western Europe, except England, was apparently under his control. France itself reached from the Baltic nearly to the Bay of Naples and included a considerable district beyond the Adriatic. The emperor of the French was also king of Italy and "protector" of the Confederation of the Rhine, which now included all of the German states except Austria and the remains of the kingdom of Prussia. Napoleon's brother Joseph was king of Spain, and his brother-in-law, Murat, king of Naples. Poland once more appeared on the map as the grand duchy of Warsaw, a faithful ally of its "restorer." The possessions of the emperor of Austria had so shrunk on the west that Hungary was now by far the most important part of Francis I's realms, but he had the satisfaction of beholding in his grandson, the king of Rome, the heir to unprecedented power. Surely in the history of the world there is nothing comparable to the career of Napoleon Bonaparte! He was, as a sage Frenchman has said, "as great as a man can be without virtue."

[1] Louis Bonaparte, the father of Napoleon III, and the most conscientious of the Bonaparte family, had been so harassed by Napoleon that he had abdicated.

SECTION 46. THE FALL OF NAPOLEON

But all Napoleon's military genius, his statesmanship, his tireless vigilance, and his absolute unscrupulousness could not invent means by which an empire such as he had built up could be held together permanently. Even if he could, by force or persuasion, have induced the monarchs to remain his vassals, he could not cope with the growing spirit of nationality among their subjects which made subordination to a French ruler seem a more and more shameful thing to Spaniards, Germans, and Italians alike. Moreover there were two governments that he had not succeeded in conquering — England and Russia. Insecurity of Napoleon's achievements

FIG. 74. THE DUKE OF WELLINGTON

The English, far from begging for peace on account of the continental blockade, had annihilated the French sea power and now began to attack Napoleon on land. Sir Arthur Wellesley (a commander who had made a reputation in India, and who is better known by his later title of the Duke of Wellington) had Wellington and the English in Spain (1808–1812) landed English troops in Portugal (August, 1808) and forced Junot and the French army to evacuate the country. While Napoleon was busy about Vienna in 1809 Wellesley had invaded Spain and gained a victory over the French there. He then retired again to Portugal where he spent the winter constructing a system of fortifications — the lines of Torres Vedras — on a rocky promontory near Lisbon. From here he could carry on his operations against the French with security and success. He and his Spanish allies continued to occupy the attention of about three hundred thousand of Napoleon's troops and some of his very best generals. So Napoleon never really conquered Spain, which proved a constant drain on his resources, a source of humiliation to him and of exultation and encouragement to his enemies.

The lines of Torres Vedras

Relations between Napoleon and Alexander I of Russia

Among the continental states Russia alone was entirely out of Napoleon's control. Up to this time the agreement of Tilsit had been maintained. There were, however, plenty of causes for misunderstanding between the ardent young Tsar, Alexander I, and Napoleon. Napoleon was secretly opposing, instead of aiding, Alexander's plans for adding the Danubian provinces to his possessions. Then the possibility of Napoleon's reëstablishing Poland as a national kingdom, which might threaten Russia's interests, was a constant source of apprehension to Alexander.

Russia could not afford to enforce the continental blockade

The chief difficulty lay, however, in Russia's unwillingness to enforce the continental blockade. The Tsar was willing, in accordance with the Treaty of Tilsit, to continue to close his harbors to English ships, but he refused to accede to Napoleon's demand that he shut out vessels sailing under a neutral flag. Russia had to dispose of her own products in some way and to obtain English manufactures, as well as coffee, sugar, spices, and other tropical and semi-tropical products which she had no hope of producing herself. Her comfort and prosperity depended, therefore, upon the neutral vessels which visited her Baltic ports.

Napoleon viewed the open Russian ports as a fatal flaw in his continental system and began to make preparations for an attack upon his doubtful friend, who was already beginning to look like an enemy. In 1812 he believed that he was ready to subdue even distant Russia. His more far-sighted counselors vainly attempted to dissuade him by pointing out the fearful risks that he was taking. Deaf to their warnings, he collected on the Russian frontier a vast army of half a million men, composed to a great extent of young French recruits and the contingents furnished by his allies.

Napoleon determines to attack Russia (1812)

The story of the fearful Russian campaign which followed cannot be told here in detail. Napoleon had planned to take three years to conquer Russia, but he was forced on by the necessity of gaining at least one signal victory before he closed the first season's campaign. The Russians simply retreated and led him far within a hostile and devastated country before they offered battle at Borodino (September 7). Napoleon won the battle, but his army was reduced to something over one hundred thousand men when he entered Moscow a week later. The town had been set on fire by the Russians before his arrival; he found his position untenable, and had to retreat as winter came on. The cold, the lack of food, and the harassing attacks of the people along the route made that retreat the most signal military tragedy on record. Napoleon regained Poland early in December, accompanied by scarcely twenty thousand men of the five hundred thousand with whom he had opened the campaign less than six months before.[1]

Napoleon's campaign in Russia (1812)

He hastened back to Paris, where he freely misrepresented the true state of affairs, even declaring that the army was in good condition up to the time when he had turned it over to Murat in December. While the loss of men in the Russian

Napoleon collects a new army

[1] This does not mean that all but twenty thousand had been killed. Some of the contingents, that of Prussia for example, did not take an active part in the war. Some idea of the horrors of the Russian campaign may be obtained from the descriptions given in the *Readings*, section 46.

campaign was enormous, just those few had naturally survived who would be most essential in the formation of a new army, namely, the officers. With their help Napoleon soon had a force of no less than six hundred thousand men with which to return to the attack. This contained one hundred and fifty thousand conscripts who should not have been called into service until 1814, besides older men who had been hitherto exempted.

What Prussia had suffered from Napoleon

The first of his allies to desert Napoleon was Prussia — and no wonder. She had felt his tyranny as no other country had. He had not only taken her lands; he had cajoled and insulted her; he had forced her to send her ablest minister, Stein, into exile because he had aroused the French emperor's dislike; he had opposed every measure of reform which might have served to strengthen the diminished kingdom which he had left to Frederick William III.

Reform of Prussia after the battle of Jena

Prussia, notwithstanding the reforms of Frederick the Great, had retained its half-feudal institutions down to the decisive defeat of Jena. The agricultural classes were serfs bound to the soil and compelled to work a certain part of each week for their lords without remuneration. The population was still divided into three distinct castes — nobles, burghers, and peasants — who could not acquire one another's land. The overwhelming defeat of the Prussian army at Jena and the provisions of the Treaty of Tilsit, which reduced Prussia to territorial insignificance, forced the leaders of that old-fashioned country to consider whether its weakness was not partly due to its medieval institutions. Neither the king nor his usual advisers were ready for thoroughgoing reform, but there were some more progressive spirits, among whom Baron vom Stein and Prince Hardenberg were conspicuous, who induced the government to alter the old system.

Prussia forced to undertake reforms

Serfdom abolished, 1807

The first step was taken in October, 1807, when a royal decree was issued which declared its purpose to be nothing less than "to remove every obstacle that has hitherto prevented the individual from attaining such a degree of prosperity as he is capable of reaching." Serfdom was abolished, and the old class system done away with, so that any one, regardless of social rank, was legally free to purchase and hold landed property, no matter to whom it had formerly belonged.

FIG. 75. STEIN

Continued influence in Prussia of the former feudal lords

It is important to note that while serfs had practically disappeared in England and France hundreds of years earlier, it was not until the opening of the nineteenth century, and then under the stress of dire calamity, that Prussia sufficiently modernized herself to abolish the medieval manor and free the peasants until then bound to the soil and sold with it. But the manorial lords, the so-called *Junkers*, remained rich and influential, and have continued down to this day, with their ancient notions of kingship by the grace of God and of military prowess, to exercise a fatal influence on the Prussian government. Moreover, the mass of the Prussian people seem to retain something of their old servile attitude toward their masters.

Origin of the modern Prussian army

The old army of Frederick the Great had been completely discredited, and a few days after the signing of the Treaty of Tilsit a commission for military reorganization was appointed. The object of the reformers was to introduce universal military service. Napoleon permitted Prussia to maintain only a small force of not more than forty-two thousand men, but the reformers arranged that this army should be continually recruited by new men, while those who had had some training should retire and form a reserve. In this way, in spite of Napoleon's restrictions on the size of the regular Prussian army, there were before long as many as a hundred and fifty thousand men sufficiently trained to fight when the opportunity should come. This system was later adopted by other European states and was the basis of the great armies of the Continent at the outbreak of the Great War in 1914.

Fichte's addresses (1807–1808)

While serfdom and the old system of social classes were being abolished in Prussia, attempts were being made to rouse the national spirit of the Germans and prepare them to fight against their French conquerors. A leader in this movement was the well-known philosopher Fichte He arranged a course of public addresses in Berlin, just after the defeat at Jena, in which he laid the foundation for the modern German arrogance from which the world has suffered so much. He told his auditors, with impressive warmth and eloquence, that the Germans were the one really superior people in the whole world. All other nations were degraded and had, he was confident, seen their best days; but the future belonged to the Germans, who would in due time, owing to their supreme natural gifts, come into their own and be recognized as the leaders of the world. The German language was, he claimed, infinitely stronger than the feeble speech of the French and Italians, borrowed from ancient Latin.

Fatal effects of the teaching of Fichte and other German writers

Unhappily, later German writers, economists, philosophers, and even the clergymen, as we shall see, have followed Fichte's lead in cultivating the Germans' self-esteem and their ill-concealed contempt for every other race.

The University of Berlin, which, before the Great War, was one of the largest institutions in the world, was founded in the interest of higher education. Four hundred and fifty-eight students registered the first year (1810–1811). A League of Virtue was formed to foster fidelity to the Fatherland and to cultivate hatred of Napoleon and the French. In this way the Prussian people were roused from their lethargy and prepared to join their leaders in an attack on their foreign oppressors.

University of Berlin opened (1810)

The Prussian contingent which Napoleon had ordered to support him in his campaign against Alexander was under the command of Yorck. It had held back and so was not involved in the destruction of the main army. On learning of Napoleon's retreat from Moscow, Yorck finally resolved to join the Russians in spite of the fact that his timid king was still afraid to declare war on Napoleon.

Yorck deserts Napoleon

This action of Yorck and the influence of public opinion finally induced the faint-hearted king, who was still apprehensive of Napoleon's vengeance, to sign a treaty with the Tsar (February 27, 1813), in which Russia agreed not to lay down arms until Prussia should be restored to a total area equal to that she had possessed before the fatal battle of Jena. It was understood that she should give up to the Tsar all that she had received in the second and third partitions of Poland and be indemnified by annexations in northern Germany. This proved a very important stipulation. On March 17 Frederick William issued a proclamation "To my People," in which he summoned his subjects — Brandenburgers, Prussians, Silesians, Pomeranians, and Lithuanians — to follow the example of the Spaniards and free their country from the rule of a foreign tyrant.

Prussia joins Russia against Napoleon (February, 1813)

Napoleon's situation was, however, by no means desperate so long as Italy, Austria, and the Confederation of the Rhine stood by him. With the new army which he had collected after his disastrous campaign in Russia the previous year, he marched to Leipzig, where he found the Russians and the

Napoleon's campaign in Saxony (1813)

Prussians under Blücher awaiting him. He once more defeated the allies at Lützen (May 2, 1813), and then moved on to Dresden, the capital of his faithful friend, the king of Saxony. During the summer he inflicted several defeats upon the allies, and on August 26–27 he won his last great victory, the battle of Dresden.

Austria and Sweden turn against Napoleon

Metternich's friendship had grown cold as Napoleon's position became more and more uncertain. He was willing to maintain the alliance between Austria and France if Napoleon would abandon a considerable portion of his conquests since 1806. As Napoleon refused to do this, Austria joined the allies in August. Meanwhile Sweden, which a year or two before had chosen one of Napoleon's marshals, Bernadotte, as its crown prince, also joined the allies and sent an army into northern Germany.

Napoleon defeated in the battle of Leipzig (October, 1813)

Finding that the allied armies of Russia, Prussia, Austria, and Sweden, under excellent generals like Blücher and Bernadotte, had at last learned that it was necessary to coöperate if they hoped to crush their ever-alert enemy, and that they were preparing to cut him off from France, Napoleon retreated early in October to Leipzig. Here the tremendous "Battle of the Nations," as it has since been known, raged for four days. No less than one hundred and twenty thousand men were killed or wounded, and Napoleon was totally defeated (October 16–19).

As the emperor of the French escaped across the Rhine with the remnants of his army the whole fabric of his vast political edifice crumbled. The members of the Confederation of the Rhine renounced their protector and joined the allies. Jerome fled from his kingdom of Westphalia, and the Dutch drove the French officials out of Holland. Wellington had been steadily and successfully engaged in aiding the Spanish against their common enemy, and by the end of 1813 Spain was practically cleared of the French intruders, so that Wellington could press on across the Pyrenees into France.

Occupation of Paris by the allies (March 31, 1814)

In spite of these disasters, Napoleon refused an offer of peace on condition that he would content himself henceforth with France alone. The allies consequently marched into France, and the almost superhuman activity of the hard-pressed emperor could not prevent their occupation of Paris (March 31, 1814). Napoleon was forced to abdicate, and the allies, in seeming derision, granted him full sovereignty over the tiny

FIG. 76. THE ABDICATION OF NAPOLEON — THE DOCUMENT IN HIS OWN HANDWRITING[1]

Napoleon abdicates and is banished to the island of Elba

island of Elba, off the coast of Tuscany, permitting him to retain his imperial title and assuring him of an annual revenue of two million francs. His mother, brothers, sisters, nephews, and nieces were allowed to retain, wherever they might be, the titles of princes of his family. But in reality Napoleon was a prisoner on his island kingdom, and the Bourbons reigned again in France.

[1] The document reads as follows: "Les puissances alliées ayant proclamé que l'Empereur Napoléon était le seul obstacle au rétablissement de la paix en Europe, l'Empereur, fidèle à son serment, déclare qu'il renonce pour lui et pour ses successeurs, aux trônes de France et d'Italie et qu'il, fidèle à son serment, n'est aucun sacrifice personnel, même celui de la vie qu'il ne soit prêt à faire aux intérêts de la France." Which, being translated, reads:

"The allied powers having proclaimed that the Emperor Napoleon was the sole obstacle to the reëstablishment of peace in Europe, the Emperor, faithful to his oath, proclaims that he renounces, for himself and his successors, the thrones of France and of Italy, and that, faithful to his oath, there is no personal sacrifice, even that of life, that he is not ready to make for the interests of France."

Return of Napoleon

Within a year, encouraged by the dissensions of the allies and the unpopularity of the Bourbons, he made his escape, landed in France (March 1, 1815), and was received with enthusiasm by a portion of the army. Yet France as a whole

FIG. 77. THE RETURN OF NAPOLEON FROM ELBA

Napoleon landed almost alone in France, but had a triumphal march to Paris. The old soldiers of the armies of the empire responded to his call, and even those sent against him yielded to the spell of his personality and joined his small but growing army. Louis XVIII fled from Paris and took refuge with the allies, until Waterloo ended this last great adventure of Napoleon, one hundred days later. The period is often known as "the Hundred Days"

was indifferent, if not hostile, to his attempt to reëstablish his power. Certainly no one could place confidence in his talk of peace and liberty. Moreover, whatever disagreement there might be among the allies on other matters, there was perfect unanimity in their attitude toward "the enemy and destroyer of the world's peace." They solemnly proclaimed him an outlaw, and proceeded to devote him to public vengeance. Battle of Waterloo, June, 1815

Upon learning that English troops under Wellington and a Prussian army under Blücher had arrived in the Netherlands, Napoleon decided to attack them with such troops as he could collect. In the first engagements he defeated and drove back the Prussians. Wellington then took his station south of Brussels, at Waterloo. Napoleon advanced against him (June 18, 1815) and might have defeated the English had they not been opportunely reënforced by Blücher's Prussians, who had recovered themselves. As it was, Napoleon lost the most memorable of modern battles. Yet even if he had not been defeated at Waterloo, he could not long have opposed the vast armies which were being concentrated to overthrow him.

FIG. 78. TOMB OF NAPOLEON

Napoleon died at St. Helena in 1821. The body was brought to Paris in 1840 and placed with great military splendor in this sarcophagus of reddish-brown granite, which was hewn in Finland out of a solid block weighing sixty-seven tons. Around it in the pavement are inscribed the names of Napoleon's greatest victories, while some sixty captured banners stand beside colossal statues of victory. The tomb is under the lofty gilded dome of the church which is connected with the old soldiers' asylum, known as the *Invalides*

The fugitive emperor hastened to the coast, but found it so carefully guarded by English ships that he decided to throw

Napoleon banished to St. Helena

himself upon the generosity of the English nation. The British government treated him, however, as a dangerous prisoner of war rather than as a retired foreign general and statesman of distinction who desired, as he claimed, to finish his days in peaceful seclusion. He was banished with a few companions and guards to the remote island of St. Helena.[1] Here he spent the six years until his death on May 5, 1821, brooding over his past glories and dictating his memoirs, in which he strove to justify his career and explain his motives.

The Napoleonic legend

"For the general history of Europe the captivity at St. Helena possesses a double interest. Not only did it invest the career of the fallen hero with an atmosphere of martyrdom and pathos, which gave it a new and distinct appeal, but it enabled him to arrange a pose before the mirror of history, to soften away all that had been ungracious and hard and violent, and to draw in firm and authoritative outline a picture of his splendid achievements and liberal designs. . . . The great captain, hero of adventures wondrous as the *Arabian Nights*, passes over the mysterious ocean to his lonely island and emerges transfigured as in some ennobling mirage."[2]

QUESTIONS

SECTION 42. Outline Bonaparte's domestic policy in general. What was the Concordat? What was the importance of the *Code Napoléon*? Why did Napoleon revive the splendors of a court? Why did France accept him as emperor?

SECTION 43. What did Napoleon consider the ideal government for Europe? Account for England's hostility to France. Describe Napoleon's foreign policy. Give the terms and state the importance of the Treaty of Pressburg. Describe the Confederation of the Rhine. When and under what circumstances did the Holy Roman

[1] An isolated rocky island lying south of the equator between Brazil and the African coast, from which it is separated by some thirteen hundred miles of water.

[2] H. A. L. Fisher in the *Cambridge Modern History*, Vol. IX, p. 757. Some historians have accepted Napoleon at his own valuation, among them J. S. C. Abbott, whose popular but misleading life of Napoleon has given thousands of readers a wholly false notion of his character and aims.

Empire cease to exist? Continue the sketch of Napoleon's foreign policy from the dissolution of the Holy Roman Empire to the alliance of Tilsit

SECTION 44. Outline the various stages in Napoleon's continental blockade. Who suffered most by it? Why was England able to endure it so well?

SECTION 45. Name some of the public works for which Napoleon was reponsible. Describe the university system which he established. What was the Legion of Honor? Describe the despotic character of the latter part of Napoleon's rule. Outline his campaigns in Portugal and Spain.

Take Spain as an example to show the manner in which Napoleon introduced the reforms of the French Revolution into the countries which came under his sway. Describe the Austrian campaign of 1809. Draw a map of Europe and on it indicate the greatest extent of Napoleon's power.

SECTION 46. Describe the relations between France and Russia which led to Napoleon's attack on the latter country. Give an account of the Russian campaign. Describe the regeneration of Prussia. Outline Napoleon's campaign of 1813 and describe the downfall of his empire. Discuss the terms offered to Napoleon by the allies. Give an account of the return from Elba and of the campaign which ended with Waterloo. Describe Napoleon's last years.

THE RECONSTRUCTION OF EUROPE AT THE CONGRESS OF VIENNA

SECTION 47. THE CONGRESS OF VIENNA AND ITS WORK

Extreme difficulty of adjusting the map of Europe after the great changes of the Napoleonic Period

The readjustment of the map of Europe after Napoleon's downfall was an extremely perplexing and delicate operation. Boundary lines centuries old had been swept away by the storms of war and the ambition of the conqueror. Many ancient states had disappeared altogether — Venice, Genoa, Piedmont, the Papal States, Holland, and scores of little German principalities. These had been either merged into France or the realms of their more fortunate neighbors, or formed into new countries — the kingdom of Italy, the kingdom of Westphalia, the Confederation of the Rhine, the grand duchy of Warsaw. Those which had survived had, with the exception of England and Russia, received new bounds, new rulers, or new institutions. When Napoleon was forced to abdicate, the princes whose former realms had vanished from the map, or who had been thrust aside, clamored to be restored to their thrones. The great powers, England, Austria, Russia, and Prussia, whose rulers had finally combined to bring about his overthrow, naturally assumed the rôle of arbiters in the settlement. But they were far from impartial judges, since each proposed to gain for itself the greatest possible advantages in the reapportionment of territory.

Some matters settled at the first Peace of Paris, May 30, 1814

The least troublesome points were settled by the allies in the first Treaty of Paris, which had been concluded in May, 1814, immediately after Napoleon had been sent to Elba. They readily agreed, for instance, that the Bourbon dynasty should be

Fig. 79. Marshal Ney Sustaining the Rear Guard of the Grand Army on the Retreat from Moscow

Fig. 80. The Congress of Vienna

restored to the throne of France in the person of Louis XVI's younger brother, the count of Provence, who took the title of Louis XVIII.[1] They at first permitted France to retain the boundaries she had had on November 1, 1792, but later deprived her of Savoy as a penalty for yielding to Napoleon after his return from Elba.[2] The powers also agreed, at Paris, upon a kingdom of the Netherlands, with increased territories, to be established under the House of Orange; the union of Germany into a confederation of sovereign states; the independence of Switzerland; and the restoration of the monarchical states of Italy. The graver issues and the details of the settlement were left to the consideration of the great congress which was to convene at Vienna in the autumn.[3]

Holland made a kingdom and given the former Austrian Netherlands

This Congress of Vienna continued the old policy of carving out and distributing states — especially the smaller ones — without regard to the wishes of the people concerned. The allies confirmed their former decision that Holland should become an hereditary kingdom under the House of Orange, which had so long played a conspicuous rôle in the Dutch republic. In order that Holland might be better able to check any encroachments on the part of France, the Austrian Netherlands (which had been seized by the French Convention early in the revolutionary wars) were joined to the new Dutch kingdom. The fact that most of the inhabitants of the Austrian Netherlands were not closely connected by language,[4] traditions, or religion with the Dutch was ignored just as it had been in former times

[1] The young son of Louis XVI had been imprisoned by the Convention and, according to reports, maltreated by the jailers set to guard him. His fate has been a fruitful theme of historical discussion, but it is probable that he died in 1795. Though he never exercised power in any form, he takes his place in the line of French kings as Louis XVII.

[2] The second Peace of Paris (November, 1815) also provided for the return of the works of art and manuscripts which Napoleon had carried off from Venice, Milan, Rome, Naples, and elsewhere. But not all were returned.

[3] On the rivalry of the rulers at the Congress of Vienna, see *Readings*, Vol. I, p. 375.

[4] About half the people of Belgium to-day speak French, while the remainder use Flemish, a dialect akin to Dutch.

when the provinces had passed to Spain by inheritance and, later, to Austria by conquest.

The consolidation of Germany leaves only thirty-eight surviving states

The territorial settlement of Germany did not prove to be so difficult as might have been expected. No one except the petty princes and the ecclesiastics desired to undo the work of 1803 and restore the old minute subdivisions which had been done away with by the *Reichsdeputationshauptschluss*. The restoration of the Holy Roman Empire could not be seriously considered by any one, but they all felt the need of some sort of union between the surviving thirty-eight German states. A very loose union was therefore created, which permitted the former members of the Confederation of the Rhine to continue to enjoy that precious "sovereignty" which Napoleon had granted them. Formerly that portion of Germany which lies on the Rhine had been so broken up into little states that it was a constant temptation to any strong power to take advantage of this disintegration and encroach upon German territory. After 1815 this source of weakness was partially remedied, for Prussia was assigned a large tract on the Rhine, while Baden, Würtemberg, and Bavaria stood by her side to discourage new aggressions from any foreign enemy.

Strengthening of Germany's western boundary

In the readjustment of Italy, Austria is assigned a predominating influence

Italy, however, was not so fortunate in securing greater unity than she had enjoyed before the French Revolution. Napoleon had reduced and consolidated her various divisions into the kingdom of Italy, of which he was the head, and the kingdom of Naples, which he had finally bestowed on Murat, while Piedmont, Genoa, Tuscany, and the Papal States he had annexed to France.[1] Naturally the powers had no reason for maintaining this arrangement and determined to restore all the former monarchical states. Tuscany, Modena, the Papal States, and Naples were given back to their former princes, and little Parma was assigned to Napoleon's second wife, the Austrian princess, Maria Louisa. The king of Sardinia returned from

[1] Nothing need be said of a half dozen petty Italian territories — Lucca, San Marino, Benevento, etc.

his island and reëstablished himself in Turin. There were few at the congress to plead for a revival of the ancient republics of Genoa and Venice. The lands of the former were therefore added to those of the king of Sardinia, in order to make as firm

FIG. 81. GENERAL BERNADOTTE, KING CHARLES XIV OF SWEDEN

The son of a lawyer in southern France, Bernadotte (1763–1844) won his way in the French army by merit and was one of Napoleon's greatest marshals. In 1810 he was surprised by the news that some Swedish statesmen were proposing him as successor to the throne, owing to his kindness to Swedish prisoners he had taken once, and also in order to secure Sweden against Russia by having a warrior king, a good friend of Napoleon. Elected, he became very popular, and after the Napoleonic wars his reign was peaceful

a bulwark as possible against France. Austria deemed the territories of Venice a fair compensation for the loss of the Netherlands, and was accordingly permitted to add Venetia to her old duchy of Milan and thus form a new Austrian province in northern Italy, the so-called Lombardo-Venetian kingdom.

Switzerland

Switzerland gave the allies but little trouble. The Congress of Vienna recognized the cantons as all free and equal, and established their "neutrality" by agreeing never to invade Switzerland or send troops through her territory. The cantons (which had been joined by the former free city of Geneva) then drew up a new constitution, which bound them together into a Swiss federation consisting of twenty-two little states.

Personal union of Sweden and Norway under the rule of the House of Bernadotte

The Congress of Vienna ratified an arrangement by which Sweden and Norway were joined under a single ruler, one of Napoleon's generals, Bernadotte (see Fig. 84). The Norwegians protested, drew up a constitution of their own, and elected a king, but Bernadotte induced them to accept him as their ruler on condition that Norway should have its own separate constitution and government. This was the origin of the "personal union"[1] of Sweden and Norway under Bernadotte and his successors, which lasted until October, 1905.[2]

Russia and Prussia agree upon the fate of the grand duchy of Warsaw and of the kingdom of Saxony

In these adjustments all was fairly harmonious, but when it came to the rewards claimed by Russia and Prussia there developed at the congress serious differences of opinion which nearly brought on war between the allies themselves, and which encouraged Napoleon's return from Elba. Russia desired the grand duchy of Warsaw, which Napoleon had formed principally out of the territory seized by Austria and Prussia in the

[1] This is the term applied in international law to describe the union of two or more independent states under a single ruler.

[2] This personal union worked very well so long as the joint king was tolerably free from control by the Swedish parliament, for the Norwegians had their own constitution and parliament, or Storthing, as it is called, and they could regard themselves as practically independent under a sovereign who also happened to be king of Sweden. However, especially near the close of the nineteenth century, the interests of the two countries diverged more and more widely. With the development of parliamentary government the diets of both countries desired to control the king's choice of ministers and the foreign policy of the two kingdoms. So, after a long period of friction, the two states agreed to separate on October 26, 1905. Sweden retained her old king, Oscar II (1872–1907), while Norway elected as king Prince Carl, second son of Frederick, king of Denmark, and gave him the title of Haakon VII. The Norwegians still retain the constitution which was drawn up in 1814, but it has been several times modified by democratic measures.

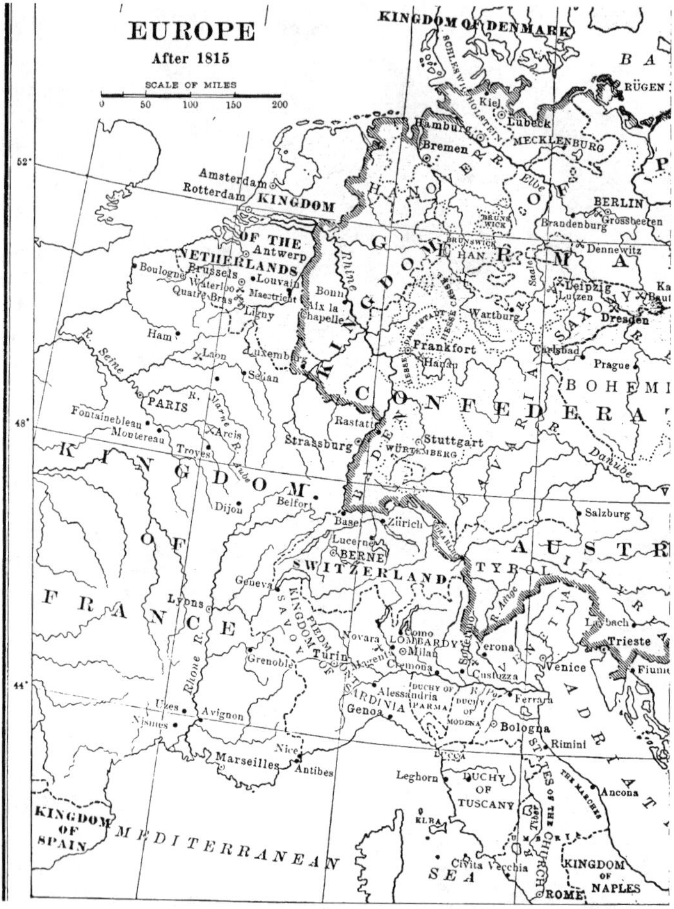
EUROPE
After 1815
SCALE OF MILES
0 50 100 150 200
KINGDOM OF DENMARK
SCHLESWIG
HOLSTEIN
Kiel
Lübeck
Hamburg
Bremen
MECKLENBURG
RÜGEN
BERLIN
Brandenburg
Grossbeeren
Dennewitz
Amsterdam
Rotterdam
KINGDOM OF THE NETHERLANDS
Antwerp
Brussels
Louvain
Waterloo
Quatre Bras
Maestricht
Ligny
Boulogne
Bonn
Aix la Chapelle
Rhine
HANOVER
BRUNSWICK
HAN.
KINGDOM OF GERMAN CONFEDERATION
Elbe
Saale
Leipzig
Lutzen
SAXONY
Dresden
Wartburg
HESSE CASSEL
HESSE DARMSTADT
Frankfort
Hanau
Carlsbad
Prague
BOHEMIA
Ham
Laon
Luxemburg
Sedan
R. Seine
PARIS
R. Marne
Fontainebleau
Montereau
Arcis
Troyes
R. Aube
Rastatt
Strassburg
Stuttgart
WÜRTEMBERG
BADEN
BAVARIA
Danube
KINGDOM OF FRANCE
Dijon
Belfort
Basel
Zürich
Lucerne
BERNE
SWITZERLAND
Salzburg
AUSTRIA
TYROL
ILLYRIA
Geneva
Lyons
Rhone R.
KINGDOM OF SARDINIA
PIEDMONT
SAVOY
Grenoble
Turin
Novara
Magenta
Como
LOMBARDY
Milan
Cremona
Verona
VENETIA
Venice
Custozza
Laibach
Trieste
Fiume
Alessandria
Genoa
DUCHY OF PARMA
DUCHY OF MODENA
R. Po
Ferrara
Bologna
Rimini
ADRIATIC
Uzes
Avignon
Nismes
Nice
Marseilles
Antibes
LUCCA
Leghorn
DUCHY OF TUSCANY
ELBA
STATES OF THE CHURCH
THE MARCHES
UMBRIA
Ancona
Tiber
Civita Vecchia
ROME
KINGDOM OF NAPLES
KINGDOM OF SPAIN
MEDITERRANEAN SEA

IC SEA
R. Niemen
Vilna
LITHUANIA
Danzig
R.
RUSSIAN EMPIRE
USSIA
Bialystock
Thorn
Vistula
Posen
Warsaw
52°
Dnieper
POLAND
VOLHYNIA
R.
Breslau
Breslau
Vistula R.
CRACOW
GALICIA
PODOLIA
R. Bug
Troppau
Dniester
R.
ION
HUNGARY
48
R.
Pruth
Pressburg
MOLDAVIA
Leitha
Komorn
R.
Raab
Buda Pesth
Debreczin
Jassy
Odessa
AN EMPIRE
Akerman
Nagy Salo
Theiss
R.
TRANSYLVANIA
Vilagos
R.
Drave
Temesvar
R.
Maros
Agram
SLAVONIA
DOBRUDSCHA
WALLACHIA
Kustendjeh
Bucharest
44°
Belgrade
BOSNIA
SERVIA
Widdin
R.
Danube
Rustchuk
OTTOMAN EMPIRE
Nicopolis
Sistova
Shumla
Varna
BULGARIA
Plevna
Tirnova
Alexinatz
HERZEGOVINA
DALMATIA
Morava
Shipka Pass
BLACK SEA
Novibazar
Bourgas
Sofia
Kazanlik
MONTENEGRO
R.
Maritza
Philippopolis
ALBANIA
SEA
Adrianople
Antivari
Dulcigno
CONSTANTINOPLE

FIG. 82. THREE IMPORTANT MEMBERS OF THE CONGRESS OF VIENNA

partitions of the previous century. The Tsar proposed to increase this duchy by the addition of a portion of Russian Poland and so form a kingdom to be united in a personal union with his other dominions. The king of Prussia agreed to this plan on condition that in return for the loss of such a large portion of his former Polish territories he should be allowed to annex the lands of the king of Saxony, who, it was argued, had deserved this punishment for remaining faithful to Napoleon after the other members of the Confederation of the Rhine had deserted him.

England, Austria, and France prepare to oppose the plans of Russia and Prussia

Austria and England, on the other hand, were opposed to this arrangement. They did not approve of dispossessing the king of Saxony or of extending the Tsar's influence westward by giving him Poland; and Austria had special grounds for objection because a large portion of the duchy of Warsaw which the Tsar proposed to take had formerly belonged to her. The great French diplomatist, Talleyrand, now saw his chance to disturb the good will existing between England, Prussia, Austria, and Russia. The allies had resolved to treat France as a black sheep and arrange everything to suit themselves. But now that they were hopelessly at odds Austria and England found the hitherto discredited France a welcome ally. Acting with the consent of Louis XVIII, Talleyrand offered to Austria the aid of French arms in resisting the proposal of Russia and Prussia, and on January 3, 1815, France, England, and Austria joined in a secret treaty against Russia and Prussia, and even went so far as to draw up a plan of campaign. So France, who had stood apart for the last quarter of a century, was received back into the family of nations, and the French ambassador joyfully announced to his king that the coalition against France was dissolved forever.

Skillful diplomacy of Talleyrand

The Tsar gets Poland, and Prussia becomes powerful on the Rhine

A compromise was, however, at length arranged without resorting to arms. The Tsar gave up a small portion of the duchy of Warsaw, but was allowed to create the kingdom of Poland on which he had set his heart. Only about one half of the possessions of the king of Saxony were ceded to Prussia, but as a further indemnity Prussia received certain districts on the left bank of the Rhine, which had belonged to petty lay and ecclesiastical princes before the Peace of Lunéville. This proved an important gain for Prussia, although it was not considered so at the time. It gave her a large number of German subjects in exchange for the Poles she lost, and so prepared the way for her to become the dominant power in Germany.

If one compares the map of Europe as it was reconstructed by the representatives of the great powers at Vienna, with the situation after the Treaty of Utrecht a hundred years before, several very important changes are apparent. A general consolidation had been effected. Holland and the Austrian Netherlands were united under one king. The Holy Roman Empire, with its hundreds of petty principalities, had disappeared and a union of thirty-eight states and free towns had taken its place. Prussia had greatly increased the extent of its German territories, although these remained rather scattered. The kingdom of Poland had reappeared on the map, but had lost its independence and been reduced in extent. Portions of it had fallen to Prussia and Austria, but the great mass of Polish territory was now brought under the control of the Tsar, who was no longer regarded by the western nations as an eastern potentate, but was regularly admitted to their councils. Austria had lost her outlying provinces of the Netherlands, which had proved so troublesome, but had been indemnified by the lands of the extinct Venetian republic, while her future rival in Italy, the king of Sardinia, had been strengthened by receiving the important city of Genoa and the adjacent territory. Otherwise, Italy remained in her former state of disruption and more completely than ever under the control of Austria.

Map of Europe in 1815 as compared with the conditions established by the Treaty of Utrecht

The gains of England resulting from the Napoleonic conflict, like all her other acquisitions since the War of the Spanish

England gains Ceylon and the Cape of Good Hope

Succession, were colonial. The most important of these were Ceylon, off the southeastern coast of the Indian peninsula, and the Cape of Good Hope. The latter had been wrested from the Dutch (1806) while Holland was under Napoleon's influence. This seemingly insignificant conquest proved to be the basis of further British expansion, which has secured for England the most valuable portions of southern Africa.[1]

Vast extent of England's colonial possessions in 1815

In spite of the loss of the American colonies on the eve of the French Revolution, England possessed in 1815 the foundations of the greatest commercial and colonial power which has ever existed. She still held Canada and all the vast northwest of the North American continent, except Alaska. Important islands in the West Indies furnished stations from which a lucrative trade with South America could be carried on. In Gibraltar she had a sentinel at the gateway of the Mediterranean, and the possession of the Cape of Good Hope afforded not only a basis for pressing into the heart of the most habitable part of Africa but also a halfway port for vessels bound to distant India. In India the beginnings of empire had already been made in the Bengal region and along the east and west coasts. Finally, in Australia, far away in the southern Pacific, convict settlements had been made which were in time to be supplanted by rich, populous, and prosperous commonwealths. In addition to her colonial strength England possessed the most formidable navy and the largest mercantile marine afloat.

The Congress of Vienna marks the condemnation of one of the most atrocious practices which Europe had inherited from

[1] England also received from France the island of Mauritius in the Indian Ocean, east of Madagascar; Tobago, a small island north of the mouth of the Orinoco River; and Saint Lucia, one of the Windward Islands. From Spain England got the island of Trinidad near Tobago, and from Denmark the island of Heligoland, commanding the mouth of the Elbe (ceded to Germany in 1890) In the Mediterranean England held Malta and, as a protectorate, the Ionian Islands off the coast of Greece, thus securing a basis for operations in the eastern Mediterranean.

The Congress of Vienna, under the influence of England, condemns the slave trade

ancient times, namely, the slave trade.[1] The congress itself did no more than declare the traffic contrary to the principles of civilization and human right; but, under the leadership of England, the various states, with the exception of Spain and Portugal, were already busy doing away with the trade in human beings. The horrors of the business had roused the conscience of the more enlightened and humane Englishmen and Frenchmen in the eighteenth century. Finally, in March, 1807, three weeks after the Congress of the United States had forbidden the importation of slaves,[2] Parliament prohibited Englishmen from engaging in the traffic. Sweden followed England's example in 1813, and Holland a year later. Napoleon, on his return from Elba, in order to gain if possible the confidence of England, abolished the French slave trade.

Disregard of nationality before the nineteenth century

Napoleon had done more than alter the map of Europe and introduce such reforms in the countries under his control as suited his purposes; he had aroused the modern *spirit of nationality*, which is one of the forces that helped to make the nineteenth century different from the eighteenth. Before the French Revolution kings went to war without consulting their subjects, and made arrangements with other monarchs in regard to the distribution, division, and annexation of territory without asking the consent of those who lived in the regions involved. Practically no attention was paid to differences in race, for kings gladly added to their realms any lands they could gain by conquest, negotiation, marriage, or inheritance, regardless of the particular kind of subjects that they might bring under their scepters.

[1] The slave trade had been greatly stimulated by the discovery that African slaves could be profitably used to cultivate the vast plantations of the New World. The English navigator, Hawkins, had carried a cargo of three hundred negroes from Sierra Leone to Hispania in 1562, and so introduced English seamen to a business in which Portugal, Spain, and Holland were already engaged. It is estimated that previous to 1776 at least three million slaves had been imported into French, Spanish, and English colonies, while at least a quarter of a million more had perished during the voyages.

[2] England abolished slavery throughout all her colonies in 1833.

The French National Assembly declares the monarch responsible to the nation, and so awakens political life among the people

However, the French Declaration of the Rights of Man in 1789 had proclaimed that the law was the expression of the general will, and that every citizen had a right, personally or through his representatives, to participate in its formation. The king and his officials were made responsible for their public acts not to God but to the people. This idea that the nation had a right to control the making of the laws and the granting of the taxes, and to choose or depose its ruler, who was responsible to it, served to rouse a general interest in political questions, which could not possibly have developed as long as people were content to believe that God had excluded them from all participation in affairs of State. Political leaders appeared, the newspapers began to discuss public questions, and political societies were formed.

The awakening of nationalism

The various nations became more and more keenly conscious that each had its own language and traditions which made it different from other peoples. Patriotic orators in Germany, Italy, and Greece recalled the glorious past of the ancient Germans, Romans, and Hellenes, with a view to stimulating this enthusiasm. National feeling may be defined as a general recognition that a people should have a government suited to its particular traditions and needs, and should be ruled by its own native officials, and that (if nations were entitled to political rights, as the French Revolution had taught) it is wrong for one people to dominate another, or for monarchs to divide, redistribute, and transfer territories with no regard to the wishes of the inhabitants, merely to provide some landless prince with a patrimony.

We shall have to reckon hereafter with this national spirit, which continued to spread and to increase in strength during the nineteenth century. It has played a great part in the unification of Italy and Germany, in the emancipation of Greece and the Balkan States from Turkish dominion, and finally in the causes of the great war of 1914.

Section 48. The Holy Alliance: Metternich becomes the Chief Opponent of Revolution

Horror of revolution and suspicion of reform after 1815

In June, 1815, the Congress of Vienna brought together the results of all the treaties and arrangements which its various members had agreed upon among themselves, and issued its "Final Act," in which its work was summed up for convenient reference.[1] A few days later the battle of Waterloo and the subsequent exile of Napoleon freed the powers from their chief cause of anxiety during the past fifteen years. No wonder that the restored monarchs, as they composed themselves upon their thrones and reviewed the wars and turmoil which had begun with the French Revolution and lasted more than a quarter of a century, longed for peace at any cost, and viewed with the utmost suspicion any individual or party who ventured to suggest further changes. The word "revolution" had acquired a hideous sound, not only to the rulers and their immediate advisers, but to all the aristocratic class and the clergy, who thought that they had reason enough to abhor the modern tendencies as they had seen them at work.

The Holy Alliance devised by Alexander I (September, 1815)

It was clear that the powers which had combined to reëstablish order must continue their alliance if they hoped to maintain the arrangements they had made and stifle the fires of revolution which were sure to break out at some unexpected point unless the most constant vigilance was exercised. Alexander I proposed a plan for preserving European tranquillity by the formation of a religious brotherhood of monarchs, which was given the name of "The Holy Alliance." This was accepted by the emperor of Austria and the king of Prussia, and published in September, 1815. In this singular instrument their majesties agreed to view one another as brothers and compatriots, as "delegates of Providence to govern three branches of the same family." All the other European powers which

[1] The chief provisions are given in the *Readings*, Vol. I, p. 381.

recognized the sacred principles of the act were to be welcomed cordially and affectionately into this "holy alliance."[1]

The Holy Alliance not a union to prevent revolution

The Tsar and Frederick William took the alliance seriously, but to most of the diplomats who had participated in the scramble for the spoils at Vienna, and who looked back upon the habits of monarchs in dealing with one another, it was an amusing vagary of the Tsar. It was not, as has often been supposed, a conspiracy of despotic monarchs to repress all liberal movements. It contained no definite allusions to the dangers of revolution or to the necessity of maintaining the settlement of Vienna. The name "Holy Alliance" came nevertheless to be applied by the more liberal newspapers and reformers to a real and effective organization of the powers opposed to change. In this case the monarchs did not unite in "the name of the Most High" to promote Christian love, but frankly combined to fight against reform, under the worldly guidance of Clement Wencelaus Nepomuk Lothaire, Prince of Metternich-Winneburg-Ochsenhausen.

Metternich's political creed

Metternich, who was destined to succeed Napoleon as the most conspicuous statesman in Europe, was born in 1773 and had followed the course of the French Revolution from the beginning, with hatred and alarm. All talk about constitutions and national unity was to him revolutionary, and therefore highly dangerous.[2]

Any development of the spirit of nationality dangerous to Austria

He was doubtless much strengthened in his hostility to reform by the situation of Austria, whose affairs he had been guiding since 1809. No country, except Prussia, had suffered more from the Revolution, which it had been the first to oppose in 1792. Should the idea of nationality gain ground the various peoples included in the Austrian Empire — Germans, Czechs, Poles, Hungarians, Italians, and the rest — would surely revolt and each demand its own constitution. Liberal ideas, whether in Austria, Italy, or Germany, foreboded the

[1] See the text of this interesting document in the *Readings*, Vol. I, p. 384.
[2] For Metternich's views on politics, see *Readings*, Vol. I, p. 386.

destruction of the highly artificial Austrian realms, which had been accumulated through the centuries by conquest, marriage, and inheritance, without regard to the great differences between the races which were gathered together under the scepter of Francis I. Consequently, to Metternich the preservation of Austria, the suppression of reformers and of agitators for constitutional government, and "the tranquillity of Europe" all meant one and the same thing.

On November 20, 1815, Austria, Prussia, England, and Russia entered a secret agreement to keep peace in Europe. In order to effect their ends the powers agreed to hold periodical meetings with a view to considering their common interests and taking such measures as might be expedient for the preservation of general order. Thus a sort of international congress was established for the purpose of upholding the settlement of Vienna.

Secret alliance of November 20, 1815

The first formal meeting of the powers under this agreement took place at Aix-la-Chapelle in 1818, to arrange for the evacuation of France by the troops of the allies, which had been stationed there since 1814 to suppress any possible disorder. France, once more admitted to the brotherhood of nations, joined Metternich's conservative league, and that judicious statesman could report with complacency that the whole conference was a brilliant triumph for those principles which he held dearest.

Congress of Aix-la-Chapelle, 1818

Section 49. Thought and Culture at the Opening of the Nineteenth Century

It must not be imagined that, because histories deal almost exclusively with the politics of the Revolutionary and Napoleonic periods, the people of that time were continually and completely immersed in wars and treaties. During all these years artisans worked at their trades, farmers gathered in their harvests and grumbled at high prices and the weather, manufacturers were

The history of a people includes other things than politics

seeking new markets, and inventors were contriving new machines to do the world's work. For instance, just as Napoleon was landing from Elba for his desperate adventure which ended at Waterloo, a poor young fireman at a Newcastle colliery, named George Stephenson, was perfecting the locomotive, by which vaster continents were to be conquered for the arts of peace than even Napoleon ever dreamed of. The changes in industry and the methods of work due to the application of science, which were taking place at that time, is so large a subject that we shall describe it by itself below.[1] But alongside the busy, unresting world of commerce and industry, there are other fields of achievement hardly less important — those of literature, art, and philosophy. In all of these, great masters were at work through the whole period just described.

The influence of France upon literature in the eighteenth century

During the eighteenth century the literatures of all Europe were profoundly under the influence of the culture of France. The poetry was stately and formal, such as Dryden and Pope wrote in England; the prose, although often witty and clever, seems to us, nowadays, rather artificial and affected. This was partly due to the fact that ever since the work of the humanists of the Renaissance, education had been largely taken up with studying the Greek and Latin classics. Ancient masters of rhetoric like Cicero were imitated by all writers of correct prose, and the tranquil dignity of Vergil's poetry furnished the model for thousands of rather monotonous lines of courtly verse. These writers used only a limited number of words, which were sanctioned by good taste as properly belonging to literature. In the choice of subjects, too, they were limited, for this lofty, "classical" style was regarded as suited only to lofty subjects. The result was that literature did not deal with the common affairs of daily life as it does now, but with somewhat unreal events and persons, generally the heroes and heroines of antiquity. In the hands of a master like Voltaire one did not feel the restraint which such formality imposed, but

The influence of the classics upon literature

[1] See the chapter on The Industrial Revolution, below.

upon the whole, the effect was to make both prose and poetry commonplace.[1] Rousseau's great success as a writer had been partly due to his passionate revolt against the stiffness and formality which French good taste had insisted upon.

Nature and naturalness in literature

Britain had no Rousseau, but the popularity of Robert Burns, the plowman poet, and of Wordsworth and his friends who sought to "get back to nature" was a sign of the same kind of revolt against artificiality. It also pointed to the rise of a less courtly audience than that of noble patrons for whose favor and gold authors used to write, namely, the great middle class now rapidly acquiring wealth and the leisure to read.

Romanticism

At the opening of the nineteenth century, and especially after the Napoleonic wars, this new reading public was entertained by a new theme — the romantic glorification of the past. During the eighteenth century and the Revolutionary era, the past had been decried, and people looked forward to the future for inspiration. Now writers turned to the despised Middle Ages and depicted in glowing terms the picturesque life of feudal times. One of the main leaders in this movement, which is called Romanticism, was Sir Walter Scott, whose poems and novels of the days of chivalry were read everywhere. The movement spread through France[2] and Germany. It fitted admirably with the conservative ideas of the period after Waterloo, and yet even its extravagant praise of the past, which, to progressive minds, seemed to obscure the duties of the present, had one important result — the rise of scientific history.

The modern historians

The past which the Romanticists wrote about was an unreal world, largely the creation of their imagination, where noble warriors and fair ladies were true heroes and heroines, with even the cruelty and triviality of their lives touched with the attraction of romance. But this attraction led others to study

[1] A clever writer like Voltaire could manage to make one see that, while pretending to talk about an ancient king, he often had the king of France and present politics in mind. In this way he could poke fun at absurdities in his own day, or denounce them roundly without being forbidden by the censor.

[2] In France one of the greatest Romanticists was Victor Hugo.

FIG. 83. THREE MEN WHOSE WORKS WERE WIDELY POPULAR IN THE EARLY NINETEENTH CENTURY

the past more critically, and scientific scholars set to work deciphering documents in dusty libraries in order to find out the truth. These historians were also animated by a deep interest in the story of politics and the rise of that most important factor in modern times — the nation. The French Revolution had, as we have seen, brought out strongly in the peoples of the Continent that national sentiment which the English had possessed for at least two centuries. Now the historians of Continental Europe began the great task of recovering the sources of their national history. As this scientific work was extended to cover the nations of antiquity as well, the later nineteenth and twentieth centuries have been enabled to know more about the history of civilization than any previous age. Such little manuals as this could not have been written but for the patient labor of these great scholars,[1] to whose works it is hoped that it may offer an introduction.

German literature

The rise of the modern German literature, which reached its climax in the works of Goethe,[2] is all the more remarkable when we recall that as recently as the days of Frederick the Great, German had not been regarded as a literary language. Frederick had written his poems and books in French. It was only after his victories had given a new self-confidence to the North Germans that they ventured to use the tongue of Luther as a rival to that of the court of Versailles. Thus the rapid rise of German literature is of great importance in the creation of that new and dangerously arrogant national feeling which has cost the world so much suffering in recent years.

[1] It should be noted that their work is by no means done. History is not an unchanging repetition of an old tale. It is, like any other branch of learning, a constantly changing body of facts, in proportion as new research and greater enlightenment bring other data to prominence. Until recently it has been largely a branch of literature, with emphasis upon the picturesque or dramatic. Now it is tending to pay more attention to economics and commonplace things.

[2] Pronounced *gė'te.* The greater part of his life (1749–1832) was spent at the small court of the Duke of Weimar. He was not much disturbed by the conquests of Napoleon, and cannot be counted among the distinctively patriotic Germans of his day. His wider outlook kept this greatest German poet from mere local sympathies and absorption in temporary problems.

FIG. 84. COUNT RUMFORD

One of the most distinguished pioneers in the development of Germany was Benjamin Thompson, who won the title Count Rumford for his services to the Elector of Bavaria in the years just before the French Revolution. Like Benjamin Franklin, he combined a scientific genius with great statesmanlike qualities, only in his case these were devoted to a foreign country. Rumford's life reads like a romance. Born in 1753, the son of a Massachusetts farmer, he left for England at the time of the Revolution. There he held public office and at the same time carried on scientific experiments. Going to fight against the Turks, he was given the post of minister by the Elector of Bavaria. He boldly advocated reforms in government so that problems of social welfare, such as the care of the poor and the treatment of criminals, or the development of the country's resources, should be met by scientific study instead of by old-fashioned remedies. It is part of the romance that when he was made a count of the Holy Roman Empire he chose as his title the name of the little village of Rumford, now Concord, New Hampshire, where his wife's home had been.

The new age of reading

It is clear that, with the rise of the middle class and the great increase in the number of readers, a new era dawned at the opening of the nineteenth century in the literatures of Europe. In addition to the histories, the poetry and novels, which for the first time began to attract thousands of readers, newspapers and other periodicals began to take the place of pamphlets. Improvements in the printing press made it possible to print as many as eight hundred pages in an hour,[1] instead of a few score, and so the great age of reading began.

The slow beginning of national education in France and England

This involved more education. In the eighteenth century the mass of the inhabitants of Europe could not read or write. Education was largely in the hands of the clergy and, beyond a grounding in the merest rudiments, was generally confined to the well-to-do. In France, as we have seen,[2] an attempt had been made during the Reign of Terror to establish a national free public-school system, but it was not carried out. In England little was done to improve matters until the second half of the nineteenth century. There had long been Church and endowed schools, which had received some financial support from the government; but in 1870 a system of compulsory free education was introduced, with free public elementary schools in every school district.

Prussian education system

In Prussia a new school system was part of the work of regeneration begun by the group of men around Stein, of whom Karl Wilhelm Humboldt was a distinguished leader. The founding of the University of Berlin in 1810 was one of the most noticeable events in this important movement. Before the opening of the Great War in 1914 the German universities attracted many foreigners. But the attitude of German professors, who have almost without exception supported and loudly defended the atrocious policy of their government, has brought German learning into disrepute among other nations.

[1] This was printed on only one side. Now there are presses which can print almost one hundred thousand newspapers an hour, consuming paper at the rate of seven hundred miles an hour.

[2] See above, p. 246.

QUESTIONS

SECTION 47. Outline the work accomplished by the Treaty of Paris. Describe the work of territorial redistribution in the Congress of Vienna. Give an account of Talleyrand's diplomacy. What was the result of the compromise between Russia and Prussia?

Draw two maps, one showing Europe in 1715, the other, in 1815. Show on a map the colonial possessions gained by England in 1815. Account for the awakening of the spirit of nationality towards the end of the eighteenth century.

SECTION 48. What was the Holy Alliance? Describe Metternich's political aims. Who were the members and what was the purpose of the quadruple alliance formed November 20, 1815?

SECTION 49. What effect did the study of the Greek and Latin classics have upon the style of authors in the eighteenth century? When and how did writers begin to write differently? What is romanticism? Describe Goethe's views.

CHAPTER XIII

EUROPE AFTER THE CONGRESS OF VIENNA

SECTION 50. THE RESTORATION IN FRANCE AND THE REVOLUTION OF 1830

The French do not oppose the restoration of the Bourbons in 1814

When, in 1814, the allies placed on the throne the brother of Louis XVI, a veteran *émigré*, who had openly derided the Revolution and had been intriguing with other European powers for nearly twenty years to gain the French crown, there was no organized opposition to the new king. There had never been a majority in France in favor of a republic. The doctrines of the Jacobins had been held by no more than a vigorous minority. The French were still monarchical at heart.

Louis XVIII is not tempted to undo the work of Napoleon and the Revolution

There was, however, no danger that Louis XVIII would undo the great work of the Revolution and of Napoleon. He was no fanatic like his younger brother, the count of Artois. In his youth he had delighted in Voltaire and the writings of the philosophers; he had little sympathy for the Church party. His sixty years, his corpulence, his gout, and a saving sense of humor prevented him from undertaking any wild schemes for restoring the old régime which might be suggested to him by the emigrant nobles, who now returned to France in great numbers.

The Constitutional Charter granted to France by Louis XVIII. June, 1814

The Constitutional Charter which he issued in June, 1814, was indeed a much more liberal form of government than that which Napoleon had permitted the French to enjoy, and suggested in some ways the English constitution.[1] There was to be a parliament consisting of two chambers — a house of peers chosen by the king, and a chamber of deputies elected

[1] The leading provisions of the Charter are to be found in the *Readings*, Vol. II, p. 2.

by the wealthier citizens. The king alone could propose laws, but the chambers could petition the sovereign to lay before them any measure which they thought desirable.

Some of the "Rights of Man" guaranteed by the charter

In addition to establishing representative government the Charter guaranteed almost all the great principles of reform laid down in the first Declaration of the Rights of Man. It proclaimed that all men were equal before the law and equally eligible to offices in the government and the army; taxation was to be apportioned according to the wealth of each citizen; personal and religious liberty was assured, although the Roman Catholic faith was to be the religion of the State; freedom of the press was guaranteed, but subject to such laws as might be passed for the purpose of checking the abuses of that freedom.

The ultra-royalists led by the count of Artois

Naturally different political parties soon appeared. The reactionary group, known as the ultra-royalists, was composed largely of emigrant nobles and clergy, who wished to undo the work of the past twenty-five years and to restore the old régime in its entirety. They clamored for greater power for the clergy, for the restriction of the liberal press, for the king's absolute control over his ministers, and for the restoration of the property that they had lost during the Revolution. This party, though small in numbers, was composed of zealots, and with the king's brother, the count of Artois, at their head, they formed an active and influential minority.

The moderate royalists

The most valuable and effective support for the king, however, came from a more moderate group of royalists who had learned something during the last quarter of a century. They knew that the age of Louis XVI and Marie Antoinette could not return, and consequently they urged the faithful observance of the Charter, and sought, on the one hand, to induce the reactionary nobility and clergy to accept the results of the Revolution, and, on the other hand, to reconcile the people to the restored monarchy. The two royalist parties — extreme and moderate — doubtless made up the greater portion of the nation.

A third party was composed of liberals, who, though loyal to the king, did not believe the Charter gave as much power to the people as it should. They favored a reduction of the amount of property which a man was required to own in order to vote, and they maintained that the king should be guided by ministers responsible to the parliament. The liberals

Then there was a large group of persons who were irreconcilable enemies of the Bourbons and everything savoring of Bourbonism. Among them were the Bonapartists, soldiers of Napoleon, who remembered the glories of Austerlitz and Wagram and were angered by the prestige suddenly given to hundreds of Frenchmen who had borne arms against their country, but who now crowded around the king to receive offices, rewards, and honors.[1] While Napoleon lived they longed for his return, and after his death in 1821 they placed their hopes upon his youthful son,[2] "Napoleon II," as they called him. The irreconcilables The Bonapartists

On the other hand, there were the republicans, who detested Bonapartism no less than Bourbonism and wished to restore the republic of 1792. The republicans

As long as Louis XVIII lived the party loyal to him grew stronger, and at the time of his death in 1824 the restored Bourbon line seemed to have triumphed completely over its enemies. Had his brother, who succeeded him as Charles X, been equally wise, he too might have retained the throne until his death. But he frankly declared that he would rather chop wood than be king on the same terms as the king of England. During the early years of his reign the clergy and Jesuits exercised a great deal of influence upon the policy of the government, and the nobles, who had been deprived of their lands Views of Charles X (1824–1830)

[1] See *Readings*, Vol. II, p. 6.

[2] The son of Napoleon and Maria Louisa, born in 1811, to whom his father gave the title "King of Rome," was taken to Vienna after Napoleon's overthrow, and given the title of "Duke of Reichstadt." He lived at his grandfather's court until his death in 1832, and is the hero of Rostand's popular drama, *L'Aiglon* (The Eaglet).

II

during the Revolution, were granted a thousand million francs by way of indemnity.

The July ordinances, July 25, 1830

Charles's policy naturally aroused violent antagonism. But he did not heed the warnings, and in July, 1830, determined upon a bold stroke. Acting under a provision of the Charter which empowered him to make regulations for the security of the realm, he and his ministers issued a series of ordinances establishing press censorship, increasing the property qualifications for voters, and confining the proposing of laws to the king.[1] These ordinances practically destroyed the last vestiges of constitutional government and left the French people without any guaranty against absolutism.

The protests of the journalists

The day following the promulgation of the ordinances, July 26, 1830, the Paris journalists published a protest, which became the signal for open resistance to the king. They declared that they would issue their newspapers in spite of the king, and that all citizens were freed from their allegiance by this attack on their rights.

The republicans start an insurrection in Paris, July 27

The revolt, however, which brought about the overthrow of Charles X was the work of the fearless though small republican party which faithfully cherished the traditions of 1792. On July 27 they began tearing up the paving stones for barricades, behind which they could defend themselves in the narrow streets against the police and soldiers.

A new candidate for the throne appears

On July 29 the entire city of Paris was in the hands of the insurgents. The king, now realizing the seriousness of the situation, opened negotiations with the members of the parliament and promised to repeal the obnoxious ordinances. It was, however, too late for concessions; a faction of wealthy

* The picture represents Louis Philippe riding through the streets of Paris after the fighting had ceased, in the revolution of July. He is going from his residence, in the center of the city, to the Hôtel de Ville, or City Hall, where the leading revolutionists, the aged Lafayette at their head, await him. Notice the barricades in the street, formed of paving stones and other obstacles.

[1] See the ordinance against the press, in the *Readings*, Vol. II, p. 11.

Fig. 85. Louis Philippe going to the City Hall, Paris, July, 1830*

FIG. 86. THE MONUMENT TO THE REVOLUTIONISTS OF JULY, 1830*

bankers and business men was busily engaged in an intrigue to place upon the throne Louis Philippe, the son of that duke of Orleans who had supported the reformers in the early days of the first revolution and had finally been executed as a "suspect" during the Reign of Terror. The son had been identified with the Jacobins and had fought in the army of the Republic at Valmy and Jemappes. He was later exiled, and spent some time in England. When he returned to France after the restoration he sought popularity by professing democratic opinions, going about like a plain citizen, and sending his children to ordinary schools instead of employing private tutors. He was therefore the logical candidate of those who wished to preserve the monarchy and yet establish the middle class in power in place of the nobles and clergy.

Charles X abdicates; Louis Philippe appointed lieutenant general

Charles X, despairing of his ability to retain the crown for himself, abdicated in favor of his grandson, the duke of Bordeaux. He then charged Louis Philippe with the task of proclaiming the young duke as King Henry V, and fled with his family to England. Though this arrangement might very well have met the approval of the nation at large, Louis Philippe was not inclined to execute the orders of Charles X. On the contrary he began to seek the favor of the republicans who had done the actual fighting, and who had already formed a provisional government with the aged Lafayette at its head.

This committee occupied the City Hall and was surrounded by the insurgents who supported it. Louis Philippe forced his way through the throng, and, in a conference with Lafayette, won him over to his cause by fair promises. The two men then went out on the balcony and Lafayette embraced his companion before the crowd as a sign of their good understanding,

* This column was erected in memory of those who fell in the street fighting in Paris in July, 1830. It stands on the site of the Bastille, which was torn down after its capture in 1789. The stones of the Bastille were used for bridges and other public works; but when the Paris subway was dug through the square recently the foundations of the old building were found, and are used as walls for a station.

while the duke on his part showed his sympathy for liberal doctrines by waving the tricolored flag, — the banner of the Revolution, — which had not been unfurled in Paris since the last days of Napoleon. The hopes of the republicans who had borne the brunt of the Revolution were now at an end, for they realized that they formed too small a party to prevent Louis Philippe's accession to the throne.[1]

The Chamber of Deputies calls Louis Philippe to the throne

Louis Philippe convoked the Chamber of Deputies on August 3 and announced the abdication of Charles X, carefully omitting any allusion to the fact that the dethroned king had indicated his grandson as his successor. Four days later the Chamber of Deputies passed a resolution — which was ratified by the Chamber of Peers — calling Louis Philippe to the throne as "king of the French"; he accepted their invitation, declaring that "he could not resist the call of his country."

[1] THE BOURBON KINGS

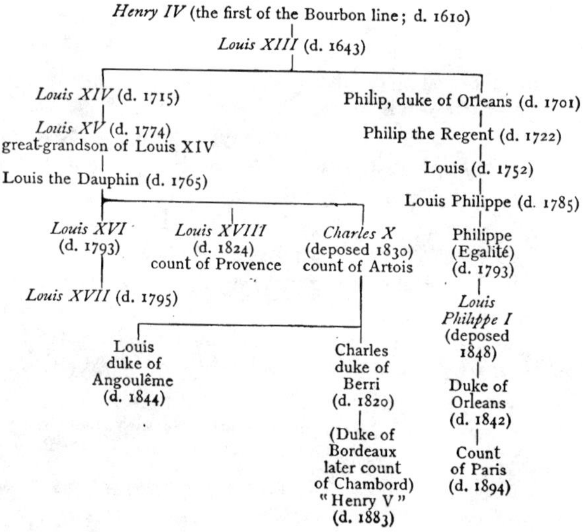

The parliament undertook to make the necessary changes in the existing Charter which Louis XVIII had granted, and required the new king to accept it before his coronation. The preamble of the Charter was suppressed because it wounded national dignity "in appearing to *grant* to Frenchmen the rights which essentially belonged to them." Freedom of the press and the responsibility of the ministers to the parliament were expressly proclaimed. Lastly, the provision establishing the Roman Catholic religion as the religion of the State was stricken out. The Charter is revised

In reality, however, the Revolution of 1830 made few innovations. One king had been exchanged for another who professed more liberal views, but the government was no more democratic than before. The right to vote was still limited to the few wealthy taxpayers, and government by clergy and nobility had given place to government by bankers, speculators, manufacturers, and merchants. The tricolored flag of the Revolution was adopted as the national flag instead of the white banner of the Bourbons, but France was still a monarchy, and the labors of the republicans in organizing the insurrection had gone for naught. The slight results of the Revolution of 1830

Section 51. Establishment of the Kingdom of Belgium

The Revolution of 1830 in France was the signal for an outbreak in the former Austrian Netherlands, where many grievances had developed since the Congress of Vienna had united the region with the Dutch Netherlands under the rule of William of Orange. In the first place, the inhabitants of his southern provinces were dissatisfied with William's government. He had granted a constitution to his entire kingdom on the model of the French Charter, but many people objected to his making the ministers responsible to himself instead of to the parliament, and also to the restricted suffrage which excluded Grievance of the Belgians against the Dutch government all but the well-to-do from the right to vote. Although the southern provinces had over a million more inhabitants than the Dutch portion of the kingdom, they had only an equal number of representatives. Moreover, the Dutch monopolized most of the offices and conducted the government in their own

FIG. 87. PALACE OF JUSTICE AT BRUSSELS

Belgium was for centuries one of the busiest and most thrifty sections of Europe. Its rich, industrial cities, like Brussels, Ghent, Bruges, and Antwerp, were nurseries of democracy during the Middle Ages. The sturdy self-dependence of the Belgians was shown in many wars against their own feudal rulers and neighboring monarchs. This picture shows how the great courthouse at Brussels towers over the roofs of the city. It is not a monument of the old days, however, but of the new kingdom of the nineteenth century

Religious dissensions arise between Protestants and Catholics

interests. There were religious difficulties too. The southern provinces were Catholic, the northern mainly Protestant. The king was a Protestant, and took advantage of his position to convert Catholics to his own faith.[1]

Louis Philippe had been seated on his throne only a few days when the agitation over these grievances broke out into

[1] For the Belgians' statement of their grievances, see *Readings*, Vol. II, p. 14.

open revolt at Brussels. The revolution spread; a provisional government was set up; and on October 4, 1830, it declared: "The province of Belgium, detached from Holland by force, shall constitute an independent state." The declaration was soon followed by the meeting of a congress to establish a permanent form of government. This assembly drew up a constitution based on the idea of the sovereignty of the people, and decided that the head of the new government should be a king constrained by oath to observe the laws adopted by the people. The Belgians were therefore very much in the same position as the English in 1688 when they made William of Orange their king on their own terms. They finally chose as their sovereign Leopold of Coburg, and in July, 1831, he was crowned king of the new state.[1]

The independent kingdom of Belgium is established

Section 52. Formation of the German Confederation

The chief effects of the Napoleonic occupation of Germany were three in number. First, the consolidation of territory that followed the cession of the left bank of the Rhine to France, as explained previously, had done away with the ecclesiastical states, the territories of the knights, and most of the free towns. Only thirty-eight German states, including four free towns, were left when the Congress of Vienna took up the question of forming a confederation to replace the defunct Holy Roman Empire.[2]

Three chief results of Napoleon's influence in Germany

1. Disappearance of most of the little states

[1] The constitution which the Belgians drew up for themselves in 1831, with some modifications, is the basis of their government to-day, and Leopold II, the son of their first king, Leopold I, was their sovereign until 1909, when he was succeeded by his nephew, King Albert.

The loss of Belgium made no important change in the government of the Netherlands. In 1848 King William II was forced to grant his subjects a new and enlightened constitution in place of the charter which he had issued some thirty years before. On the death of William III in 1890 his daughter, Wilhelmina, came to the throne, and as the grand duchy of Luxemburg was hereditary only in the male line it passed to a relative of the deceased king, the duke of Nassau.

[2] The leading provisions of the Act of Confederation are given in the *Readings*, Vol. II, pp. 16 ff.

2. Advantageous position of Prussia

Secondly, the external and internal conditions of Prussia had been so changed as to open the way for it to replace Austria as the controlling power in Germany. A great part of the Slavic possessions seized in the last two partitions of Poland had been lost, but as an indemnity Prussia had received half of the kingdom of Saxony, in the very center of Germany, and also the Rhine provinces on the west, where the people were thoroughly imbued with the revolutionary doctrines that had prevailed in France. Prussia now embraced all the various types of people included in the German nation and was comparatively free from the presence of non-German races. In this respect it offered a marked contrast to the heterogeneous and mongrel population of its great rival, Austria.

The internal changes in Prussia were equally great. The reforms carried out after the battle of Jena by the distinguished minister Stein and his successor, Hardenberg, had done for Prussia somewhat the same service that the first National Assembly had done for France. The abolition of the feudal social castes and the liberation of the serfs made the economic development of the country possible. The reorganization of the whole military system prepared the way for Prussia's victories in 1866 and 1870, which led to the formation of a German Empire under her headship.

3. Demand for constitutional government

Thirdly, the agitations of the Napoleonic Period had aroused the national spirit.[1] The appeal to the people to aid in freeing their country from foreign oppression, and the idea of their participation in a government based upon a written constitution, had produced widespread discontent with the old absolute monarchy.

The German Confederation of 1815

When the form of union for the German states came up for discussion at the Congress of Vienna, two different plans were advocated. Prussia's representatives submitted a scheme for a firm union, in which the representatives chosen by the several states should form a central government and control the individual states in all matters of general interest. This idea was successfully

[1] See above, p. 322.

opposed by Metternich, supported by the other German rulers. Austria realized that her possessions, as a whole, could never be included in any real German union, for even in the western portion of her territory there were many Slavs, while in Hungary and the southern provinces there were practically no Germans at all. On the other hand, she felt that she might be the leader

FIG. 88. NAPOLEON AT THE BATTLE OF JENA
After the picture by Meissonier

in a very loose union in which all the members should be left practically independent. Her ideal of a union of sovereign princes under her own headship was almost completely realized in the constitution adopted.

The German Confederation a union of rulers and free towns

The confederation was not a union of the various *countries* involved, but of "The Sovereign Princes and Free Towns of Germany," including the emperor of Austria and the king of Prussia for such of their possessions as were formerly included in the Holy Roman Empire; the king of Denmark for Holstein;

and the king of the Netherlands for the grand duchy of Luxemburg. The union thus included two sovereigns who were out-and-out foreigners, and, on the other hand, did not include all the possessions of its two most important members.[1]

The insignificant diet at Frankfort

The assembly of the confederation was a diet which met at Frankfort. It was composed (as was perfectly logical) not of representatives of the people, but of plenipotentiaries of the rulers who were members of the confederation. The diet had very slight powers, for it could not interfere in the domestic affairs of the states, and the delegates who composed it could not vote as they pleased, since they had to obey the instructions of the rulers who appointed them, and refer all important questions to their respective sovereigns. So powerless and so dilatory was this assembly that it became the laughingstock of Europe.

Weakness of the German union

The members of the confederation reserved to themselves the right of forming alliances of all kinds, but pledged themselves to make no agreement threatening the safety of the union or of any of its members, and not to make war upon any member of the confederation on any pretense whatsoever. The constitution could not be amended without the approval of *all* the governments concerned. In spite of its obvious weaknesses, the confederation of 1815 lasted for half a century, until Prussia finally (in 1866) expelled Austria from the union by arms, and began the formation of the later German federation.

Political associations of German students

The liberal and progressive party in Germany was much disappointed by the failure of the Congress of Vienna to weld Germany into a really national state. The university students denounced the reactionary party in their meetings, and drank to the freedom of Germany. On October 18, 1817, they held a celebration in the Wartburg to commemorate both Luther's revolt[2] and the anniversary of the battle of Leipzig. Speeches were made in honor of the brave who had fallen in the war against Napoleon.

[1] Observe the boundary of the German Confederation as indicated on the map, pp. 318–319.

[2] The tercentenary of the outbreak.

This innocent burst of enthusiasm excited great anxiety in the minds of the conservative statesmen of Europe, of whom Metternich was, of course, the leader. The murder by a fanatical student of a newspaper man, Kotzebue, who was supposed to have influenced the Tsar to desert his former liberal policy, cast further discredit upon the liberal party. It also gave Metternich an opportunity to emphasize the terrible results which he anticipated would come from the students' associations, liberal governments, and the freedom of the press.

The murder of Kotzebue

Metternich called together the representatives of the larger states of the confederation at Carlsbad in August, 1819. Here a series of resolutions were drawn up with the aim of checking the free expression of opinions in newspapers and universities hostile to existing institutions, and of discovering and bringing to justice the revolutionists who were supposed to exist in dangerous numbers. These "Carlsbad Resolutions" were laid before the diet of the confederation by Austria and adopted, though not without protest.[1]

The "Carlsbad Resolutions," 1819

The attack upon the freedom of the press, and especially the interference with the liberty of teaching in the great institutions of learning, which were already beginning to pride themselves on their scholarship and science, scandalized some of the progressive spirits in Germany; yet no successful protest was raised, and Germany as a whole acquiesced for a generation in Metternich's system of discouraging reform of all kinds.

Nevertheless, important progress was made in southern Germany. As early as 1818 the king of Bavaria granted his people a constitution in which he stated their rights and admitted them to a share in the government by establishing a parliament. His example was followed within two years by the rulers of Baden, Würtemberg, and Hesse. Another change was the gradual formation of a customs union, which permitted goods to be sent freely from one German state to another without the payment of duties at each boundary line. This

The southern German states receive constitutions, 1818–1820

Formation of a customs union — *Zollverein* — with Prussia at its head

[1] See *Readings*, Vol. II, p. 20, for the "Carlsbad Resolutions."

yielded some of the advantages of a political union. This economic confederation, of which Prussia was the head and from which Austria was excluded, was a harbinger of the future German Empire (see Chapter XVIII, below).

Section 53. Restoration in Spain and Italy

State of Spain under Joseph Bonaparte

The restoration in Spain after Napoleon's downfall was more thoroughgoing than in any other country involved in the revolutionary conflicts. Napoleon's efforts to keep his brother Joseph on the Spanish throne had led to a war which brought misery and demoralization upon the country until the autumn of 1812, when Wellington drove the French invaders over the Pyrenees. During this entire period the Spanish people steadily resisted French dominion and maintained the semblance of an independent government.

The Cortes, or parliament, was loyal to the dethroned Bourbon, Ferdinand VII, but it took advantage of his absence to draw up a liberal constitution in 1812.

Ferdinand VII abolishes the constitution

When Ferdinand VII (who had spent the previous six years in France surrounded by Napoleon's guards) was, in 1814, restored to power by the strength of English arms, he repudiated entirely this liberal government. He declared that the Cortes which had drawn up this instrument had usurped his rights by imposing on his people "an anarchical and seditious constitution based on the democratic principles of the French Revolution." He accordingly annulled it and proclaimed those who continued to support it guilty of high treason and worthy of death.[1] With the old absolute government, he restored the Inquisition, feudal privileges, and the religious orders. The Jesuits returned, the books and newspapers were strictly censored, free speech was repressed, monastic property was returned to the former owners, and the liberals were imprisoned in large numbers or executed.

[1] This manifesto is printed in the *Readings*, Vol. II, p. 23.

Turning to Italy, we find that the Congress of Vienna had left it, as Metternich observed, merely "a geographical expression"; it had no political unity whatever. Lombardy and Venetia, in the northern part, were in the hands of Austria, while Parma, Modena, and Tuscany belonged to members of the Austrian family. In the south the considerable kingdom of Naples was ruled over by a branch of the Spanish Bourbons. In the center, cutting the peninsula in twain, were the Papal States, which extended north to the Po. The presence of Austria, and the apparent impossibility of inducing the Pope to submit to any government but his own, seemed to preclude all hope of making Italy into a true nation. Italy only "a geographical expression" after 1815

Although Napoleon had governed Italy despotically, he had introduced many important reforms. The vestiges of the feudal régime had vanished at his approach; he had established an orderly administration and had forwarded public improvements. But his unscrupulous use of Italy to advance his personal ambitions disappointed those who at first had received him with enthusiasm, and they came to look eagerly for his downfall. Reforms introduced in Italy during the Napoleonic occupation

The king of Sardinia, Victor Emmanuel I, entered his capital of Turin on May 20, 1814, amid great rejoicing, but immediately proceeded to destroy with a stroke of his pen all the reforms which the Revolution had accomplished in Piedmont during his absence. He gave back to the nobility their ancient feudal rights; he restored to the clergy their property, their courts, and their press censorship; religious freedom was suppressed. Abolition of reforms in Piedmont

The same policy was adopted in the States of the Church, where, in 1814, an edict was issued which swept away French legislation and restored the old order. In the zeal to destroy the work of the French, root and branch, vaccination and street lighting at Rome were abolished as revolutionary innovations. The clergy resume the temporal power in the Papal States

In Lombardy and Venetia, where Austrian sovereignty was established, the reforms instituted during the Napoleonic Period were practically nullified. In order to fasten securely their The Austrian possessions in Italy government on these provinces, the Austrians set up a public and secret police system, which constantly interfered with individual liberty in the most arbitrary fashion.

Austrian influence in Italy

In addition to his Lombardo-Venetian kingdom in the northern part of Italy, the Austrian emperor enjoyed a protectorate over Modena; by treaty the duke of Tuscany practically surrendered his duchy to him; Maria Louisa of Parma turned the administration of her domain over to his officers; and Ferdinand of Naples was bound to him in a defensive and offensive alliance. In short, only Sardinia and the Papal States retained their freedom from "German" domination.

The work of the French not entirely undone

Though dismembered and subjected to a foreign yoke, the Italy of 1815 was not the Italy which Napoleon had found when he first entered it at the head of the French army in 1796. Despite the restoration, traces of the Revolution were everywhere apparent, not only in law and government but, above all, in the minds of men. National aspirations had been awakened which the Austrian police could not stamp out; Italians, high and low, came to know and appreciate French reforms at first hand, though they might loathe the memory of Napoleon as a conqueror and a tyrant.

Section 54. The Spanish-American Colonies and the Revolution of 1820

The very thoroughness with which Metternich's ideas were carried out in Spain and Italy led to renewed attempts on the part of the liberals to abolish despotism. It was not, therefore, in Germany or France, as the allies had feared, but in Spain and then in Italy, that the spirit of revolution was first to reawaken.

Spain itself was, of course, but a small part of the vast Spanish empire, which included Mexico (and the regions to the northwest later acquired by the United States), Central America, and large portions of South America, besides her island possessions. The Spanish colonies had from the first been the victims of the selfish commercial policy of the mother country, which forced them to carry on all their trade with one or two favored Spanish ports. The success of the North American colonies in throwing off the yoke of England suggested ideas of independence to the Spanish colonies. These suddenly broke out into revolt when the news reached the colonies that

The Spanish colonies in North and South America begin to dream of independence

FIG. 89. BOLIVAR

Napoleon had placed his brother on the Spanish throne and proposed to control the Spanish commerce in his own interests.

Revolt of the Spanish colonies, 1810–1825

Beginning in 1810, the colonies of Mexico, New Granada (now Colombia), Venezuela, Peru, Buenos Ayres, and Chile, while they still professed to be loyal to Ferdinand VII, took their government into their own hands, drove out the former Spanish agents, and finally rejected Spanish rule altogether. At first the revolt was put down with great cruelty, but in 1817, under the leadership of Bolivar, Venezuela won its independence, and during the following five years the Spaniards lost

New Granada, Peru, Ecuador, Çhile, Mexico, and lastly (1825) Upper Peru, which was renamed Bolivia after its liberator.

England opposes reconquest of the Spanish colonies

Ever since his restoration Ferdinand VII had been sending thousands of men to die of fever and wounds in the vain attempt to subdue the insurgents. He had called upon the other powers to help him, on the ground that his colonies were guilty of revolutionary crimes which it was to the interest of all the allied monarchs to aid in suppressing. He was disappointed however. England did not wish to lose the trade which had grown up with South American ports since they were freed from the restrictions of the mother country.

Restoration of the constitution of 1812 in Spain, 1820

At last, in January, 1820, the soldiers who were waiting in Cadiz to be sent to America, well aware of the sufferings of the regiments which had preceded them, were easily aroused to revolt by two adventurous officers. The revolutionists proclaimed the restoration of the constitution of 1812, which Ferdinand had abolished on his return. Their call was answered by the liberals in the larger towns, including Madrid, where a mob surrounded the palace (March 9), and forced the king to take the oath to the constitution of 1812.

News of the Spanish revolution reaches Italy

News of the Spanish revolt spread quickly throughout Italy, where the spirit of insurrection had been at work among the secret societies which had everywhere been organized. By far the most noted of these was that which called itself the Carbonari, that is, charcoal burners. Its objects were constitutional government and national independence and unity. When the Neapolitans heard that the king of Spain had been forced by an insurrection to accept a constitution, they made the first attempt on the part of the Italian people to gain constitutional liberty by compelling their king (July, 1820) to agree to accept this same Spanish constitution of 1812. The king, however, at once began to cast about for foreign assistance to suppress the revolution and enable him to return to his former ways.

He had not long to wait. The alert Metternich invited Russia, Prussia, France, and England to unite, in order to check the development of "revolt and crime." "Revolution" appeared to him and his sympathizers as a fearful disease that not only destroyed those whom it attacked directly, but spread contagion wherever it appeared. Therefore prompt and severe measures of quarantine were justified, in view of the necessity of stamping out the devastating plague.

Metternich regards revolution as a terrible disease

A conference was called in January, 1821,[1] for the purpose of taking practical measures to restore absolutism in southern Italy. To this conference King Ferdinand of Naples was summoned, and once safely away from the reformers, he heartily concurred in the plan to send an Austrian army to Naples to abolish the noxious constitution. The leaders of the revolt were executed, imprisoned, or exiled, and the king was freed from the embarrassments of the constitution.

Austrian intervention in Italy

Meanwhile the revolution in Spain had developed into a civil war, and the representatives of the great powers, Russia, Austria, Prussia, France, and England, met at Verona in 1822 to discuss their common interests and decide what should be done about the Spanish crisis.[2] England refused to interfere in any way; so finally it was left to Louis XVIII, urged on by the clerical and ultra-royalist party, to send an army across the Pyrenees "with the purpose of maintaining a descendant of Henry IV on the throne of Spain." This interference in the affairs of a neighboring nation which was struggling for constitutional government disgusted the French liberals, who saw that France, in intervening in favor of Ferdinand VII, was doing just what Prussia and Austria had attempted in 1792 in the interests of Louis XVI. But, unlike the duke of Brunswick, the French commander easily defeated the revolutionists and placed Ferdinand in a position to stamp out his enemies in such a ferocious and bloodthirsty manner that his French allies were heartily ashamed of him.

The Congress of Verona, 1822

France aids Ferdinand VII to suppress reform, 1823–1825

While France was helping to restore absolutism in Spain the Spanish colonies, as we have seen, were rapidly winning their

[1] It met at Laibach. [2] See *Readings*, Vol. II, p. 38.

II

Question of the revolted Spanish colonies

independence, encouraged by the United States and England. At the Congress of Verona all the powers except England were anxious to discuss a plan by which they might aid Spain to get the better of her rebellious colonies, since it was the fixed purpose of the allies to suppress "rebellion in whatever place and under whatever form it might show itself."

The Monroe Doctrine

The threats of Metternich and his friends led President Monroe, in his message to Congress, December, 1823, to call attention to the dangers of intervention as practiced by the European alliance of great powers, and clearly state what has since become famous as the "Monroe Doctrine,"[1] namely, that the United States would consider any attempt on the part of the European allies to extend their system to any portion of this hemisphere as dangerous to the peace and safety of the United States and as an unfriendly act.

England recognizes the independence of some Spanish colonies

About the same time the English foreign secretary, Canning, informed the French ambassador in London that any attempt to bring the Spanish colonies again under their former submission to Spain would prove unsuccessful; and that while England would remain neutral in the troubles between the mother country and her American dominions, it would not tolerate the intervention of a third party. Toward the close of 1824 England recognized the independence of Buenos Ayres, Mexico, and Colombia, and paid no heed to the remonstrance of the continental powers that such an action "tended to encourage the revolutionary spirit which it had been found so difficult to restrain in Europe."

Portugal

A word may be said here of Spain's little neighbor Portugal. It will be remembered that when Napoleon dispatched his troops thither in 1807 the royal family fled across the Atlantic to their colony of Brazil. After the expulsion of the French by the English, the government was placed in the hands of an English general, Beresford, who ruled so despotically that

[1] See *Readings*, Vol. II, p. 42, for an extract from President Monroe's famous message.

he stirred up a revolt in 1820, at the time when the insurrection in Spain was in progress. The insurgents demanded the return of the royal family from Brazil and the granting of a constitution. The king, John VI, accordingly set sail for Portugal, leaving his elder son, Pedro, to represent him in Brazil.[1]

Metternich's international police system fails

It will have become apparent that Metternich's international police system, designed to prevent innovation and revolution, was for all practical purposes a failure. The action of Great Britain and the United States had weakened it. The struggle of the Greek revolutionists against Turkey for independence,[2] which finally involved Russia in a war with the Sultan and ended in victory for the Greeks, demonstrated that even Russia would not hesitate to aid and abet revolution if she could thereby advance her own interests. The climax was reached in 1830 by the revolution in France described above, which deposed the older Bourbon line and established a liberal government, thus violating the principles for which Metternich had fought with so much determination. In fact, the Holy Alliance, as such, never accomplished any great work, and it went to pieces as much through its own inherent weakness as through the growth of revolutionary spirit.

QUESTIONS

SECTION 50. Account for the fact that the French people did not oppose the restoration of 1814. Describe the Constitutional Charter granted to France, June, 1814. Account for the origin of political parties in France. State the principles for which they stood.

Contrast the political views of Charles X with those of his brother Louis XVIII. What were the July ordinances? Describe the way in which Louis Philippe secured the title of king. Give the terms of the revised Charter. What gains were made by the Revolution of 1830?

[1] In 1822 Pedro proclaimed the independence of Brazil and took the title of emperor. In 1831 he abdicated in favor of his son, who retained the crown until he was deposed by the revolution of 1889, which established the United States of Brazil as a republic.

[2] See below, p. 577.

SECTION 51. State the objections of the Belgians to the Dutch government. Describe the government established in the new kingdom of Belgium.

SECTION 52. What were the most important results of Napoleon's influence in Germany? What plans for German union were discussed in the Congress of Vienna? What objections were made to any of these plans? Describe the plan adopted in the German Confederation of 1815. Point out the weaknesses of this union. Mention two important changes in the government of the German states during the first quarter of the nineteenth century.

SECTION 53. Describe the condition of Spain from 1812 to the restoration of Ferdinand VII. Draw a map showing the territory held by Austria in Italy. What was the kingdom of Sardinia?

SECTION 54. Describe the revolt of the Spanish-American colonies. In what way did Spain regain the constitution of 1812? What was the effect of the Spanish revolt upon the people of Italy? What hindrances were placed in the way of constitutional government in Spain from 1823 to 1825?

Who was Bolivar? What is the Monroe Doctrine? When and why was it first stated? Give a brief outline of the history of Portugal from 1807 to the restoration of the House of Braganza.

CHAPTER XIV

THE INDUSTRIAL REVOLUTION

SECTION 55. INVENTION OF MACHINERY FOR SPINNING AND WEAVING

The Industrial Revolution due to mechanical inventions

In the preceding chapters we have reviewed the startling changes and reforms introduced by the leaders of the French Revolution and by Napoleon Bonaparte, and the reconstruction of Europe at the Congress of Vienna. These were mainly the work of statesmen, warriors, and diplomats — who have certainly done their part in making Europe what it is to-day. But a still more fundamental revolution than that which has been described had begun in England before the meeting of the Estates General.

The chief actors in this never stirred an assembly by their fiery denunciation of abuses, or led an army to victory, or conducted a clever diplomatic negotiation. On the contrary, their attention was concentrated upon the homely operations of everyday life — the housewife drawing out her thread with distaff or spinning wheel, the slow work of the weaver at his primitive loom, the miner struggling against the water which threatened to flood his mine. They busied themselves perseveringly with wheels, cylinders, bands, and rollers, patiently combining and recombining them, until, after many discouragements, they made discoveries destined to alter the habits, ideas, and prospects of the great mass of the people far more profoundly than all the edicts of the National Assembly and all the conquests of Napoleon taken together.

The Greeks and Romans, notwithstanding their refined civilization, had, as has been pointed out, shown slight aptitude for

Few new inventions added to the old stock before the eighteenth century

mechanical invention, and little had been added to their stock of human appliances before the middle of the eighteenth century. Up to that time the people of western Europe for the most part continued to till their fields, weave their cloth, and saw and plane their boards by hand, much as the ancient Egyptians had done. Merchandise was still transported in slow, lumbering carts, and letters were as long in passing from London to Rome as in the reign of Constantine. Could a peasant, a smith, or a weaver of the age of Cæsar Augustus have visited France or England eighteen hundred years later, he would have recognized the familiar flail, forge, distaff, and hand loom of his own day.

FIG. 90. DISTAFF AND SPINDLE

Suddenly, however, a series of ingenious devices were invented, which in a few generations eclipsed the achievements of ages and revolutionized every branch of business. This *Industrial Revolution* serves to explain the world in which we live, with its busy cities, its gigantic factories filled with complicated machinery, its commerce and vast fortunes, its trade-unions and labor parties, its bewildering variety of plans for bettering the lot of the great mass of the people. This story of mechanical invention is in no way inferior in importance to the more familiar history of kings, parliaments, wars, treaties, and constitutions.

Improvements in spinning and weaving

The revolution in manufacture which has taken place in the last hundred and fifty years can be illustrated by the improvement in making cloth, which is so necessary to our comfort and welfare. In order to produce cloth one must first *spin* (that is, twist) the wool, cotton, or flax into thread; then by means of a loom the thread can be *woven* into a fabric. A simple way of spinning thread was discovered thousands of years ago, but it was possible by the old methods for a person to make only a single thread at a time.[1] By 1767 James Hargreaves, an English spinner, invented what was called a spinning jenny, which enabled a single workman, by turning a wheel, to spin eight or ten threads at once, and thus do the work of eight or ten spinners. A year later a barber, Richard Arkwright,[2] patented a device for drawing out thread by means of rollers, and made a large fortune — for his time — by establishing a great factory filled with power-driven machines. In 1779 Samuel Crompton made a happy combination of Hargreaves's spinning jenny and Arkwright's roller machine, which was called the mule. Before the end of the eighteenth century, machines spinning two hundred threads simultaneously had been invented, and as they were driven by power and required only one or two watchers, the hand workers could by no means

FIG. 91. THE FIRST SPINNING JENNY

1 The hand spinner had bunches of wool, which had been combed into loose curls, on the end of a stick, or distaff, and then pulled and twisted this with her fingers into a yarn, which she wound on the spindle (see Fig. 90). By whirling the spindle around she could help twist. The spinning wheel was invented to give a better twist to the spindle. It was used by our great-grandmothers, and became common in the sixteenth and seventeenth centuries. By means of the spinning wheel it was possible in some cases for one person to make two threads, one in one hand and the other in the other.

2 See picture opposite page 366. Arkwright is often spoken of as the founder of the factory system. He was not only an inventor but also a clever business man, and knew how to make large profits from the machines he set up.

compete with them. Such inventions as these produced the factory system of manufacture.

The power loom and cotton gin

The enormous output of thread and yarn on these new machines made the weavers dissatisfied with the clumsy old hand loom, which had been little changed for many centuries until the eighteenth century. At length, in 1738, John Kay invented a fly shuttle, a contrivance by which the weaver, without

FIG. 92. SPINNING MULE

This huge frame is in principle much like Hargreaves's, though now the long row of spindles — which the boy is touching — moves in and out instead of the spinner with the wool. The combed wool is held on the frame behind, to be pulled out and spun from the spindle tops

any assistant, could drive the shuttle to and fro, by means of a handle placed conveniently near his stool. This improved hand loom was in use during the entire eighteenth century, although in 1784 Dr. Cartwright, a clergyman of Kent, patented a new loom, which automatically threw the shuttle and shifted the weft. Cartwright's self-acting loom, however, did not supplant the hand loom for almost fifty years, when its mechanism was so perfected that the hand workers could no longer compete with it. It was steadily improved during the nineteenth century until now a single machine watched by one workman can do as much weaving in a day as two hundred weavers could do with old-fashioned hand looms. Other inventions followed. The time required for bleaching was reduced from several months to a few days by the use of acids, instead of relying principally upon the sunlight. In 1792 Eli Whitney, in the United States, invented a power "gin," which enabled one man to take the seeds out of over a thousand pounds of cotton a day instead of five or six pounds, which had been the limit for the hand worker.

The effect of these inventions in increasing the amount of cloth manufactured was astonishing. In 1764 England imported only about four million pounds of raw cotton, but by 1841 she was using nearly five hundred million pounds annually. At the close of the Napoleonic wars Robert Owen, a distinguished manufacturer and philanthropist (see below), declared that his two thousand workmen at New Lanark could do as much work with the new machinery which had been invented during the past forty years as all the operators of Scotland could do without it.

Section 56. The Steam Engine

Iron and power necessary for the development of machinery

In order that inventions could further develop and become widely useful, two things were necessary: In the first place, there must be available a sufficiently strong material out of which to construct the machinery, and for this purpose iron and steel have, with few exceptions, proved the most satisfactory. In the second place, some adequate power had to be found to propel the machinery, which is ordinarily too heavy to be run by hand or foot. Of course windmills were common, and waterfalls and running streams had long been used to turn water wheels, but these forces were too restricted and uncertain to suffice for the rapid development of machinery which resulted from the beginnings we have described. Consequently while Arkwright, Hargreaves, and Crompton were successfully solving the problem of new methods of spinning and weaving, other inventors were improving the ways of melting and forging iron for the machines and of using steam to run them.

Although iron had been used for tools, weapons, and armor for hundreds of years, the processes of reducing the iron from the ore and of working it up were very crude. It was not until 1750 that coal began to be used instead of charcoal for melting, or softening, the metal. The old-fashioned bellows gave way to new ways of producing the blast necessary for melting iron, and steam hammers were invented to pound out the iron instead of doing it by hand.

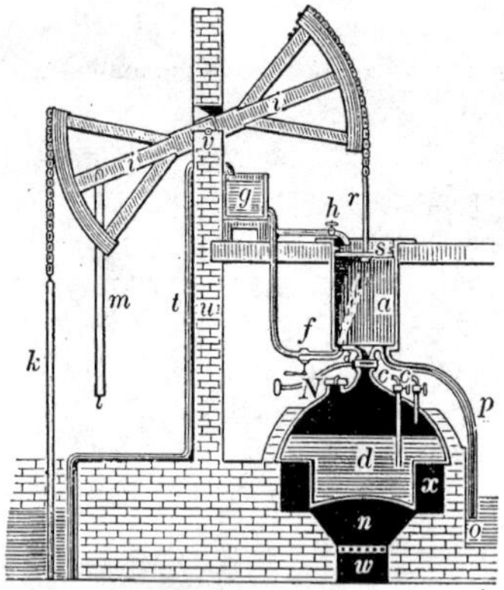

FIG. 93. NEWCOMEN'S STEAM ENGINE

Newcomen's steam engines were run by condensing the steam in the cylinder (*a*) by cold water (*g*), so that the air on the piston (*s*) pressed it down on the vacuum. Watt covered both ends of the cylinder and used steam instead of air to push the piston

Contrary to popular impression, James Watt did not invent the steam engine. Important parts of the engine — the boiler, the cylinder, and the piston — had been invented before he was born, and crude engines had been employed for a long time in pumping water. Indeed, Watt's interest in the steam engine seems to have been awakened first during the winter of 1763–1764, when, as an instrument maker in Glasgow, he was called upon to repair the model of a steam engine which had been invented sixty years before by an ingenious mechanic named Newcomen. Watt, however, was a brilliant and industrious experimenter, and, building upon the work of Newcomen and other men, he was able to make the steam engine a practical machine for furnishing power to the new factories. In 1785 the steam engine was first applied to run spinning machinery in a factory in Nottinghamshire. Arkwright adopted

FIG. 94. JAMES WATT

Watt was enabled to make his invention a success by securing the financial support of a rich iron manufacturer of Birmingham. The firm to Boulton and Watt soon supplied most of the engines for the whole country. Their first use was as a pump in the mines

it in 1790, and by the end of the century steam engines were becoming as common as wind and water mills.

The Industrial Revolution in France

England was the first country to develop the modern use of machinery for manufacturing. It was not until after the establishment of peace in 1815 that the Industrial Revolution really began in France. Napoleon endeavored to foster and protect French industries and stimulate the employment of machinery in manufacturing; but in spite of his best efforts, French industry remained in a backward state. On the eve of his downfall there was only one small steam engine employed in French industry — at a cotton factory in Alsace; but by 1847 France had nearly five thousand steam engines with a capacity of sixty thousand horse power. Germany was also much behind England.

The consumption of raw cotton was multiplied fivefold in thirty years, and in 1847 there were over one hundred thousand spinning machines with three and a half million spindles at work. By 1848 France had many important manufacturing centers. Paris alone had three hundred and forty-two thousand working people, and other cities, such as Lyons, Marseilles, Lille, Bordeaux, and Toulouse, had their great factories and whole quarters peopled by factory laborers. And the working class had begun by that time to form unions and organize strikes against their employers for the purpose of increasing wages and reducing the hours of labor.

Section 57. Capitalism and the Factory System

The "domestic system" of industry

Having seen how machinery was introduced into England in the latter part of the eighteenth century and how steam came to be utilized as a motive power, we have now to consider the important results of these inventions in changing the conditions under which people lived and worked. Up to this time the term "manufacture" still meant, as it did in the original Latin (*manu facere*), "to make by hand." Artisans carried on trades with their own tools in their own homes or in small shops, as the cobbler does to-day. Instead of working with hundreds of others in great factories and being entirely dependent upon his wages, the artisan, in England at least, was often able to give some attention to a small garden plot, from which he derived a part of his support. This "domestic system," as it is called, is graphically described by the journalist Defoe, as he observed it in Yorkshire during a journey through England in 1724–1726:

Defoe's description of Yorkshire artisans about 1725

"The land was divided into small enclosures of from two acres to six or seven acres each, seldom more, every three or four pieces having a house belonging to them; hardly a house standing out of speaking distance from another. We could see at every house a tenter and on almost every tenter a piece of cloth, or kersie, or shalloon. At every considerable house there was a manufactory. Every clothier keeps one horse at least to carry his manufactures to market, and every one generally keeps a cow or two, or more, for his family. By this means the small pieces of enclosed land about each house are occupied, for they scarce sow corn [that is, grain] enough to feed their poultry. The houses are full of lusty fellows, some at their dye vat, some at their looms, others dressing the cloth; the women and children carding or spinning, all being employed from the youngest to the eldest."

Principle of the "factory system"

As the Industrial Revolution progressed, these hand workers found themselves unable to compete with the swift and tireless machines. Manufacturing on a small scale with the simple old tools and appliances became increasingly unprofitable. The workers had to leave their cottages and spend their days in great factories established by capitalists who had enough money to erect the huge buildings and install in them the elaborate and costly machinery and the engines to run it.

Chief results of the introduction of machinery

1. Division of labor

One of the principal results of this factory system[1] is that it makes possible a minute division of labor. Instead of working at the whole process, each worker concentrates his attention upon a single stage of it, and by repeating a simple set of motions over and over again acquires wonderful dexterity. At the same time the apprenticeship is shortened, because each separate task is comparatively simple. Moreover the invention of new machinery is increased, because the very subdivision of the process into simple steps often suggests some way of substituting mechanical action for that of the human hand.

[1] For an account of the way in which Arkwright founded the factory system, see *Readings*, Vol. II, p. 63.

2. Examples of the increased production of goods by machinery

An example of the greatly increased output rendered possible by the use of machinery and the division of labor is given by the distinguished Scotch economist, Adam Smith, whose great work, *The Wealth of Nations*, appeared in 1776. Speaking of the manufacture of a pin in his own time, Adam Smith says: "To make the head requires two or three distinct operations; to put it on is a peculiar business, to whiten the pin is another. It is even a trade by itself to put them into the paper, and the important business of making a pin is, in this manner, divided into about eighteen distinct operations." By this division, he adds, ten persons can make upwards of forty-eight thousand pins in a day. This was when machinery was in its infancy. A recent writer reports that an English machine now makes one hundred and eighty pins a minute, cutting the wire, flattening the heads, sharpening the points, and dropping the pins into their proper places. In a single factory which he visited seven million pins were made in a day, and three men were all that were required to manage the mechanism.

Printing

Another example of modern mechanical work is found in printing. For several centuries after Gutenberg printed his first book, the type was set by hand, inked by hand, each sheet of paper was laid by hand upon the type and then printed by means of a press operated by a hand lever. Nowadays our newspapers, in the great cities at least, are printed almost altogether by machinery, from the setting up of the type until they are dropped, complete, and counted out by hundreds, at the bottom of a rotary press. The paper is fed into the press from a great roll and is printed on both sides and folded at the rate of five hundred or more newspapers a minute.

3. Growth of great manufacturing towns

Before the coming of machinery, industry was not concentrated in a few great cities, but was scattered more or less evenly over the country in the hands of small masters, or independent workmen, who combined manufacturing with agriculture on a small scale. For example, the metal workers of West Bromwich and the cutlers of Sheffield (already famous

FIG. 95. RICHARD ARKWRIGHT

Arkwright was one of the first men to acquire wealth from the use of machinery in the factories, and so is sometimes termed the father of the Factory System

Fig. 96. Adam Smith

in Chaucer's day) lived in cottages with small plots of land around them, and in dull seasons, or to change their occupation, engaged in gardening. The factory system put an end to all this. The workmen now had to live near their work; long rows of houses, without gardens or even grassplots, were hastily built around the factory buildings, and thus the ugly tenement districts of our cities came into existence.

4. Appearance of a capitalist class

This great revolution in the methods of manufacturing produced also a sharp distinction between two classes of men involved. There were, on the one hand, the capitalists who owned the buildings and all the mechanism, and, on the other, the workmen whom they hired to operate the machines. Previous to the eighteenth century those who owned large estates had been, on the whole, the most important class in political and social life. But, alongside of the landed aristocracy, a powerful mercantile class had arisen, whose wealth, gained by commerce and trade, gave them influence in the affairs of the nation.[1] With the improvements in machinery there was added the new class of modern capitalists, who amassed fortunes by establishing great manufacturing industries.[2]

5. The workman becomes dependent upon the capitalist

The workingman necessarily became dependent upon the few who were rich enough to set up factories. He could no longer earn a livelihood in the old way by conducting a small shop to suit himself. The capitalist owned and controlled the necessary machinery, and so long as there were plenty of workmen seeking employment in order to earn their daily bread, the owner could fix a low wage and long hours. While an individual employee of special ability might himself become a capitalist, the ordinary workman would have to remain a workman. The question of the proportion of the product which should

[1] See Defoe's description of eighteenth-century merchant princes, *Readings*, Vol. II, p. 67.

[2] The industrial capitalist began to appear even before the days of Arkwright and Watt, for there were employers earlier, who in some cases collected ten, twenty, or more looms in a town and employed workmen who had no tools of their own, thus creating something like the later factory system.

Problem of labor vs. capital

go to the workers, and that which may properly be taken by the capitalist, or manager, who makes a successful business possible, lies at the basis of the great problem of capital and labor.

6. Women and children in the factories

The destruction of the domestic system of industry had also a revolutionary effect upon the work and the lives of women and children. In all except the heaviest of the mechanical industries, such as ironworking or shipbuilding, the introduction of simple machines tended greatly to increase the number of women and children employed compared with the men. For example, in the textile industry in England during the fifty years from 1841 to 1891, the number of males employed increased fifty-three per cent, and the number of females two hundred and twenty-one per cent. Before the invention of the steam engine, when the simple machines were worked by hand, children could be employed only in some of the minor processes such as preparing the cotton for spinning. But in the modern factory labor is largely confined to watching machines, piecing broken threads, and working levers, so that both women and children can be utilized as effectively as men, and much more cheaply.

The Industrial Revolution relieves some women of their former duties

Doubtless the women were by no means idle under the old system of domestic industry, but their tasks were varied and performed at home, whereas under the new system they must flock to the factory at the call of the whistle, and labor monotonously at a speed set by the foreman. This led to many grave abuses which, as we shall see,[1] the State has been called upon to remedy by factory legislation, which has served to save the women and children from some of the worst hardships, although a great deal still remains to be done. On the other hand, thousands of women belonging to the more fortunate classes have been relieved of many of the duties which devolved upon the housewife in the eighteenth century, when many things were made at home which can now be better and more cheaply produced on a large scale.

[1] See below, p. 512.

to the prosperous middle class of merchants and manufacturers, and they assumed that their doctrines were not only sound and productive of the greatest happiness, but partook of the character of "natural laws" which could not be broken by governments or by organizations of workingmen without disastrous consequences.

Sad results of the Industrial Revolution

The chief trouble with this political economy was that it did not work well in practice. On the contrary, the great manufacturing cities, instead of being filled with happy and prosperous people, became the homes of a small number of capitalists who had grown rich as the owners and directors of the factories and multitudes of poor working people with no other resources than their wages, which were often not enough to keep their families from starvation. Little children under nine years of age working from twelve to fifteen hours a day and women forced to leave their homes to tend the machines in the factories were now replacing the men workers. After their long day's work they returned to miserable tenements in which they were forced to live.

Attempts to secure laws to help the working classes

After the close of the Napoleonic wars as things got worse rather than better, there were increasing signs of discontent in England. This led to various attempts to improve matters. On the one hand there were those who hoped to secure reforms by extending the right to vote, in order that the working classes might be represented in Parliament and so have laws passed to remedy the worst evils at least. In this movement some of the wealthier class often joined, but the working people were naturally chiefly interested and they embodied their ideas of reform in a great "people's charter," which is described below in Chapter XXI.

Origin of trade-unions

In addition to this attempt to secure reform by political action, the workingmen formed unions of their own in the various trades and industries, in order to protect themselves by dealing in a body with their employers. This trade-union movement is one of the most important things in modern times. It began in the early part of the nineteenth century.[1] At first the formation of unions was forbidden by English law, and it was regarded as a crime for workingmen to combine together to raise wages. Men were sentenced to imprisonment or deportation as convicts because they joined such "combinations," or unions. In 1824 Parliament repealed this harsh law, and trade-unions increased rapidly. They were hampered, however, by various restrictions, and even now, although they have spread widely all over the world, people are by no means agreed as to whether workingmen's unions are the best means of improving the conditions of the laboring classes.

Socialism

The third general plan for permanently bettering the situation of the working people is what is known as socialism. As this has played a great rôle in the history of Europe during the past fifty years we must stop to examine the meaning of this word.

Section 58. The Rise of Socialism

The social ownership of the means of production

Socialism teaches that "the means of production" should belong to society and not be held as the private property of individuals. "The means of production" is a very vague phrase, and might include farms and gardens as well as tools; but when the Socialist uses it he is generally, thinking of the *machines* which the Industrial Revolution has brought into the world and the factories which house them, as well as the railroads and steamships which carry their goods. In short, the main idea of the Socialists is that the great industries which have arisen as a result of the Industrial Revolution should not be left in private hands. They claim that it is not right for the capitalists to own the mills upon which the workingman must depend for his living; that the attempt of labor unions to get higher wages

[1] The craft guilds described in a previous chapter (see above, p. 126) somewhat resembled modern labor unions, but they included both capitalists and laborers. Our labor unions did not grow out of the medieval guilds but were organized to meet conditions that resulted from the Industrial Revolution.

does not offer more than a temporary relief, since the *system* is wrong which permits the wealthy to have such a control over the poor. The person who works for wages, say the Socialists, is not free; he is a "wage slave" of his employer. The way to remedy this is to turn over the great industries of the

FIG. 97. ROBERT OWEN

Robert Owen rose from a mill worker to be a rich factory owner. He was convinced that mankind is naturally good and that the evil in society comes from bad surroundings. One of the worst influences, he thought, was the competitive system, which makes people try to get the best of one another; while common ownership would, he thought, make each interested in the other's welfare

capitalists to national, state, or local ownership, so that all should have a share in the profits. This ideal state of society, which, they say, is sure to come in the future, they call the Coöperative Commonwealth.

The first Socialists relied on the kind hearts of the capitalists to bring the change, once the situation was made clear. They dreamed of a future civilization which would be without The early Socialists poverty, idleness, or ugliness.[1] Of these early Socialists the most attractive figure was Robert Owen, a rich British mill owner, who had much influence in England in the period of hard times after Waterloo. To him, probably, is due the word "socialism." There were also Socialist writers and teachers in France who exercised a great influence over the working classes there during the second quarter of the century (see next chapter).

Later socialism a working-class movement

Modern Socialists, however, regard these early Socialists as dreamers and their methods as impracticable. They do not think that the rich will ever, from pure unselfishness, give up their control over industries. So they turn to working people only, point out the great advantage to them of socialism, and call upon them to bring it about in the face of the opposition of the capitalists. They claim that wealth is produced by labor, for which capital but furnishes the opportunity, and that labor is justified in taking what it produces.[2]

Karl Marx

The great teacher of this modern doctrine of socialism was Karl Marx, a German writer who lived most of his life in London. He was a learned man, trained in philosophy and political economy, and he came to the conclusion from a study of history that just as the middle class or capitalists[3] had replaced feudal nobles, so the working class would replace the capitalists in the future. By the working class he meant those who depend upon their work for a living. The introduction of the factory system had reduced the vast majority of artisans to a position in which the capitalist was able to dictate the conditions upon which this work should be done. Marx, in an eloquent appeal to them

[1] Among these dreamers may be mentioned Sir Thomas More, who, in the time of Henry VIII, wrote the famous little book called "Utopia," or "the land of nowhere," where everything was arranged as it should be, and where men lived together in brotherly love and prosperity. Since his day those who advocate any fundamental revolution in society have commonly been called Utopians.

[2] This does not mean that Socialists would divide up all private property. Socialists claim only that there shall be no unearned wealth in private hands, controlling, as now, the industries of the country. Brain workers are also "workers."

[3] The French term *bourgeoisie* is often used by Socialists for this class.

in 1847,[1] called upon the members of this "proletariat," "who have nothing to lose but their chains," to rise and seize the means of production themselves. His appeal had almost

FIG. 98. KARL MARX

Karl Marx was born in 1818 in Treves, reared in an enlightened home, and educated at the universities of Bonn and Berlin. He had early decided upon the career of a university professor, but the boldness of his speech and his radical tendencies barred his way, and consequently he entered journalism. His attacks on the Prussian government led to the suppression of his paper in 1843, and he soon migrated to Paris. He was, however, expelled from France, and after some wanderings he finally settled in London, where he studied and wrote until his death, in 1883

no effect at the time, but it has been an inspiration to later generations of Socialists and is frequently quoted by them.

Socialism and democracy

Modern, or "Marxian," socialism is therefore a movement of the working class. As such, it must be viewed as part of

[1] The *Communist Manifesto*, written jointly with Frederick Engels. Marx used the word "communism" to distinguish his plan from the socialism of Owen and the "dreamers" who looked to capitalists to help.

the history of democracy. It is never satisfied with partial reforms so long as the conditions remain which make possible the control of the work of one man by another for the latter's benefit. So it insists that the workers shall keep one aim clearly in mind and not be drawn into other political parties until the Coöperative Commonwealth is gained.

Socialism an international movement

There is one other important element in socialism. It is international. It regards the cause of workers in different countries as a common cause against a common oppressor — capitalism. In this way socialism was a force for peace between nations until the war of 1914.

QUESTIONS

SECTION 55. What do you mean by the Industrial Revolution? Describe the contribution to the Industrial Revolution of each of the following men, giving dates of their inventions: Kay, Hargreaves, Arkwright, Crompton, Cartwright, Whitney.

SECTION 56. Give an account of the invention of the steam engine. Give a short sketch of the Industrial Revolution in France.

SECTION 57. What was the domestic system of industry? Contrast this system with the factory system. Outline the main results of the factory system. What is political economy? What is meant by individualism?

SECTION 58. What is meant by socialism? Give a brief account of the life of Karl Marx. What difference is there between the socialism of Marx and that of the earlier Socialists?

CHAPTER XV

REVOLUTION OF 1848 IN FRANCE

Section 59. Unpopularity of Louis Philippe's Government

Character of Louis Philippe

The Revolution of 1830 gave the final blow in France to the divine right of kings. The sovereignty of the people was proclaimed in the revised Charter which Louis Philippe accepted from the parliament. He added to the former title — "King of the French by the Grace of God" — the significant phrase "and the Will of the Nation." But in spite of these externals, only a small fraction of the nation had any part in the new government. The revised election law, which reduced the voting age from forty to thirty years and the property qualification by one third, still excluded the majority of Frenchmen from political life. The king himself announced that his policy would be the golden mean between conservatism and liberalism.

The Legitimists

The so-called "July monarchy" was therefore stoutly opposed by two types of extremists — the adherents of the older Bourbon line (or Legitimists, as they were called) and the Republicans. The former regarded as their lawful king a grandson of Charles X whom they called Henry V (see table, p. 340). This party was numerically small; it was mainly recruited from the nobility and the clergy, and was not given to violent measures, such as throwing up barricades and seizing public buildings.

The Republicans

It was an altogether different matter with the Republicans, who cherished the memories of 1793 and continued to threaten France with another violent revolution. This party carried on its work mainly through secret societies, similar to the Carbonari in Italy, which spread rapidly in the new manufacturing towns. Remembering the ease with which they had shaken a monarch off the throne in 1830, the Republicans made several

FIG. 99. LOUIS PHILIPPE

Louis Philippe lived without the pomp of royalty, and was fond of going shopping, almost unattended, carrying his green umbrella under his arm. He was cautious, grasping, and avaricious, and as time wore on he grew more and more conservative. His reign of eighteen years was a period of political stagnation

futile attempts to organize insurrections, which were speedily put down, however, by Louis Philippe's troops.

The government takes measures to suppress the Republican party

In addition to their other efforts to destroy the monarchy, the Republicans published a number of papers which attacked the government and even ventured to make sport of the king. The administration thereupon determined to suppress entirely this revolutionary party by strict police supervision of societies and by press censorship. By the use of these vigorous and tyrannical methods the Republicans, as a political party, were reduced for the time being to insignificance.

The Socialists

Meanwhile there was growing up in the large industrial cities a socialistic party, which no mere change of rulers or extension of the suffrage would satisfy. Its members had seen the republic, the empire, and the Bourbon monarchy come and go, and constitutions made and unmade, leaving the peasants and workingmen in the same poverty as before. On the other hand, they had seen the nobles deprived of their privileges and the clergy of their property, and it was only natural that bold thinkers among them should demand that the triumphant middle class, who owed their wealth to commerce and the new machinery, should in turn be divested of some of their riches and privileges in the interest of the working classes.

Babœuf advocates a socialistic system during the Reign of Terror

Denunciations of private property and of the unequal distribution of wealth had been heard during the first French Revolution and even earlier, but they had attracted little attention. Babœuf (1760–1797) had declared in the days of the Terror that a *political* revolution left the condition of the people practically unchanged. What was needed, he claimed, was an *economic* revolution. "When I see the poor without the clothing and shoes which they themselves are engaged in making, and contemplate the small minority who do not work and yet want for nothing, I am convinced that government is still the old conspiracy of the few against the many, only it has taken a new form." His proposal to transfer all property to the State and so administer it that every one should be assured employment, speedily found adherents, and a society was formed to usher in the new order. The organization was soon suppressed and Babœuf himself executed; but his writings were widely circulated, and after the July revolution in 1830 several groups of Socialists began to agitate their plans of social revolution.

"Utopian" Socialists

Some of these were dreamers, like Fourier, who wished to establish groups of coöperative workers in well-arranged settlements, living by themselves, where all would be happy in each other's welfare. Fourier relied, as Robert Owen did, upon the kind hearts of philanthropists to start the movement. Of a different character, however, was the practical program of Louis Blanc, whose volume on *The Organization of Labor*, published in 1839, gave definiteness to the vague aspirations of the reformers.[1] Blanc proclaimed the right of all men to employment and the duty of the State to provide it. He proposed that the government should furnish the capital to found national workshops which should be managed by the workmen, who were to divide the profits of the industry among themselves, thus abolishing the employing class altogether. The "organization of labor" became the battle cry of the labor leaders; it was heard even in the Chamber of Deputies. Nevertheless, there was no well-organized socialist party ready to enter the political field or to work for a definite aim.

Louis Blanc's *Organization of Labor*, 1839

Views of Thiers and Guizot

The political power at this time was really in the hands of two groups of statesmen, one headed by Thiers, and the other by Guizot, both famous as historians and men of letters. Thiers wished to have a constitution like that of England, where, as he was wont to say, "the king reigns but does not rule." Guizot wished the king to exercise real power; he did not want the throne to become an "empty armchair," and regarded further changes in the constitution as undesirable. In 1840 he became prime minister, and he and the king together ruled France for eight years. Though personally honorable, Guizot placed the government on a thoroughly corrupt basis and then attempted to stifle protest by police measures and the prosecution of newspaper editors. He steadily refused to undertake any legislation for the benefit of the working classes and opposed all efforts to extend the suffrage, maintaining that there were not more than one hundred thousand persons in all France "capable of voting with good judgment and independence." This extreme conservatism, which checked reform, brought instead a revolution.

[1] For Blanc's labor program, see *Readings*, Vol. II, p. 76.

Section 60. The Second French Republic

The February revolution in Paris

In spite of Guizot's strong position, there were, in February, 1848, disturbances in the streets of Paris which frightened Louis Philippe and led to the resignation of the unpopular minister. But this did not restore quiet, for the leaders in the street disturbances wanted far more than a change in the ministry. During the evening of the twenty-third they made a formidable demonstration before the Foreign Office, where Guizot resided; thereupon the soldiers on guard fired upon and killed several of the rioters. This roused the anger of the populace to fever heat; the bodies of the victims were placed on a cart and carried through the boulevards in a weird torchlight procession. Before the dawn of February 24 the eastern part of the city was covered with barricades. In the narrow winding streets a cart or two and a heap of cobblestones formed an effective fortification, while the tall houses on either side enabled a few defenders to check a considerable body of soldiers.

Abdication of Louis Philippe, February 24, 1848

The entire city was soon in the hands of the insurgents, and Louis Philippe in despair abdicated in favor of his grandson, the count of Paris. Both the Republicans and the labor party were determined to have no more royalty, so they proclaimed a republic on the afternoon of the twenty-fourth, subject to the ratification of the people in a national assembly to be summoned immediately.

A republic proclaimed

How the labor party was able to control the provisional government

The moderate Republicans were quite satisfied with merely abolishing the monarchy, but the workingmen, whose active coöperation had put the revolutionists in power, had set their hearts on introducing the whole scheme advocated by Louis Blanc. So they induced the provisional government to issue a decree establishing "national workshops," and empowering the minister of public works to put the plan into execution.

As a further concession to the labor element the provisional government established in the Luxembourg palace, the former meeting place of the House of Peers, a committee charged

A labor commission established at the Luxembourg

with the special task of looking after the interests of the working classes. This was really a shrewd move on the part of the opponents of the "Socialists," for it sent the latter away from the City Hall to waste their time in making fine speeches and expounding theories for carrying out which no money had been appropriated.

The labor parliament assembles in the hall hitherto occupied by the House of Peers

The Luxembourg committee, headed by Louis Blanc and a leader of the workingmen named Albert, began its sessions on March 1, and at once proceeded to organize a labor parliament composed of delegates from each trade. This was opened on March 10 with a speech by the eloquent Blanc. He declared that as he beheld the workmen assembled in the Hall of the Peers, hitherto the sanctuary of privilege, in which so many laws directed against them had been made, he felt an emotion which he could with difficulty repress. "On these same seats," he exclaimed, "once glittering with embroidered coats, what do I see now? Garments threadbare with honorable toil, some perhaps bearing the marks of recent conflict." The labor parliament, however, accomplished very little, for the government had furnished them with no money, and consequently Louis Blanc and his supporters were powerless to carry out their plan for coöperative workshops, which they regarded as the most vital of all their reforms.[1]

The national workshops a mere temporary expedient unworthy the name

The provisional government had, it is true, ordered the establishment of national workshops and issued a decree guaranteeing employment to all, but with very different motives from those of the labor committee. Louis Blanc and his followers sought to organize the various trades into permanent, self-supporting coöperative industries, financed in the beginning by the State, but managed by the workingmen themselves. The provisional government, on the contrary, merely desired to allay the restlessness of the unemployed by fair promises. It opened relief works accordingly, which offered more or less useless occupation to the idle men who thronged to Paris. It attempted

[1] Blanc's version of this experiment is given in the *Readings*, Vol. II, p. 82.

no more than merely to organize into brigades those who applied for work, and set them to digging ditches and building forts at a uniform wage of two francs a day. In fact the minister placed in charge of these so-called "national workshops" was opposed to the whole scheme.

This crude temporary expedient was put into operation March 1, and in fifteen days six thousand men had enrolled in the government employ. In April the number reached a hundred thousand, and several million francs were being expended to pay these labor gangs. The plan, however, realized the original object of the government — it kept the idle busy and prevented disorder until the conservative classes could regain their usual ascendency.

The National Assembly exhibits no sympathy for socialism

On May 4 the provisional government gave way to a National Assembly elected by practically universal manhood suffrage, which was called upon to draft a new republican constitution for the country. The majority of the deputies were moderate Republicans who were bitterly opposed to all socialistic tendencies. The rural districts which had taken no part in the Revolution could now make themselves felt, and it was clear enough that the representatives of the peasants did not sympathize in any way with the projects and demands of the Paris workingmen.

The terrible "June days" of 1848

Before it could proceed to consider seriously the form of the new constitution the National Assembly was forced to take decisive measures in regard to the "national workshops," to which crowds continued to flock, draining the treasury to pay for their useless labor. It soon resolved to close the "workshops," and ordered the men either to join the army or leave the city. The people at once set up the cry of "bread or lead," and the most terrible street fighting that Paris had ever witnessed ensued. The streets of the districts inhabited by the working classes were again torn up for barricades, and from Friday, June 23, until the following Monday a desperate conflict raged. The Assembly, fearing the triumph of the labor party, invested General Cavaignac with dictatorial power to crush the revolt. Victory was inevitably on the side of the government troops, who were well disciplined and well equipped, while the insurgents fought irregularly and were half-starved. In its hour of triumph the government's retaliation was most unjustifiably severe; for about four thousand citizens were transported without trial, thirty-two newspapers were suppressed, and the leading writers among the radicals imprisoned. Order was restored, but the carnage of the "June days" left a heritage of undying hatred between the workingmen and the capitalists of Paris.

FIG. 100. CONFLICT BETWEEN WORKINGMEN AND THE TROOPS IN PARIS, JUNE, 1848

After this cruel "solution" of the labor problem the Assembly turned to the work of drawing up a constitution. In spite of a strong royalist minority, the Assembly had declared itself in favor of a republic on the very first day of meeting. It revived the motto of "Liberty, Equality, and Fraternity," and urged all Frenchmen to forget their former dissensions and "to constitute henceforth but a single family."

After six months of debate a new constitution was promulgated. It proclaimed the sovereignty of the people and guaranteed religious freedom and liberty of the press. The government was vested in a single chamber elected by popular vote, and in a president, to be chosen, also by popular vote, for a term of four years.

The candidates for the presidency

After the establishment of the constitution, interest centered in the first presidential election, held on December 10, 1848. Three leading candidates entered the contest, Ledru-Rollin, representing the labor party, General Cavaignac, who had so ruthlessly suppressed the June insurrection, and Louis Napoleon, a nephew of Napoleon I.

Checkered career of Louis Napoleon

The last of these candidates had up to this time led a varied and interesting life. He was born in Paris while his father, Louis Napoleon, was king of Holland. After his uncle's downfall, when he was six years old, he was expelled from France with his mother, who wandered about with him for some time. She continually impressed upon his youthful mind the fact that one who bore the great name of Bonaparte was destined to accomplish something in the world, and he came firmly to believe that it was his mission to reëstablish the Napoleonic dynasty on the throne of France.

After the death of Napoleon I's son in 1832[1] he put himself forward as the direct claimant to the imperial crown, and four years later he attempted to provoke a military uprising at Strassburg, designed to put him on the throne of France. This proved a miserable failure. He then settled in England, where he published in 1839 a volume on *Napoleonic Ideas*,[2] in which

1 Chief members of the Napoleonic House.

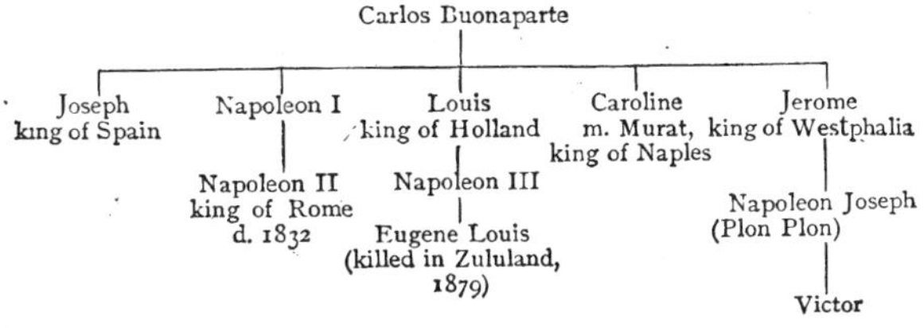

2 Extracts from this work are printed in the *Readings*, Vol. II, p. 84.

The caricaturist represents Louis Napoleon fallen upon evil times. But as he sits in his London lodgings despondent over his past failures to make himself master of France, his pet eagle alights upon the bust of his famous uncle, Napoleon I, and prophesies a great future for his nephew.

FIG. 101. ENGLISH CARICATURE OF LOUIS NAPOLEON (1848)

he represented Napoleon as the servant of the principles of the Revolution, his empire as the guardian of the rights of the people, and his fondest desire, the progress of democracy. In short, he created a fictitious Napoleon who hoped and labored only for the good of the people, and who was overthrown by tyrants.

Louis Napoleon's work on *Napoleonic Ideas*

In 1840 it seemed to Louis Napoleon that the time was ripe for another attempt to win the coveted crown. He landed with a few companions at Boulogne, bringing with him a tame eagle as an emblem of the empire. This second enterprise, like the first, proved a fiasco, and the unhappy leader was shut up in a fortress, from which, in 1846, he escaped to England to await the good fortune to which he still firmly believed himself destined.

Louis Napoleon returns to France in 1848

The insurrection in 1848 offered just the opportunity he desired, and four days after the proclamation of the republic he announced his presence in Paris to the provisional government, pledged himself to support it, and declared that he had no other ambition than that of serving his country. Shortly afterward he was elected a member of the National Assembly and soon found favor with the populace.

He conciliates the favor of all classes and is elected president of the French Republic

He had for years professed himself a democrat and proclaimed his belief in the sovereignty of the people.[1] He had written several essays in which he had expressed sympathy with the working classes, and he was known to have interested himself in the projects of Louis Blanc. He now offered himself as a candidate for the presidency and issued a campaign manifesto, as adroitly worded as many of his famous uncle's proclamations, in which he promised the working classes special laws for their benefit; but, on the other hand, he distinctly repudiated all socialistic schemes and reassured the middle classes by guaranteeing order and the security of property. This time his plans worked admirably, for he was elected president by an overwhelming majority of five and a half million votes to less than one million and a half cast for the two other candidates combined.

[1] An interesting characterization of Louis Napoleon by one who knew him is given in the *Readings*, Vol. II, p. 92.

Section 61. Louis Napoleon and the Second French Empire

It soon became clear that the man whom the French had put at the head of their second republic was bent on making himself emperor.

How Louis Napoleon began to work toward reëstablishing the empire

He speedily began to work for a revision of the constitution that would extend his term of office from four to ten years. He selected his ministers from among his personal friends, courted the favor of the army and the government officials, and by journeys through the country sought to arouse the enthusiasm of the people for the restoration of the empire.

Coup d'état of December 1–2, 1851

As the Assembly refused to coöperate in his plans he finally determined to risk a *coup d'état*, which he had been meditating for some time. After a social function held in his palace on the evening of December 1, 1851, he gathered about him a few of his most trusted advisers and confided his designs to them. When the morning of December 2 — the anniversary of the glorious victory of Austerlitz — broke, the walls of Paris were placarded with copies of a decree issued by the president, dissolving the Assembly, reëstablishing universal suffrage, and ordering a new election.[1]

The president is given dictatorial power by a plebiscitum

Finally, he submitted to the people of France the following proposition: "The French people desire the maintenance of the authority of Louis Napoleon Bonaparte and delegate to him the necessary powers in order to make a constitution on the basis announced in his proclamation of December 2." Every Frenchman twenty-one years of age was permitted to vote "yes" or "no" on this proposition, and the result was officially estimated at 7,740,000 for the measure and 646,000 against it. The figures were doubtless quite inaccurate, but the *coup d'état* was approved by the people, and what may be called the constitutional absolutism of the first Napoleon was again introduced into France.

[1] For Louis Napoleon's appeal to the French, see *Readings*, Vol. II, p. 88.

Save for a little bloodshed in Paris on December 4, this revolution was accomplished very quietly. About a hundred thousand opponents of Napoleon throughout the country, including the leaders of the opposition in the Assembly, were arrested, and nearly ten thousand were exiled from France, but the people at large accepted the situation without protest. The workingmen generally rejoiced in the overthrow of the politicians who had waged war on them in the bloody June days of 1848.

Peaceful character of the revolution of December, 1851

The president was now master of France. He appointed officers, proposed laws, declared war, made peace, and in fact himself constituted the real power in the government. Though already an emperor in reality, he was not satisfied until he secured the title, and it was evident that the country was ready for the fulfillment of his hopes, for wherever he went he was greeted with cries of "Long live the Emperor." Part of this public sentiment was doubtless inspired by the president's officials, but the name of Napoleon awakened glorious memories, and there was a genuine desire throughout France to see the empire reëstablished.

Reëstablishment of the empire, November, 1852

Toward the close of 1852 Louis Napoleon, in a speech at Bordeaux,[1] at last openly announced his belief that France was ready for the abolition of the second republic. Inasmuch as the members of the senate were chosen by Louis Napoleon himself they readily agreed to pass a decree making him Napoleon III, emperor of the French. This decree was submitted to popular vote (November, 1852) and ratified by an overwhelming majority. The dream of Louis Napoleon's life was at last realized — the Napoleonic dynasty was restored.

For over ten years his government was a thinly veiled despotism. Though the imperial constitution confirmed the great principles of the Revolution, a decree abolishing the liberty of the press was immediately issued. No periodical or newspaper treating of political or social economy could be published without previous authorization on the part of the government.

Despotic character of Napoleon III's government

1 *Readings*, Vol. II, p. 91.

Moreover the government officers could suppress journals at will. Napoleon III had promised liberty of instruction, but he compelled the teachers in the university to take an oath of allegiance to himself. Instruction in history and philosophy was discouraged, and the university professors were directed to shave their moustaches "in order to remove from their appearance, as well as from their manners, the last vestiges of anarchy."

FIG. 102. NAPOLEON III

Prosperity of France under the second empire, 1852–1870

Notwithstanding this autocratic régime, the country was prosperous and the people fairly contented. If the emperor was a despot, he endeavored — and with no little success — to be an enlightened one. Benevolent institutions increased in number. Railway construction was rapidly pushed forward, and great trunk lines which had been begun under Louis Philippe were completed. The city of Paris was improved and beautified; the narrow streets were widened and broad avenues laid out. The great exposition of 1855 testified to the industrial and scientific advance of France; and if little of all this progress is to be attributed to the emperor's initiative, it nevertheless remains a fact that it was accomplished under his rule. Moreover, in 1870, he yielded to the imperative demand of the liberals for a reform of the constitution, and established the responsibility of his ministers to parliament. If it had not been for a series of foreign events which weakened his reputation at home, Napoleon III might have remained securely on his throne until his death.

QUESTIONS

SECTION 59. Give a sketch of the two parties which opposed the "July monarchy." Discuss the work of Babœuf and Blanc. Contrast the political views of Thiers and Guizot.

SECTION 60. Give an account of the February revolution in Paris. Describe the part taken in the provisional government by the labor party. What were the "June days of 1848"? Describe the constitution of the Second French Republic. Sketch the life of Louis Napoleon to the year 1848.

SECTION 61. What means did Louis Napoleon take to reëstablish the empire? Characterize the government of Napoleon III. What did the empire do for France?

Section 62. The Fall of Metternich

The issues of the Revolution of 1848 broader than those of the First French Revolution

When Metternich heard of the February revolution in France all his old fears were revived. "Europe finds herself to-day," he declared, "in the presence of a second 1793." Great changes had, however, taken place during the fifty-five years which had elapsed since France first offered to aid other nations to free themselves from their "tyrants" and throw off the trammels of feudalism. In 1848 the principles proclaimed in the Declaration of the Rights of Man were accepted by the liberal parties which had come into existence in every state of Europe, and which were actively engaged in promoting the cause of popular government, a free press, equality of all before the law, and the abolition of the vestiges of the feudal system. Moreover the national spirit which had awakened during the Napoleonic Period was at work, and served more than anything else to excite opposition to the existing order. Lastly, the Industrial Revolution was beginning to quicken the thought and arouse the aspirations of the great mass of the population. Those who lived by the labor of their hands and were employed in the new industries which were rapidly developing, now had their spokesmen, especially in France and England, and claimed the right to vote and to mold the laws to meet their particular interests. So in 1848 the rights of nations and of the laborer were added to the rights of man, which had constituted the main issue in 1793.

In nearly every European country the liberals were encouraged by the successful February revolution in Paris to undertake

The agitation of 1848 general throughout western Europe

to win, by violence if necessary, the reforms which they had so long been advocating. In England a body of workingmen, known as "Chartists," made a desperate though futile effort to wring from Parliament the right to vote.[1] The Swiss, who had just passed through a civil conflict, swept away the constitution which had been adopted in 1814, and drew up a new one.[2] But the chief agitations of 1848, outside of France, were directed against the governments of Germany, where Metternich had for forty years been doing his best to prevent any hint of change.

Extraordinary mixture of peoples under Austrian rule

But before proceeding it will be necessary to consider more carefully than we have hitherto done the singular composition of the realms of the House of Hapsburg. The regions west of Vienna, extending to Switzerland and Bavaria, were inhabited chiefly by Germans. To the south, in the provinces of Carniola, Styria, Carinthia, and Istria, there were many Slavs; and to the north, in Bohemia and Moravia, were the Czechs, interspersed among twice their number of Germans. On the borders of Russia dwelt the Poles, whose territories the emperor had received at the partition of their kingdom. The

1 See below, p. 497.

2 The settlement of 1815 in Switzerland, like that in Germany, Italy, and other European countries, met with opposition from the liberals. It had left the internal government of each canton in the hands of a small minority of the wealthy classes, and had modeled the diet on that of Germany, making it merely a congress of ambassadors with slight powers. Agitation for a revision of this system was begun immediately after its establishment, but it was opposed especially by the Catholics, who were in a slight minority and feared that a stronger central government would be used by the Protestants to restrict their rights. In 1841 the government of Aargau precipitated a civil conflict by suppressing the monasteries within its jurisdiction. Although the Swiss constitution guaranteed the monasteries in their rights, the federal government refused to interfere with the domestic concerns of Aargau. Thereupon the Catholic cantons, under the leadership of Lucerne, Uri, and Zug, formed a Catholic alliance, or *Sonderbund*, which defied the entire democratic and nationalist party. After some skirmishes which scarcely deserve the name of war, this party of disunion was suppressed, and in 1848 a new federal constitution was drawn up. Instead of a diet of ambassadors it provided for a senate representing the states, and for deputies elected by the people at large on the plan of the government of the United States. This constitution was revised in 1874, when still larger powers were given to the federal government.

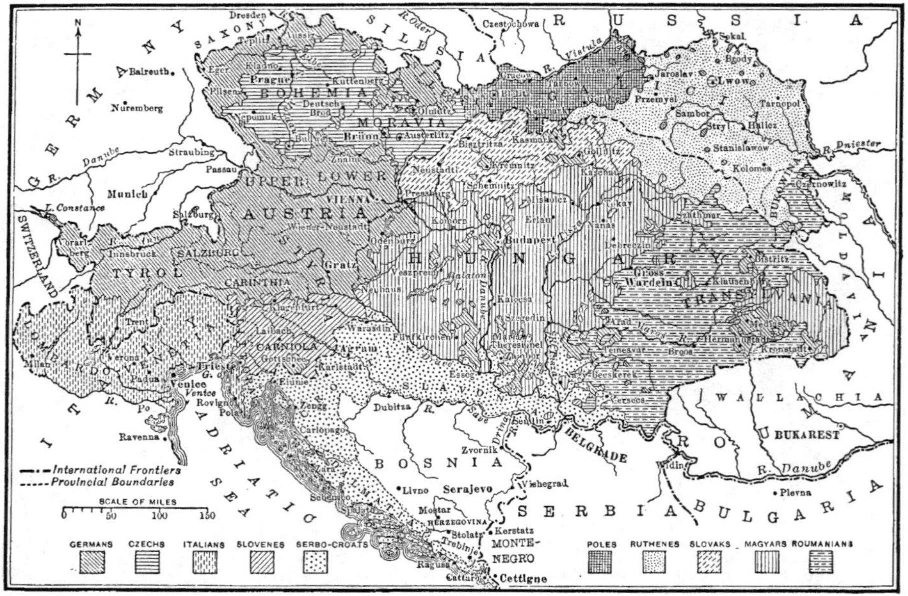

ETHNOGRAPHIC MAP OF AUSTRIA-HUNGARY

inhabitants of the kingdom of Hungary included, besides the Magyars, or Hungarians proper, who dwelt in the vast plains of the Danube valley, Roumanians in the south and east, and the independence-loving Croats (Croatians) in the south and west. Beyond the Alps was the Lombardo-Venetian kingdom inhabited by Italians. Among this mass of people of different tongues and traditions, the most important were the Germans of Austria, the Czechs of Bohemia, the Magyars of Hungary, and the Italians in Lombardy and Venetia.

The government of Austria

In the provinces of the Austrian Empire, Ferdinand I ruled personally through ministers whom he appointed and dismissed. Laws were made, taxes levied, and revenues spent without consulting the people. Newspapers, books, theaters, and teachers were watched closely by the police to prevent the introduction of any new ideas. Travel abroad was restricted by a decree which required every citizen leaving the realm to have a government passport. Scholars were therefore largely cut off from the thought of western Europe, and Metternich boasted that the scientific spirit had been kept out of even the universities. The nobles still enjoyed their ancient authority over their serfs, including the right to prevent their leaving the villages without permission, and to exact from them the old feudal services. The clergy were as powerful as they had been before the French Revolution, and non-Catholics were excluded entirely from government offices.

Hungary controlled by the Magyar nobles

In the kingdom of Hungary the government was under the control of the proud and tyrannical Magyar nobles, who still enjoyed their old feudal privileges. There was a diet, or parliament, composed of an upper house of nobles, and a lower house of representatives chosen by the smaller landlords. Although the Magyars, or Hungarians proper,[1] constituted less than one

[1] The Hungarians — who belong to a very different race from the Slavic peoples, more akin to the Mongolian or Tartar, and speak the Magyar tongue — invaded the Danube valley in the year 895, and wedged themselves in between the Slavic Russians and Poles on the north and the "South Slavs" composed of Croats, Slovaks, Montenegrins, and Serbians.

half of the population, they held their neighbors, the Croats, Roumanians, and Slovaks, in contempt, and denied them all national rights. There were, however, enlightened liberals in Hungary, whose program included the admission of the public to the discussions in the diet; a parliamentary journal in which the debates should be published in full; regular yearly meetings of the diet; equal taxation of all classes; the abolition of the forced labor required of the peasant, and all other vestiges of serfdom.

Kossuth (1802–1894)

The government did all it could to suppress these tendencies. The publication of reform speeches was forbidden, and a prominent Hungarian leader, Kossuth, was imprisoned for circulating them in manuscript. Undaunted by this punishment, however, Kossuth, on his release, established a newspaper at Pesth and began to advocate radical reforms in the Hungarian government itself, as well as greater freedom from Austrian interference. With fiery zeal he wrote and spoke on the abolition of feudal privileges, the introduction of trial by jury, revision of the barbarous criminal law, and similar questions which had long agitated the rest of Europe.

Causes of discontent in Lombardo-Venetia

The Italians in Lombardo-Venetia were no less dissatisfied than the Hungarians. The Austrian government there was in the hands of police officials and judges who arrested and imprisoned freely all advocates of Italian rights. Tariffs were so arranged as to enrich the emperor's treasury and check Italian industries in favor of those of Austria. The forts were garrisoned with Austrian troops which the government employed to suppress any violent demonstrations.

March revolution in Vienna

The ground was therefore thoroughly prepared for the seeds of insurrection when the overthrow of Louis Philippe encouraged the opponents of Metternich in Germany, Austria, Hungary, and Italy to hope that they could destroy his system at once and forever. On March 13, 1848, a number of students proceeded to the assembly hall in Vienna where the local diet was in session, and, supported by the crowd that quickly gathered, invaded the building. Outside, the mob continued to increase, barricades were built, street fighting began, and shouts of "Down with Metternich!" penetrated the imperial palace. The aged minister, convinced that it was no longer possible to check the rising torrent of revolution, tendered his resignation. Fall of Metternich

FIG. 103. LOUIS KOSSUTH

Kossuth was a wonderful orator, speaking with passionate, fiery eloquence. He was largely responsible for the Magyars' revolt in 1848, and became their virtual dictator during it. After it was crushed he fled to Turkey, then visited France, England, and the United States. He had learned in prison the tongue of Shakespeare and the King James Bible, and surprised everyone by his eloquent command of English. His great popularity was later clouded by the protests of other refugees that he was claiming altogether too much for himself. From 1859 to his death, in 1894, he lived in Italy, refusing to return home while a Hapsburg was ruling over Hungary

He fled from Austria and found refuge in England, where he was heartily welcomed by his old friend, the duke of Wellington, who was himself occupied with a threatened uprising in London. After the flight of Metternich a new ministry was formed, which began to draft a constitution.

Reform measures in Hungary

Two days after the uprising in Vienna the Hungarian diet at Pressburg, by a unanimous vote, dispatched a delegation to the emperor, demanding a responsible ministry, freedom of the press, trial by jury, and a national educational system. Then the Hungarian diet, under the influence of the zealous patriot, Kossuth, swept away the old offices through which the emperor had ruled in Hungary, and established its own ministries of finance, war, and foreign affairs — a first step toward independence. It also emancipated the peasants without providing compensation to the landlords, leaving that as a "debt of honor" to be paid in the future. The king, owing to the insurrection in Vienna, was in no position to reject even these revolutionary measures.

Revolution in Prague

His troubles were, moreover, not yet at an end, for on March 15 the patriotic Czechs in the city of Prague held a mass meeting at which a petition for civil liberty and the abolition of serfdom was drawn up. Solemn mass was then said, and a delegation bearing the petition left by special train for Vienna amid the cheers of the crowd and the waving of Czech flags. The emperor addressed the Bohemian delegates, to their great joy, in their own language, and approved most of their proposals. It will be observed that so far neither in Hungary nor in Bohemia had the patriots shown any desire to throw off their allegiance to their Austrian ruler.

Revolution throughout Italy, March, 1848

In Italy, however, the Austrian rule was thoroughly hated. Immediately on hearing the news of Metternich's fall the Milanese expelled the imperial troops from their city, and the Austrians were soon forced to evacuate a great part of Lombardy. The Venetians followed the lead of Milan and set up once more their ancient republic, which Napoleon had suppressed. The Milanese, anticipating a struggle, appealed to Charles Albert, king of Sardinia, for aid. By the middle of March a great part of Italy was in revolt, and constitutions had been granted by the rulers in Naples, Rome, Tuscany, and Piedmont. The king of Sardinia was forced by public opinion to assume the leadership in the attempt to expel Austria from Italy and ultimately perhaps to found some sort of an Italian union which would satisfy the national aspirations of the Italian people. Pope Pius IX, who was just beginning his long and celebrated pontificate of more than thirty years, and even the Bourbon king of Naples, were induced to consent to the arming of troops in the cause of Italian freedom, and thus Italy began her first war for independence.

The Prussians demand a constitution

The crisis in Vienna and the war in Italy now made it impossible for Austria to continue to exercise the control over the German states which she had enjoyed for more than thirty years. Consequently there were almost simultaneous risings in Baden, Würtemberg, Bavaria, and Saxony. The news of the February revolution in Paris caused great excitement also in Berlin, where deputations were sent to the king, asking him to grant Prussia a constitution. On March 18 a crowd gathered before the royal palace and the police tried to disperse it; fighting ensued, and barricades were constructed after the Paris fashion in the districts in which the working people lived. Frederick William IV, hoping to avoid more disorder and bloodshed, promised to summon an assembly to draft the desired constitution.

A national assembly convoked at Frankfort to draw up a new constitution for Germany, May, 1848

Now that Metternich was overthrown there was some hope of reorganizing the weak German confederation and forming a new and firm union which would at last make a real nation of the Germans. At the instigation of the liberals the diet of the confederation convoked a national assembly made up of representatives chosen by popular vote in all the states. This met at Frankfort, May 18, 1848, amid high hopes, and proceeded to take up the difficult question of drafting a constitution which should please at once the German princes and their liberal-minded subjects.[1]

1 The events of the year 1848 moved so rapidly that one is likely to be at first confused by them. But it must be remembered that the revolutionary movements in the various countries of Germany, such as Austria and Prussia, were quite different from the attempt to reform the whole confederation, which has just been referred to.

Section 63. Failure of the Revolution in Bohemia and Hungary

Bright outlook for reform in March, 1848

By the end of March, 1848, the prospects of reform seemed bright indeed. Hungary and Bohemia had been granted the rights which they had so long desired; a committee in Vienna was busy drawing up a constitution for the Austrian provinces; Lombardy and Venetia had declared their independence; four other Italian states had obtained their longed-for constitutions; a Prussian convention to reform the government had been promised; and, lastly, a great national assembly was about to be convened at Frankfort to prepare a constitution for Germany.

How the radicals aided the conservatives to regain their power

The reformers who had gained these seeming victories had, however, only just reached the most difficult part of their task. For, as in France, so also in the other countries, the revolutionists were divided among themselves, and this division enabled the reactionary rulers and their supporters to recover from the extraordinary humiliations which they had suffered during the various uprisings in March.

Divergent views of the Czechs and Germans in Bohemia

The first notable victory for the reaction was in Bohemia, where race rivalry proved favorable to the reëstablishment of the emperor's former influence. The Czechs hated the Germans, while the Germans, on their part, feared that they would be oppressed if the Czechs were given a free hand. They therefore opposed the plan of making Bohemia practically independent of the government at Vienna, for it was to German Vienna that they were accustomed to look for protection against the enterprises of their Czechish fellow countrymen. The German element in Bohemia also wanted to send delegates to the Frankfort convention and were very anxious that Bohemia should not be excluded from the reorganized German confederation.

The Czechs, on the other hand, determined to offset the movement toward German consolidation by a Pan-Slavic congress, which should bring together the various Slavic peoples comprised in the Austrian Empire. To this assembly, which met at Prague early in June, 1848, came representatives of the Czechs, Moravians, and Ruthenians in the north, and the Serbians and Croatians in the south. Unfortunately the several Slavonic languages differ from one another quite as much as English, Swedish, Dutch, and German, and after trying French as a common tongue, the delegates had to fall back upon German, which was the only language with which they were all familiar.

The Pan-Slavic congress forced to carry on its debates in German

The congress accomplished nothing and was about to dissolve on June 12, when some of the more radical students and workingmen began singing Bohemian songs and denouncing General Windischgrätz, the Austrian commander of the troops in Prague, who was especially hated on account of his aristocratic bearing and sentiments. A street fight broke out between the crowd and his soldiers, which was followed by an attack on his residence. On June 17 he retaliated by bombarding the town, which caught fire. The next day he entered the flaming streets and announced that the revolution in Bohemia was at an end. This was Austria's first real victory over her rebellious subjects.

Windischgrätz puts an end to the Bohemian revolution, June 18, 1848

In Vienna affairs were going from bad to worse. Frightened by the growing disorder, the incompetent emperor fled to Innsbruck (May 18). A provisional government was set up and an assembly called to draft a new constitution, but nothing was accomplished. Meantime the turmoil increased. The emperor's government was helpless, and finally Windischgrätz announced his intention of marching on Vienna and, with the emperor's approval, putting an end to revolution there as he had done in Prague. The Viennese attempted to defend the city, but all in vain. After a cruel bombardment Windischgrätz entered the capital on October 31, and once within the walls, he showed little mercy on the people.[1]

Windischgrätz bombards and takes Vienna, October 31, 1848

A reactionary ministry was soon formed, and a new Metternich discovered in the person of Schwartzenberg, who forced

[1] An account by an eyewitness is given in the *Readings*, Vol. II, p. 101.

Francis Joseph emperor of Austria

the weak Ferdinand to abdicate, December 2, in favor of his youthful nephew, Francis Joseph, who ruled for nearly sixty-eight years.

It will be remembered that after the fall of Metternich the emperor had not been in a position to refuse the demands of

FIG. 104. FRANCIS JOSEPH AT HIS ACCESSION

Francis Joseph (1830–1916) witnessed the revolutions of 1848 at the age of eighteen and the great war of 1914 at the age of eighty-four. Pictures of him as an old man are familiar; but this one of him at his accession recalls to us his long reign

Dissension between the Magyars and Slavs

the Hungarians, and that they had succeeded in gaining practical independence for their kingdom. But the spirit of nationalism had also been awakened in the other races which the Magyars had so long dominated. The Slavs in Hungary, southern Austria, and the neighboring Turkish Empire had long meditated on the possibility of a united Slavic kingdom in the south, and when the Magyars attempted to force their language on the Croats, one of the Slav leaders hurled back at them: "You Magyars are only an island in an ocean of Slavs. Take heed that the waves do not rise and overwhelm you." Indeed, the Croats and Serbians were, on the whole, friendly to the Vienna government, and ready to fight the Hungarians.

Austria, with Russia's aid, crushes the Hungarian rebellion, August, 1849

The emperor finally threw off the mask and, in a manifesto on October 3, declared the Hungarian parliament dissolved and its acts void. In December Windischgrätz, the conqueror of Prague and Vienna, crossed into Hungary at the head of an army, and on January 5 entered Pesth. The war seemed for a time at an end, but the Hungarians, inspired by Kossuth, rallied in a mighty national uprising against the Austrians, and on April 19, 1849, they declared their complete and eternal separation from the Vienna government. They might have succeeded in maintaining their independence had not the Tsar, Nicholas I, placed his forces at the disposal of Francis Joseph. Attacked by an army of a hundred and fifty thousand Russians, who marched in from the east, the Hungarians were compelled, by the middle of August, to give up the contest. Austria took terrible vengeance upon the rebels. Thousands were shot, hanged, or imprisoned, and many, including Kossuth,[1] fled to England or the United States. The ancient kingdom of Hungary seemed about to be reduced to the state of an insignificant Austrian province, but, as we shall see,[2] within less than twenty years she was able to secure substantially the coveted independence.

Section 64. Austria regains her Power in Italy

Defeat of the Italians under Charles Albert of Sardinia, July, 1848

Austria was no less successful in reëstablishing her power in Italy than in Hungary. The Italians had been unable to drive out the Austrian army which, under the indomitable general, Radetzky, had taken refuge in the neighborhood of Mantua, in the so-called Quadrilateral, where it was protected

[1] Kossuth's version of the revolution is given in the *Readings*, Vol. II, pp. 103 ff. [2] See below, p. 439.

by four great fortresses.[1] Charles Albert of Sardinia found himself, with the exception of a few volunteers, almost unsupported by the other Italian states. The best ally of Austria was the absence of united action upon the part of the Italians and the jealousy and indifference which they showed as soon as war had actually begun. Pius IX decided that his mission was one of peace, and that he could not afford to join in a war against Austria, the stanchest friend of the Roman Church. The king of Naples easily found a pretext for recalling the troops that public opinion had compelled him to send to the aid of the king of Sardinia. Charles Albert was defeated at Custozza, July 25, and compelled to sign a truce with Austria and to withdraw his forces from Lombardy.

Policy of the Italian republicans

The Italian republicans were undismayed, however, and now attempted to carry out their own program. Florence followed the example of Venice and proclaimed itself a republic. At Rome the liberal and enlightened Rossi, whom the Pope had placed at the head of affairs, was assassinated in November just as he was ready to promulgate his reforms. Pius IX fled from the city and put himself under the protection of the king of Naples. A constitutional assembly was then convoked by the revolutionists, and in February, 1849, under the influence of Mazzini, it declared the temporal power of the Pope abolished, and proclaimed the Roman Republic.

Austria defeats the king of Sardinia at Novara, March, 1849

While these local insurrections were weakening the already distracted Italy, the truce between Piedmont and Austria expired, and in March, 1849, Charles Albert renewed the war which had been discontinued after the disaster at Custozza. The campaign lasted but five days and closed with his crushing defeat at Novara (March 23), which put an end to the hopes of Italian liberty for the time being. Charles Albert abdicated in favor of his son, Victor Emmanuel II, who was destined before many years to exchange the title of "King of Sardinia" for that of "King of Italy."

Accession of Victor Emmanuel II as king of Sardinia

[1] See the map of Napoleon I's campaigns in this country, p. 257.

Austria reëstablishes the former conditions in Italy, except in Piedmont

After bringing the king of Sardinia to terms, Austria pushed southward, reëstablishing the old order as she went. The newly established Italian republics were unable to offer any effectual resistance. The former rulers were restored in Rome, Tuscany, and Venice, and the new constitutions were swept away from one end of the peninsula to the other, except in Piedmont, the

FIG. 105. PIUS IX

most important part of the king of Sardinia's realms. There Victor Emmanuel not only maintained the representative government[1] introduced by his father, but, by summoning to his councils men known throughout Italy for their liberal sentiments, he prepared to lead the Italian states once more against their foreign oppressors.

[1] Extracts from the constitution are given in the *Readings*, Vol. II, p. 109.

Section 65. Outcome of the Revolution of 1848 in Germany

Question of the extent of the proposed German union

In Germany, as elsewhere, Austria profited by the dissensions among her opponents. On May 18, 1848, the national assembly, consisting of nearly six hundred representatives of the German people, had met at Frankfort. It immediately began the consideration of a new constitution that should satisfy the popular longings for a great free German state, in which the people should have a voice. But what were to be the confines of this new German state? The Confederation of 1815 did not include all the German inhabitants of Prussia, and did include the heterogeneous western possessions of Austria — Bohemia and Moravia, for example, where many of the people were Slavs. There was no hesitation in deciding that all the Prussian territories should be admitted to the new union. As it appeared impossible to leave out Austria altogether, the assembly agreed to include those parts of her territory which had belonged to the confederation formed in 1815. This decision rendered the task of founding a real German state practically impossible; for the new union was to include two great European powers which might at any moment become rivals, since Prussia would hardly consent to be led forever by Austria. So heterogeneous a union could only continue to be, as it had been, a loose confederation of practically independent princes.

Impossibility of a German state which should include both Austria and Prussia

The assembly at Frankfort gives Austria time to recover

The improbability that the assembly at Frankfort would succeed in its undertaking was greatly increased by its unwise conduct. Instead of proceeding immediately to frame a new form of government, it devoted several months to formulating the general rights of the individual citizen. Consequently by the time that the constitution itself came up for discussion, Austria had begun to regain her influence and was ready to lead the conservative forces once more. She could rely upon the support of the rulers of the states of southern Germany, for they were well satisfied with the old confederation and the degree of independence that it gave them.

The assembly asks the king of Prussia to become emperor of Germany

In spite of her partiality for the old union, Austria could not prevent the assembly from completing its new constitution. This provided that there should be an hereditary emperor at the head of the government, and that exalted office was tendered to the king of Prussia. Frederick William IV had been alienated from the liberal cause, which he had at first espoused, by the insurrection in Berlin. He was, moreover, timid and conservative at heart; he hated revolution and doubted whether the national assembly had any right to confer the imperial title. He also greatly respected Austria, and felt that a war with her, which was likely to ensue if he accepted the crown, would be dangerous to Prussia. So he refused the imperial title and announced his rejection of the new constitution (April, 1849).

Frederick William IV refuses the imperial crown

This decision rendered the year's work of the national assembly fruitless, and its members gradually dispersed. Austria now insisted upon the reëstablishment of the old diet and Germany returned once more to its old ways.

The national assembly disperses and the old diet is restored

Prussia granted a constitution by Frederick William IV (January, 1850)

Yet amid the meager results of the Revolution of 1848 there was one gain of seeming importance for the future of Germany; Prussia emerged from the turmoil of the period with a written constitution which established a legislative assembly and admitted a portion of the people to a slight share in the government. As we have seen, the news of the revolution in France caused great excitement in Berlin, and the king, fearing a continuance of violence, promised to convoke an assembly to formulate a constitution. This convention met at Berlin in May of the same year, and, amid prolonged debates, advocated many radical measures which displeased the king. It proposed to abolish the nobility and to strike from the royal title the phrase "King by the Grace of God." Meanwhile there was disorder in the quarters occupied by the working class, and on June 14 a mob stormed the arsenal. This situation frightened the king, and he withdrew to Potsdam. He then ordered the assembly to adjourn to Brandenburg, some distance away, and on its refusal, he dissolved it in spite of its protests. After getting rid of the popular assembly, the king, in 1849, submitted a constitution of his own to a more tractable convention of carefully selected subjects. This document, which was promulgated in January, 1850, remained, with some minor changes, the constitution of the Prussian state.

The Prussian constitution disappoints the liberals

It proved, however, a great disappointment to the liberals, who had hoped for a really democratic form of government. It provides for a ministry, but makes it responsible to the king rather than to the diet. The latter comprises a house of lords — consisting of princes, nobles, life peers selected by the king, representatives of the universities, and burgomasters of the large towns — and a house of deputies.

System of voting by classes in Prussia

All men over twenty-five years of age may vote for the electors, who in turn select the deputies to the lower house, but the constitution carefully arranges to give the rich a predominating influence in the election. Those who stand first on the tax list, and pay together one third of the total taxes, are permitted to choose one third of the electors. The second third on the list also choose a third of the electors, and, finally, the great mass of the poorer people, whose small contributions to the treasury make up the remaining third of the revenue, are entitled to cast their votes for the remaining third of the electors assigned to the district. It may happen that a single wealthy man, if he pays a third of the taxes, has as much influence in electing representatives from his district as all the working people combined.[1]

QUESTIONS

SECTION 62. Show the effect of the February revolution upon the English and the Swiss. Over what lands and peoples did the House of Hapsburg rule in 1848? Describe the government of Austria; of Hungary. Who was Kossuth? What were the objections of the Italians in Lombardo-Venetia to Austrian rule? Describe

[1] For further discussion of the Prussian constitution, see below, pp. 445 f.

the March revolution in Vienna. Give an account of the reform legislation of the Hungarian diet. What were the demands of the Bohemians in March, 1848? Trace the course of the revolution in Italy. What were the demands of the Prussians at this period? How were they met?

SECTION 63. With what two groups of people were the reformers of 1848 forced to deal? Describe the manner in which the different revolutionary movements were put down.

SECTION 64. Account for the defeat of the Italians at Custozza, July, 1848, by the Austrian forces. Describe the result of the defeat by Austria of the king of Sardinia at Novara.

SECTION 65. What problem faced the members of the national assembly which met at Frankfort, May, 1848? Account for the refusal of Frederick William IV to accept the imperial title offered to him by the national assembly. What was the effect of his act upon the work of this assembly? What permanent gain was made by Prussia as a result of the Revolution of 1848? Describe the Prussian constitution.

SECTION 66. CAVOUR AND ITALIAN UNITY

Italy in 1850

The efforts of the Italian liberals to expel Austria from the peninsula and establish constitutional governments in the various Italian states had failed, and after the battle of Novara it seemed as if the former political conditions were to be restored. The king of Naples broke all the promises which he had made to his subjects, revoked the constitution which he had granted, and imprisoned, exiled, or in some cases executed the revolutionists. The Pope, with the assistance of France, Austria, Naples, and Spain, was able to destroy the Roman Republic which had been set up and to place the government again in the hands of the clergy. In northern Italy Austria was once more in control, and she found faithful adherents in the rulers of Modena, Parma, and Tuscany, who looked to her for continued support. The leading spirits of the revolution who had escaped prison or death fled to foreign countries to await a more auspicious opportunity to secure their ends, for they did not surrender the hope that Austria would sometime be driven from their country, and all the Italian states brought together in a federation or perhaps united into a single monarchy or republic.

Divergent views of those intent on unifying Italy

However, those who, since the fall of Napoleon I, had been interested in promoting Italian independence and liberty differed among themselves as to the best way in which to make Italy a nation. There were the republicans, who became more and more disgusted with monarchy and believed that nothing could be accomplished until the various rulers should give way

VICTOR EMMANUEL II

Fig. 106

Fig. 107. Victor Emmanuel's Entrance to Florence in 1860

to a great democratic republic, which should recall the ancient glories of Rome; others were confident that an enlightened Pope could form an Italian federation, of which he should be the head; lastly, there was a practical party, whose adherents placed their hopes in the king of Sardinia, who seemed to them to be the natural leader in the emancipation of Italy. Little as

FIG. 108. MAZZINI

the Revolution of 1848 had accomplished, it had at least given Sardinia a young and energetic king and a new constitution.

Among the republican leaders the most conspicuous was the sensitive and highly endowed Giuseppe Mazzini. Born in 1805, he had, as he tells us, become a republican from hearing his father discuss the achievements of the French Revolution, and had read eagerly the old French newspapers which he found hidden behind the medical books in his father's library. He joined the secret society of the Carbonari, and in 1830 was caught by the police and imprisoned in the fortress of Savona,

Mazzini, 1805–1872

west of Genoa. Here he arranged a secret code, which enabled him to keep in communication with the revolutionists.

"Young Italy"

Becoming disgusted with the inefficiency and the silly mystery of the Carbonari, Mazzini planned a new association, which he called "Young Italy." This aimed to bring about the regeneration of Italy through the education of young men in lofty republican principles. Mazzini had no confidence in princes or in foreign aid. He urged that all the Italians should be brought together into a single republic, for he feared that any form of federation would leave the country too weak to resist the constant interference of neighboring nations. Mazzini was not a man to carry through a successful revolution, for he lacked the necessary practical, business sense, but he inspired the young Italians with almost religious enthusiasm for the cause of Italy's liberation.[1] Still other patriots, however, who dreamed of a new Italy, placed their hopes, not in a republic in which the common man should have a voice in the conduct of the government, but in a federation of princes under that most ancient of all Italian princes, the bishop of Rome.

Progressive government of Victor Emmanuel

The future, however, belonged neither to the republicans nor to the papal party, but to those who looked to the king of Sardinia to bring about the salvation of Italy. Only under his leadership was there any prospect of ousting Austria, and until that was done no independent union could possibly be formed. Practical men therefore began to turn to the young Victor Emmanuel, whose devotion to the cause of freedom in the war with Austria in 1848, and whose frank acceptance of the principles of constitutional government, distinguished him from all the other rulers of Italy. His father, Charles Albert, had granted Piedmont a constitution in 1848, which provided for a parliament with two houses and a responsible ministry. This constitution (which was later to become that of a united Italy) Victor Emmanuel maintained in spite of Austria's demands that he suppress it.

[1] For Mazzini's doctrines, see *Readings*, Vol. II, pp. 115 ff.

Count Cavour, 1810–1861

Victor Emmanuel was wise enough to call to his aid one of the most distinguished of modern statesmen, Count Cavour, who had long been an advocate both of constitutional government and of Italian unity.[1] Cavour, however, did not believe that unity could be secured without foreign aid, for Sardinia was a rather insignificant kingdom when compared with the more important countries of Europe. It had a population of

FIG. 109. CAVOUR

less than five millions and consisted of four distinct regions which were more or less hostile to one another. In view of this fact Cavour held that it was impossible to disregard the other powers of Europe, who had so long interfered freely in Italian affairs. In particular he looked to France. He early declared, "Whether we like it or not, our destinies depend upon France; we must be her partner in the great game which will be played sooner or later in Europe."

[1] *Readings*, Vol. II, pp. 119 ff.

Sardinia joins France in the Crimean War

An opportunity soon offered itself for Sardinia to become the ally of France. The Crimean War[1] had broken out in 1854 between England and France on the one side, and Russia on the other, and in 1855 Cavour signed an offensive and defensive alliance with France and sent troops to her aid in the Crimea. This gave him an opportunity to take part in the European congress which met in Paris in 1856 to conclude a peace. There he warned the powers that Austrian control in northern Italy was a menace to the peace of Europe, and succeeded in enlisting the interest of Napoleon III in Italian affairs; — it will be remembered that in his younger days the French emperor had sympathized with the Carbonari, and he had a number of Italian relatives who besought his aid in forwarding the cause of Italian unity.

Position and policy of Napoleon III

There were other reasons, too, why Napoleon was ready to consider interfering in Italy. Like his distinguished uncle, he was after all only a usurper. He knew that he could not rely upon mere tradition, but must maintain his popularity by deeds that should redound to the glory of France. A war with Austria for the liberation of the Italians, who like the French were a Latin race, would be popular, especially if France could thereby add a bit of territory to her realms and perhaps become the protector of the proposed Italian confederation. A conference was arranged between Napoleon and Cavour. Just what agreement was reached we do not know, but Napoleon no doubt engaged to come to the aid of the king of Sardinia, should the latter find a pretense for going to war with Austria. Should they together succeed in expelling Austria from northern Italy, the king of Sardinia was to reward France by ceding to her Savoy and Nice, which belonged to her geographically and racially.

Victories at Magenta and Solferino

By April, 1859, Victor Emmanuel had managed to involve himself in a war with Austria. The French army promptly joined forces with the Piedmontese, defeated the Austrians at

[1] See below, pp. 578 f.

ITALY
1814-1859
GERMAN FEDERATION
FRANCE
SWITZERLAND
EMPIRE OF AUSTRIA
KINGDOM OF HUNGARY
Danube
SAVOY Ceded to France 1860
KINGDOM OF SARDINIA
PIEDMONT
LOMBARDY-VENETIA
Chiavenna
Bormio
Trent
Udine
Trieste
Varese
Como
Bergamo
L. Garda
Treviso
R. Piave
Magenta
Brescia
Vicenza
Venice
Vercelli
Milan
Solferino
Verona
Padua
Lodi
Villafranca
R. Adige
Legnago
R. Po
Casale
Turin
Alessandria
Pavia
Piacenza
Mantua
Rovigo
Parma
Reggio
Ferrara
Novi
DUCHY OF PARMA
Modena
Bologna
Comacchio
DUCHY OF MODENA
Ravenna
Pontremoli
Imola
Forli
Genoa
Fivizzano
S. Marino
Ceded to France 1860
Nice
Monaco
Carrara
Massa
DUCHY OF LUCCA
Lucca
Florence
R. Arno
Urbino
Pesaro
Pisa
GRAND DUCHY OF TUSCANY
STATES OF THE CHURCH
Ancona
Castelfidardo
Jesi
Loreto
Arezzo
C. di Castello
Siena
Perugia
Umbria
Orvieto
Spoleto
ISTRIA
Fiume
KINGDOM
TURKEY
Adriatic Sea
Lissa I.
Aquila
Corsica (To France)
Viterbo
Civita Vecchia
Mentana
Rome
R. Tiber
Velletri
Foggia
Barletta
Trani
Bari
Capua
Benevento
Gaeta
R. Volturno
KINGDOM OF THE TWO SICILIES
NAPLES
Naples
Salerno
Taranto
Otranto
La Maddalena I.
Caprera I.
SARDINIA
Part of Kingdom of Sardinia
Cagliari
TYRRHENIAN SEA
Calabria
Aspromonte
Scylla
Messina
Reggio
Palermo
Milazzo
Trapani
Marsala
Calatafimi
SICILY
Catania
Girgenti
Syracusa
AFRICA
Malta (To Great Britain)
0 50 100
Scale of Miles
Longitude East from Greenwich
M.-N. ENG., BUFFALO

Magenta, and on June 8 Napoleon III and Victor Emmanuel entered Milan amid the rejoicings of the people. The Austrians managed the campaign very badly and were again defeated at Solferino (June 24).

Napoleon III unexpectedly consents to a truce

Suddenly Europe was astonished to hear that a truce had been concluded and that the preliminaries of a peace had been arranged which left Venetia in Austria's hands, in spite of Napoleon III's boast that he would free Italy to the Adriatic. The French emperor was shocked, however, by the horrors of a real battlefield; he believed, moreover, that it would require three hundred thousand soldiers to drive the Austrians from their strongly fortified Quadrilateral, and he could not draw further upon the resources of France. Lastly, he had begun to fear that, in view of the growing enthusiasm which was showing itself throughout the peninsula for Piedmont, there was danger that it might succeed in forming a national kingdom so strong as to need no French protector. By leaving Venetia in the possession of Austria and agreeing that Piedmont should only be increased by the incorporation of Lombardy and the little duchies of Parma and Modena, Napoleon III hoped to prevent the consolidation of Italy from proceeding too far. He had, however, precipitated changes which he was powerless to check. Italy was now ready to fuse into a single state.

Parma, Modena, Tuscany, and the Romagna request to be annexed to Sardinia (August–September, 1859)

During the months of August and September, 1859, the people in the three duchies of Parma, Modena, and Tuscany declared in favor of the permanent expulsion of their respective rulers and for annexation to the kingdom of Sardinia. An assembly in the Romagna, the papal territory lying north of the Apennines, repudiated the temporal rule of the Pope and also expressed the wish to be joined to Sardinia. The customs lines were thereupon abolished between these countries, they adopted the Sardinian constitution and placed their postal service under the control of Sardinian officials. They were, therefore, of their own accord, preparing the way for a united state in northern Italy.

Garibaldi, 1807–1882

In southern Italy, on the contrary, the king of Naples stubbornly refused either to form any kind of an alliance with the king of Sardinia or to grant his people a constitution. Garibaldi, an ardent disciple of Mazzini, thereupon determined to

FIG. 110. GARIBALDI

Garibaldi shares with Victor Emmanuel the national enthusiasm of Italy, and his monument, one of the finest in Rome, looks proudly over the Eternal City from a high hill. He was a republican, a convert of Mazzini, and had lived a restless life, having fought in South America and living for a time in New York (where his house is preserved as a memorial). At the head of his "legion" of volunteers, clad in their gay red blouses, he was a most picturesque figure, and his rapid success in the south lent an element of romance to the unification of Italy

bring him to terms and prepare the way for the union of southern Italy and Sicily with the expanding Sardinia. This bold sailor, warrior, and revolutionist accordingly set sail from Genoa for Sicily in May, 1860, on his own responsibility, with a band of a thousand "Red Shirts," as his followers were called from their rough costume.[1] He gained an easy victory over the few troops that the king of the Two Sicilies was able to send against him, and made himself dictator of the island in the name of Victor Emmanuel. He then crossed over to the mainland, and after a slight skirmish he was received in Naples with enthusiasm on September 6.

Napoleon III intervenes to prevent the annexation of Rome to the kingdom of Italy

Garibaldi now proposed to march on Rome and proclaim there the kingdom of Italy. This would have imperiled all the previous gains, for Napoleon III could not, in view of the strong Catholic sentiment in France, possibly permit the occupation of Rome and the destruction of the political independence of the Pope. He agreed that Victor Emmanuel might annex the outlying papal possessions to the north and reëstablish a stable government in Naples instead of Garibaldi's dictatorship. But Rome, the imperial city, with the territory immediately surrounding it, must be left to its old master. Victor Emmanuel accordingly marched southward and occupied Naples (October). Its king capitulated and all southern Italy became a part of the kingdom of Italy.

In February, 1861, the first Italian parliament was opened at Turin, and the process of really amalgamating the heterogeneous portions of the new kingdom began. Yet the joy of the Italians over the realization of their hopes of unity and national independence was tempered by the fact that Austria still held one of the most famous of the Italian provinces, and that Rome, which typified Italy's former grandeur, was not included in the new kingdom.

Section 67. The Kingdom of Italy since 1861

Attitude of the Pope toward the new Italian kingdom

The fact that Italian unification was not complete did not cause the patriots to lose hope. In a debate in the very first parliament held in the new kingdom of Italy, Cavour directed the thoughts and energies of the nation to the recovery of the

[1] *Readings*, Vol. II, p. 126.

"Eternal City and the Queen of the Adriatic." Meanwhile, however, Pius IX excommunicated the king of Sardinia and his ministers and declared the new constitution to be a creation of revolution, which was a thing to be struck down like a mad dog wherever it showed itself. And Napoleon III, at the

MAP OF THE UNIFICATION OF ITALY

instigation of the French Catholics, sent a French garrison to Rome with a view to protecting the Pope from attack.

How Venetia was added to the kingdom of Italy, 1866

Help, however, soon came from an unexpected quarter. In the early months of 1866 Prussia and Austria were on the eve of war, and in order to gain the support of Italy, Prussia concluded a treaty with Victor Emmanuel in April of that year. When the war came in July the Italians as well as the Prussians attacked Austria. The Italians were worsted in the battle of Custozza, but the Prussians more than made up for this defeat by their memorable victory at Sadowa. Thereupon Austria consented to cede Venetia to Napoleon III, with the understanding that he should transfer it to Italy. The efforts of the Italians to wrest Trent and Trieste from Austria failed, however, for their fleet was defeated, and they were forced to content themselves with Venetia, which they owed rather to the victories of others than to their own.

Rome occupied by the king of Italy, 1870

Four years later, in 1870, when war broke out between France and Prussia, Napoleon III was forced to withdraw the French garrison from Rome, and Victor Emmanuel, having nothing further to fear from French intervention, demanded of Pius IX that he make terms with the kingdom of Italy. The Pope refused, whereupon the Italian troops blew open a gate of the city and, without further violence, took possession of Rome, while the Pope withdrew to the Vatican palace and proclaimed himself the prisoner of the Italian government. The inhabitants, however, welcomed the invaders, and, by a vote of one hundred and thirty thousand to fifteen hundred, Rome and the remaining portions of the Papal States were formally annexed to the kingdom of Italy in January, 1871.

Rome becomes the capital of the kingdom of Italy, 1871

Italy was at last free and united from the Alps to the sea, and, as King Victor Emmanuel said at the opening of the parliament of 1871, "It only remains to make our country great and happy." The capital, which had been transferred from Turin to Florence in 1865, was moved to Rome in 1871, and the king made his solemn entry into the city, announcing to the people, "We are at Rome and we shall remain here." The Sardinian constitution became the constitution of the kingdom of Italy.

Position of the Pope

It was a difficult problem to determine the relations which should exist between the new government and the head of the Christian Church, who for a thousand years had regarded the city of Rome as his capital. By a law of May, 1871, the Pope was declared to enjoy perfect freedom in all his spiritual functions, and his person was made sacred and inviolable like that of the king. He was to continue to enjoy the honors and dignity of a sovereign prince, and to send and receive diplomatic agents like any other sovereign. Within the trifling domain

FIG. 111. THE PAPAL GARDENS AT THE VATICAN, ROME

These few acres, along with a summer residence which the Popes never use, and the two churches of the Vatican and the Lateran in Rome, are all that is left of the temporal sovereignty of the Papacy. The Pope refuses to leave this little territory, claiming that he is practically a prisoner of the Italian government, and has never given up his claim to rule Rome. He maintains a small guard of picturesque Swiss soldiers, who keep watch along the garden walls with bayonets fixed on their rifles, as if they were in perpetual siege. The Vatican palace has over a thousand rooms and galleries, many of them decorated by the greatest artists, like Raphael and Michael Angelo. The dome of the church rises directly over the shrine, or tomb, of St. Peter

which was left to him, he may live as an independent ruler, since no officer of the Italian government is permitted to enter these precincts on any business of State. In order to indemnify him decently for the loss of his possessions, the Italian government assigned him something over six hundred thousand dollars a year from the State treasury. The Pope, however, has not only always refused to accept this sum, but he persistently declines, down to the present day, to recognize the Italian government, and continues to consider himself the prisoner of a usurping power.[1]

Italy becomes a European power

In order to maintain the dignity of her new position, Italy adopted the expensive policy of rapidly increasing her army and navy. Modern warships were constructed, the principle of universal military service was introduced, and the army was reorganized. The building of ships and the equipment of the increased army nearly doubled the military expenses and served to produce a deficit, which amounted in 1887 to $83,000,000.

Italy joins the Triple Alliance

Nevertheless, Italy cherished ambitions of expansion and colonial empire. Just across the Mediterranean lay the ancient territory of Carthage, modern Tunis, and from sentimental as well as practical reasons, Italy coveted it. But in 1882, before it could act, France seized the land, which bordered on its province of Algeria. This increased Italy's bitterness toward France, and Bismarck used the occasion to win Italy over to sign the famous triple alliance with Germany and Austria-Hungary[2] — an alliance which lasted until the great war of 1914.

Italy's colonial policy in Africa

Frustrated in northern Africa, the Italians next turned their attention to winning colonial domains in the region of Abyssinia, near the outlet of the Red Sea. An army of occupation was dispatched thither in 1887, and after some fifteen years of intermittent warfare, treaties, negotiations, and massacres of the Italian troops by the natives, the Italians were able to make themselves masters of an area about twice the size of the state of Pennsylvania, inhabited by half a million of nomad peoples. More recently the Italians have waged war on the Turks for the purpose of securing dominion in northern Africa by the conquest of Tripoli.[3]

[1] For Pius IX's protest, see *Readings*, Vol. II, p. 136.

[2] This triple alliance was renewed in 1902.

[3] See below, p. 588.

Political parties in Italy

It is clear that the old ideals of Cavour and King Victor Emmanuel have been left far behind. The heavy burden of taxation which the Italians have had to bear, in order to play the part of a European power and pay for the very expensive luxury of colonization, has roused deep discontent among the peasants and workingmen. The patriotic feelings which had nerved the people to heroic service in behalf of unity and independence gave way later to a spirit of selfishness in the various provinces, the interests of which were by no means identical, for the conditions in Naples were essentially different from those of Venetia or Piedmont. The republicans, who still clung to the ideas of Mazzini and Garibaldi, continued to oppose the monarchy, while the ideals of socialism, as elsewhere in Europe, appealed strongly to the workingmen. Lastly there were the defenders of the Pope's political power, who were among the bitterest enemies of the new government.

Progress of Italy

Notwithstanding these adverse circumstances, the kingdom has made remarkable progress during the last generation. Italy is rapidly becoming an industrial state, and to-day more than one third of its population is engaged in manufacturing and commercial pursuits. Silk, cotton, and woolen mills export large quantities of goods to foreign markets.

Improvements in education

Many laws have been passed for the improvement of the public schools, in the hope of diminishing the illiteracy which is a reproach to the kingdom. The republicans and socialists are not satisfied, however, with the amount of money voted for education; they admit that there has been a steady reduction in the number of persons over twenty years of age who are unable to read and write, — from 73 per cent in 1862 to 52 per cent in 1901, — but they contend that it is a disgrace for the nation to spend six or eight times as much a year on the army and navy as it does for the schools.[1]

[1] In 1901, 28 per cent of the population of northern Italy over six years of age could not read or write, and in southern Italy, whence a large proportion of the American immigrants come, 70 per cent were illiterate.

Burden of taxation

In proportion to its wealth, the Italian nation has had the largest debt and the heaviest taxation of any country in Europe.[1] It has had to pay the land tax, the income tax, the house tax, the inheritance tax, the stamp tax, the excise, the customs duties, in addition to the government monopolies of tobacco, lotteries, salt, and quinine. These are so distributed that the most burdensome of them fall on the workingmen and the peasants, who receive very low wages, so that it is estimated that the poor pay over one half of the revenue of the government.

The heaviest taxes are imposed on the necessities of life, such as grain and salt; and in times of scarcity this has been a source of serious bread riots in the towns. As for the salt, the government in 1900 was charging eight dollars for a quintal (two hundred and twenty pounds) of salt, which cost it only thirty cents. An Italian economist estimated in 1898 that the family of a Florentine workingman was forced to pay in local and national taxes no less than one fourth of its income, whereas in England the government demanded less than one twentieth of the earnings of a workman in a similar position.

Yet it should be remembered that in most of the Italian states before the union, there was as heavy taxation, combined with bad government. United Italy has at least spent much of its money on national improvements, on railways and public buildings, as well as on colonial enterprises.

Assassination of King Humbert

Victor Emmanuel died in 1878. His son and successor, Humbert I, although personally courageous and faithful to the constitution, was not the man to undertake the reforms necessary to relieve the prevailing discontent. He did not control the government either for or against reform; nevertheless the anarchists marked him as one of their victims, and on July 29, 1900, he was assassinated while distributing prizes at a great public meeting. He was succeeded by his son, Victor Emmanuel III,[2] who has continued the general policy of his father.

[1] *Readings*, Vol. II, p. 141.

[2] The title is reckoned from the former kingdom of Sardinia.

Emigration from Italy

The discontent continues, and if emigration can be taken as in any sense a measure of it, the year after the assassination of Humbert was a period of exceptional distress. In 1888 Italy lost by emigration one hundred and nineteen thousand subjects; this had increased by 1900 to three hundred and

FIG. 112. MONUMENT TO VICTOR EMMANUEL, AT ROME

On the northwestern slope of the Capitoline Hill the Italians have erected the most imposing monument in Europe, to commemorate the unification of Italy. Its size is indicated in the picture by the relative size of people and buildings. A colossal statue of Victor Emmanuel adorns the center, while a vast colonnade surmounts the hill. The Forum of ancient Rome lies just behind it; but it faces in the opposite direction down a broad, busy street of the modern city, which is growing rapidly. Electric cars now connect the seven hills, and arc lights shine beside the Colosseum (cf. *Outlines*, Part I, pp. 250 and 273)

fifty-two thousand, and in 1901 to over half a million. Italy had never come into possession of any of those new territories which her sons, Columbus, Cabot, and Verrazano, had laid claim to in the name of other European nations, and her acquisitions in Africa were entirely uninviting to her discontented peasants and workingmen. Those who leave Italy, therefore, go to foreign lands — to Brazil, Argentina, Uruguay, and Paraguay; while hundreds of thousands settle in the United States. In 1910, however, no less than 147,000 returned from abroad.

This enormous emigration does not appear to relieve the discontent. In 1905 the strength of the socialists became so alarming that Pope Pius X instructed faithful Catholics to aid in the struggle against socialism by taking part in the elections, from which they had hitherto been admonished by the Church to abstain. Others, on the contrary, have reached the conclusion that the socialist party is an effective instrument for arousing the more conservative people to undertake important reforms.

QUESTIONS

SECTION 66. Describe the political condition of Italy in 1850. What were the views of those who desired the unification of Italy? Describe the government of Victor Emmanuel. What was the foreign policy of Cavour? What was the outcome of the participation of Sardinia in the Crimean War? Outline the war waged by Sardinia and France against Austria. What gains were made by Sardinia as a result of this war?

Describe the changes which took place in Parma, Modena, Tuscany, and the Romagna in 1859. What part was played by Garibaldi in the unification of Italy? What prevented the complete unification of Italy in 1860? Draw a map of Italy in 1848 showing the chief political divisions. Draw a map of Italy in 1861 showing the changes effected between these two periods.

SECTION 67. Describe the attitude of Pope Pius IX toward the new Italian kingdom. By what means did the kingdom of Italy gain possession of Venetia in 1866? When and in what way was Rome finally made the capital of Italy? What has been the position of the Pope in Italy since 1871? Describe Italy's colonial policy. Discuss the advantages to Italians of a united Italy. How is the burden of taxation injuring the country?

CHAPTER XVIII

FORMATION OF THE GERMAN EMPIRE AND THE AUSTRO-HUNGARIAN UNION

SECTION 68. PRUSSIA ASSUMES THE LEADERSHIP IN GERMANY

Industrial Revolution in Germany

The failure of the liberals to bring about a true German state at the congress at Frankfort in 1848 was largely due to the tenacity with which the numerous German rulers clung to their sovereignty and independence. However, industry and commerce were silently but surely welding the German people into a nation. In 1835 the first railway line had been built and the era of steam transportation begun; a network of telegraph lines quickly brought the separate states into close and constant touch with one another; and the growth of machine industry compelled them to seek wider markets beyond their borders. A solid foundation for unity was thus laid by steam, electricity, and machinery, and the growth of common business interests.

Commercial disadvantages of the division of Germany into practically independent states

Statesmen as well as leaders in commerce and industry began, shortly after the settlement of 1815, to realize the disastrous effects of the existing division of Germany into numerous independent countries. Each of the thirty-eight states had its own customs line, which cut it off from its German neighbors as well as from foreigners. How this hampered trade can be readily seen by examining the map of Germany at that time. One who traveled in a straight line from Fulda to Altenburg, a distance of some one hundred and twenty-five miles, crossed on the way thirty-four boundary lines and passed through the dominions of nine sovereign and independent monarchs.

A merchants' association complained to the diet of the Confederation in 1819 that in order to trade from Hamburg to Austria, or from Berlin to Switzerland, one had to cross ten states, study ten different customs systems, and pay ten tariff charges.

In January, 1834, a *Zollverein*, or tariff union, was formed, which was composed of seventeen states with a combined

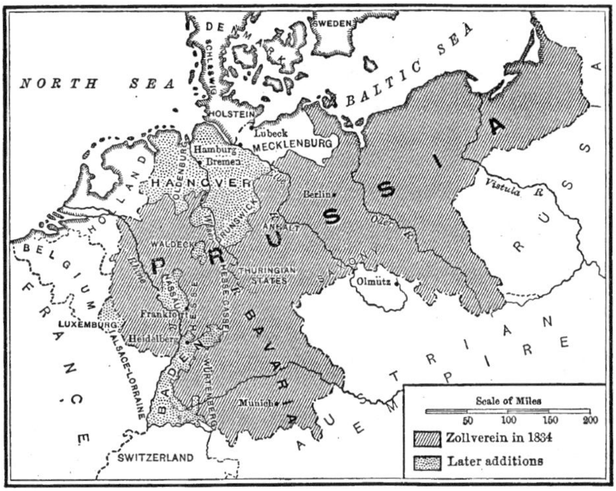

THE *Zollverein*

population of twenty-three millions. Goods were allowed to pass freely from one of these states to another, while the entire group was protected against all outsiders by a common tariff frontier. Austria, after some hesitation, decided not to join this union, but other German states were from time to time compelled by their own interests to do so.

The customs union (*Zollverein*)

As the center of this commercial reorganization of Germany, Prussia gathered strength for the coming conflict with her great rival, Austria; and with the accession of William I in

Accession of William I, 1858 (1861)

1858,[1] a new era dawned for Prussia. The chief aim of the new emperor was to expel Austria from the German Confederation, and out of the remaining states to construct a firm union under the leadership of Prussia, which would then take its place among the most powerful nations of Europe. He believed that war must come sooner or later, and therefore made it his first business to develop the military resources of his realms.

The strengthening of the Prussian army

The German army, which owes much of its power to the reforms of William I, has proved so fatal to the peace of the world that its organization merits attention. Fifty years before, the necessity of expelling Napoleon had led Scharnhorst to revolutionize the military strength of the kingdom by making military service compulsory for all healthy male citizens, who were to be trained in the standing army in all the essentials of discipline and then retired to the reserve, ready for service at need. The first thing that William I did was to increase the annual levy from forty to sixty thousand men and to see that all the soldiers remained in active service three years. They then passed into the reserve, according to the existing law, where for two years more they remained ready at any time to take up arms should it be necessary. William wished to increase the term of service in the reserve to four years. In this way the State would claim seven of the years of early manhood and have an effective army of four hundred thousand, which would permit it to dispense with the service of those who were approaching middle life. The lower house of the Prussian parliament refused, however, to make the necessary appropriations for thus increasing the strength of the army.

Bismarck sets out to Prussianize Germany

The king proceeded, nevertheless, with his plan, and in 1862 summoned to his side a Prussian statesman who would carry out that plan despite all opposition. It was an evil moment in the world's history when Otto von Bismarck was called to the

[1] He ruled until 1861 as regent for his brother, Frederick William IV, who had become incapacitated by disease.

presidency of the Prussian cabinet. He was a Prussian of the Prussians, and dedicated his great abilities to the one supreme object of Prussianizing all Germany — and with such success that his country became a fearful menace against which a great part of the civilized world was summoned to fight. Bismarck firmly believed in the divine right of the Hohenzollerns; he hated parliaments and freely displayed his contempt for the ideas of the liberal party which had attempted to unify Germany in 1848. He had every confidence in the mailed fist and shining sword, by which he foresaw he must gain his ends. He belonged to the highly conservative class of Prussian landed proprietors, — the so-called Junkers, — the same group who had so much to do with precipitating and prolonging the war of 1914. To accomplish his purposes he started three wars, and by his policy prepared the way for a fourth, which after his death involved the whole globe.

Four elements in the accomplishment of Bismarck's plan

In order to raise Prussia to the position of a dominating European power Bismarck perceived that four things were essential: (1) The Prussian army must be greatly strengthened, for without that he could not hope to carry out his audacious program. (2) Austria, hitherto so influential in German affairs, must be pushed out of Germany altogether, leaving the field to Prussia. (3) Prussian territory must be enlarged and consolidated by annexing those German states that separated the eastern possessions of the Hohenzollerns from the Rhine districts. (4) And, lastly, the large South German states, which disliked Prussia and suspected her motives, must in some way be induced to join a union under her headship. The task seemed hopeless, for attempts to consolidate Germany had failed from the times of Otto the Great down to those of William I. Nevertheless, within ten years Bismarck had, by a combination of diplomacy, deceit, and violence, succeeded in uniting Germany under the Hohenzollerns.

The first obstacle Bismarck encountered was the refusal of the lower house of the Prussian parliament to grant the money

Bismarck overrides the Prussian parliament

necessary for increasing the army. But Bismarck was not the man to be stopped. In defiance of the lower house and of the newspapers he carried on the strengthening of the army without formal appropriations by parliament, on the theory that the constitution had made no provision in case of a deadlock between the upper and lower houses and that consequently the king, in such a case, might exercise his former absolute power.[1] In one of his first speeches in parliament he said with brutal frankness, "The great questions of the time are to be decided not by speeches and votes of majorities, but by blood and iron." For a time it seemed as if Prussia was returning to a pure despotism, for there was assuredly no more fundamental provision of the constitution than the right of the people to control the granting of the taxes. Yet after Bismarck had succeeded in his policy of "blood and iron," he was eventually fully forgiven by the Germans, on the ground that the end had justified the means.

The Schleswig-Holstein affair

Prussia now had a military force sufficient to encourage hope of victory should she undertake a war with her old rival. In order to bring about the expulsion of Austria from the Confederation, Bismarck took advantage of a knotty problem that had been troubling Germany, known as the Schleswig-Holstein affair. The provinces of Schleswig and Holstein, although inhabited largely by Germans, had for centuries belonged to the king of Denmark. They were not considered a part of Denmark, however, any more than Hanover had been a part of Great Britain. But in 1847 the king of Denmark proclaimed that he was going to incorporate these provinces into the Danish kingdom in spite of the large proportion of Germans in the population. This aroused great indignation throughout Germany. The controversy over the relation of these provinces to Denmark continued, and finally, in 1863, just after Bismarck's ascension to power, Schleswig was definitely united with the Danish kingdom.

[1] *Readings*, Vol. II, p. 143.

Bismarck's shrewd game

Bismarck saw a way of settling the whole matter by annexing the Danish provinces to his dear Prussia and at the same time securing an excuse for a fight with Austria, for which he now felt himself ready. His first step was politely to ask Austria to coöperate with Prussia in an effort to settle the question of the provinces. The king of Denmark refused to make any concessions, and so the two great German powers declared war on him (February, 1864). The little Danish army was no match for them, and a few months later Denmark ceded the duchies to Austria and Prussia. They were to make such disposition of the provinces as they saw fit. Bismarck did everything to prevent any permanent rearrangement, for he was anxious to fall out with Austria and at the same time get both the Danish provinces for Prussia. He boldly began to turn Kiel, on the Baltic coast of Holstein, into a Prussian naval station, and did all in his power to irritate Austria.[1]

The victory over Denmark, 1864

Section 69. The War of 1866 and the Formation of the North German Federation

Prussia declares the German Confederation dissolved, June, 1866

In April, 1866, Bismarck made a treaty with Italy that, should the king of Prussia take up arms during the following three months, it too would immediately declare war on Austria, with the hope, of course, of obtaining Venetia. The relations between Austria and Prussia grew more and more strained, until finally, in June, 1866, Austria was compelled to call out the forces of the Confederation to protect herself against Prussia. Prussia's representative in the diet declared that this act put an end to the existing union.

[1] Prussia definitely annexed the provinces in 1866. Later the Germans built a canal across Holstein from Kiel to the mouth of the Elbe and so connected the two stretches of German coast which are separated by the Danish peninsula. The Danes of northern Schleswig were promised the right to say whether or no they desired to be united with Denmark. But Prussia paid no attention to this pledge, and these Danes sent to the German parliament a deputy who took every opportunity to protest against the ugly efforts of the Prussian government to compel them to adopt the German language.

War declared between Austria and Prussia

On June 14 Prussia formally declared war on Austria. With the exception of Mecklenburg and the small states of the north, all Germany sided with Austria against Prussia. Bismarck immediately demanded of the rulers of the larger North German states — Hanover, Saxony, and Hesse-Cassel — that they stop their warlike preparations and agree to accept Prussia's plan of reform. On their refusal, Prussian troops immediately occupied these territories and war actually began.

Prussia wins the battle of Sadowa, July 3, 1866

The Prussian army promptly prevented all resistance on the part of the states of the north; Austria was miserably defeated on July 3 in the decisive battle of Königgrätz, or Sadowa,[1] and within three weeks after the severance of diplomatic relations the war was practically over. Austria's influence was at an end, and Prussia was in a position to dictate to the rest of Germany.

The North German Federation

Prussia was aware that the larger states south of the river Main were not ripe for the union that she desired. She therefore organized a so-called North German Federation, which included all the states north of the Main. Prussia had seized the opportunity to increase considerably her own boundaries and round out her territory by annexing the North German states (with the exception of Saxony) which had opposed her in the war. Hanover, Hesse-Cassel, Nassau, and the free city of Frankfort, along with the duchies of Schleswig and Holstein, all were added to the kingdom of the Hohenzollerns.

Requirements of the proposed constitution

Prussia, thus enlarged, summoned the lesser states about her to confer upon a constitution that should accomplish three ends. First, it must give to all the people of the territory included in the new union, regardless of the particular state in which they lived, a voice in the government. A popular assembly satisfied this demand. Secondly, the predominating position of Prussia must be secured; but at the same time, thirdly, the self-respect of the other monarchs whose lands were included must not be sacrificed. The king of Prussia was therefore

[1] Bismarck's account of the battle is given in the *Readings*, Vol. II, p. 147.

made "president" of the federation but not its sovereign. The chief governing body was the Federal Council (*Bundesrat*). In this each ruler, however small his state, and each of the three free towns — Hamburg, Bremen, and Lübeck — had at least one vote; thus it was arranged that the other rulers should not become *subjects* of the king of Prussia. The real sovereign

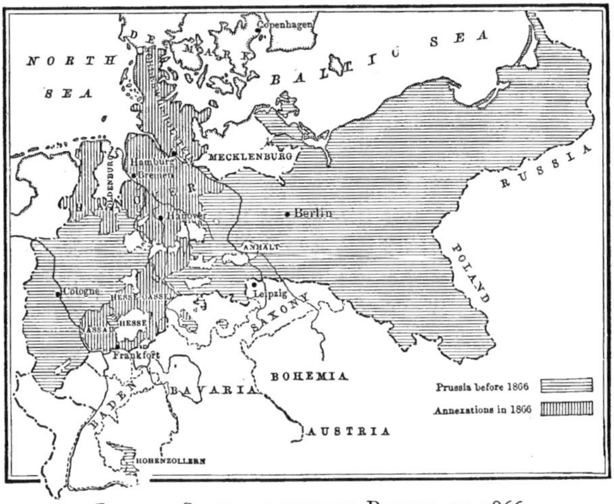

GERMAN STATES SEIZED BY PRUSSIA IN 1866

of the North German Federation was not the king of Prussia, but "all of the united governments." At the same time, by distributing the votes as in the old diet, Prussia, including the territory she seized in 1866, enjoyed seventeen votes out of forty-three. Moreover, Prussia could count upon the support of some of the lesser states. Lastly, the constitution was so arranged that when the time came for the southern states — Bavaria, Würtemberg, Baden, and South Hesse — to join the union, there would be little need of change.

II

Section 70. The Franco-Prussian War and the Foundation of the German Empire

Foreign policy of Napoleon III

No one was more chagrined by the abrupt termination of the war of 1866 and the victory of Prussia than Napoleon III. He had hoped that both combatants might be weakened by a long struggle, and that in the end he might have an opportunity to arbitrate, and incidentally to gain something for France, as had happened after the Italian war. His disappointment was the more keen because he was troubled at home by the demands of the liberals for reform, and had recently suffered a loss of prestige among his people by the failure of a design for getting a foothold in Mexico.[1] Napoleon was further chagrined by his failure to secure the grand duchy of Luxemburg, which its sovereign, the king of Holland, would have sold to him if it had not been for the intervention of Prussia. In other diplomatic negotiations also it was believed that Napoleon had been outwitted by Bismarck, and a war fever developed both

[1] This Mexican episode is one of the most curious incidents in the checkered career of Napoleon III. He desired to see the Latin peoples of the western world develop into strong nations to offset the preponderance of the Anglo-Saxons in North America; and furthermore, like his uncle, he cherished imperial designs outside of the confines of Europe. What appeared to him to be an excellent opportunity to build up a Latin empire under his protection was afforded by disorders in Mexico. In the summer of 1861, at the opening of the great Civil War in America, the republic of Mexico suspended payments on its debts. England, France, and Spain made a joint demonstration against Mexico in favor of their subjects who held Mexican bonds. Napoleon then entered into negotiations with some Mexicans who wanted to overthrow the republic, and he offered to support the establishment of an empire if they would choose as their ruler Archduke Maximilian, brother of the Austrian emperor, to which they agreed. Little realizing how few of the Mexican people wanted him for their ruler, Maximilian landed in his new realm in 1864, strongly supported by French troops. As soon as the Civil War in the United States was brought to a close, the American government protested, in the name of the Monroe Doctrine, against foreign intervention in Mexican affairs, and as Napoleon III was in no position to wage war with so formidable a power, he withdrew his soldiers and advised Maximilian to abdicate and return to Europe. The new emperor, however, refused to leave Mexico, and shortly afterwards he was captured and shot (June, 1867). The whole affair cost France a great deal of money and the lives of many soldiers, and discredited Napoleon's ability as a statesman.

in France and Germany, which was fostered by the sensational press of Paris and Berlin. Frenchmen began to talk about "avenging Sadowa," and the Prussians to threaten their "hereditary enemy" with summary treatment for past wrongs.

Question of the succession to the throne of Spain

In the midst of this irritation a pretext for war was afforded by the question of the Spanish throne, then vacant as the result of the expulsion of Queen Isabella in 1868. After the flight of the queen a national Cortes was summoned to determine upon a form of government, and after long deliberations it finally tendered the crown to Leopold of Hohenzollern, a distant relative of William I of Prussia. This greatly excited the journalists of Paris, who loudly protested that it was only an indirect way of bringing Spain under the influence of Prussia. The French minister of foreign affairs declared that the candidacy was an attempt to reëstablish the empire of Charles V. This belief was unfounded, for, in spite of the apprehensions of the French, the mass of the Spanish people were more anxious to see the restoration of the Bourbon line in the person of Alfonso, the son of Queen Isabella, than they were to have as their ruler Leopold of Hohenzollern, or Amadeus (the son of the king of Italy), who was finally induced in 1870 to accept the crown.[1]

[1] Amadeus was an enlightened prince, and endeavored to rule according to the wishes of his new subjects, but he found himself opposed by the Carlists, who supported a grandson of Don Carlos as their candidate; by the clergy, who opposed the new constitution because it granted religious liberty; and by the moderate royalists, who favored placing Isabella's son, Alfonso, on the throne. After little more than two years' experience, Amadeus laid down his crown, and the revolutionists proclaimed a republic (February 12, 1873), which lasted only about a year. At last, in 1875, the crown was given to Isabella's son, who took the title of Alfonso XII, and after a short civil war with the Carlists a new constitution was drawn up in 1876 providing for a parliament of two houses — a senate composed of grandees, appointed dignitaries, and elected persons, and a lower house of representatives chosen by popular suffrage. (By the electoral law of 1890 all male Spaniards twenty-five years of age are entitled to vote.) This is the present constitution of Spain. Alfonso XII died in 1885, and was succeeded by the present king, Alfonso XIII, who was born a few months after his father's death.

Attitude of France toward the candidacy of Leopold of Hohenzollern

But the war parties in France and Prussia were looking for a pretext for a conflict, and consequently the candidacy of Prince Leopold was given an exaggerated importance. In June, 1870, with the consent of the king of Prussia, Leopold accepted the proffered crown; but when the French government protested he withdrew his acceptance, also with the approbation of the Prussian king. The affair now seemed to be closed, but the French ministry was not satisfied with the outcome and demanded that the king of Prussia should pledge himself that the candidacy should never be renewed. This William refused to do, and Bismarck, anxious both to force a war and to throw the blame for it upon the French, with gleeful malice, so edited the account given to the German newspapers of the refusal as to make it appear that the French ambassador had insulted King William, and had been rebuffed.[1] This excited the "jingoes" in both countries to a state of frenzy, and although the war party in France was a small minority, that country nevertheless declared war against Prussia on July 19, 1870.

France declares war on Prussia, July 19, 1870

Disastrous opening of the war for France

The French minister proclaimed that he entered the conflict with a "light heart," but it was not long before he realized the folly of the headlong plunge. The hostility which the South German states had hitherto shown toward Prussia had encouraged Napoleon III to believe that so soon as the French troops should gain their first victory, Bavaria, Würtemberg, and Baden would join him. But that first victory was never won. War had no sooner been declared than the South as well as the North Germans ranged themselves as a nation against a national assailant. The French army, moreover, was neither well equipped nor well commanded. The Germans hastened across the Rhine and within a few days were driving the French before them. In a series of bloody encounters about Metz, one of the French armies was defeated and finally shut up within the fortifications of the town. Seven weeks had not

[1] For Bismarck's version of the affair, see *Readings*, Vol. II, pp. 158 ff.

elapsed after the beginning of the war before the Germans had captured a second French army and made a prisoner of the emperor himself in the great battle of Sedan, September 1, 1870.

Siege of Paris and close of the Franco-Prussian War

The Germans then surrounded and laid siege to Paris. Napoleon III had been completely discredited by the disasters about Metz and Sedan, and consequently the empire was abolished and France for the third time was declared a republic.[1] In spite of the energy which the new government showed in arousing the nation against the invaders, prolonged resistance was impossible. The capital surrendered on January 28, 1871, after a memorable siege, and an armistice was concluded.

The Germans require the cession of Alsace-Lorraine

In arranging the terms of peace their exultation led the Germans to make a mistake for which they had to pay dearly in the war of 1914. When Bismarck concluded the war with Austria he wisely took precautions to leave as little bitterness behind as possible. With France it was different. The Germans wished a visible sign that they had had their revenge. They forced the French to cede to them two provinces — Alsace and northeastern Lorraine.[2] In this way France was cut off from "the German Rhine," and the crest of the Vosges Mountains became the frontier. Many of the Alsatians, it is true, spoke a German dialect, but they had no desire to become a part of the German Empire. The people felt themselves to be an integral part of the French nation, and rather than submit to the hated rule of the Germans many of them left their homes and settled in France. Those who remained have never ceased to protest against the harsh attempts of the German government to prevent the expressions of their resentment.

[1] See below, Chapter XX.

[2] Alsace had, with certain reservations, — especially as regarded Strassburg and the other free towns, — been ceded to the French king by the Treaty of Westphalia at the close of the Thirty Years' War. During the reign of Louis XIV all of Alsace had been annexed to France (1681). The duchy of Lorraine had fallen to France in 1766, upon the death of its last duke. It had previously been regarded as a part of the Holy Roman Empire. The part of Lorraine demanded by Germany in 1871 included about one third of the original duchy, in which was the fortified city of Metz.

The Germans exacted a heavy war indemnity from France—a billion dollars—and proclaimed that German troops would remain in France until the sum was paid. The French people made pathetic sacrifices to hasten the payment of the indemnity in order to free their country from the presence of the detested "Prussians." The bitter feeling between France and Germany dates from this war. The natural longing of the French for their "lost provinces," and the suspicions of the Germans, not only prevented the nations from becoming friends but had much to do with the sudden and inexcusable attack which Germany made on France in August, 1914. The fate of Alsace-Lorraine has been from the first one of the crucial issues of the Great War. It is one of the most troublesome questions that will have to be decided at the peace table now the awful struggle is over.

Proclamation of the German Empire, January 1, 1871

As Bismarck had hoped, the successful war against France completed his work, begun in 1866, of creating a German empire. The southern states,—Bavaria, Würtemberg, Baden, and South Hesse,—having sent their troops to fight side by side with the Prussian forces, consented, after their common victory over France, to join the North German Federation. By a series of treaties it was agreed, among other things, that the name "North German Federation" should give way to that of "German Empire" and that the king of Prussia, as president of the union, should be given the title of "German Emperor." Surrounded by German princes, William, king of Prussia and president of the North German Federation, was proclaimed German Emperor in the former palace of the French kings at Versailles, January 18, 1871.

French politicians and newspaper men certainly played into Germany's hands when, imposed upon by Bismarck's garbled edition of the Ems dispatch, they urged a declaration of war against their neighbor. France had to pay for this terrible mistake by losing her provinces and watching Germany increase in population and wealth until Prussian ambition and insolence reached such a point that, forty-three years later, the German armies once more swept into France, this time without any plausible excuse whatsoever. In 1870 Europe and the United States observed strict neutrality during the conflict. In 1914, on the contrary, the despicable conduct of Germany speedily aroused the hostility of most of the other nations of the world, and they gradually formed a gigantic alliance against her and her allies.

SECTION 71. AUSTRIA–HUNGARY SINCE 1866

Problems facing Austria in 1866

The defeat at Sadowa and the formation of the North German Federation had served to cut off Austria from Germany altogether, and she was left to solve as best she might the problems of adjusting her relations with Hungary, reconciling the claims of the various races within her borders, and meeting the demands of the liberals for constitutional government and reforms in general.

The Austro-Hungarian dual monarchy established in 1867

An attempt had been made in 1861 to unite all the possessions of Francis Joseph into a single great empire with its parliament at Vienna, but the Hungarians obstinately refused to take part in the deliberations and, by encouraging the Bohemians, Poles, and Croats to withdraw, caused the plan to fail.

Soon after the defeat of Austria by Prussia in 1866 the relations between the Austrian Empire and the kingdom of Hungary were finally settled by a compromise (*Ausgleich*, as the Germans call it).[1] Francis Joseph agreed to regard himself as ruling over two separate and practically independent states: (1) the Austrian Empire, which includes seventeen provinces, — Upper and Lower Austria, Bohemia, Moravia, Carinthia, Carniola, and the rest; and (2) the kingdom of Hungary, including Croatia and Slavonia. While each of these had its own constitution and its own parliament, one at Vienna and the other at Pesth, and managed its own affairs under the guidance of its own ministers, the two governments, in dealing with

1 See *Readings*, Vol. II, pp. 165 ff., for extracts.

foreign nations, declaring war, and concluding treaties, were to appear as one state, to be called Austria-Hungary. They were to have a common army and navy and to be united commercially by using the same coins, weights, and measures, and agreeing upon a common tariff. Although this particular kind of union between two states was a new thing in Europe, it proved to be strong enough to last until 1918.

The government of the Austro-Hungarian dualism consisted of a common sovereign, three ministries, and the *Delegations*

In order to manage the affairs common to the two states, their joint monarch appointed three ministers — of foreign affairs, war, and finance. These ministers were responsible to a curious kind of joint parliament, called the *Delegations*, one section of which was chosen by the Austrian parliament, and the other by the Hungarian diet. These Delegations consisted of sixty members each and held their sessions alternately at Vienna and at Pesth, in order to avoid all jealousy. They sat as separate bodies, one carrying on its discussions in German and the other in Hungarian, and ordinarily communicated with each other in writing, except in cases of disagreement, when the two Delegations came together and voted as a single body, but without debate.

Continued difficulties due to the mixture of races

The problem of satisfying the various races, with their differing languages and their national aspirations, was the most serious difficulty which both Austria and Hungary had to face. In 1867 there were in Austria 7,100,000 Germans, 4,700,000 Czechs, 2,440,000 Poles (in Galicia), 2,580,000 Ruthenians (in eastern Galicia), 1,190,000 Slovenians (principally in Carniola), 520,000 Croats (in Dalmatia and Istria), 580,000 Italians (in Trieste and southern Tyrol), and 200,000 Roumanians (in Bukowina).[1] The Germans held that the German town of Vienna, the old seat of the court, was the natural center of all the provinces, and that the German language, since it was spoken more generally than any other in the Austrian provinces and was widely used in scientific and literary works, should be given the preference everywhere by

[1] See map, p. 394.

the government. The Czechs and Poles, on their part, longed for their old freedom and independence, wished to use their own language, and constantly permitted their dislike of the Germans to influence their policy in the parliament at Vienna.[1]

Power of the Church reduced in Austria

The three most noteworthy achievements in Austria during the past fifty years were the establishment of a constitutional system in 1867, the readjustment of the relations between Church and State in 1867–1868, and the extension of the suffrage in 1906. After the settlement of 1867 the German liberal party forced through the Austrian parliament a series of laws which restricted the time-honored prerogatives of the Catholic clergy.[2] Every individual was given the right to choose his own religion and to worship as he pleased. Government offices and positions in the schools were thrown open to all citizens, regardless of creed; the State, not the Church, was thereafter to manage the schools; civil marriage was instituted for those who did not wish to have a priest officiate at their marriage, as well as for those whom the priests refused to unite. The Pope vigorously condemned the constitutional laws of 1867, which had guaranteed complete religious liberty; the laws of 1868 he pronounced "abominable," and null and void. Nevertheless the reforms which Joseph II had striven to introduce before the French Revolution were at last secured.

Question of the suffrage

Austria, like the other European states, had been profoundly affected by the Industrial Revolution. The ever-increasing numbers of workingmen began to urge that the old system of voting, which permitted the richer classes to choose the members of the parliament, should be changed so as to allow the great mass of the people to send representatives to Vienna.[3]

[1] In the newspapers we read of the "Young" Czechs, who agree with the "Old" Czechs in working for Bohemian independence, but are more progressive than their fellow representatives.

[2] *Readings*, Vol. II, pp. 169 ff.

[3] The system adopted in 1867, according to which the local diets of the provinces elected the deputies, was later abolished, and the right to select the 425 deputies was put into the hands of four classes: the landowners were assigned 85 seats; the chambers of trade and commerce, 21; the towns, 118; the rural districts, 129. The adult males were permitted to choose the remaining 72.

At last, in 1906, the suffrage was extended to all males over twenty-four years of age. The first election under the new law took place in May, 1907.[1] The socialists gained over fifty seats, many of which they secured at the expense of the Czechs. But, on the other hand, the conservative clerical party also gained. It remains to be seen whether the various little parties formed on the basis of race issues will give way in time to those representing grave economic and social problems such as exist in the other European states.

FIG. 113. FARMING SCENE IN HUNGARY

The vast plains of Hungary are now farmed much like the prairies of America, with implements made by American firms. But the peasants on the great feudal estates are still dressed in quaint costumes, the kilts of the men being almost indistinguishable from women's skirts

The Magyars predominate in Hungary

The history of Hungary after 1867 resembled that of Austria in some respects. The Magyars have, however, been more successful than the Germans in maintaining their supremacy. The population of Hungary proper in 1911 was about eighteen millions, of which the Magyars formed something over half. Croatia and Slavonia had together slightly more than two and a half millions. In the lower house of the diet four hundred and thirteen deputies were chosen in Hungary, and only forty in Croatia and Slavonia. Magyar was naturally the language chiefly used in the diet, and by government officials and railway employees, and in the universities. The government

[1] *Readings*, Vol. II, pp. 171 ff.

Longitude East
10°
12°
14°
16°
50°
48°
46°
44°
GERMAN EMPI
Eger R.
Carlsbad
Eger
Elbe
Prague
Königgratz
Glatz
SUDETIC MTS.
Main
Nuremberg
BOHEMIA
Pilsen
Moldau R.
Tabor
Troppau
Olmütz
MORAVI
Brunn
Budweis
LITTLE CARPATHIAN MTS.
BAVARIA
Danube R.
Ulm
Augsburg
Passau
Gmünd
LOWER
AUSTRIA
Vienna
Schönbrunn
Pressburg
Munich
Inn R.
Salzach
UPPER AUSTRIA
Linz
Danube R.
L. of Constance
Gmunden
Salzburg
Bregenz
VORARLBERG
LIECHTENSTEIN
Innsbruck
BRENNER PASS
SALZBURG
Bad Gastein
GR. GLOCKNER
Enns
STYRIA
STYRIAN ALPS
Raab R.
Papa
Stuhlweissen
Platten See
TYROL
SWITZERLAND
RHAETIAN ALPS
Brixen
Botzen
CARNIC ALPS
CARINTHIA
Gratz
Klagenfurt
Mur R.
Drave
Nagy-Kaniz
Trent
JULIAN ALPS
Laibach
TRENTINE ALPS
Lake of Garda
Goerz
CARNIOLA
Agram
Trieste
CROATIA and SLAVONIA
Verona
Padua
Venice
Gulf of Venice
Istria
Fiume
Karlstadt
Mantua
Save
Modena
Bologna
Zara
BOS
Rimini
Florence
San Marino
Pisa
Ancona
DALMATIA
Livno
ITALY
ADRIATIC SEA
MEDITERRANEAN SEA
HERZEG
Lissa
Ragu
THE MATTHEWS-NORTHRUP WORKS

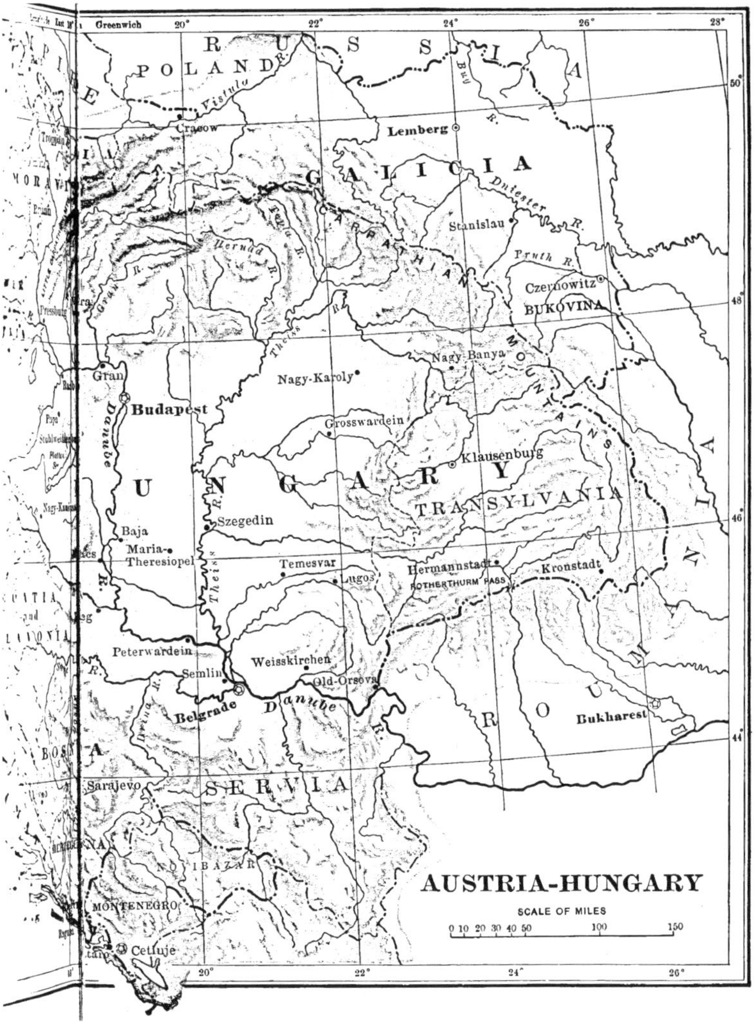
AUSTRIA-HUNGARY
SCALE OF MILES
0 10 20 30 40 50 100 150
Greenwich
20°
22°
24°
26°
28°
50°
48°
46°
44°
RUSSIA
POLAND
Vistula R.
Cracow
Lemberg
Bug R.
GALICIA
Dniester R.
Stanislau
CARPATHIAN MOUNTAINS
Pruth R.
Czernowitz
BUKOVINA
Hernad R.
Theiss R.
Gran R.
Pressburg
MORAVIA
Troppau
Nagy-Banya
Nagy-Karoly
Gran
Budapest
Danube R.
Grosswardein
Klausenburg
HUNGARY
TRANSYLVANIA
Szegedin
Baja
Maria-Theresiopel
Temesvar
Lugos
Hermannstadt
ROTHERTHURM PASS
Kronstadt
Peterwardein
Semlin
Weisskirchen
Old-Orsova
Belgrade
Danube
ROUMANIA
Bukharest
SERVIA
BOSNIA
Sarajevo
HERZEGOVINA
NOVIBAZAR
MONTENEGRO
Cettuje

encouraged the migration of the people to the cities, especially to Budapest, for it is the rapidly growing cities which are the strongholds of the Magyars, and the number of those who speak their language is steadily increasing.

Race discontent in Hungary

Croatia and Slavonia were dissatisfied with the way they were treated in the national parliament at Budapest. The Serbians were discontented, and some of the extremists among them cherished the hope that the region they inhabited would be annexed some day to the kingdom of Serbia; while the Roumanians looked longingly to the independent kingdom of Roumania, of which they felt they should form a part.[1] It was this racial discontent which furnished the cause for the events leading to the great war of 1914 and for the disruption of the monarchy in 1918.

QUESTIONS

SECTION 68. What was the effect of the Industrial Revolution upon the German states? Describe the *Zollverein* of 1834. By what means was Prussia enabled to assume the leadership of the German states? Describe the way in which the Prussian army was strengthened. Give an account of Bismarck's views and aims.

SECTION 69. What use did Bismarck make of the Schleswig-Holstein question? Show on a map the position taken by the different German states in the Austro-German war of 1866. Trace on a map the extent of the North German Federation, indicating the gains made by Prussia as a result of the war with Austria. Contrast the constitution of the North German Federation with that of the German Confederation.

SECTION 70. Describe the foreign policy of Napoleon III. Describe the situation which led to the war between France and Prussia in 1870. Outline the main events of this war. What were the terms of peace? Discuss the effect of this war upon German unity.

SECTION 71. Show the result of Austria's war with Prussia, in 1866, on the relations between Austria and Hungary. Describe the government of the dual monarchy. What are the internal problems which confront Austria at the present day?

[1] For the annexation of Bosnia and Herzegovina, see below, p. 586.

SECTION 72. THE GERMAN CONSTITUTION

The war of 1914 makes the German government a world issue

Few persons outside of Germany knew much about the German constitution and methods of government before the opening of the Great War in 1914. Then suddenly these became a matter of world-wide interest. The ravaging of a helpless, blameless little country like Belgium, with no further excuse than that it suited the interests of the German high military command to pass through that country in order to crush France, woke other nations to the dangers that lurked in the German system.

President Wilson's arraignment of the German government

When, in April, 1917, the policy of the German military authorities finally forced the United States into the war, President Wilson explained to Congress that Germany had "an irresponsible government which has thrown aside all considerations of humanity and of right and is running amuck"; that "the Prussian autocracy was not and could never be our friend"; that, with its control of the German military machine, it was the "natural foe to liberty"; that "no autocratic government could be trusted to keep faith"; and that since the German Empire had become a menace to the peace and freedom of the world the United States should combine with other democratic nations against it and, if necessary, "spend the whole force of the nation to check and nullify its pretensions and its power."

Prussian origin of the German constitution

In the previous chapter the origin of the German Empire was described. Its constitution was originally drawn up after Prussia defeated Austria in 1866, and was designed to secure Prussian predominance in Germany. Even if some little influence was granted to the representatives of the people, we might be sure that Bismarck, with his autocratic ideas and his confidence in kings and armies, would not consent to any essential weakening of the monarch's power or of the control enjoyed by the military and landowning classes (*Junkers*).

Predominance of Prussia

In the North German Federation of 1866 Prussia, with the German states she had seized, constituted nearly the whole union. In spite of the addition of the states south of the Main River in 1870–1871, Prussia still formed nearly two thirds of the empire, and her citizens amounted to nearly two thirds of the population of Germany.

The Prussian constitution of 1850

So before considering the constitution of the empire, we must see the nature of the Prussian government under which a majority of the Germans lived — a government that existed until the end of the great war of 1914. The autocratic Prussian government was overthrown in 1918, and at the present writing it is yet too early to say whether or not any of its outer forms will be retained in the new German state. When, in 1850, the king of Prussia "granted" his people a constitution, Bismarck heartily opposed the measure; and, when, as we have seen, in 1862, he decided that the army must be increased he paid no attention to the refusal of the Prussian lower house to grant him the necessary money. The king of Prussia and the Austrian monarch were the last of the old-fashioned autocrats to reign in Europe. By the end of 1918 the ruler "by the grace of God" had become a thing of the past. Until then the militaristic landowning class were in control of the upper house of the Prussian parliament, or diet. The method of electing members to the lower house was so arranged as to give the richer classes an overwhelming influence.

"The three-class system" of voting

The members of the lower house were elected *indirectly*, that is, by conventions, the delegates to which were chosen in each electoral district. Every man who had reached the age of twenty-five years was permitted to vote, but care was taken that if he were poor and discontented with the government his vote should count for practically nothing. This was effected by dividing the voters into three classes, according to the amount of taxes they paid. Those who were richest and together paid a third of the taxes had a third of the votes; those who paid the second third had a third; and, finally, the great mass of the people who made up the other third had a right to select a third of the deputies to the electoral convention, which met to select representatives of the district to sit in the diet.

Character of Prussian elections

Sometimes it happened that a single rich *Junker*, or even a Berlin sausage manufacturer, might elect a third of the delegates in his district. In 1900 the Social Democrats cast a majority of votes for members of the conventions and found themselves with only seven seats in the diet out of nearly four hundred, the rest having been filled by the richer, conservative classes. But not satisfied with the workings of "the three-class system," the Prussian government made every one vote aloud, so that the government officials could tell what his sentiments were. Moreover, it shamelessly interfered with the elections, as one of the Prussian chancellors frankly admits in his memoirs, to prevent the election of deputies opposed to the plans of the small group which controlled the policy of Prussia.

Powerlessness of the lower house

Even when the lower house got together, it had little power. The king was in control of the upper house, the members of which were elected as he wished. He initiated all laws and had an absolute veto on all measures passed by the parliament. He managed the administration, which was in the hands of a permanent bureaucracy of the most conservative militaristic type. The members of the lower house could talk, so far as they thought prudent, and could refuse to approve appropriations; but there were various forms of pressure that could be brought to bear on them to support the king and his advisers. These facts justified one in calling Prussia, which was the predominating state of the German Empire, autocratic, or highly aristocratic, in its frame of government and methods. We must now turn to the federal constitution and note the ingenious manner in which the control of Prussia and its king was extended over the whole empire.

Position of the German Emperor

It will be remembered that the constitution of the North German Federation had been drawn up with the hope that the South German states would consent in time to join this union which Prussia arranged in 1866. Consequently, when the German Empire was proclaimed, four years later, fewer changes needed to be made than might have been expected. The ancient title "German Emperor" (*Deutscher Kaiser*) was bestowed on King William I of Prussia and his successors on the throne of the Hohenzollerns forever. He was not, however, regarded as the sovereign of Germany, for this would have offended the pride of the various German kings and princes, like the kings of Bavaria and Würtemberg, who would not consent to be subkings under the chief king of Prussia. So the Kaiser was only given the "presidency" of the empire. It is true that William II was accustomed to talk as if he ruled Germany by the grace of God, but he had no constitutional right to make this claim.

Powers of the Kaiser

The emperor did not have the right directly to veto the measures passed by the imperial parliament, but he exercised many of the powers that would fall to an absolute monarch. He appointed and dismissed the chancellor of the empire, who, with his "all-highest" self, was the chief official spokesman of Germany. What was most dangerous for the rest of the world, the Kaiser commanded the unconditional obedience of all German soldiers and sailors and appointed the chief officers in the army and navy. He had only to say that the fatherland was attacked and he could hurl the German army against any innocent neighbor he chose without asking any one's approval. This he did when he ordered the invasion of Belgium and France in 1914.

The *Bundesrat*

The sovereignty of the empire was theoretically vested not in the Kaiser but in a sort of composite monarch called the Federal Council (*Bundesrat*), the most peculiar, important, and least understood feature of the German system. This was made up of the personal representatives of the twenty-two monarchs and of the three free cities included in the federation (see above, p. 433). The *Bundesrat* consisted of representatives of the individual states of the union, but its members were agents of their respective governments, which they represented, and not of the people of the several states. They had to vote as their rulers commanded rather than as the people of their respective states might desire. The king of Prussia had seventeen votes, to which he added the three assigned to Alsace-Lorraine, which he controlled; this insured him twenty out of a total of sixty-one. The king of Bavaria had six, the ruler of Saxony four, the ruler of Würtemberg four, and a great part of the smaller countries only one.[1]

[1] Composition of the German Empire

Names of the States	Population Dec. 1, 1910 (in Round Numbers)	Number of Members in the Bundesrat	Present Number of Representatives in the Reichstag
Kingdom of Prussia	40,100,000	17	236
Kingdom of Bavaria	6,800,000	6	48
Kingdom of Saxony	4,800,000	4	23
Kingdom of Würtemberg	2,400,000	4	17
Grandduchy of Baden	2,100,000	3	14
Grandduchy of Hesse	1,200,000	3	9
Grandduchy of Mecklenburg-Schwerin	639,000	2	6
Grandduchy of Saxe-Weimar	417,000	1	3
Grandduchy of Mecklenburg-Strelitz	106,000	1	1
Grandduchy of Oldenburg	482,000	1	3
Duchy of Brunswick	494,000	2	3
Duchy of Saxe-Meiningen	278,000	1	2
Duchy of Saxe-Altenburg	216,000	1	1
Duchy of Saxe-Coburg-Gotha	257,000	1	2
Duchy of Anhalt	331,000	1	2
Principality of Schwarzburg-Sondershausen	89,000	1	1
Principality of Schwarzburg-Rudolstadt	100,000	1	1
Principality of Waldeck	61,000	1	1
Principality of Reuss, elder line	72,000	1	1
Principality of Reuss, junior line	152,000	1	1
Principality of Schaumburg-Lippe	46,000	1	1
Principality of Lippe	150,000	1	1
Free town of Lübeck	116,000	1	1
Free town of Bremen	298,000	1	1
Free town of Hamburg	1,015,000	1	3
Imperial territory of Alsace-Lorraine	1,800,000	3	15
Total (details added)	64,903,423	61	397

The *Reichstag*, or House of Representatives

The democratic element in the government was the *Reichstag*, or House of Representatives, which consisted of about four hundred members distributed among the various states according to their population. The constitution provided that every German citizen twenty-five years of age might vote for members of the Reichstag. The representatives were elected for a term of five years, but the house might at any time be dissolved by the emperor with the consent of the Bundesrat. Members of the Reichstag, under a law of May, 1906, were paid for their services.

The chancellor

The chief minister of the empire was the chancellor, who was appointed by the Kaiser from among the Prussian delegates in the Bundesrat and might be dismissed by him at will without regard to the rise and fall of parties in the Reichstag. The chancellor was not bound by any resolutions or votes of the Reichstag; he was entirely at the command of the emperor, from whom alone he derived his authority. He presided over the Bundesrat, appointed the federal officers in the name of the emperor, and supervised the discharge of their duties.

No cabinet system in the German Empire

In short, Germany had never introduced the cabinet system of government which prevails in other European countries.[1] The Kaiser exercised, through the chancellor and in view of his position as king of Prussia, a power unrivaled by any of the constitutional rulers of Europe, and the Reichstag served rather as a critic of, and a check on, the government than as the directing force.

Necessity for uniform laws for the whole empire

When German unity was finally achieved in 1871 by the formation of the empire, the new nation was still in a very uncertain position, and individual preferences bade fair to jeopardize a real union. A federation had been entered into by states bound together by ties of a common race and language, but its permanence was by no means assured. The various German rulers were zealous in safeguarding their dignity and their own

[1] See above, pp. 56, 168. See *Readings*, Vol. II, pp. 176 ff., for Bismarck's view.

particular rights, and they were not altogether pleased with the preëminence assumed by the king of Prussia. Each state has its own traditions of independence, its own peculiar industrial interests, and its own particular form of government. Realizing the strength of these local tendencies, the imperial government undertook to establish stronger national ties through the introduction of uniform laws for the whole German people, to supplant the diverse laws of the various states.

Powers of the imperial government

The leadership in this nationalizing movement fell naturally to Bismarck, chancellor of the empire and president of the Prussian ministry. Fortunately for him the constitution conferred on the federal legislature wide powers in regulating many economic matters instead of reserving these entirely to the states. The imperial parliament was given the power to regulate commerce and intercourse between the states and with foreign nations, to coin money, to fix weights and measures, and to control the banking system, railways, telegraph, and post office, besides other general powers. But, more than this, the federal government in Germany was empowered by the constitution to make uniform throughout the empire the criminal and civil law, the organization of the courts, and judicial procedure. No individual state could define crimes, regulate the form of contracts, and so forth. Consequently the Prussian chancellor could proceed to direct the reform of all Germany according to his ideas of what was best for her.

Imperial legislation

The parliament at once set to work to exercise the important powers conferred upon it. In 1873 a uniform currency law was passed, and the bewildering variety of coins and paper notes of the separate states was replaced by a simple system of which the *mark* (about twenty-five cents) is the basis. The new coins bore on one side the effigy of the emperor and on the other the arms of the empire, "to preach to the people the good news of unity." In 1871 a uniform criminal code was introduced; in 1877 a law was passed regulating the organization of the courts, civil and

Longitude East 12° from
NORTH SEA
HELGOLAND
Copenhagen
Schleswig
Kiel Bay
FEHMARN
Kiel
Kaiser Wilhelm Canal
Schleswig-Holstein
Lübeck Bay
Cuxhaven
Lübeck
MECKLENBURG SCHWERIN
Schwerin
Altona
Hamburg
Harburg
Elbe R.
Bremen
Oldenburg
OLDENBURG
NETHERLANDS
Zuider Zee
Amsterdam
The Hague
Hanover
Weser R.
Aller R.
Ems R.
Osnabrück
Schaumburg Lippe
Brunswick
BRUNSWICK
Magdeburg
Lippe
Hildesheim
Münster
Detmold
Halberstadt
Bernburg
Anhalt
Westphalia
Essen
Dortmund
Nordhausen
Halle
Krefeld
Düsseldorf
Barmen
Elberfeld
Cassel
Waldeck
Mühlhausen
Brussels
BELGIUM
Cologne
Mülheim
Rhine Prov.
Aachen
Bonn
Nassau
Hesse
Gotha
Erfurt
THURINGIA
Plauen
Coblenz
Frankfort
Hanau
Coburg
Wiesbaden
Mayence
Sedan
LUXEMBURG
Luxemburg
Treves
Moselle
Darmstadt
Worms
Mannheim
Main R.
Würzburg
Bamberg
Bayreuth
Reims
Kaiserslautern
Palatinate (To Bavaria)
Heidelberg
Fürth
Nuremberg
Metz
LORRAINE
Wörth
Karlsruhe
Heilbronn
Ratisbon
Pforzheim
Nancy
Strassburg
Stuttgart
WÜRTEMBERG
Danube
Ulm
Augsburg
Hohenzollern
Lech R.
Isar
Inn
Munich
ALSACE
Freiburg
BADEN
FRANCE
BAVARIA
Belfort
Mülhausen
Lake of Constance
Constance
Basel
SWITZERLAND
Tyrol
THE MATTHEWS-NORTHRUP WORKS

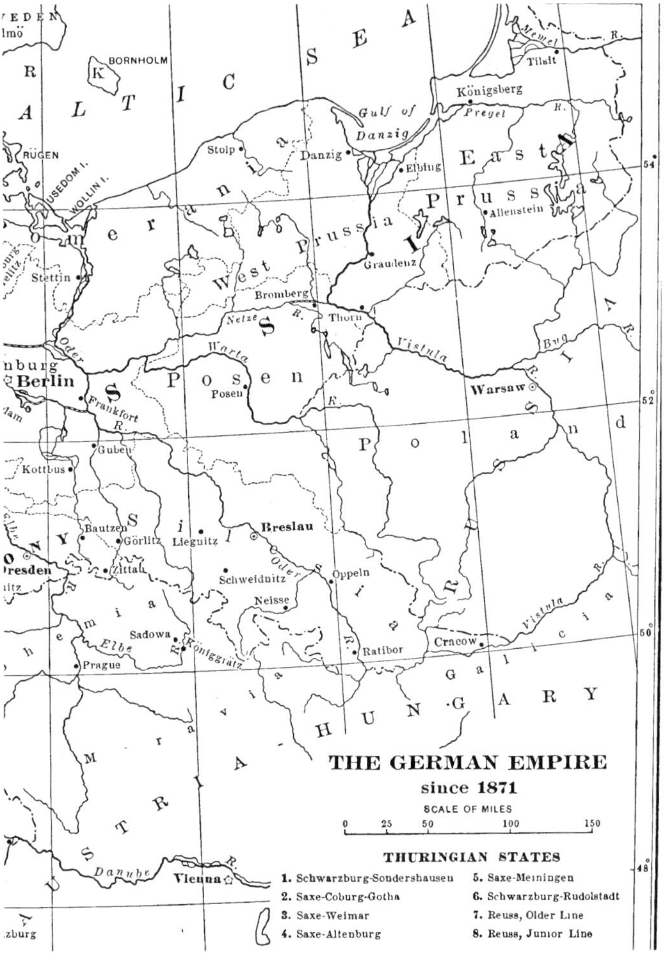
THE GERMAN EMPIRE
since 1871
SCALE OF MILES
0 25 50 100 150
THURINGIAN STATES
1. Schwarzburg-Sondershausen
2. Saxe-Coburg-Gotha
3. Saxe-Weimar
4. Saxe-Altenburg
5. Saxe-Meiningen
6. Schwarzburg-Rudolstadt
7. Reuss, Older Line
8. Reuss, Junior Line
BALTIC SEA
BORNHOLM
RÜGEN
USEDOM I.
WOLLIN I.
Gulf of Danzig
Pomerania
West Prussia
East Prussia
Posen
Silesia
Poland
Galicia
HUNGARY
AUSTRIA
Moravia
Bohemia
Königsberg
Tilsit
Memel
Pregel R.
Stolp
Danzig
Elbing
Allenstein
Graudenz
Bromberg
Thorn
Netze R.
Vistula
Bug R.
Warsaw
Stettin
Oder
Warta
Berlin
Frankfort
Posen
Guben
Kottbus
Bautzen
Görlitz
Liegnitz
Breslau
Dresden
Zittau
Schweidnitz
Oppeln
Neisse
Sadowa
Königgrätz
Elbe
Prague
Ratibor
Cracow
Danube R.
Vienna
54°
52°
50°
48°

criminal procedure, bankruptcy, and patents; and from 1874 to 1887 a commission was busy drafting the civil code, which went into effect in 1900.

The *Kulturkampf*

Although the champions of states' rights looked with disfavor upon Bismarck's policy of strengthening the imperial government and making uniform laws for the whole empire, the greatest opposition came from the Catholics, who feared the growing influence of Protestant Prussia. At the first imperial elections in 1871 the Catholics returned sixty-three members to parliament, and in this the chancellor saw, or pretended to see, a conspiracy of clerical forces against the state. The decrees of the Vatican Council, issued in 1870, definitely asserted that the secular governments might not interfere with the Pope in his relations with the clergy or with lay Catholics in church matters. Bismarck insisted on the supremacy of the civil law, and, mainly over a question of control of schools, began what was called the *Kulturkampf*, or "war in defense of civilization," by laws expelling the Jesuits and other religious societies and imposing penalties upon the clergy for any criticism of the government.[1] This was followed by other harsh legislation in Prussia; and the Pope and German clergy in general were moved to resist Bismarck's anti-clerical policy. Instead of submitting, the Catholics were welded into one party, and elected ninety-one members to the Reichstag in 1874.

Bismarck makes terms with the Catholic party

Finding the Catholic opposition growing stronger, and discovering a new danger to his policy in the rapid rise of a socialistic party, Bismarck came to terms with the Church, repealed nearly all of the measures directed against the clergy, and established cordial relations with the Vatican. The Catholic political party — whose representatives in the Reichstag are called the Center — was not, however, broken up by the reversal of the government policy; and the attempt to destroy the Socialist party, which Bismarck was now free to make, proved no more successful.

[1] See *Readings*, Vol. II, p. 183.

Section 73. Bismarck and State Socialism

Beginnings of socialism in Germany

The Socialist party had grown up in Germany practically within Bismarck's own time. In 1842 a German professor had declared that Germany had nothing to fear from that movement since the country had no distinct working class. But within less than a quarter of a century Germany, like England and France, underwent a radical industrial revolution. Large manufacturing towns sprang up; railways were built; the working classes inevitably combined to protect and advance their own interests; and all the problems of capital and labor were suddenly thrust upon the German people.

Karl Marx

The Socialist view of the labor problems and their solution had been elaborated by a German scholar, Karl Marx, before the Revolution of 1848,[1] but it was not until nearly twenty years later that a party championing his doctrines entered German politics. Under the leadership of Lassalle, a radical thinker and a brilliant orator, a General Workingmen's Association was formed at a labor congress in Leipzig in 1863. After more than a year's vigorous agitation Lassalle had, however, mustered less than five thousand members for his association, and he was thoroughly discouraged when he met his end in a duel over a love affair in 1864.

Lassalle

The Social Democrats organize in 1869

Notwithstanding the death of Lassalle, the campaign which he had begun continued to be prosecuted with greater vigor than before, although by no means all of the workingmen believed in his program. Some of the more radical among them, under the influence of the teachings of Marx, founded at Eisenach, in 1869, a new association, which bore the name of the Social Democratic Labor Party of Germany. The two groups worked side by side until 1875, when, at a general labor congress held at Gotha, they combined and issued an important statement of the views and purposes of the party.[2] In the elections of that year for the Reichstag the Socialists

[1] See above, p. 375. [2] See *Readings*, Vol. II, p. 493.

polled three hundred and forty thousand votes and began to arouse the apprehension of the government, which was naturally suspicious of them.

Bismarck determines to crush out socialism. 1878

Bismarck resented the attitude of the Socialists, and after two attempts had been made upon the life of the emperor, which he ascribed without justification to Socialist conspiracies, he had a law passed in 1878 designed to suppress socialistic agitation altogether. It prohibited meetings, publications, and associations having for their purpose "the overthrow of the social order" or the promotion of socialistic tendencies dangerous to the public peace, and authorized the government to proclaim martial law in any city threatened by labor disturbances. This repressive law remained in force for twelve years and completely disorganized the party as far as national politics were concerned. It failed, however, in accomplishing its full purpose, for the Socialists continued to form local societies in spite of the precautions of the police, and to spread their doctrines by secret propaganda in the factories and the army and by means of papers smuggled in principally from Switzerland.[1]

Origin of the "State socialist" party

While these attempts were being made to suppress the Social Democrats, there was growing up in Germany a new school of political economists known as "State socialists," who maintained that the government should adopt a number of the socialistic schemes for the benefit of the working classes in order to remove the causes of their discontent. The practical proposals of the State socialists were exceedingly numerous. They advocated providing steady employment for the working classes, reduction of the hours of labor, improvement of the sanitary and moral conditions in factories, restriction of the labor of women and children, and adequate precautions against accidents and sickness. They proposed to equalize the distribution of wealth by taxing those whose incomes were derived from rents, interest, or speculation, and favored government ownership

[1] See *Readings*, Vol. II, pp. 185 ff.

of railways, canals, and all means of communication and transport, water and gas works, a large portion of the land within city limits, markets, and the business of banking and insurance.

Attitude of Bismarck toward socialism and the working classes

Bismarck himself took a deep interest in the theories of the State socialists, and from 1878 to the close of his administration he advocated a number of reforms for the benefit of the working people and carried out a few of them. In undertaking these measures he frankly admitted that he was only renewing the old Brandenburg policy of paternal interest in the welfare of the people and in increasing the power and prosperity of the State. He accepted the capitalist system of industry and the division of society into rich and poor as a natural and permanent arrangement, but considered it the duty of the State to better the condition of the working people by special laws, as well as to encourage industry by protective tariffs.

State insurance in the interest of the working classes

He looked upon certain reforms in favor of the working classes as the best means of undermining the influence of the Socialists. In 1882 the government introduced two bills providing for accident and sickness insurance, which were given their final form after two years of deliberation and went into effect in 1885. According to the provisions of the first law, employers are obliged to provide a fund to insure their employees against accidents. From this fund the workmen are compensated when partially or totally disabled, and in case of death provision is made for the family of the deceased. The sickness insurance law compels working men and women to insure themselves against sickness, but helps them to bear the burden by requiring the employer to pay a portion of the premium and to be responsible for carrying out the law.

Accident and sickness insurance

Insurance for the aged and incapacitated

These measures were supplemented in 1889, after the accession of William II, by an old-age insurance law which compels every employee with an income under five hundred dollars a year to pay a certain proportion into a State fund which provides an annual pension for him after he has reached the age of seventy years. In case he is incapacitated earlier in life he may begin to draw the pension before he reaches that age. As in other forms of workingmen's insurance, the employers pay a portion of the premium; and the State also makes a regular contribution to every annuity paid.[1] In 1913 over twenty-five million persons were insured under these laws.

State socialism criticized by Socialists

These measures by which the government assumes a large degree of responsibility for the welfare of the working class constitute what is known as State socialism. Socialists, however, insist that one most important element of socialism is lacking, namely, democratic control. It is a revival and extension of the paternalism so familiar to Prussia in the days of Frederick the Great, and, however important as philanthropy, Socialists claim that it still leaves the *system* of capitalist ownership which keeps the poor from a fair share of what they earn. However, the State has kept enlarging its ownership of railways and of mines, and has engaged in other forms of productive employment.[2]

Section 74. Germany's Policy of Protection and Colonization; Foreign Affairs

Demand for protection of German industries

Closely connected with Bismarck's paternal attitude toward the working classes was his policy of protecting German industries against foreign competition. The successful war with France, the establishment of the empire, and, above all, the payment of the French indemnity had created a great "boom" in Germany. New enterprises multiplied; in Prussia alone the number of joint-stock companies increased from 410 in 1870 to 2267 in 1874; wages rose rapidly and times were "good" until the inevitable reaction due to overspeculation set in. Prices and wages then began to fall, companies failed, and factories closed. The manufacturers then commenced to demand that they be protected from foreign competition, and the farmers asked that high duties be placed upon the grain that was being shipped into the country from the United States and

[1] See *Readings*, Vol. II, pp. 189 ff.

[2] See below, p. 651.

Russia. It was urged that the German "infant" industries (of which we have heard so much in the United States) could not maintain themselves without aid from their government when rival nations, especially England, were so much better equipped with machinery, experience, and natural resources.

Germany establishes a protective system in 1879

It was under these circumstances that the imperial chancellor presented to the Reichstag in 1878 a program of tariff revision embodying two main points: (1) protective duties designed to give German industries the advantage over foreign producers; (2) a reduction of duties on raw materials not produced within the empire. In the following year the Reichstag adopted the new tariff laws by a large majority and thus initiated a system under which Germany became a great manufacturing country.

African colonization

German manufacturers were, however, not satisfied with securing preference over foreign competitors in their domestic trade; they soon began to demand government aid in finding new markets abroad. In spite of many misgivings about the ultimate value of distant colonies peopled by barbarous races, Bismarck was induced to take steps toward the acquisition of territory in Africa.

Togoland and Kamerun

He sent out Dr. Gustav Nachtigal in 1884 for the purpose of establishing German control at certain points along the western coast of Africa. In a short time the German agent had induced native chiefs to acknowledge a German protectorate over two large provinces, Togoland in Upper Guinea, a region about the size of the state of Indiana, and Kamerun, adjoining the French Congo — in all an area of over two hundred thousand square miles.[1] In the same year Herr Lüderitz, a Bremen merchant, acting under orders from Bismarck, raised the German flag at Angra Pequena (a point on the west coast a short distance above the English possessions at the Cape), where German merchants and traders had been active for some time. Within a few years the German government carved out a block of territory

[1] See map of Africa below, p. 622.

estimated at over three hundred and twenty thousand square miles, an area far greater than that of the entire German Empire. This colony was given the name of German Southwest Africa, but its entire European population is less than fifteen thousand.

German East Africa

Even larger territories were secured by Germany in East Africa. In 1884 the Society for German Colonization sent Dr. Karl Peters to determine what could be done in that region. The sultan of Zanzibar was induced in 1888 to lease a narrow strip of territory over six hundred miles long to the Germans, and in two years transferred all his rights to the German Empire for a million dollars. The few German settlers then established plantations of cocoa palms, coffee, vanilla, tobacco, caoutchouc, sugar, tea, etc., and the government founded several experiment stations for determining the possibilities of profitable agriculture.[1]

Bismarck and foreign affairs

In foreign affairs Bismarck was very active. Russia had been a valued friend during the formation of the empire, and for some years afterwards the three emperors of Germany, Russia, and Austria stood together against any chance of war between France and Germany. But in 1878 Austria turned against Russia to check the latter's successful career in the Balkans.[2] Bismarck then sided with Austria, making an alliance with it the next year. This alliance was joined by Italy[3] in 1882, and was known as the Triple Alliance. In the summer of 1914 Germany's friendly attitude toward Austria was one of the direct causes of the outbreak of the world war, as we shall see. But Italy, soon after the conflict began, repudiated the unnatural Triple Alliance and joined Germany's enemies.

The Triple Alliance

[1] About the same time German agents found their way into the Pacific and occupied a region in New Guinea to which the name of "Kaiser Wilhelm's Land" was given. The Caroline Islands (except Guam, which belongs to the United States) and a part of the Solomon group were also acquired. German merchants and investors also developed railways in Asia Minor, Syria, and Mesopotamia with a view to opening up the natural resources. Their activities in Morocco brought them into conflict with the French, who believed that they possessed special rights there, and for a time there was talk of war, but matters were adjusted in 1906 at a congress of European powers held at Algeciras on the Strait of Gibraltar and later (in 1911) by a special arrangement between France and Germany (see Chapter XXVII). [2] See below, p. 581. [3] See above, p. 421.

Section 75. Reign of William II

Accession of William II, 1888

With the accession of the third emperor, William II,[1] in 1888, Prince Bismarck lost his power. He had been implicitly trusted by the old Kaiser, William I, who had been content to leave the practical management of the empire largely in the hands of the chancellor. The new emperor proved a very different man. He was fond of making speeches[2] in which he had much to say of the power which God had given him; indeed, he seemed to be a stout adherent of that conception of kingship which Bossuet extracted from the Holy Scriptures and urged upon the willing Louis XIV.[3] On his accession to the throne he expressed himself as follows: "Summoned to the throne of my fathers, I have taken up the reins of government, looking for aid to the King of kings. I have sworn to God to follow the example of my fathers and be to my people a just and firm ruler, to nurture piety and the fear of God, to cherish peace, and to be a helper of the poor and oppressed, and a faithful guardian of justice."

Bismarck resigns, March, 1890

It is not strange that Bismarck should have found it hard to tolerate the intervention of the inexperienced young emperor. In March, 1890, he presented his resignation, and, amid a great demonstration of popular feeling, the "Iron Chancellor" retired to private life. Upon the announcement of Bismarck's resignation William II declared, with his usual unction: "I am as much afflicted as if I had lost my grandfather anew, but we must endure whatever God sends us, even if we should have to die for it. The post of officer of the quarterdeck of the ship of state has fallen to me. The course remains unchanged. Forward, with full steam!"

[1] William II is the eldest son of Frederick (who succeeded his father, William I, in March, 1888, and died in June of the same year) and of Victoria, the daughter of Queen Victoria of England. Frederick was the third of that name in the royal line of Prussia.

[2] See *Readings*, Vol. II, pp. 193 ff., 198 ff.

[3] See *Readings*, Vol. I, pp. 5 ff.

FIG. 114. THE LAST CARTRIDGE

An incident at Sedan, September 1, 1870. From a painting by De Neuville

FIG. 115. A VIEW OF THE CITY OF SEDAN

The scene of the defeat and capture of Napoleon III in 1870. After being held for over four years by the Germans in the Great War (1914–1918), Sedan was retaken during the last few days of the fighting in the victorious advance of the Allies

Attitude of William II toward socialism

For a time it seemed as if William II proposed to conciliate the Socialist party, although he could not possibly have had any real sympathy with its aims. The legislation against the Socialists which Bismarck had inaugurated in 1878 was allowed to lapse in 1890, and they now carried on their agitation openly and with vigor and success. The emperor pledged himself to continue the social legislation begun by his grandfather, since he deemed it one of the duties of the State to relieve poverty; and he declared that the welfare of the workingman lay close to his heart. Irritated, however, at his failure to check the expression of discontent on the part of the working classes,[1] he grew angry and pronounced the Social Democrat as "nothing better than an enemy of the empire and his country."

Germany in the Far East

United Germany, as we have seen, embarked on a colonial policy, and William II showed himself very ready to participate in world politics. At the close of the war between China and Japan, in 1895, he joined with Russia and France in preventing Japan from occupying the Liaotung peninsula. Two years later the Germans seized the port of Kiaochow on the Shantung peninsula opposite Korea.

Doubtful value of Germany's experiments in colonization

Notwithstanding Germany's extensive colonial dominion and commercial adventures in the Far East, the whole enterprise proved of doubtful value. None of the lands acquired were really suitable for settlement by German people who wish to emigrate from the fatherland.[2] Especially in Africa the native races under the German flag were very warlike, and in 1905–1906 the government spent the sum of nine million dollars in suppressing local uprisings, while the value of the exports and imports of the provinces scarcely exceeded two million dollars. (When the Great War began Germany lost all her colonies. It is impossible to say whether they will ever be returned or not.)

[1] See table below, p. 460, note.

[2] In 1910 there were only 340 Germans in Togoland, 1132 in Kamerun, about 10,000 in German Southwest Africa, and 2700 in East Africa.

Sources of dissatisfaction on the part of the liberals and Socialists

However, both the colonial policy and the system of autocratic government represented by the Kaiser were not without powerful opponents, for in spite of the fact that the imperial government was founded on a written constitution and the Reichstag was elected by popular vote, the German government was the least democratic in western Europe. The emperor was not controlled by a ministry representing the majority in parliament, and public criticism of the government was liable to cause the arrest and imprisonment of the offender. Furthermore, the Reichstag could scarcely be regarded as really representing the views of the nation. The government refused to revise the apportionment of representatives as arranged in 1871, although great changes took place after that year. As a result Berlin, for instance, had only six members in the Reichstag, although its population of two million inhabitants entitled it to twenty. This accounts for the relatively small number of Socialists and the large number of conservatives in the parliament, for in 1907 the Socialists, although they could muster 3,250,000 voters, returned only 43 members, whereas the conservatives secured 83 seats with less than 1,500,000 supporters, mainly in the country districts. In the elections of 1912 the Socialists made large gains in spite of the unequal distribution of seats.[1]

There was no large liberal party in Germany to oppose the ancient Prussian despotism and militarism. This task fell to the Social Democrats, who in general talked freely against militarism and imperialism and derided the Kaiser's solemn nonsense about his partnership with God. But when the war came, in 1914, only a minority of the Socialists were proof against the war spirit; in the Reichstag the Socialist members gave loyal

[1] The steady increase of socialism is shown by the following table:

Year of election	Socialist votes	Members elected	Year of election	Socialist votes	Members elected
1877	493,288	12	1903	3,008,000	81
1881	311,961	12	1907	3,251,009	43
1887	763,000	11	1912	4,250,300	110
1890	1,497,298	36			

support to the government's military program. Some of them, however, bravely continued to assert that the fearful conflict was a criminal enterprise of the *Junkers* and generals.[1]

QUESTIONS

SECTION 72. What powers were given to the German emperor by the constitution of the German Empire? Give an account of the legislative branch of the imperial government. Who were permitted to vote for members of the Reichstag? Describe the office of imperial chancellor. Outline the powers of the imperial government. What was the *Kulturkampf*?

SECTION 73. Give an account of the Socialist movement in Germany through the year 1875. What was the purpose of the legislation of 1878 with reference to socialism? What is meant by State socialism? What were the proposals of the State Socialists of Germany? Discuss Bismarck's attitude toward socialism. Describe the system of State insurance for the working classes.

SECTION 74. Account for the policy of protection of German industries. Describe the tariff adopted in 1879. What was the effect of the development of German industries upon colonization in Africa? in other parts of the world?

SECTION 75. Under what circumstances did Bismarck resign the chancellorship? What was the attitude of William II toward socialism? Discuss the German colonial policy in the Far East. What criticism of the government was made by the Socialists?

[1] For more recent developments in Germany, see below, pp. 648 f.

CHAPTER XX

FRANCE UNDER THE THIRD REPUBLIC

SECTION 76. ESTABLISHMENT OF THE THIRD FRENCH REPUBLIC

The Third French Republic proclaimed, September 4, 1870

On September 3, 1870, Napoleon III telegraphed from Sedan to Paris, "The army is defeated and captured, and I am a prisoner."[1] This meant an immediate collapse of the empire which he had established some twenty years before. The Chamber of Deputies was invaded by a mob shouting for the republic, and a motion was made to dethrone Napoleon and his dynasty. Next day Gambetta, a fiery young orator from the south of France, and the deputies representing the city of Paris betook themselves to the old revolutionary storm center, the City Hall, and there proclaimed the reëstablishment of a republic. This was sanctioned by an overwhelming majority of the Parisians. Meanwhile other large cities, such as Bordeaux, Marseilles, and Lyons, took similar action.

The Germans invade France and lay siege to Paris

The terrible defeat at Sedan and the capture of the emperor did not, as we know, bring the war to a close. The German invaders pressed on; city after city was taken; the strongly fortified Strassburg fell at the end of September after a terrific bombardment, and the fortress of Metz a month later. Paris itself was surrounded by an immense German army, and the king of Prussia took up his quarters at Versailles. Gambetta, escaping from Paris in a balloon, floated safely over the lines of the besieging Germans and reached Tours. Here he invoked the memories of 1793 and sought to organize a national army

[1] After the conclusion of peace between France and Germany the Germans set Napoleon III free and he retired to England, where he died in 1873.

of volunteers; but the raw French battalions were easily defeated by the disciplined German regiments which had been set free by the surrender of Metz. In January, 1871, the French made their last effort to bring the enemy to terms by endeavoring to cut off his communications with Germany, but the attempt failed and a considerable part of the French forces were compelled to take refuge in the neutral territory of Switzerland, whither the Germans could not pursue them. Paris, reduced after a terrible siege to the point of starvation,[1] capitulated on January 28, and an armistice was concluded.

The National Assembly elected February, 1871, proves to be strongly monarchical

Since the fall of the government of Napoleon III early in September, France had had no opportunity to work out a new constitution, and had drifted on under a provisional "Government of the Public Defense," which Gambetta and others among the former deputies had improvised. There was some doubt whether this revolutionary body was authorized to conclude a peace, and accordingly it was arranged, upon the surrender of Paris, that the French should elect a national assembly which would legally represent the nation in dealing with the victorious enemy. The result of the elections was surprising, for only two hundred republican candidates were chosen as against five hundred monarchists of various kinds, namely, Legitimists, who adhered to the grandson of Charles X, Orleanists, who were in favor of the grandson of Louis Philippe, and a few Bonapartists. This was largely due to the fact that Gambetta and other prominent republicans had talked so fervidly of continuing the war at any cost that the mass of the people was fearful lest if put in power they might prolong the disastrous conflict which was ruining the country. The National Assembly, aware that Paris was strongly republican in its sentiments, determined to meet in Bordeaux, where it held its first session on February 12.

Adolphe Thiers

Foremost among the brilliant men who composed this body was Adolphe Thiers, the historian, journalist, and politician, who

[1] For a description by an eyewitness, see *Readings*, Vol. II, pp. 208 ff.

for more than forty years had been a prominent figure both in literature and in affairs of State. In the grave crisis in which France found herself in February, 1871, he appeared to be the natural leader. His popularity was demonstrated by the

FIG. 116. GAMBETTA

Gambetta, who was only thirty-two years old in 1870, was a lawyer and journalist from southern France, who had already become prominent before the war by his attacks upon the empire. After the war he became the leader of the republicans against the monarchists and an emphatic opponent of *cléricalisme*. He also advocated a policy of social reform. He died suddenly at the age of forty-four

fact that in the elections for the National Assembly he had received over two million votes. The National Assembly therefore appointed him "Head of the Executive Power of the French Republic" and provided that he should exercise his authority through ministers of his own choice. This was, of course, a temporary arrangement, and the vital question whether

France was to remain a republic or to be reconverted into a monarchy was deferred until the hated Germans should be got rid of. Thiers declared that in the face of the trying situation

FIG. 117. THIERS

Thiers, as a young man, had been one of the leaders of the Revolution of 1830, a minister of Louis Philippe, then a strong opponent of his policy. He was also partly responsible for the Revolution of 1848. After Sedan he visited the various courts of Europe in the vain effort to win help for France. Then, as president of the French Assembly, he had to make the treaty which closed the war and arrange to pay the German indemnity. The title "liberator of the country" is applied to him by the middle classes of France, but the working class charge him with much cruelty in the suppression of the Commune

in which France found herself, all enlightened and patriotic citizens, whatever their individual views of government, should unite to free their country from the invader and restore her to her former prosperity.

The conclusion of peace with the Germans. Treaty of Frankfort, May 10, 1871

The first step in the realization of this policy was the conclusion of a final peace with the Germans, for the armistice which had been agreed upon at the capitulation of Paris had almost expired. On February 21 Thiers hurried to Versailles to open negotiations with the German emperor and Bismarck, and on the twenty-sixth, after many stormy scenes, the terms of the preliminary treaty were formulated. France was to renounce Alsace and a part of Lorraine, which together included a population of almost 1,600,000; pay an enormous indemnity of five billion francs; and submit to the presence of German troops until the last payment was made. The Assembly, convinced that a renewal of the war would be futile, accepted the terms imposed by the victorious Germans, and the peace documents were formally signed at Frankfort on May 10.[1]

The National Assembly moves to Versailles, March, 1871

As soon as peace had been duly concluded with Germany the republican minority urged that the National Assembly should dissolve itself, since it had now fulfilled its purpose. The majority, however, insisted upon continuing to govern France and proceeding to draft a constitution. The Assembly refused to remove to Paris, where the monarchists had good reason to fear the strong republican sentiment, so they chose Versailles as their place of meeting.[2] Louis Blanc warned the members that if they thus neglected the claims of Paris as the seat of government, there might arise "from the ashes of a horrible war with the foreigner a still more horrible civil conflict." His fears proved only too well founded, for Paris rose in revolt against an assembly which it regarded as made up of obstinate and benighted "rustics" who still clung to monarchy and had no sympathy with the needs of the great cities.

[1] The Germans were disappointed in their hope that the indemnity would seriously cripple France, for the first loan of two billion francs was secured in 1871 with ease, and the next year the second loan of three billions was subscribed twelve times over — thus demonstrating both the patriotism and the credit of the French people. In the autumn of 1873 the amount was paid in full and the last German soldier left the soil of France.

[2] Not until 1879 did the French legislature again return to Paris.

Paris resolves to bid defiance to the National Assembly

Trouble had been brewing in Paris for several months. The siege had thrown tens of thousands out of work and had produced general demoralization. The revolutionary group, which was speedily formed and which now attempted to govern Paris, included republicans, socialists, communists, anarchists, and some who could scarcely be said to have had much interest in anything except disorder. Many of the leaders were honest men of high ideals, who were determined to defend the republic, even by the sacrifice of their lives, as the "only form of government compatible with the rights of the people and the development of a free society." They all agreed in demanding that every *commune*, or municipality, should be left free to manage its own affairs in the interests of its own people. France would then become a sort of federation of communes, each community electing its own officers and introducing freely such social reforms as suited local conditions. It was this exalted confidence in the commune, or local government, that gained for the leaders the name of "Communards."[1]

Views of the Communards

The Commune suppressed with terrible loss of life and property, April-May, 1871

The doctrines of the Communards failed, however, to gain any considerable support in the other cities of France, and the Assembly at Versailles determined to reduce rebellious Paris to subjection. Toward the close of April, Thiers ordered a bombardment of the fortifications on the outskirts of the city preparatory to its capture. This was the beginning of a desperate struggle; the Versailles troops, under orders, refused to accord to the Communards the rights of soldiers, and shot, as traitors and rebels, all who fell into their hands. After three weeks of fighting on the outskirts, the forces of the Assembly entered Paris by an unguarded gate on May 21, and then began a terrible period of war, murder, and arson in the city itself. For a

[1] The word "communist" is often unhappily applied to the Communards. But "communist" is best reserved for those who advocate the more or less complete abolition of private property and maintain that society as a whole should own and control, in the interests of all, the capital which is now left in the hands of individuals. Many of the Communards were communists, but the terms are not synonymous.

whole week the fratricidal strife raged, until finally, on May 28, Marshal MacMahon, who was in command of the troops, was able to announce the close of the conflict and the restoration of order. The slaughter, however, was not yet at an end, for the monarchists set up courts-martial and, with scarcely the semblance of a trial, shot hundreds of the prisoners that had been taken. Unlike the government of the United States after the close of the Civil War, that of France under the leadership of Thiers — once a revolutionist himself — forgave no one. Seventy-five hundred of the insurgents were sent to the penal colony in New Caledonia and thirteen thousand were condemned to imprisonment at hard labor or sent into exile.

Dissensions between Legitimists and Orleanists in the National Assembly

The National Assembly was at last free to turn to the vexed question of settling upon a permanent form of government for the distracted country. There would have been little difficulty in reëstablishing the monarchy if the monarchists had not been hopelessly divided among themselves. Some of them, known as the Legitimists because they regarded the older Bourbon line as the lawful one, were in favor of bestowing the crown on the count of Chambord, a grandson of Charles X, who had been deposed by the Orleanist revolution in 1830. The Orleanists, who wished to see a restoration of the House of Orleans which had been overthrown in 1848, had a strong candidate in the person of the count of Paris, a grandson of Louis Philippe. These two groups of monarchists had nothing in common but their opposition to a republic; their hatred of each other was bitter and uncompromising.

Thiers (elected president of the republic) undertakes to strengthen the French army

In view of these divisions all factions were willing to postpone for a time the final solution of the problem, each hoping meanwhile to gain strength by delay. This policy was sanctioned by Thiers, who, elected president of the republic in August, 1871, urged the Assembly to devote its attention to the pressing task of strengthening the army and restoring the prosperity of France. Smarting under the humiliation of their defeat by the Germans, the Assembly passed a new army law which bound every Frenchman to military service for five years in the active service and fifteen years in the reserve force.[1] The frontier defenses were strengthened, the army equipped with the most improved instruments of war, and the war department completely reorganized.

Thiers overthrown and MacMahon elected president, 1873

At last, in December, 1872, Thiers, who had been an Orleanist, declared himself for the republic, arguing that its overthrow would mean a new revolution. His conservative republicanism, however, did not save him from attacks by Gambetta and the radical republicans of the extreme left; while the monarchists, angered by his defection, determined on his downfall. In May, 1873, they secured a majority vote in the Assembly for a resolution condemning Thiers's policy, and he thereupon resigned, leaving the government in the hands of the monarchists, who chose Marshal MacMahon as president and formed a coalition ministry representing Orleanists, Legitimists, and Bonapartists.

The Legitimists and Orleanists agree on a compromise, 1873

The various monarchist parties soon saw that they must arrange a compromise if they wished to restore the monarchy. Accordingly the Orleanists and Legitimists agreed that the count of Chambord should be recognized as Henry V, and that since he had no children he should be succeeded by the count of Paris, the candidate of the Orleanists. The thorny question whether France should cling to the tricolored flag, which suggested revolution, or adopt the ancient white banner of the Bourbons was deferred until the monarchy should be securely established.

The count of Chambord refuses to abandon the white flag of the Bourbons

In this adjustment of affairs the parties had not reckoned with the character of the count of Chambord. He was then over fifty years of age and had spent most of his life as an exile in Scotland, Germany, Austria, and Italy. He had been educated by pious Catholics and ardent supporters of the Legitimist cause, who had imbued him with a passionate devotion to

[1] This was gradually reduced later to two years in active service and eleven years in the reserve. In 1913, however, the term of active service was lengthened to three years, in order to keep pace with the increasing German army. See below, section 116.

the ancient rights of his house and with an equally passionate hatred of revolution in every form. Immediately after the suppression of the Paris Commune he had issued a manifesto in which he declared, "France will come to me, and I to her, just as I am, with my principles and my flag." He consented to negotiate with the count of Paris only on condition that he himself should be recognized as the legitimate head of the family and the lawful king. He then published an open letter in which he declared that he would not renounce the white flag which had so long been the standard of his house.

MacMahon's term prolonged to seven years

The Orleanists, enraged by the conduct of the fusion candidate, determined that he should not ascend the throne upon his own terms and took measures to prevent his coronation, although he had come to Versailles to superintend the preparations. They turned to the Bonapartists and republicans with a proposition to prolong the term of Marshal MacMahon, as president of the republic, for a period of seven years, in the hope that by the time his term expired they could gain sufficient strength to place their own candidate on the throne.

The Assembly at last agrees to sanction a republican form of government, January, 1875

The Assembly meanwhile continued its confused and heated debates, the republicans demanding the establishment without further delay of a republican constitution; the Legitimists, the retirement of Marshal MacMahon in favor of the count of Chambord; and the Orleanists, the president's continuance in office until 1880. Finally, at the beginning of the year 1875, four years after the election of the Assembly, it at last took up seriously the consideration of a permanent form of government, and on January 29 a motion was carried by a majority of one, providing that the president of the *republic* should be elected by the Senate and Chamber of Deputies meeting in a joint assembly. Thus the republicans finally, by the narrowest possible margin, secured the statement in the constitution itself that France was to be a republic.

The restoration of the monarchy having now become impossible, for the time being at least, the Assembly proceeded with the work of completing a form of government, not by drafting an elaborate constitution but by passing a series of laws. These separate laws, supplemented by later amendments, form the constitution of the Third Republic, which consequently differs in many fundamental ways from all the previous French constitutions. It contains no reference to the sovereignty of the people; it includes no bill of rights enumerating the liberties of French citizens; and it makes no definite provision for maintaining a republican form of government. It, in fact, bears throughout the marks of hasty compilation, designed as it was to tide the nation over a crisis until one of the contending parties in the Assembly could secure a triumphant majority. Nevertheless, despite the expectations of many who took part in its making, it has lasted longer and provided a more stable government than any of the numerous constitutions France has had since 1789. Indeed many students of politics now regard it as one of the best constitutions in existence.

Peculiar form of the present constitution of France

Under this new constitution the president of the French republic occupies a position rather more like that of the king of England than that of the president of the United States — he presides over the government but leaves the conduct of affairs to a premier and cabinet; he is more an ornamental than an active head of the State, representing it in great official functions, but exercising little of the power he outwardly seems to possess. He is elected for a term of seven years, not by the people at large but by the Senate and Chamber of Deputies, which meet as one body in Versailles for the purpose. There is no vice president, and in case of the death or resignation of the president a new one is immediately chosen for the full term of seven years. He selects his cabinet principally from among the members of the chambers, and the ministers thus chosen exercise a powerful control over his policy and appointments. The real head of the government is the prime minister, as in England. The president has no veto, but may return a measure to the Chamber and Senate for reconsideration.

Position of the president of the French republic

The Senate and Chamber of Deputies

The parliament consists of two houses, differing in this respect from the legislative bodies established in 1791 and 1848. The members of the Chamber of Deputies (about 600 in number) are chosen for a term of four years directly by the people, and every man over twenty-one years of age — unless he be in active service in the army — is permitted to vote. The three hundred senators are chosen indirectly for a term of nine years — one third of them each three years — by a small group of local government officers in each department.

Exceptional powers of the French parliament

It will be observed that the French parliament is more powerful than the Congress of the United States. It not only elects the president, who is under the control of a ministry representing the majority in the chambers, but it may by meeting in joint session amend the constitution without the necessity of submitting the changes to the people for their ratification. There is no supreme court in France to declare the measures of parliament unconstitutional, and the president cannot veto them. Like the members of the English cabinet, the French ministers resign when they find their policy is no longer supported by a majority in the Chamber of Deputies.

Section 77. The Third French Republic since 1875; the Dreyfus Affair

Strength of the republicans causes MacMahon to resign, 1879

The National Assembly, after completing the laws which now serve France as a constitution, dissolved on December 31, 1875, and a regular election was held throughout France for the purpose of choosing the members of the Senate and Chamber of Deputies. This resulted in an overwhelming majority for the republicans in the Chamber, and even in the Senate there were enough of them to give them the balance of power among the conflicting royalist factions. The Orleanist president, Marshal MacMahon, found himself unable to work in harmony with the deputies, and in 1877 he dissolved the Chamber with the hope that by meddling in the elections and

FIG. 118. PARIS

Paris is a beautiful city. It was largely rebuilt in the nineteenth century, mainly according to the plans of Napoleon III's engineers, with broad, shaded streets and many fine public buildings. South of the river is the Latin Quarter, where are the University and the art schools. Along the northern bank stretches the vast palace of the Louvre, the greatest art gallery in the world, from the roof of which this picture was taken. On the island, beyond the chapel of the Palace of Justice (see p. 241), rises the majestic cathedral of Notre Dame manipulating the returns he could secure at last a monarchical majority. This *coup d'état* failed. The new election left the republicans still in power; they denounced the president's policy and refused to approve the budget that he presented. After continuing the struggle until 1879, MacMahon resigned and was succeeded by an unmistakable republican, Jules Grévy.

Freedom of the press and of public assemblies

Still further strengthened by the elections of 1881, the republicans undertook a number of urgent reforms. The press had been declared free in 1789 and in 1815, but the government had constantly watched the newspapers and punished editors who offended it by too frank criticism. At last, in 1881, the licenses previously required of those who wished to undertake new publications were abolished, publishers were no longer forced to make deposits in order to insure their respectful treatment of the government, and the police courts were deprived of their right to try those accused of defaming government officials. Akin to this reform was the right extended to any group of citizens to hold public meetings, on condition that they should merely announce their intention to the authorities. In 1884, after nearly a hundred years of harsh repressive legislation directed against all labor associations, a law was passed permitting workingmen to form unions. Finally, the government undertook a series of measures with a view of freeing the schools from the influence of the clergy, who were accused of undermining the loyalty of the children to the republic. These measures will be considered presently.

Disappearance of the monarchical parties

Year by year the French republic gained in the number of its adherents and in the confidence of the other powers of Europe. The death of the son of Napoleon III in 1879 was a fatal blow to the already declining hopes of the Bonapartists, and the death of the childless count of Chambord in 1883 left the Legitimist faction without a head. A few Orleanists clung to their candidate, the count of Paris, until his death in 1894, but the elections of the preceding year, which resulted in the choice of only seventy-three royalist deputies, — Legitimists,

Orleanists, and Bonapartists, — had shown that France was at last irrevocably committed to the republic.

Boulanger's attempt to overturn the republic

Only twice since the formation of the republic has it been seriously threatened by political disturbances. Gambetta was in favor of a policy of reform, with the aim of winning the support of the working class. But there were many republicans who, in such matters, were as conservative as the monarchists, and these succeeded in frustrating Gambetta's program. After his death, in 1881, the government attempted by colonial enterprises abroad, particularly in Tonkin, China, to turn people's minds away from conditions at home. But the working class was discontented, and, encouraged by this situation, a popular officer, General Boulanger, began courting the favor of the army and the workingmen in somewhat the same way that Napoleon III had done when he was planning to make himself master of France. In 1889 he was reëlected to the Chamber of Deputies by an overwhelming majority, and it seemed for a time that he might be able to gain sufficient popularity to enable him to get control of the government.[1] His enemies charged him with threatening the safety of the State, and he was tried and condemned to life imprisonment. He escaped from France, however, and in 1891 committed suicide, leaving his party to go to pieces. This episode served rather to discredit the monarchists than to weaken the republic.

The opening of the Dreyfus affair, 1894

France had scarcely settled down after the Boulanger episode before a singular incident rent the country into angry factions and stirred up the most bitter animosity which had distracted the nation since the Franco-German War and the suppression of the Commune. In 1894 Captain Alfred Dreyfus, a Jew from Alsace, in the French artillery service, was charged with having been a spy in the pay of the German army. He was secretly tried by a military tribunal, condemned to life imprisonment, degraded from his rank, and sent into solitary confinement on the lonely Devil's Island off the coast of French Guiana.

[1] For a defense of Boulanger, see *Readings*, Vol. II, pp. 216 ff.

Dreyfus protested all the time that he was entirely innocent of the charge, and his friends began to work for a new trial. Prominent military officers, however, were determined that the Dreyfus affair should not be reopened for fear, apparently, that something discreditable to the army might be unearthed.

France roused to frenzy over the affair

The supporters of Dreyfus charged the army officers with unscrupulousness and corruption; his opponents, on the other hand, appealed to the country in the name of the honor of the army; churchmen attacked him as a Jew and as an enemy of Christian France. Government officials in general maintained his guilt, but many politicians, journalists, and prominent radicals declared their belief in his innocence and accused those in power of shielding criminal injustice. Monarchists cited the whole scandal as conclusive evidence of the failure of republican government. Thus the Dreyfus affair became a military, religious, and political question, which created a sort of frenzy in France and aroused the interest of the whole civilized world.[1]

Dreyfus at last declared innocent 1906

The controversy reached a crisis in 1898 when the well-known novelist, Émile Zola, published an article[2] accusing all the officials connected with the trial and conviction of Dreyfus not only of wanton injustice but of downright dishonesty. Zola's charges greatly increased the excitement, and distinguished scholars and men of letters raised their voices in defense of Dreyfus. Zola was tried and condemned for his bold indictment,[3] but the reconsideration of the whole case could not be postponed any longer, and a new trial was ordered, which began at Rennes in the summer of 1899. This resulted in the condemnation of Dreyfus to six years' imprisonment, but he was immediately pardoned by President Loubet. It was hoped that the credit of those who had originally condemned Dreyfus might in this way be saved and yet no penalty be imposed on

[1] There was clear evidence that somebody had been a traitor to France; the only point at issue was whether Dreyfus was the guilty one or not.

[2] An extract is given in the *Readings*, Vol. II, pp. 219 ff.

[3] He escaped punishment by retiring to England.

an innocent man. Naturally enough, however, this did not satisfy Dreyfus, who wanted not freedom as a pardoned criminal but a judicial declaration of his innocence. Consequently his numerous sympathizers continued to work for a new trial, and finally, in 1906, the highest court in France completely exonerated Dreyfus.

Effects of the controversy

The affair was thus at an end, but the effects of the controversy on the political situation in France could not be undone. It produced an alliance, called the "*bloc*," among the republicans of all shades, including the Socialists, for the purpose of reducing the political importance of the army and the Church. The army was republicanized by getting rid of the royalist officers; the destruction of the political power of the clergy was by no means so easy a matter.

The formation of the "*bloc*"

Section 78. The Separation of Church and State

Natural hostility of the clergy to the French republic

The Catholic clergy had from the first been hostile to the republic, for they had reason to fear that the new government, composed largely of anti-clericals, insisting upon freedom of the press and public schools, would sooner or later undermine their authority. The head of the Church, Pius IX, in a solemn statement called the Syllabus of 1864, had denounced in no uncertain terms what he regarded as the great dangers and errors of the age. Among these were religious toleration, liberty of conscience, freedom of the press and of speech, separation of Church and State, and secular education. The republicans were therefore pledged to just those things which the Pope condemned. It was inevitable, therefore, that the clerical party should do all in its power to discredit the republic and bring about a restoration of the monarchy. The Jesuits and other religious orders who maintained schools aroused in the children's minds a distrust of the government, and the clergy actively engaged in electioneering whenever there was hope of electing deputies who would favor their cause. The religious newspapers represented the republic as an unfortunate accident which had put ungodly men in power but which would doubtless speedily give way to a more legitimate form of government.

The republicans become anti-clerical

This attitude on the part of the clergy naturally made the republicans more strongly anti-clerical than ever. They came to hate the clergy and all they stood for. Gambetta declared that clericalism was "*the* enemy." Indeed, it was not until 1892 that Leo XIII admonished the French bishops and priests to "accept the republic, that is to say, the established power which exists among you; respect it and submit to it as representing the power which comes from God."

Main objects of the anti-clericals during the past twenty-five years

In spite of this peaceful advice on the part of the head of the Church, peace did not follow. On the contrary the struggle between Church and State in France grew in bitterness, until finally the republic proved the victor and succeeded in depriving the Church of a great part of those sources of political influence which remained to it after the losses it suffered during the French Revolution. The opponents of the Church have had two main objects in view: (1) to take the schools from the control or influence of the clergy and thus prevent the children of France from being brought up as monarchists, and (2) to relieve the government from the burden of paying the salaries of the clergy and to bring about the complete separation of Church and State.

Establishment of public schools under purely secular influence

The first step was to increase the number of public schools which might serve to attract pupils away from the convent and other Church schools. Over two hundred millions of dollars have been appropriated for this purpose during the past thirty years. By laws passed in 1881–1886 instruction was made free in the primary public schools, no clergyman was to be employed as a teacher in them, and compulsory education for children between six and thirteen years was established. The private schools were also placed under strict government supervision.

Opposition to the religious associations

Many of the monastic orders and various other religious associations which had lost their property and then been abolished during the first revolution had been reëstablished, and new ones had been created. Most of them were devoted to charitable work or to education. The Jesuits, however, were accused of working in the interests of the Pope, and the Dominicans of preaching openly against the republic, while the innumerable schools in the convents and elsewhere were reproached with instilling monarchical and reactionary ideas into the tender minds of the children committed to their charge.

The Associations Law of 1901

From time to time some anti-clerical deputy would propose the abolition of all the religious associations, and finally, in 1900, Waldeck-Rousseau, then prime minister, committed himself and his cabinet to a measure for greatly reducing their number, declaring, "There are too many monks in politics and too many monks in business."[1] The following year the Associations Law was passed. This provided that no religious order could continue to exist in France without a specific authorization from the parliament, and that no one belonging to a nonauthorized association should be permitted to teach or to conduct a school. At the time of the passage of the law there were about one hundred and sixty thousand members (mainly women) in the various religious associations, which maintained about twenty thousand establishments. The parliament refused to grant most of the applications made by the many unauthorized associations, and as a result numerous teaching, preaching, and commercial societies which had been organized under the auspices of the Catholic Church were broken up, and within two years ten thousand religious schools were closed. In the year 1909–1910 there were over five million French children in the public and other secular schools

[1] Sometimes the orders carried on a little industry in the interests of their convent. For example, the monks of the great Carthusian monastery above Grenoble manufactured the famous liqueur known as Chartreuse. The labor parties denounced the monks for thus going into business and competing with other manufacturers.

and less than one hundred thousand enrolled in those connected with religious associations. A law of 1904 provided that within ten years all teaching by religious associations should cease.

The Concordat of 1801 established a close relation between Church and State

The attack on the religious orders was only the prelude to the complete separation of Church and State which had been advocated for a century by the opponents of the Church. It will be remembered that the French Convention proclaimed this separation in 1795 and refused longer to pay the salaries of the clergy, or in any way to recognize the existence of the Church except as a voluntary association which should be supported by those who wished to belong to it. Bonaparte, however, partially restored the old system in the Concordat which he arranged with the Pope in 1801.[1] This, with a supplementary act, remained the basis of the relations between Church and State in France down to 1906.[2] Bonaparte did not give back the property of the Church of which it had been deprived by the first French Assembly in 1789, but he agreed that the government should pay the salaries of the bishops and priests whose appointment it controlled. Although the Catholic religion was recognized as that of the majority of Frenchmen, the State also helped support the Reformed and Lutheran churches and the Jewish religious community.

Power of the clergy during the nineteenth century

From the standpoint of the government this was in many ways an excellent arrangement, for it was thus enabled profoundly to influence public opinion through its control over the clergy. Consequently, amid all the later political changes, the settlement reached by Bonaparte was retained essentially unaltered. Louis XVIII, Charles X, Louis Philippe, and Napoleon III had no desire to do away with the Concordat which afforded them such great political power.

[1] See *Readings*, Vol. II, pp. 224 f.

[2] The policy of the leaders of the French Revolution and of Bonaparte in regard to the clergy and the religious associations has already been carefully described with a view of preparing the way for an understanding of the recent important legislation in France affecting the Church. See above, pp. 211 ff., 225, and 276 ff.

Final separation of Church and State in 1905

But with the establishment of the republic all this was changed, owing to the strong monarchical sympathies of the clergy. There were, moreover, large numbers of Frenchmen who, if not actively opposed to the Church, had no interest in religion. To this class it seemed wrong that the government should be paying forty million francs a year to clergymen for teaching the people what they did not believe in, especially since they were so openly opposed in politics. Nevertheless, it was no easy task to put asunder Church and State, which had been closely associated with each other from the times of Constantine and Theodosius the Great. It was not until December, 1905, that the Separation Law was promulgated.

Main provisions of the Separation Law

The main provisions of the new law were relatively simple. It suppressed all government appropriations for religious purposes, but provided pensions for clergymen of long service and the gradual extinction of the salaries of others. It declared that cathedrals, churches, the residences of bishops, and other ecclesiastical buildings belonged to the government, but should be placed at the disposal of congregations and their pastors free of charge. The management of these edifices and the control of other property of the Church were vested in "associations for religious worship" (*associations cultuelles*) composed of from seven to twenty-five persons according to the size of the commune. The Concordat concluded in 1801 was, of course, expressly abolished.[1]

The Pope and clergy oppose the new law

It soon became evident that the Pope and a large Catholic party were determined not to accept these provisions. Crowds collided with the soldiers sent to guard the churches while inventories were being made of the property to be handed over to the "associations for religious worship." In February, 1906, the Pope condemned the entire law in a long letter to the archbishops and bishops of France in which he protested

[1] The statesman who had most to do in framing and applying this law was Aristide Briand, who won a great reputation for combined tact and firmness. He has been premier several times, especially during the Great War, from 1915.

especially against the religious associations for which it provided.[1] Unfortunately he did not advise the French clergy just how to get out of the predicament in which they found themselves.

National elections uphold the government

The clergy, obedient to the commands of the head of the Church, refused to countenance the formation of associations, and most of them declined the proffered pensions. The nation at large, however, evidently supported the government in its plans, for the elections held in May, 1906, returned a large majority of radicals, Socialists, and progressives committed to the full execution of the law.

The government permits the continuance of public worship by a new law, December, 1906

When the year allowed for the formation of the religious associations expired in December, 1906, the Church property which had no legal claimants passed into the hands of the government. However, the minister of public worship, M. Briand, a former Socialist, unwilling to stop religious services, took steps to allow the churches to remain open in spite of the failure to comply with the law. At his instigation the French parliament passed a very important supplementary measure, which provided that buildings for public worship and their entire furniture should remain at the disposal of priests and their congregations even if the associations required by the original law were not formed.

In January, 1907, the Pope again denounced the government, which, he declared, was confiscating Church property and attempting to destroy Christianity in France; and he has not yet been reconciled to the policy of the government. Nevertheless, it is quite clear that the republic means to render permanent the separation of Church and State. Subsidies to the clergy are no longer provided, although the promised pensions are paid to such clergymen as apply for them. In the budget of 1912 only about $50,000 was set aside for "the assistance of retired clergymen." The government leaves the Church to choose its own bishops and priests and hold

[1] The protest is printed in the *Readings*, Vol. II, pp. 226 ff.

conventions when and where it wishes. It has converted the palaces of the bishops, the parsonages, and the seminaries into schools, hospitals, or other public institutions, although it still permits the churches to be used for public worship.

Section 79. Political Parties in France

Parties in the French parliament

The parties and factions in the French parliament are bewildering in number. The election of 1906 sent to the Chamber of Deputies representatives of the following groups: radicals, socialist radicals, dissident radicals, independent socialists, unified socialists, republicans of the left, progressivists, nationalists, monarchists and Bonapartists, and a few other minor factions. With the exception, of course, of the monarchists and Bonapartists, they all agree that the republic shall be maintained, and they have been able to unite upon many important measures, such as those relating to education and the relations of the State to the Church, but they differ on other questions of reform which are constantly coming up. Some are pretty well satisfied with things as they are, while others, especially the various socialist groups, would like to see the government undertake a complete social and economic revolution for the benefit of the laboring classes. The State should, they believe, take possession of lands, mines, mills, and other sources of wealth and means of production, and see that they are used for the benefit of those who do the work and no longer serve to enrich men who seem to them to sit idly by and profit by the labor of others.

Socialism reappears under the Third Republic

The socialistic party, which figured so prominently in the Revolution of 1848 and the revolt of the Paris Commune, disappeared for a time after the suppression of the insurrection in 1871, but again reappeared shortly after the final establishment of the republic. In 1879 the Socialists held their first congress under the republic at Marseilles, where they may be said to have initiated the present socialist movement in France.

The following year a general amnesty was granted to all who had been connected with the Commune, and a great labor convention was immediately held in Paris, where the doctrines of Karl Marx were accepted as the fundamental principles of French socialism.

Divisions among the Socialists — Marxians and "Possibilists"

Notwithstanding their general agreement as to their ends, the French Socialists have from the very first been divided over the question of the best methods of attaining their aims. Broadly speaking, there have been two groups, each with varying shades of opinion. In the first place there have been the Marxians, — who are in general strongly opposed to voting for candidates of other parties, though willing to wring concessions from them in the Chamber of Deputies, — who expect socialism to be ushered in by a crisis in which the workingmen will seize the supreme power and use it for their own benefit, as the middle class did in the previous revolutions. The second, and more numerous, socialist group goes by the name of the "Possibilists," because they do not believe that socialistic ideas can be carried into effect as the result of a violent revolution, but hope to see them realized by a gradual process in which the government will assume control and ownership of one industry after another.

The Socialists become a political factor

The various socialistic factions, numbering six or seven at times, united at the general election in 1893, and by remarkable energy succeeded in returning about fifty members to the Chamber of Deputies, thus inaugurating a new era in French politics. The socialist vote steadily increased until in 1899 the prime minister, Waldeck-Rousseau, was forced to accept a Socialist, M. Millerand, as Minister of Commerce in order to control enough votes in the Chamber to carry on the government. Since then the Possibilists have from time to time been represented in the cabinet, and they have worked for their ends by combining with other parties.[1]

[1] For a speech by the former prime minister, Clémenceau, on socialism, see *Readings*, Vol. II, pp. 233 ff.

In England and the United States there are two great parties, one of which is ordinarily in unmistakable control. In France there are so many parties that no single one can ever long command a majority of votes in the Chamber of Deputies. As a result measures cannot be carried simply because the leaders of one party agree on them, but they must appeal to a number of groups on their own merits. Minorities, consequently, have an opportunity to influence legislation in France, and there is little chance for machine politics to develop. It is true that French ministries rise and fall at very short intervals, but nevertheless the laws which do pass receive more careful attention, perhaps, than they would if pushed through as party measures.[1]

Contrast between the French parties and those in England and the United States

The opponents of a ministry in the Chamber of Deputies take advantage of the privilege of asking the ministers questions in regard to their policy and thus force them to explain their motives. When a deputy formally announces that he is going to "interpellate" the ministers, he must be given an opportunity to do so within a certain period at a regular session of the Chamber. These "interpellations" are more common in France than elsewhere, but are not unknown in other governments.

"Interpellations"

Section 80. Expansion of France

While solving grave problems at home the Third Republic has pushed forward its commercial, exploring, and military enterprises until it has built up a colonial dominion vaster than that lost during the eighteenth century in the conflicts with England, though less valuable and less inviting to French emigrants. When the Third Republic was established French colonial possessions consisted of Algeria in northern Africa, the Senegal region on the west coast of Africa, some minor posts scattered along the Gulf of Guinea down to the Congo

French colonial dominion in 1870

[1] For recent social legislation in France, see below, p. 657.

River, a foothold in Cochin China, and a number of small islands in various parts of the world. The basis of territorial expansion had thus been laid, and after the quick recovery which followed the reverses of the German War, the French government frankly committed itself to a policy of imperialism.

The French annex Algeria

After the defeat of France by Germany in 1870, there was a serious revolt in the African province of Algeria, which had been seized in 1830 on account of the refusal of the native ruler to give satisfaction for having slapped the French consul general in the face at a public reception. This insurrection was not put down until more than two hundred battles and skirmishes had been fought. The great province of Algeria is only slightly smaller than France itself, and has a population of over five millions, of whom only about eight hundred thousand are of European origin.[1] To the east of Algeria lies the province of Tunis, equaling in area the state of New York and having a population akin to that of Algeria in race and religion. Tunisian tribes were accused by the French of disturbing the peace of the Algerian border, and in 1881 France dispatched troops into Tunis. After some serious fighting the province was occupied and the Bey was virtually forced to surrender the administration of his possessions to the French government, in whose hands it remains.[2]

The French in Senegal

While these enterprises were bringing northern Africa under French dominion, a series of daring explorations and conquests in western and central Africa were adding vast regions and millions of African natives to the French colonial domain. France had taken formal possession of the province of Senegal on the west coast as early as 1637, but no serious efforts to extend her control inland were made until the annexation of Algeria called attention to the possibility of joining the two provinces. After the middle of the nineteenth century steady pressure inland began and Timbuktu was conquered in 1894.

[1] The French have also been mapping out and occupying the vast desert to the south.

[2] See above, p. 421.

French Congo

A post on the equator at the mouth of the Gabun River, bought in 1839, became the base for celebrated expeditions headed by du Chaillu and de Brazza, which added a vast region north of the Congo River more than twice the size of France and now known as French Congo.[1] The vast extent of the French possessions in northwestern Africa will become apparent as one glances at the map, p. 622, below.

The annexation of Madagascar, 1896

While the French explorers were pushing their way through the jungles of the Senegal and Congo regions, or braving the sand-storms of the Sahara,[2] French missionaries and commercial agents were preparing the way for the annexation of the island of Madagascar. Using as a pretext the murder of some French citizens by the natives, the French waged war on the ruler of Madagascar (1882–1885), and succeeded in establishing a protectorate over the entire island. Later they accused Queen Ranavalona III of bad faith and of inability to suppress brigandage. A second war which broke out in 1895 ended in the deposition and expulsion of the queen.

The "Fashoda incident"

In the year 1898 Marchand, a French explorer, pressed eastward across the Sahara desert from the French possessions on the west and reached the Nile region, where he raised the French flag at Fashoda, in the Sudan, over lands claimed by the English. An English force, however, compelled Marchand to lower the flag, and for a time it looked as if the two countries might come to blows. Fortunately, however, the French withdrew, and the two nations arranged the disputed boundaries between them. Indeed, the "Fashoda incident," as it was called, which threatened to plunge the two nations into war, thus became the basis of an "understanding," or "entente,"

[1] In addition to their larger African dependencies the French control French Guiana, south of Senegal, the Ivory Coast, and the native kingdom of Dahomey.

[2] In the contest for the east coast of Africa the French have taken little part. In 1862 they purchased from a native chief the post of Obock, but it was not actually occupied until 1884. Since that time, however, slight additions of land have been made, and the post has grown into French Somaliland, a province of about six thousand square miles.

as the French call it, between England and France. For while France withdrew from Egypt and the Sudan, England withdrew from any claims upon Morocco, which was the next tempting bit of Africa to divide up. France then was free, apparently, to round out its great empire of northwest Africa. But one neighbor had been left out of account in this agreement between England and France, namely Germany, and no sooner had France started to penetrate Morocco than Germany protested, as we shall see.[1]

FIG. 119. THE "FASHODA INCIDENT"

The English expedition, which has just come up the Nile in the steamboats, is surprised to find the tricolor of France floating at Fashoda. Colonel Marchand is just receiving the Sirdar, as the English commanding officer in Egypt was termed

The Third Republic also has extensive colonial dominions in Asia, where French missionaries and traders had been attracted under Colbert's administration. Interest in the province of Anam was renewed about 1850, when some French missionaries were murdered there. Napoleon III waged war on the king in 1857, forcing from him the payment of an indemnity and the cession of a small portion of his territory. The foothold thus obtained formed the basis for rapid expansion in every direction; a protectorate was extended over

[1] See below, section 115.

the kingdom of Cambodia in 1864; and in 1867 Cochin China was entirely annexed. An attempt in 1873 to force the opening to navigation of the Red River in Tonkin led to a war with the ruler of that province which resulted in the extension of a protectorate over all of Anam, of which Tonkin was a district. This defiance of the Chinese emperor's claims at length stirred him to resistance; but the war of 1884 which resulted cost him all his rights over Tonkin and the remainder of Anam. In 1893 France extended her authority over the territory of Laos to the south. The French possessions are thus in close contact with the provinces of southern China, into which French influence is already penetrating in the form of railways and mining concessions.[1]

COLONIES AND DEPENDENCIES OF FRANCE

IN ASIA: Five towns in India, Anam, Cambodia, Cochin China, Tonkin, and Laos.

IN AFRICA: Algeria, Tunis, Sahara, Senegal, Upper Senegal and Niger, French Guinea, Ivory Coast, Dahomey, Congo, Somaliland, Mauretania, Madagascar, the islands of Réunion and Mayotte, and the Comoro Isles.

IN AMERICA: Guiana, Guadeloupe, Martinique, St. Pierre, and Miquelon.

IN OCEANIA: New Caledonia and dependencies. Various stations in the Pacific.

Total area, 4,776,126 square miles. Population, 41,653,650.

QUESTIONS

SECTION 76. Under what circumstances did the Third French Republic come into existence? Outline the course of the Franco-Prussian War from the battle of Sedan to the capitulation of Paris. For what purpose was the National Assembly elected in 1871? Describe the means by which the Assembly accomplished this purpose. What was the cause of the ill feeling between the people of Paris and the National Assembly in March, 1871?

[1] On the recent tendencies in French thought and society see Chapter XXVI, below.

Who were the Communards and what were their views on government? Describe the suppression of the Commune. What parties were to be found in the National Assembly? What was the effect of their inability to agree upon the form of government established in France in August, 1871? Describe the means taken in 1871 to strengthen the position of France.

What led to the resignation of Thiers? Who succeeded Thiers as president of France? Upon what problem were the monarchist parties at work from 1873 to 1875? Describe the constitution of France. Compare the position of the president of the French republic with that of the king of England and the president of the United States. Describe the legislative branch of the French government, contrasting it with that of the United States.

SECTION 77. Under what circumstances did Marshal MacMahon resign the presidency? Mention the reforms instituted by the republicans in the years 1881–1884. Outline the Dreyfus case. What effect did it leave upon the political situation in France?

SECTION 78. Account for the hostility between Church and State in France. What has been the program of the anti-clerical party during the last twenty-five years? Outline the relations of Church and State in France from 1901 to 1905. What was the nature of the public-worship law passed in December, 1906?

SECTION 79. Give a brief account of the history of political parties in France. In what way does the party system of France differ from that of England and the United States? What is an "interpellation"?

SECTION 80. Locate on a map the colonial possessions of France before 1870. Trace on maps the colonial expansion of France since the establishment of the Third Republic. Sketch the whole of the "Fashoda incident."

SECTION 81. PARLIAMENTARY REFORM

Political situation in England at the opening of the nineteenth century

In the eighteenth century the English government had been extolled by students of politics as by far the most liberal and enlightened in Europe. Although they had no written constitution, the English had won two important safeguards for their liberties — a parliament, free from royal interference, to make their laws, and a good system of courts, equally free from royal interference, to see that the laws were properly carried out. But in the nineteenth century it became apparent that there was great need of reform in both branches of the government, and that the mass of the people, if free from the tyranny of a king, were, after all, not trusted with the right of self-government.

"Rotten boroughs"

The reform of Parliament was the most pressing need; for Parliament had ceased to represent the nation at large and had become a council of wealthy landlords and nobles. This was due to two things. In the first place there were the so-called "rotten boroughs." Such towns as had in earlier times been summoned by the king to send their two representatives each to Parliament, continued to do so at the opening of the nineteenth century, regardless of the number of their inhabitants, and no new boroughs had been added to the list since the reign of Charles II. Dunwich, which had been buried under the waters of the North Sea for two centuries, was duly represented, as well as the famous borough of Old Sarum, which was only a green mound where a town had once stood. On the other hand, mere villages had grown into great cities, and the newer towns which had developed under the influence of the Industrial Revolution, like Birmingham, Manchester, and Leeds, had no representatives at all. Moreover it was not only in the towns that representation was wholly unequal. The county of Cornwall, with a population of a quarter of a million, had forty-four representatives, while all Scotland, with eight times that population, was entitled to only one more member.

Few persons permitted to vote

In the second place, few persons had a right to vote, even in the towns which had representation in Parliament. In some boroughs all taxpayers had the right to take part in elections, but this varied greatly. In one of these — Gatton — there were only seven voters. In other boroughs the right of choosing the members of Parliament was exercised by the mayor and town council, who were often not elected by the people at all.

Many seats controlled by Lords

Many of the boroughs were owned outright by members of the House of Lords or others, who easily forced the few voters to choose any candidate they proposed.[1]

Situation in the country districts

In the country districts matters were no better. It is true that every person owning land which brought in forty shillings a year was permitted to vote for members of Parliament, but the disappearance of most of the small farmers had reduced the voters to the few who owned large estates. To take an extreme case, in the Scottish county of Bute, with its population of fourteen thousand inhabitants, there were twenty-one voters, of whom all but one were nonresidents.

Prevalence of bribery

Bribery was prevalent and was fostered by the system of public balloting. The election was held in the open air. The sheriff, presiding, read off the list of candidates and the voters

[1] The duke of Norfolk chose eleven members of the House of Commons, Lord Lonsdall, nine, and Lord Darlington, seven; while other peers had one or more representatives in the Commons. In 1828 the duke of Newcastle evicted over five hundred of his tenants because they refused to vote for his candidate, and when this led to a protest in Parliament he replied, "Have I not a right to do as I like with my own?"

shouted and raised their hands to show their choice. A defeated candidate might then demand a roll call, and each voter had then to sign his name in a poll book so that every one might know how he voted. Naturally there was much intimidation and electioneering as well as bribery.[1]

England really governed by an oligarchy

Thus, through the gross inequalities in apportioning the members, the curious methods of balloting, open bribery, and ownership of boroughs, the House of Commons was ordinarily under the control of a comparatively few men. A very cautious scholar of our own day estimates that not more than one third of the representatives in the House of Commons were fairly chosen.

Proposals for reform before the nineteenth century

The whole system was so obviously preposterous that it is not surprising that objections to it had long been common. As early as the middle of the eighteenth century the abuses were severely attacked, and during the democratic agitation which preceded and accompanied the French Revolution several attempts were made to induce Parliament to reform itself. The elder Pitt (Lord Chatham), in 1770, and later his distinguished son, the younger Pitt, proposed changes. But the French Revolution came before anything was done, and the excesses of the French Convention during the Reign of Terror put an end to all hope of reform for some time. Even the more cool-headed and progressive among the English statesmen were discouraged by the apparently disastrous results in France of permitting the people at large to vote. Indeed, until 1830 England was under Tory rule, and the government adopted harsh measures to prevent all agitation for reform.

The French Revolution puts an end for a time to hopes of reform in England

The "Peterloo massacre," 1819

After the overthrow of Napoleon, orators, writers, and agitators redoubled their efforts to arouse the working classes to action. Hampden clubs were founded to propagate reform doctrines, and monster demonstrations and parades were organized

[1] Hogarth, the great artist, shows the humorous side of such an election in the picture which is reproduced on page 170 above. The crippled, the sick, and the old are brought to the election booth, where they are being persuaded to vote one way or another. The secret ballot was established in 1872; see below, p. 501.

to prove to the government the strength of the popular feeling. At one of these meetings in Manchester in 1819, the police and soldiers charged the populace without provocation and killed

FIG. 120. THE PARLIAMENT BUILDINGS, LONDON

This massive pile stands on the site of an old royal palace, between Westminster Abbey, which is not shown but is just across the street at the right, and the river Thames, which runs along the other side. The House of Commons met in the chapel of this palace — St. Stephens — from the middle of the sixteenth century until 1834, when the palace was burned down, with the exception of the great hall with the plain roof in the foreground. The new building, completed in 1867, is richly ornamented. From its main tower, 340 feet high, a flag is flown by day when Parliament is in session, and by night a light shines over the clock tower, which stands by Westminster Bridge

and wounded a large number.[1] The government was frightened by the popular outcry and passed a series of laws, known as the Six Acts, which restricted the rights of free press, free speech, and public meeting.

[1] This assault, known as the "Peterloo massacre," occurred in St. Peter's Field, then on the outskirts, but now in the heart, of Manchester.

Merchants and manufacturers begin to urge reform

This attempt at repression could not last, however, for it was not only the working classes but the rich and powerful merchants and manufacturers as well who demanded the revision of a system which excluded them from political power. The Whigs, under the leadership of Lord John Russell, urged parliamentary reform again and again in the Commons. The Revolution of 1830 in France added impetus to the agitation in England, and that stanch Tory, the duke of Wellington, was obliged to resign his premiership under pressure of a growing public opinion that seemed verging on open violence.

The passage of the Reform Bill of 1832

The Whigs, or "Reformers," then were called to power, and in March, 1831, Lord John Russell introduced a reform bill into the House of Commons,[1] where it was violently opposed. A new election was then held, resulting in a triumph for the reform party, which then carried the bill through the Commons by a substantial majority. It was, however, rejected by the House of Lords. The Commons then replied by passing another bill of the same character as the first, and the country awaited with breathless anxiety the action of the peers. Finally, King William IV gave way to the Reformers and granted permission to the prime minister "to create such a number of peers as will insure the passage of the reform bill." The lords, realizing that further opposition was useless, gave way, and in June, 1832, the long-debated bill became a law.

Provisions of the Reform Bill of 1832

According to its provisions fifty-six "rotten boroughs," each containing less than two thousand inhabitants, were entirely deprived of representation; thirty-two more, with less than four thousand inhabitants, lost one member each; and forty-three new boroughs were created with one or two members each, according to their respective populations. The counties were divided into election districts and assigned a representation corresponding more nearly than heretofore with the number of their inhabitants. The suffrage was given in the towns

[1] For Lord John Russell's speech on parliamentary reform, see *Readings*, Vol. II, pp. 239 ff. A speech in opposition is printed on pp. 242 ff.

to all citizens who owned or rented houses worth ten pounds (about fifty dollars) a year, and to *renters* as well as *owners* of lands of a certain value in the country. In this way the shopkeepers and manufacturers and some of the more prosperous people in the country were given the right to vote, but nearly all workingmen and agricultural laborers were still excluded from the franchise.

The Reform Bill of 1832 far from a democratic measure

The great Reform Bill of 1832 was therefore not really a triumph for democracy. It was estimated from official returns in 1836 that out of a total number of 6,023,752 adult males there were only 839,519 voters. The thousands whose parades and demonstrations had frightened the duke of Wellington and the king into yielding were naturally dissatisfied with the outcome. The fact that those who came into power under the new bill — mostly representing the new capitalistic class — showed little inclination to relieve the condition of the working classes, whose wages were pitiably low and whose homes were miserable hovels, added bitterness to their disappointment.

The demands of the Charter

The Reform Bill had scarcely been signed before a veritable flood of pamphlet literature appeared, proposing more radical measures.[1] Translations of Magna Carta and reprints of the Bill of Rights and the acts of the Long Parliament abolishing the House of Lords and the kingship were circulated as leaflets among the working classes. At last six demands were embodied in a "charter"; to wit, universal suffrage, vote by secret ballot, annual election of Parliament, payment of members of Parliament, abolition of property qualifications for members of Parliament, and equal electoral districts.

The Chartist movement

In the opening year of Queen Victoria's reign,[2] this charter won thousands of adherents, to whom the name of "Chartists"

[1] For extracts from contemporary pamphlets on the extension of the suffrage, see *Readings*, Vol. II, pp. 245 ff.

[2] George III died in 1820. He had been insane for some years, during which his son, afterward George IV, was regent. George IV's reign lasted from 1820 to 1830, when his brother, William IV, succeeded. Their niece, Victoria, succeeded in 1837, reigning until 1901.

was given. Local Chartist clubs were founded in every manufacturing town, and in 1840 a national Charter Association was organized for the purpose of federating the various clubs. Leaders of remarkable oratorical ability sprang into prominence; papers were established; Chartist songs and poems were composed, and national conventions assembled. Great meetings and parades were held all over England; the charter was transformed into a petition to which it was claimed that over a million signatures were obtained. This petition was presented to Parliament in 1839 only to be rejected by a large vote.

Some of the Chartists advocate violence

Despairing of securing reforms by peaceful means, some of the leaders began openly to advocate revolutionary violence, and rioting spread to such an extent that the government had to resort to extraordinary police measures to suppress it. The disorders did not amount to much, however, considering the size of the Chartist movement, and the main agitation continued on peaceful lines.[1] Several Chartist members were elected to Parliament, and another petition was submitted to that body.

Final Chartist petition of 1848

The Revolution of 1848 in France and the establishment of the Second Republic gave the signal for the last great outburst of Chartist enthusiasm. Owing to the hard times in that year, thousands of workmen were unemployed, and the poor were roused to bitter hatred for a government that replied to demands

[1] The Chartists were violently attacked by the opponents of their democratic proposals, which seem harmless enough to-day. The statements of these conservative people, on the contrary, seem very absurd. In 1840 the Reverend E. Jenkins issued a book called *Chartism Unmasked*, in which he made the following observations: "What would you gain by universal suffrage? I am certain that you would gain nothing but universal confusion, universal setting of workmen against each other.... All workmen would then become politicians — they would neglect their vocations in life — spend their time, their strength, their talents in what would increase their poverty. Vote by ballot would be nothing but a law for rogues and knaves, nothing but a cloak for dishonesty, insincerity, hypocrisy and lies.... With respect to having members of Parliament paid and void of property qualifications — really this is too absurd for an idiot to be the author of it.... The famous Chartist doctrine of Equality is diametrically opposed to Nature and the word of God; it is a doctrine taught only by lying prophets — men who are of their father the Devil, for his works they do."

for reform by police measures. Preparations were made to present another gigantic petition to the House of Commons, to which it was claimed that six million names had been secured, and the Chartist leaders determined to overawe Parliament by a march on London. Though this show of force was frustrated by the aged duke of Wellington, then commander of the troops policing London, the petition was finally presented to the House of Commons. It was there referred to a committee, which reported that there were less than two million names and that many of these were evident forgeries, such as "Victoria Rex," "the Duke of Wellington," "Pugnose," and "Snooks." The petition was thereby greatly discredited, and Parliament refused to take any action on it. Chartism, as an organized movement, thereupon collapsed.

Gladstone espouses the cause of parliamentary reform in 1866

The cause of parliamentary reform was not, however, lost with the failure of the Chartist movement. The doctrines of democracy had been spread among the people by the agitation, and from time to time advocates were found to introduce reform measures in the House of Commons. Although these proposals were easily defeated, there was a steadily growing recognition that some changes were inevitable, and at length,

* Victoria was much beloved by the British, and her name was connected with the proudest age of the British empire. English literature and art of the last half of the nineteenth century are often spoken of as belonging to the Victorian age, and it was in her reign that the colonies became real, self-governing "dominions." The celebration of the Diamond Jubilee of the queen's reign in 1897 was the most magnificent spectacle of modern times. It was attended by practically all the other sovereigns of Europe, including Victoria's grandson, the German emperor, and it brought together, for the first time, the statesmen of the widely scattered "dominions beyond the seas." One should have in mind all this splendor and power of the empress-queen when one looks at this picture of the young girl who was roused from her sleep on June 20, 1837, by the Archbishop of Canterbury and another official, to be told of the death of her uncle, William IV, and her accession to the throne. Victoria received them with quiet dignity, although clad with wrapper and shawl, with her hair falling over her shoulders and her feet hurriedly thrust into slippers.

Plate V. Queen Victoria notified of her Accession to the Throne*

in 1866, Gladstone, as leader of the House of Commons, made the question an issue of practical politics. Mr. Gladstone was then fifty-seven years old. He had entered Parliament as a Tory at the first election after the Reform Bill of 1832, and had quickly shown himself a commanding orator and a capable politician. At the end of a few years his views on public questions began to change, and at length he broke with the conservative traditions of his youth. In a debate on parliamentary reform in 1864 he maintained that the burden of proof rested on those "who would exclude forty-nine fiftieths of the working classes from the franchise." The very next year the veteran reformer of 1832, Lord Russell, now elevated to the peerage, was called upon to form a new ministry, and he selected Gladstone as leader of the lower house.

Disraeli succeeds Gladstone as leader of the House of Commons

At the opening of Parliament in 1866 Gladstone proposed a moderate extension of the franchise, which was still based on property qualifications. This measure displeased many of Gladstone's followers because it went too far, and others because it did not go far enough. Consequently the cabinet felt compelled to resign, and a Conservative ministry was formed under the leadership of Lord Derby, who was represented in the House of Commons by Benjamin Disraeli (afterwards created Lord Beaconsfield), one of the most striking figures in the political life of England during the nineteenth century. When a young man of twenty-two he had sprung into prominence as the author of a successful novel, *Vivian Grey*, and at the age of thirty-three he entered upon his political career as a Conservative member of Parliament. His Jewish origin, his obtrusive style of dress, and his florid oratory immediately brought him into conspicuous notoriety; but those who laughed at him at first soon came to recognize him as a leader of great force and a politician of remarkable ability.

The Conservatives, as the old Tory party had come to be called, were alarmed by the general demand for reform and some rioting which took place in Hyde Park, but Disraeli was

Disraeli's reform bill of 1867 doubles the number of voters

able to secure the passage of a reform bill in spite of the denunciations of some of his fellow Conservatives and the smiles of the Liberals,[1] who taunted him with advocating changes which he had long opposed.[2] The new law of 1867 granted the right to vote to every adult male in the larger towns who occupied for twelve months, either as owner or tenant, a dwelling within the borough and paid the local poor tax; also to lodgers who

FIG. 121. DISRAELI

paid ten pounds or more a year for unfurnished rooms. In the country it permitted those to vote who owned property which produced an income of at least five pounds net a year, and all renters paying at least twelve pounds annually. This served to double the previous number of voters.[3]

[1] The followers of Gladstone were termed Liberal rather than Whig, from which party most of them came. The old name "Reformer," however, persisted.

[2] Extracts from a contemporary speech against giving the vote to workingmen are given in the *Readings*, Vol. II, pp. 251 ff.

[3] It may be said here, once for all, that in England, as in most European countries, it is customary to exclude from the suffrage all paupers, criminals, the insane, and certain other classes of persons.

A further reform was the adoption of the secret ballot in 1872, instead of the old, disorderly method of public elections, described above.[1]

In 1884 the Liberal party, again under Gladstone's leadership, resolved to carry still further the reforms of 1832 and

FIG. 122. MEN RIOTING FOR THE SUFFRAGE IN HYDE PARK (1866)

The great reforms in England in the nineteenth century were achieved with little disorder, but there would have been more if the government had not yielded in time

Extension of the franchise in 1884

1867, for over two million men, chiefly agricultural laborers, were denied the right to vote.[2] By extending the suffrage to them the Liberals hoped to gain their support to offset the control of the rural districts which had hitherto been enjoyed

[1] See p. 493. The form of ballot used was copied from that in use in the colony of Victoria, Australia, and is known as the Australian ballot. It has been adopted in many countries.

[2] For Gladstone's speech on suffrage in 1884, see *Readings*, Vol. II, pp. 255 ff.

by the Conservatives. The new law which they succeeded in passing provided that the franchise established for the larger towns in 1867 should be extended to all towns, and to the country districts as well, thus introducing general uniformity throughout the United Kingdom. While this measure seemed to establish something approaching the manhood suffrage already common on the Continent, many men are still excluded from voting, especially unmarried laborers who, owing to the low rents in England, do not pay as much as ten pounds (fifty dollars) a year for unfurnished lodgings.

The question of woman suffrage

For twenty years the matter of the franchise excited little attention, for the Conservatives were in power and were satisfied to leave things alone. But when the Liberal party was again called to the helm in 1906, it had to face not only the question of including more *men* among the voters but the much more novel demand that *women* also should be allowed to vote. The Industrial Revolution, by opening up new employments to women, has given them a certain kind of independence which they never before had. During the latter part of the nineteenth century women were admitted to universities, and colleges began to be established for them as well as for men. All these things have produced the demand that women be given the right to vote.

In 1870 the women of England were given the right to vote for members of the newly created school boards, and in 1888

* Royalty in England keeps up its splendor for the most part upon social occasions, when distinguished or wealthy people are "presented at court," which means that they pass in line before the monarchs and bow their way out. But the monarchs also appear in state upon one political occasion, — outside of royal marriages, funerals, coronations, and the like, — and this is when they go to open Parliament in the midst of a pageant, which this picture represents. When the king mounts the throne in the House of Lords, however, and all the members of Parliament are summoned to hear "the king's speech," he has to read the words set before him by the prime minister and cabinet. The Houses then meet and debate it with little regard for the feelings of the real authors.

Plate VI. The King and Queen going in State to open Parliament*

and 1894 they were admitted to the franchise in certain local government matters. In 1893 women were enfranchised in New Zealand. Shortly after the establishment of the new Commonwealth of Australia in 1901 full parliamentary suffrage was granted to them. In 1906 the women of Finland, and in 1907, 1912, and 1915 the women of Norway, Sweden, and Denmark respectively, were given the vote on the same terms as men. The British government, however, steadily refused to grant woman suffrage. As a result, some leaders of the suffrage movement, notably Mrs. Pankhurst, resorted to violent demonstrations, but this apparently alienated lukewarm supporters, and Parliament finally, in 1913, rejected a bill proposing a general reform of the suffrage, in which women should share.

Steady extension of the suffrage to women

Section 82. The English Cabinet

These reforms, which permit a large number of voters to select the members of the House of Commons, have left untouched, so far as appearances are concerned, the ancient and honorable institutions of the king and the House of Lords.[1] The sovereign is crowned with traditional pomp; coins and proclamations still assert that he rules "by the grace of God"; and laws purport to be enacted "by the king's most excellent Majesty, by and with the advice and consent of the Commons in Parliament assembled."[2] Justice is executed and the colonies are governed in the name of the king. The term "royal" is still applied to the army, the navy, and the mail service, reserving, as a wit once remarked, the word "national" only for the public debt.

The position of the English sovereign

There was a time, of course, when sovereign power was really exercised by the king of England. Henry VIII, for example, appointed his own ministers and dismissed them at

[1] For recent attacks on the Lords, see below, pp. 644 f.

[2] Prior to the Parliament Act of 1911 the formula ran "by and with the consent of the Lords Spiritual and Temporal and Commons in Parliament assembled."

Parliament really controls the English government

will. He made war and peace at his pleasure, and exercised such an influence on the elections that Parliament was filled with his supporters. The long struggle, however, between the king and the Parliament in the seventeenth century, and the circumstances of the Revolution of 1688 which placed William and Mary on the throne, made Parliament the predominant element in the English government. The king is still legally empowered to veto any bill passed by Parliament, but he never exercises this power. He has in reality only the right to be consulted, the right to encourage, and the right to warn. He cannot permanently oppose the wishes of the majority in Parliament, for should he venture to do so, he could always be brought to terms by cutting off the appropriations necessary to conduct his government.

The cabinet

The king of England must now act through a ministry composed of the heads of the various departments of the government, with the prime minister as their head.[1] The development of this ministry, which is known as the cabinet, has been described in an earlier chapter.[2] It was pretty firmly established under George I and George II, who were glad to let others manage the government for them. While the king nominally appoints the members of the cabinet, that body is in reality a committee selected from the party which has a majority in the House of Commons. The leader of the party which secures the majority in a parliamentary election is charged by the king with the task of naming the other cabinet ministers, who may be selected from among the lords as well as the commons.[3] Thus, unlike the president of the United States and his cabinet, who in general communicate with Congress through written messages, reports, or other indirect means, the prime minister and the heads of

How the members of the cabinet are chosen

[1] Gladstone's description of the cabinet system is given in *Readings*, Vol. II, pp. 258 ff.

[2] See above, pp. 55 ff.

[3] He may choose some distinguished man not in Parliament at the time, but in that case the nominee must be immediately elected a member. This can be done by inducing some obscure member to resign so as to have a by-election.

departments in England themselves sit in Parliament and are obliged therefore to present and defend their own proposals.

The cabinet drafts the more important measures to be laid before Parliament and presents its general program at the opening of each session of Parliament in the form of "the king's speech," which is read by the sovereign or his representative. In all matters the cabinet acts as a unit, and whenever a member cannot agree with the majority on an important point he is bound to resign. The cabinet, therefore, presents a united front to Parliament and the country.[1]

FIG. 123. THE RESIDENCE OF THE PRIME MINISTER, 10 DOWNING STREET, LONDON

The official residences of the prime minister of England and of the Chancellor of the Exchequer, respectively, are these two plain-looking buildings on a little street near the Parliament buildings, named after a Sir George Downing, who was a nephew of Governor John Winthrop of Massachusetts and a graduate of Harvard College. Downing was a strong partisan of Cromwell, but on the restoration of Charles II abandoned the principles "he had sucked in" in America and was rewarded for services by a gift of this land

Whenever it happens that the House of Commons expresses its disapproval of the policy of the ministry, either by defeating an

[1] An interesting illustration of this is to be found in the story told of a prime minister of the middle of the century, Lord Melbourne. His cabinet was divided on the question of the duty on grain, and with his back against the door, he declared to them: "Now, is it to lower the price of corn, or is n't it? It does not matter much what we say, but mind, we must all say the same thing."

important measure or by a direct vote of censure, the cabinet is bound to do one of two things. It may resign in a body and thus give way to a new ministry made up from the opposite party. If, however, the ministers feel that their policy has popular support outside of Parliament, they may "go to the country"; that is, they may ask the king to dissolve the existing Parliament and order a new election in the hope that the people may indicate its approval of their policy by electing their supporters. The further action of the ministry is then determined by the outcome of the election. A failure to gain a majority is the signal for the resignation of the entire ministry and the transference of power to their opponents.

The English government more under the influence of public opinion than that of the United States

As the members of the House of Commons are not elected for a definite term of years (though according to a law passed in 1911 elections must be held *at least* every five years), that body may be dissolved at any time for the purpose of securing an expression of the popular will on any important issue. It is thus clear that the British government is more sensitive to public opinion than are governments where the members of the legislatures are chosen for a definite term of years. For example, in the United States, Congressmen are elected for two years and Senators for six; consequently when a crisis arises it usually has to be settled by men who were not chosen according to their views on that particular question, while in England a new election can be held with direct reference to the special issue at hand.

The House of Lords

Nevertheless, the reader will naturally ask how it is that the British government could be so democratic and yet retain, in its upper house, a body of hereditary peers responsible to no constituents. The explanation is that the House of Commons, by reason of its ancient right of initiating all money bills, could control the king and force him, if necessary, to create enough new peers to pass any measure blocked by the House of Lords. In practice the king has not had to do more than threaten such a measure to bring the House of Lords to terms.

Unpopularity of the House of Lords

Although many bills have been defeated in the House of Lords during the nineteenth century, a sort of constitutional understanding has grown up that the upper house must yield to an unmistakable and definite expression of public opinion in favor of a measure which it has previously opposed. However, the House of Lords is increasingly unpopular with a large class in England. Its members for the most part take little or no interest in their duties and rarely attend the sessions. The opposition of the peers to an educational bill introduced in 1906, and also to the budget of 1909, again raised the question of the abolition or complete reorganization of the upper house, and the result was the important Parliament Act of 1911, by which, under certain circumstances, the House of Commons may force a bill through in spite of the Lords.[1]

Section 83. Freedom of Speech and Opinion, and Reform of the Criminal Law

While England was transforming herself into a democracy by remodeling her Parliament, the people gradually gained the right freely to discuss political questions in the newspapers and in public meetings, and to express religious opinions differing from those sanctioned by the government without thereby sacrificing the possibility of holding office.

Taxes on newspapers and other publications

Freedom of the press from governmental censorship is commonly regarded as having been established in 1695 by the refusal of Parliament to renew an old law providing for such

[1] According to the terms of this important act, any bill relating to raising taxes, or making appropriations, which the House of Commons passes and sends up to the House of Lords at least one month before the close of a session may become a law even if the House of Lords fails to ratify it. Other bills passed by the Commons at *three* successive sessions and rejected by the Lords may also be presented to the king for his signature and become laws in spite of their rejection by the upper house. In this way control of the financial policy of the government is practically taken out of the hands of the House of Lords, and in the case of all other laws the House of Commons is able, by a little patience and waiting a couple of years, to do what it pleases without regard to the sentiments of the peers.

control. However, in times of disturbance the government adopted repressive measures, as, for instance, during the French Revolution and in 1819, when there was extensive popular unrest. Moreover the stamp duties on newspapers and advertisements hampered the publication of cheap journals spreading political information among the masses. The necessity of paying an eight-cent tax on each copy made the average price of a newspaper fourteen cents, while the price of the *London Times* was eighteen cents. In addition to these stamp duties there was a special tax on paper, which increased its cost about fifty per cent.

Freedom of the press

These "taxes on knowledge," as they were called, were attacked by those who advocated popular education, and by the political reformers who wanted cheap newspapers through which to carry on agitation.[1] At length, in 1833, the tax on advertisements, and in 1836 the stamp taxes, were reduced, bringing the price of most London papers down to ten cents. Twenty years later these taxes were swept away altogether, and in 1861 the duty on printing paper was removed, and thus England secured a free press. The government, however, does not give low postal rates to the newspapers as in the United States.

Freedom of speech

No less important to democracy than freedom of the press is the right to hold public meetings and to criticize the government. Although during the eighteenth century English laws were less oppressive than those on the Continent,[2] it was not until the middle of the nineteenth century that full liberty of speech was attained. Now England is very proud of this necessary institution of a free people, and every one agrees that it does no harm to let people talk.[3]

[1] For Bulwer-Lytton's speech in favor of a free press, see *Readings*, Vol. II, pp. 270 ff.

[2] See above, p. 140.

[3] A somewhat amusing illustration of the extent of this tolerance is the way the British police will protect from his audience an anarchist or a republican attacking the monarchy.

It was natural that, in the midst of this general movement for political liberty and freedom of the press, the Dissenters and Catholics should have put in a claim for the abolition of the laws which placed them under many disabilities. The Dissenters, although they enjoyed a certain liberty of religious Religious liberty

FIG. 124. WESTMINSTER ABBEY, LONDON

Westminster Abbey is the famous church in which are buried the most distinguished statesmen, authors, artists, and scientists of England. It stands on the site of a church founded in Anglo-Saxon times, but the present building dates mainly from later centuries, the last notable addition having been added by the fifteenth century. The tombs of Chatham, Pitt, Beaconsfield, Gladstone, and other great statesmen lie just inside the door shown in the picture. The Parliament buildings stand just across the street from the church, to the left of the picture

worship, were excluded from municipal offices and from all places of trust, civil and military, in the government, although, curiously enough, they were not forbidden to sit in Parliament — a disability imposed on Catholics in addition to exclusion from public offices. The rapid increase of the dissenting sects in wealth, numbers, and influence, especially after the appearance of the Methodists, at last forced Parliament to respect their demand, and in 1828 the old laws against them were repealed, and they were admitted freely to public offices on condition that they would take an oath "upon the true faith of a Christian" not to use their influence to injure or weaken the Established Church. The following year the Catholics secured the passage of the famous Emancipation Act, which admitted them to both houses of Parliament and to practically all municipal and government offices, upon condition that they would take an oath renouncing the *temporal* supremacy of the Pope and disclaiming any intention of injuring the Protestant religion.[1]

Religion and the schools

These reforms by no means took religious controversies out of politics in England, for the religious sects are still at war over the question as to who shall control the schools. Anglicans, Catholics, and Dissenters during the nineteenth century built schoolhouses and maintained schools of their own, and when the demand for free popular education became so strong that in 1870 the government provided for the erection and equipment of schools at public expense, religious bodies began to contend among themselves for a representation on the school boards having charge of the government schools. All of the sects agreed that education without religious instruction was bad, but they differed hotly on the particular kind of religious instruction that should be given. The problem of how to satisfy the demands of the several bitterly contending sects has constituted one of the main issues of English politics up to the present time. Nevertheless, the efficiency of the schools has steadily increased, and there has been a corresponding decline in illiteracy. In 1843 thirty-two per cent of the men and forty-nine per cent of the women had to sign their names in the marriage registers with a cross. In 1903 only two per cent of the men and three per cent of the women were unable to write their own names in the registers.

[1] For speeches for and against religious toleration, see *Readings*, Vol. II, pp. 274 ff.

While some reformers were busy with securing freedom of the press and removing religious disabilities, others were attacking the criminal law, which, at the opening of the nineteenth century, as an English writer has observed, sacrificed the lives of men with a reckless barbarity worthier of an Eastern despot than of a Christian state.[1] This drastic code included no less than two hundred and fifty offenses for which the death penalty was imposed. It is estimated that between 1810 and 1845 there were fourteen hundred executions for acts which were not regarded as capital offenses after the latter date.

The criminal law

FIG. 125. THE RUINS OF MELROSE ABBEY

It required many years of agitation, however, to move the British Parliament, and although some of the worst abuses were gotten rid of in the third decade of the century, the list of capital offenses was not reduced to three until 1861. In 1835, after a parliamentary investigation had revealed the horrible conditions of prisons, a law was passed providing for government inspection and the improvement of their administration, and this marked the beginning of prison reform, which

Reform of the criminal law

[1] See *Readings*, Vol. II, pp. 279 ff.

includes sanitary buildings, separation of the sexes, separation of the hardened criminals from the younger offenders, and a more enlightened treatment of criminals generally, with a view to reforming them[1] while protecting society.

Section 84. Social Reforms

Wretchedness of life in the English factories

The cruelty of the criminal law had its origin in the Middle Ages, but with the coming of the Industrial Revolution in the reign of George III new forms of inhumanity had arisen. These were the result of the factory system, which brought untold misery to the working classes of England.[2] Great factory buildings were hastily erected by men ignorant of the most elementary principles of sanitary science, and often too avaricious to care for anything but space enough to operate the machines and light enough to enable the laborers to do their work. To these industrial centers flocked thousands of landless and homeless men and women entirely dependent upon the factory owners for the opportunity to earn their daily bread. Fluctuations in trade caused long periods of enforced idleness, which resulted in great uncertainty in the life of the workman.

Child labor

The introduction of steam-driven machinery had made possible the use of child labor on a large scale, and it was the condition of the children which first attracted the attention of philanthropists and reformers. Thousands of little paupers were taken from the poorhouses and nominally apprenticed, but practically sold, to the proprietors of the mills. Necessity or greed on the part of parents, and the demand for "cheap labor" on the part of manufacturers, brought thousands of other children into industrial life.

[1] It should be stated that the attitude of the English toward such matters as crime and its punishment was shared by the other nations as well, although no place can be found in this history to describe them. The proper treatment of criminals and the causes of crime are still subjects but little understood.

[2] For extracts from parliamentary reports on conditions in the factories, see *Readings*, Vol. II, pp. 282 ff.

The conditions of adult labor, save in the most skilled classes, were almost as wretched as those of child labor. Women and girls were employed in great numbers in mills and even in the dark and dangerous recesses of the mines, which were badly ventilated and perilous to work in; dangerous machinery was not properly safeguarded, and the working time was excessively prolonged. The misery of the poor is reflected in Mrs. Browning's poem, "The Cry of the Children," in the bitter scorn which Carlyle poured out on the heads of the factory owners, in the impassioned pages of Kingsley's *Alton Locke*, and in the vivid word pictures of Dickens.

General misery of the factory hands and operatives in the mines

The working classes were excluded from representation in Parliament, they were denied opportunities for education, and the statesmen of the time refused to take action in their behalf until after long and violent agitation. In this refusal Parliament was supported by the economic theorists, who defended the rights of mill owners as Bossuet had defended the divine right of kings. These theorists believed that government interference with industry or commerce would only make matters worse,[1] since the business men knew what was good for their business better than members of Parliament. If capitalists were obliged to shorten hours of labor, they claimed that it would make profits impossible, thus closing the factories and bringing still greater hardships for the workers.

Opposition of economists and statesmen to factory legislation

The result of such a theory was that during the first thirty years of the nineteenth century the government did almost nothing to remedy conditions. In 1802 an act reduced the hours of pauper children in cotton mills to seventy-two per week and made some other reforms, such as compelling employers to furnish at least one suit of clothes a year. But even this act was not enforced and conditions remained as bad as ever. From 1815 to 1819 Robert Owen, the great philanthropist,[2] labored to secure a better law for the protection of children. He had shown by the conduct of his own factories the

Early agitation for factory laws

[1] See above, p. 160. [2] See above, p. 373.

advantage of treating employees well, and appealed to other manufacturers to help secure such conditions in the mills as would produce healthier and happier workers. But his appeal fell on deaf ears, and the bill he finally got passed was but a slight part of his demands. It only forbade the employment of children under nine in the cotton mills, and limited the working time of those between nine and sixteen to twelve hours per day.

Parliament at last begins to adopt reforms

During the following years, however, ardent reformers disregarding the advice of the theorists, and discontented workmen filling the country with unrest, at last forced Parliament to undertake to improve conditions. Indeed, the bad ventilation, scanty food, long hours, and lack of sanitation led to the spread of epidemics in the factory districts, and action could not longer be delayed without endangering the health of the well-to-do.

The report of the factory commission appointed by Parliament in 1832

A group of men, aroused by these conditions, of whom the most notable was Lord Ashley, by unselfish and untiring labors so stirred public opinion that Parliament in 1832 appointed a select commission for the purpose of investigating the whole question of factory legislation. The appalling disclosures of this commission resulted in a new bill still further reducing the working hours for children and providing for the first time for regular factory inspectors. In 1842 Lord Ashley carried through Parliament a mining law which forbade the employment of women and children in underground occupations.

Agitation for a ten-hour day for women and children

These laws did not satisfy the reformers, and they now began to work for another measure, restricting the labor of women and children in mills to ten hours per day exclusive of meal times. This proposition gave rise to a heated contest in the House of Commons between manufacturers and landed proprietors. In vain did John Bright (champion of the abolition of slavery in the United States) denounce the proposition as "most injurious and destructive to the best interests of the country," "a delusion practiced upon the working classes," and "one of the worst measures ever passed."[1] Nevertheless,

[1] Extracts from Bright's speech are given in *Readings*, Vol. II, pp. 285 f.

in 1847 the ten-hour bill for women and children became a law. In practice it applied to all adults as well, for the mills could not run after the women and children had stopped working.

John Morley's description of England's measures for protecting the laboring classes

With this great victory for the reformers the general resistance to state interference was broken down, and year after year, through the long reign of Queen Victoria (1837–1901), and those of her successors, new measures were carried through Parliament, revising and supplementing earlier laws, until to-day England does more than any other European country to protect the factory operatives. In the language of Lord Morley, England has "a complete, minute, voluminous code for the protection of labor; buildings must be kept clear of effluvia; dangerous machinery must be fenced; children and young persons must not clean it while in motion; their hours are not only limited but fixed; continuous employment must not exceed a given number of hours, varying with the trade, but prescribed by law in given cases; a statutable number of holidays is imposed; the children must go to school, and the employer must every week have a certificate to that effect; if an accident happens, notice must be sent to the proper authorities; special provisions are made for bakehouses, for lacemaking, for collieries, and for a whole schedule of other special callings; for the due enforcement and vigilant supervision of this code of minute prescriptions, there is an immense host of inspectors, certifying surgeons, and other authorities, whose business it is to 'speed and post o'er land and ocean' in restless guardianship of every kind of labor, from that of the woman who plaits straw at her cottage door to the miner who descends into the bowels of the earth, and the seaman who conveys the fruits and materials of universal industry to and fro between the remotest parts of the globe."

Important as are the measures thus summarized, far more revolutionary legislation for the working class has been enacted during the last decade than during the entire nineteenth century.[1]

[1] See below, Chapter XXVI.

Section 85. Free Trade

Policy of protection in England before the nineteenth century

From the fourteenth century onward England endeavored, by high tariffs, navigation laws, and numerous other measures, to protect her manufacturers, farmers, and ship owners against foreign competition. Special tariffs were imposed on the manufactured goods of other countries; bounties were paid from the government treasury to encourage various forms of commercial enterprise; Englishmen were obliged to import their goods from the colonies in English ships, no matter how much cheaper they could get them carried by Dutch merchantmen; and high duties were imposed on grain.

Manufacturers demand a repeal of the duties on grain

Adam Smith and other economists denounced this system of protection, claiming that it hampered commerce and so injured industry as well. However, the free-trade movement which in the middle of the nineteenth century opened British markets freely to the products of all nations was mainly the work of the owners of the new factories, who objected to the tariffs on grain, which, they argued, made the bread of their workmen dear. They contended, as well, that undeveloped countries like Russia or America would be happy to buy English cloth, shoes, and cutlery if they could freely send to England, in return, a portion of their great crops of wheat, rye, oats, and barley. Having little fear of foreign competition in their industries, and owning no land, they wanted no protection for themselves or the farmers.

The Corn Laws

The manufacturers began, therefore, to attack the Corn Laws,[1] as the tariff acts protecting grain were called. The duties on grain had been made especially high after 1815, when the fall of the inflated war prices threatened to ruin the farmers.

To secure the repeal of these duties on grain and to propagate the principles of free trade generally, the manufacturers

[1] The term "corn," usually confined to Indian corn, or maize, in the United States, is commonly used in England to mean grain in general.

founded in 1838 the Anti-Corn-Law League, and for almost ten years this organization, under the brilliant leadership of Richard Cobden[1] and John Bright, carried on one of the most thoroughgoing campaigns of popular education in the history of democracy, expending in one year over a million dollars in publications and meetings. The attack was concentrated on the Corn Laws because it was easier to rouse feeling against the landlords than in favor of any abstract theories of political economy. It was a war on the landed aristocracy.

The Anti-Corn-Law League, 1838

The agitation was brought to a crisis in 1845 by a failure of crops in England and a potato famine in Ireland, which raised the price of food stuffs enormously and brought thousands to the verge of starvation, especially in Ireland. In the midst of such distress it appeared to thinking men nothing short of criminal to maintain high prices of grain by law. Consequently Sir Robert Peel, then prime minister, determined that the Corn Laws must go, in spite of the fact that he had hitherto defended them, and in 1846 he succeeded in carrying through Parliament a law which led to their practical repeal. Though compelled to resign immediately after the passage of this bill, Peel had given the whole protective system in England its death blow, since it was chiefly the tariff on grain that could claim any really active defenders.

Sir Robert Peel carries the repeal of the Corn Laws, 1846, and opens the way to free trade

Within ten years all of the old navigation laws were abolished and English ports opened freely to the ships of other nations. Gladstone, as Chancellor of the Exchequer in 1852, removed the duties on one hundred and twenty-three articles entirely, and reduced them on one hundred and thirty-three more. On his return to office, some fifteen years later, he made a clean sweep of all *protective* duties, retaining, for revenue purposes, those on tea, wines, cocoa, and a few other articles.

Free trade established, 1852–1867

The tendency toward free trade was not confined to England. Indeed, until the seventies, it looked as if a network of

[1] Some of Cobden's arguments against the Corn Laws are given in the *Readings*, Vol. II, pp. 287 ff.

Tendency toward free trade in Europe followed by a reaction in the seventies

commercial treaties, combined with low tariffs, would carry all Europe into a free-trade policy. The liberals in France under Napoleon III favored it, and, as we have seen, Germany had accepted it in a modified form until Bismarck's tariff law of 1879. At last, however, a reaction set in. The protectionists rose to power in the continental countries; the United States converted what was once regarded as a temporary policy of encouraging infant industries and of increasing the revenue during the Civil War into a permanent policy of high protection; and foreign competitors, having free access to England's markets, began to undersell her at home as well as abroad.

Growing dissatisfaction with free trade in England

This radical change in the economic conditions in the continental countries and the United States has convinced many Englishmen that some alteration will have to be made in England's free-trade policy. In the election of 1906 Mr. Chamberlain sought to make the establishment of some form of a protective tariff the leading campaign issue. Although the free traders carried the day and the possibility of a change in policy seemed remote, yet the arguments of the protectionists have gained a new force through the war of 1914, and the continuance, to some degree, of tariffs adopted during the war finds many adherents.

Section 86. The Irish Question

In addition to the important problems the English have had to solve at home, they have been constantly involved in perplexities in their dealings with the Irish, who belong to the Celtic race and the Roman Catholic faith and differ essentially from their English neighbors in sentiments and traditions. The principal troubles with Ireland have been over the land question, religious differences, and Home Rule.

The land question

The first of these questions, the land question, grew out of the fact that Ireland had been frequently invaded by the English, and Irish estates had been handed over to English warriors, fortune hunters, and royal favorites. These invasions dated back to the twelfth century, when, under Henry II (1154–1189), certain eastern districts around Dublin, known as the "Pale," were wrested from the Irish. In the sixteenth century, during the reign of Queen Elizabeth, revolts of the Irish led to new conquests, particularly of Ulster in the north. Under James I Protestant colonists from Scotland and England were settled in Ulster, adding a permanent element of discord. A little later, when the Puritans in England were fighting Charles I, the Catholic Irish rose in revolt, but as they were hopelessly divided into factions, Oliver Cromwell's well-disciplined army crushed them all. Cromwell took terrible and bloody vengeance, scourging the country with fire and sword and confiscating more land. During the English Revolution of 1688 the Irish again rose for their Catholic king, James II, and drove the Protestants out or into a few strongholds.[1] Finally William III defeated James at a battle by the river Boyne, July 1, 1690. The Ulster Protestants annually celebrate this deliverance by "William of Orange," and their lodges of "Orangemen" keep alive the spirit of opposition to the Irish Catholics and the fear of what might happen if they got control of the country.[2]

Conquests and settlements

Under Elizabeth

Under James I

Under Cromwell

Under William III

The result of these unsuccessful rebellions was that still more lands were taken from the Irish. Now the English landlords, to whom these estates were given, and their descendants, for the most part, lived in England. In the nineteenth century millions of pounds yearly were drained away from Ireland to pay absentee landlords, who rarely set foot in that country and took little or no interest in their tenants beyond the collection of their rents. If the tenants did not pay or could not pay, they were speedily evicted from their

Evil of absentee landlordism

[1] One of these, Londonderry, held out heroically, with but slight resources, till help came. The town owes its name to the settlement of Derry by Protestants from London.

[2] The first Orange lodges date from 1795, but the movement began earlier.

cottages and lands. It was estimated in 1847 that about one third of the entire rental of Ireland was paid to absentee landlords.

The condition of the peasantry

Throughout large portions of Ireland the peasants were constantly on the verge of starvation. They were deprived of nearly all incentive to work at the improvement of their little holdings, because they were liable to be evicted and lose the results of their own labors. Whenever there was a failure of the potato crop, on which from one third to one half the population depended for food, there were scenes of misery in Ireland which defy description. This was the case in the

The potato famine

"Black Year of Forty-Seven," when the potato crop failed almost entirely and thousands died of starvation in spite of the relief afforded by the government.[1] It was in the midst of this terrible famine that the stream of emigration began to flow toward America. Within half a century four million emigrants left the shores of Ireland for other countries, principally the United States, taking with them their bitter resentment against England.

The Protestant Established Church in Ireland

The second source of trouble in Ireland was the Established Church. When England adopted the Protestant faith an attempt was made to force it upon the Irish, who however clung steadfastly to the Pope and their ancient Church. The monasteries were suppressed and their lands confiscated. Catholic clergy were expelled from their parishes and Protestant priests installed in their places, to be supported by tithes collected from a people still loyal to their old faith. Even in the darkest days of the nineteenth century, when Irish peasants were starving, the Established Church in Ireland continued to draw its ample revenues from the tithes and endowments, although its members numbered but one tenth of the population. These tithes, however, were collected from the peasants only with the utmost difficulty and pitched battles were sometimes fought between

[1] For contemporary accounts of suffering during famines in Ireland, see *Readings*, Vol. II, pp. 297 ff.

them and the police when the latter undertook to drive off the last cow to pay the dues to the hated priest of an alien faith.[1]

Disestablishment of the English Church

It is small wonder, therefore, that the Irish were deeply embittered on the religious question and began a movement to overthrow the Anglican Church in their midst. By the Catholic Emancipation Act, mentioned above, Irish Catholics, along with the English Catholics, had been admitted to Parliament,

FIG. 126. DUBLIN

The fine buildings along this beautiful street were badly injured in the street fighting in 1916, mentioned at the end of the chapter. The slums of Dublin furnish a sad contrast with the impressive public buildings in the main street, and most of the rebels were from the very poor

as well as to other public offices; and they carried on an agitation which ended in 1869 in the passage of an act by Parliament which disestablished the English Church in Ireland and abolished its tithes.[2] The Anglicans, however, were allowed to retain the beautiful buildings which had been seized during the period of the Reformation, and the clergy were recompensed

[1] For extracts from parliamentary reports showing the difficulties of collecting tithes, see *Readings*, Vol. II, pp. 293 ff.

[2] For John Bright's plea for disestablishment, see *Readings*, Vol. II, pp. 295 f.

for the loss of the tithes, which they found it difficult to collect, by a large grant of money from the government.

Although the burden of the tithes was thus removed from the peasants, the evils of absentee landlordism remained; and finding themselves victorious in the struggle against the Anglican Church they undertook an agitation for a drastic land reform.

Parnell and the Land League, 1879

In 1879 a great Land League, with Charles Stewart Parnell, a member of Parliament, at its head, was established with the aim of securing three things for the Irish peasant — fair rent, fixed holding, and fair sale; that is to say, they asked for legislation providing that the rent should not be fixed by the landlord at any amount he thought he could get, but by a court taking into consideration the fair value of the land; that the tenant should hold his land as long as he paid the rent so fixed; and finally that, in case he surrendered his holding, he should be allowed to sell his improvements to the tenant who succeeded him.

The Irish land acts, 1881–1903

Parnell, with the support of the Irish members in Parliament, resorted to "filibustering" until that body was forced in 1881 to pass a land act granting these three demands. This measure has been supplemented by land-purchase acts by which the government puts at the disposal of the tenants money to buy their holdings, with the privilege of repayment on the installment plan. One of these acts, passed in 1903, appropriates a practically unlimited amount for this purpose, and offers a considerable inducement to landlords to sell, so that the land question seems in a fair way to be settled to the satisfaction of the peasantry.[1]

The third source of trouble between England and Ireland has been the contest over Home Rule. Until 1801 Ireland

[1] The Land-Purchase Act of 1885, passed by Lord Salisbury, set apart twenty-five million dollars; that of 1888, a second sum of the same amount; that of 1891 devoted one hundred and seventy million dollars to the purchase of lands, and that of 1903 an almost unlimited sum.

had maintained a separate parliament of her own; but in that year the English government determined to suppress it, as a result of an uprising in 1798 led by Wolfe Tone, a Protestant who had imbibed socialistic principles in France. The Act of Union of 1801 abolished the Irish parliament and provided that Ireland should be represented by one hundred members in the House of Commons and, in the House of Lords, by

Act of Union, 1801

FIG. 127. IRISH COTTAGES

The pictures show the contrast between the quaint, but filthy and unsanitary, old thatched cottages of Ireland and the clean and comfortable, if unpicturesque, new ones. The American traveler often regrets the disappearance of these old houses from the landscape of the Old World, but wherever the peasantry of Europe is prosperous, as in Ireland now, it is replacing picturesqueness by comfort. Hence much of the Old World looks as new as America

twenty-eight peers chosen by the Irish baronage. This Act of Union was resented by the Irish patriots. Accordingly, they at once began an agitation for Home Rule, that is, for a parliament of their own in which they can legislate on their own affairs instead of being forced to rely upon the British Parliament, where the English and the Scotch have an overwhelming majority.

Home Rule agitation

The repeal of the Act of Union was warmly urged by Daniel O'Connell after the emancipation of 1829, and at the general election of 1834 forty members of Parliament favored Home

Daniel O'Connell

Rule. A Repeal Association was organized, monster meetings were arranged by O'Connell, and the examples of Belgium and Greece in winning independence were cited as indications of what the Irish might do. All Ireland seemed on the verge of rebellion, and Irish Americans planned an invasion of Canada. The British government met this agitation by stationing thirty-five thousand troops in the island, and O'Connell, in spite of his violent and inflammatory speeches, shrank from the test of civil war.

Gladstone espouses the cause of Irish Home Rule, 1886

O'Connell died in 1847, but the cause of Home Rule did not perish with him, for it was taken up by the Fenians and the Land League, who inaugurated a reign of terror for the landlords and thus kept steadily before the people. In 1882 the shocking murder of Lord Frederick Cavendish, the chief minister for Ireland, and his secretary took place in Phœnix Park, Dublin. This deed aroused the horror of the civilized world and convinced Gladstone that nothing short of Home Rule could solve the perennial Irish problem. After the parliamentary election of 1886, which gave him a small majority in the Commons and made him dependent upon the Irish members for their support, he undertook to secure the repeal of the Act of Union.[1] Many of his followers, who did not believe in the policy of Home Rule, broke away from his leadership and formed the party of the Liberal Unionists, thus defeating the bill by about thirty votes. Seven years later Gladstone brought forward a new Home Rule bill providing that the Irish should have a parliament of their own at Dublin and also retain representation in that of the United Kingdom. This bill, though passed by the Commons, was rejected by the House of Lords.

The Home Rule Bill of 1914

For some years thereafter the issue almost dropped out of English politics, but the majority of the Irish members of Parliament continued to agitate the question, and in 1914 the Liberal government passed a Home Rule bill which almost

[1] Extracts from Gladstone's speech on Home Rule in 1886 are given in the *Readings*, Vol. II, pp. 301 f.

threatened to plunge Ireland into civil war. The inhabitants of Ulster, in northern Ireland, are mainly Protestant and they have been the bitterest opponents of Home Rule, fearing the rule of a Catholic majority. When the bill was on the point of becoming law, they prepared to rebel, and openly armed and drilled a small army of volunteers. Protestant army officers declared that they would refuse to put down the "Ulsterites," and the government, to avoid bloodshed, modified the bill so as to allow the various divisions of Ulster to decide for themselves whether they would send their members of parliament to London or to Dublin.[1] This did not suit extreme Home Rulers or extreme Unionists, but the Liberals sought to calm them by proposing a federal system for other parts of the United Kingdom as well, with parliaments for Wales and Scotland, much like the system in use in Canada. The European war, however, put an end to these plans, and the actual application of Home Rule, along with other such schemes, was postponed.

The protest of Ulster

Meanwhile, although the old discontent burst out in the spring of 1916 into a revolt which was not crushed without serious damage to Dublin and heavy loss of life, new prosperity has come to the island since the British government, some half-dozen years ago, voted money to aid the Irish peasant to buy his land instead of holding it as a tenant. Much progress has been made in establishing coöperative dairies and farmers' banks. Ireland is now probably more prosperous than she has ever been before.

Revolt of 1916

New prosperity in Ireland

QUESTIONS

SECTION 81. Give an account of the political situation in England at the opening of the nineteenth century. What were the "rotten boroughs"? Who enjoyed the right to vote? Describe an election before the introduction of the secret ballot. Discuss the attempts made to secure parliamentary reform before 1832.

[1] At the end of six years all should send members to Dublin, and so Home Rule would be gradually established.

Describe the passage of the Reform Bill of 1832. State the provisions of the bill. Outline the history of the Chartist movement. Sketch the course of parliamentary reform from 1848 to 1884, giving the terms of the bills of 1867 and 1884. What problems connected with the extension of the franchise are yet to be solved?

SECTION 82. What powers does the king of England possess? What is the English cabinet? Describe the method of selecting cabinet officers; the manner in which the cabinet acts. What is meant by the "rise and fall of ministries"?

For what reason is the English government said to be more under the influence of public opinion than that of the United States? What effect did the Parliament Act of 1911 have upon the power of the House of Lords?

SECTION 83. What were the "taxes on knowledge"? When were they abolished? When and by what means was religious liberty secured by Dissenters and Roman Catholics? Describe the criminal-law system at the beginning of the nineteenth century and the reforms instituted after the parliamentary investigation of 1835.

SECTION 84. Give a brief account of the abuses of the factory system. Account for the opposition to factory legislation. Outline the history of factory legislation.

SECTION 85. Discuss the policy of protection in England. Give the arguments of those who favored free trade. Indicate the steps by which free-trade was established. What is the present-day feeling in England about the free-trade policy?

SECTION 86. Outline the history of England's relations with Ireland from the twelfth to the eighteenth century. What have been the three sources of trouble between England and Ireland in the nineteenth and twentieth centuries? What attempts have been made to remove these causes of discontent in each case?

* W. E. Gladstone was one of the greatest orators and statesmen of England. He began as a Tory, but grew more and more liberal and forced along much reform legislation. The picture shows him, at the age of eighty-two, introducing the Home Rule Bill of 1893. The House of Commons is crowded with the most distinguished men of the day. Note how it is divided into opposing rows of benches, the party in power holding those on the right, the opposition party those on the left, of the Speaker, who sits in the thronelike chair, clad in quaint robes and wearing a wig, as do the clerks in front of him. On this occasion the aisle in the foreground is as crowded as the benches.

FIG. 128. GLADSTONE ADDRESSING THE HOUSE OF COMMONS ON THE HOME RULE BILL *

FIG. 129. THE IMPERIAL DURBAR, INDIA *

CHAPTER XXII

THE BRITISH EMPIRE IN THE NINETEENTH CENTURY

SECTION 87. THE EXTENSION OF BRITISH DOMINION IN INDIA

The British extend their empire while making reforms at home

The story of the British struggles for colonial dominions and world markets — the rivalry with the Dutch in the Spice Islands, the wars for Spanish trade, the struggle with France in India and North America — we have brought down to the settlement at Vienna, which left England foremost among the commercial and colonial powers of all time. The task of developing the resources acquired in India, Africa, Canada, and Australasia, was one of the important problems which the eighteenth century bequeathed to the nineteenth.

British dominion in India at the opening of the nineteenth century

Turning first to India, the British rule, in the opening years of the nineteenth century, extended over the Bengal region and far up the Ganges valley beyond Delhi. A narrow strip along the eastern coast, the southern point of the peninsula, and the island of Ceylon had also been brought under England's control, and in the west she held Bombay and a considerable area north of Surat.[1] In addition to these regions which the English administered directly, there were a number of princes, such as the Nizam of Hyderabad, over whom they exercised the right of "protection." They had secured a foothold which made it evident that the Mogul emperor, who retained but the shadow

* In a great ceremonial gathering, or *durbar*, the princes of India meet to offer allegiance to the British ruler upon his accession. The last imperial durbar was a scene of great magnificence, as this procession of bejeweled princes and elephants shows. The actual ceremony was upon too vast a scale to be reproduced in a single picture.

[1] See map above, p. 106.

of power at Delhi, could never recover the shattered dominions of the great Aurangzeb. The French and Portuguese possessions had declined into mere trading posts along the coast, and in the heart of India only one power disputed the advance of the English toward the complete conquest of the peninsula.

FIG. 130. SCENE ON THE GANGES

Benares, the religious center of Hinduism, rises from the curving shore of the sacred Ganges River, its many domes and minarets giving it an appearance of great splendor. Along the river are many richly ornamented landing places built by pious devotees. The narrow streets behind are crowded with Brahmans and religious pilgrims

The Mahratta wars

This one political power was a union of native princes, known as the Mahratta Confederacy. The country occupied by this confederation extended inward from the Bombay coast and was inclosed on the western border by mountain ranges. The ruling princes, however, who had formed the confederation, were usually warring with one another, except when dangers from without compelled them to unite. If it had not been for the jealousy amongst these princes, they might have checked the growing power of the English and seized India for themselves as it fell from the relaxing grasp of the Great Mogul. But they were generally contending among themselves, and where their territory bordered on British dominion the people were kept in constant turmoil by their restless and unsettled life. At length the English determined to suppress them altogether and in a great war (1816–1818) they were finally conquered, a large part of their territories was annexed, and some of the princes were transformed into feudal lords under British sovereignty — a position which they retain to-day.

While pacifying the interior of India the British were also occupied with the defense and extension of their frontiers on the north, east, and west. For six hundred miles along the northern frontier, where the foothills of the Himalayas gradually sink into the valley of the Ganges, there was chronic disorder fomented by the Gurkhas — a race composed of a mixture of the hill men and the Hindu plain dwellers. Periodically the Gurkha chieftains, like the Highlanders of Scotland or the Mahrattas of western India, would sweep down into the valley, loot the villages of the defenseless peasants, and then retire to their mountain retreats. A few of the most powerful of these chieftains succeeded in building up a sort of confederation under a rajah in whose name they governed Nepal, as their kingdom was called. They then sought to extend their sway at the expense of the British in the Ganges valley, but were badly beaten in a two years' war (1814–1816) and compelled to cede to the British empire a vast northern region, which brought the Anglo-Indian boundary at that point to the borders of Tibet, high up in the Himalaya mountains.

The British advance to the borders of China

While the British were busy with the Mahrattas and Nepalese, the Burmese were pressing into the Bengal districts from the east, and as they had never met the disciplined Europeans in armed conflict, they were confident that they would be able to expand westward indefinitely. Their ambitions were, however, checked by the British (1824–1826), and they were compelled

Annexation in Burma, 1826–1885

to cede to the victors a considerable strip of territory along the east coast of the Bay of Bengal. Having thus made their first definite advance beyond the confines of India proper, the British, after twenty-five years of peace with the Burmese, engaged in a second war against them in 1852 and made themselves masters of the Irawadi valley and a long narrow strip of coast below Rangoon.[1]

Conquest of the Sindh and Punjab regions

After the gains made at the expense of the Burmese, the northwestern frontier next attracted the attention of the conquering British. In the valley of the Indus, where the soldiers of Alexander the Great had faltered on their eastward march, there was a fertile region known as the Sindh, ruled over by an Ameer, who seems to have shown an irritating independence in his dealings with the British. On the ground that the Ameer's government was inefficient and corrupt, the British invaded his territory in 1843, and after some brilliant campaigning they wrested his domain from him and added it to their Indian empire, thus winning a strong western frontier. This enterprise was scarcely concluded when a war broke out with the Sikhs in the northwest, which resulted in the addition of the great Punjab region farther up the valley of the Indus, northeast of Sindh, and the extension of the boundary of the Anglo-Indian empire to the borders of Afghanistan.[2] In addition to this policy of annexation through war with the natives, a process of "peaceful assimilation" was adopted under the governorship

[1] Additional annexations were made after another Burmese war in 1884–1885.

[2] The province of Baluchistan on the northwest has been brought under British dominion by gradual annexations beginning in 1876 and extending down to 1903. Several of the districts were formally organized as British Baluchistan in 1887. In attempting to extend their authority over the neighboring Afghanistan, the British have waged two wars with the ruler of that country, one in 1837–1843 and the last in 1878–1880. The problem how to maintain control over Afghanistan and use it as a protecting state against Russia's southeasterly advance has constituted one of the fundamental issues of Anglo-Indian politics. Recently, however, Russia and England have come to terms on the question of the boundaries, and they have proceeded to divide up Persia, Russia taking the north and Britain the south, leaving only a strip of autonomous territory between. See map, p. 610.

of Lord Dalhousie (1848–1856), who quietly transformed "protected" states into British provinces whenever the direct line of the ruling houses became extinct.[1]

Causes of discontent in India

It was inevitable that the conquest and annexation of so many native Indian states should stir up intense hatred against the British aggressors. In the provinces which were under the direct administration of the British, ruling families and the official classes attached to them had been set aside, and in those which were merely under the suzerainty of the conquerors as feudal states, the rulers chafed at their vassalage. The Mohammedans cherished a religious abhorrence for the Christian intruders in addition to their bitterness at the loss of their former power. The native Mahrattas had good reason to feel that only the advent of the British had prevented them from transforming the peninsula into a Mahratta empire.[2]

Introduction of greased cartridges causes trouble

There were embers of discontent everywhere, and they were fanned into a consuming flame in 1857 by several military reforms undertaken by the English government. The year before, the British had become impressed with the advantages of a new rifle invented by a Frenchman. It was loaded with a paper cartridge containing powder and ball, which was slipped into the barrel and then rammed down into place. In order to slide more easily into the gun the paper was greased, and the soldier had to tear off one end of it with his teeth so that the powder would take fire when the cap was exploded.

The sepoys mutiny in 1857

The introduction of this new rifle seemed innocent enough, but the government had not taken into account certain religious scruples of the sepoys, as the native troops were called. The Hindu regarded touching the fat of a cow as contamination worse than death, and to Mohammedans the fat of swine was almost as horrifying. The government soon heard of this grievance and promised not to use the objectionable grease. Peace was thus maintained for a time, but in May, 1857, some

[1] For Dalhousie's justification for annexations, see *Readings*, Vol. II, pp. 307 f.

[2] For a summary of Indian grievances, see *Readings*, Vol. II, pp. 310 ff.

soldiers at Meerut, in the broad plain between the Jumna and the Ganges, refused to receive the cartridges served out to them and were thereupon sentenced to prison for ten years. Their native companions rallied to their support and rose in rebellion; the next day, May 11, the soldiers mutinied at Delhi, massacred the English inhabitants of the city and besieged the garrison; in a few days the entire northwest was in full revolt. Lucknow, with its population of seven hundred thousand natives, rose against the British and besieged them in their fortifications. At Cawnpore, about forty miles to the south, a thousand British men, women, and children were cruelly massacred after they had surrendered, and by the middle of July all Oudh and the northwest seemed lost.

The rebellion crushed

Immediately after the insurrection at Meerut the governor general telegraphed to Bombay, Madras, and Ceylon for instant help. Though there were as yet no railroads in the rebellious provinces, the telegraph helped to save the empire. Aid was at once sent to Lucknow under the command of General Colin Campbell, a hero of the Napoleonic and Crimean wars, and in November he succeeded in relieving the brave garrison, which had held out for nearly six months. Many of the sepoys remained loyal, and with aid from the coast provinces city after city was wrested from the mutineers until by the end of November British India was saved, but at a frightful cost. In the punishment of the rebels the frenzied English showed themselves as cruel as the natives had been in their treatment of English prisoners.

Queen Victoria assumes the East India Company's political power, 1858

After the suppression of the sepoy rebellion the Parliament of Great Britain revolutionized the government of India. The administration of the peninsula was finally taken entirely out of the hands of the East India Company, which had directed it for more than two hundred and fifty years, and vested in the British sovereign, to be exercised under parliamentary control. In November, 1858, a royal proclamation[1] announced to the

[1] For the proclamation, see *Readings*, Vol. II, pp. 312 ff.

inhabitants of British India that all treaties made under the authority of the East India Company would be maintained, the rights of feudatory princes upheld, and religious toleration granted. The governor general of the company in India was supplanted by a viceroy, and the company's directors in London surrendered their power into the hands of the Secretary of State for India. The Mogul of Delhi, successor of the great Aurangzeb, was expelled from his capital, but when, nearly twenty years later (on January 1, 1877), Victoria was proclaimed Empress of India amid an illustrious gathering of Indian princes and British officials, the pomp and magnificence of the ancient Moguls were invoked to bind their former subjects more closely to their English conquerors. George V, Emperor of India, now rules over about three hundred millions of Indian subjects inhabiting a domain embracing 1,773,000 square miles.

Queen Victoria proclaimed Empress of India, 1877

Progress in India since the mutiny

Since the great mutiny the British government in India has been concerned chiefly with problems of internal reform and administration and with the defense of the frontiers, especially in the northwest. The proportion of natives to white men in the army was greatly reduced and the artillery placed almost entirely in charge of the latter. Codes of law and of criminal procedure were introduced in 1860 and 1861. The construction of railway lines was pushed forward with great rapidity for military and economic purposes, so that the vast interior might be quickly reached by troops, and an outlet opened for its crops of cotton, rice, wheat, indigo, and tobacco. Cotton mills are rising by the tombs of ancient kings, cities are increasing rapidly in population, and the foreign trade by sea has multiplied twenty-fold in the past seventy years. About eight hundred newspapers, printed in twenty-two languages, including Burmese, Sanskrit, and Persian, are published; educational institutions have been provided for nearly five million students. In short, an industrial and educational revolution is taking place in India, and the Indians are beginning to be discontented with a government in which they have little share.

Railroads and newspapers

Section 88. The Dominion of Canada

The French in Canada obtain a liberal government by the Quebec Act, 1774

When the English government was established in Canada after the capture of Montreal in 1760, only about two hundred of the sixty-five thousand inhabitants were of English origin; the rest were French. Barriers of race, language, laws, and religion separated the conquerors from the conquered. For a few years the English administration, not unnaturally, was badly adapted to the needs of its new subjects, but in 1774, on the eve of the war with the American colonies, the British Parliament, in order to insure the allegiance of the Canadians, passed the famous Quebec Act — one of the most remarkable enactments in the history of English law. In an age of intolerance it recognized the Catholic faith, allowed the clergy to collect their tithes, perpetuated the French civil law, and left French customs and traditions undisturbed.

Loyalists settle in Canada during the American Revolution

Under this act the new colony stood patriotically by England during the American Revolution, and though France was herself allied with the revolting colonies, the Canadians repulsed their advances and received fugitive loyalists in great numbers. The latter, known as the United Empire Loyalists, settled in what are now the Maritime Provinces and also in Upper Canada — the region lying along the Great Lakes, which was to become the province of Ontario. It is estimated that by 1806 about eighty thousand loyalist immigrants had crossed the frontier from the United States — the British government offering lands and subsidies to encourage their coming.

Canada divided into two provinces, Ontario and Quebec

The influx of an English population necessitated a change in the government, which had been designed especially for the French. Consequently, in 1791, representative government was established in Canada by a new act of Parliament. The country was divided into two provinces — an upper one, Ontario, lying mainly along the Great Lakes, which was being rapidly settled by the English, and a lower one, Quebec, which had long been the home of the French.

Under this new government the English and French inhabitants once more showed their loyalty to England when the armies of the United States prepared to invade Canada during the War of 1812; for the old loyalists in Ontario still remembered with bitterness their expulsion during the American Revolution. The French Canadians likewise flocked to the support of the English cause. The invasion failed, and the result of the conflict was merely to increase the ill will already felt for the neighboring republic, whose designs of annexation were regarded with distrust and aversion.

French Canadians loyal to Britain in the War of 1812

Amicably as the Canadians in the two provinces coöperated against the United States, they were troubled by domestic dissensions. In Upper Canada (now Ontario), United Empire Loyalists were in control of the government. They were mostly Tories, and the ruling group was known as the "Family Compact" because it was largely composed of relatives or intimate friends. The Liberals became exasperated at the lack of responsible government, and a section of them took up arms in rebellion in 1837. In Lower Canada (now Quebec) rebellion broke out as well, due to irritation of the French at British rule. Both rebellions were easily crushed, but the British sent over an investigator, Lord Durham, whose report (1840), advocating self-government for the colonies, marks a turning point in the attitude of England toward the treatment of her possessions beyond the seas. From that time on, it has been a matter of principle in British politics to give self-government to the colonies so far as it can be done. This is one of the most important revolutions in the history of government. The British self-governing colonies even make their own treaties, and are practically free nations.

The Canadian rebellion of 1837 and Durham's Report

Self-governing colonies

The report was followed by a union of the two provinces under one government, which was responsible to the people.[1]

Act of Union

[1] In Nova Scotia, New Brunswick, and Prince Edward Island there were demands for more local rights, and about the middle of the century they were granted self-government through responsible ministries.

Canadian provinces federated in 1867

This was an important step in the direction of the Canadian federation, which was organized a few years later. By the British North America Act of 1867 Ontario, Quebec, New Brunswick, and Nova Scotia were united into the Dominion of Canada, with the provision that the remaining provinces and territories might be admitted later. This federation was given a constitution providing for a governor general representing the sovereign of England, who is a mere figure head; a Senate, the members

FIG. 131. THE PARLIAMENT BUILDINGS, OTTAWA

Parliament Hill is beautifully situated beside the Ottawa River. The main building was burned, February, 1916

of which are appointed for life by the governor general; and a House of Commons, which is the real governing body, elected by popular vote. The new plan of federation went into effect on July 1, 1867 — a day which is celebrated as the Canadian national holiday, like the Fourth of July in the United States.

New provinces admitted to the federation

Since the formation of the federation, the history of the dominion has been characterized by rapid material development and the growth of a national spirit among the Canadian people. The great western regions have been divided into territories and then into provinces, just as the western part of the United States has been organized into territories and then into states. In 1869 the extensive rights which the Hudson Bay Company had possessed for more than two hundred years over vast regions encircling Hudson Bay were purchased. The province of Manitoba was laid out in 1870; in 1871 British Columbia, which had been occupied after the settlement of the Oregon controversy with the United States, was admitted to the federation; Prince Edward Island followed two years later; and in 1905 the great provinces of Alberta and Saskatchewan came into the union, leaving only Newfoundland outside. The tide of immigration has slowly risen, and the population, which was a little over half a million in 1820, was more than five millions at the close of the century, and is now nearly eight millions.

Growth of national spirit in Canada

The development of Canadian industries under the encouragement of protective tariffs and government bounties is intimately connected with the growth of a feeling that Canada constitutes a nation by herself, in spite of her position as a member of the British empire. The close trading relations which were once fostered between Canada and the United States by reciprocity treaties, guaranteeing mutual interests, were long hampered by the protective policy which the government at Washington followed after the close of the Civil War. As a result, Canada was driven to look more and more to Great Britain as her industrial ally rather than to the neighboring republic. In the seventies Sir John MacDonald, leader of the Conservative party, made the idea of a "national policy," or protection for Canadian interests, a current political issue, and since that time both the Conservative and Liberal parties have labored to make Canada an independent manufacturing nation. In the fostering of this "colonial nationalism," as it is aptly called, there has been found no more ardent advocate than the former premier, Sir Wilfrid Laurier,[1] who, as a

[1] Extracts from one of Laurier's speeches on his attitude toward England are given in the *Readings*, Vol. II, pp. 320 ff.

Liberal, had once been for free trade. The way in which Canada rejected the plan for trade reciprocity with the United States in 1911 shows that there is little support for anything that has the faintest resemblance to annexation to the republic. In the election of that year the Conservative party, which stands for closer ties with the mother country and a protective tariff against the United States, was returned to power with a very large majority. Sir Robert Borden, its leader, as premier, has been prominent in imperial conferences held from time to time in England.

Section 89. The Australasian Colonies

The British did not have to contend with many natives in Australasia

The Australasian colonies of Great Britain — Australia, Tasmania, New Zealand, and some of the minor islands — were practically unoccupied when the English colonists began to flock there in the nineteenth century. The aborigines of Australia and Tasmania were never very numerous or warlike. The English were therefore free, in these vast regions, to work out in their own way a democratic government suited to the conditions in which they found themselves. They have neither been forced into conflict with other European peoples, as in Canada, nor have they had to control alien races, as in India.

The extent and natural resources of Australasia

The continent of Australia, with the neighboring island of Tasmania, somewhat exceeds in extent the area of the United States, while New Zealand alone is somewhat larger than the island of Great Britain. Although a great part of Australia lies in the temperate zone, the northern region nearest the equator is parched in summer, and the whole central portion suffers from a scarcity of water, which makes vast areas of the interior permanently uninhabitable unless some means of irrigation on a large scale can be introduced. The eastern and southern coasts have always been the chief centers of colonization. Melbourne, in the extreme south, lies in a latitude

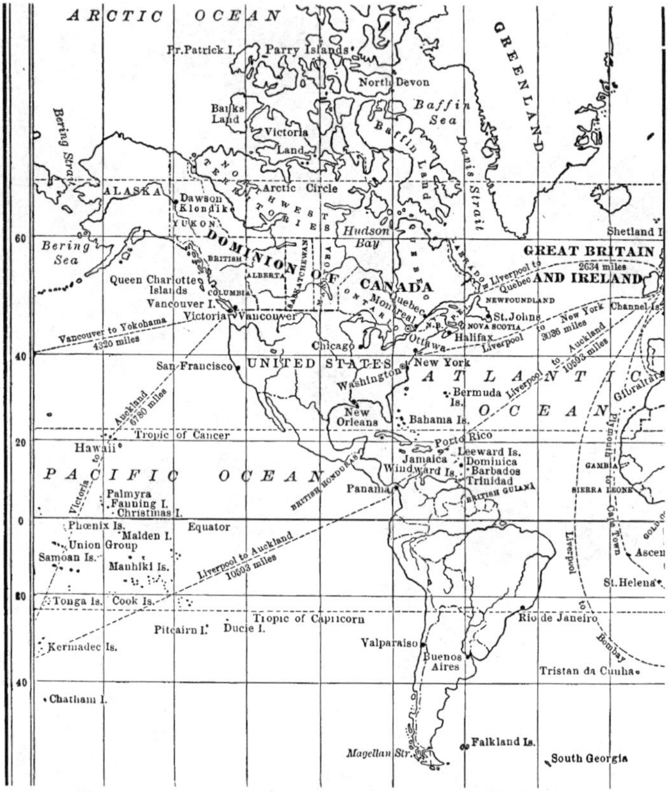
ARCTIC OCEAN
Pr.Patrick I.
Parry Islands
North Devon
GREENLAND
Baffin Sea
Banks Land
Victoria Land
Baffin Land
Davis Strait
Bering Strait
Arctic Circle
ALASKA
Dawson
Klondike
NORTHWEST TERRITORIES
YUKON
Hudson Bay
QUEBEC
LABRADOR
Shetland I.
60
Bering Sea
DOMINION OF CANADA
BRITISH COLUMBIA
ALBERTA
SASKATCHEWAN
MANITOBA
ONTARIO
GREAT BRITAIN AND IRELAND
Liverpool to Quebec 2634 miles
Queen Charlotte Islands
Vancouver I.
Victoria
Vancouver
Quebec
Montreal
NEWFOUNDLAND
St.Johns
Channel Is.
N.B.
NOVA SCOTIA
Halifax
Ottawa
Liverpool to New York 3036 miles
Vancouver to Yokohama 4320 miles
Chicago
40
San Francisco
UNITED STATES
New York
Washington
Liverpool to Auckland 10503 miles
ATLANTIC OCEAN
Gibraltar
Bermuda Is.
Auckland 6780 miles
New Orleans
Bahama Is.
Tropic of Cancer
Porto Rico
20
Hawaii
Victoria to
Leeward Is.
Jamaica
Dominica
Windward Is.
Barbados
Trinidad
GAMBIA
PACIFIC OCEAN
BRITISH HONDURAS
Panama
BRITISH GUIANA
SIERRA LEONE
Plymouth to Cape Town
Palmyra
Fanning I.
Christmas I.
0
Phœnix Is.
Equator
Malden I.
Union Group
Samoan Is.
Manhiki Is.
Liverpool to Auckland 10503 miles
Ascen
St.Helena
20
Tonga Is.
Cook Is.
Tropic of Capricorn
Rio de Janeiro
Liverpool to Bombay
Pitcairn I.
Ducie I.
Valparaiso
Kermadec Is.
Buenos Aires
Tristan da Cunha
40
Chatham I.
Falkland Is.
Magellan Str.
South Georgia

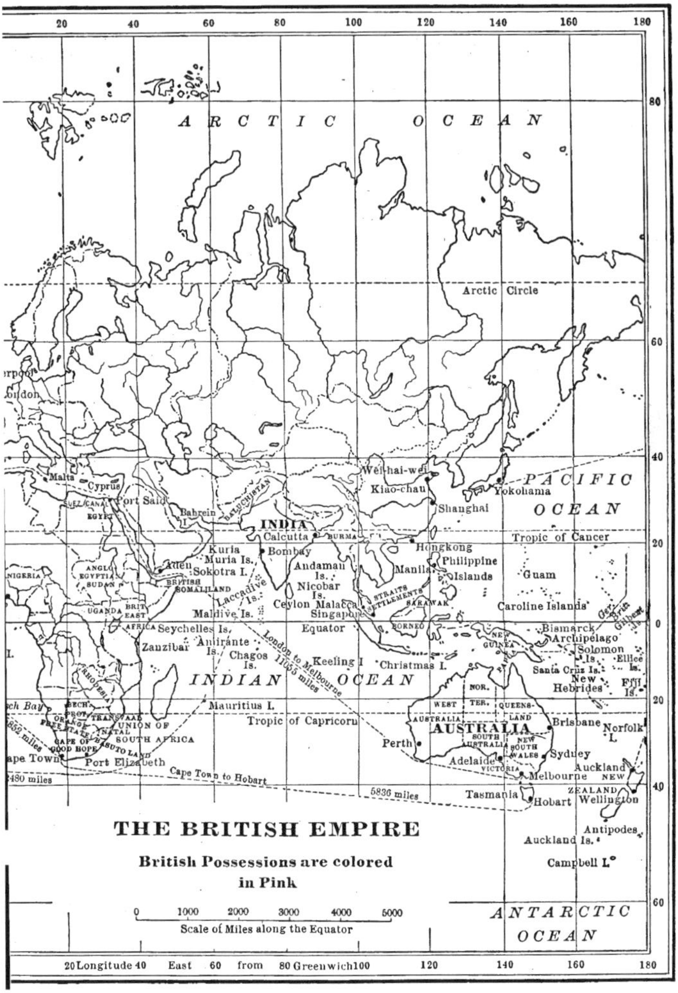
ARCTIC OCEAN
Arctic Circle
PACIFIC OCEAN
INDIAN OCEAN
ANTARCTIC OCEAN
INDIA
AUSTRALIA
Malta
Cyprus
Port Said
Bahrein I.
Calcutta
Bombay
Aden
Kuria Muria Is.
Sokotra I.
Laccadive Is.
Maldive Is.
Ceylon
Andaman Is.
Nicobar Is.
Malacca
Singapore
Wei-hai-wei
Kiao-chau
Shanghai
Hongkong
Manila
Philippine Islands
Yokohama
Guam
Caroline Islands
Bismarck Archipelago
Solomon Is.
Santa Cruz Is.
New Hebrides
Fiji Is.
Ellice Is.
Seychelles Is.
Amirante Is.
Chagos Is.
Zanzibar
Mauritius I.
Keeling I
Christmas I.
Equator
Tropic of Cancer
Tropic of Capricorn
London to Melbourne 11055 miles
Cape Town to Hobart
5836 miles
480 miles
Perth
Adelaide
Melbourne
Sydney
Brisbane
Norfolk I.
Tasmania
Hobart
Auckland
Wellington
NEW ZEALAND
Antipodes
Auckland Is.
Campbell I.
Cape Town
Port Elizabeth
UNION OF SOUTH AFRICA
Liverpool
London
THE BRITISH EMPIRE
British Possessions are colored in Pink
0 1000 2000 3000 4000 5000
Scale of Miles along the Equator
20 Longitude 40 East 60 from 80 Greenwich 100 120 140 160 180

corresponding to that of Washington, St. Louis, and San Francisco in the northern hemisphere. The country affords gold, silver, coal, tin, copper, and iron. Tasmania and New Zealand are more fortunate than Australia in the diversity of their scenery and the general fertility of their soil, while their climate is said to possess all the advantages of the mother country without her fog and smoke.

Early explorations in Australasia — Captain Cook's voyages

The English occupation of Australasia belongs to the nineteenth century. The Portuguese, in their eager hunt for the Spice Islands, may perhaps have come upon Australia, but it long remained an unknown portion of the globe, as shown by the rude outline of *Terra Australis* (or Southern Land) which appears on the maps of the Elizabethan age. In 1642 a Dutch seaman, Tasman, discovered the island which now bears his name (originally called Van Dieman's Land). He also sighted in the same year the islands to the east, which, in spite of their almost Alpine character, were named New Zealand, after the low-lying meadows at the mouth of the Rhine. The Dutch did not, however, occupy these lands, which were later brought to the attention of the English by the famous voyages of Captain Cook. He skirted around the entire coast of New Zealand in 1769–1770, and then sailed westward to Australia, reaching land at a point which, owing to its luxuriant foliage, he called Botany Bay. He took possession of the continent in the name of the English sovereign, and it was called New South Wales, on account of its fancied resemblance to the Welsh shore line.

Founding the Australian colonies

In 1787 England began the colonization of Australia by transporting to Botany Bay a number of convicts. Just north of Botany Bay lies an excellent harbor, and the town of Sydney, which grew up on its shores, became the chief city of New South Wales, the first of six sister states, which now form the Australian federation. Tasmania, with the town of Hobart established in 1804, and Western Australia also began as penal stations. Some settlements which had grown up around the town of Melbourne were united in 1851 to form the colony of Victoria. Shortly after, the region to the north of Sydney was organized into the colony of Queensland. South Australia, with its town of Adelaide, sprang up as an independent settlement of free men, never having had the misfortune of being used as a station for criminals. The discovery of gold in Australia in 1851 brought in many settlers, and as the colonies advanced in wealth and prosperity, protest was made against the transportation of criminals, and the British government finally abandoned it. Civil government supplanted the military rule which had been exercised over the penal stations, and each colony at length secured self-government, that is, a parliament and a ministry of its own, under the general sovereignty of the British crown.

The Australian Commonwealth formed by the union of six colonies

It was natural that in time the people of these colonies, speaking the same language and having the same institutions, should seek a closer union. The question of a federation was long discussed, and at last, in 1891, a general convention composed of delegates from all the states drafted a federal constitution, which was submitted to the people for their ratification. In 1900 the British Parliament passed an act constituting the Commonwealth of Australia on the basis of this draft.[1] The six states — New South Wales, Tasmania, Victoria, Queensland, South Australia, and Western Australia — are now formed into a union similar to that of the United States. The king is represented by a governor general; the federal parliament is composed of two houses, a Senate, consisting of six senators from each state, and a House of Representatives chosen in the same way as in the United States. This body has extensive power over commerce, railways, currency, banking, postal and telegraph service, marriage and divorce, and industrial arbitration.

The settlement of New Zealand

To the southeast of Australia, twelve hundred miles away, lie the islands of New Zealand, to which English pioneers began to go in the early part of the nineteenth century. In 1840 the

[1] Extracts from the constitution are given in the *Readings*, Vol. II. pp. 326 f.

English concluded a treaty with the native Maoris, by which the latter were assigned a definite reservation of lands on condition that they would recognize Queen Victoria as their sovereign. The English settlers established the city of Auckland on North Island, and twenty-five years later New Zealand became a separate colony, with the seat of government at Wellington. Under the auspices of the New Zealand Company colonization was actively carried on, and before long the whites began to press in upon the reservations of the Maoris. This led to two revolts on the part of the natives (1860 and 1871), which were, however, speedily repressed and have not been repeated.

Social reform in New Zealand

New Zealand has recently become famous for its experiments in social reform.[1] During the last decade of the nineteenth century the workingmen became very influential, and they have been able to carry through a number of measures which they believe to be to their advantage. Special courts are established to settle disputes between employers and their workmen; a pension law helps the poor in their old age. Various measures have been adopted for discouraging the creation of large estates, which are heavily taxed, while small farms pay but little. The right to vote is enjoyed by women as well as by men.[2]

Victoria attempts to maintain standard wages for workingmen

The colony of Victoria has vied with New Zealand in respect to social reform. The government has attempted to stop "sweating" in the poorly paid industries, and public boards composed of employers and workmen have been established for the purpose of fixing the minimum wages and standards of work, so that these matters are no longer arranged by private bargaining between individuals. The system of secret voting which originated in Australia — the so-called "Australian ballot" — is one of the reforms which has already spread beyond Australasia, and is in use both in England and in the United States.

[1] For a summary of the principles of reform, see *Readings*, Vol. II, pp. 322 ff.

[2] In Australia women are also permitted to vote for members of the federal parliament and in the local elections of all the states.

Section 90. Growth of the British Empire in Africa

Early conflict between the British and Dutch in South Africa

The chief centers of British advance in Africa have been two — the Cape of Good Hope at the extreme south and Egypt[1] in the north. The Cape Colony was permanently acquired, as we have seen, at the Congress of Vienna in 1814, some eight years after its actual seizure from the Dutch during the war with Napoleon. When this colony passed into the hands of the British it contained slightly over twenty-five thousand people of European descent, mainly Dutch, and it is from this original Dutch stock that the majority of the present white inhabitants are derived, although immigration from England set in after the fall of Napoleon. These Dutch settlers were a sturdy, resolute people, strongly attached to their customs, including slavery, and though of peaceable spirit, they were unwilling to submit to interference. It was just these characteristics which the new rulers overlooked. Shortly after their occupation the British reconstructed the system of local government and the courts; they insisted on the use of the English language; and finally, in 1833, they abolished slavery.

Many thousand Boers leave Cape Colony for the interior

Owing to these grievances, about ten thousand of the Boers[2] left the Cape during the years 1836 to 1838, and, pressing northeastward beyond the Orange River into the interior, partly inhabited by warlike savages, set up a new colony. During the succeeding years large numbers of the Boers pushed farther eastward and northward into the regions now known as Natal and the Transvaal. For a time they had their own way in these barren wildernesses.

Natal, however, was on the seacoast, and the British had no desire to see a strong unfriendly state established there.

[1] The circumstances which led England to interfere in Egyptian affairs will be considered below, pp. 627 ff.

[2] This is the Dutch word for "farmer" and has come to be especially applied to the Dutch population of South Africa.

Consequently they sent troops over to occupy Durban (then called Port Natal), which had formerly been the seat of some English settlers. These troops came into conflict with the Dutch there in 1842 and drove them out — adding more bitterness to the ill will which the Boers already felt for the English. The conquerors cared little, however, for Dutch opinion, and six years later (in 1848) they seized the Orange River Colony, which the Boers had founded between the Orange and Vaal rivers.

The British seize Natal (1842) and the Orange River Colony (1848)

Once more a great Boer migration began, this time into the region beyond the Vaal, where pioneers had already broken the way. There the Transvaal Colony was founded. The British believed that the vast inland wilderness was good only for cattle raising and rude agriculture and was therefore not worth the trouble of annexation and defense. Accordingly, in 1852, by a treaty known as the Sand River Convention, they recognized the independence of the Boers in the Transvaal region, guaranteeing them the right "to manage their own affairs and to govern themselves according to their own laws, without any interference on the part of the British government." This was followed, two years later, by the recognition of the independence of the Orange River Colony under the name of the Orange Free State, until the recent war brought it again under British sovereignty.

The Transvaal Colony founded and its independence recognized by the British, 1852

Independence of the Orange Free State recognized, 1854

In the Transvaal the Dutch lived a rude wild life, having little government and desiring little. They were constantly embroiled with the natives, and as time went on the British began to complain, as they had previously of the Orange River Colony, that their disorders constituted a standing menace to the peace of the neighboring colonies. Whether or not there was any justification for this claim, Great Britain in 1877 annexed the Transvaal Republic,[1] whose independence it had recognized twenty-five years before. The government thus imposed upon the Boers was extremely galling, and in 1880 they organized an insurrection and destroyed at Majuba Hill (1881) a small detachment of English troops.

The British annex the Transvaal Republic, 1877

[1] See *Readings*, Vol. II, pp. 328 ff.

But Gladstone grants Dutch independence again

At that time Gladstone was in office, and turning a deaf ear to the demands of the imperialists for vengeance, he determined to grant to the Dutch that independence for which they had fought. Consequently he concluded a convention with the Transvaal provisional government by which autonomy under the suzerainty of the queen of England[1] was granted to the Boers, except that their foreign affairs were to be subject to British control. Regarding this measure not as an act of magnanimity on the part of the British government but as a concession wrung from it by force of arms, the Boers determined to secure complete independence, and succeeded in 1884 in obtaining a new convention recognizing the Transvaal as free and independent in all respects except the conclusion of treaties with foreign powers. They thus regained, for all practical purposes, the freedom which they had enjoyed before the annexation of 1877.

The discovery of gold in the Transvaal

The very next year (1885) gold was discovered in the southern part of the Transvaal, and wild lands which the negroes had despised and from which the Boers could scarcely wring a scanty living now became exceedingly valuable. Thousands of miners, prospectors, speculators, and the customary rabble of the mining camp began to flow into the Transvaal, and within a short time the population had trebled. The Boers were now outnumbered by the newcomers, the *Uitlanders*, or foreigners, as they were called. The Dutch, in order to retain their supremacy, put all sorts of obstacles in the way of the newcomers who wished to acquire citizenship and the right to vote.

It was now the turn of the Uitlanders (who were largely English) to protest.[2] They declared that their energy and

[1] Just what "suzerainty" meant was to be a matter of dispute. The term comes from feudal days when a lord was the suzerain of his vassal, leaving him free to do much as he wanted to, so long as the vassal recognized his dependence and complied with the conditions.

[2] For a summary of English grievances against the Boers, see *Readings*, Vol. II, p. 332.

enterprise had transformed a poor and sparsely settled country into a relatively populous and prosperous one; that they had enriched the treasury of an almost bankrupt government; and that since they also had a stake in the country, they should be allowed a voice in making the laws and in the administration of justice. They tried to effect a change in the Transvaal constitution, and, failing that, they planned in 1895 an insurrection against the Boer authorities.

The British in the Transvaal protest against the government as managed by the Dutch

The conspiracy was encouraged by Cecil Rhodes, prime minister of Cape Colony and head of the British South Africa Company. It is alleged that he was supported in this by some of those who were then in control of the home government. Dr. Jameson, an agent of the company, who was much interested in promoting some of Rhodes's great schemes, started for the interior of the Transvaal at the head of an armed band of the company's forces with the intention of coöperating with those who were preparing for an uprising at Johannesburg. The enterprise miscarried, however, and the insurgents were captured by the Boers.

The Jameson raid, 1895

This "Jameson raid," as it is called, only served further to embitter the Boers and afforded them a pretext for collecting large military supplies in self-defense. The president of the Transvaal Republic, Paul Kruger, was firmly opposed to all compromise with the British.[1] He was practically master of the little oligarchy that controlled the republic; he persistently disregarded the petitions of the Uitlanders, and entered into an offensive and defensive alliance with the Orange Free State to the south.

President Kruger refuses to conciliate the British

The English now began to claim that the Boers would not be satisfied until they had got control of all the British possessions in South Africa. The Boers with more reason, as it seemed to the rest of the world, declared that England was only trying to find an excuse for annexing the two republics which the

The Boer War, 1899

1 For Kruger's appeal to the Boers to resist the British, see *Readings*, Vol. II, pp. 333 f.

II

Dutch farmers had built up in the wilderness after a long fight with the native savages. Finally, in 1899, the weak Transvaal and the Orange Free State boldly declared war on England. The Boers made a brave fight and the English managed the war badly. Many Englishmen thought it a shame to be fighting Paul Kruger and his fellow farmers, and although the greater number of foreign nations were in sympathy with the Boers,

FIG. 132. GENERAL LOUIS BOTHA

no one of the powers intervened. Finally, England, after some humiliating defeats, was victorious and annexed the two Boer republics.

Formation of the South African Union

With a wise liberality toward the conquered Boers, Britain proceeded to give them self-government like other parts of the empire. In 1910 an act of Parliament formed a South African Union on the model of Canada and Australia. This includes the flourishing Cape Colony, with its great diamond mines about Kimberley, Natal to the northeast, and the two Boer republics — the Orange Free State and the Transvaal. These are now managed as a single federation by a representative of the British ruler and a parliament which makes laws for the whole union. When war broke out between England and Germany in 1914 the Germans expected the Boers to rise against England, but they were disappointed. The prime minister of the South African Union, General Botha, who had been the best Boer general in the war against England fifteen years before, not only easily suppressed a rising of some of his old comrades but conquered German Southwest Africa for the British empire. In addition, South African troops have invaded German East Africa and have fought on the main battle line in France. The British look with much natural pride upon this tribute to their wisdom in granting freedom and self-government to the Boers.[1]

FIG. 133. BRIDGE ACROSS THE ZAMBESI RIVER, NEAR VICTORIA FALLS

Built in 1905 on the "Cape to Cairo" railway, this bridge crosses the great cañon in which for 40 miles the river runs below the falls. The falls are twice the height of Niagara and over a mile wide. They occur about midway in the 2000-mile course of the river

[1] There are about six millions of people in the South African Union, but a large portion of these are colored. The white population, including both those of English and those of Dutch descent, do not equal in number the inhabitants of Philadelphia.

Other British possessions in Africa

In addition to these colonies Great Britain has three enormous provinces in Africa occupied almost entirely by negroes. North of the Cape lies the Bechuanaland protectorate, inhabited by peaceful native tribes. Beyond Bechuanaland and the Transvaal is Rhodesia, which was acquired through the British South Africa Company by two annexations in 1888 and 1898 and, with subsequent additions, brought under the protection of the British government. On the east coast, extending inland to the great lakes at the source of the Nile, lies the valuable ranching land of British East Africa. It is of especial value as controlling the southern approach to the Sudan and Egypt, which are so important to Britain.

In addition to these colonies in Africa, British Somaliland was secured on the Straits of Bab-el-Mandeb in 1884 in connection with the establishment of the English power in Egypt. Along the west coast Great Britain has five centers, Gambia, Sierra Leone, the Gold Coast, Lagos, and Nigeria — the beginnings of which date back to the days of Drake and Hawkins, when the British were ravaging the coast for slaves to carry to the New World. The English now, however, are making atonement for the past by helping the natives to become civilized, sending physicians to fight tropical diseases and governing well.

Several railways have been built in South Africa, one running through the whole country from Cape Town to the northern border of Rhodesia. There was once much talk of an "all British line from the Cape to Cairo" across Africa, but the extension of the Belgian Congo Free State on the northwest, and especially of German East Africa on the northeast, blocked this plan. The hope was revived, however, by the victories of the Boer armies fighting for England against the Germans in Africa during the great war of 1914. The fate of these sections of Africa will be one of the most important matters to be settled after the war.

TABLE OF PRINCIPAL BRITISH POSSESSIONS

IN EUROPE: The United Kingdom, Gibraltar, and Malta.

IN ASIA: Aden, Perim, Sokotra, Kuria Muria Islands, Bahrein Islands, British Borneo, Ceylon, Cyprus, Hongkong, India and dependencies, Labuan, the Straits Settlements, the Federated Malay States, Weihaiwei.

IN AFRICA: Ascension Island, Basutoland, Bechuanaland Protectorate, British East Africa, Cape of Good Hope, Nyasaland Protectorate, Zanzibar, Mauritius, Natal, Orange River Colony, Rhodesia, St. Helena, Tristan da Cunha, Seychelles, Somaliland, Transvaal Colony, Swaziland, Northern Nigeria, Southern Nigeria, the Gold Coast, Gambia, Sierra Leone.

IN NORTH AND SOUTH AMERICA: Bermudas, Canada, Falkland Islands, British Guiana, British Honduras, Newfoundland and Labrador, the West Indies, including Bahama Islands, Barbados, Jamaica, Leeward Islands, Trinidad, and Windward Islands.

IN AUSTRALASIA AND THE PACIFIC ISLANDS: The Commonwealth of Australia (including New South Wales, Victoria, Queensland, South Australia, Western Australia, and Tasmania), New Zealand, New Guinea (British), Fiji Islands, Tonga or Friendly Islands, and other minor islands in the Pacific.

Total area, 11,447,954 square miles. Population, 419,401,371.

QUESTIONS

SECTION 87. Describe the position of the British in India at the opening of the nineteenth century. Show on a map the extension of British control over India in this century. Mention the causes of discontent in India prior to the Indian mutiny. What was the immediate cause of the mutiny of 1857? What change in government resulted from this uprising? Show the progress which has been made in India since 1857.

SECTION 88. Outline the history of the British in Canada from 1760 to 1812. What was the cause of the Canadian rebellion of 1837? Describe the federation of the Canadian provinces in 1867. Draw a map of Canada, showing the additions to the federation down to the year 1905.

SECTION 89. Give a short account of Australian exploration and colonization. Describe the Australian Commonwealth. Give an account of social reform in New Zealand.

SECTION 90. How did the British gain possession of the Cape of Good Hope? Describe the relations between the Boers and the British down to 1848, and from that date to 1881. What was the result of Gladstone's South African policy? Show the effect of the discovery of gold upon the relations of the British and the Dutch in South Africa from 1885 to 1899.

Give a brief account of the Boer War. What colonies make up the South African Union? Describe the form of government of the South African Union. Draw a map showing the British possessions in South Africa.

FIG. 134. A REVIEW OF THE BRITISH FLEET IN JULY, 1914

FIG. 135. TSAR NICHOLAS II AT THE OPENING OF THE FIRST DUMA *

CHAPTER XXIII

THE RUSSIAN EMPIRE IN THE NINETEENTH CENTURY

SECTION 91. THE REIGNS OF ALEXANDER I (1801–1825) AND NICHOLAS I (1825–1855)

Relations between Russia and western Europe becoming more intimate

During the past century Russia has been coming into ever closer relations with western Europe. Although still a backward country in many respects, she has been busily engaged for fifty years in modernizing herself; and shortly after the opening of the twentieth century it looked as if a popular government would be established by violence. The works of some of her writers are widely read in foreign lands, especially those of Leo Tolstoy. The music of Rubinstein and Tschaikowsky is as highly esteemed in London or New York as in Petrograd or Moscow. Even in the field of science such names as that of Mendelyeev, the chemist, and of Metchnikoff, the biologist, are well known to their fellow workers in Germany, France, England, and America. And among the vast millions of Russians many more are sure to contribute to our civilization in the future. It becomes, therefore, a matter of vital interest to follow the changes which are turning the tide of modern civilization into eastern Europe.

* The picture represents the religious ceremony at the opening of Russia's first parliament (see p. 571). The Tsar, his wife, and mother stand facing an altar before which the richly robed clergy are officiating. The altar stands just at the steps leading to the throne, which is therefore not shown in the picture, and the religious ceremony is taking place while the Tsar is on his way up the aisle to the throne, where he is to preside. The Russians are a very religious nation and the Church has therefore great influence.

Participation of Alexander I in European affairs

When, in 1815, Tsar Alexander I returned to St. Petersburg after the close of the Congress of Vienna, he could view his position and recent achievements with pride. He had participated in Napoleon's overthrow, and had succeeded in uniting the rulers of western Europe in that Holy Alliance which he

FIG. 136. THE KREMLIN, MOSCOW

The Kremlin is a walled inclosure occupying a hill of about 100 acres in the heart of Moscow. Five gates surmounted with towers open into its picturesque courts, where some three cathedrals, a convent and a monastery, a palace of the Tsars, and various other remarkable buildings are found, in which are priceless treasures of art as well as sacred relics venerated through all Russia. Note the peculiar architecture of the churches, due largely to oriental and Byzantine influence

had so much at heart. But his chief interests lay, of course, in his own vast empire. He was the undisputed and autocratic ruler of more than half of the whole continent of Europe, not to speak of the almost interminable reaches of northern Asia which lay beneath his scepter.

Under Alexander's dominion there were many races and peoples, differing in customs, language, and religion — Finns,

Heterogeneous character of the Russian empire

Germans, Poles, Jews, Tartars, Armenians, Georgians, and Mongols.[1] The Russians themselves, it is true, had colonized the southern plains of European Russia and had spread even into Siberia. They made up a large proportion of the population of the empire, and their language was everywhere taught in the schools and used by the officials. The people of the grand duchy of Finland, speaking Swedish and Finnish, did not like their incorporation with Russia; and the Poles, recalling the time when their kingdom far outshone the petty duchy of Moscow among the European powers, still hoped that the kingdom of Poland might form an independent nation with its own language and constitution.

In the time of Alexander I the Russians had not begun to flock to the cities, which were small and ill-constructed compared with those of western Europe. The great mass of the population still lived in the country, and more than half of them were serfs, as ignorant and wretched as those of France or England in the twelfth century.

Absolute powers of the Tsar

Alexander I had inherited, as "Autocrat of all the Russias," a despotic power over his subjects as absolute as that to which Louis XIV laid claim. He could make war and conclude peace at will, freely appoint or dismiss his ministers, order the arrest, imprisonment, exile, or execution of any one he chose, without consulting or giving an account to any living being. Even the Russian national Church was under his personal control. There was no thought of any responsibility to the people, and the Tsar's officials ruled corruptly and tyrannically.

During his early years Alexander entertained liberal ideas, but after his return from the Congress of Vienna he began to dismiss his liberal advisers.[2] He became as apprehensive of

[1] The Cossacks, or light cavalry, who constitute so conspicuous a feature of the Russian army, were originally lawless rovers on the southern and eastern frontiers, composed mainly of adventurous Russians with some admixture of other peoples. Certain districts are assigned to them by the government, on the lower Don, near the Black Sea, the Urals, and elsewhere, in return for military service.

[2] For a contemporary account of Alexander's liberal ideas, see *Readings*, Vol. II, pp. 338 ff.

How Tsar Alexander became the enemy of revolution and of liberal ideas

revolution as his friend Metternich, and threw himself into the arms of the "Old Russian" party, which obstinately opposed the introduction of all Western ideas. The Tsar was soon denouncing liberalism as a frightful illusion which threatened the whole social order. He permitted his officials to do all they could to stamp out the ideas which he had himself formerly done so much to encourage. The censorship of the press put an end to the liberal periodicals which had sprung up, and professors in the universities were dismissed for teaching modern science. The attraction of the new ideas was, however, too strong for the Tsar to prevent some of his more enlightened subjects from following eagerly the course of the revolutionary movements in western Europe and reading the new books dealing with scientific discoveries and questions of political and social reform.

The "Decembrist" revolt of 1825

Alexander I died suddenly on December 1, 1825. The revolutionary societies seized this opportunity to organize a revolt known as the "Decembrist conspiracy." But the movement was badly organized; a few charges of grapeshot brought the insurgents to terms, and some of the leaders were hanged.

Polish rebellion, 1830–1831

Nicholas I never forgot the rebellion which inaugurated his reign, and he proved one of the most despotic of all the long list of autocratic rulers. His arbitrary measures speedily produced a revolt in Poland. The constitution which Alexander I had in his liberal days granted to the kingdom was violated. Russian troops were stationed there in great numbers, Russian officials forced their way into the government offices, and the petitions of the Polish diet were contemptuously ignored by the Tsar. Secret societies then began to promote a movement for the reëstablishment of the ancient Polish republic, which Catherine II and her fellow monarchs had destroyed. Late in 1830 an uprising occurred in Warsaw; the insurgents secured control of the city, drove out the Russian officials, organized a provisional government, and appealing to the European powers for aid, proclaimed the independence of Poland, January 25, 1831.

Europe, however, made no response to Poland's appeal for assistance. The Tsar's armies were soon able to crush the rebellion, and when Poland lay prostrate at his feet, Nicholas gave no quarter. He revoked the constitution,[1] abolished the diet, suppressed the national flag, and transferred forty-five thousand Polish families to the valley of the Don and the mountains of the Caucasus. To all intents and purposes Poland became henceforth merely a Russian province, governed, like the rest of the empire, from St. Petersburg.[2]

Nicholas crushes the revolt and deprives Poland of its constitution

Nicholas I sincerely believed that Russia could only be saved from the "decay" of religion and government, which he believed to be taking place in western Europe, by maintaining autocracy, for this alone was strong enough to make head against the destructive ideas which some of his subjects in their blindness mistook for enlightenment. The Russian-Greek Church [3] and all its beliefs must be defended, and the Russian nation preserved as a separate and superior people who should maintain forever the noble beliefs and institutions of the past.[4] Certainly a great many of his advisers were well content with the system, and his army of officials were loath to recommend reform.

Nicholas I's belief that autocracy alone could save Russia

[1] His proclamation is printed in the *Readings*, Vol. II, pp. 343 f.

[2] Thirty years later, in 1863, the Poles made another desperate attempt to free themselves from the yoke of Russia, but without success. Napoleon III refused to assist them, and Bismarck supported the Tsar in the fearful repression that followed.

[3] The Russians were converted to Christianity by missionaries from Constantinople, the religious capital of the Eastern, or Greek, Church, which had gradually drifted away from the Latin, or Roman Catholic, Church in the seventh and eighth centuries. For many centuries the Russian Church remained in close relations with the patriarch of Constantinople, but after that city fell into the hands of the infidel Turks it occurred to the Russian rulers that the Tsars must be the divinely appointed successors of the Eastern emperors. Old Rome, on the Tiber, and new Rome, on the Bosporus, had both fallen on account of their sins. Russia thus became the "third Rome," and the Tsar, the head of all true Christians who accepted the only orthodox faith, that of the Greek Church. Under Peter the Great the Russian Church was brought completely under the control of the government.

[4] Nicholas introduced into the schools a catechism which recalls that of Napoleon I: "*Question.* What does religion teach us as to our duties to the Tsar? *Answer.* Worship, fidelity, the payment of taxes, service, love, and prayer — the whole being comprised in the words worship and fidelity."

Stern efforts of Nicholas to check liberalism

Accordingly, in the name of Russian nationality, the Tsar adopted strong measures to check the growth of liberalism. The officials bestirred themselves to prevent in every way the ingress into Russia of western ideas. Books on religion and science were carefully examined by the police or the clergy; foreign works containing references to politics were confiscated or the objectionable pages were blotted out by the censors. The government officials did not hesitate freely to open private letters committed to the post. It may be said that, except for a few short intervals of freedom, this whole system has been continued down to the present time.

Section 92. The Freeing of the Serfs and the Growth of the Spirit of Revolution

In 1854 the efforts of Russia to increase her influence in Turkey led to a war with France and England. The Russians were defeated, and their strong fortress of Sebastopol, in the Crimea, was captured by the allies.[1] Nicholas I died in the midst of the reverses of the Crimean War, leaving to his son, Alexander II, the responsibility of coming to terms with the enemy, and then, if possible, strengthening Russia by reducing the flagrant political corruption and bribery which had been revealed by the war and by improving the lot of the people at large.

Accession of Alexander II, 1855

Situation of the Russian serfs

Nearly one half of the Tsar's subjects were serfs, whose bondage and wretched lives seemed to present an insurmountable barrier to general progress and prosperity. The landlord commonly reserved a portion of his estate for himself and turned over to his serfs barely enough to enable them to keep body and soul together. They usually spent three days in the week cultivating their lord's fields. He was their judge as well as their master and could flog them at will. The serf was viewed as scarcely more than a beast of burden.[2]

[1] See next chapter.

[2] For an account of Russian serfdom, see *Readings*, Vol. II, pp. 345 ff.

From time to time the serfs, infuriated by the hard conditions imposed upon them, revolted against their lords. During the reign of Catherine the Great a general uprising had taken place which grew to the proportions of a civil war and was only put down with terrible bloodshed and cruelty. Under Nicholas I over five hundred riots had occurred, and these

Peasant revolts

FIG. 137. RUSSIAN PEASANT'S HOME

seemed to increase rather than decrease, notwithstanding the vigilance of the police and the severity of the government.

Emancipation of the serfs, March, 1861

Alexander II, fearful lest the peasants should again attempt to win their liberty by force, decided that the government must undertake the difficult task of freeing forty millions of his subjects from serfdom. After much discussion he issued an emancipation proclamation, March 3, 1861,[1] on the eve of the great

[1] See *Readings*, Vol. II, pp. 348 ff. According to the Russian calendar the date is February 19, for Russia has never followed the example of the western nations and rectified her mode of indicating dates by adopting the Gregorian calendar.

Civil War, which was to put an end to negro slavery in the United States. In his anxiety to prevent any loss to the landowners, who constituted the ruling class in the Russian government, the Tsar did his work in a very half-hearted manner. It is true the government deprived the former lord of his right to force the peasants to work for him and pay him the old dues; he could no longer flog them or command them to marry against their will; but the peasants still remained bound to the land, for they were not permitted to leave their villages without a government pass. The landlords surrendered a portion of their estates to the peasants, but this did not become the property of *individual* owners, but was vested in the *village community* as a whole. The land assigned to each village was to be periodically redistributed among the various families of the community so that, aside from his hut and garden, no peasant could lay claim permanently to any particular plot of land as his own.

The village community, or *mir*

The government dealt very generously with the landlords, as might have been anticipated. It not only agreed that the peasants should be required to pay for such land as their former masters turned over to them, but commonly fixed the price at an amount far greater than the real value of the land — a price which the government paid and began to collect from the serfs in installments. His new freedom seemed to the peasant little better than that enjoyed by a convict condemned to hard labor in the penitentiary. Indeed, he sometimes refused to be "freed" when he learned of the hard bargain which the government proposed to drive with him. There were hundreds of riots while the readjustments were taking place, which were sternly suppressed by the government. The peasants were compelled by force of arms to accept their "liberty" and pay the land tax which emancipation imposed upon them.

Naturally, if the people in a given community increased, the size of the individual allotments inevitably decreased, and with that the chances of earning a livelihood. At present, more than fifty years after the "freeing" of the serfs, the peasant has, on the average, scarcely half as much land as that originally assigned to him. Although he lived constantly on the verge of starvation, he fell far behind in the payment of his taxes, so that in 1904 the Tsar, in a moment of forced generosity, canceled the arrears, which the peasants could, in any case, never have paid. A little later the Tsar issued an order permitting

FIG. 138. ALEXANDER II

the peasants to leave their particular village and seek employment elsewhere. They might, on the other hand, become *owners* of their allotments. This led to the practical abolition of the ancient *mir*, or village community.[1]

Original meaning of "nihilism"

Alexander II's despotic régime developed among the more cultivated classes a spirit of opposition, known as *nihilism*.[2] This

[1] These village communities had long existed in Russia, since the lords had usually found it convenient to have the village redistribute the land from time to time among the serfs as the number of inhabitants changed.

[2] The term "nihilist" was first introduced in Russia by Turgenev in his novel, *Fathers and Children*. It was applied to the chief character on account of his denial of the authority of all tradition. See *Readings*, Vol. II, p. 353.

was not in its origin a frantic terrorism, as commonly supposed, but an intellectual and moral revolt against tyranny in the State, bigotry in the Church, and all unreasonable traditions and unfounded prejudices. In short, the nihilist would have agreed with Voltaire, Diderot, and the Encyclopedists in exalting reason as man's sole guide in this mysterious world.

Origin of terrorism

The government officials regarded the reformers with the utmost suspicion and began to arrest the more active among them. The prisons were soon crowded and hundreds were banished to Siberia. The Tsar and his police seemed to be the avowed enemies of all progress, and any one who advanced a new idea was punished as if he had committed a murder. The peaceful preparation of the people for representative government could not go on so long as the police were arresting men for forming debating clubs. It seemed to the more ardent reformers that there was no course open to them but to declare war on the government as a body of cruel, corrupt tyrants who would keep Russia in darkness forever merely in order that they might continue to fill their own pockets by grinding down the people. They argued that the wicked acts of the officials must be exposed, the government intimidated, and the eyes of the world opened to the horrors of the situation by conspicuous acts of violent retribution. So some of the reformers became *terrorists*, not because they were depraved men or loved bloodshed, but because they were convinced that there was no other way to save their beloved land from the fearful oppression under which it groaned.

Terrorism, 1878–1881

The government fought terrorism with terrorism. In 1879 sixteen suspected revolutionists were hanged and scores sent to the dungeons of St. Petersburg or the mines of Siberia.[1] The terrorists, on their part, retaliated by attacks on the Tsar and his government. A student tried to kill the Tsar as the head and representative of the whole tyrannical system.

[1] For a description of the horrors of Siberian exile life, see *Readings*, Vol. II, pp. 354 ff.

Attempts were made to blow up a special train on which the Tsar was traveling, and, in another effort to kill him, the Winter Palace in St. Petersburg was wrecked by a revolutionist disguised as a carpenter.

Alexander II consents to permit the representatives of the people to give their opinion on proposed laws

In short, the efforts of the Tsar's officials to check the revolutionists proved vain, and the minister, to whom the Tsar had given almost dictatorial powers to suppress the agitation, finally saw that the government must make some concessions in order to pacify its enemies; so he advised Alexander II to grant a species of constitution, in which he should agree to convoke an assembly elected by the people and thereafter ask its opinion and counsel before making new and important laws. The Tsar finally consented, but it was too late. On the afternoon that he gave his assent to the plan he was assassinated as he was driving to his palace (March, 1881).[1]

Assassination of Alexander II, 1881

The Balkan War, 1877-1878

The reign of Alexander II had not been entirely given up to internal reforms and repression, however. In 1877 Russia was again at war with Turkey, aiding the "south Slavs"— Serbians, Montenegrins, and Bulgarians — in their attempt to throw off the Turkish yoke. Successful in arms, Russia was, however, obliged to relinquish most of her gains and those of her allies by a congress of the European powers held at Berlin in 1878. But all this is described in the next chapter.

Terrorism rapidly declines after the death of Alexander II

While the body of the murdered Tsar, Alexander II, was still lying in state, the executive committee of the revolutionists issued a warning to his son and successor, Alexander III, threatening him with the evils to come if he did not yield to their demand for representative government, freedom of speech and of the press, and the right to meet together for the discussion of political questions.[2] The new Tsar was not, however, moved by the appeal, and the police redoubled their activity. The plans of reform were repudiated, and the autocracy settled back into its usual despotic habits. The terrorists realized that, for the time being, they had nothing to gain by further acts

[1] See *Readings*, Vol. II, pp. 362 f.

[2] See *Readings*, Vol. II, pp. 364 ff.

of violence, which would only serve to strengthen the government they were fighting. It was clear that the people at large were not yet ready for a revolution.

Belief of the reactionaries that Russia must be kept "frozen"

The reign of Alexander III (1881–1894) was a period of quiet, during which little progress seemed to be made. The people suffered the oppression of the government officials without active opposition. Their occasional protests were answered by imprisonment, flogging, or exile, for Alexander III and his intimate advisers believed quite as firmly and religiously in autocracy as Nicholas I had done. Freedom and liberalism, they agreed, could only serve to destroy a nation.

SECTION 93. THE INDUSTRIAL REVOLUTION IN RUSSIA

The Industrial Revolution overtakes Russia

It became increasingly difficult, however, to keep Russia "frozen," for during the last quarter of the nineteenth century the spread of democratic ideas had been hastened by the coming of the steam engine, the factory, and the locomotive, all of which served to unsettle the humdrum agricultural life which the great majority of the people had led for centuries. In spite of her mineral resources Russia had lagged far behind her western neighbors in the use of machinery. She had little capital and no adequate means of transportation across the vast stretches of country that separated her chief towns, and the governing classes had no taste for manufacturing enterprises.[1]

The liberation of the serfs, with all its drawbacks, favored the growth of factories, for the peasants were sometimes permitted to leave their villages for the manufacturing centers which were gradually growing up. The value of the products of the chief industries doubled between 1887 and 1897; and the number of people employed in them increased from 1,318,048 to 2,098,262. If Napoleon could come once more to Moscow, he would not recognize the city which met his gaze in 1812. It has now become the center of the Russian textile industries,

Rapid growth of Russian industries, 1887–1897

[1] See *Readings*, Vol. II, pp. 368 ff.

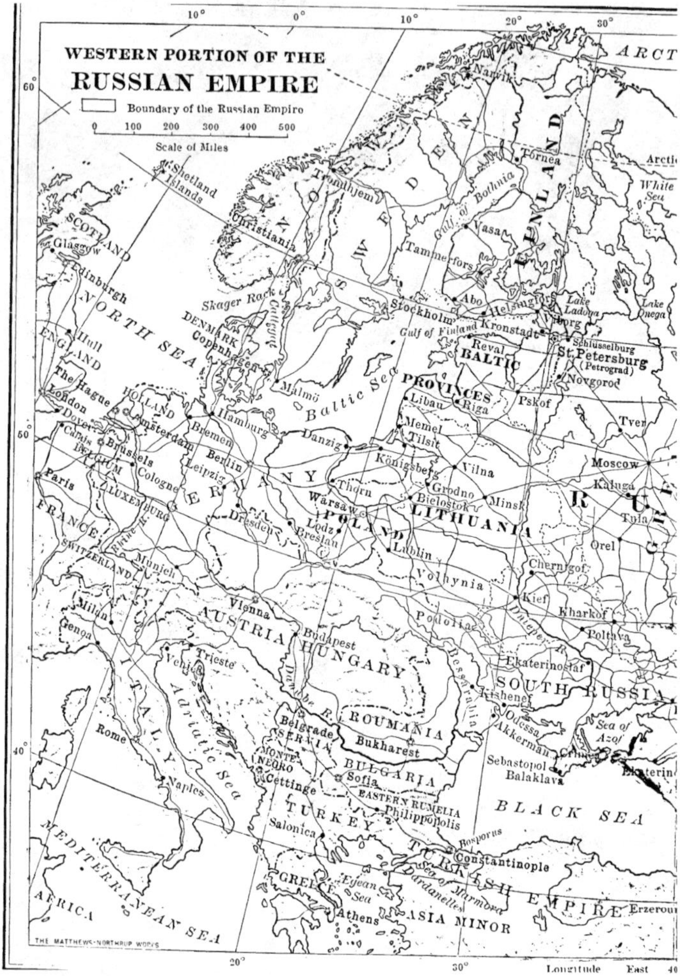
WESTERN PORTION OF THE
RUSSIAN EMPIRE
Boundary of the Russian Empire
0 100 200 300 400 500
Scale of Miles
ARCTIC
Narvik
SWEDEN
FINLAND
NORWAY
Tornea
Arctic
White Sea
Trondhjem
Gulf of Bothnia
Shetland Islands
Christiania
Vasa
SCOTLAND
Glasgow
Tammerfors
Edinburgh
NORTH SEA
Skager Rack
Cattegat
Abo
Helsingfors
Lake Ladoga
Lake Onega
Stockholm
Gulf of Finland
Kronstadt
Viborg
DENMARK
Copenhagen
Schlusselburg
Hull
ENGLAND
Reval
BALTIC
St. Petersburg
(Petrograd)
Novgorod
The Hague
Malmö
Baltic Sea
PROVINCES
London
HOLLAND
Libau
Riga
Pskof
Dover
Amsterdam
Hamburg
Bremen
Memel
Tilsit
Tver
Calais
Brussels
BELGIUM
Danzig
Berlin
Königsberg
Moscow
Paris
Cologne
Leipzig
GERMANY
Vilna
Kaluga
LUXEMBURG
Thorn
Grodno
Minsk
Warsaw
Bielostok
Tula
FRANCE
Dresden
POLAND
LITHUANIA
Rhine R.
Lodz
Breslau
Orel
SWITZERLAND
Munich
Lublin
Chernigof
Volhynia
Milan
Vienna
Kief
Kharkof
Genoa
AUSTRIA
Budapest
Podolia
Dnieper R.
Poltava
Venice
Trieste
HUNGARY
Bessarabia
Ekaterinoslaf
SOUTH RUSSIA
ITALY
Adriatic Sea
Danube R.
Kishenef
ROUMANIA
Odessa
Akkerman
Sea of Azof
Belgrade
SERVIA
Bukharest
Crimea
Rome
MONTENEGRO
BULGARIA
Sebastopol
Balaklava
Cettinge
Sofia
Naples
EASTERN RUMELIA
Philippopolis
BLACK SEA
TURKEY
Salonica
Bosporus
Constantinople
MEDITERRANEAN SEA
GREECE
Egean Sea
Sea of Marmora
Dardanelles
TURKISH EMPIRE
Erzeroum
AFRICA
Athens
ASIA MINOR
THE MATTHEWS-NORTHRUP WORKS
Longitude East

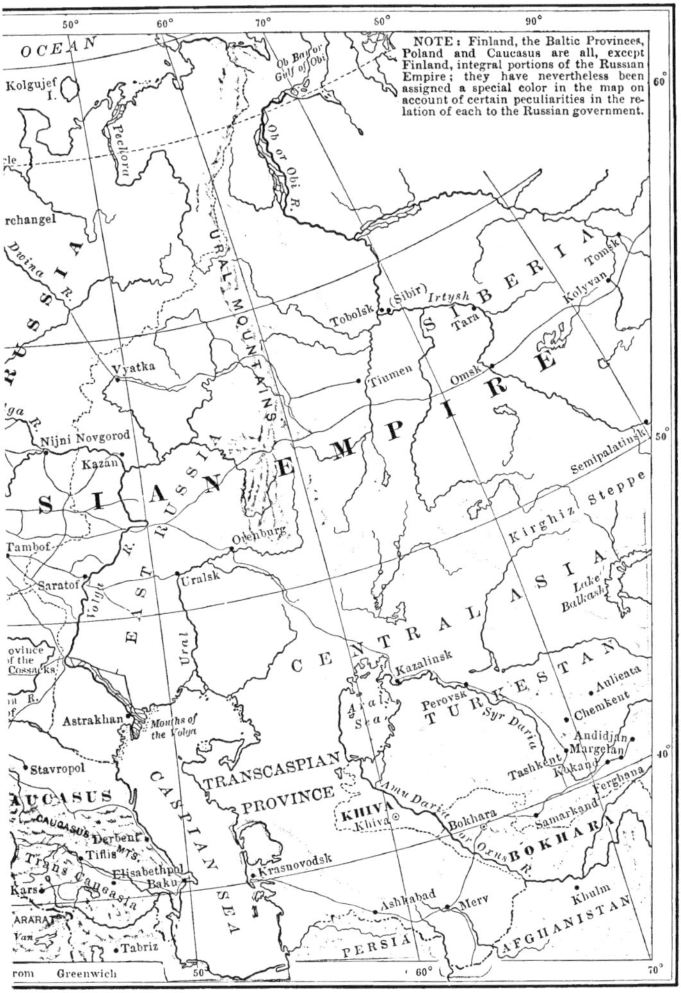

NOTE: Finland, the Baltic Provinces, Poland and Caucasus are all, except Finland, integral portions of the Russian Empire; they have nevertheless been assigned a special color in the map on account of certain peculiarities in the relation of each to the Russian government.
OCEAN
Kolgujef I.
Pechora
Ob Bay or Gulf of Obi
Ob or Obi R.
rchangel
Dwina R.
URAL MOUNTAINS
SIBERIA
Tomsk
Kolyvan
Tobolsk
(Sibir)
Irtysh
Tara
Vyatka
Tiumen
Omsk
RUSSIAN EMPIRE
Nijni Novgorod
Kazan
Semipalatinsk
EAST RUSSIA
Kirghiz Steppe
Orenburg
Tambof
Saratof
Uralsk
Volga
Ural
CENTRAL ASIA
Lake Balkash
Kazalinsk
TURKESTAN
Aral Sea
Perovsk
Syr Daria
Aulieata
Chemkent
Astrakhan
Mouths of the Volga
Andidjan
Margelan
Tashkent
Kokand
Ferghana
Stavropol
TRANSCASPIAN PROVINCE
CAUCASUS
CAUCASUS MTS.
CASPIAN SEA
Amu Daria or Oxus R.
KHIVA
Khiva
Bokhara
Samarkand
BOKHARA
Derbent
Tiflis
Trans Caucasia
Elisabethpol
Baku
Krasnovodsk
Kars
Ashkabad
Merv
Khulm
ARARAT
Van
Tabriz
PERSIA
AFGHANISTAN
Greenwich
50°
60°
70°
80°
90°
40°

and the sound of a thousand looms and forges announces the creation of a new industrial world. There are in Russia to-day twenty-five cities with a population of one hundred thousand or more, and two of them — Petrograd and Moscow — have over a million each. The industrial cities have developed especially in the densely populated Polish, or central western, part of Russia.

Railway construction in Russia

Along with this industrial development has gone the construction of great railway lines, built largely by the government with money borrowed from capitalists in western Europe. Some of the railroads have been constructed chiefly for political and military purposes, but others are designed to connect the great industrial centers. Railway building was first seriously under- en in Russia after the disasters of the Crimean War, when soldiers suffered cruel hardships in consequence of the diffi- y of obtaining supplies. By 1878 upward of eight thousand s had been built, connecting the capital with the frontiers European Russia. In 1885 the railway advance toward the ntiers of India[1] was begun, and within a short time Afghan- was reached and communication opened to the borders of China. Important lines have also been built in the region een the Black Sea and the Caspian.

[1] The expansion of Russia to the southeast has been very rapid. In 1846 the southern boundary ran along the lower edge of the Aral Sea. In 1863 Russia, claiming that the Turkestan tribesmen pillaged caravans and harried her frontiers, sent forces which captured the cities of Turkestan, Chemkent, and Tashkent, and two years later organized the region into the new province of Russian Turkestan. Shortly afterward the Ameer of Bokhara declared war on the Tsar, only to have the Russians occupy the ancient city of Samarkand (where Alexander the Great had halted on his eastward march) and later establish a protectorate over Bokhara, which brought them to the borders of Afghanistan. In 1872 the Khan of Khiva was reduced to vassalage. During the following years (1873–1886) the regions to the south, about Merv, down to the borders of Persia and Afghanistan, were gradually annexed. In 1876 the province of Kokand on the boundary of the Chinese empire was seized and transformed into the province of Ferghana. By securing railway concessions and making loans to the Shah, the Russians have become powerful in Persia, and thus all along their southeastern frontiers they are struggling for predominance against British influence. In 1907 the British and Russian governments marked off their spheres of influence in Persia. See above, p. 530, and map, p. 610, also Chapter XXVI, below.

The Trans-Siberian railroad

The greatest of all railway undertakings was the Trans-Siberian road, which was rendered necessary for the transportation of soldiers and military supplies to the eastern boundary of the empire. Communication was established between St. Petersburg and the Pacific in 1900, and a branch line from Harbin southward to Port Arthur was soon finished.[1] One can now

FIG. 139. HARBIN, A CITY ON THE TRANS-SIBERIAN RAILWAY

Cities have sprung up along the great Russian railway just as they did along the transcontinental lines in the United States or Canada. This Western-looking town is northeast of Peking, in the farming country of Manchuria, nominally a part of the Chinese republic but in reality held by Russia

travel in comfort, with few changes of cars, from Havre to Vladivostok, via Paris, Cologne, Berlin, Warsaw, Moscow, Irkutsk on Lake Baikal, and Harbin, a distance of seventy-three hundred miles. In addition to the main line, some important branches have been built, and more are planned. By means of these the vast plains of central Asia may, before long, be peopled as the plains of America have been. Russian migration has been moving eastward.

[1] See map below, p. 610.

Section 94. The Struggle for Liberty under Nicholas II

Nicholas II speedily dispels the hopes of the liberals

When Nicholas II succeeded his father, Alexander III, in 1894,[1] he was but twenty-six years old and there was some reason to hope that he would face the problems of this new industrial Russia in a progressive spirit. He had had an opportunity in his travels to become somewhat familiar with the enlightened governments of western Europe, and one of his first acts was to order the imprisonment of the prefect of police of St. Petersburg for annoying the correspondents of foreign newspapers. Nicholas, however, quickly dispelled any illusions which his more liberal subjects entertained. "Let it be understood by all," he declared, "that I shall employ all my powers in the best interests of the people, but the principle of autocracy will be sustained by me as firmly and unswervingly as it was by my never-to-be-forgotten father."

Censorship of the press

The censorship of the press was made stricter than ever, one decree alone adding two hundred books to the already long list of those which the government condemned.[2] The

[1] On page 163 we have indicated the line of Russian rulers from Peter the Great to Catherine II. From Catherine to the present the line runs as follows:

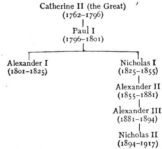

Catherine II (the Great)
(1762–1796)
|
Paul I
(1796–1801)
|
Alexander I (1801–1825) — Nicholas I (1825–1855)

Nicholas I
(1825–1855)
|
Alexander II
(1855–1881)
|
Alexander III
(1881–1894)
|
Nicholas II
(1894–1917)

[2] Among the books which the government prohibits in public libraries are the Russian translation of Mill's *Political Economy*, Green's *History of the English People*, Bryce's *American Commonwealth*, and Fyffe's *Modern Europe*.

distinguished historian, Professor Milyoukov, was dismissed from the University of Moscow on the ground of his "generally noxious tendencies," and other teachers were warned not to talk about government.[1]

Attempt to Russify Finland given up

Nowhere did the Tsar show his desire for absolute control more clearly than in his dealings with Finland. When Alexander I had annexed that country in 1809 he had permitted it to retain its own diet and pass its own laws, although it of course recognized the Tsar as its ruler under the title of Grand Duke. The Finns cherished their independence and have in recent times shown themselves one of the most progressive peoples of Europe. In 1899, however, Nicholas began a harsh and determined *Russification* of Finland. He sent heartless officials, like von Plehve, to represent him and crush out all opposition to his changes. He placed the Finnish army under the Russian minister of war, deprived the diet of the right to control the lawmaking, except in some minor and purely local matters, and undertook to substitute the Russian language so far as possible for the Finnish.

Finally, on June 17, 1904, the Russian governor of Finland was assassinated by the son of one of the senators, who then killed himself, leaving a letter in which he explained that he had acted alone and with the simple purpose of forcing on the Tsar's attention the atrocities of his officials. The new governor permitted the newspapers to be started once more and forbade the Russian officials to interfere in the elections. A year later the Tsar, under the influence of revolution at home and disaster abroad, consented to restore to Finland all her former rights.

Harsh policy of von Plehve

We must now trace the history of the terrible struggle between the Russian people and their despotic government,

[1] One may judge of the sober, high-minded scholars upon whom the Russian autocracy believed it essential to make war by reading Professor Milyoukov's *Russia and its Crisis*, which is based on a series of lectures which he delivered in the United States during the year 1903–1904.

which began openly in 1904. In 1902 an unpopular minister of the interior had been assassinated, and the Tsar had appointed a still more unpopular man in his place, namely, von Plehve, who was notorious for his success in hunting down those who criticized the government and for the vigor with which he had carried on the Russification of Finland.

Massacres of the Jews

Von Plehve connived at the persecution of those among the Tsar's subjects who ventured to disagree with the doctrines of the Russian official Church, to which every Russian was supposed to belong. The Jews suffered especially. There were massacres at Kishinef[1] and elsewhere in 1903 which horrified the western world and drove hundreds of thousands of Jews to foreign lands, especially to the United States. There is good reason to believe that von Plehve actually arranged these massacres.

The liberals, or constitutional democrats

Von Plehve was mistaken, however, in his belief that all the trouble came from a handful of deluded fanatics. Among those who detested the cruel and corrupt government which he represented were the professional men, the university professors, the enlightened merchants and manufacturers, and the public-spirited nobility. These were not at first organized into a distinct party, but in time they came to be known as the *constitutional democrats*. They hoped that a parliament elected by the people might be established to coöperate with the Tsar and his ministers in making the laws and imposing the taxes. They demanded freedom of speech and of the press, the right to hold public meetings to discuss public questions, the abolition of the secret police system, of arbitrary imprisonment and religious persecutions, and the gradual improvement of the condition of the peasants and workingmen through the passage of wise laws.

The social democrats

In the towns a socialistic party had been growing up which advocated the theories of Karl Marx.[2] It desired, and still desires, all the reforms advocated by the constitutional democrats

[1] See *Readings*, Vol. II, pp. 371 f. [2] See above, pp. 375 ff.

just described, but looks forward to the time when the workingmen will become so numerous and powerful that they can seize the government offices and assume the management of lands, mines, and industries, which shall thereafter be used for the benefit of all rather than for the small class of rich men who now own them. Unlike the reformers next to be described, they do not believe in terrorism or in murderous attacks upon unpopular government officials.

The socialist revolutionary party

In contrast with these were those Russian agitators who belonged to the socialist revolutionary party, which was well organized and was responsible for the chief acts of violence during the years of the revolution. They maintained that it was right to make war upon the government which was oppressing them and extorting money from the people to fill the pockets of dishonest officeholders. Its members selected their victims from the most notoriously cruel among the officials, and after a victim had been killed they usually published a list of the offenses which cost him his life. Lists of those condemned to death were also prepared, after careful consideration, by their executive committee. They did not practice, or in any way approve of, indiscriminate assassination, as is sometimes supposed.

Great unpopularity of the war with Japan, which began in February, 1904

The more von Plehve sought to stamp out all protest against the autocracy, the more its enemies increased, and at last, in 1904, the open revolution may be said to have begun. On February 5 of that year a war commenced with Japan, which was due to Russia's encroachments in Korea and her evident intention of permanently depriving China of Manchuria. The liberals attributed the conflict to bad management on the part of the Tsar's officials, and declared it to be inhuman and contrary to the interests of the people.

Russian reverses

The Japanese succeeded in beating back the Russians, destroying their vessels, and besieging their fortress of Port Arthur, which they had cut off from any aid or supplies. The liberal-minded among the Russians regarded these disasters with a certain satisfaction. The reverses, they held, were due to the incompetence and corruption of the Tsar's officials, and served to make plain how very badly autocracy really worked in practice.

Von Plehve continued, however, in spite of the rising indignation, to encourage the police to break up scientific and literary meetings, in which disapprobation of the government was pretty sure to be expressed, and to send men eminent in science and literature to prison or to Siberia, until, on July 28, 1904, a bomb was thrown under the minister's carriage by a former student in the University of Moscow and his career was brought to an abrupt close.

Assassination of von Plehve, July, 1904

Meanwhile disasters and revolt met the government on every hand. The Japanese continued to force back the Russians in Manchuria in a series of terrific conflicts south of Mukden. In one long battle on the Sha-ho River sixty thousand Russians perished. Their fleets in the East were annihilated, and on January 1, 1905, Port Arthur fell, after the most terrible siege on record. The crops failed and the starving peasants burned and sacked the houses and barns of the nobles, arguing that if the buildings were destroyed, the owners could not come back, and the Tsar's police could no longer make them their headquarters.

General disorder

The war had produced a stagnation of commerce and industry, and strikes became common. It became known that the government officials had been stealing money that should have gone to strengthen and equip the armies; rifles had been paid for that had never been delivered, supplies bought which never reached the suffering soldiers, and — most scandalous of all — high Russian dignitaries had even misappropriated the funds of the Red Cross Society for aiding the wounded.

On Sunday, January 22, 1905, a fearful event occurred. The workingmen of St. Petersburg had sent a petition to the Tsar and had informed him that on Sunday they would march to the palace humbly to pray him in person to consider their sufferings, since they had no faith in his officials or ministers. When

"Red Sunday," January 22, 1905

Sunday morning came, masses of men, women, and children, wholly unarmed, attempted to approach the Winter Palace in the pathetic hope that the "Little Father," as they called the Tsar, would listen to their woes. Instead, the Cossacks tried to disperse them with their whips, and then the troops which guarded the palace shot and cut down hundreds, and wounded thousands in a conflict which continued all day.[1] "Red Sunday"

FIG. 140. THE WINTER PALACE, PETROGRAD
The massacre took place just in front of the palace

was, however, only the most impressive of many similar encounters between citizens and the Tsar's police and guards.

Protest of the men of letters

The day after "Red Sunday" all the leading lawyers and men of letters in St. Petersburg joined in the following declaration: "The public should understand that the government has declared war on the entire Russian people. There is no further doubt on this point. A government which is unable to hold intercourse with the people except with the assistance of sabers and rifles is self-condemned. We summon all the vital energies of Russian society to the assistance of the workingmen who began the struggle for the common cause of the whole people."

[1] For a contemporary newspaper account, see *Readings*, Vol. II, pp 373 ff.

Finally, the Tsar so far yielded to the pressure of public opinion that on August 19 he promised to summon a *Duma*, or council, which should meet not later than January, 1906.[1] It was to represent all Russia, but to have no further power than that of giving to the still autocratic ruler advice in making the laws.

The Tsar promises to summon the Duma (August 19, 1905)

This was a bitter disappointment to even the most moderate liberals. It was pointed out that both the workingmen and the professional men were excluded by the regulations from voting. A more effective measure in bringing the Tsar and his advisers to terms was a great general strike in the interest of reform which began late in October. All the railroads stopped running; in all the great towns the shops, except those that dealt in provisions, were closed; gas and electricity were no longer furnished; the law courts ceased their duties, and even the apothecaries refused to prepare prescriptions until reforms should be granted.

The great general strikes, October and November, 1905

The situation soon became intolerable, and on October 29 the Tsar announced that he had ordered "the government" to grant the people freedom of conscience, speech, and association, and to permit the classes which had been excluded in his first edict to vote for members of the Duma. Lastly, he agreed "to establish an immutable rule that no law can come into force without the approval of the Duma."

The Tsar promises (October 29, 1905) that no law shall go into force without the Duma's assent

The elections for the Duma took place in March and April, 1906, and, in spite of the activity of the police, resulted in an overwhelming majority for the constitutional democrats. The deputies to the Duma assembled in no humble frame of mind. Like the members of the Estates General in 1789, they felt that they had the nation behind them. They listened stonily to the Tsar's remarks at the opening session, and it was clear from the first that they would not agree any better with their monarch than the French deputies had agreed with Louis XVI and his courtiers.

The Duma received by the Tsar, May 10, 1906

The Tsar's ministers would not coöperate with the Duma in any important measures of reform, and on July 21 Nicholas II

[1] For the manifesto calling the first Duma, see *Readings*, Vol. II, pp. 375 ff.

The Duma freely discusses the vices of the Tsar's government

declared that he was "cruelly disappointed" because the deputies had not confined themselves to their proper duties and had commented upon many matters which belonged to him. He accordingly dissolved the Duma,[1] as he had a perfect right to do, and fixed March 5, 1907, as the date for the meeting of a new Duma.

Atrocities and disorder continue

The revolutionists made an unsuccessful attempt in August to blow up the Tsar's chief minister in his country house and continued to assassinate governors and police officials. The "Black Hundreds," on the other hand, murdered Jews and liberals while the government established courts-martial to insure the speedy trial and immediate execution of revolutionists. In the two months, September and October, 1906, these courts summarily condemned three hundred persons to be shot or hanged. During the whole year some nine thousand persons were killed or wounded for political reasons.

Famine added to the other disasters

A terrible famine was afflicting the land at the end of the year, and it was discovered that a member of the Tsar's ministry had been stealing the money appropriated to furnish grain to the dying peasants. An observer who had traveled eight hundred miles through the famine-stricken district reported that he did not find a single village where the peasants had food enough for themselves or their cattle. In some places the peasants were reduced to eating bark and the straw used for their thatch roofs.

Dissolution of the village communities, November, 1906

In October a ukase permitted the peasants to leave their particular village community and join another, or to seek employment elsewhere. On November 25 the peasants were empowered to become owners of their allotments, and all redemption dues were remitted. This constituted the first step toward a practical abolition of the system of common ownership by village communities, described above, which was finally achieved by a law of June 27, 1910. This was the beginning of the great social changes that are taking place in Russia.

[1] For the decree dissolving the first Duma, see *Readings*, Vol. II, pp 377f.

The Tsar continued to summon the Duma regularly, but so changed suffrage that only the conservative sections of the nation were represented, and his officials did all they could to keep out liberal deputies. In spite of this the fourth Duma, elected in 1912, showed much independence in opposing the oppressive rule of the Tsar's ministers. Although parliamentary government is by no means won in Russia, many important reforms have been achieved. The Tsar continued to retain the title of "Autocrat of all the Russias," and his officials went on violating all the principles of liberty and persecuting those who ventured to criticize the government, until the revolution of March, 1917, deprived them of all power.

The Dumas oppose the Tsar's ministers

QUESTIONS

SECTION 91. Explain the racial problem which confronts the Russian government. Why have the Tsars of Russia borne the title of "Autocrat of all the Russias"? Account for the changed attitude of Alexander I after 1815. Tell of the revolt of the Poles under Nicholas I.

SECTION 92. Describe the life of the Russian serfs. What change in their condition resulted from the emancipation proclamation of 1861? Define nihilism. Account for the origin of terrorism.

SECTION 93. What were the effects of the Industrial Revolution in Russia? Show on a map the advance of Russia to the southeast and the line of the Trans-Siberian railroad.

SECTION 94. Describe the attempt to russify Finland. Outline the platforms of the three great political parties of Russia. Describe the Russo-Japanese War of 1904–1905. What was "Red Sunday"? Mention the other important events of the year 1905.

Describe the first session of the Duma. What change in the life of the peasant resulted from the ukase of November, 1906? Describe the session of the second Duma. What changes in the election regulations were made before the third Duma assembled?

CHAPTER XXIV

TURKEY AND THE EASTERN QUESTION

SECTION 95. THE GREEK WAR OF INDEPENDENCE

European Turkey the source of many dissensions among the powers

In our narrative reference has been made now and again to the Sultan of Turkey, and especially to his troubles with his neighbors, Russia and Austria. In order to understand this "Eastern question," — which has involved the gradual expulsion of the Turks from Europe, the interminable quarrel over the Sultan's government and finances, and the formation of the new states of Serbia, Roumania, Greece, and Bulgaria, — it is necessary to turn back, for the moment, to the origin of the Turkish empire in Europe.

The advance and decline of Turkish power in Europe

Although there had been an almost steady conflict between the Cross and the Crescent ever since the days of Mohammed, it was not until the fourteenth century that southeastern Europe was threatened by a Mohammedan invasion. Under Othman (died 1326) a Turkish tribe from western Asia established itself in Asia Minor, across the Bosporus from Constantinople. From their leader they derived the name of Ottoman Turks, to distinguish them from the Seljuk Turks, with whom the Crusaders had in earlier centuries come in contact. Under successive sultans the Ottoman Turks extended their dominion

* The colored picture opposite shows the Bosporus as one looks across it to Asia, from a point near the grounds of Robert College, Constantinople. The towers in the foreground form part of "the Castle of Europe," built by the Turkish invaders when attacking Constantinople, 1452. On the opposite shore is "the Castle of Asia," so that the Turks who held both sides could soon control Constantinople. The towers are now in ruins, and American teachers play lawn tennis almost under their shadow.

Plate VII. The Bosporus, at the Point where the Turks crossed into Europe*

into Asia Minor, Syria, Arabia, and Egypt, while to the west they conquered the Balkan regions and Greece. In 1453 the capital of the Eastern Empire, Constantinople, fell into their hands, and for two hundred and fifty years thereafter they were a source of serious apprehension to the states of western Europe.

The Turks pushed up the valley of the Danube almost to the borders of the German Empire, and for nearly two centuries the republic of Venice and the House of Hapsburg were engaged in an almost continuous war with them. In 1683 they laid siege to Vienna, but were defeated by the Polish king, John Sobieski, who came to the relief of the Austrians. The following year, the Emperor, Poland, and Venice formed a Holy League, which for fifteen years waged an intermittent war against the infidels (in which Peter the Great joined) and which, by 1699, succeeded in forcing the Turks out of Hungary.

Catherine the Great wins territory on the Black Sea

While Turkey ceased, thereafter, to be dangerously aggressive, she was able for several decades to resist the efforts of Russia and Austria to deprive her of further territory. In 1774 Catherine the Great managed to secure the Crimea and the region about the Sea of Azof, thus giving Russia a permanent foothold on the Black Sea. Moreover the Porte, as the Turkish government is commonly called, conceded to Russia the right to protect the Sultan's Christian subjects, most of whom were adherents of the Orthodox Greek Church, the State Church of Russia.[1]

Russian influence in Turkey

These and other provisions seemed to give the Russians an excuse for intervening in Turkish affairs, and offered an opportunity for fomenting discontent among the Sultan's Christian subjects. In 1812, just before Napoleon's march on Moscow, Alexander I forced Turkey to cede to him Bessarabia on the Black Sea, which still remains the last of Russia's conquests toward the southwest.

[1] See above, p. 555, note 3.

Serbia becomes a tributary principality in 1817

Shortly after the Congress of Vienna, the Serbians, who had for a number of years been in revolt against the Turks, were able to establish their practical independence (1817), and Serbia, with Belgrade as its capital, became a principality tributary to Turkey. This was the first of a series of states which have emerged, during the nineteenth century, from beneath the Mohammedan inundation.

The national spirit is awakened in Greece

The next state to gain its independence was Greece, whose long conflict against Turkish despotism aroused throughout Europe the sympathy of all who appreciated the glories of ancient Greece. The inhabitants of the land of Plato, Aristotle, and Demosthenes were, it is true, scarcely to be regarded as descendants of the Greeks, and the language they spoke bore little resemblance to the ancient tongue. At the opening of the nineteenth century, however, the national spirit once more awoke in Greece, and able writers made modern Greek a literary language and employed it in stirring appeals to the patriotism of their fellow countrymen.

The independence of Greece declared, January, 1822

In 1821 an insurrection broke out in Morea, as the ancient Peloponnesus is now called. The revolutionists were supported by the clergy of the Greek Church, who proclaimed a savage war of extermination against the infidel. The movement spread through the peninsula; the atrocities of the Turk were rivaled by those of the Greeks, and thousands of Mohammedans — men, women, and children — were slaughtered. On January 27, 1822, the Greek National Assembly issued a proclamation of independence.[1]

Sympathy of western Europe for the cause of Greek independence

To Metternich this revolt seemed only another illustration of the dangers of revolution, but the liberals throughout Europe enthusiastically sympathized with the Greek uprising, since it was carried on in the name of national liberty. Intellectual men in England, France, Germany, and the United States held meetings to express sympathy for the cause, while to the ardent Christian it seemed a righteous war against infidels

[1] See *Readings*, Vol. II, pp. 384 ff.

and persecutors. Soldiers and supplies poured into Greece. Indeed, the Greeks could scarcely have freed themselves had the European powers refused to intervene.

The powers intervene in the war for Greek independence

It is needless to follow the long negotiations between the various European courts in connection with Greek affairs. In 1827 England, France, and Russia signed a treaty at London providing for a joint adjustment of the difficulty, on the ground that it was necessary to put an end to the sanguinary struggle which left Greece and the adjacent islands a prey "to all the disasters of anarchy, and daily causes fresh impediments to the commerce of Europe." The Porte having refused to accept the mediation of the allies, their combined fleets destroyed that of the Sultan at Navarino in October, 1827. Thereupon the Porte declared a "holy war" on the unbelievers, especially the Russians. But the latter were prepared to push the war with vigor, and they not only actively promoted the freedom of Greece, but forced the Sultan to grant practical independence to the Danubian principalities of Wallachia and Moldavia, which came thereby under Russian influence and later were to become the kingdom of Roumania. Turkey was no longer able to oppose the wishes of the allies, and in 1832 Greece became an independent state, choosing for its king Prince Otto of Bavaria.

The Turks defeated at Navarino in 1827

Wallachia and Moldavia (Roumania)

Establishment of the kingdom of Greece, 1832

Section 96. The Crimean War (1854–1856)

The international controversy over the protection of Christians in Turkey

A fresh excuse for interfering in Turkish affairs was afforded the Tsar in 1853. Complaints reached him that Christian pilgrims were not permitted by the Turks (who had long been in possession of the Holy Land and Jerusalem) freely to visit the places made sacred by their associations with the life of Jesus. Russia seemed the natural protector of those, at least, who adhered to her own form of Christianity, and the Russian ambassador rudely demanded that the Porte should grant the Tsar a protectorate over all the Christians in Turkey.

France and England declare war on Russia

When news of this situation reached Paris Napoleon III, who had recently become emperor and was anxious to take a hand in European affairs, declared that France, in virtue of earlier treaties with the Porte, enjoyed the right to protect Catholic Christians. He found an ally in England, who feared that if Russia took Constantinople it would command the route to India, and who accordingly advised the Sultan not to accede to Russia's demands. When the Tsar's troops marched into the Turkish dominions France and England came to the Sultan's assistance and declared war upon Russia in 1854.

The Crimean War, 1854

The Crimean War, which followed, owes its name to the fact that the operations of the allies against Russia culminated in the long and bloody siege of Sebastopol, in the southern part of the Crimean peninsula. Every victory won by the allies was dearly bought. The English soldiers suffered at first in consequence of the inefficiency of the home government in sending them the necessary supplies. The charge of the light brigade at Balaklava, which has been made famous by Tennyson's poem, and the engagement at Inkerman were small compensation for the immense losses and hardships endured by both the French and the English. Russia was, however, disheartened by the sufferings of her own soldiers, the inefficiency and corruption of her officials, and the final loss of the mighty fortress of Sebastopol.[1] She saw, moreover, that her near neighbor, Austria, was about to join her enemies. The new Tsar, Alexander II, therefore, consented in 1856 to the terms of a treaty drawn up at Paris.[2]

Terms of the Treaty of Paris, 1856

This treaty recognized the independence of the Ottoman empire and guaranteed its territorial integrity. The "Sublime Porte" was also included within the scope of the international law of Europe, from which it had hitherto been excluded as a

[1] For a description of scenes in the storming of Sebastopol, see *Readings*, Vol. II, pp. 391 ff.

[2] It will be remembered that Sardinia had joined the allies against Russia, and in this way forced the powers to admit it to the deliberations at Paris, where Cavour seized the opportunity to plead the cause of Italy. See above, p. 414.

barbarous government, and the other powers agreed not to interfere further with the domestic affairs of Turkey. The Black Sea was declared neutral territory and its waters were thrown open to merchant ships of all nations, but no warships

The Black Sea declared neutral

FIG. 141. FLORENCE NIGHTINGALE

The most famous of nurses was a wealthy English woman who, having studied medicine and directed a hospital of her own, took with her some forty nurses to the Crimea, where the soldiers were suffering from cholera as well as from wounds. Her heroic work won her the devotion of the soldiers. The Red Cross organization for nursing soldiers dates only from an international convention at Geneva in 1864, which arranged that such nurses should not be fired on in battle

were to pass through the Bosporus or Dardanelles. In short, Turkey was preserved and strengthened by the intervention of the powers as a bulwark against Russian encroachment into the Balkan peninsula, but, although the Sultan made liberal promises, nothing was really done to reform the Turkish administration or to make the lot of the Christian subjects more secure.

Section 97. Revolts in the Balkan Peninsula

Terrible conditions in Bosnia and Herzegovina under Turkish rule

Some idea of the situation of the people under the Sultan's rule may be derived from the report of an English traveler (Mr. Arthur Evans) in 1875. In the Turkish provinces of Bosnia and Herzegovina he found that outside the large towns, where European consuls were present, there was no safety for the honor, property, or lives of the Christians, because the authorities were blind to any outrage committed by a Mohammedan. The Sultan's taxes fell principally on the peasants, in the form of a tenth of their produce. It was a common custom for the collectors (who were often not Mohammedans but brutal Christians) to require the peasant to pay the tax in cash before the harvesting of the ripe crop, and if he could not meet the charges, the taxgatherer simply said, "Then your harvest shall rot on the ground till you pay it." When this oppression was resisted the most cruel punishments were meted out to the offenders.

The Bulgarian atrocities (1876)

In 1874 a failure of crops aggravated the intolerable conditions and an insurrection broke out in Bosnia and Herzegovina which set the whole Balkan peninsula aflame. The Bulgarians around Philippopolis, incited to hopes of independence by the events in the states to the west, assassinated some of the Turkish officials and gave the Ottoman government a pretext for the most terrible atrocities in the history of Turkish rule in Europe, murdering thousands of Bulgarians in revenge.

Gladstone pleads with his countrymen to aid the Balkan Christians

While the European powers, in their usual fashion, were exchanging futile diplomatic notes on the situation, Serbia and Montenegro declared war on the Sultan, and the Christians in the Balkan region made a frantic appeal to the West for immediate help. A good deal naturally depended on the position taken by England, which was in alliance with Turkey. Gladstone, then leader of the Liberals, urged his countrymen to break the unholy alliance between England and "the unspeakable Turk." But Gladstone's party was not in power, and

Lord Beaconsfield was fearful that English encouragement to the Slavic rebels in the Sultan's dominions would only result in their becoming independent and allying themselves with England's enemy, Russia. The English believed that in the interest of their trade they must continue to resist any movement which might destroy the power of the Sultan, who was not likely to hamper their eastern commerce.

Russia overwhelms the Sultan in a short war, 1877–1878

The negotiations of the powers having come to nothing, Russia determined, in 1877, to act alone. Her declaration of war was shortly followed by Russian victories, and in 1878 a Russian army entered Adrianople — which was equivalent to an announcement to the world that Ottoman dominion in Europe had come to an end. England protested, but the Sultan was forced to sign the Treaty of San Stefano with the Tsar and to recognize the complete independence of Serbia, Montenegro, and Roumania,[1] while Bulgaria was made independent except for the payment of tribute to the Sultan.

England forces a settlement of Turkish affairs in the Berlin Conference in 1878

England and Austria had naturally serious objections to this treaty, which increased the influence of Russia in the Balkans. They therefore forced Tsar Alexander II to submit the whole matter to the consideration of a general European congress at Berlin, where, after prolonged and stormy sessions, the powers agreed that Serbia, Roumania, and little Montenegro should be entirely independent and that Bulgaria should also be independent except for the payment of a tribute to the Sultan.[2] The Tsar was permitted to annex a district to the east of the Black Sea, including the towns of Batum and Kars. The provinces of Bosnia and Herzegovina were to be occupied and administered by Austria-Hungary.[3]

[1] In 1862 the so-called "Danubian provinces" of Moldavia and Wallachia had formed a voluntary union under the name "Roumania." In 1866 the Roumanians chose for their ruler a German prince, Charles of Hohenzollern-Sigmaringen, who in 1881 was proclaimed King of Roumania as Carol I. He died in 1914 and was succeeded by his nephew Ferdinand.

[2] For extracts from the Treaty of Berlin, see *Readings*, Vol. II, pp. 397 f.

[3] They were finally annexed by Austria-Hungary in 1908. See below, pp. 690 ff., and *Readings*, Vol. II, p. 401.

The Bulgarians discontented with the Berlin Treaty

The territorial settlement at Berlin, like that at Vienna half a century before, disregarded many national aspirations. The Bulgarians were especially disappointed with the arrangement, for, instead of being all united in one state, as they had hoped, only the region between the Danube and the Balkans, with some slight additions, was recognized as the principality of Bulgaria. Those dwelling just south of the Balkans were left under the Turkish province, Eastern Roumelia, although under a Christian governor general. As for Macedonia and the region about Adrianople, where there were also many Bulgarians, it was left under the direct administration of Turkish officials.

Union of Bulgaria and Eastern Roumelia, 1885

Under the terms of the treaty the inhabitants of the Bulgarian principality proceeded to frame a constitution and chose, as their prince, Alexander of Battenberg (succeeded by Ferdinand of Coburg in 1886). They adopted as their watchword "Bulgaria for the Bulgarians," and took the first step toward the reunion of their race by a bloodless revolution in 1885 which joined Eastern Roumelia and Bulgaria. At length, in 1908, they refused to pay the Sultan's tribute and took their place among the independent nations of the world.

Turkish dominion in Europe restricted to the Macedonian region inhabited by Greeks, Bulgarians, Serbians, Roumanians, and Albanians

Thus the Turkish Empire in Europe was cut down to a narrow strip of territory — less in extent than the state of Missouri — extending from the Black Sea to the Adriatic, to the main part of which the name Macedonia is generally applied. This area is broken everywhere by mountain ranges and is inhabited by such a complicated mixture of races that it has been aptly called "a perfect ethnographic museum." Along the coast line of the Ægean Sea and the borders of Greece the Greeks, numbering roughly three hundred thousand, predominate. To the north and east, over against Bulgaria and Eastern Roumelia, dwell the Macedonian Bulgarians. In the north are the Serbs, a nation of sturdy peasant farmers, owning their own farms. They resemble the thrifty Bulgarians of the northeast in somewhat the same way as the Irish resemble the

Scotch. They speak somewhat similar languages but are rivals of each other in the Macedonian regions.[1] In the west, bordering on the Adriatic, are the Albanians, a wild people, primitive in their civilization and lawless in their habits. Almost two thirds of them have accepted Mohammedanism, and they are often used by the Sultan to overawe their Christian neighbors in the rest of Macedonia. Scattered through all this Balkan region, there are also, naturally, some Turks.

Disorders in Macedonia

Clearly a population representing so many races, and varying in stages of culture from wild mountain outlaws to orderly industrial communities, would present grave problems even to a government which was entirely honest and efficient. Unfortunately the Turkish rule over Macedonia was neither. Christian bandits would carry off other Christians into the mountains and hold them for ransom; isolated uprisings often resulted in the assassination of the Mohammedan officials in the district; and constant friction between the two faiths made orderly government impossible. The Turkish administration in Macedonia was bound to excite opposition and disorder, in which it cannot be denied that many of the Christians delighted to share.[2]

Section 98. The Independent Balkan States

Unhappy as the Macedonian peoples have been who remained under direct rule of the Turks, it can scarcely be said that the success of the independent states — Greece, Serbia, Roumania, and Montenegro — has been such as to encourage greatly those who advocate self-government for the minor nations in the Balkan regions.

Development of Greece since independence

The Greeks found their Bavarian king, Otto, inclined to be a despot and, after considerable trouble, expelled him from his kingdom in 1862 and chose in his stead George I, son of

1 Throughout the central districts there are also Macedonian "Roumans," of old native stock, but roughly latinized in language and civilization by the Roman colonists who settled in this country after the Roman conquest of Greece.

2 For recent revolutionary events in Turkey, see below, pp. 586 ff.

the former king of Denmark.[1] The country has made progress slowly. In the mountain regions bands of brigands were long so powerful as to defy the police and make traveling dangerous. The fertile soil of the valleys is badly tilled by an ignorant peasantry overburdened with taxes, and the persistent efforts of the government to educate the people still leave about one third of the population illiterate.

Efforts to bring all Greeks within the kingdom have so far failed

Nothwithstanding adverse circumstances, the Greeks are ambitious to become a great and enlightened nation, and they have driven themselves almost into bankruptcy in the construction of canals, railways, and roads, and in the maintenance of a large army. They have regarded themselves as morally bound to free, as soon as possible, their fellow Greeks still under Ottoman rule in Macedonia, Asia Minor, Crete, and the other islands in the eastern Mediterranean, and in 1897 they declared war on Turkey in the hope of accomplishing their long-cherished designs. Though sadly worsted in this war, they continued to encourage agitation in Crete, where disorders became so common that Great Britain, France, Russia, and Italy undertook to guard it in the name of the Sultan, finally, in 1906, allowing the king of Greece to name the governor of the island. Still discontented, in 1908 Crete declared its annexation to Greece in spite of the powers, and in 1913 Turkey formally gave it up.

Revolutions in Serbia

The experiment of self-government in the kingdom of Serbia, which was declared independent in 1878 after about sixty years of practical exemption from Turkish authority, has not proved as much of a success as its advocates had hoped for. Its ruler, who, in 1882, assumed the title of King Milan I, proved to be both despotic and immoral, and the radicals among his subjects forced him to call a national assembly, which drew up a new constitution in 1889. Angered at this interference, Milan abdicated,

[1] After the expulsion of Otto the Greeks drew up a constitution (1864), which provided for a parliament of one chamber elected by popular vote. In 1911 it was modified and a sort of second chamber established. George I was assassinated in 1913 and was succeeded by his son, Constantine I, who was expelled in 1917 and was succeeded by his second son, Alexander.

declaring that he would not be a puppet king. His son, Alexander, proved even less acceptable to the nation, for he suspended the new constitution and recalled his father from exile. In 1903 King Alexander was assassinated by some discontented army officers, and the Serbians then chose for their ruler Peter Karageorgevitch, the grandson of Kara George, or "Black George," who in the early part of the nineteenth century had led the struggle for independence and become a national hero.

Roumania troubled with agrarian disorders

Although the Roumanian kingdom has undergone no palace revolutions like the neighboring Serbia, it has suffered from political agitations and agrarian disorders. The constitution is so arranged as to vest nearly all political power in the hands of those possessing considerable property; and this state of affairs rouses the constant protests of a rapidly growing radical party. Even more serious, however, than the political agitation is the unrest among the peasants, who compose the vast majority of the nation. They claim that ever since the emancipation of the serfs, in 1864, they have been the victims of grasping money lenders and tyrannical landlords. Roumania, however, suffered less than the other countries from the Balkan wars of the last few years, as we shall see.

Bulgaria gaining in prosperity

The new state, Bulgaria, which secured its independence in 1908, was very progressive in many respects. It had a population of over four millions, and until the war of 1914 a democratic constitution maintained good order. Through the growing trade at the ports on the Black Sea the wealth of the kingdom was increasing rapidly.

Montenegro secures constitutional government in 1905

The petty kingdom of Montenegro, smaller in area than the state of Connecticut and with a population of about two hundred and thirty thousand, has caused Europe more trouble than its size warrants. From 1878, when it became independent, until 1905 it was governed by an absolute prince, but he was at last forced to adopt the fashion of western Europe and establish constitutional government with a parliament elected by popular vote. In 1910 the prince assumed the title of king.

Section 99. Extinction of Turkey in Europe

The massacres in Macedonia

Turkey was naturally anxious to hold on to Macedonia, the last remnant of her once large dominion in Europe, but she did not mind the subject people fighting one another when they were so inclined. The European powers were well aware of the horrible local massacres, assassinations, and robberies that were constantly going on in Macedonia, but they dreaded the general war that might come if any attempt was made to take the region from Turkey and divide it up among the independent Balkan states, — Greece, Serbia, and Bulgaria, — for each of these countries declared that Macedonia rightfully belonged to it.

The Turkish revolution of 1908

In recent years a small party of reformers, known as Young Turks, developed, especially in the army, for as officers they had had to study the methods of Western nations. In 1908 a so-called "Committee of Union and Progress" was formed in the Turkish port of Salonica. In July this committee declared that Turkey must have a constitution and that the reformers would march on Constantinople if the Sultan did not yield. The aged Sultan, Abdul Hamid, did not feel himself in a position to oppose the movement, and so even Turkey got a constitution at last. The election of representatives to the Turkish parliament took place, and the assembly was opened by the Sultan with great pomp in December, 1908. This "bloodless revolution" attracted the attention of Europe, and every one wondered whether the Young Turks, who were few in number and impracticable in their notions of government, would really succeed in reforming such a thoroughly corrupt government as that of Abdul Hamid, who had hated and cruelly suppressed every tendency toward betterment during his long reign.

Austria annexes Bosnia and Herzegovina

Bulgaria immediately seized the occasion to declare itself entirely independent of Turkey. Next Austria proclaimed the annexation of Bosnia and Herzegovina, two Slavic provinces of Turkey which she had been managing since the settlement

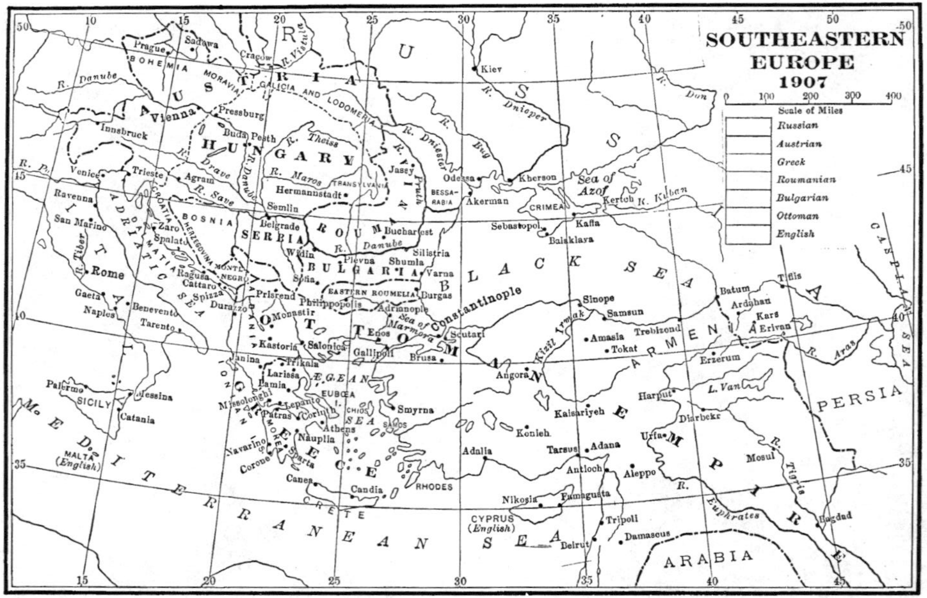
SOUTHEASTERN
EUROPE
1907
Scale of Miles
0 100 200 300 400
Russian
Austrian
Greek
Roumanian
Bulgarian
Ottoman
English
AUSTRIA
HUNGARY
RUSSIA
ROUMANIA
SERBIA
BULGARIA
EASTERN ROUMELIA
MONTENEGRO
BOSNIA
HERZEGOVINA
CROATIA
DALMATIA
BOHEMIA
MORAVIA
GALICIA AND LODOMERIA
TRANSYLVANIA
BESSARABIA
CRIMEA
ALBANIA
GREECE
MOREA
ITALY
SICILY
MALTA (English)
CYPRUS (English)
CRETE
RHODES
EUBŒA
CHIOS
SAMOS
OTTOMAN EMPIRE
ARMENIA
PERSIA
ARABIA
BLACK SEA
CASPIAN SEA
MEDITERRANEAN SEA
ADRIATIC SEA
ÆGEAN SEA
IONIAN SEA
Sea of Azof
Sea of Marmora
L. Van
R. Danube
R. Vistula
R. Dniester
R. Dnieper
R. Bug
R. Don
R. Kuban
R. Pruth
R. Theiss
R. Maros
R. Drave
R. Save
R. Tiber
R. Po
Kizil Irmak
R. Aras
R. Tigris
R. Euphrates
Prague
Sadowa
Cracow
Vienna
Pressburg
Innsbruck
Buda Pesth
Venice
Trieste
Agram
Hermannstadt
Jasey
Semlin
Belgrade
Bucharest
Widin
Plevna
Shumla
Silistria
Varna
Sofia
Burgas
Philippopolis
Adrianople
Constantinople
Scutari
Enos
Gallipoli
Brusa
Prisrend
Monastir
Durazzo
Spizza
Cattaro
Ragusa
Spalato
Zaro
Kastoria
Salonica
Janina
Trikala
Larissa
Lamia
Missolonghi
Lepanto
Patras
Corinth
Athens
Nauplia
Sparta
Navarino
Corone
Canea
Candia
Smyrna
Kiev
Odessa
Kherson
Akerman
Sebastopol
Balaklava
Kaffa
Kertch
Ravenna
San Marino
Rome
Gaeta
Naples
Benevento
Tarento
Palermo
Messina
Catania
Sinope
Samsun
Amasia
Tokat
Trebizond
Batum
Ardahan
Tiflis
Kars
Erivan
Erzerum
Angora
Konieh
Kaisariyeh
Harput
Diarbekr
Urfa
Mosul
Bagdad
Adalia
Tarsus
Adana
Antioch
Aleppo
Nikosia
Famagusta
Tripoli
Beirut
Damascus
10
15
20
25
30
35
40
45
50

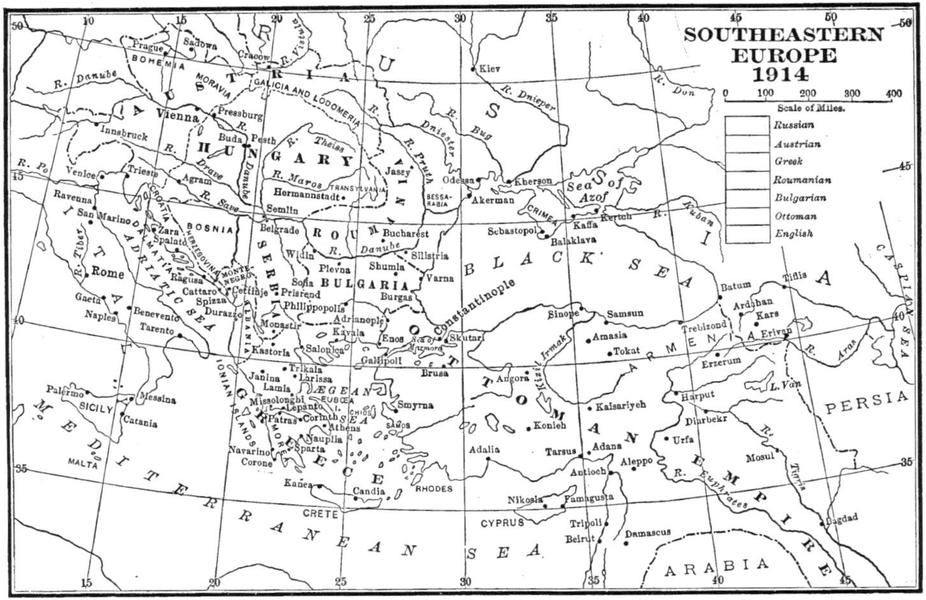
SOUTHEASTERN
EUROPE
1914
0 100 200 300 400
Scale of Miles.
Russian
Austrian
Greek
Roumanian
Bulgarian
Ottoman
English
AUSTRIA
HUNGARY
RUSSIA
ROUMANIA
BULGARIA
SERBIA
GREECE
ITALY
OTTOMAN EMPIRE
ARMENIA
PERSIA
ARABIA
BOHEMIA
MORAVIA
GALICIA AND LODOMERIA
TRANSYLVANIA
BESSARABIA
CROATIA
BOSNIA
HERZEGOVINA
DALMATIA
MONTENEGRO
ALBANIA
CRIMEA
MOREA
BLACK SEA
ADRIATIC SEA
ÆGEAN SEA
MEDITERRANEAN SEA
CASPIAN SEA
Sea of Azof
Sea of Marmora
IONIAN ISLANDS
SICILY
MALTA
CRETE
RHODES
CYPRUS
EUBŒA
CHIOS
Samos
R. Danube
R. Vistula
R. Dniester
R. Dnieper
R. Bug
R. Don
R. Pruth
R. Theiss
R. Maros
R. Drave
R. Save
R. Po
R. Tiber
R. Kuban
R. Aras
R. Kizil Irmak
R. Euphrates
R. Tigris
L. Van
Prague
Sadowa
Cracow
Vienna
Pressburg
Buda
Pesth
Innsbruck
Venice
Trieste
Agram
Hermannstadt
Semlin
Belgrade
Jasey
Bucharest
Silistria
Varna
Shumla
Plevna
Widin
Sofia
Prisrend
Burgas
Philippopolis
Adrianople
Kavala
Enos
Gallipoli
Constantinople
Skutari
Brusa
Smyrna
Salonica
Monastir
Kastoria
Trikala
Larissa
Janina
Lamia
Missolonghi
Lepanto
Patras
Corinth
Athens
Nauplia
Sparta
Navarino
Corone
Kanea
Candia
Zara
Spalato
Ragusa
Cattaro
Cettinje
Spizza
Durazzo
Ravenna
San Marino
Rome
Gaeta
Naples
Benevento
Tarento
Palermo
Messina
Catania
Kiev
Odessa
Kherson
Akerman
Sebastopol
Balaklava
Kaffa
Kertch
Batum
Tiflis
Ardahan
Kars
Erivan
Trebizond
Erzerum
Sinope
Samsun
Amasia
Tokat
Angora
Konieh
Kaisariyeh
Adalia
Tarsus
Adana
Antioch
Aleppo
Harput
Diarbekr
Urfa
Mosul
Bagdad
Nikosia
Famagusta
Tripoli
Beirut
Damascus

of 1878 at the Congress of Berlin. She set to work to Germanize them as completely as possible and suppress all tendencies to join their Slavic relatives in Serbia. A glance at the map will show how important these provinces are for Austria, since they connect her other main possessions with Dalmatia and her ports on the Adriatic. It was in the capital of Bosnia that the event occurred which gave the pretext for the World War.

FIG. 142. TURKISH PARLIAMENT BUILDINGS

A representative parliament in Turkey would naturally include Armenians, Greeks, Bulgarians, Albanians, and Arabs. But the Young Turk party managed it so that the Turks should rule

Difficulties of the Young Turks

The Young Turks encountered ever-increasing difficulties. They naturally thought that it would be a wise thing to deprive the unruly populations of Albania and Macedonia of their arms. This led to a vast amount of trouble, for the people were attached to their guns and swords, and besides they might need them any minute either to kill their neighbors or defend themselves. The Albanians had always been willing to fight for the Turks, but on their own terms, and they had no inclination to join the regular army or to pay taxes, as the new government wished. So there were successive revolts in Albania and Macedonia, and the disorder under the new constitution was worse than under the old despotism. Then the officials and politicians who liked the old ways of doing things organized a revolt in Constantinople which had to be put down. Old Abdul Hamid was deposed and imprisoned, and his brother was made Sultan under the title of Mohammed V. In spite of this the Young Turks found it increasingly difficult to maintain their position against their many opponents.

War between Italy and Turkey

In September, 1911, Italy determined to declare war on Turkey, on the ground that Italian subjects in Tripoli were not properly treated. All Europe protested against this "high-handed" action by Italy; but Italy replied that she was merely following the example set by other countries — protecting the lives and property of her citizens by annexing a country beset by chronic disorders. Turkey was no match for Italy. There was not a great deal of fighting, but Italy took possession of such portions of Tripoli as she could hold with her troops, and also captured the island of Rhodes. The Young Turks did not feel that they could face the unpopularity of ceding these to Italy, but after the war had dragged on for a year they were forced in October, 1912, by the oncoming of a new Balkan war, to cede Tripoli, reserving only a vague Turkish suzerainty. Italy continued to hold Rhodes too.

The Balkan alliance against Turkey

Venizelos, who had been reorganizing Greece with the ability of a Cavour, secretly arranged an alliance with Bulgaria, Serbia, and little Montenegro for a war with Turkey, which began in October, 1912. The Turkish army disappointed every one, and the Bulgarians were able in a few days to defeat it, invest the important fortress of Adrianople, and drive the Turkish forces back close to Constantinople. The Greeks advanced into Macedonia and Thrace, and the Montenegrin and Serbian army defeated the Turkish army sent against them and attacked Albania.

The first Balkan War, 1912

Austria now began to get very nervous lest the Serbians should establish themselves on the Adriatic. She forbade Serbia to hold the port of Durazzo. Had Russia been inclined to support Serbia at that moment the general European war would probably have broken out at the end of 1912 instead of two

Austria balks Serbia

THE RIVAL CLAIMS OF THE BALKAN POWERS

Each of the Balkan powers claims that it should hold the land where members of its nation or race live. Since these are intermingled, there is constant source of quarrel, especially in Macedonia, where Bulgars, Serbs, and Greeks are all found, along with Turks. The Ægean islands and parts of the coast of Asia Minor are also claimed by Greece

years later. Serbia, however, backed down. A truce was arranged and representatives of the Balkan states and of Turkey met in London to see if peace could be arranged. The powers advised Turkey to give up everything in Europe except Constantinople and the region immediately to the west. The Young Turks decided, however, to fight a little longer, and the war was resumed in January. Everything went against them, and in May

Treaty of London

preliminaries of peace were signed in London in which Turkey turned over Macedonia and Crete[1] to the Balkan allies.

Second Balkan War, 1913

But Serbia, Bulgaria, and Greece were all jealous of one another, and the division of the booty led immediately to Bulgaria's turning around to wage war on Greece and Serbia. There was a month of frightful war (July, 1913) and then the Bulgarians,

FIG. 143. TREES FROM WHICH WAR VICTIMS HAVE EATEN THE BARK

Most of the atrocities of the Balkan wars are too horrible even to repeat. This grove of trees, on a small island, was stripped of bark by the starving victims imprisoned there without food. Each side seems to have been guilty of cruelty and murder

defeated on all sides, — for even the Turks recovered Adrianople and the Roumanians invaded on the east, — agreed to consider peace, and delegates met in Bucharest, the capital of Roumania.

Treaty of Bucharest

The treaties concluded at Bucharest between the Balkan kingdoms disposed of practically all of Turkey's possessions in Europe. The Sultan was left with Constantinople and a small area to the west including the important fortress of Adrianople.

[1] This island had revolted from Turkey in 1908 and raised the Greek flag.

The great powers, particularly Austria, had insisted that Albania should be made an independent state, so as to prevent Serbia's getting a port on the Adriatic. The rest of the former Turkish possessions were divided up between Greece, Serbia, Bulgaria, and Montenegro. Greece got the important port of Salonica and the island of Crete as well as a considerable area in Macedonia. Bulgaria was extended to the Ægean Sea on the south. Serbia was nearly doubled in area, and Montenegro as well. (See map.)

QUESTIONS

SECTION 95. Outline the rise and fall of Turkish power in Europe. Describe the relations between Russia and Turkey in the eighteenth and nineteenth centuries. What state in Europe first freed itself from the yoke of Turkey? Give a short history of the Greek struggle for independence. Describe the part played in this war by Great Britain, France, and Russia. Which of the Balkan states owes its origin to the war of Greek independence?

SECTION 96. What circumstances led to the Crimean War? Give the terms of the Treaty of Paris, 1856.

SECTION 97. Describe conditions in Bosnia and Herzegovina under Turkish rule. What was Gladstone's attitude on the Turkish question? State the terms of the Treaty of San Stefano. Mention the most important changes made in the treaty by the Congress of Berlin, 1878. What are the two most important events in Bulgarian history since this date?

SECTION 98. Trace the history of Greece as an independent state. Outline the history of Serbia from 1878 to the present war. What have been Roumania's problems in the past half century? What change has taken place in Montenegro in the past few years?

SECTION 99. Give a short account of the Turkish revolution of 1908. In what way did Bulgaria and Austria take advantage of the situation in Turkey in 1908? Mention some of the difficulties which confronted the Young Turks. What reason did Italy give for making war on Turkey? What was the outcome of the war?

Outline the history of the Balkan states from the formation of the Balkan alliance to the Treaty of Bucharest. Show on a map the territory in Europe under Turkish rule; the territorial changes in the Balkans since the Treaty of Bucharest.

CHAPTER XXV

THE EXPANSION OF EUROPE AND THE SPREAD OF WESTERN CIVILIZATION

SECTION 100. THE GROWTH OF INTERNATIONAL TRADE AND COMPETITION: IMPERIALISM

The foreign trade of Europe

As a result of the Industrial Revolution, Europe has become a busy world of shops and factories, which produce much more than Europeans can use. So new markets are constantly sought in distant parts of the world. The trade with the Far East, which, as we have seen, led to the discovery of America, has grown in the nineteenth century to enormous extent, scattering the wares of London, Paris, or Hamburg through China and India and the islands of the Pacific. This world trade is one of the great facts of history; for it has led the European nations to plant new colonies and to try to monopolize markets in Asia and Africa and wherever else they could. This has brought rivalries between the nations at home, and it was one of the causes of the great European war.

Beginnings of steam navigation

This prodigious expansion of commerce was made possible by the discovery that steam could be used to carry goods cheaply and speedily to all parts of the earth. Steamships and railways have made the world one great market place.

Robert Fulton

The problem of applying steam to navigation had long occupied inventors, but the honor of making the steamship a success commercially belongs to Robert Fulton. In the spring of 1807 he launched his *Clermont* at New York, and in the autumn of that year the "new water monster" made its famous trip to Albany. Transoceanic steam navigation began in 1819 with the voyage of the steamer *Savannah* from Savannah to

Liverpool, which took twenty-five days, sails being used to help the engine. The *Great Western*, which startled the world in 1838 by steaming from Bristol to New York in fifteen days and ten hours, was a ship of 1378 tons, 212 feet long, with a daily consumption of 36 tons of coal.[1] Now a commercial map of the world shows that the globe is crossed in every direction by definite routes which are followed by innumerable freight and

Steady increase in the size and speed of ocean vessels

FIG. 144. THE *SAVANNAH*

passenger steamers passing regularly from one port to another, and few of all these thousands of ships are as small as the famous *Great Western*.

The East and the West have been brought much nearer together by the piercing of the Isthmus of Suez, which formerly barred the way from the Mediterranean Sea to the Indian Ocean. This enterprise was carried out under the

The Suez Canal completed in 1869

[1] Compare this with the *Lusitania*, which had a tonnage of 32,500 tons, engines of 68,000 horse power, was 785 feet long, and carried a supply of over 5000 tons of coal for its journey across the Atlantic, which lasted less than five days. A German vessel, the *Imperator*, was launched in 1912, having a tonnage of over 50,000 tons.

direction of the great French engineer Ferdinand de Lesseps. After ten years of work the canal was opened to traffic in November, 1869. Now annually over five thousand vessels take advantage of it, thus avoiding the long voyage around the Cape of Good Hope.

Panama Canal

The construction of a canal through the Isthmus of Panama was undertaken in 1881 by a French company organized by de Lesseps. But those promoting the enterprise were guilty of wholesale bribery of members of the French parliament, and the work itself was mismanaged. This was disclosed in 1892, and the scandal led to the dissolution of the company. In 1902 the Congress of the United States authorized the President to purchase for forty million dollars the property in which the French investors had sunk so much money. Arrangements with the republic of Colombia for the construction of the canal by the United States having come to naught, the state of Panama, through which the line of the proposed canal passes, seceded from Colombia in 1903, and its independence was immediately recognized by President Roosevelt. A treaty in regard to the canal zone was then duly concluded with the new republic, and after some delays the work of the French company was resumed by the United States and practically completed in 1915.

The beginnings of steam locomotion on land

Just as the gigantic modern steamship has taken the place of the schooner for the rapid trade of the world, so, on land, the merchandise which used to be dragged by means of horses and oxen or carried in slow canal boats is being transported in long trains of capacious cars, each of which holds as much as fifteen or twenty large wagons. The story of the locomotive, like that of the spinning machine or steam engine, is the history of many experiments and their final combination by a successful inventor, George Stephenson.

In 1814 Stephenson built a small locomotive, known as "Puffing Billy," which was used at the mines, and in 1825, with the authorization of Parliament, he opened between Stockton and

Darlington, in the northern part of England, a line for the conveyance of passengers and freight. About this time a road was being projected between Liverpool and Manchester, and in an open competition, in which five locomotives were entered, Stephenson's "Rocket" was chosen for the new railroad, which was formally opened in 1830. This famous engine weighed about seven tons and ran at an average speed of thirteen miles an hour — a small affair when compared with the giant locomotive of our day, weighing a hundred tons and running fifty miles an hour.[1] Within fifteen years trains were running regularly between Liverpool, Manchester, Birmingham, and London, and at the close of the century Great Britain had twenty-two thousand miles of railway carrying over a billion passengers annually.

George Stephenson (1781–1848) and the development of railways in England

FIG. 145. A LOCOMOTIVE BUILT BY GEORGE STEPHENSON

Stephenson forced the exhaust steam up the smokestack to get a hot fire

The first railway was opened in France in 1828; the first in Germany in 1835, but the development of the system was greatly hindered by the territorial divisions which then existed. Now Europe is bound together by a network of over two hundred thousand miles of railway.

Railways in Germany and France

Railway construction is also rapidly advancing in Africa and Asia, preparing cheap outlets for the products of Western

[1] It will be noted that this is the average speed on regular runs. For short distances the "Rocket" made thirty-five miles an hour, while the modern locomotive, as is well known, sometimes runs over a hundred miles an hour.

Railways as pioneering enterprises

mills and mines. As we have seen, the Trans-Siberian road has connected Europe overland with the Pacific,[1] and Russia has also pushed lines southward toward Persia and Afghanistan; British India has some thirty-five thousand miles. Even Africa has been penetrated, and now trains run many thousands of miles through forest, plain, and jungle, where no white man had ever gone before the nineteenth century. These railroads are of the greatest importance, for those who own them are placed in a position to control, to a very large degree, the economic or even the political life of the regions through which they pass. Therefore, as we shall see, the various European nations have been jealous of each other's railroad enterprises in the undeveloped countries. For instance, the importance of the new railroads in China and Turkey was so great as to involve the rival European nations interested in them, and so contribute a cause of war.[2]

The penny post

Quite as essential to the world market as railway and steamship lines are the easy and inexpensive means of communication afforded by the post, telephone, telegraph, and cable. The English "penny post" is now so commonplace as no longer to excite wonder, but to men of Frederick the Great's time it would have seemed impossible. Until 1839 in England the postage on an ordinary letter was a shilling for a short distance, and the cost varied with the distance sent. In that year a reform measure long advocated by Rowland Hill was carried, establishing a uniform penny post throughout Great Britain. The result of reducing the rate of postage to this nominal sum surprised every one, in vastly increasing the frequency with which people wrote to one another. Moreover, in cheapening the rate for sending mail, the isolation of the past was broken up, and

[1] See above, p. 564.

[2] See below, p. 690. The Japanese and Russians have used the railways of Manchuria to establish themselves along the route. The German concession from Turkey of a railroad from Constantinople to Bagdad was very unwelcome to English and Russians. The United States has the greatest railroad systems in the world, extending over two hundred and fifty thousand miles.

people were able to lead more intelligent lives. Other European countries followed the example of Great Britain in reducing postage, and now the world is moving rapidly in the direction of a universal two-cent rate. Already letters may be carried from China to New York for two cents in less time than it took news to cross the Atlantic when penny postage was begun.

Telegraph and telephone

No less wonderful is the development of the telegraph and telephone systems, the former an invention of 1837, the latter as recent as 1876.[1] Distant and obscure places in Africa and Asia are being brought into close touch with one another and with Europe. China now has lines connecting all the important cities of the republic and affording direct overland communication between Peking and Paris. In October, 1907, Marconi established regular communication across the Atlantic by means of the wireless system of telegraphy discovered some years before; and now the wireless telephone can carry the voice from Washington to Paris, and perhaps twice as far.

Competition for foreign markets

The industrial revolution which enables Europe to produce far more goods than it can sell in its own markets, and the rapid transportation which permits producers to distribute their commodities over the whole surface of the globe, have combined to produce a keen competition for foreign markets. The European nations have secured the control of practically all the territory occupied by defenseless peoples in Africa and Asia, and have introduced Western ideas of business into China and Japan, where steamships now ply the navigable rivers, and railroads are being rapidly built.

The process of colonization and of Westernizing the oriental peoples has been further hastened by European and American

[1] The electric-telegraph instrument was invented in America by Morse, and in England by Cooke and Wheatstone at the same time. Alexander Graham Bell invented the telephone just in time to exhibit it at the Centennial Exposition, celebrating one hundred years of American independence, in Philadelphia, 1876. Now the combined length of wire used for messages in the United States is about fifteen million miles. Telegrams are cheaper in Europe than in the United States and therefore more frequently used.

capitalists investing in railroads and mines in backward countries. Great Britain alone is said to have about ten billion dollars invested abroad; one fifth of Russian industrial enterprises are financed by foreigners, who are also to a considerable extent constructing the railroads in China. The Germans supply the money for large banking concerns in Brazil, Buenos Aires, and Valparaiso, which in turn stimulate industry and the construction of railways.

Various forms of imperialism

These two powerful forces — factories seeking markets and capital seeking investment — are shaping the foreign and commercial policies of every important European country. They alone explain why the great industrial nations are embarking on what has been termed a policy of *imperialism*, which means a policy of adding distant territories for the purpose of controlling their products, getting the trade with the natives, and investing money in the development of natural resources. Sometimes this imperialism takes the form of outright annexation at the desire of the natives, such as the acquisition of Hawaii by the United States. Again, it assumes the form of a "protectorate," which is a declaration on the part of a nation somewhat as follows: "This is our particular piece of land; we are not intending to take all the responsibility of governing it just now; but we want other nations to keep out, for we may annex it sooner or later." Sometimes imperialism goes no farther than the securing of concessions in undeveloped countries, such as foreigners have obtained in China or citizens of the United States in Mexico.[1]

The missionary as an agent of imperialism

The way for imperialism had been smoothed by the missionaries.[2] There have always been ardent Christians ready to obey the command, "Go ye into all the world and preach the gospel to every creature" (Mark xvi, 15). No sooner was a new country brought to the attention of Europeans than missionaries

[1] For an argument in favor of imperialism, see *Readings*, Vol. II, pp. 411 ff.

[2] See *Readings*, Vol. II, pp. 415 ff. On the explorations of Jesuits in America, see above, p. 105.

flocked thither with the traders and soldiers. When America was discovered and the sea route opened to the East, the Franciscan and Dominican friars braved every danger to bring the gospel to them that sat in darkness. They were reënforced about 1540 by the powerful Jesuit order.

The Roman Catholic missionary movement

In 1622 the great missionary board of the Roman Catholic Church was given its final organization and the name it still retains — *Congregatio de propaganda Fide.* It has its headquarters at Rome and is composed of twenty-nine cardinals and their assistants. In its colleges and schools missionaries are trained for their work and taught the requisite languages. The Roman Catholic Church now reckons millions of adherents in Turkey, Persia, Arabia, India, Siam, Indo-China, Malaysia, the Chinese republic, Korea, Japan, Africa, and Polynesia.

Protestant missions

For a long time after the Protestant Revolt the reformed churches showed little ardor for foreign missions. The Dutch undertook to Christianize the East Indies in 1602, and their rivals, the English, also did something to promote missions. Among the earliest Protestant missionary associations was the Society for the Promotion of Christian Knowledge, founded in 1695 and conducted under the auspices of the Church of England. In the eighteenth century the Methodists and Baptists joined in the efforts to convert the heathen. The United States entered the field in 1810, when the American Board of Foreign Missions was organized. As time went on, practically all the Protestant denominations established each its board of foreign missions, and the United States has rivaled Europe in the distinction and energy of the missionaries it has sent out and in the generous support its people have given them. Bible societies have been engaged in translating the Scriptures into every known language and scattering copies of them broadcast.

Missionaries as civilizers and teachers

Missionaries have not alone spread the knowledge of the Christian religion, but have carried with them modern scientific ideas and modern inventions. They have reduced to writing the languages of peoples previously ignorant of the existence of an alphabet. They have conquered cruel superstitions, extirpated human sacrifices and cannibalism, and done much to make the lot of woman more tolerable. Their physicians have introduced rational methods of treating the sick, and their schools have given an education to millions who without them would have been left in complete barbarism. Finally, they have encouraged thousands of Japanese, Chinese, and representatives of other peoples to visit Europe and America, and thus prepare themselves to become apostles of Western ideas among their fellows. The explorations and investigations carried on by the missionaries have vastly increased the knowledge of the world and its inhabitants. Their maps and their scientific reports on languages and customs have often proved of the highest value. They have also created a demand for Western goods and opened the way for trade.

How missions have led to the extension of European control in Asia and Africa

In some instances injudicious missionaries have doubtless shown too little appreciation of the ancient culture of India, China, and Japan, and have rudely denounced the cherished traditions and the rooted prejudices of the peoples to whom they came. Even the most prudent and sagacious among them could hardly have avoided arousing the hostility of those whose most revered institutions they felt it their duty to attack. So it has come about that the missionaries have often been badly treated, have undergone great hardships, and have even been murdered by infuriated mobs.

This has generally led to the armed interference of their respective governments, and has more than once, as we shall see, served the none too religious ambitions of these governments as an excuse for annexing the territory in which these outrages have happened, or at least establishing protectorates and spheres of influence. Some illustrations of the rôle of the missionaries will be found in the following sections. We shall turn first to the development of Europe's interest in China.

SECTION 101. RELATIONS OF EUROPE WITH CHINA

Early knowledge of China

The relations of Europe to China extend back into ancient times. Some of the Roman emperors, including Marcus Aurelius, sent embassies to the Chinese monarch, and in the Middle Ages some missionaries labored to introduce Christianity into China. It was not, however, until after the opening of the water route around the Cape of Good Hope that European trade with China became important. Early in the sixteenth century Portuguese merchants appeared in Chinese harbors, offering Western merchandise in exchange for tea and silks. In 1537 the Portuguese rented a trifling bit of land of Macao, off Canton — a post which they hold to-day.

Europeans excluded from China

However, the Chinese did not welcome foreign interference. Their officials regarded the European merchants as barbarians. When, in 1655, the Dutch sent two envoys to the Chinese emperor, they were received only on condition that they would prostrate themselves before his throne and strike their heads nine times on the earth as evidence of their inferiority. In spite of this treatment Dutch and English merchants flocked to Canton, the sole port at which the Chinese emperor permitted regular commerce with foreign countries.

The "Opium War"

Repeated efforts were made, particularly by the English, to get into direct communication with the government at Peking, but they were steadily rebuffed and were only able to establish the commercial relations which they sought by an armed conflict in 1840, known as the "Opium War." The Chinese had attempted to prevent all traffic in this drug, but the English found it so profitable that they were unwilling to give up the trade. When, in 1839, the Chinese government seized many thousand chests of opium and informed the British that the traffic would have to stop, war broke out.

The opening of treaty ports

The British, of course, with their modern implements of warfare, were speedily victorious, and the Chinese were forced to agree, in the Treaty of Nanking, to pay a heavy indemnity, to cede to the British the island of Hongkong, which lies at the mouth of the Canton River, and to open to foreign commerce the ports of Amoy, Foochow, Ningpo, and Shanghai on the same terms as Canton. The United States, taking advantage of this war, secured similar commercial privileges in 1844.

FIG. 146. THE GREAT WALL OF CHINA AT THE NANKOW PASS

This great wall, 15 to 30 feet high and 15 to 25 feet broad, extends for 1400 miles along the northern borders of China. Part of it was built in the third century B.C., part in the fourteenth century A.D., as a barrier to the Tartar tribes. The civilization of China is very old and the Chinese have been proudly disdainful of Western ways and inventions until recently, when nations supplied with these inventions have been threatening the very independence of China

The French and others in China

From the Opium War to the present date China has been troubled with foreign invasions. Napoleon III, supported by the English, waged war on China in 1858 and forced the emperor

* The picture opposite shows how the thrifty Chinese have terraced the hills so that not a drop of water is wasted nor a foot of the fertile ground left uncultivated.

FIG. 147. IRRIGATED CHINESE RICE FIELDS ON HILLSIDES *

FIG. 148. CHINESE COOLIES HAULING A BOAT *

to open new ports to European trade, including Tientsin, which was dangerously near the imperial city of Peking. Recently China has been thrown open to the foreign merchants to a very great extent, and the "concessions" demanded by the great powers have caused some fear that the whole country might be divided among them.[1]

Section 102. Japan becomes a World Power; Intervention in China

The extraordinary history of Japan

To the northeast of China lies a long group of islands which, if they lay off the eastern coast of North America, would extend from Maine to Georgia. This archipelago, comprising four main islands and some four thousand smaller ones, is the center of the Japanese Empire. Fifty years ago Japan was still almost completely isolated from the rest of the world; but now, through a series of extraordinary events, she has become one of the conspicuous members of the family of nations. American newspapers deal as fully with her foreign policy as with that of France or Germany; we are familiar with the portraits of her statesmen and warriors, and her exquisite art has many enthusiastic admirers in England and America. Her people, who are somewhat more numerous than the inhabitants of the British Isles, resemble the Chinese in appearance and owe to China the beginnings of their culture and their art, for it was Buddhist missionaries from Korea who, in the sixth century, first aroused Japan from its previous barbarism.

The feudal period in Japan

Little is known of the early Mikados (emperors) of Japan, and during the twelfth century the *shogun*, or commander in chief of the empire, was able to bring the sovereign powers

* The picture opposite gives an example of cheap Chinese labor. Each coolie received one fourteenth of one cent for hauling the ship up the rapids. Now the rocks have been cleared away by dynamite, and steamboats have displaced the coolies. See below, p. 612.

[1] See below, p. 610.

into his own hands (somewhat as the mayor of the palace had done in the Frankish kingdom), while the emperor began to live in retirement in his capital of Kyoto. Conditions in Japan resembled those in western Europe during the same period. Scattered about the country were the castles of powerful feudal lords (the *daimios*), who continued, until the

FIG. 149. JAPANESE FEUDAL CASTLE

Contrast this stronghold of feudal days in Japan with the grim castles of Europe in the Middle Ages. Rival parties among the Japanese nobles now contend only in parliament

nineteenth century, to enjoy powers similar to the vassals of the medieval European kings.

Brief period of intercourse with Europeans in the late sixteenth and early seventeenth centuries

Rumors of the existence of Japan reached Europe through the Venetian traveler, Marco Polo, at the end of the thirteenth century, but the Portuguese navigator Pinto appears to have been the first European to reach Japan, in the year 1542. Some years later the great Jesuit missionary, Francis Xavier, accompanied by some Japanese who had been converted to Christianity at Goa, made the first attempt to preach the Christian faith in the island. Spanish missionaries from Manila carried on the work, and it is reported that within thirty years two hundred Christian churches had been erected and fifty thousand converts made.

Persecution of Christian missionaries and expulsion of foreigners

The arrogance of the bishops, however, led the Japanese government to issue an edict, in 1586, forbidding the Japanese to accept Christianity, and ten years later some twenty thousand converts are said to have been put to death. For a time the shoguns favored the few Dutch and English merchants who came to their shores and permitted factories to be opened at Yedo and elsewhere, but the quarrels between the Dutch and English and the constant drain of silver paid out for foreign merchandise led the Japanese to impose restrictions on foreigners, so that in the time of Louis XIV all of them had departed, except a few Dutch on the island of Deshima. From that time on, for nearly two hundred years, Japan remained a nation apart, with practically no intercourse with foreigners.

Commodore Perry opens negotiations with the shogun in 1853

In 1853 Commodore Perry visited Yokohama with a message from the United States government to the "Sovereign of Japan," asking that arrangements be made to protect the property and persons of Americans wrecked on the coasts, and that the right be extended to Americans to dispose of their cargoes at one or more ports.[1] Supposing that the shogun was the ruler of Japan, Commodore Perry presented his demands to him. These led to a long and earnest discussion in the shogun's council, as to whether foreigners should be admitted or not, but their demands were finally conceded, and two ports were opened to American and English ships.

Foreigners attacked in the name of the Mikado

Within the next few years several of the European powers had arranged to trade at three or four of the ports (Hakodate, Yokohama, Nagasaki, and a little later at Kobe). Attacks,

[1] See *Readings*, Vol. II, pp. 424 ff.

however, were made upon foreigners in the name of the emperor, who disapproved the shogun's action. An Englishman by the name of Richardson was killed in 1862, on the great highroad between Yedo and Kyoto, by the retainers of the powerful daimio of Satsuma, whereupon the English bombarded Kagoshima, the stronghold of the Satsuma clan.

FIG. 150. JAPANESE WARRIORS

The men who led the Japanese armies in the great war with Russia had learned, as boys, to fight in armor with sword and spear, like these warriors

This produced an extraordinary change of heart in this leading clan, one of the most powerful in Japan, for it saw that the foreigners were much more powerful than the Japanese, and that Japan would suffer as China had done unless she acquainted herself with foreign science and inventions. The next year English ships bombarded another port (Shimonoseki), on account of the refusal of its feudal ruler to permit them to pass freely through the Inland Sea. This produced an effect similar to the bombardment of Kagoshima, and public opinion in Japan gradually changed in favor of the admission of foreigners.

In 1867 the late Mikado, Mutsuhito (d. 1912), then fifteen years of age, ascended the throne. In March of the next year, he invited Sir Harry Parkes, a representative of Great Britain, as well as the representatives of France and the Netherlands,

FIG. 151. JAPANESE HOUSE OF REPRESENTATIVES IN SESSION

This drawing, by a Japanese artist, shows the extent to which Japan is being Westernized. In spite, however, of the extremely modern character of the scene, one has a glimpse of the native artistic skill which, in old Japan, produced drawings now prized the world over. The figures are accurate, but not dull and wooden, and the whole scene is enlivened by the gay tapestry. No Western artist would have drawn quite like this

The Mikado orders his people to cease maltreating Europeans, 1868

to Kyoto. He was deeply chagrined by an attack made upon the retinue of Sir Harry Parkes and publicly declared that any one who committed any deed of violence toward foreigners would be acting in opposition to his Majesty's express orders. With this episode the period of resistance to the foreigners, their trade and their religion, may be said to have closed.

Revolution in Japan. Disappearance of the shogunate and of feudalism

Meanwhile a great revolution was taking place in Japan; the power of the shogun was rapidly declining, and in October, 1867, he was forced to resign his office. This left the Mikado not only the nominal but the real ruler of Japan. He emerged from his ancient seclusion in the sacred city of Kyoto, and removed the capital to Yedo, which was given the new name of Tokyo, or "northern capital." The feudal princes, who had, in general, sided with the Mikado against the shogun, now agreed peacefully to surrender their titles and prerogatives in the interests of their country, and in July, 1871, feudalism was formally abolished throughout the empire. Serfdom was also done away with and — a fact of great importance — the army and navy were reformed in accordance with Western models.

The Industrial Revolution in Japan

Since that date the modernizing of Japan has progressed with incredible rapidity. Although the Japanese still continue to carry on their ancient industries, kneeling on their straw mats, with a few simple implements and no machinery, Western industries have been introduced side by side with the older arts. Students were sent abroad to investigate the most recent achievements in science, a university was established at Tokyo, and the system of education completely revolutionized. There was not a steam mill in the islands when Commodore Perry cast anchor there; now there are about a hundred great cotton factories, with over two million spindles. Since the railroad between Tokyo and the neighboring port of Yokohama was opened in 1872, several thousand miles of railways have been constructed, and the Japanese, who are very fond of travel, can go readily from one end to the other of their archipelago. Great towns have sprung up. Tokyo has over two million inhabitants, and the manufacturing city of Osaka more than a million. The total population of the islands is now about fifty-four millions, more than one half that of the United States, but crowded into an area of about one hundred and sixty thousand square miles.

Constitutional government established in Japan, 1890

With this progress came inevitably a demand for representative government, and as early as 1877 petitions for a constitution were laid before the emperor. Four years later he announced that a parliament would be established in 1890, and a commission was sent to Europe to study constitutional government there. In 1889 a constitution was completed which vested the powers of government in the Mikado and a parliament of two houses.[1]

Section 103. War between Japan and China and its Results

Japan seeks an outlet for her products

After carrying out the various reforms mentioned above, Japan found herself confronted, like the Western nations, with the necessity of extending her trade and securing foreign markets. Her merchants and her ships became the rivals of the Europeans in the neighboring seas, where her commerce has increased far more rapidly than that of the Western nations.

The Chino-Japanese War over Korea, 1894–1895

On the opposite side of the Sea of Japan lies Korea, a land which has become well known throughout the world on account of the two bloody wars to which the question of its possession has given rise. For a long time China and Japan were rival claimants to the Korean kingdom. When Japanese trade developed, the question of control in Korea became an important one, and in 1894 it led to war between the two countries. But the Chinese, with their ancient weapons and organization, were no match for the Japanese, who had eagerly adopted every device of Western warfare, and in a short time the Chinese armies had been driven from Korea and the campaign was transferred

[1] For extracts, see *Readings*, Vol. II, pp. 431 ff.

to the neighboring Manchuria, where the Japanese took Port Arthur. China then called upon the Western powers for assistance, but they did not take action until Japan, in the Treaty of Shimonoseki, had forced China's representative, Li Hung Chang, to recognize the complete independence of Korea (which practically meant opening it up to the Japanese) and to cede to Japan Port Arthur, the Liaotung peninsula on which it lies, and the island of Formosa.

Russia, France, and Germany drive Japan from the mainland

Russia, France, and Germany had watched the course of events with jealous eyes, and now intervened to prevent Japan from securing a foothold on the mainland. Russia was the real leader in this intervention, for she coveted just the region which had been ceded to Japan. Japan was exhausted by the war with China and at that time had no adequate navy. Therefore the Mikado, at the demand of the three powers, withdrew from Manchuria.

Russia thereupon gains valuable concessions in China

The result of this compromise was to throw China into the arms of Russia, which proceeded to take every advantage of the situation. China had been forced to pay a heavy indemnity to Japan in order to get the Liaotung peninsula back again; and when the Chinese government attempted to borrow a large sum from England to meet this obligation, Russia interfered and herself loaned China eighty million dollars without security. In this way China became dependent upon her as a creditor. The Russians were permitted by the Chinese emperor to build their great Trans-Siberian railroad across his territory, which would enable them to reach Vladivostok by a direct line from Irkutsk. Moreover, in order to guard the railway line, Russian soldiers were to be introduced freely into Manchuria. It is clear that these arrangements gave Russia a great advantage over the other European powers, since she controlled the Chinese government through its debt and occupied Manchuria with her soldiers.

Meanwhile the Germans found an excuse for strengthening themselves in the same region. A German missionary having

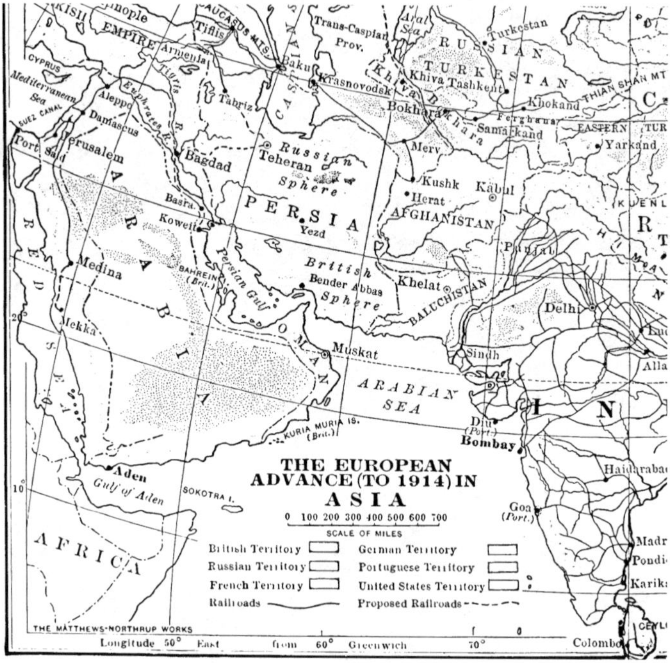
THE EUROPEAN ADVANCE (TO 1914) IN ASIA
0 100 200 300 400 500 600 700
SCALE OF MILES
British Territory
German Territory
Russian Territory
Portuguese Territory
French Territory
United States Territory
Railroads
Proposed Railroads
THE MATTHEWS-NORTHRUP WORKS
Longitude 50° East from 60° Greenwich 70°
EMPIRE
CYPRUS
Mediterranean Sea
SUEZ CANAL
Port Said
Aleppo
Damascus
Armenia
Tiflis
CAUCASUS MTS.
Baku
Tabriz
Trans-Caspian Prov.
Aral Sea
Turkestan
RUSSIAN TURKESTAN
Khiva
Tashkent
Krasnovodsk
Bokhara
Khokand
THIAN SHAN MT
Ferghana
Samarkand
EASTERN
Yarkand
Merv
Euphrates R.
Tigris
Bagdad
Russian Sphere
Teheran
PERSIA
Yezd
Kushk
Kabul
Herat
AFGHANISTAN
Basra
Koweit
ARABIA
Medina
Mekka
RED SEA
BAHREIN (Brit.)
Persian Gulf
British Sphere
Bender Abbas
Khelat
BALUCHISTAN
Delhi
OMAN
Muskat
Sindh
ARABIAN SEA
KURIA MURIA IS. (Brit.)
Diu (Port.)
Bombay
Aden
Gulf of Aden
SOKOTRA I.
AFRICA
Goa (Port.)
Haidarabad
Colombo

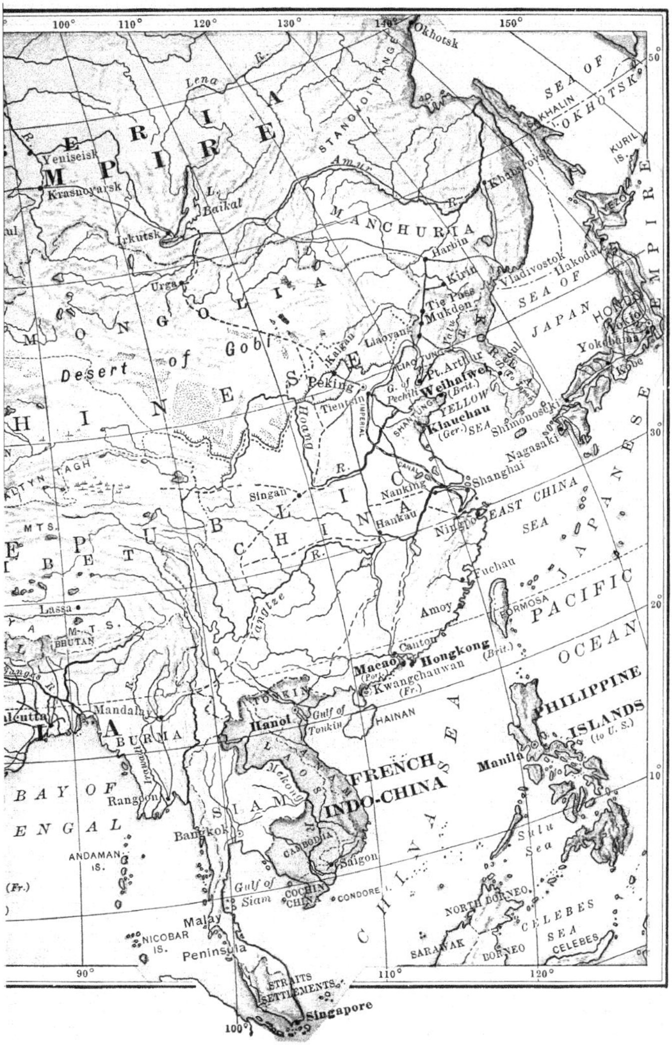
Okhotsk
SEA OF OKHOTSK
SAKHALIN
KURIL IS.
STANOVOI RANGE
Lena R.
Yeniseisk
Krasnoyarsk
L. Baikal
Irkutsk
Amur R.
Khabarovsk
MANCHURIA
Harbin
Kirin
Vladivostok
Hakodate
YEZO
Urga
MONGOLIA
Desert of Gobi
Tie Pass
Mukden
Liaoyang
Kalgan
Peking
Tientsin
Pt. Arthur
Weihaiwei (Brit.)
G. of Pechili
YELLOW SEA
Kiauchau (Ger.)
Seoul
SEA OF JAPAN
HONDO
Tokio
Yokohama
Kobe
Shimonoseki
Nagasaki
JAPANESE EMPIRE
ALTYN TAGH
TIBET
Lassa
BHUTAN
Singan
Nanking
Shanghai
Hankau
Ningpo
CHINA
EAST CHINA SEA
Yangtze R.
Hoang R.
Fuchau
Amoy
FORMOSA
PACIFIC OCEAN
Canton
Hongkong (Brit.)
Macao (Port.)
Kwangchauwan (Fr.)
TONKIN
Hanoi
Gulf of Tonkin
HAINAN
Calcutta
Mandalay
BURMA
Irawadi R.
Rangoon
BAY OF BENGAL
ANDAMAN IS.
NICOBAR IS.
LAOS
ANNAM
Mekong
FRENCH INDO-CHINA
SIAM
Bangkok
CAMBODIA
Saigon
COCHIN CHINA
Gulf of Siam
CONDORE
Malay Peninsula
STRAITS SETTLEMENTS
Singapore
CHINA SEA
PHILIPPINE ISLANDS (to U. S.)
Manila
Sulu Sea
NORTH BORNEO
SARAWAK
BORNEO
CELEBES SEA
CELEBES

been murdered in the province of Shantung, which lies opposite Korea, a German squadron appeared in Kiaochow Bay, in November, 1897, landed a force of marines, and raised the German flag. As a compensation for the murder of the missionary, Germany demanded a long lease of Kiaochow, with the right to build railways in the region and work mines. Upon acquiring Kiaochow the Germans built harbors, constructed forts, military barracks, machine shops, etc. In short, a model German town was constructed on the Chinese coast, which, with its defenses, constituted a fine base for further extension of Germany's sphere of influence.

Germany seizes territory in the Shantung peninsula

At first the Tsar hoped to balk the plans of Germany, but decided, instead, to secure additional advantages for himself. Accordingly Port Arthur and the waters adjacent to the Liaotung peninsula, upon which it lies, were leased by China to Russia, in March, 1898, for a period of twenty-five years, subject to renewal by mutual consent. Port Arthur was to be open only to Chinese and Russian vessels, and Russia immediately began to build fortifications which were believed to render the town impregnable. A railway was constructed to Harbin,[1] connecting Port Arthur with Vladivostok and the Trans-Siberian railway. This at last gave Russia a port on the Pacific which, unlike Vladivostok, was free from ice the year round.

Russia leases Port Arthur

Great Britain, learning of the negotiations, sent a fleet northward from Hongkong to the Gulf of Chihli (or Pechili), and induced China to lease to her Weihaiwei, which lay just between the lands acquired by Germany and Russia. England, moreover, believed it to be for her interest to be on good terms with Japan, and in 1902 an offensive and defensive alliance was concluded between the two powers, binding each to assist the other in case a third party joined in a conflict in which either was involved. For example, under the provisions, England had to aid Japan in a war with Russia, should France or Germany intervene.

The British lease Weihaiwei and conclude a treaty of alliance with Japan

[1] See picture of Harbin, p. 564.

Section 104. Changes in China; the Boxer Rising

The Europeans begin to develop the natural resources of China

The foreigners were by no means content with establishing trading posts in China; they longed to develop the neglected natural resources of the empire, to open up communication by railroads and steamships, and to Westernize the Orientals, in order that business might be carried on more easily with them and new opportunities be found for profitable investments.

Railroads built in China

The first railroad in China was built by British promoters in 1876, from Shanghai to a point some fifteen miles to the north of that city. The Chinese, however, were horrified by this innovation, which they felt to be a desecration of the graves of their ancestors. Yielding to popular prejudice the government purchased the railroad, only to destroy it and throw the locomotives into the river. Nevertheless, five years later, the Chinese themselves, with the aid of British capital, began the construction of an imperial railroad system, and in 1895 other foreigners besides the Russians were once more permitted to undertake the construction of railway lines, and there are now several thousand miles of road open for traffic. The French and Germans are also interested in opening up the regions within their spheres of influence, and the British are planning to push into the interior of China a line running northward from Rangoon through Mandalay. Thousands of miles of railway are now projected, one of the most important running south from Peking, through Hankow to Canton, thus for the first time linking north China with the south, which is quite different in many ways. The result will be to help unify the Chinese and develop a stronger nationality. Doubtless within half a century China will be covered with a network of lines which cannot fail to do much to revolutionize her ancient habits and civilization.

Steamships, post, and telegraph

In 1898 the internal waterways of China were opened to foreign ships. Several lines of well-equipped steamships now ply on the Canton River and follow the waters of the Yangtze

River for a thousand miles inland. Many thousand miles of telegraph lines are in operation, affording overland connection with Europe, while wireless stations have been planted even in the inland cities. The post office, organized in 1897, has branches throughout the country.

China begins a great series of reforms

It was inevitable that intercourse with European nations should affect the whole policy and ideals of the Chinese government. In 1889 a decree was issued establishing an annual audience in which the emperor might show his "desire to treat with honor all the foreign ministers resident in Peking." A few years later the cumbersome ancient ceremonial was abolished, and foreigners were received in a manner which indicated the recognition of their equality with Chinese of the same rank. In 1898, when Prince Henry of Prussia visited Peking, he was cordially greeted by the emperor, who shook hands with him in Western fashion and conversed with him on a familiar footing.

In the same year a series of decrees was issued with the object of reforming the army on models offered by those nations that had given so many proofs of their military superiority. New schools and colleges were planned with a view of starting the country on the road to progress. Chinese students were sent to Europe to study foreign methods of government, agricultural schools were built, patent and copyright laws were introduced, and a department of mines and railroads was established, in order that China might no longer be obliged to leave these matters entirely in the hands of foreigners. Journalists were even encouraged to write on political questions.

The conservatives oppose reforms in China

These abrupt reforms aroused the superstitious horror of the conservative party. They found a sympathetic leader in the Dowager Empress, who had been regent during the early years of the emperor's reign. She succeeded in regaining her influence and in putting an end, for the time being, to the distasteful reforms. The Europeans, both missionaries and business men, nevertheless continued their activities, and the conservatives believed it necessary, therefore, to organize a great movement to drive out the "foreign devils," who had been, in their eyes, steadily undermining the ancient traditions of China.

The "Boxers"

Among those hostile to the foreigner none were more conspicuous than the secret society of the "Boxers," or, as they appear to have called themselves, the "Order of the Patriotic Harmonious Fists." They were quite willing to coöperate with the Dowager Empress in carrying out her designs against foreign influence. They proclaimed that the Western nations were "lacerating China like tigers"; and summoned every patriotic Chinaman to rise in defense of his country.

The Peking insurrection of 1900

The party in favor of meeting the "Christian Peril" by violence rapidly increased. The Boxers, who were arming and drilling, knew very well that neither the Chinese officials nor the imperial troops would interfere with them. Missionaries and traders were murdered in the provinces, and although the government at Peking always declared that it was doing all it could to suppress disorder, the representatives of foreign nations in the capital became thoroughly alarmed. On June 20, 1900, the Boxers, supported by the troops, killed the German ambassador, Baron von Ketteler, while on his way to the palace to expostulate with the government. The Europeans were then besieged in the several legations and in the Catholic cathedral, but, for some reason which is not clear, the Chinese did not murder them all, as they might easily have done.

The powers intervene and settle affairs in China

The powers determined upon immediate intervention, and in August a relief expedition, made up of Japanese, Russian, British, American, French, and German troops, fought its way from Tientsin to Peking, and brought relief to the imprisoned foreigners. The Chinese court left Peking, and the royal palace was shamefully desecrated and pillaged. The scandalous conduct of the Germans, in particular, disgraced the Western world. Negotiations were now opened, and the aged Li Hung Chang rendered his last services by concluding an agreement in which China made certain reparations, including the payment of an indemnity of three hundred and twenty million dollars, and promised to repress all anti-foreign societies.[1]

The Chinese reform movement renewed

Although the Dowager Empress still retained her power, the work of reform was again undertaken. The work of reorganizing the army was renewed, and students were again sent abroad in large numbers to investigate Western methods of industry and government. By one of the most momentous decrees in the intellectual history of the world, the ancient classical system of education, which had for centuries been deemed an essential preparation for public office, was abolished in 1905.[2] Students preparing for the government service are no longer examined upon Confucius and asked to write essays on such subjects as "How the moonlight sleeps on the lake"; for the new examination questions deal with the history of the West, with politics and economics, and with such grave questions as the relation of capital to labor and the methods of stimulating modern industry. Even the Dowager Empress was obliged to yield to the progressive party, and in September, 1906, she went so far as to announce that China should prepare herself for the introduction of representative government and of a parliament.[3]

Section 105. The Russo-Japanese War; the Revolution in China

Russo-Japanese rivalry in Korea and Manchuria leads to war, February, 1904

Scarcely had the troubles due to the Boxer rising been adjusted when a new war cloud appeared in the East. The interest of Japan in finding markets has already been mentioned. The occupation of Manchuria and Port Arthur by the Russians seriously threatened Japanese extension in that direction; and when Russia secured from Korea a lumber cession in the

[1] For an account of the Boxer rising, see *Readings*, Vol. II, pp. 436 ff. The United States returned its share of the indemnity, and China, in gratitude, is spending it to educate students in America.

[2] See *Readings*, Vol. II, pp. 441 ff.

[3] For the revolution of 1911–1912 in China, see below, p. 618.

Yalu valley and sent Cossacks to build forts in that region, Japan, which regarded Korea as lying within her sphere of influence, could hardly fail to protest. Russia had agreed repeatedly to withdraw from Manchuria, but had always failed to keep her promises when the time came. She had, moreover, guaranteed the integrity of Korea, upon whose territory she was now encroaching. Accordingly, the Japanese, determined to have Korea for themselves, after spending some months in futile negotiations with the Tsar's government, broke off diplomatic relations on February 5, 1904, and opened hostilities with Russia.

Japan far better prepared for war than Russia

Japan was well prepared for war and was, moreover, within easy reach of the field of conflict. The Russian government, on the contrary, was rotten to the core and was already engaged in a terrible struggle with the Russian nation.[1] The eastern boundary of European Russia lay three thousand miles from Port Arthur and the Yalu River, and the only means of communication was the single line of badly constructed railroad that stretched across Siberia to the Pacific.

Early reverses of the Russians on the seas

Three days after the war opened the Japanese fleet surprised the Russian battleships lying off Port Arthur, sank four of them, and drove the rest into the harbor, where they succeeded, in the main, in keeping them "bottled up." A second fleet which had been stationed at Vladivostok was defeated early in May, thus giving Japan control of the seas. At the same time the Russians were driven back from the Yalu, and the Japanese under General Oku landed on the Liaotung peninsula, cut off Port Arthur from communication with Russia, and captured the town of Dalny, which they made their naval headquarters. General Oku then began pushing the Russians northward toward Mukden, while General Nogi was left to besiege Port Arthur. For months the world watched in suspense the heroic attacks which the Japanese, at deadly cost to themselves, made upon the Russian fortress. Meanwhile fighting continued to

Siege of Port Arthur

[1] See above, pp. 567 ff.

the north along the line of the railroad. In October the Japanese were victorious in a fearful battle which raged south of Mukden for days, thus putting an end to General Kuropatkin's designs for relieving Port Arthur. As winter came on, the Japanese redoubled their efforts and the fortress at last surrendered, on January 1, 1905, after a siege of seven months, the horrors of which were then perhaps without a parallel.

Mukden captured by the Japanese, March, 1905

The conduct of the war on the part of the Japanese affords one of the most extraordinary examples on record of military organization and efficiency. By means of an ingenious system of telephones they kept every division of the army in direct communication with the war office in Tokyo, and by the strictest discipline they checked disease and contagion in the hospitals. The Russian sanitary service was also of high order, as compared with previous wars. Late in February fighting again began, and for three weeks the Russians struggled against the combined Japanese armies; but on March 9 they deserted Mukden and moved northward, after forty thousand of them had been killed and over a hundred thousand wounded.

Togo destroys the Russian fleet in the Straits of Korea, May 27, 1905

On learning of the destruction of the fleets in the Pacific the Russian government determined to dispatch its Baltic squadron to the Orient. After some strange adventures, which aroused both the amusement and the disgust of those who were following the war,[1] the fleet arrived in May in the Straits of Korea, where Admiral Togo was waiting for it. In a few hours he sank twenty-two of the Russian vessels and captured six. The Tsar's fleet was practically annihilated, with terrible loss of life, while the Japanese came out of the conflict almost unscathed.[2]

Lest the war should drag on indefinitely, President Roosevelt, acting under the provisions of the Hague Convention,[3] took

[1] As the squadron was passing through the North Sea the Russians fired upon a fishing fleet off Dogger Bank, and alleged later that they mistook the poor fishermen for Japanese. This is but one of numerous examples of the incompetence which was shown by the Russians throughout the war.

[2] For Admiral Togo's account of the battle, see *Readings*, Vol. II, pp. 445 f.

[3] See below, p. 682.

The Treaty of Portsmouth, 1905

measures which brought about a peace. After consulting the representatives of Japan and Russia at Washington and ascertaining the attitude of the neutral powers, he dispatched notes to the Tsar and Mikado, urging them to open negotiations.[1] This invitation was accepted, and on August 9 the first session of the conference was held at Portsmouth, New Hampshire. On September 5 the Treaty of Portsmouth was signed. This recognized the Japanese influence as paramount in Korea, which, however, was to remain independent.[2] Both the Japanese and Russians were to evacuate Manchuria; the Japanese were, however, given the rights in the Liaotung peninsula and Port Arthur which Russia had formerly enjoyed. Lastly, the southern part of the Russian island of Sakhalin was ceded to Japan.

China becomes a republic

Thus this great conflict produced by the friction of the powers in the East was brought to an end, but the wealth of China and the fact that it has not yet organized a strong army or navy leave it as a tempting prize for further aggression. Nevertheless, China has been changing as rapidly during the last five years as Japan ever did. Students of Western countries returning home determined to overthrow the Manchu (or Manchurian) dynasty, which had ruled for two hundred and sixty-seven years, and their corrupt officials. After a heroic and bloody struggle they forced the court, on February 12, 1912, to declare the abdication of the boy-emperor then on the throne and the creation of a republic. But the emperor's prime minister, Yuan Shih-kai, skillfully had himself granted full power to establish the republic which the revolutionists had won. In this way he prevented the ardent republicans, who had done the

[1] See *Readings*, Vol. II, p. 447.

[2] The Japanese have not left Korea independent. They immediately took control of the administration, and in the summer of 1907 forced the Korean emperor most unwillingly to abdicate. Finally, by the treaty of August 23, 1910, Korea was annexed to the Japanese empire and named "Chosen." There are now many thousand Japanese colonists in it, and the country, which was very backward, is being rapidly developed.

fighting, from carrying out their program of immediate reform. Instead, he secretly thwarted their plans, and when he had a sufficient pretext he lessened the powers of the new Chinese parliament so that it was unable to oppose his will. Having thus prepared the way for a *coup d'état*, he announced in the autumn of 1914 that he would assume the title of "Emperor of China." The protest of Japan, and possibly of other powers,

President Yuan Shih-kai attempts a *coup d'état*, but fails to become emperor

FIG. 152. YUAN SHIH-KAI

against this move led him to postpone the actual assumption of the crown; for Japan feared that with a strong emperor China might defend itself successfully, and even become a dangerous rival. Then the republicans revolted, and Yuan Shih-kai finally, March, 1916, fearing to lose all, declared that he would never accept the title "emperor," and that the whole incident had been a mistake. This did not satisfy the republicans, however, who rose in revolt against a president who seemed to them to be steadily violating the principles of republican rule. During the spring of 1916 their movement grew, especially through the south, which has been more progressive than the north. Finally, in June, Yuan Shih-kai died suddenly and the vice president, Li Yuan Hung, became president. The revolutionary republicans have apparently shown that they are the real power in China. If so, it means rapid advance.

Section 106. Occupation of Africa by the European Powers

The ancients knew little of the main body of the African continent

The vast continent of Africa, the northeastern corner of which was the seat of perhaps the first highly civilized people, was the last of the great divisions of the earth's surface to be explored and appropriated by the European nations. The lower valley of the Nile and the coasts which bound the Mediterranean on the south were well known to the ancients, and were included in the Roman Empire, but the upper reaches of that great river and the main body of the continent to the south of the desert of Sahara, were practically unknown to them, and they had no suspicions that the land extended for five thousand miles to the south of Carthage.

How the Mohammedans conquered northern Africa

Shortly after the death of Mohammed in 632, his followers began the conquest of Egypt and northern Africa, and in less than a hundred years they had subdued all the region which had formerly been ruled from Rome. From Cape Guardafui on the extreme east, to Cape Verde, lying on the Atlantic, nearly five thousand miles to the west, they introduced their civilization and religion, so that to-day in the towns of Tunis and Morocco one sees many things to remind him of the conditions in Palestine or Arabia. The Mohammedans built up a flourishing trade with the interior; they traversed the deserts and opened caravan routes through the sandy wastes; they pushed their trading settlements down the east coast as far as a point opposite Madagascar; they made maps of that portion of the continent with which they had become familiar, and described its climate and appearance. The knowledge which the Mohammedans had acquired naturally spread into Spain, which long formed a part of their dominions, and it appears probable that the Portuguese, who began to explore the west coast of Africa in the fifteenth century, also received such information as they possessed from the Moors.

Slow advance of the Europeans in Africa

Europe was, however, a long time taking advantage of such knowledge of Africa as it secured through the Mohammedans. Although the Portuguese rounded the Cape of Good Hope in 1486, they found traffic in the East Indies too profitable to warrant their spending any time exploring and settling the uninviting interior of Africa. The most important trade which sprang up with that continent was the slave traffic, which was soon undertaken by the English, whose enterprising slavers made enormous fortunes at that cruel business. The Europeans generally were too busy settling the more inviting portions of the New World to undertake serious colonization in Africa. The Dutch post, established at the Cape of Good Hope in 1652, did not prove to be very successful and had a population of only ten thousand at the opening of the nineteenth century. The French station, St. Louis, founded at the mouth of the Senegal River in the seventeenth century, was nothing more than a trading station; but it was destined to become important in the nineteenth century as a basis for the extension of French power in northwest Africa.

The situation in 1815

No serious attempts had been made by any of the European powers to colonize any portion of Africa before the close of the Napoleonic wars in 1815. Indeed, the suppression of the slave trade had discouraged further activity for a time,[1] for this traffic had been more profitable than the combined trade in gold, ivory, gum, and other African commodities.

The situation in 1815 may be summed up as follows: In northern Africa the Sultan of Turkey was the nominal suzerain of Egypt and the so-called Barbary States, that is, Tripoli,

[1] See above, pp. 322 f.

Tunis, and Algeria. Morocco was, however, an independent state, as it still is nominally, under the sultan of Morocco. France maintained her foothold at the mouth of the Senegal; the most important Portuguese possessions were in Lower Guinea and on the east coast opposite the island of Madagascar; the British held some minor posts along the west coast, and had wrested Cape Colony from the Dutch during the Napoleonic wars. The heart of Africa was still unknown; no European power contemplated laying claim to the arid waste of the Sahara desert, and the more attractive regions of the upper Nile were ruled by semicivilized Mohammedan chiefs.

Advance of France and England in Africa during the first half of the nineteenth century

For fifty years after the Congress of Vienna the advance of European powers in Africa was very slow indeed. England and France were, it is true, gradually extending their spheres of influence, and explorers were tracing the rivers and mountain chains of the interior. France, as has been explained, conquered Algiers during this period,[1] and formally annexed it in 1848. The Dutch Boers, disgusted with English rule, had migrated to the north, and laid the foundations of the Transvaal and Orange River colonies.[2]

Explorations of Livingstone and others

The latter half of the nineteenth century was, however, a time of active exploration in Africa. It is impossible here even to name all those adventurers who braved the torrid heat and fevers and the danger from savages and wild beasts. Under the auspices of the Royal Geographical Society of England a search was begun for the mysterious sources of the Nile, and a lake lying just south of the equator was discovered in 1858 and named Victoria Nyanza. In 1864 Sir Samuel Baker discovered another lake, Albert Nyanza, to the northwest, and explored its connections with the Nile River. Livingstone had visited Bechuanaland twenty years before, and pushed up the valley of the Zambesi River, tracing it nearly to its source. In 1866 he explored the regions about the lakes of Nyasa and

[1] See above, p. 486. [2] See above, pp. 542 ff.

Tanganyika, and reached a point on the upper Congo. This expedition attracted general attention throughout the civilized world. His long absence roused the fear that he was, perhaps, the prisoner of some savage tribe, and on his return to Lake Tanganyika he was met by Henry Stanley, another explorer, who had been sent out by the *New York Herald* to search for him.[1] Livingstone, who was both missionary and explorer, continued his work until his death in 1873.

Stanley's discoveries

Two years later Stanley set out upon an expedition which is regarded as the most important in the annals of African exploration. After visiting lakes Victoria Nyanza and Tanganyika, he journeyed across the country to the headwaters of the Congo, down which he found his way to the Atlantic. Meanwhile other explorers, French and German, as well as English, were constantly adding to the knowledge of a hitherto unknown continent.

Rapid partition of Africa

Stanley's famous journey through the heart of "Darkest Africa" naturally aroused the intense interest of all the European powers, and within ten years after his triumphant return to Marseilles in 1878, the entire surface of Africa had been divided up among the powers, or marked out into "spheres of influence." A generation ago a map of Africa was for the most part indefinite and conjectural, except along the coast. To-day its natural features have been largely determined, and it is traversed by boundary lines almost as carefully drawn as those which separate the various European countries. The manner in which the English, French, and Germans have asserted their claims in Africa has been briefly explained in preceding chapters.

French possessions

The northwestern shoulder of the continent, from the mouth of the Congo to Tunis, belongs, with some exceptions, to France.[2] It must be remembered, however, that a very considerable portion of the French claim is nothing but a desert,

[1] For Stanley's account of the meeting, see *Readings*, Vol. II, pp. 449 ff.
[2] See above, p. 488.

totally useless in its present state. On the east coast of Africa France controls French Somaliland, and her port of Jibuti, which lies at the mouth of the Red Sea, gives her somewhat the same advantages that Aden affords the English. The French also hold the island of Madagascar. Their attempt to penetrate Morocco, mentioned above, was one of the remoter causes of the war of 1914.[1]

German possessions

Between 1884 and 1890 Germany acquired four considerable areas of African territory, which included together nearly a million square miles: Togoland, Kamerun, German Southwest Africa, and German East Africa. The Germans made heroic efforts to develop these regions by building railways and schools and expending enormous sums in other ways, but the wars with the natives and the slight commerce which had been established left the experiment one of doubtful value.

The Belgian Congo

Wedged in between German East Africa and the French Congo is the vast Belgian Congo, the history of which began with a conference held in Brussels in 1876 under the auspices of the king of Belgium. Representatives of most of the European countries were invited to attend, with a view to considering the best methods of opening up the region and of stopping the slave trade which was carried on by the Mohammedans in the interior. The result was the organization of an international African Association with its center at Brussels. The enterprise was, however, in reality the personal affair of King Leopold, who supplied from his own purse a large portion of the funds which were used by Stanley in exploring the Congo basin, establishing posts, and negotiating hundreds of treaties with the petty native chiefs.

The Berlin conference on the Congo territory

The activity of the African Association aroused the apprehensions of the European powers interested in Africa, especially England and Portugal, and a congress was called at Berlin to consider the situation. This met in November, 1884, and every

[1] See below, pp. 625 f.

European state except Switzerland sent delegates, as did the United States. The congress recognized the right of the African Association to the vast expanse drained by the Congo River, and declared the new territory a neutral state, the Congo Free State, open to the trade of all nations.

The following year King Leopold announced to the world that he had assumed sovereignty over the Congo Free State, and that he proposed to unite it in a personal union with Belgium. He gradually filled the government offices with Belgians and established customs lines with a view to raising revenue.

Alleged cruel treatment of the natives in the Congo Free State

During the opening years of the twentieth century the Belgians were charged with practicing atrocious cruelties on the natives.[1] There is reason to think that the hideous reports published in the newspapers were much exaggerated; but there is little doubt that the natives, as commonly happens in such cases, have suffered seriously at the hands of the European invader. King Leopold claimed ownership over the vacant land, and in this way roused the hatred of the peoples who had been used to roaming freely in every direction. By a system of "apprenticeship" many of the blacks had been reduced to the condition of slaves. Labor was hard to secure, for the natives, accustomed to a free life in the jungle, did not relish driving spikes on railways or draining swamps for Belgian capitalists. The government therefore required native chiefs to furnish a certain number of workmen, and on their failure to supply the demand it had been customary to burn their villages. The government also required the natives to furnish a certain quantity of rubber each year; failure to comply with these demands had also brought summary punishment upon them. Finally, protests in England and America led the Belgian ministry to take up the question of the Congo, and at length, in 1908, the government assumed complete ownership of the Free State, which then took the name of the Belgian Congo.

[1] See *Readings*, Vol. II, pp. 453 f.

African possessions of Portugal, Italy, and Spain

The Portuguese still control remnants of the possessions to which they laid claim when South Africa was first brought to the attention of Europe, namely, Guinea, Angola, and East Africa. Italy has the colony of Eritrea on the coast of the Red Sea, and Italian Somaliland to the south of Cape Guardafui, and in 1912 wrested Tripoli from Turkey by a costly war.[1] Spain's two colonies, one on the Strait of Gibraltar, the other on the Gulf of Guinea, only serve to remind her of the vast colonial empire which she has lost.

Morocco

Morocco still remains nominally independent of European powers, but has been an object of contention among them. Its population, which is a curious mixture of Berbers, Arabs, and negroes, has not materially changed its civilization during the past thousand years. The fierce tribesmen often defy the rule of their sultan at Fez. A bandit leader, Raisuli, seized an English envoy to the sultan, Sir Harry McLean, during the summer of 1907 and held him a prisoner for several months. This is but one of many instances which illustrate the inability of the sultan of Morocco to control his subjects and protect foreigners.

The conference at Algeciras

The French, who are neighbors of the Moors on the east, have, in spite of many difficulties, gradually been developing relations with Morocco. They carry on a trade in almonds, gum, and the famous Moroccan goatskin, and have also lent money to the sultan. It will be recalled that, after the settlement of the "Fashoda incident," Britain allowed France a free hand, so far as Britain was concerned, in dealing with Morocco. The French soon found either the necessity or the pretext for intervention, and were proceeding to deal with "the Moroccan problem" as though it were their own affair when Germany protested that it too had interests in Morocco. The result was a conference of the powers, including the United States, at Algeciras, Spain (just across the bay from Gibraltar), in 1906. Their representatives agreed on the formation of a police force under French

[1] See above, p. 588.

and Spanish officers, and the organization of a state bank, which should be controlled by the powers.[1]

The English in Africa

The English, as we have seen already, have built up a great federal dominion in South Africa, which is the most important of all the European colonies in Africa. They also hold valuable territories on the east coast, running inland to the great lakes. But much more interesting to the historian is their control over Egypt.

Mehemet Ali establishes himself and his successors as rulers of Egypt

This ancient center of civilization had, as we have seen, been conquered by the Arabs in the seventh century. Through the late Middle Ages it was ruled by a curious military class known as the Mamelukes, and only fell to the Ottoman Turks in 1517. With the decline of the Sultan's power the country fell under the domination of Mameluke beys, or leaders; and it was against these that Bonaparte fought in 1798. Shortly after Nelson and the English had frustrated Bonaparte's attempt to bring Egypt under French rule, a military adventurer from Albania, Mehemet Ali, compelled the Sultan to recognize him as governor of Egypt in 1805. A few years later he brought about a massacre of the Mamelukes and began a series of reforms. He created an army and a fleet, and not only brought all Egypt under his sway, but established himself at Khartum where he could control the Sudan,[2] or region of the Upper Nile. Before his death in 1849 he had induced the Sultan to recognize his heirs as rightful rulers, khedives,[3] of Egypt.

The importance of Egypt for the Western powers was greatly increased by the construction of the Suez Canal, begun in 1859,[4] for both Port Said on the Mediterranean and Suez on the Red Sea are Egyptian ports. The English were able to get a foothold

[1] A continuance of disorder in Morocco enabled France to use the situation for further penetration, which led to a second German protest. But this belongs rather to the history of Europe than of Africa, as it was one of the causes of the great war of 1914.

[2] The term "Sudan" (see map) was applied by the Mohammedans to the whole region south of the Sahara desert, but as now used it commonly means Anglo-Egyptian Sudan only.

[3] This title was assumed with the consent of the Sultan.

[4] See above, p. 593.

The khedive Ismail I (1863–1879) becomes hopelessly involved in debt

in Egypt through the improvidence of the Egyptian ruler, Ismail I, who came to the throne in 1863, and by reckless extravagance involved his country in a heavy debt which forced him to sell a block of his canal shares to the British government at a low price. Still heavily in debt, however, Ismail was forced by his English and French creditors to let them oversee his

FIG. 153. GORDON COLLEGE, KHARTUM

This college, named for their murdered general, was erected by the British to teach the sons of their former enemies the arts of civilization. On the campus is a mosque, for the British do not interfere with the religion of these Sudanese tribesmen

financial administration. This foreign intervention aroused discontent in Egypt, and the natives revolted in 1882, demanding "Egypt for the Egyptians." Inasmuch as France declined to join in suppressing the rebellion, England undertook it alone, and after putting down the uprising assumed a temporary occupation of the country and the supervision of the army and finances of Egypt. The British continued their "temporary" occupation, until shortly after the opening of the war of 1914, when Britain assumed a permanent protectorate over Egypt, which was declared independent of Turkey.[1]

[1] The khedive, remaining loyal to the Turks, was dethroned, the title abolished, and the new ruler acclaimed as sultan.

The Mahdi and the death of Gordon

Shortly after the British conquest of Egypt, a revolt arose in the Sudan, under the leadership of Mohammed Ahmed, who claimed to be the Messiah, and found great numbers of fanatical followers who called him El Mahdi, "the leader."[1] General Gordon was in charge of the British garrison at Khartum. Here he was besieged by the followers of the Mahdi in 1885, and after a memorable defense fell a victim to their fury, thus adding a tragic page to the military history of the British empire. This disaster was avenged twelve years later, when in 1897–1898 the Sudan was reconquered and the city of Khartum was taken by the British under General Kitchener.

Results of the British occupation of Egypt

During the occupation of Egypt by the British the progress of the country has been unquestioned; industry and commerce are growing steadily, public works have been constructed, and financial order has been reëstablished under the supervision of the British agent, whose word is law. A large dam has been built across the Nile at Assuan to control the floods, and also to increase greatly the fertility of the valley. There is strict honesty in the government, and, in spite of some racial irritation against the European "unbelievers" who are running the country, Egypt has never, in all its long history, been so prosperous.

Section 107. Decline of the Spanish World Empire; Portugal

Decline of Spain as a colonial power

In striking contrast to the colonial expansion of the other powers of Europe stand the two which, in the era of discovery, led them all in enterprise and achievement — Spain and Portugal. Spain, who could once boast that the sun never set on her empire, was already in decline from the days of Philip II. After losing her colonies on the American continents in the early nineteenth century,[2] she made no compensating gains in other parts of the world, and at the close of the nineteenth century received the final blow in a war with the United States.

[1] See *Readings*, Vol. II, pp. 456 ff.

[2] See above, pp. 350 ff.

The Spanish-American War, 1898

The cause of this war was the chronic disturbance which existed in Cuba under Spanish government and which led the United States to decide upon the expulsion of Spain from the western hemisphere. In 1895 the last of many Cuban insurrections against Spain broke out, and sympathy was immediately manifested in the United States. Both political parties during the presidential campaign of 1896 declared in favor of the Cubans, and with the inauguration of McKinley a policy of intervention was adopted. The American government demanded the recall of General Weyler — whose cruelty had become notorious — and a reform in the treatment of prisoners of war. In February, 1898, the battleship *Maine* was mysteriously blown up in the harbor of Havana, where it had been sent in American interests. Although the cause of this disaster could not be discovered, the United States, maintaining that the conditions in Cuba were intolerable, declared war on Spain in April.

Spain loses her remaining colonies

The war was brief, for the American forces were everywhere victorious. Cuba and Porto Rico were lost to Spain, and by the capture of the city of Manila in May, the Philippine Islands also fell to the United States. Peace was reëstablished in August, and representatives were shortly sent to Paris to arrange the final terms. Cuba was declared independent; Porto Rico, with the adjoining islands of Vieques and Culebra, and the Philippines were ceded to the United States.[1] The following year the Caroline and Pelew islands were transferred to Germany, and thus the territory of Spain was reduced to the Spanish peninsula, the Balearic and Canary islands, and her small holdings in Africa.

By the Spanish-American War, therefore, Spain lost its colonial empire and the United States began its career as a world power.

The possessions of Portugal

As for Portugal, which had lost its greatest possession, Brazil, about the same time as Spain had lost its South American colonies, it still retains considerable stretches of

[1] Spain also ceded to the United States the island of Guam in the Ladrone archipelago.

Africa, as a glance at the map will show, but its holdings in Asia are reduced to the posts of Macao in China, Goa in India, and two small islands. In foreign affairs it is closely allied with England.

Assassination of King Carlos

The chief event in recent Portuguese history, however, took place at home. The attempt of the king, Carlos I, to establish a dictatorship and squander the revenues without accountability, raised up a party determined upon his overthrow, and on February 1, 1908, King Carlos and the Crown Prince, while riding in the streets of Lisbon, were assassinated. The late king's eighteen-year-old son was at once proclaimed as Manuel II, but he found that he had received a troublesome heritage. The little realm was disturbed by party dissensions; finances were in a bad way; workingmen were discontented; the radicals were waging war against the clergy and the monks; and the republicans daily gained in strength in spite of the promises of reform made by the young ruler.

The establishment of the Portuguese republic, 1910

Early in October a revolt broke out at the capital. After some serious street fighting and the bombardment of the royal palace, the king fled to England, protesting that his hasty flight did not mean abdication. The republicans at once set up a provisional government and began the expulsion of the monks and nuns and the confiscation of their property.[1] In May, 1911, elections were held for a constitutional convention, which met in June. This convention drafted a constitution providing for a legislative body of two chambers, one elected directly by universal manhood suffrage and the other indirectly by the municipalities; for a president to be elected for four years by the legislature; and for a ministry responsible to parliament.

Troublesome times for the new republic

The government under the new constitution began the difficult task of conciliating the factions which the revolution had left behind. The Catholic priests and bishops were offered pensions, but they declined to receive them. The Pope issued

[1] Monastic establishments were suppressed in 1834, and the new republic reënforced the old law.

an encyclical condemning the anti-clerical measures of the republic, which granted toleration to all religions; and the republic replied by confiscating the government securities held by the clergy to the amount of $25,000,000. The finances of the government have been in critical shape; there has been some unrest among the workingmen of the industrial centers; but the young republic seems to have gained in stability in spite of the continued efforts of the monarchists to overturn it.

QUESTIONS

SECTION 100. Contrast the commercial position of Great Britain in 1815 with that of the other nations of Europe and the United States. Describe the earliest attempts at steam navigation. Give a brief account of the construction of the two great interoceanic canals. Outline the history of railroad development in Europe, Asia, and Africa.

Sketch the history of each of the following: the post; the telephone; the telegraph; the cable. What is meant by imperialism? Describe the work of missionaries. What is the connection between the Industrial Revolution and imperialism?

SECTION 101. What were the relations between China and Europe prior to the nineteenth century? Show on a map the ports opened to Western commerce as a result of the Opium War of 1840, and the war waged by England and France against China in 1858.

SECTION 102. Outline the early history of Japan through the twelfth century. Describe the relations of Japan with Europe in the sixteenth and seventeenth centuries. Give a brief account of the relations of the United States and Japan in 1853.

Why did Great Britain bombard certain of the Japanese ports in 1863–1864? Describe the revolution which took place in Japan after the accession of the Mikado Mutsuhito. What was the effect of the Industrial Revolution on the form of government of Japan?

SECTION 103. What gave rise to the war between China and Japan in 1894–1895? Give the terms of the Treaty of Shimonoseki. What changes were made in this treaty as a result of the intervention of Russia, France, and Germany? What did Russia gain as a result of the compromise effected? In what way and when did Germany get possession of territory in the Shantung peninsula?

What compensation did Russia seek in 1898? What was the importance of this acquisition to Russia? How did Great Britain secure possession of Weihaiwei? What arrangement was made by Great Britain and Japan in 1902? Draw a map of the east coast of Asia and on it show the territory leased to foreigners by China.

SECTION 104. What led to the Boxer uprising? Describe the Peking insurrection and the intervention of the powers to restore order.

SECTION 105. Describe the circumstances which led to the Russo-Japanese War. Outline the history of the war and give the terms of the Treaty of Portsmouth. Give a short account of the history of China since 1912.

SECTION 106. Outline the history of Africa to 1815. Describe the situation in Africa in the year 1815. What progress in the opening up of Africa during the first half of the nineteenth century was made by France and England? Indicate on a map the parts of Africa explored by Livingstone and Stanley.

Describe the development of the Belgian Congo and discuss the problems involved. What has England had to do with the French occupation of Morocco? Briefly sketch the history of Egypt to the middle of the nineteenth century. In what way did Great Britain gain a foothold in Egypt?

What was the position of Great Britain in Egypt from 1882 to 1914? What has been Great Britain's position in Egypt since 1914? Describe the revolt in the Sudan in 1885 and the conquest of the territory in 1897–1898. What are the results of the British occupation of Egypt?

SECTION 107. Review the story of Spain in the nineteenth century. How did it lose its colonies? What colonial possessions has Portugal? Sketch conditions in Portugal during the last ten years.

CHAPTER XXVI

THE TWENTIETH CENTURY IN EUROPE, PRIOR TO THE GREAT WAR

SECTION 108. REVIEW OF THE PREVIOUS CHAPTERS

Review of the preceding chapters

In the preceding twenty chapters we have tried to bridge the gap which separates the Europe of Louis XIV from the world of to-day. We have seen how, in the eighteenth century, the European monarchs light-heartedly made war upon one another in the hope of adding a bit of territory to their realms, or of seating a relative or friend on a vacant throne. Such enterprises were encouraged by the division of Germany and Italy into small states which could be used as counters in this royal game of war and diplomacy. But nevertheless in the eighteenth century European history was already broadening out. The whole eastern half of the continent was brought into relation with the West by Peter the Great and Catherine, and merchants and traders were forcing the problem of colonial expansion upon their several governments. England succeeded in driving France from India and America and in laying the foundation of that empire, unprecedented in extent, over which she rules to-day. Portugal and the Netherlands, once so conspicuous upon the seas, had lost their importance, and the grasp of Spain upon the New World was relaxing.

We next considered the condition of the people over whom the monarchs of the eighteenth century reigned — the serfs, the townspeople with their guilds, the nobility, the clergy, and the religious orders. We noted the unlimited authority of the kings and the extraordinary prerogatives and privileges enjoyed by the Roman Catholic clergy. The origin of the Anglican Church and of the many Protestant sects in England was explained. We next showed how the growing interest in natural science served to wean men from their reverence for the past and to open up vistas of progress; how the French philosophers, Voltaire, Diderot, Rousseau, and many others, attacked existing institutions, and how the so-called enlightened despots who listened to them undertook a few timid reforms, mainly with a view of increasing their own power. But when at last, in 1789, the king of France was forced to call together representatives of his people to help him fill an empty treasury, they seized the opportunity to limit his powers, abolish the old abuses, and proclaim a program of reform which was destined to be accepted in turn by all the European nations.

The wars which began in 1792 led to the establishment of a temporary republic in France, but a military genius, the like of which the world had never before seen, soon brought not only France but a great part of western Europe under his control. He found it to his interest to introduce many of the reforms of the French Revolution in the countries which he conquered and, by his partial consolidation of Germany and the consequent extinction of the Holy Roman Empire, he prepared the way for the creation later of one of the most powerful European states of recent times.

Since the Congress of Vienna, which readjusted the map of Europe after Napoleon's downfall, a number of very important changes have occurred. Both Germany and Italy have been consolidated and have taken their places among the great powers. The Turk has been steadily pushed back, and a group of states unknown in the eighteenth century has come into existence in the Balkan peninsula. Everywhere the monarchs have lost their former absolute powers and have more or less gracefully submitted to the limitations imposed by a constitution. Even the Tsar, while still calling himself "Autocrat of all the Russias," had to promise to submit new laws and the provisions of his yearly budget to a parliament, upon which he and his police, however, kept a very sharp eye.

Alongside these important changes an Industrial Revolution has been in progress, the influence of which upon the lives of the people at large has been incalculably greater than all that armies and legislative assemblies have accomplished. It has not only given rise to the most serious problems which face Europe to-day but has heralded an imperialism which carries European civilization through all the world. During the latter half of the nineteenth century the European powers, especially England, France, Germany, and Russia, have been busy opening up the vast Chinese Empire and other Asiatic countries to European influences, and in this way the whole continent of Asia has, in a certain sense, been drawn into the current of European history. Africa, the borders alone of which were known in 1850, has, during the past fifty years, been explored and apportioned out among the European powers. It will inevitably continue for many years to be completely dominated by them. These are perhaps the most striking features of our study of the past two hundred years.

It remains for us to see what Europe itself was like in the opening years of the twentieth century, to examine how it took over the heritage of the past and what further contributions it offered to civilization.

Section 109. The Social Revolution in England, 1906–1914

England long conservative

At the close of the nineteenth century England was, to all appearances, as conservative as any nation in western Europe. The enthusiasm for the extension of the suffrage and for the reform of ancient abuses, which had stirred the country for a hundred years, seemed to have died away. Contentment with the existing order, and interest in great imperial enterprises in South Africa and other parts of the world, characterized English politics. During the twenty years from 1886 to 1906 (except for a short period in 1892–1895) the Conservative party was in control of the House of Commons and the government. Liberalism appeared to be dead, and the agitation of the Socialists apparently made no impression on the workingmen.

But the general election of 1906 brought a startling change. The Conservatives were completely defeated by the Liberals, and no less than fifty labor representatives were elected to Parliament. Several of these were avowed Socialists.[1] In the next ten years the Liberals, with their radical and laborite colleagues, made such sweeping reforms as to amount to a real revolution in British society and politics.

Social reform now the issue in England

The change in English sentiment was clearly expressed by a Liberal, Mr. Winston Churchill, in a political speech at Nottingham, on January 30, 1909: "The main aspirations of the British people are at the present time social rather than political. They see around them on every side, and almost every day, spectacles of confusion and misery which they cannot reconcile with any conception of humanity or justice. They see that there are in the modern state a score of misfortunes that can happen to a man without his being at fault in any way. They see, on the other hand, the mighty power of science, backed by wealth and power, to introduce order, to provide safeguards, to prevent accidents, or at least mitigate their consequences. They know that this country is the richest in the world; and in my sincere judgment the British democracy will not give their hearts to any party that is not able and willing to set up that larger, fuller, more elaborate, more thorough

1 Socialism made very little progress in Britain during the nineteenth century. In 1883 a Social Democratic Federation had been formed to promote the teachings of Marx, but it had little success. The Independent Labor party appeared in 1893, under the leadership of Keir Hardie, a miner who was elected to Parliament. It was moderately socialistic and grew slowly. The Fabian Society, of which Sidney and Beatrice Webb, G. B. Shaw, and H. G. Wells have been members, believes in reaching the socialists' goal by going slowly (like the old Roman general, Fabius, who gained his end by going slowly). So it has advocated municipal or national ownership of land and industrial capital. But the Fabians do not form a political party. It was not until the trade-unions "entered politics" in 1905, coöperating with the Independent Labor party, that anything much was accomplished.

social organization, without which our country and its people will inevitably sink through sorrow to disaster and our name and fame fade upon the pages of history."

Recent English labor laws

In this spirit the Liberal government began, shortly after its accession to power in 1906, a series of laws designed to mitigate, at least, if not to abolish, the evils of poverty, sweating, unemployment, and industrial accidents. The provisions of the Workmen's Compensation Act of 1897 were extended to agricultural laborers and domestic servants. Under this law employers in the industries covered are required to pay compensation to workmen injured in their employ, except when the accident is due to the "serious and willful misconduct of the injured workman himself." At the same time (1906) a law was passed exempting the funds of trade-unions from the liability of being attached for damages caused by their officials in strikes and industrial conflicts generally. Two years later (1908) Parliament passed an act providing that, subject to certain incidental reservations, "a workman shall not be below ground in a mine for the purpose of his work and of going to and from his work, for more than eight hours during any consecutive twenty-fours hours."

Booth's survey of London poverty

Measures for the benefit of trade-unionists, miners, and injured workmen, however important they may be, do not solve the problem of poverty, due to low wages, uncertain employment, illness, and causes other than those which may be ascribed to individual faults. Undoubtedly poverty on a large scale has been one of the inevitable accompaniments of the Industrial Revolution, and in England the amount of depressing poverty is only too apparent. Several years ago Mr. Charles Booth, a wealthy shipowner, feeling that there was no accurate information available in regard to the condition of the working people of London, undertook a house-to-house canvass at his own expense. With a large corps of helpers he set about ascertaining the "numerical relations which poverty, misery, and depravity bear to regular earnings and comparative comfort," and published, as the result of his survey, *The Life and Labor of the People of London*, in sixteen volumes. In the district of East London, embracing a population of nearly a million, he found that more than one third of the people belonged to families with incomes of a guinea (about $5.15) or less a week; that forty-two per cent of the families earned from about $5.50 to $7.50 a week; and that only about thirteen per cent had more than $7.50 a week to live on. His studies further revealed terrible overcrowding in squalid tenements which were badly lighted, poorly equipped with water and sanitary arrangements, and conducive to disease. He reached the startling conclusion that throughout the vast city of London nearly one third of the people were in poverty; that is, lived on wages too low to provide the necessaries for a decent physical existence, to say nothing of comforts or luxuries.

Indications that the poverty in London is not exceptional

It might at first sight seem that the poverty of London is exceptionally great, but Mr. Rowntree, in an equally careful survey, proved that in the city of York, with its population of less than eighty thousand inhabitants, toward one third of the people are also, as in London, in dire poverty.[1] He showed, too, that the physical development of the children, the prevalence of disease, and the death rate corresponded with the rate of wages; in short, that health, happiness, and well-being increased as wages increased. There is reason to believe that conditions are essentially the same in many other modern cities, not only in England but throughout the world, although this has not as yet been demonstrated by scientific investigations.

Possibility of abolishing poverty

Formerly it was generally assumed that poverty was inevitable and that little could be done to remedy it, since there was not enough wealth in any given community to make everybody comfortable; but the progress of practical inventions and of scientific discovery has roused the hope in the minds of many that if industries were reorganized in a way to avoid waste and to promote efficiency, if the idle were set to work and

[1] See *Readings*, Vol. II, pp. 487 f.

precautions taken to distribute the wealth in such a way that a few could not, as they can now, appropriate vast fortunes, there might sometime be enough for all who were willing to do their part, so that all could live in comfort and bring up their children in healthful surroundings, thus greatly reducing vice and disease. As the kindly Pope Leo XIII well said, "There can be no question that some remedy must be found, and that quickly, for the misery and wretchedness which press so heavily at this moment on a large majority of the very poor."

The English government declares war on poverty

The English government boldly grappled with the situation and proceeded to "make war on poverty" a part of its official program. In 1908 it passed an old-age pension law, the leading provisions of which follow: The recipient of a government pension must be seventy years of age, a British subject, neither a pauper nor in receipt of a private income of more than $150 (£31 10 s.). Criminals and those who have not honestly worked for their self-support are debarred. The maximum pension allowed is about $1.25 per week (5 s.) to those having incomes not exceeding about $100 (£21 4 s.) a year.

Government employment bureaus

To help in reducing the large amount of unemployment, Parliament passed an act in 1909 authorizing the establishment of labor exchanges throughout the country to collect information as to employers requiring working people and as to laborers seeking employment. Provisions were also made whereby the government may advance loans to laborers to pay their traveling expenses to the places where employment may be found for them by the labor exchanges.

Regulation of wages in "sweated" trades

Parliament has sought to raise the level of wages in some industries which do not pay the employees enough to uphold a fairly decent standard of life. By an act passed in 1909, provision is made for the establishment of trade boards in certain of the "sweated" trades, such as tailoring, machine lace-making, and box-making industries, or any other trade which may fall below decent standards of wages or conditions of labor. These trade boards consist of representatives of the working people and of the employers and also persons appointed by the government, and are empowered to fix minimum rates of wages for time work and general minimum rates for piece work in their respective trades. Agreements for wages lower than those fixed by the board are forbidden, and employers paying under the minimum are liable to heavy fines.

The House of Lords blocks reform

Meanwhile the opposition to these sweeping reforms was becoming intense among the Conservatives. As they were in a minority in the House of Commons, however, they were unable to do more than to protest that the country was going to ruin and that the upper and middle classes would be submerged by the rising power of democracy. The Conservatives, however, were firmly intrenched in the House of Lords, where they had a large majority, and there they began to take up arms against measures which were, in their opinion, nothing short of revolutionary. In December, 1906, the Lords mutilated a bill which the Commons had passed for the support of a system of national, free secular schools — like those of America — at a disadvantage to those of the Established Church, and a few days later they threw out a plural-voting bill abolishing the ancient practice of allowing a man to vote in all counties in which he had the requisite property to entitle him to the ballot. Such action angered the Commons, which claimed that the principles of representative government were violated by it.

The "revolutionary" budget of 1909

The real clash between the Lords and Commons came in 1909 over the budget — that is, over the taxes which the Liberals proposed to lay and the expenses they proposed to incur. In April of that year, Mr. Lloyd George, Chancellor of the Exchequer in Mr. Asquith's government, laid before the House of Commons a scheme of taxation which stirred up a veritable hornets' nest. In this "revolutionary budget" he proposed a high tax on automobiles, a heavy income tax with a special additional tax on incomes over £5000, — heavier on unearned than on earned incomes, — and an inheritance tax on a new scale, varying according to the amount of the inheritance up to fifteen per cent of estates over £1,000,000. He also proposed a new land tax, distinguishing sharply between landowners who actually worked their lands and the owners of mineral lands and city lots who exacted royalties and made large profits from growth in land values. The budget also included a twenty per cent tax on unearned values in land, payable on its sale or transfer, so that any one who sold property at a profit would have to pay a good share of the gain to the public treasury. The chancellor also proposed a special tax on undeveloped and on mineral lands.

A budget for war on poverty

These special taxes, in addition to the other taxes, made a heavy budget; but the chancellor defended it on the ground that it was a war budget for "waging implacable war against poverty." He concluded his opening speech in defense of his policy by expressing the hope "that great advance will be made during this generation toward the time when poverty with its wretchedness and squalor will be as remote from the people of this country as the wolves which once infested the forests."

The Conservatives attack the budget

The budget was at once hotly attacked by the Conservatives as socialistic and revolutionary. They claimed that the distinction between "earned" and "unearned" incomes was an unwarranted and invidious attack on the rights of property. "If a man," asked one, "is to be more heavily taxed on an income that he has not earned than on an earned income, on the ground that he does not have the same absolute right to both incomes, why may not the government advance step by step until it takes away all unearned incomes on the theory that their possessors have no right to them at all?" Some of the more conservative defenders of the budget shrank from answering this question, and contented themselves by replying that it was a matter of degree, not of fundamental principles. Other supporters of the budget frankly declared that a man's right to his property depended upon the way in which he got it.

Speaking on this point, Mr. Winston Churchill said: "Formerly the question of the taxgatherer was, 'How much have you got?' . . . Now a new question has arisen. We do not only ask to-day, 'How much have you got?' we also ask, 'How did you get it? Did you earn it by yourself, or has it been left to you by others? Was it gained by processes which are in

A new question in taxation

FIG. 154. DAVID LLOYD GEORGE

The son of a Welsh school-teacher, Mr. Lloyd George knew himself the meaning of that poverty he has tried to lessen in Britain. Studying law he entered politics, and was elected to Parliament at the age of twenty-seven. He bitterly opposed the Boer War, and was noted as a fearless radical, as well as the leader of Welsh nationalism. Becoming a cabinet minister when the Liberals came to power in 1905, he continued his radical attacks on "property" but combined with them much far-seeing statesmanship. It was mainly due to him that England went so far in the "war against poverty." When the great war of 1914 came Lloyd George was the one whose energy and skill did most to awaken England to her danger and to prepare to meet it

themselves beneficial to the community in general, or was it gained by processes which have done no good to anyone, but only harm? Was it gained by the enterprise and capacity necessary to found a business, or merely by squeezing and bleeding the owner and founder of the business? Was it gained by supplying the capital which industry needs, or by denying, except at extortionate price, the land which industry requires? Was it derived by active reproductive processes, or merely by squatting on some piece of necessary land till enterprise and labor, national interests and municipal interests, had to buy you out at fifty times the agricultural value? Was it gained by opening new minerals to the service of man, or by drawing a mining royalty from the toil and adventure of others? . . . How did you get it?' That is the new question which has been postulated, and which is vibrating in penetrating repetition through the land."

The Lords reject the budget

The arguments in favor of the budget convinced the House of Commons, and it was carried by a handsome majority. In the House of Lords, however, it was defeated by a vote of 350 to 75.

The Commons protest

The Liberals immediately took up the gage thus thrown down. On December 2, Mr. Asquith moved in the House of Commons a resolution "That the action of the House of Lords in refusing to pass into law the financial provision made by the House for the services of the year is a breach of the Constitution and a usurpation of the rights of the House of Commons." This resolution was carried by a vote of 349 to 134, showing that there was little hope for a compromise on the issue. Then, to test the feeling of the country upon the matter, a new election was held, January, 1910.

The campaign for the election of January, 1910

The election campaign was unusually bitter, being marked by open violence in some places. The Socialists, radicals, and Irish demanded the speedy abolition of the House of Lords, but the moderate Liberals were content to lessen its power. The election still gave the Liberals a majority, although they lost almost one hundred seats. Their majority was so small, however, that for working purposes they had to cultivate friendly relations with the Labor and Irish members.

The Lords pass the budget

When Parliament met, the Lords, threatened with loss of their powers, passed the obnoxious budget. But the Liberals were determined, none the less, to render that ancient seat of privilege harmless to thwart the will of the Commons in future.

The election (December, 1910) on the House of Lords' issue

In the midst of this constitutional crisis, King Edward VII died (May 6, 1910), and a sort of truce was made between the leaders. This was followed by conferences between the representatives of the Liberals and Conservatives, at which attempts were made to arrive at a compromise. These efforts failed, and at the opening of Parliament in November it was found that the deadlock was as fast as ever. Thereupon the Liberals dissolved Parliament and appealed to the country in a new election that closed on December 19, 1910. The result of this campaign was as unsatisfactory as that of the preceding January, for the Liberals only made slight gains in spite of a hard fight.

The House of Lords conquered

Shortly after the opening of the new Parliament in February, 1911, a bill designed to check the exercise of the "veto" power by the Lords was introduced in Commons and passed by a good round majority. The measure was then sent to the House of Lords, and Mr. Asquith announced that he had received the consent of King George V to create enough new peers to insure its passage in case the Conservative opponents were able to defeat it. Thus intimidated, the upper house, on August 18, 1911, passed the Parliament Act, or the Lords' Veto Bill as it was called, the leading provisions of which follow.

The Lords' Veto Bill

If any money bill — that is, a bill relative to raising taxes and making appropriations — is passed by Commons and sent up to the Lords at least one month before the end of a session, and is not passed by the Lords within one month without amendment, the bill may be presented to the king for his signature and, on being approved, becomes a law notwithstanding the fact that the Lords have not consented to it. Any public bill (other than a money bill, or a bill changing the provision for a maximum term of five years for a parliament), passed by the House of Commons at three successive sessions and rejected by the Lords at each of the three sessions, may be presented to the king and, on receiving his approval, will become a law without the consent of the Lords — provided that two years have elapsed between the date of the second reading of the bill in the Commons in the first of those sessions and the date on which it passes the Commons in the third of those sessions. The veto bill also fixed five years instead of seven years as the time which any parliament may last. That is, under the law of August 18, a new parliamentary election must be held at least every five years, although of course a dissolution may be ordered at any time by the cabinet. Provision was also made in 1911 to pay members of the House of Commons £400 a year. Thus one more demand of the Chartists was realized.

National insurance against ill health and unemployment

With the House of Lords curbed, the Liberal government proceeded with further reforms. The most comprehensive of all recent measures is the National Insurance Act of 1911, which went into effect in July, 1912. One part of this law requires the compulsory insurance of nearly all employees (except those not engaged in manual labor and enjoying an income of more than £160 a year) against ill health of every kind. The insured persons, the employers, and the government are all contributors to the fund. Among the benefits for the insured are medical treatment and attendance, sanatorium treatment for tuberculosis, payments during sickness, disablement allowances, and the payment of 30s. to each mother on the birth of a child. A second portion of the act requires employers and employees in certain trades to contribute a small sum weekly to a fund for insurance against unemployment, and provides government assistance as well.

Great Britain finally a democracy in politics though retaining social aristocracy

By these measures we can see that political democracy has at last been achieved in Great Britain. The British are still attached to their monarch, and they retain a genuine respect for the nobility in social life. But political power has passed into the hands of the great majority, who are using it with but slight regard for the feelings or pockets of the aristocracy. Even the so-called upper classes accept this transformation of British politics as a settled fact, and have confined their efforts to preventing further change. But the program of social legislation in the hands of Asquith and Lloyd George has been as progressive as ever, down to the outbreak of the great war of 1914.[1] Indeed, the Liberal government has been charged by the Conservatives with having been so absorbed with these problems of social reform at home — or, as they call it, with confiscating their property — as to have been blind to the danger of war, until it suddenly burst upon an unprepared country. This charge seems hardly fair, however, for not only had Sir Edward Grey, the foreign minister, been energetic, as we shall see in the next chapter, in keeping on terms of close friendship with France and arranging a friendly understanding with Russia, but the minister in charge of naval defense kept the British fleet, the real protector of England's liberty, ready for immediate action at any time.

Local reforms; municipal ownership of public utilities

Parallel with these measures of Parliament for the nation as a whole, there has gone on a movement for civic betterment. Local self-government for the cities as well as for the country districts was reorganized in 1835, when representative bodies replaced the old authorities whose offices had lasted down from the Middle Ages. In recent years there has been much increase in municipal enterprise and ownership of public utilities. Cities, like Manchester and Birmingham, as well as London, have undertaken great public works. Most of them own their street railways as well as gas and electric-light plants and experiments in the development of model suburbs or workmen's houses, and are proud of the success of their enterprises. There is still much poverty in Britain, and until the war of 1914 little had been done to check the evil of intemperance, but the nation has been awakened to new possibilities.

1 Among Lloyd George's further plans was a heavy tax on the land, arranged so as to hit the great landowners, mainly nobles, very hard, and so perhaps bring back under cultivation the vast parks which have formed many of the beauty spots of England but do not help feed the people nor pay much to the State. The war taxes since 1914 promise to accomplish this in any case.

Prosperity in Great Britain

Finally, in spite of the prophecies, by conservative people, of financial disaster if the country were to meet the burden of these taxes for social regeneration, Great Britain kept steadily increasing in prosperity. Its commerce, just before the war, reached stupendous figures, the imports into the United Kingdom in 1913 being worth over three and a half billion dollars and the exports about three billion. Industries have prospered in like manner. The total output of the main textile industries, in which, it will be recalled, the Industrial Revolution largely began, has grown in a century from slightly over a hundred million to almost a billion dollars a year, and in 1913 was supporting over five million people.

Section 110. Recent History in Germany

Germany becomes a world menace

The Great War which opened in 1914 has completely altered the attitude of the rest of the world toward Germany. No one can view the history of that country in the same way that he did before the Prussian military party precipitated the terrific conflict which is described in a later chapter. The chief interest of Germany's development after the dismissal of Bismarck in 1890 is likely to lie hereafter in the manner in which her government reached a degree of power and insolence which tempted them to defy the world, and which made her such an international menace that even our great republic, separated from her by the broad Atlantic, was forced finally to array its whole strength against her.

German prosperity

The iron and steel industries

During the reign of William II, Germany grew astonishingly in wealth as well as in population. The foundations for this prosperity lay partly in the fact that the country had been unified politically into an empire. But almost as important has been the development of German manufactures, which in its turn has largely depended upon the growth of the great iron and steel industries that center in western Prussia, along the Rhine, and in Saxony. Strangely enough, it was a young

English engineer, Mr. Sidney G. Thomas, who invented in 1878 the process upon which much of this vast industry and, therefore, also, much of the might of modern Germany rests. The iron ore of Germany, particularly that in the great deposits along the Moselle River, in Lorraine, which was seized by Germany in 1871, contained a good deal of phosphorus, and the system of making steel then most in use, the Bessemer system, did not convert this into steel satisfactorily. Hence England, whose iron industry did not suffer from the handicap of too much phosphorus in the ore, had developed great steel works much more successfully than Germany could. Mr. Thomas solved the problem, however, and his invention, introduced in the cities along the Rhine, enabled Germany ultimately to surpass the English, whose supply is more limited. At the beginning of the war Germany stood next to the United States in the output of her iron industries.

Growth of Germany in numbers and wealth

Parallel with the increase in wealth has come an increase in population. The population in 1870 was about 40,000,000; in 1914 it was almost 68,000,000, — a larger increase than was shown in any other country in western Europe. Vast new cities therefore grew up; old ones did away with their narrow streets, destroyed their slums, and spread out along miles of wide boulevards as new as those of Chicago.

Municipal socialism in Germany

A number of municipalities, like Berlin, Munich, Leipzig, and Hanover, have purchased enormous areas of land so as to gain the profit arising from the increase in value and make it easier to prevent congestion. Several cities are laid out into zones, and the building in each zone is restricted by law, to stop overcrowding. Some of the more progressive towns own their street-car lines, gas works, electric-light plants, and slaughter-houses, manage theaters, operate pawnshops, build houses for workingmen, and attempt to plan their growth in such a way as to obviate the hideous and unsanitary features which have too often been supposed to be quite unavoidable in factory towns.

The German business men controlled by the State

Germany's trade increased surprisingly. German steamship lines, heavily subsidized by the government, developed rapidly, and their vessels were soon sailing on every sea. The farmers and manufacturers flourished owing to the new markets throughout the world opened by the new German merchant marine. Workmen stopped emigrating to the United States

FIG. 155. BRIDGE ACROSS THE RHINE AT MAINZ

This long bridge spans the Rhine where, over nineteen hundred years before, Julius Cæsar built a bridge to subdue the barbarian Germans of that day. Wooden stakes and iron spikes of Cæsar's bridge are kept in the museum at Mainz

and South America because times were good everywhere in Germany and it was easy to get enough to do at home.

But Germany did not play the game fairly. Individual Englishmen and individual English companies had built up England's world commerce. But German business men were generally backed by the German government, which put its power and money at their disposal. So they did not work simply for themselves, but the State saw to it that they worked for the aggrandizement of the German government.

Ugly spirit of German competition

From a relatively poor country in 1871 Germany became rich and insolent. Commercial spies were everywhere on the alert to gain some advantage for *Germans as Germans.* Instead of acting in a spirit of decent competition they formed a sort of gigantic conspiracy utterly regardless of the rights of others. Although the Germans were freely received by all other nations, including England and France, they abused the hospitality granted them by their neighbors. They judged others by themselves. They imagined that they were surrounded on all sides by an "iron ring" of enemies. When by peaceful means they were becoming a highly important commercial nation they nevertheless began to denounce England as a pirate and to talk of making "a place in the sun" for themselves by crushing her as their chief enemy.

How the unexpected happened

Unfortunately the other nations did not take this German talk seriously. Few imagined that the old Prussian spirit of the Great Elector, Frederick the Great, and Bismarck and the silly talk of Fichte and other German philosophers, historians, and economists about German superiority would take the form of an armed attempt to put the theories into practice. Nevertheless this did happen. The German conception of the State is quite different from that which prevails in democratic countries. Lincoln once defined democracy as "the government of the people, by the people, for the people." But in Germany the people are taught by their officials that the State is something more precious than the interests of all those who compose it. And it is the duty of the people not to control the State in their own interests but to obey the government officials and believe what the government tells them. There has been no large liberal party in Germany to oppose ancient Prussian despotism and militarism. The Social Democrats, it is true, have often talked against autocracy and militarism and the Kaiser's nonsense about his partnership with God. But few of them were proof against the war spirit when the Kaiser and his advisers precipitated the great conflict in 1914.

The Germans taught to revere the State and its officials

Constant strengthening of the German army

Germany's astonishing growth in wealth and commercial importance produced in some classes a spirit of arrogant self-confidence. Her military leaders fostered pride in her "invincible" army; they recalled the victories of the past, especially those of 1866 and 1870–1871, and suggested that "the next war" might give her further opportunities for subduing her jealous neighbors and enhancing her power and glory. The Reichstag was induced in 1913 to grant money to increase the army in time of peace. There was no intermission in warlike preparations. Great attention was given to the manufacture of improved artillery and the invention of high explosives, to the development of gigantic dirigible balloons (Zeppelins), and to the opening possibilities of undersea warfare. When the Germans considered that they possessed an army of four million men, more carefully trained and more fully and ingeniously equipped than those of any other State, and that they had, besides, six million men who could be summoned in case of war to fill gaps or guard the fatherland, it seemed impossible that they could suffer defeat, no matter who should attack them.

The German navy

But they were not satisfied with their superior army; they must have a powerful navy as well,—one that would vie with the sea power of Germany's chief rival, Great Britain. Accordingly, urged on by the Kaiser, Germany began in 1898 to construct a huge modern navy. She added cruiser to cruiser and dreadnaught to dreadnaught, until she was second only to England in the size and equipment of her marine. She has two stretches of seacoast, separated by the Danish peninsula. By means of a canal (opened in 1895) between her war port of Kiel and the mouth of the Elbe River she connected her coasts from the Dutch to the Russian boundary, and her ships passed easily back and forth between the Baltic and the North Sea. But when the war really came England promptly blockaded Germany's ports on the North Sea, and except for one sally with doubtful results a great part of the German navy remained during the entire war peacefully ensconced in her own ports.

The Prussian crown prince certainly expressed the views of many German leaders and writers when he said, in 1913: "Our country is obliged more than any other country to place all its confidence in its good weapons. Set in the center of Europe, it is badly protected by its unfavorable geographic frontiers, and is regarded by many nations without affection. Upon the German Empire, therefore, is imposed more emphatically than upon any other people of the earth the sacred duty of watching carefully that its army and its navy be always prepared to meet any attack from the outside. It is only by reliance upon our brave sword that we shall be able to maintain that place in the sun which belongs to us, and which the world does not seem very willing to accord us."

Views of the Prussian crown prince

But to many Germans the "safety" and "defense" of the fatherland means the right to expand in various ways at the expense of its neighbors. Other countries must be weakened, especially England, before Germany is really safe. She must have European dependencies as well as colonial possessions in Africa, Asia, and South America. It would be quite impossible here to set down all the schemes of national aggrandizement suggested by German writers during the past twenty years.[1] Before the war little attention was paid to these seemingly wild projects. As President Wilson said in June, 1917, most people "regarded what German professors expounded in their classrooms, and German writers set forth to the world . . ., as the dream of minds detached from practical affairs, as preposterous private conceptions of German destiny." But since the opening of the war and Germany's occupation of Belgium, northern France, and large portions of Russia, it has been necessary to take account of that fierce party in Germany which seems willing to cast aside every obligation of international law and humanity in order to make Germany a "world power."

German idea of the safety and defense of the fatherland

1 The United States government has published for free distribution an invaluable selection of extracts from German writers, called *Conquest and Kultur; Aims of the Germans in their Own Words.*

German application of Darwin's theory

Many Germans hold that Darwin's idea that the fittest survive in the constant struggle for existence should be applied to modern States. War, or its equivalent, they argue, has always been nature's way of eliminating the weak and inferior and leaving the field to the strong and resourceful. But the German might be reluctant to welcome war if he was not assured by his philosophers, clergymen, and government leaders that his race is superior to all others and his civilization unequaled elsewhere. German victories in the past, German science and art and learning, all combine to prove to the German's satisfaction that his people are undoubtedly the "fittest." They should therefore welcome war, not only because they think that they are sure to win but because it is their natural duty and prerogative, as they assume, to spread their civilization (*Kultur*) among the inferior peoples about them.[1]

The supreme issue of the war

Their opponents in the Great War were bent on showing the Germans that this theory is the result of criminal self-delusion. The fact that a country has a big army is no sign that it is "fittest" to play a part in our modern world. Germany was able to crush little Belgium in 1914 and to sink the *Lusitania* in 1915, but the world refused to think these were proofs of her superior civilization. Nothing but overwhelming defeat could force the Kaiser and the Prussian war party to conclude that military glory and conquest are outworn ambitions which the present world cannot tolerate.

Section III. France in the Twentieth Century

The contribution of France to civilization

Perhaps no country in Europe has contributed more to the history of civilization than France. A home of new ideas, of freedom in thinking and experiment in politics, it has also been the main center, through most of the modern period, for the development of art.

[1] The ideas that the Germans harbor of themselves and their mission are somewhat more fully stated in the supplementary chapter, in the section dealing with the problem of reëstablishing peace.

Paris is the painters' city. Not only do its vast galleries contain priceless treasures of the world's masterpieces, but its schools of art draw students from every country. In this way it has influenced the taste and ideals of the whole art world. Paris the "art capital" of Europe

FIG. 156. THE OPERA HOUSE, PARIS

The Opera House stands in the very center of the city. It is the most magnificent building devoted to music in the world, and was begun by Napoleon III but completed under the Third Republic. On opening nights high officials of the government come in state. But once a month free performances by the best artists are given, open to the people of Paris; for the French government, like other European governments, supports art by national subsidies

It is also a great musical center. The great masters and geniuses in music, of other countries as well as of France, regard the manner of the reception of their work in the great opera house in Paris as a matter of the first importance.

Although France stands so high in the realm of art and has made contributions to science not less phenomenal,[1] yet, until the war of 1914 revealed the courage and moral devotion of France misunderstood by foreigners

[1] See next section.

the people, it was the custom for foreigners to refer to the France of the Third Republic as an outworn country, which was already in decline. The main reason for this was that those who wrote about modern France did not really know their subject. The serious, hard-working, thrifty Frenchmen and Frenchwomen, of which the nation is mainly composed, have not interested pleasure-seeking travelers who write about their experiences abroad. These writers have been struck by small things, differences in ways and manners, and have failed to see beneath the quick wit and lively expression the real seriousness of the French people.

The conservativism of the French

The modern history of France, if studied superficially, adds to this impression of "the volatile French." Paris is "the home of revolutions." But Paris is not France, and the country as a whole is rather conservative in many ways. It is mainly a country of prosperous peasant farmers, who own their land and invest their savings at interest rather than spend them on such luxuries as automobiles or piano players. They are quite happy to leave things as they are, and object to reforms that increase the taxes. The shrewd, well-to-do merchants of the towns are of much the same mind. Hence when really vital reforms are proposed they are likely to meet with sufficient opposition to bring about some sort of a political crisis.[1]

The French parliament controls its cabinet

During the earlier years of the history of the Third Republic the cabinet was defeated every few months, and a new prime minister would be called to power. This was regarded in England and America as a sign of political instability. But if one examines the situation more closely, one sees that the change of cabinet did not matter in France as it would have mattered in England or America. For in most cases the policy was

[1] See above, p. 485. On the other hand, this also explains the success of revolutions in which apparently so few people took part. The mass of the nation was rather indifferent to politics so long as things went along about as they had been going; and the successive governments, republic or monarchy, generally made little change in the great *administrative* structure, which dates from Napoleon and the Revolution, or even from the old régime.

unchanged. The new cabinet would often be just a more competent group of men to accomplish the same end. The point to be kept in mind is that, whereas in the English system the cabinet tends to run the Parliament, in the French system the parliament controls the cabinet.

The group system of parties

This is the result of the "group system" of political parties. The government is faced with the possibility of a hostile coalition of the various groups at any time, whereas with the bi-party system the government is practically sure of the support of its party, which, in the nature of the case, is in the majority.

Social insurance

As we have intimated above, France has been a little slow to follow the example of other European countries in matters of social reform, partly because the problems of poverty have not been so pressing there. But in 1910, building upon earlier laws, it established a thorough-going system of old-age and disability pensions. The law requires all wage workers and salaried employees to be insured, and permits certain other workers to take advantage of the law if they wish. Employers and employees make equal contributions to the fund, and the government also lends its aid. The pension begins at the age of sixty-five — five years earlier than in England — and will normally amount to about $75 per annum for men and $60 per annum for women. Provisions are also made for those disabled through sickness or accident; and widows and orphans receive certain death benefits. In 1913 over eight million persons were registered under this scheme.

France follows the example of England

The Third Republic becomes pacific

The Napoleonic tradition of military glory was the worst handicap of France during the nineteenth century. The memories of the empire, when Paris was the capital of most of Europe, continued to haunt a certain section of the people, mainly the aristocracy, down to the disastrous war of 1870. During the Third Republic the military party, particularly the Bonapartists, tried to keep up the old spirit by insisting upon the need for reconquering Alsace-Lorraine from Germany. Demonstrations in Paris were held before the statue representing the lost city of Strassburg. But in recent years the jingoes have had little support either in parliament or out of it. The demonstrations have been witnessed by smaller and smaller crowds of bystanders, and a strong pacifist movement has been noticeable in the republic.[1] The growth of the Socialist party, which was strongly antimilitarist, was a definite sign of the new spirit, and the government, at least in the eyes of the militarists, did not support a consistent policy of preparedness.

The effect of the Morocco affair

This attitude was changed, however, by the trouble with Germany over Morocco in 1911.[2] After that, France was thoroughly alarmed, and all but the Socialists were for increasing the army. The great Socialist leader, Jaurès, one of the greatest orators and statesmen in Europe, continued, even up to the outbreak of the war, to argue against any yielding to a warlike policy. But upon the actual outbreak of the war in 1914, many people thought his idealism no longer patriotic. He was assassinated just as the invasion of France began.

Section 112. Progress and Effects of Natural Science

This story of politics and social reform, and of achievement in producing wealth and penetrating continents, which has been our main theme during the last twenty chapters, has, however, left almost unmentioned a phase of the history which is perhaps of more lasting importance than anything else that has taken place — indeed, more important than anything else that has ever been accomplished by mankind in all its long history — the rise of modern science.

In Chapter VI the extraordinary advance of natural science in the eighteenth century was briefly described. Through careful observation and experimentation, and the invention

[1] As an illustration of the popular outlook see the vote for Pasteur referred to below, p. 674.

[2] See below, p. 686.

of scientific instruments like the microscope and telescope, and by laborious watching, musing, and calculating, men of science — Newton, Linnæus, Buffon, Lavoisier, and hundreds of others — laid the foundations of our modern sciences, astronomy, botany, zoölogy, chemistry, physics. Their researches greatly increased man's knowledge of himself, of the animals and plants about him, of the minerals and gases which he had hitherto so ill understood, of the earth itself, and of the universe in which it revolves. These scientific discoveries have not served merely to gratify a noble curiosity; they have deeply affected the lives even of those who never heard of oxygen and hydrogen or the laws of motion. Scarcely any human interest has escaped the direct influence of natural science, for it has not only begotten a spirit of reform but is supplying the means for infinitely improving our human lot by bettering the conditions in which we live.[1]

Great importance of scientific research on the lives of men

Great as were the achievements of the eighteenth century, those of the nineteenth were still more startling. In order to appreciate this we have only to recollect that the representatives of the European powers who met together at Vienna after Napoleon's fall had not only never dreamed of telegraphs, telephones, electric lights, and electric cars, which are everyday necessities to us, but they knew nothing of ocean steamships or railways, of photography, anæsthetics, or antiseptics. Such humble comforts as matches, kerosene oil, illuminating gas, and our innumerable India-rubber articles were still unheard of. Sewing machines, typewriters, and lawn mowers would have appeared to them wholly mysterious contrivances whose uses they could not have guessed. Probably none of them had ever heard of the atomic theory; certainly not of the cellular theory, the conservation of energy, evolution, the germ theory of disease — all these, which every college boy and girl now finds in the textbooks, would have been perfectly strange to Stein or Alexander I.

Some examples of scientific advance during the nineteenth century

1 Unfortunately, it is also capable of heightening the horrors of war.

Possibility of scientific progress appears almost limitless

The progress of science in the twentieth century bids fair, with our ever more refined means of research, to solve many another deep mystery and add enormously to man's power and resources. Yet, so far, each discovery has suggested problems hitherto unsuspected. The universe is far more complicated than it was once believed to be, and there seems, therefore, to be no end to profitable research. It should be the aim of every student of modern history to follow the development of science and to observe the ways in which it is constantly changing our habits and our views of man, his origin and destiny. It will be possible here to do no more than suggest some of the more astonishing results of the scientific research which has been carried on during the past hundred years with ever-increasing ardor, both in Europe and America.

Former conception of creation and of the age of the earth

To begin with the earth itself, practically every one in Europe fifty years ago believed that it had existed but five or six thousand years, and that during the successive days of a single week God had created it and all the creatures upon it and had set the sun and moon in the firmament to light it. For this conception of creation the geologist, zoölogist, paleontologist, anthropologist, physicist, and astronomer have been substituting another, according to which all things have come to their present estate through a gradual process extending through millions, perhaps billions, of years.

The tremendous period during which life has probably existed on the earth

The earth is now commonly believed to have once been a gaseous ball which gradually cooled until its surface became hardened into the crust upon which we live.[1] Geologists do not agree as to the age of the earth in its present state, and there appears to be no means of definitely settling the question.

[1] Some distinguished scientists hold that there are weighty reasons for supposing that this crust is not more than thirty or forty miles thick, and that the volcanoes are openings which reach down to the molten and gaseous interior. Other geologists, however, either believe that the globe is solid, or humbly confess that we can form no satisfactory conclusions as to its interior, since we have no means of determining the condition of matter under such a tremendous pressure. Recently the theory has been advanced that the earth was gradually built of particles previously flying about in space, and was never a molten mass.

They infer, however, that it must have required from a hundred to a thousand millions of years for the so-called sedimentary rocks to be laid down in the beds of ancient seas and oceans. Many of these rocks contain fossils which indicate that plants and animals have existed on the earth from the very remote periods when some of these older strata were formed. Accordingly it seems possible that for at least a hundred million years the earth has had its seas and its dry land, differing little in temperature from the green globe familiar to us.

Even if we reduce this period by one half, it is impossible to form more than a faint idea of the time during which plants and the lower forms of animals have probably existed on the earth. Let us imagine a record having been kept during the past fifty million years, in which but a single page should be devoted to the chief changes occurring during each successive five thousand years. This mighty journal would now amount to ten volumes of a thousand pages each; and scarcely more than the last page, Volume X, page 1000, would be assigned to the whole recorded history of the world from the earliest Assyrian and Egyptian inscriptions to the present day.

As for the starry universe of which our sun and his little following of planets form an infinitesimal part — that seems to our poor minds to have existed always and to be boundless in extent. Nevertheless the revelations of the spectroscope and the samples of substances which reach the earth in the form of meteoric dust and stones indicate that heavenly bodies are composed of the same chemical constituents with which we are familiar — hydrogen, oxygen, nitrogen, carbon, sodium, iron, and so forth.

Lyell's *Principles of Geology* first appears in 1830

As early as 1795 the Scotch geologist, James Hutton, published his conclusion that the earth had gradually assumed its present form by slow natural processes; and he roused a storm of protest by declaring that he found "no traces of a beginning and no prospect of an end." In 1830 Sir Charles

Lyell published his famous *Principles of Geology*, in which he explained at great length the manner in which the gradual contraction of the globe, the action of the rain and the frost, had, through countless æons, and without any great general convulsions or cataclysms, formed the mountains and valleys and laid down the strata of limestone, clay, and sandstone. He showed, in short, that the surface of the earth was the result of familiar causes, most of which can still be seen in operation. The work of more recent geologists has tended to substantiate Lyell's views.

Buffon, 1707–1788, discovers signs of a gradual evolution of vegetable and animal life

And just as the earth itself has slowly changed through the operation of natural forces, so plants and animals appear to have assumed their present forms gradually. Buffon, a French naturalist who was busy upon a vast *Natural History* at the time that Diderot's *Encyclopædia* was in the course of publication, pointed out that all mammals closely resemble each other in their structure, unlike as they may appear to the casual observer. If a horse be compared point by point to a man, "our wonder," he declares, "is excited rather by the resemblances than by the differences between them." As he noted the family resemblances between one species and another he admitted that it looked as if Nature might, if sufficient time were allowed, "have evolved all organized forms from one original type."

The idea of evolution adopted by a very few advanced thinkers in the first half of the nineteenth century

In other passages Buffon forecast the great theory of evolution, and in the opening decade of the nineteenth century his fellow countryman, Lamarck, published a work in which he boldly maintained that the whole animal world has been gradually developed. He was half a century in advance of his times in this conviction, although the causes of development which he assigned would not seem at all adequate to modern zoölogists. Nevertheless other investigators were impressed by the same facts which had led Buffon and Lamarck to their conclusions, and in 1852 Herbert Spencer, in one of his very earliest works, gave many strong and seemingly unanswerable arguments to support the idea that the whole visible universe — the earth, the plants and animals, even man himself and all his ideas and institutions — had slowly developed by a natural process.

Seven years later (1859) Charles Darwin's *The Origin of Species by Means of Natural Selection* — the result of years of the most patient study of plants and animals — finally brought the whole theory of evolution to the attention of the world at large. Darwin maintained that the various species of animals and plants — all the different kinds of monkeys, sparrows, and whales, of maple trees, blackberries, and violets — were

Darwin's theory of natural selection

FIG. 157. DARWIN

Charles Darwin (1809–1882), after college days and a trip around the world (1832–1836) as naturalist to a scientific exploration, spent a secluded but studious and busy life in an English village. He published many books; one of the best known was "The Descent of Man" (1871) not descendants from original separate and individual species created in a certain form which they had always kept, but that these species as they exist in the world to-day were the result of many changes and modifications which have taken place during the millions of years in which plants and animals have lived upon the earth.[1]

The nature of "the struggle for existence"

Darwin pointed out that if any animal or plant were left free to multiply it would speedily fill the earth. For instance, a single pair of robin redbreasts, or sparrows, if allowed to live and breed unmolested, would under favorable circumstances increase to more than twenty millions in ten years. Consequently since the number of plants and animals shows no actual general increase, it is clear that by far the greater portion of the eggs of birds and fishes, the seeds of plants, and the young of mammals are destroyed before they develop. Heat and cold, rain and drought, are largely responsible for this, but organisms also kill one another in a thousand different ways, often by merely crowding out one another and consuming all the available food. There is thus a perpetual struggle for existence among all organisms, whether of the same or different species, and few only can possibly survive — one in five, or in ten, or in a thousand, or, in some cases, in a million.

Variation and the survival of the fittest

"Then comes the question, Why do some live rather than others? If all the individuals of each species were exactly alike in every respect, we could only say that it is a matter of chance, but they are not alike. We find that they vary in many different ways. Some are stronger, some swifter, some hardier in constitution, some more cunning. An obscure color may render concealment more easy for some; keener sight may enable others

[1] In the introduction to his book he says: "Although much remains obscure, I can entertain no doubt, after the most deliberate and dispassionate judgment of which I am capable, that the view which most naturalists till recently entertained, and which I formerly entertained, — namely, that each species has been independently created, — is erroneous. I am fully convinced that species are not immutable, but that those belonging to what are called the same genera are lineal descendants of some other and generally extinct species."

to discover prey or escape from an enemy better than their fellows. Among plants the smallest differences may be useful or the reverse. The earliest and strongest shoots may escape the slugs; their greater vigor may enable them to flower and seed earlier in wet autumn; plants best armed with spines or hair may escape being devoured; those whose flowers are most conspicuous may be soonest fertilized by insects. We cannot doubt that, on the whole, any beneficial variation will give the possessor of it a greater probability of living through the tremendous ordeal they have to undergo. There may be something left to chance, but on the whole *the fittest will survive*."[1]

Darwin's theory was, in short, that species did not endure unchanged, but, owing to the constant variations, those best fitted to survive escaped destruction in the constant struggle for existence and transmitted their advantageous characteristics to their offspring. This idea that all plants and animals, and even man himself, had *developed* instead of being created in their present form, and that man belonged, physically, to the "primates," the group of animals which includes the apes, shocked a great many people, and the subject began to be discussed with no little heat and sometimes with much indignation by men of science, theologians, and the cultivated public in general.

The theory of evolution finds defenders and is now accepted by most scientists

Among those who enthusiastically welcomed Darwin's book were Spencer, Alfred Wallace (who had reached the same conclusion before he knew of Darwin's work), Huxley, and the American botanist, Asa Gray, all of whom devoted their gifted pens to the defense and explanation of the new ideas. Evolution, although far more disturbing to the older ideas of the world than the discovery of Copernicus that the earth revolves around the sun, made its way far more rapidly into general acceptance, and to-day a large majority of zoölogists, botanists, geologists, and biologists, and indeed a great part of those who have received a scientific training, accept the general theory of

1 Alfred Wallace, *Darwinism*, chap. i.

evolution as confidently as that of universal gravitation or the fact that water is composed of oxygen and hydrogen.[1]

Evolution may be viewed as raising the dignity of man

The opponents of the theory of evolution have slowly decreased in numbers. At first the clergy, both Protestant and Catholic, could find no words too harsh to apply to the patient and careful Darwin, who seemed to them to contradict the express word of God and to rob man of all his dignity. But as time went on many religious leaders became reconciled to the new view. For on further thought it seemed to them to furnish a more exalted notion of God's purposes and methods than that formerly universally entertained, and they came to feel that instead of being degraded by being put on a level with the brutes man still remains as before the goal toward which all Nature's work through the ages is directed.

The atomic theory

While the zoölogist, the botanist, and the geologist were elaborating the theory of evolution, the chemists, physicists, and astronomers were busy with the problems suggested by matter and energy — heat, light, electricity, the nature and history of the sun and stars. Early in the nineteenth century an Englishman, Dalton, suggested that all matter acted as if it consisted of *atoms* of the various elements, which combined with one another to form the molecules, or little particles of the innumerable compound substances. For example, an atom of carbon combined with two atoms of oxygen to form the gas commonly called carbonic acid. Moreover as twelve parts by weight of carbon always combined with thirty-two parts of oxygen, it might be inferred that the carbon atom weighed twelve units and each of the two oxygen atoms sixteen. This

[1] Many investigators feel, however, that Darwin's explanation of evolution is, as he himself freely admitted, only a partial one and quite inadequate to account for the existing forms of animals and plants. Recently the Dutch naturalist, de Vries, has proved that the marked variations known as "sports," or freaks of nature, may sometimes be perpetuated from generation to generation. These sudden developments are known as "mutations." They would seem to indicate that the species we know, including perhaps man himself, have come into existence more rapidly than would be possible in the slow process of ordinary variation and natural selection. For a summary of recent discussions, see Kellogg, *Darwinism To-day* (1907).

formed the basis of the atomic theory which, after being very carefully worked out by a great many celebrated investigators, has become the foundation of modern chemistry.

Great importance of the chemist to-day

The chemist has been able to analyze the most complex substances and discover just what enters into the make-up of a plant or the body of an animal. He has even succeeded in properly combining ("synthesizing") atoms in the proper proportions so as to reproduce artificially substances which had previously been produced only by plants or in the bodies of animals; among these are alcohol, indigo, madder, and certain perfumes. The chemist has given us our aniline dyes and many useful new drugs; he has been able greatly to improve and facilitate the production of steel. The Bessemer process is estimated to have added to the world's wealth no less than two billion dollars annually. The chemist, since he knows just what a plant needs in its make-up, can, after analyzing a soil, supply those chemicals which are needed to produce a particular crop. He is able to determine whether water is pure or not. He is becoming ever more necessary to the manufacturer, mine owner, and agriculturist, besides standing guard over the public health.

Nature of light

During the nineteenth century the nature of heat and light was at last explained. Light and radiant heat are transmitted by minute waves produced in the *ether*, a something which it is assumed must everywhere exist, for without some medium the light would not reach us from the sun and stars.

Fundamental importance of electricity

Electricity, of which very little was known in the eighteenth century, has now been promoted to the most important place in the physical universe. It appears to be the chemical affinity, or cement, between the atoms of a molecule which serves to hold them together.[1] Light is believed to be nothing more

1 The chemist was long satisfied with his idea of an atom as the smallest particle of matter of whose existence there was any indication. He gradually added to the list of different kinds of atoms and has now named some eighty elements, each of which has its special atomic weight, hydrogen being the lightest. The physicist has, however, discovered a method of breaking up the

than electric forces traveling through the ether from a source of electrical disturbance, namely, the luminous body. Matter itself may ultimately be proved to be nothing more than electricity. The practical applications of electricity during the past thirty years are the most startling and best known of scientific achievements.

Radio-activity suggests that the elements are not permanent and immutable

As early as the seventeenth century the chemists reached the conclusion that the attempts of the alchemists to change one metal into another were futile, since each element had its particular nature, which so long as it was unmixed with other substances remained forever the same. Within the last ten years even this idea has been modified by the strange conduct of the so-called radio-active bodies, of which radium is the most striking. This new substance was extracted with the utmost difficulty from a mineral, pitchblende, by Professor Curie of Paris and his distinguished wife and fellow worker, Madame Curie. Although a ton of pitchblende yielded only the seventh part of a grain of radium in an impure state,[1] and although there are as yet perhaps only a hundred or so grains in the world, this minute quantity has served by its extraordinary properties to indicate that an atom can change its character and become a different substance. So it may be that all matter, as well as all life, has been gradually evolved.

Radium

Great energy within the atom

Radium gives out heat enough in an hour to raise its own weight of water from the freezing to the boiling point, yet it wastes away so gradually that it has been estimated that it would require well-nigh fifteen hundred years to lose half its

atom into bits which are only a thousandth part of the mass of a hydrogen atom. Moreover these inconceivably minute particles act as if they were pure negative electricity wholly free from matter. The atom is shown in this way, and by the use of the spectroscope, to be a tremendously complex affair. The "electrons" which compose it appear to revolve within the atom in somewhat the same way that the planets revolve about the sun.

[1] The Associated Press reports, November 23, 1907, that experiments made by the Vienna Imperial Academy of Sciences promise greatly to cheapen radium. Some forty-six grains have been extracted from a ton of pitchblende, thus reducing the estimated cost of an ounce from three million dollars to one million dollars.

weight. This extraordinary display of energy must be due to something within the atom itself and not to the breaking up of the molecule, which is called chemical change and of which we take advantage when we burn coal or explode gasoline vapor in order to run our engines. Some optimistic spirits have begun to dream of a time when the energy of the atoms may be utilized to take the place of the relatively weak chemical processes upon which we now rely. But as yet no means has been discovered of hastening, retarding, or in any way controlling the operations which go on within the atoms of radium and other radio-active substances.

The cell theory

In the world of plants and animals the discoveries have been quite as astonishing as in the realm of matter and electricity. About 1838 two German naturalists, Schleiden and Schwann, one of whom had been studying plants and the other animals, compared their observations and reached the conclusion that all living things were composed of minute bodies, which they named *cells*. The cells are composed of a gelatinous substance, to which the name of *protoplasm* was given by the botanist Mohl in 1846. All life was shown to have its beginning in this protoplasm, and the old theory that very simple organisms might be generated spontaneously from dead matter was shown to be a mistake. As Virchow, the famous German physiologist, expressed it, only a cell can produce another cell — *omnis cellula a cellula*. The cell corresponds, in a way, to the molecules which form inanimate substances.[1]

Protoplasm

[1] Many very low organisms, like the bacteria, consist of a single cell. The human body, on the other hand, is estimated to contain over twenty-six billions of cells, that is, of minute masses of protoplasm, each of which is due to the division of a previous cell, and all of which sprang from a single original cell, called the ovum, or egg. "All these cells are not alike, however, but just as in a social community one group of individuals devotes itself to the performance of one of the duties requisite to the well-being of the community and another group devotes itself to the performance of another duty, so too, in the body, one group of cells takes upon itself one special function and another, another." (McMurrich, *The Development of the Human Body*, 1907, p. 2.)

Importance of modern biology

The cell theory underlies the study of biology and is shedding a flood of light upon the manner in which the original egg develops and gradually gives rise to all the tissues and organs of the body. It has helped to explain many diseases and in some cases to suggest remedies, or at least rational methods of treatment. Indeed it is most important for our happiness and efficiency, as Dr. Osler well says, that the leaves of the tree of knowledge are serving for the healing of the nations. The human body and the minute structure of its tissues in health and disease, the functions of its various organs and their relations to one another, digestion, assimilation, circulation, and secretion, the extraordinary activities of the blood corpuscles, the nerves and their head and master, the brain — all these subjects and many others have been studied in the ever-increasing number of laboratories and well-equipped hospitals which have been founded during the past century. It is clear enough, in the light of our present knowledge, that the physicians of the eighteenth and most of the nineteenth centuries relied upon drugs and other treatment which were often far worse than nothing.

Vaccination, 1796

In 1796 Edward Jenner first ventured to try vaccination and thus found a means of prevention for one of the most terrible diseases of his time. With the precautions which experience has taught, his discovery would doubtless rid the world of smallpox altogether if vaccination could be everywhere enforced. But there are always great numbers of negligent persons as well as some actual opponents of vaccination who will combine to give the disease, happily much diminished in prevalence, a long lease of life.

Discovery of anæsthetics, 1846–1847

Just fifty years after Jenner's first epoch-making experiment, Dr. Warren performed, in the Massachusetts General Hospital in Boston, the first serious operation upon a patient who had been rendered unconscious by the use of an anæsthetic, namely, ether. The following year chloroform began to be used for the same purpose in Edinburgh. Before the discovery of anæsthetics few could be induced to undergo the terrible experiences of an operation; even the most unsympathetic surgeon could not bring himself to take the necessary time and care as the agonized victim lay under his knife. Now operations can be prolonged, if necessary, for an hour or more with no additional pain to the patient.[1]

Joseph Lister advocates antiseptic surgery

But even after a means was discovered of rendering patients insensible and operations could be undertaken with freedom and deliberation, the cases which ended fatally continued to be very numerous by reason of the blood poisoning, erysipelas, or gangrene which were likely to set in. To open the head, chest, or abdomen was pretty sure to mean death. Joseph Lister, an English professor of surgery, finally hit upon the remedy. By observing the most scrupulous cleanliness in everything connected with his operations and using certain antiseptics, he greatly reduced the number of cases which went wrong. The exact reason for his success was not, however, understood in the early sixties, when his work first began to attract attention; but a new branch of science was just being born which was not only to reveal the cause of infection in wounds but to explain a number of the worst diseases which afflict mankind. Medicine must have remained a blundering and incomplete science had bacteriology not opened up hitherto undreamed-of possibilities in the treatment and prevention of disease.

Bacteriology

Bacteria named in 1863

As early as 1675 the microscope had revealed minute organisms (*animalcula*) in putrefying meat, milk, and cheese, and a hundred years later Plenciz of Vienna declared that he was firmly convinced that both disease and the decomposition of animal matter were due to these minute creatures. But another hundred years elapsed before a Frenchman, Pasteur, claimed (in 1863) that the virulent ulcer called anthrax was due to little rod-shaped bodies, which he named *bacteria*.

[1] During the five years before Dr. Warren performed his famous operation but thirty-seven persons on the average consented annually to undergo an operation in the Massachusetts General Hospital. Fifty years later thirty-seven hundred went through the ordeal in the same hospital in a single year.

Researches of Pasteur, 1822–1895

Pasteur was a French chemist who made many important discoveries besides the treatment for hydrophobia, with which his name is most commonly associated. He proved that bacteria were very common in the air, and that it was they that gave rise to what had previously been mistaken for spontaneous generation. He was sent by the government to the south of France to study the disease of the silkworm, the ravages of which were impoverishing the country. He found the bodies and eggs of the silkworms full of bacteria and suggested the proper remedy. His study of fermentation enabled him to prevent great losses also among the wine growers.

Germ theory of disease

Koch of Berlin discovered the "bacillus" of tuberculosis, which produces the most common, perhaps, of all diseases, consumption of the lungs. Other workers have found the germs which cause pneumonia, diphtheria, lockjaw, the bubonic plague, etc.[1]

Struggle against disease-producing bacteria

It would, at first sight, seem hopeless to attempt to avoid bacteria, since they are so minute and so numerous, but experience has shown that they can be fended off in surgical cases by a scrupulous sterilization of everything that enters into the operation. That typhoid fever is due ordinarily to impure water or milk, that tuberculosis is spread mainly through the dried sputum of those afflicted with it, that the germs of yellow fever

[1] These bacteria are minute plants, rodlike, beadlike, or spiral in shape, which multiply by dividing into two parts, or by forming a germ or spore. They are very tiny. Four thousand of the *larger* kinds put end to end would extend only an inch, whereas the smaller are but one four-hundred-thousandth of an inch in length, and it is possible that some diseases are due to those too small to be seen under the most powerful microscopic lenses. They would do little harm were it not for their tremendous powers of multiplication. Under favorable circumstances the offspring of a single bacillus dividing itself into two every hour would amount to seventeen millions at the end of twenty-four hours. It has been calculated that if the proper conditions could be maintained a little rodlike bacterium which would measure only about a thousandth of an inch in length would, in less than five days, form a mass which would completely fill all the oceans on the earth's surface to the depth of a mile. They are well-nigh everywhere — in air, water, milk, on the bodies of men and animals, and in the earth. Many kinds are harmless, and some even appear to be absolutely necessary for the growth of certain most useful plants. Only a few species cause infectious diseases.

and malaria[1] are transmitted by the mosquito — all suggest obvious means of precaution, which will greatly reduce the chances of spreading the diseases. Moreover remedies are being discovered in addition to these preventive measures. Pasteur found that animals could be rendered immune to hydrophobia by injections of the virus of the disease. So-called *antitoxins* (counter poisons) have been discovered for diphtheria and lockjaw, but none has yet been found for tuberculosis or pneumonia.

Metchnikoff and his theory of the white blood corpuscles

The Russian Metchnikoff, a scientist working at the institute erected in honor of Pasteur in Paris, demonstrated that the white blood corpuscles keep up a constant warfare on the bacteria which find their way into the body, and devour them. Methods of helping these white corpuscles to increase and to make a good fight against the noxious bacteria are now occupying the attention of scientists. So the enemies of mankind are one by one being hunted down, and the means of warding them off or of rendering our bodies able to cope with them are being invented.

Necessity of giving more attention to natural science

It is clear, however, that two things are essential if the struggle against disease, and suffering, and inconvenience of all kinds is to make the progress that the achievements of the past would warrant us in hoping. Far more money must be appropriated by states or given by rich individuals than has been the case hitherto that an army of investigators with their laboratories and the necessary delicate and costly apparatus may be maintained. In the second place, our schools, colleges, and universities must give even more attention than they now give to spreading a knowledge of natural science and of its uses. A famous English scientist has recommended not only that many more institutions be established in which nature searching shall be the chief aim, but that a political party should be formed which should make a proper scientific training a test

[1] Malaria is not caused by bacteria, nor is the terrible sleeping sickness in Africa, but both are due to minute animal organisms.

question in all elections. No candidate for Parliament would receive the votes of the party "unless he were either himself educated in the knowledge of Nature or promised his support exclusively to ministers who would insist on the utilization of nature-knowledge in the administration of the great departments of State, and would take active measures of a financial character to develop with far greater rapidity and certainty than is at present the case, that inquiry into and control of Nature which is indispensable in human welfare and progress."[1]

Possibility of a new kind of history, in which kings and warriors will give place to men of science

In 1906 a popular newspaper in France asked its readers to give a list of notable Frenchmen of recent times in the order of their greatness. Pasteur the scientist came first in the estimation of his countrymen, receiving several million votes more than the soldier Napoleon Bonaparte, who came fourth. It may well be that men of science, not kings or warriors or even statesmen, are to be the heroes of the future. Perhaps during the twentieth century the progress of science and its practical applications will be recognized as the most vital element in the history of the eighteenth and nineteenth centuries. Our histories will have to be rewritten. Diderot's *Encyclopædia* will receive more space than the wars of Frederick the Great, and the names of Lyell, Darwin, Lister, Koch, and Curie will take their place alongside those of Metternich, Cavour, and Bismarck.

For, after all, the real progress of civilization depends less upon statesmen who control the fate of nations than upon the scientist and discoverer, who gives us control of nature and, to some extent, of life itself. From his laboratory comes much of the wealth and power of modern nations. The statesmen of the future must, therefore, reckon with these new contributions as the statesmen of the past have had to reckon with the new sea routes which changed the fate of the Mediterranean, or the Industrial Revolution which readjusted the nations of Europe and led to their expansion throughout the whole world.

[1] E. Ray Lankester, *The Kingdom of Man*, pp. 60–61, note.

QUESTIONS

SECTION 108. What are the main topics treated of so far? Would it be possible to write a parallel volume of modern European history, emphasizing different things? What is the main heritage of the twentieth century?

SECTION 109. Describe the political temper of England at the close of the nineteenth century. What political change occurred in 1906? Trace briefly the history of socialism in England. Review the history of labor legislation in England from 1897 to 1908. Mention the most important points made by Mr. Charles Booth in his survey of London poverty.

What is the modern view regarding the possibility of abolishing poverty? State the provisions of the old-age pension law of 1908. What means have been taken to lessen the amount of unemployment? In what way has an attempt been made to regulate wages in "sweated" trades? By what measures did the House of Lords seek to block the reforms of the Liberals? What was the "revolutionary" budget of 1909?

For what purpose were the special taxes to be used? Discuss the opposition of the House of Lords to the budget of 1909 and the protest of the House of Commons. Under what circumstances was the budget finally passed? Outline the Parliament Act of 1911. Give the main provisions of the National Insurance Act of 1911. In what sense is Great Britain both a democracy and an aristocracy?

What progress has been made in local reforms during the nineteenth and twentieth centuries? What was the commercial and industrial condition of Great Britain at the opening of the war in 1914?

SECTION 110. What are the chief explanations of Germany's recent wealth and importance? What measures were to be taken to make her a "world power"? Describe some of the activities of the German government, federal and local. What application do certain German writers make of Darwin's idea of the survival of the fittest?

SECTION 111. What have been the contributions of France to civilization? Account for our misunderstanding of the French of the Third Republic. Contrast the position of the French cabinet with that of the cabinet in England. Describe the French system of social insurance. Has militarism grown or decreased during the Third French Republic?

SECTION 112. How did the growth of the science of geology affect the perspective of historians? What is meant by the theory of evolution? When was it first advanced? What contribution did Darwin make to it? Why was it opposed? What has the chemist contributed to civilization? How did the discovery of radium affect our views of matter? What is the cell theory in biology? Describe various steps in the development of the science of medicine.

* Before the germ theory of disease, which Pasteur did so much to establish, medicine was hardly a genuine science. It was impotent in some of the commonest diseases and generally used haphazard cures. Now it is confidently saving human life and so adding to the possibilities of happiness more than any other science. This service of the scientists to make men live is to be contrasted with the terrible power they have also acquired over the engines of death, as the Great War, described in the next chapter, has shown. But wars will pass away and the arts of peace and the science of life will remain.

FIG. 158. PASTEUR IN HIS LABORATORY *

FIG. 159. THE SURRENDER OF THE GERMAN FLEET

A view taken from one of the boats of the British navy, showing the arrival of the German fleet when it surrendered to the Allied fleet in accordance with the terms laid down in the armistice

ORIGIN OF THE WAR OF 1914

SECTION 113. THE ARMIES AND NAVIES OF EUROPE

The incredible war of 1914

In August, 1914, the most terrible and destructive war in the history of the world broke out. Never before had millions and millions of men been ready to march against an enemy at a moment's notice; never before had any European army been supplied with such deadly weapons; never before had any war, however serious, so disturbed the affairs of the whole globe. The war confronted most thoughtful people as a horrible surprise. They could not believe that the European governments would dare take the fearful responsibility of entering upon a war which they all knew would involve untold woe and destruction. Nevertheless war was declared, and since it is, perhaps, the most important single event in the whole history of the world, we must endeavor to see how it came about and what were the great questions involved.

The growth of militarism in Europe

After Germany defeated France in 1870–1871, nearly fifty years passed without any of the Western powers coming to blows with one another. This was a long and hopeful period of peace; but meanwhile all the powers had been spending vast sums each year to train soldiers and supply them with arms. Prussia was the chief promoter of militarism. As we have seen, it began to aspire more than two hundred years before to become a great power through the might of its army. Frederick the Great was the chief military aggressor of the eighteenth century; but the modern Prussian army dates from the period when Napoleon defeated Prussia at Jena, for after that her statesmen had to rely upon "the nation in arms" rather than

The origin of the Prussian army system

an old-fashioned standing army. This had to be done at first in such a way as not to arouse the suspicions of the Corsican, so she hit upon the idea of giving her men a brief period of training in the army and then sending them into the reserve forces. In this way, without increasing the number of troops under the colors at any one time, she secured a very much larger force upon which she could call when war came. The defeat at Jena revealed also to Prussia the need for officers who should be trained, and not chosen for their positions because of their family or wealth as many had been up to that time. Military schools were established where the future Prussian officers underwent careful and intensive training after the manner of officers of other nations.

As we know, this army of Prussia was able to take an important part in the conflict which led to Napoleon's final defeat. Her idea of "the nation in arms" was not forgotten. The law passed in Napoleon's time making every able-bodied male subject of Prussia liable to military service in the army was not repealed. When, fifty years later, William I and Bismarck were preparing to Prussianize all Germany and foresaw a war with Austria, the annual levy of recruits was increased, the period of active service lengthened from two to three years, and the term of service in the reserve to four years. Thus Prussia secured an effective army of four hundred thousand troops, and with these she defeated Austria in 1866, led in the successful war against France, and gained her end of consolidating Germany into the German Empire, of which the king of Prussia became the head.[1]

Other nations adopt universal training

Not long after the war of 1870–1871 all the European powers, except England, adopted the plan of building up an army by requiring all able-bodied men that the government could afford to train to enter the army for two or three years, after which they were sent into the reserve to be ready in case of war. A large number of permanent officers had to be

[1] See above, sections 69–70.

FIG. 160. THE MUNITION WORKS, LE CREUSOT, FRANCE

France relied much upon its artillery for defense, since Germany had more soldiers, but in the great war of 1914 the Germans had prepared more heavy cannon than the French, who used mainly a lighter gun. The Creusot works are among the largest and most important munition works in Europe. This picture of them is from an etching by the American artist Mr. Joseph Pennell

maintained to see that the military education of the soldiers was properly conducted, and a vast amount had to be spent on rifles, cannon, and other arms, which were being constantly improved and rendered more and more deadly.

The burden of militarism

The result of this competition in armaments was a tremendous increase in the size of the continental armies and a fearful burden of taxation, which the people had to bear. When the war broke out, Germany and France had each over four millions of men in their armies, Russia had six or seven millions, and Austria-Hungary had over two and a half millions. England's forces, on the other hand, numbered less than two hundred thousand, and of these only a very small number were kept in the British Isles. Her army was needed mainly as a matter of protection for her distant colonies. The English army, like that of the United States, was recruited by voluntary enlistment and not built up by national conscription.

FIG. 161. THE BURDEN OF MILITARISM

A cartoon by Robert Carter in the New York *Sun*

England's fleet

England, however, relied for her protection upon her unrivaled navy, which she has maintained at a strength equal to that of any two other powers. There are two reasons for this great navy. England has a much larger population than it is possible to feed from her own farms, and so has to import most of her food. Then, too, England is almost wholly a manufacturing country, and her industrial welfare is vitally dependent upon her commerce. If, therefore, England should be defeated at sea, she would be utterly overcome.

Germany especially was unwilling to grant this supremacy of England at sea, although it was essential to her existence. Then, too, Germany was jealous of the ability of England to plant and maintain such widely scattered dominions, and was as anxious as the English to capture the commerce of distant markets and to protect that commerce by powerful fleets. She spent millions in her vain endeavor to surpass England commercially. Kaiser William II was from the first interested in the navy, and repeatedly declared that Germany's future lay upon the ocean. So in 1897 a bill was passed for the development of the German navy, which was built up so rapidly that it became a menace to the commercial peace and security of all other nations, and they, for protection, had to increase their navies. So to the crushing cost of armies European nations added the cost of navies, in which the rapid progress of invention made battleships worthless if they were but a few years old.

The naval ambition of Germany

Section 114. Movements for Peace: the Hague Conferences; Pacifism; Socialism

The enormous cost of armaments, combined with horror at the thought of a war in which so many millions would be fighting provided with such terrible weapons as modern science supplies, led many earnest people to try to prevent war altogether.

Movements for peace

The first notable movement toward arranging for a lessening of armaments originated with the Tsar, Nicholas II, when in 1898 he proposed a great conference of the powers at The Hague to discuss the problem.[1] Unlike the Congress of Vienna or Berlin, this Peace Conference of 1899 did not meet to bring a war to a close; it came together in a time of European peace to consider how the existing peace might be maintained and military expenditures reduced.

The Tsar calls a conference to lessen militarism, at The Hague

[1] For the Tsar's rescript calling the conference, see *Readings in Modern European History*, Vol. II, pp. 463 ff.

Hague conferences, 1899 and 1907

The Hague Conference did nothing to limit armaments. It is significant in view of later events that Germany strongly and successfully opposed any such action. The Conference did, however, in spite of German opposition, establish a permanent Court of Arbitration to which difficulties arising between nations "involving neither honor nor vital interests" might be submitted. But there was no way of compelling a nation to submit its grievances, and just those very sources of war that make most trouble were excluded from consideration. At the second conference, held in 1907, the question of the limitation of armaments was again proposed and championed by England, but the opposition to such a movement shown by Germany at the earlier conference had not diminished in the meantime. That country and Austria, for reasons much more clearly revealed seven years later, again caused a postponement of any action on the question. However, certain rules were established in regard to laying mines, the bombardment of unfortified towns, and the rights of neutrals in war, to which no attention was paid by Germany after the war began, when she repeatedly violated her pledged word.

Peace treaties between nations

Since the first Hague Conference more than one hundred and thirty treaties have been made between nations, pledging them to submit to arbitration all disputes which "do not affect the vital interests, the independence, or the honor of the contracting parties, and do not concern the interests of third parties." Recently some nations have gone further and proposed treaties binding themselves to submit to arbitration "all questions which are in their nature justiciable in character."

There were many other signs besides the Hague conferences and the different arbitration treaties which encouraged the hope that there would not be another great European conflict. The number of international societies and congresses was steadily increasing before the war, and there was a general recognition that peoples of different nations had innumerable common interests which they should help one another to promote.

Among the other forces making for international peace, one of the strongest has been socialism, which is an international movement of working people with the common aim of getting rid of the private ownership of the "means of production."[1] The socialists have had great international congresses and refer to each other as "comrades." They have constantly criticized governments which have embarked on "imperialistic" policies,[2] for they claim that only the rich man profits from investments in distant lands and that the wars which ensue are not the affair of the working class. Above all, socialists have insisted that the poor suffer most in war. Extreme socialists have therefore been antimilitarist. This means that they have objected to serving in the armies of Europe, and so have sometimes been imprisoned for what was viewed as treason. However, a great majority of the socialists of all countries were carried away by the ardor of the vast conflict which began in 1914, and while they still profess to detest imperialism and wars of conquest, they nevertheless fought against each other in the Great War.

Socialism as an international movement

SECTION 115. MATTERS OF DISPUTE: NATIONAL RIVALRIES

Two of the conditions which made the Great War possible have been outlined in the last two chapters — on the one hand "imperialism," and on the other the "Near-Eastern question." We have seen how the nations of Europe began in the latter part of the nineteenth century, as rivals for the world's trade, to seize colonies and trading posts in Africa and Asia, and we have also seen how they stood eying each other suspiciously as to which was to profit most from the decline of Turkey. Now we must see how these conditions — which for almost fifty years had somehow been adjusted peacefully — helped, in the summer of 1914, to precipitate the war.

"Imperialism" and the "Near-Eastern question"

[1] See above, pp. 372 ff.

[2] See above, p. 598.

Review of imperialistic policies in Africa

First, let us recall the exploration and partition of Africa. France has taken most of the Mediterranean shore, and in so doing has incurred, at different times, the rivalry of Italy, England, and Germany. Its province of Algeria, conquered in 1830 and thoroughly subdued in 1870–1874, had two native states as neighbors — Tunis and Morocco. Claiming that the Tunisian tribesmen were raiding the border, France conquered Tunis in 1881 and thus forestalled Italy, which had intended taking the site of ancient Carthage for itself. This threw Italy into the hands of Bismarck, and it became a member of the Triple Alliance with Germany and Austria.

France turns Italy against her by taking Tunis

France and England in Egypt

France and England fell out, as we have seen, over Egypt. France backed out when England got financial control in Egypt, and this was bitterly resented by the French. When the English, under General Kitchener, had conquered the Sudan in 1898, at the cost of many lives, a French explorer, Colonel Marchand, rapidly crossed the heart of Africa from the west and planted the French tricolor at Fashoda, in the upper Sudan, before Kitchener could reach there. When word of this reached Paris and London, war seemed inevitable, and it would have come had not the French given way. The "Fashoda affair" estranged the English and French still more — a fact emphasized by outspoken French sympathy with the Boers in their war with England two years later. There was a great deal of war talk, but more judicial minds triumphed.

The "Fashoda affair"

Edward VII and the *entente cordiale*

Inside of four years the change in feeling was complete. King Edward VII, who had succeeded to the throne of England upon the death of his mother, Victoria, in 1901, was personally fond of France — and the French, of him. Skillful statesmen made the most of the new situation, and in 1904 France and England came to a "cordial understanding" — or, to use the French phrase, *entente cordiale* — concerning all their outstanding sources of quarrel. This *Entente*, as it is generally called, has turned out to be one of the most important facts in the world's history. France was to recognize British interests in Egypt, and

England those of France in Morocco, which country France had begun to penetrate from the Algerian border.[1] The *Entente* was hailed with great delight on both sides; Englishmen cheered French marines marching on a friendly visit through London streets, and Frenchmen began to admire traits of character in the Anglo-Saxon which they had not appreciated before.

France to have free hand in Morocco

England's isolation had been ended even before the *entente* with France, by an alliance with Japan in 1902.[2] Then, when, after the Russo-Japanese War, the Japanese and Russians decided, instead of fighting over Manchuria, to join together and help each other "penetrate" it, and so became friends, England made terms with Russia also. This seemed almost incredible, for England had long been suspicious of Russian designs upon India, where it had detected Russian agents causing border uprisings. Moreover, the English bitterly hated Russian autocracy, and London was a place of refuge for Russian revolutionists. The incredible happened, however. In 1907 England and Russia settled their Asian boundary disputes by agreeing to limit their ambitions in Persia.[3]

Alliance of England and Japan

Entente with Russia

In addition to its alliance with Japan and its *entente* with France and Russia, England had as friends Denmark — resentful of Germany since the war of 1864 — and Portugal,[4] while English princesses became queens of Norway and Spain.[5]

The small states

[1] In addition, fishery troubles off the coast of Newfoundland were adjusted.

[2] According to this alliance England was to support Japan if attacked by a third power. The alliance was, therefore, strictly limited, but was strengthened in 1905, after the Russo-Japanese War, to be a mutually defensive alliance to safeguard the integrity of eastern Asia and India.

[3] See map, p. 610. Britain was to have as its "sphere of influence" a southern zone, Russia a northern, and neither was to interfere in the center. This left Persia itself only the central strip. There was much protest in both England and America over the cruel way in which the Russians treated the natives, but Sir Edward Grey, the British foreign minister, refused to interfere, since the only way to keep the Russians out of the boundary he had taken was for the English to stay out of Russian Persia.

[4] Its tyrannical king, Carlos I, and the crown prince were murdered in Lisbon in 1908, and Portugal became a republic, but this has not altered its foreign policy.

[5] On the other hand, the royal houses of Sweden, Roumania, Greece, and Bulgaria were closely connected with the Hohenzollerns.

Germany suspicious of the *ententes*

One great power did not become a member of this circle of friends — Germany. Although the Kaiser, William II, was the nephew of King Edward VII,[1] the two monarchs were personally never on cordial terms, and the two nations, rivals in wealth and power, distrusted each other also. The Germans pretended to believe that the defensive group of alliances and *ententes* which Edward had encouraged was formed with designs hostile to the Triple Alliance of the central powers, — Germany, Austria, and Italy, — and resolved if possible to break it up.

Germany opposes France in Morocco

In 1905, therefore, Germany, supported by Austria, objected to the agreement between England and France by which the latter was to have a free hand in Morocco. Germany claimed to have interests there too, and the emperor spoke in such a way as to bring on a general "war scare." France agreed to the conference at Algeciras, which gave the French police power in Morocco but guaranteed the latter's independence. In 1911 Germany interfered again in Morocco. Because there were a few Germans in that country she sent a cruiser to Agadir and boldly demanded that France consult her in Moroccan matters and change her policy of policing the country. War was very narrowly averted. France gave up some of its possessions on the Congo to Germany in order to be allowed a free hand in Morocco.

Algeciras Conference, 1905

The Agadir incident, 1911

Europe on the brink of war

The Agadir incident alarmed statesmen in England as well. Every one saw how near Europe had come to the brink of war. Imperialists in Germany said the Agadir incident had been a failure for Germany, since France was left in possession of Morocco, and they demanded stronger action in future. Imperialists in France and England were angered at the bold way Germany had apparently tried to humble them before the world and were bitter that Germany got any satisfaction at all. The result was that all nations increased their warlike preparations.

[1] Edward died in 1910 and was succeeded by George V.

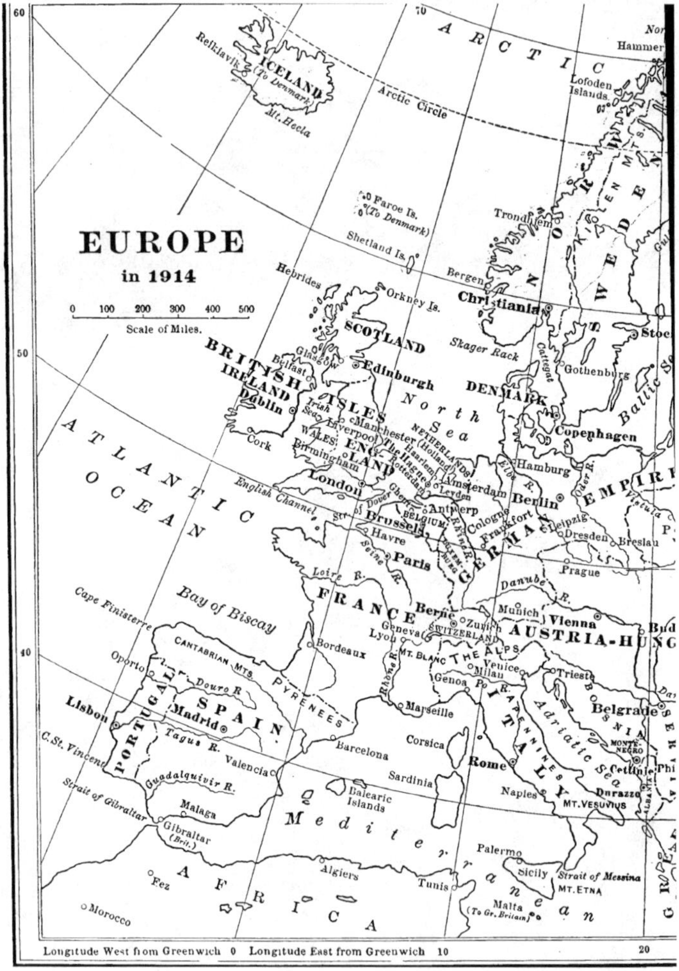
EUROPE
in 1914
0 100 200 300 400 500
Scale of Miles.
ARCTIC
Arctic Circle
ICELAND
(To Denmark)
Reikiavik
Mt. Hecla
Faroe Is.
(To Denmark)
Shetland Is.
Orkney Is.
Hebrides
SCOTLAND
Edinburgh
Glasgow
Belfast
BRITISH
IRELAND
Dublin
ISLES
Irish Sea
Cork
Liverpool
Manchester
WALES
ENGLAND
Birmingham
London
North Sea
Lofoden Islands
Hammer
Trondhjem
Bergen
Christiania
Skager Rack
Cattegat
Gothenburg
DENMARK
Copenhagen
Baltic Sea
NETHERLANDS (Holland)
Haarlem
The Hague
Rotterdam
Leyden
Amsterdam
Hamburg
Berlin
Elbe R.
Oder R.
EMPIRE
Vistula
Breslau
Leipzig
Dresden
Prague
Cologne
Frankfort
Antwerp
Ghent
BELGIUM
Brussels
Rhine R.
GERMAN
English Channel
Str. of Dover
Havre
Seine R.
Paris
Loire R.
FRANCE
ATLANTIC
OCEAN
Bay of Biscay
Cape Finisterre
Bordeaux
Berne
Zurich
Geneva
Lyon
SWITZERLAND
MT. BLANC
THE ALPS
Munich
Danube R.
Vienna
AUSTRIA-HUNG
Trieste
Venice
Milan
Genoa
Po R.
Rhone R.
Marseille
CANTABRIAN MTS.
PYRENEES
Oporto
Douro R.
PORTUGAL
SPAIN
Madrid
Lisbon
Tagus R.
C. St. Vincent
Valencia
Barcelona
Guadalquivir R.
Strait of Gibraltar
Malaga
Gibraltar (Brit.)
Corsica
Sardinia
Balearic Islands
Rome
ITALY
APENNINES
Adriatic Sea
Naples
MT. VESUVIUS
BOSNIA
Belgrade
MONTE-NEGRO
Cettinje
Durazzo
ALBANIA
Mediterranean
Palermo
Sicily
Strait of Messina
MT. ETNA
Malta
(To Gr. Britain)
AFRICA
Fez
Morocco
Algiers
Tunis
60
50
40
Longitude West from Greenwich 0 Longitude East from Greenwich 10
20

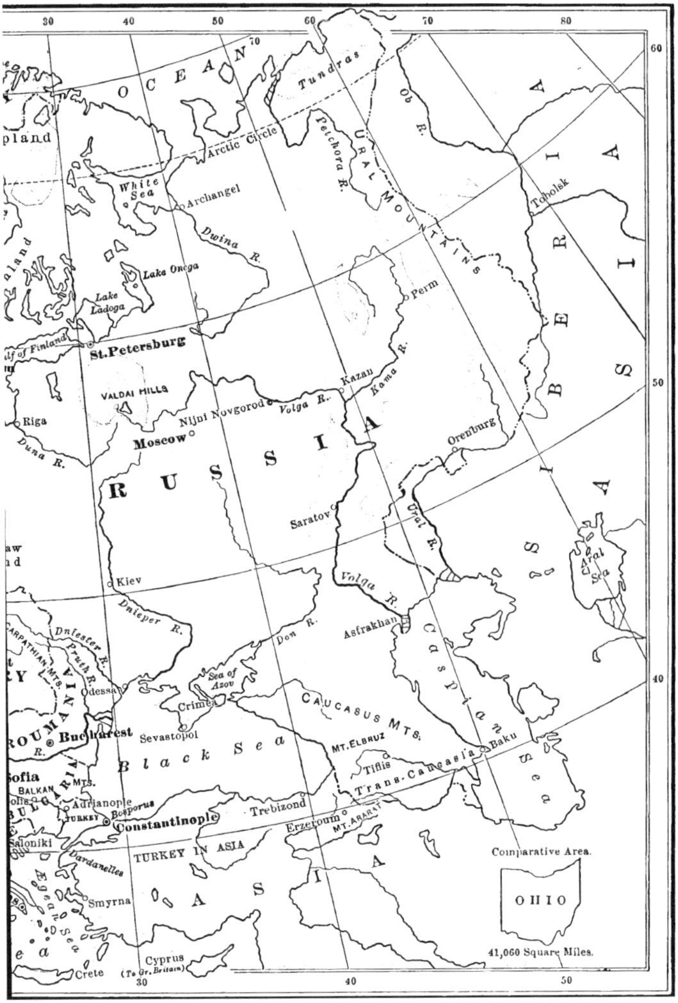
OCEAN
White Sea
Archangel
Arctic Circle
Tundras
Petchora R.
URAL MOUNTAINS
Ob R.
Tobolsk
SIBERIA
Dwina R.
Lake Onega
Lake Ladoga
Perm
St. Petersburg
Gulf of Finland
VALDAI HILLS
Kazan
Kama R.
Nijni Novgorod
Volga R.
Riga
Duna R.
Moscow
RUSSIA
Orenburg
Saratov
Ural R.
Aral Sea
ASIA
Kiev
Dnieper R.
Volga R.
Astrakhan
Dniester R.
CARPATHIAN MTS.
Pruth R.
Don R.
Caspian Sea
Odessa
Sea of Azov
Crimea
CAUCASUS MTS.
ROUMANIA
Bucharest
Sevastopol
Black Sea
MT. ELBRUZ
Baku
Tiflis
Trans-Caucasia
Sofia
BALKAN MTS.
BULGARIA
Adrianople
Bosporus
TURKEY
Constantinople
Trebizond
Erzeroum
MT. ARARAT
Saloniki
Dardanelles
TURKEY IN ASIA
Comparative Area.
OHIO
41,060 Square Miles.
Ægean Sea
Smyrna
Cyprus
(To Gr. Britain)
Crete
ASIA

Section 116. The Near-Eastern Question

Although war between Germany and England and France over the occupation of Morocco was avoided in 1911, another great danger appeared in the strained relations between Austria and Russia. The wars in the Balkan region described in a previous chapter (section 99) had revived old rivalries between these two great powers and speedily precipitated a general European conflict. In order to understand the situation we must first briefly review the history of Austria since she was defeated by Prussia in 1866 (see above, pp. 439–443). It will be remembered that Bismarck excluded her from his new North German Confederation and left her to arrange her affairs as best she could.

The races of the Hapsburg dominions

The Hapsburg dynasty with its capital at Vienna ruled over a great number of countries and provinces which it had brought together since the days of Rudolph of Hapsburg in the thirteenth century. One of its greatest difficulties was to reconcile the interests of the German population in Austria proper (and the regions to the west) with those of the Hungarians on the one hand and of the various Slavic peoples — such as the Bohemians, Poles, and Croats — on the other. It will be recollected that this difficulty had caused revolts in 1848 which led to civil war, in which both the Bohemians and the Hungarians were defeated (see above, p. 398). In 1867, the year after the unsuccessful war with Prussia, an arrangement was made between Austria and Hungary which divided the Hapsburg empire into two practically independent parts. The western provinces, together with Galicia and Dalmatia forming the Austrian Empire (the regions colored red on the map, p. 442), were to have their government carried on in Vienna; the southeastern portion, consisting of the kingdom of Hungary and some outlying provinces (colored green on the map), was to have its capital in Budapest. The emperor of Austria was also king of Hungary, but there were to be two parliaments — one

Formation of Austria-Hungary

meeting in Vienna, the other in Budapest. In this way a federation of two states was created — the so-called dual monarchy of Austria-Hungary. The common interest of these two states in matters of tariff, negotiations with foreign nations, and military arrangements were in the hands of a curious sort of joint house, known as the "Delegations."[1] Even this arrangement was made only for a few years at a time. For the great feudal lords of Hungary — a proud, unyielding nobility — had seen in Austria's necessity their opportunity, and they not only gained their own independence but generally aimed to control as well the policy of the dual monarchy.

Discontent of the Slavs in Austria-Hungary

The Slavic subjects of the Hapsburgs bitterly resented this arrangement, which kept them in an inferior political position. Moreover, since these Czechs, Croats, Ruthenians, and Slovenians cannot understand one another's language, it was a favorite policy for the government to play one over against another, or, as the phrase goes, "divide and rule." The result was great racial bitterness.

The "South Slav" neighbors of Austria aided by Russia

This difficult situation at home was made still more difficult by the fact that the "South Slav" peoples (Jugo-Slavs) extended beyond the borders of Austria-Hungary and formed the majority of the population of the whole Balkan region. With the decline of the Turkish Empire, Russia came forward as the rightful protector of these Balkan peoples, and so she naturally came into conflict with the policies of Austria-Hungary. This was especially clear in 1878, when Austria, supported by England and Germany, checked victorious Russia by the Congress of Berlin.

Austria checks Russia

Austria annexes Bosnia and Herzegovina, 1908

As a result of that congress Austria was allowed to occupy the Turkish provinces of Bosnia and Herzegovina. Austria governed these provinces well for the next thirty years, while the rest of Turkey continued to suffer from misrule. When the Turkish revolution took place in 1908, however, and

[1] The three ministers of finance, war, and foreign affairs were responsible to the Delegations, which sat as separate bodies of sixty members each (one debating in German, the other in Hungarian), and ordinarily communicated with each other in writing. If they disagreed, they could meet together and vote, but without debate.

there seemed to be some chance of a new and strong Turkey, Austria determined to prevent Bosnia and Herzegovina from ever entering into it, and unscrupulously annexed them to the dual empire. The neighboring state of Serbia was alarmed and indignant at this, since the annexed provinces were peopled with South Slavs,[1] and the Serbians had cherished the ambition of uniting with them and the Montenegrins in a new south Slavonic state which would reach from the Danube to the Adriatic. Russia also was angered, but when Germany, Austria's ally, declared that it would support Austria, in arms if need be, Russia, which had not yet recovered from the war with Japan and its own revolutions, was obliged to submit to the humiliation, as she viewed it, of being unable to protect those of her own race in the Balkans.

Serbia angry, but Russia acquiesces

For Serbia, indeed, the annexation was a serious blow. It was now apparently shut in from the sea for all time to come, and so would be dependent for a market for its farm products upon its enemy across the Danube, Austria-Hungary. This would reduce it to the condition of a weak and somewhat dependent state, which was what Austria wanted.

Serbia, victor in Balkan wars, is thwarted again by Austria

In the wars of 1912–1913, however, Serbia burst its boundaries upon the south and all but reached the Adriatic through Albania. Again Austria interfered, and had an independent prince set up in Albania to shut Serbia in. The Serbians felt that the natural rewards of their victories had been denied them by their powerful but jealous neighbor, and bitter hatred resulted.

Serbia's gains in the Balkan wars

The situation at the end of the Second Balkan War augured ill for the peace of Europe. Although Austria had managed to frustrate Serbia's hope of getting a port on the Adriatic, and had succeeded in having Albania made an independent principality under a German prince,[2] Serbia had nearly doubled her territory, and there was every probability that she would

Critical condition at the close of the Balkan wars, 1913

[1] They are mainly Croats, professing the Catholic religion, while the Serbs are of the Orthodox Greek Church; but they have common traditions.

[2] William of Wied, who was soon driven out by insurrections of the inhabitants.

undertake to carry out her former plan of uniting the discontented Southern Slavs in the neighboring provinces of Austria-Hungary — Bosnia, Croatia, and Slavonia. Germany was in hearty sympathy with the plans of Austria, while Russia was supposed to be ready to support Serbia and the Southern Slavs, their distant kinsmen.

Germany's position

Germany pretended to be much afraid that Russia would dominate the Balkan regions and perhaps seize Constantinople. This would put an end to a cherished plan of Germany — a railroad from Berlin to Bagdad and the Persian Gulf, which would control a vast trade with the Orient. The political aspects of such a controlling line through Middle Europe were revealed strikingly after the outbreak of the Great War. Germany had already arranged a "concession" from Turkey to construct this road, which was well under way when Serbia, through whose territory the trains from Germany must pass, became a danger.

The Bagdad railroad

Pan-Germanism

Pan-Germanism, which is perhaps best explained as an exaggerated race consciousness of the German people, had been for some time an active though unofficial force in German imperialism, but it came into prominence when the war party directed its energies against what they termed Pan-Slavism.

Feverish military preparations, 1913

The year 1913, therefore, brought renewed activity in military "preparedness." Germany took the lead by increasing its standing army, and the Reichstag voted about a billion marks for unusual military expenses (June, 1913). France replied by increasing the term of active service in the army from two to three years. Russia made heavy appropriations, and General Joffre, the French commander in chief, was called in to make suggestions in regard to reorganizing the Russian army. Austria-Hungary strengthened herself with improved artillery; England devoted heavy sums to her navy; and even Belgium introduced universal military service on the ground that Germany had been constructing railroad tracks up to her borders, which could only be explained by her purpose to pass through Belgium when the fight began.

Ethnographic Map of Austria-Hungary

Section 117. The Outbreak of the War

Last efforts for peace, 1914

Meanwhile the friends of peace did not despair. The English statesmen did all they could to end the misunderstandings between the great powers. England was willing to agree to let Germany develop its railroad to Bagdad and thus dispel the false impression, fostered in Germany, that England was weaving her *ententes* with a view of hemming in and weakening that country. Some of Germany's statesmen, including their ambassador at London, seemed anxious to reach a peaceful settlement, but they were frustrated by the German war party, who were eager for a conflict. Had it not been for their criminal activity peace might have been maintained indefinitely.

The murder of the Austrian archduke, Francis Ferdinand, June 28, 1914

On June 28, 1914, occurred the event which served as a pretext for war. Archduke Francis Ferdinand, heir to the throne of Austria-Hungary, and his wife were assassinated while upon a visit to Bosnia. The Serbian government had warned the archduke not to go there, because it feared that hot-headed pro-Serbian conspirators might attempt an assassination. Austria nevertheless asserted that Serbia had favored such conspiracies and was therefore responsible for the assassination. It allowed a month to pass, however, before making formal protest. Then, on July 23, it sent to Serbia not a protest but an ultimatum.

The Austrian ultimatum to Serbia, July 23, 1914

It gave Serbia forty-eight hours in which to agree to suppress anti-Austrian propaganda in press, schools, or by societies; to dismiss from the army or civil office any one obnoxious to Austria; and to allow Austrian officials to sit in Serbian courts in order to bring the guilty to justice. Serbia agreed to all these humiliating conditions except the last, and offered to refer even that to the Hague Tribunal. This Austria refused to do, and this decision was cheered in Vienna.

Germany's attitude toward the Austro-Serbian conflict

The last week of July, 1914, was perhaps the most momentous in the world's history. It was clear that Russia would not stand by and see Serbia conquered by Austria. Germany, on the other hand, declared that she would assist Austria in every way if attacked by Russia. She resisted the efforts of the Russian, French, and English diplomats, who urged that the difficulties between Austria and Serbia be referred to the Hague Tribunal, and insisted that it was Austria's affair, which she must be allowed to settle for herself. In short, Germany's unused war machine was beginning to be a burden, and Serbia offered an excuse to put it into action. She did nothing to stop the impending war as she might have done. Her leaders seem to have felt that they were ready for war, no matter on how large a scale; and they well knew that Russia had not finished her preparations, nor France either. As for England, she had only a trifling army.

How Germany began the world war

As soon as Austria declared war on Serbia, July 28, Russia began rapidly to mobilize, and Germany, pretending this to be an attack on her, declared war on Russia, August 1. On the same day she demanded of France, Russia's ally, what she proposed to do. The French government replied that France would take such action as her interests might require; whereupon Germany declared war on France, August 3. But Germany was in such a hurry to strike first that her troops were marching on France a day before war was declared. On August 2 they occupied the neutral country of Luxemburg, in spite of the protests of its ruler. Germany issued an ultimatum to Belgium, giving her twelve hours, from 7 P.M. to 7 A.M., to decide whether she would permit the German troops to cross the little kingdom on their way to France. If she consented, Germany promised to respect her territory and people; if she refused, Germany would treat her as an enemy. Now others as well as the Belgians could see why Germany had constructed such an abundance of railroad sidings close to the Belgian boundary. The Belgian government replied to the German demand with great firmness and dignity, urging that her neutrality had been at once decreed and guaranteed by the powers, including Germany, and that she should resist any attempt to violate it.

Ultimatum to Belgium, August 2, 1914

It was almost inevitable that Great Britain should be drawn

How Great Britain entered the war, August 4, 1914

into the conflict. She was not pledged to come to the assistance of France and Russia, but on August 2 she informed Germany that she could not permit the German fleet to attack the coasts of France, — for this would bring war close home to England. Two days later, learning that German troops were making their way into Belgium, Sir Edward Grey sent an ultimatum to Germany demanding assurances within twelve hours that she would respect Belgian neutrality. The German chancellor replied that military necessity required that the German armies cross Belgium. He told the English ambassador in Berlin that England ought not to enter the war just for the sake of "a scrap of paper." This contemptuous reference to the solemn treaties by which the European powers had guaranteed the neutrality of Belgium roused the anger of the entire outside world. It was the invasion of Belgium which arrayed the English people solidly behind the government, although England had made no financial preparations, had but a tiny army, and was forced at first to rely almost solely on her vast sea power.

Belligerents in 1914

Japan speedily declared war on Germany, and early in November Turkey decided to join the Central Powers. So within three months Germany, Austria-Hungary, and Turkey were pitted against Serbia, Russia, France, Belgium, England, Montenegro, and Japan. Italy declared herself neutral and not bound to help Austria and Germany, since in the Triple Alliance of 1882 she had pledged her aid only in case they were attacked; she considered that they were now the aggressors and that she was consequently free to keep out of the struggle.

The Germans pretend that England was responsible for the world war

Immediately upon the public announcement that a state of war existed between England and Germany the Germans turned all their pent-up hatred upon England and accused[1] her of being

[1] On September 5, 1917, the German chancellor, Michaelis, said: "Germany was obliged to enter a most serious struggle for the defense of her existence, because she was threatened by her neighbors France and Russia, who were eager for booty and power, who were bent on destroying her, and who were urged on by the Island Empire." This was Germany's official explanation of the cause of the war, as repeatedly stated by her government.

responsible for the war. Even German statesmen supported the absurd lie. Bethmann-Hollweg informed the Reichstag that England could have made the war impossible if she had plainly told the Russians that she would not permit the trouble between Austria and Serbia to involve the rest of Europe. Because England upheld her honor and her pledged word to a smaller nation Germany tried desperately to shove onto England her own criminal responsibility for all the incalculable loss of life and property in the war.

The English view

In regard to this responsibility the *London Times* observed, December 5, 1914: "If the British government had made the declaration to the Russians [which the Germans desired] it would have meant simply that England declared for Germany and Austria against Russia. But according to that argument all of the great powers at war are equally responsible because they did not do something different from what they did do. France, for instance, could have prevented the war if she had declined to support Russia; Russia could have prevented it if she had taken no interest in the fate of Serbia; and finally Germany could have prevented it if she had refused to support Austria; while, as for Austria, she could have prevented it if she had never presented her ultimatum [to Serbia]."

A German ambassador refutes the accusation of the German war party

The assertions of German leaders that England desired war and was responsible for it are, of course, as the rest of the world knows, clear and well-planned lies. Certain brave Germans have dared to confess this freely. Indeed, the chief witness against the Kaiser and his advisers is no less a person than the German ambassador in London at the time that the war began, Prince Lichnowsky. He published in 1918 an account of his negotiations with English statesmen during the fatal days just preceding the outbreak of the war, and makes his own country, together with Austria, not England or France, responsible for the criminal decisions which produced it.

Lichnowsky found the English statesmen highly reasonable and eager by every means to adjust matters without recourse

English diplomats did all they could to prevent war

to the sword. He says that England had harbored no ideas of fighting Germany either because she was increasing her fleet or extending her trade, and that English diplomats left no stone unturned to prevent the war when it became imminent.

Lichnowsky's denunciation of the German military spirit

In a remarkable passage he sums up the whole ancient Prussian spirit as eloquently as any enemy of Germany's might: "Is it not intelligible that our enemies declare that they will not rest until a system is destroyed which constitutes a permanent threatening of our neighbors? Must they not otherwise fear that in a few years they will again have to take up arms, and again see their provinces overrun and their towns and villages destroyed? Were these people not right who prophesied that the spirit of Treitschke and of Bernhardi dominated the German people — the spirit which glorifies war as an aim in itself and does not abhor it as an evil; that among us it is still the feudal knights and Junkers and the caste of warriors who rule and who fix our ideals and our values — not the civilian gentleman; that the love of dueling, which inspires our youths at the universities, lives on in those who guide the fortunes of the people?"

QUESTIONS

SECTION 113. Show the historical connection between nationalism and militarism in Europe. What advantage has America had over Europe, owing to European militarism?

SECTION 114. What resulted from the first Hague Conference? from the second? What movements are there making for peace?

SECTION 115. How has the partition of Africa bred international rivalries? What change did Edward VII make in the foreign affairs of England? What countries were friendly to England in 1914? Sketch the history of the Triple Alliance. Trace the history of the Morocco affair.

SECTION 116. What interests have Russia and Austria in the Balkans? How did the Balkan wars of 1912–1913 affect Germany, France, and Russia?

SECTION 117. Trace the events of the summer of 1914.

Plate VIII. General Foch

SUPPLEMENTARY CHAPTER

CHAPTER XXVIII

THE GREAT WAR

Section 118. Course of the War in 1914 and 1915

The Germans close to Paris, September 1, 1914

The vast German army advanced on France in three divisions, one through Belgium, one through Luxemburg (also a neutral state) down into Champagne, and the third approached from Metz toward Nancy. The Belgians offered a determined resistance to the advance of the northern division and hindered it for ten days — a delay of vital importance to the French. But the heavy German guns proved too much for the forts around Liège, which were soon battered to pieces, and Brussels was occupied by the enemy, August 20. The central army advancing down the Meuse met with no serious opposition. The French, reënforced by English forces hastily dispatched across the Channel, made their first stand around Namur. This famous fortress however immediately collapsed, and the French and English rapidly retreated southward. The western division of the German army had come within twenty-five miles of Paris by September 1. The French government fled to Bordeaux, and the capital prepared for a siege.

Battle of the Marne, September, 1914

South of the Marne the French general, Joffre, halted his retreating forces, added to them a fresh army which had been quietly collected around Paris and rushed to his support, and attacked the Germans on the west. This now famous battle of the Marne put an end to the danger that threatened Paris, and Joffre became the idol of his country, which bestowed on him the baton of a marshal of France in recognition of his services to her. The Germans, under Von Kluck, were now compelled to retreat to a line of hills running from Soissons to Rheims.

There they intrenched themselves before the French and English could drive them farther back.

Conquest and ill-treatment of Belgium

After the Germans had given up their hope of surrounding Paris they proceeded to overrun Belgium. They captured Antwerp, October 10, and conquered the whole country, except a tiny corner southwest of Ostend. It was their hope to push on to Calais and occupy this port nearest to England as a base of attack against the British Isles, but they were checked at the Yser River. They treated the Belgians as a conquered people, exacted huge tributes, partially burned the city of Louvain, brutally executed many civilians, and seized any machinery or supplies that they desired. This treatment of a peaceful little neighbor, whose safety from invasion they themselves had solemnly guaranteed, did more to rouse the anger of the rest of the world than any other act of the German government.

The German occupation of northeastern France

The southernmost of the German armies, and the only one which had ventured to advance directly on France without taking the unfair advantage of a neutral boundary line, was at first unable to make much headway. But before long it succeeded in establishing its lines within French territory just east of the Meuse on a line running east of Verdun and St. Dié (see map). The French, however, invaded southern Alsace and occupied a little German territory there. Thus the first three months of the war saw the Germans in practically complete possession of Belgium and Luxemburg, together with a broad strip of northeastern France, filled with prosperous manufacturing towns, farms and vineyards, and invaluable coal and iron mines.

Permanence of the battle line in France

The lines established after the battle of the Marne and the check on the Yser did not change greatly in four years, in spite of the constant fighting and the sacrifice of hundreds of thousands of men on both sides. The Germans were not able to push very much farther into France, and the Allied forces were almost equally unsuccessful in their repeated attempts, at terrible sacrifice of life, to force the Germans more than a few miles back. Both sides "dug themselves in" and

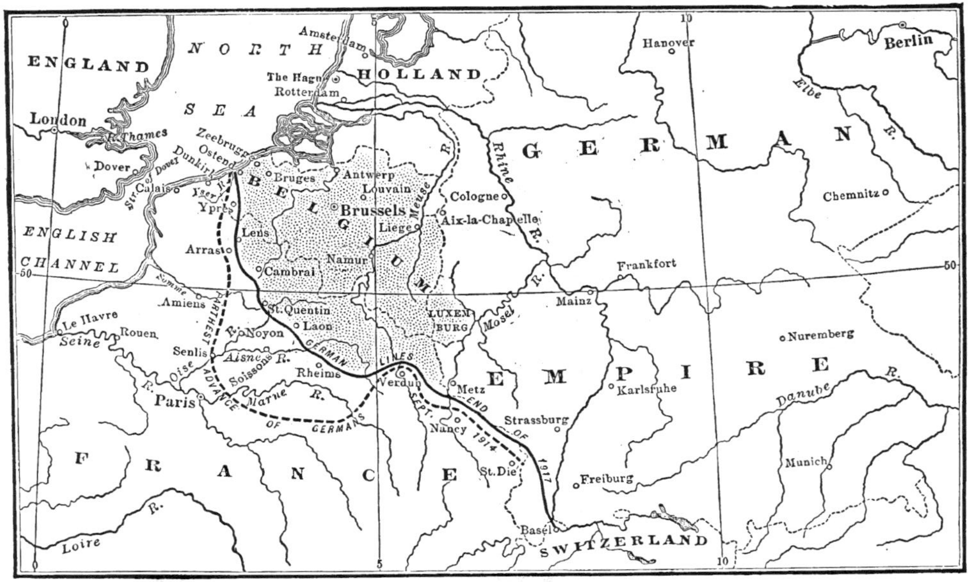

THE WESTERN FRONT, 1914–1917

trench warfare went on almost incessantly, with the aid of machine guns, shells, and huge cannon. Airplanes flew hither and thither, observing the enemy's positions and operations and dropping bombs in his midst. Poisonous gases and liquid fire, introduced by Germany, added their horrors to the situation.

The Russians fail in Galicia and lose Poland and Lithuania, 1915

On the Eastern Front the Russians at first advanced far more rapidly than had been expected. They succeeded in invading East Prussia but were soon driven out by Hindenburg and his army. They made their main attack on the Austrians in Galicia but were forced to withdraw, owing to the operations of the German and Austrian armies in Poland. These had combined in a drive on Warsaw and thus threatened the Russians on the north. During the winter of 1915 the Russians made fierce attempts to pass the Carpathians and invade Austria-Hungary. They failed, however, on account of lack of supplies, and hundreds of thousands of lives were sacrificed in vain. In August, 1915, Russia was forced to surrender Warsaw and other large Polish towns to the Germans, who pushed on beyond Poland and occupied Courland, Livonia and Esthonia. They therefore held, August, 1918, very important Russian territories in addition to their control of Poland.[1]

[1] Inasmuch as the fate of Poland is one of the problems raised by the war we may recall the following facts: At the end of the eighteenth century the ancient kingdom of Poland disappeared in a series of three partitions arranged by Prussia, Russia, and Austria. (See above, section 16, The Three Partitions of Poland.) After Napoleon succeeded in defeating both Austria and Prussia, 1805–1806, he erected the Grand Duchy of Warsaw out of the territory which Austria and Prussia had received in the third partition of Poland and what Prussia had acquired in the second. As he was on good terms with Russia at that time he left her in undisturbed possession of her part of the old Polish kingdom. At the Congress of Vienna the Grand Duchy of Warsaw was turned over to the Tsar, who promised to give it a constitutional form of government. But the region around Posen was given back to Prussia, and the Prussian government has roused constant irritation and opposition by its efforts to stamp out the Polish language in the province of Posen and to Germanize the people. As for the Kingdom of Poland created by the Congress of Vienna, that has given the Russians much trouble. The term "Poland," as now used, includes but a small part of the ancient kingdom of Poland as it existed before the three partitions. It comprises Napoleon's Grand Duchy of Warsaw, less Posen, and, to the south, Cracow, which has fallen into Austrian hands.

Germany-Austria-Hungary and their Allies
Countries at War with Teutonic Allies

THE EASTERN FRONT, 1914–1917

Germany loses all her colonies

The war early began to show an irresistible tendency to envelop the whole world. Japan quickly captured the German port of Kiau Chau and took possession of the German stations in the northern Pacific, while the Australians and New Zealanders captured those in the southern Pacific. Troops from the South African Union, with the hearty coöperation of the Boers, Britain's late enemies, occupied German Southwest Africa. The remaining German colonies, Togoland, Kamerun, and German East Africa, gradually fell into the hands of the English or French. So while Germany was able, as we shall see, to conquer important portions of central Europe as the war proceeded, she lost all her colonies. The question whether she should have them back or be indemnified for them was one of the great problems developed by the war.

Turkey joins the Central Powers, November, 1914

In November, 1914, the Teutonic allies were reënforced by Turkey. The Sultan issued a call to all faithful Mohammedans to wage a Holy War on the "enemies of Islam." But, contrary to the hopes of Germany, there was no general rising of the Mohammedans in India and Egypt against the British rule. Nor were the plans announced for capturing the Suez Canal carried out. England seized the opportunity to declare Egypt altogether independent of Turkey, December, 1914, and established a new ruler, who was given the title of Sultan of Egypt and accepted an English protectorate over his country. The English also invaded Mesopotamia and later Syria, and finally captured the famous old city of Bagdad, in March, 1917, and then the holy city of Jerusalem, in December, 1917.

The Gallipoli disaster

An attempt of the English and French in 1915 to take Constantinople proved, however, a terrible failure. In April of that year their forces, greatly strengthened by contingents from Australia and New Zealand, who had come to the Mediterranean by way of the Red Sea, tried to force their way up the Dardanelles. The Turks, well supplied with German commanders and equipment, defended themselves with such success that the Allies, in spite of the sacrifice of a hundred thousand men, killed and wounded, were unable to hold their positions on the peninsula of Gallipoli, where they had secured a footing. After some months the English government was obliged to recognize that it had made a tragic mistake, and the attempt was given up.

Italy enters the war, 1915

In May, 1915, Italy finally decided that she could no longer remain out of the war. Her people believed in the principles for which the Allies were fighting and had no love for Austria. Then too it seemed that the opportunity had come to win "Italia Irredenta,"—those portions of the Italian people still unredeemed from Austrian rule, who live around Trent, in Istria and the great seaport of Trieste, and along the Dalmatian coast. So this added another "front" which the Central Powers had to defend.

The belligerents at the opening of the second year of the war

So the line-up at the opening of the second year of the war consisted of the Central Powers,—Germany, Austria-Hungary, and Turkey,—opposed to Russia, France, Italy, Great Britain (including Canadians, Australians, New Zealanders, South Africans, and East Indian troops, all ready to shed their blood in the cause of the British Empire), Belgium, Serbia, Japan, and the tiny countries of Montenegro and San Marino,—twelve belligerents in all, scattered over the whole globe. But the war was not destined to stop at this point. Hundreds of millions of people who were at that time still neutral later took up arms against German *Kultur*.

Extinction of German commerce

It was the war on the sea that raised the chief problems for the world at large. At the beginning of the war many people supposed that there would soon be a great and perhaps decisive naval engagement between the German and British fleets, but no such thing happened.[1] The Germans kept their dreadnaughts safe in their harbors, protected by cruisers and

[1] On May 31, 1916, a portion of the German fleet ventured out of the Baltic and fell in with a strong detachment of the British fleet. After a few hours the mist, smoke, and darkness put an end to the fight. The Germans claimed a victory, but the fact that their ships retired to a fortified base from which no one of them came forth again until the entire fleet came out to surrender to the English fleet, without having fired a single shot, successfully repudiates any claim they may have asserted to a victory at this battle of Jutland.

mines. The German merchant ships took shelter at home or in neutral ports, and the few cruisers that remained at large, and for a time scoured the seas and sunk English vessels, were captured or sunk. So German commerce was soon cut off altogether, and England ruled the ocean. Had it not been for the recently discovered and rapidly improved submarines, or U-boats, as they are popularly called, the Germans would have been helpless against the British control of the seas. It is this new kind of warfare that has largely determined the course of the conflict of the nations.

Rôle of the submarine

It was easy for England to block the German ports of Hamburg and Bremen, the egress from the Kiel Canal, and the outlet from the Baltic without violating the established principles of international law. But the German submarines could still steal out and sink English merchant ships and manage now and then to torpedo a great war vessel. Great Britain claimed the right under these new conditions of naval warfare to force all neutral ships bound for the neutral ports of Holland, Norway, and Sweden to stop and be inspected at Kirkwall, in the Orkney Islands, to see if they were carrying contraband of war — namely, munitions and materials to be used directly or indirectly for military ends — and if their cargoes were really destined for Germany. When, February 1, 1915, the German government ordered the confiscation of all grain in private hands with a view of keeping its great armies well fed, England declared that thereafter all shipments of foodstuffs to Germany would be deemed absolute contraband of war, since feeding her fighting men was even more necessary than supplying them with munitions.

The Germans greatly extend the zone of marine war

This was regarded by the Germans as an obvious attempt "through starvation to doom an entire nation to destruction." The German government thereupon declared that the waters around England should be regarded as within the zone of war, that within this zone all enemy merchant vessels would be sunk, whether it were possible to save the passengers and crews or not. Neutrals were warned that they would be in great danger if they entered the zone. In former days it was possible for a man-of-war to hold up a vessel, and if the cargo was found to be contraband to capture or sink the vessel after taking off the people on board. But the submarine has no room for extra persons, and the Germans found it much more convenient to torpedo vessels without even the warning necessary to enable the passengers and crew to take to the lifeboats.

Sinking of the *Lusitania*, May, 1915

In February, 1915, German submarines began to sink not only enemy vessels but neutral ones as well, sometimes giving the people on board warning, but often not. The most terrible example of the ruthlessness of the U-boats was the sinking, without warning, of the great liner *Lusitania*, May 7, 1915, involving the loss of nearly 1200 men, women, and children, including over a hundred American citizens. The Germans hailed this as a heroic deed. They claimed that the vessel was armed and laden with shells, and that the Americans had no business to be on it, since a notice in the New York papers had warned them against traveling on the fated boat. But after careful investigation an American court decided that the vessel was not armed and did not carry any explosives and that her destruction was nothing less than an act of piracy. This crime aroused the greatest horror and indignation not only in England and the United States but throughout the rest of the world.[1]

English drive, late autumn, 1915

On the Western Front the English forces had steadily increased, until, by the end of September, 1915, Sir John French had a million men under his command. The English had also been very busy producing arms and munitions of war, in which they had been sadly deficient at the opening of the war, and they had greatly added to their supplies by purchases in the United States. They therefore resolved upon a drive northeast of Arras. After a period of terrific fighting they succeeded in

[1] The questions of the rights of neutrals, of contraband, and the rights of search, are very complicated, and only the main issues in the long and heated discussions can be suggested here.

forcing back the German lines two or three miles on a front of fifteen or twenty miles. This gave the world some notion of the difficulty the Allies would have to meet in their attempt to oust the German armies from France and Belgium.

Invasion of Serbia, October, 1915

In spite of the English drive, the Germans, who had succeeded in forcing back the Russians in Galicia, now undertook the invasion of Serbia. This encouraged Serbia's bitter enemy, Bulgaria, to declare in favor of the Central Powers and join vigorously in the cruel punishment of her neighbor. In spite of heroic resistance on the part of the Serbians, their country, attacked on two sides, quickly fell into the hands of their enemies. From this time on they were able to regain very little of their lost territory.

Bulgaria joins in the war

Neutrality of Greece

The British and French had landed troops at the Greek port of Salonica but were unable to prevent the disaster. There was a grave difference of opinion in Greece as to the proper attitude for it to take. The royal family was strongly pro-German, but many, especially Greece's chief statesman, Venizelos, favored siding with the Allies. King Constantine managed to maintain the nominal neutrality of his country until the year 1917, when his well-known German sympathies and intrigue led to his expulsion from Greece.

Section 119. The Campaigns of 1916

The attempt to break through at Verdun, February-July, 1916

After the small success of the English drive at the end of 1915 the Germans resolved to show what they could do on the Western Front. They decided to attack the ancient fortress of Verdun, the loss of which would greatly discourage the French, for it was popularly regarded as one of the country's chief strongholds. The fact that Metz, a very important center of German supplies, lies not far east of Verdun served to increase the German chances for breaking through the French lines at this point. Great masses of troops, under the general command of no less a personage than the German Crown Prince, were brought together, and the attack began February 21, 1916.

For a time the French lines gave way, and those throughout the world who favored the Allies held their breath, for it seemed as if the Germans were about to crush the French defense and again threaten Paris. But the French recovered and held their own once more. The English troops were now numerous enough to hold the lines to the north. A series of terrible encounters followed, but the French under General Joffre were able during May and June to push the Germans back from the points occupied in the first onrush. The danger of a German victory was now past, and by July all danger of collapse at that point seemed to be over. It was a great source of satisfaction to the Allies and their sympathizers to behold the insolent Crown Prince repulsed after a supreme effort to distinguish himself in the longest and bloodiest of all the fearful combats that had yet occurred.

Repulse of the Crown Prince at Verdun

At the opening of the war England had an available force of less than a hundred thousand men, "a contemptible army," as the Kaiser is reported to have scornfully denominated it. Germany, Russia, France, had their millions of trained men, owing to their long-established system of universal military service, — conscription, as it is called — which makes every able-bodied man liable to service. For a time England tried to increase its army by voluntary enlistments, and on the whole succeeded very well. But after much discussion and opposition she introduced (May, 1916) a system of universal compulsory military service, which included all able-bodied men between the ages of 18 and 41. (The limits were extended later to include men from 18 to 50 years of age, with limited service also for those between 50 and 55.)

England adopts conscription, May, 1916

Shortly after, the long-talked-of Anglo-French drive, the Battle of the Somme, began, which was fought for four months, from July to November, east and northeast of Amiens. Here a new English military invention made its first appearance, the so-called "tanks," — huge heavily armored motor cars so built as to break through barbed-wire entanglements and crawl over great holes and trenches. The English had also their fifteen-inch

Battle of the Somme, July-November, 1916

mortars for hurling big shells. The Germans retreated a few miles, but the cost was terrible, since each side lost six or seven hundred thousand men in killed or wounded.

The Italians repulse the Austrian drive and gain Gorizia, August, 1916

While the battle of Verdun was raging, the Italians, who had made but little progress against the strong Austrian fortifications, were suddenly pushed back by a great Austrian drive in May, 1916. By the middle of June they had not only lost the little they had gained but had been forced to evacuate some of their own territory. At this point the Russians, in spite of the loss of Poland, attacked Austria once more and again threatened to press into Hungary. So Austria had to give way in Italy in order to defend her Galician boundary, and the Italians were able not only to regain what they had lost but to capture the important town of Gorizia on their way, as they hoped, to Trieste.

Russian drive fails

Roumania joins the Allies and is invaded

The Russians had sacrificed more than a million men, yet treachery in the government made it impossible for them to hold their conquests, but their momentary success encouraged Roumania to join in the war on the side of the Allies, who seemed to be getting the better of the Central Powers. She invaded Transylvania, which she had long claimed as properly hers. The Germans, notwithstanding the pressure on the Somme, immediately sent two of their best generals and with the help of the Bulgarians attacked Roumania from the west and south and captured Bucharest, the capital, in December, 1916. About two thirds of Roumania was soon in possession of her enemies, and the Germans could supplement their supplies from her rich fields of grain and abundant oil wells.

Estimated losses of men up to January 1, 1917

It is estimated that by January 1, 1917, somewhere between five and seven millions of men had been killed, and a far greater number had been wounded or taken prisoner. Russia had lost the greatest number, but France the greatest in proportion to her population. The casualty lists in the war were enormous; yet, owing to the excellently organized medical care now possible on the battlefield, a greater proportion of those wounded in this war will be cured than has been possible in earlier wars.

For the first time in the history of war men have been able to fly high above the contending forces, making observations and engaging in aërial battles. Airplanes are now among the essentials of war, and they bring new horrors in their train. The Germans made repeated air raids on England, apparently with the foolish notion that they were going to intimidate the people. They first used the huge dirigible balloons called Zeppelins; but these were later replaced by airplanes of various kinds. They killed two or three thousand English civilians — men, women, and children — in town and country and destroyed some property. Without accomplishing any important military aims, they increased their reputation for needless brutality and forced the English for the safety of their unfortified towns to make reprisals. English and French airmen dropped bombs on the more accessible German towns, Freiburg, Karlsruhe, and Mannheim, and many military places. **Aërial warfare**

Section 120. The World against Germany, 1917

Early in the year 1917 Germany's submarine policy and reckless sinking of neutral ships finally involved her in war with a new antagonist, the great and powerful republic across the Atlantic. The government of the United States had been very patient and long-suffering. When the war broke out President Wilson declared that the government would observe strict neutrality, and he urged American citizens to avoid taking sides in a conflict that did not directly concern them. But it was impossible to remain indifferent when such tremendous events were being reported day by day. The German newspapers in the United States eagerly defended the Central Powers and laid the responsibility for the war at England's door. On the other hand, the great body of the American people were deeply shocked by the invasion of Belgium, by the burning of Louvain, by the needless destruction of Rheims Cathedral by German guns. They disliked the arrogant talk of the Kaiser, and they **Division of opinion in the United States** felt a quick sympathy for France, who had lent such essential aid in the American Revolution. Those of English descent naturally found themselves drawn to her side in the great struggle.

Activity of German agents

So the bitter feelings engendered by war began to show themselves immediately in the United States. German agents and spies were everywhere active, eagerly misrepresenting the motives of England and her allies and doing everything in their power to prejudice the people of the United States against Germany's foes. The German government stooped to the most shameful expedients. It even sent to its ambassador, Count von Bernstorff, funds with which to attempt to bribe Congress. The minister of Austria-Hungary had to be sent off at the opening of the war for informing his home government that he had a plan for so disorganizing the great steel factories that they would be unable for months to supply England and France with arms and ammunition.[1]

President Wilson expostulates with Germany

As time went on President Wilson dispatched note after note to Germany expostulating against the merciless and indiscriminate manner in which the submarines sent vessels to the bottom, not only British ships, like the *Lusitania*, carrying American passengers but American ships and those of other neutral nations. There was often no warning until the torpedo actually struck the ship, and no sufficient time even to take to the lifeboats and face the hazards of a troubled sea. The anger of the American people as a whole against Germany became hotter and hotter, and President Wilson began to be denounced for tolerating any diplomatic relations with the German imperial government.

[1] There was a very bitter difference of feeling between the pro-Germans and the friends of the Allies in regard to the exportation of arms and munitions. Since Germany had no way of getting supplies from the United States, owing to the English control of the Atlantic, she maintained that it was *unneutral* for the manufacturers in the United States to sell arms to the Allies. Yet it has always been considered the right of neutrals to sell to any belligerent anything they are in a position to furnish. When the Germans succeeded in getting a freight submarine, the *Deutschland*, over to New London, Connecticut, the captain found people willing enough to sell warlike supplies to Germans. But the German government's idea of "neutrality" is taking sides with it.

In January, 1917, England, in order completely to cut off supplies from Germany, extended the area which she declared to be in a state of blockade. Germany then proclaimed to the world that in order to make head against "British tyranny" and England's alleged plan to starve Germany she proposed to establish a vast barred zone extending far to the west of Great Britain, in which sea traffic with England would be prevented by every available means. In this way she flattered herself that England, who draws much of her food from distant regions, would soon be reduced to starvation and the war brought to a speedy end. One of the most insulting features of Germany's plan was that a narrow lane was to be left through which the United States was to be permitted to send one ship a week provided it was painted with bright stripes of color and carried no contraband. By these measures Germany reserved a vast area of the high seas for her murderous enterprises, utterly regardless of every recognized right of neutral nations (see map, p. 712).

Intensification of submarine warfare, February, 1917

On February 1, 1917, the Germans opened their unrestricted submarine warfare in this great barred zone, and many vessels were sunk. President Wilson broke off diplomatic relations with the German government February 3, and Count von Bernstorff was sent home, to the great relief of those who had criticized the President for being too patient. The sinkings went on, and popular opinion was more and more aroused against Germany. The hostility was intensified by the publication of a letter from the German minister of foreign affairs to the Mexican government, which proposed that if war broke out between the United States and Germany, Mexico should attack the United States and should take Texas, New Mexico, and Arizona as its reward.

The United States severs relations with Germany, February 3, 1917

It was finally evident that war was unavoidable. President Wilson summoned a special session of Congress and on April 2, 1917, read a memorable address to its members in which he said that Germany had to all intents and purposes declared war on the United States. "Our object," he maintained, "is to

The United States declares war, April 6, 1917

vindicate the principles of peace and justice in the life of the world, as against selfish and autocratic power." The free and self-governed peoples of the world must combine, he urged, "to

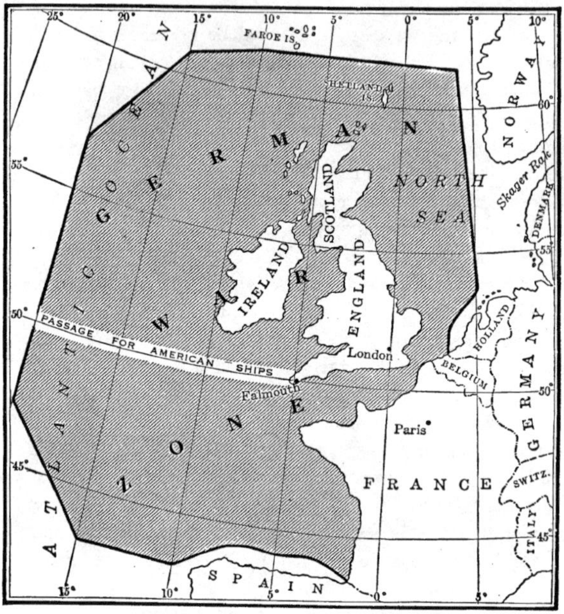

GERMAN WAR ZONE OF FEBRUARY 1, 1917

Late in the year 1917 and early in 1918 the German government extended the barred zone so as to include the islands off the coast of Africa, Madeira, the Cape Verde Islands, and the Azores, in order to cut the routes between Europe and South America

make the world safe for democracy," for otherwise no permanent peace is possible. He proposed that the United States should fight side by side with Germany's enemies and aid them with liberal loans. Both houses of Congress approved by large majorities the proposed resolution that the United States had been forced into war. Provisions were made for borrowing vast sums; old forms of taxation were greatly increased and many new ones added. In May, 1917, conscription was introduced, and all able-bodied men between the ages of twenty-one and thirty-one were declared liable to military service. Preparations were made for training great bodies of troops to be sent across the Atlantic to aid the cause of the Allies and measures taken for building ships to replace those destroyed by German submarines. The people of the United States showed themselves eager to do their part in the war on autocracy and militarism.[1]

The United States begins gigantic preparations

One result of the entrance of the United States into the war was a great increase in the number of Germany's enemies during the year 1917. Cuba and Panama immediately followed the example set by the great North American Republic; Greece, after much internal turmoil and dissension, finally, under the influence of Venizelos, joined the Allies; in the latter half of the year Siam, Liberia, China, and Brazil proclaimed war on Germany. The war had become literally a world conflict. The governments of nearly a billion and a half of the earth's population were involved in the amazing struggle. Thirteen hundred and forty millions of people were committed by their rulers to the side of the Allies, and the countries included in the Central European alliance had a total population of about one hundred and sixty millions. So nearly seven eighths of the population of the globe were nominally at war, and of these nine tenths were arrayed against one tenth, led by Prussia. Of course the vast population of India and China play a great part in these figures but had little or no part in the active prosecution of the war. And after the Russian revolution destroyed the old

The conflict becomes a world war, 1917

1 When the unrestricted submarine sinkings began, February 1, 1917, the German newspapers informed their readers that England would speedily be brought to her knees. But while hundreds of ships were sunk, thousands came and went from English ports, managing in various ways to escape the U-boats. Then by economy, raising more food, and building more ships England, with America's help, successfully offset the damage done by the Germans.

government, that country, with its millions of inhabitants, by the end of 1917 could no longer be reckoned an active factor. Keeping these facts in mind, the following tables will make the situation clear.

THE WORLD WAR AT THE OPENING OF 1918

The Allies and their Colonies and Dependencies

Country	Date of Entrance	Population	Men under Arms [1]
	1914		
Serbia	July 28	4,550,000	300,000
Russia	August 1	175,000,000	9,000,000 [2]
France	August 3	87,500,000	6,000,000
Belgium	August 4	22,500,000	300,000
British Empire	August 4	440,000,000	5,000,000
Montenegro	August 7	516,000	40,000
Japan	August 23	74,000,000	1,400,000
	1915		
Italy	May 23	37,000,000	3,000,000
San Marino	June 2	12,000	1,000
	1916		
Portugal	March 10	15,000,000	200,000
Roumania	August 27	7,500,000	320,000
	1917		
United States	April 6	113,000,000	1,000,000(?)
Cuba	April 8	2,500,000	11,000
Panama	April 9	427,000	
Greece	July 16	5,000,000	300,000
Siam	July 22	8,150,000	36,000
Liberia	August 7	1,800,000	400
China	August 14	320,000,000	540,000
Brazil	October 26	25,000,000	25,000
		1,339,455,000	27,473,400

[1] The population is only approximate and in round numbers. The strength of the armies given is based on an estimate of the United States War Department, October, 1917.

[2] The Russian armies at the end of 1917 were in a state of complete dissolution.

CENTRAL POWERS, WITH COLONIES AND DEPENDENCIES AT THE OPENING OF THE WAR

COUNTRY	DATE OF ENTRANCE	POPULATION	MEN UNDER ARMS
	1914		
Austria-Hungary	July 28	50,000,000	3,000,000
Germany . . .	August 1	80,600,000	7,000,000
Turkey	November 3	21,000,000	300,000
	1915		
Bulgaria. . . .	October 4	5,000,000	300,000
		156,600,000	10,600,000

As for the countries which remained neutral, they included a population of perhaps one hundred and ninety millions. Holland, Switzerland, Denmark, Norway, and Sweden were far too close to Germany to risk breaking with her, although it would seem that many of their people abhorred her conduct. Spain and a number of Latin-American states, including Mexico and Chile, held aloof. But no country could escape the burdens and afflictions of a war of such magnitude. Real neutrality was almost impossible. Everywhere taxes and prices rose, essential supplies were cut off, and business was greatly dislocated. Position of the few neutral countries

In addition to the increase in Germany's enemies the chief military events of 1917 were the following: In March the Germans decided to shorten their lines on the Western Front from Noyon on the south to Arras on the north. They withdrew, devastating the land as they went, and the French and English were able to reoccupy about one eighth of the French territory that the enemy had held so long. The Germans were disturbed by fierce attacks while establishing their new line of defense, but in spite of great sacrifices on the part of the French and English, and especially of the Canadians, this "Hindenburg" line was so well fortified that it held, and with slight exceptions continued to hold during the year. The English made some progress in forcing back the enemy on The Western Front, 1917 the Belgian coast, with the hope of gaining Zeebrugge, the base from which German submarines made their departure to prey on English commerce. Attempts to take St. Quentin, the important mining town of Lens, and the city of Cambrai were not successful for another year, but the terrible slaughter went on and tens of thousands were killed every week.

Russia out of the war by the end of 1917

On the Eastern Front it will be remembered that the Russian attack in the summer of 1916 failed and that the Central Powers got control of two thirds of Roumania. After the great Russian revolution of March, 1917,[1] in which the Tsar was deposed, the new popular leader, Kerensky, made a last attempt to rally the Russian armies, but his efforts came to naught. He was supplanted in November, 1917, by the leaders of the extreme socialists, the Bolsheviki,[2] who were opposed to all war except that on capital. They took immediate steps to open negotiations with the Germans and their allies (see below, p. 729).

Section 121. The Question of Peace

Grave problems antedating the war

The war rendered acute every chronic disease which Europe had failed to remedy in the long period of general peace. France had never given up hopes of regaining Alsace-Lorraine, which had been wrested from her after the war of 1870–1871. The Poles continued to aspire to appear on the map as an independent nation. Both the northern Slavs of Bohemia and the southern Slavs in Croatia, Bosnia, and Slavonia were discontented with their relations to Austria-Hungary, of which they formed a part. The Irredentists of Italy had long laid claim to important coast lands belonging to Austria. Serbia and Bulgaria were bitterly at odds over the arrangements made at the close of the Second Balkan War.[3] Roumania longed for

[1] See below, p. 727.

[2] This name, meaning "majority men," was given to the faction at an earlier time, when they constituted the majority of the Russian socialists. It was at first wrongly explained in the American press as "those who want more," and mistranslated "Maximalists."

[3] See above, pp. 590 and 691.

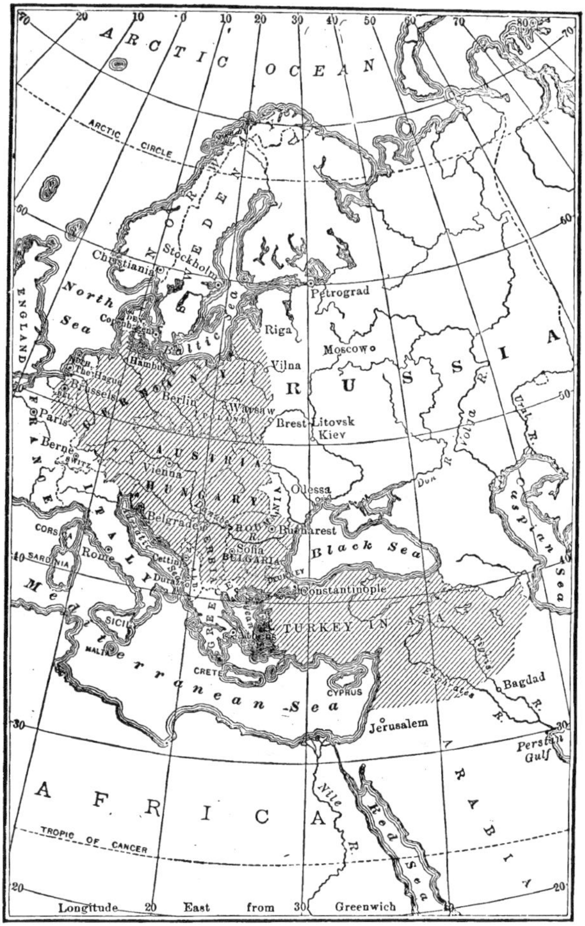

"Middle Europe," under the Control of the Teutonic Allies at the End of 1917

Transylvania and Bukowina. Then there were the old questions as to whether Russia should have Constantinople, what was to be done with the remaining vestiges of the Turkish empire, and who was to control Syria and Mesopotamia. In the far East, Japan's interests in China offered an unsolved problem. The Germans emphasized the necessity of meeting the discontent with British rule in India and Ireland.

New problems due to the war

The progress of the war added new territorial perplexities. The Central Powers at the end of 1917 were in military possession of Belgium, Luxemburg, northeastern France, Poland, Lithuania, Courland, Serbia, Montenegro, and Roumania (see map, p. 717). Great Britain had captured Bagdad and Jerusalem. In Africa all the German colonies were in the hands of her enemies, and in Australasia her possessions had been taken over by Japan and Australia. Were all these regions conquered by one or the other of the belligerent groups to be given back or not? Then what about Belgium, whose people were mulcted and abused and pillaged by their conquerors; and what of northeastern France wantonly devastated? Was not reparation due to these unhappy victims of the war?

War on war

But all these questions seem of minor importance compared with the overwhelming world problem. How shall mankind conspire to put an end to war forever? The world of to-day, compared with that of Napoleon's time, when the last great international struggle took place, is so small, the nations have been brought so close together, they are so dependent on one another, that it would seem as if the time had come to join in a last, victorious *war on war.* It required a month or more to cross the Atlantic in 1815; now less than six days are necessary, and airplanes may soon be soaring above its waves far swifter than any steamer. Formerly the oceans were great barriers separating America from Europe, and the Orient from America; but, like the ancient bulwarks around medieval cities, they have now become highways on which men of all nations hasten to and fro. Before the war, express trains were regularly traversing Europe from end to end at a speed of forty to fifty miles an hour, and the automobile vies with the locomotive in speed; whereas at the time of the Congress of Vienna no one could get about faster than a horse could travel. The telegraph and telephone enable news to be flashed to the most distant parts of the earth more quickly than Louis XVIII could send a message from one part of Paris to another. The wireless apparatus keeps vessels, no matter how far out at sea, in constant touch with the land.

Interdependence of the nations

Nations depend on one another for food, clothes, and every sort of necessity and refinement. Britain hoped to end the war by cutting off Germany from her usual communication with other countries; and Germany flattered herself she could starve England by sinking the thousands of vessels which supplied her tables with bread and meat. Even the rumor of war upsets the stock exchanges throughout the world. Nations read one another's books, profit by one another's scientific discoveries and inventions, and go to one another's plays. Italians, French, Russians, and Germans contribute to musical programs listened to in New York, Valparaiso, or Sydney. We continue to talk of *independent* nations; but only a few isolated, squalid savage tribes can be said any longer to be independent of other peoples. In an ever-increasing degree America is a part of Europe and Europe a part of America; and their histories tend to merge into the history of the whole world.

International agreements and enterprises before the war

The war only greatly emphasized all these things, which were being recognized in the previous quarter of a century. The Hague conferences, the establishment of the Hague international tribunal, the various arbitration treaties, had all been directed toward the suppression of the ancient plague of war. International arrangements in regard to coinage, postal service, commerce, and transportation had encouraged good understanding and coöperation. Innumerable international societies, congresses, and expositions had brought foreign peoples together and illustrated their manifold common interests.

Cost of preparedness greatly increased by recent inventions

The old problem of armaments, the possibility of getting rid of the crushing burden and constant peril of vast standing armies and the competition in dreadnaughts and cruisers, has assumed a somewhat new form. The progress of the deadly art of killing one's fellow men has advanced so rapidly, with the aid of scientific discovery and the stress of the world war, that what was considered adequate military preparedness before the war now seems absurdly inadequate. Giant guns, air craft, "tanks," and poisonous gases have, among other things, been added to the older devices of destruction, and the submarine suggests a complete revolution in naval strategy. So there is some hope in the fact that, since no nation can longer afford the luxury of military preparedness, it is clearer than ever before that war as a means of settling international disputes must become a thing of the past.

Issue of "militarism" fundamental

The great issue of the war was really "militarism," which includes two closely associated problems: first, shall diplomats be permitted any longer to carry on secret negotiations and pledge their respective nations to secret agreements which may involve war? and, secondly, shall a government be permitted to declare war without the approval of the great mass of its citizens? Now those opposed to Germany are all in hearty agreement in regarding her as representing the most dangerous form of militarism, which plunged the whole world into a horrible war and would, unless destroyed, remain a constant menace to future peace. Let us first see how the Germans seem to view their own institutions and ideals and then we shall be in a better position to understand the attitude of their adversaries.

The German view of Germany

The Germans have been taught, during the past hundred years, by their philosophers, teachers, clergymen, and government officials to regard themselves as the leading nation of the world. They have been told that their natural ability, virtue, insight, and prowess exceed those of all other peoples, whom they were taught to look upon as decadent, barbarians, or hypocrites. German leaders declared an invincible army must be built up to protect the Empire from its neighbors, and a powerful navy must be developed to be used when the right moment should come[1] to extend Germany's confines at the expense of England and to enable her to spread her vaunted *Kultur*. In spite of this militaristic teaching the Germans persisted in claiming to be a peace-loving people with a peace-loving emperor who had done everything to avoid war! Yet no one denied that their army was an essential part of their national constitution and that unqualified obedience and unquestioning deference to military authorities was part and parcel of their bounden duty to the State. No interest of the individual subject was allowed to conflict with its claims, since it was "of infinitely more value than the sum of all the individuals within its jurisdiction."[2]

Position of the Hohenzollern rulers of Germany

The visible head of the State, the king of Prussia as emperor of Germany, demanded the absolute fidelity of every German. He was descended from the Hohenzollern line under which first Prussia and then the German Empire was laboriously built up, under the Great Elector, Frederick the Great, Kaiser William I, and William II.

Crime of lese majesty

These were the officially accepted views in regard to the German nation, the German State, the German army, and the German Kaiser. Those who, before the war, indiscreetly questioned the claims of the Kaiser frequently found themselves imprisoned for lese majesty, the crime of insulting "The All-Highest." At the beginning of the war, the popularity of the Kaiser appeared to have greatly increased; but it is impossible to say whether the socialists and other critics of the government really changed their opinion of the Hohenzollern rule or merely

1 German officers were accustomed to drink to this future moment as "The Day" (*Der Tag*).

2 So writes Eduard Meyer, a well-known historian. He adds, "This conception of the State, which is as much a part of our life as is the blood in our veins, is nowhere to be found in the English Constitution, and is quite foreign to English thought, and to that of America as well." Quoted by Veblen, *On the Nature of Peace*, p. 86 n.

kept still from patriotic and prudential motives. There can be no doubt that the great landholders of Prussia[1] and the military class are still ardent supporters of the ancient monarchy. When the war broke out the Germans and their "peace-loving" emperor assumed no responsibility for it. On the contrary, the Kaiser declared that his enemies had forced the sword into his reluctant hand.

View of Germany taken by other peoples

It is needless to say that the rest of the world entertains a very different notion of the Germans and of the origin of the war from that just given. It is generally recognized that Germany has been in some respects a progressive country; that its scientists and scholars have played their part in modern investigation and discovery. But other nations have made vast contributions too in all the sciences, and in ingenious inventions, literature, and art other peoples outshine the Germans.

Ruthlessness of German militarism

Before the war the utterances of the Kaiser and his talk about his German God merely amused or disgusted foreigners. The plans of the Pan-Germanists were known to few, but a book by the German general, Bernhardi, called *Germany and the Next War*, which appeared in 1911, made clear their program. "We must not," Bernhardi says, "hold back in the hard struggle for the sovereignty of the world."[2] France and England had grown increasingly suspicious of German power, but nevertheless the war came as a hideous surprise to even the best informed people. Every one knew that Germany had the strongest and best organized and equipped army in Europe, but when it was suddenly hurled against Belgium, in August, 1914, the world was aghast. The spoliation of Belgium, the shooting down of civilians, the notorious atrocities ot the German soldiers, the cold-blooded instructions to the officers to intimidate the civil population by examples of cruel punishments

[1] These are popularly known as the *Junkers* (pronounced "yōōnkers"), or country squires. They are the successors of the manorial lords who controlled the land until the abolition of serfdom in Prussia at the opening of the nineteenth century. They do not confine themselves to agriculture but invest their money in industries and so merge into the capitalistic class.

[2] English translation, p. 79.

(*Schrecklichkeit*), the scandalous and criminal activities of German spies, the ruthless submarines, the slaughter of noncombatants in the air raids over England, the destruction of the noble cathedral of Rheims by German gunners, the "Song of Hate" in which a German poet summoned his fellow countrymen to execrate England with undying animosity, — all these things combined to produce world-wide horror and apprehension. To their adversaries the Germans were "Huns" led by a modern Attila,[1] ready to deluge the world in blood in order to realize the dream of world domination.

"Militarism" and "autocracy"

The fatal readiness of the German military force for instant action was also thoroughly impressed on the world. The Kaiser had but to say, "the country is attacked," — and he was the judge of what constituted an attack, — posters appeared everywhere ordering those liable to service to be at a certain railroad station at a given hour, under penalty of imprisonment or death, to be dispatched anywhere the general staff ordered. When mobilization was proclaimed, the civil government immediately gave way to military rule throughout the length and breadth of the land. At the opening of August the German people knew that they were going to war with Russia; but the soldiers sent to the Belgian boundary had no idea where *they* were going. This is what the world calls *militarism* and *autocracy*.

Germany's peace offer, December, 1916

The great difficulty of reëstablishing peace between the two great hostile alliances is well brought out in the various peace suggestions made during the third year of the war. In December, 1916, after the Central Powers had occupied Poland,

[1] When a German expedition was starting for China in July, 1900, after the Boxers had killed the German ambassador, the Kaiser addressed the troops as follows: "You know very well that you are to fight against a cunning, brave, well-armed and terrible enemy. If you come to grips with him, be assured quarter will not be given. Use your weapons in such a way that for a thousand years no Chinese shall dare to look upon a German askance. Be as terrible as Attila's Huns." While the last sentence was deleted in the later official issues of the speech, the public did not forget the impressions they got from the Kaiser's exhortation to act like *Huns*. And the German soldiers by no means neglected his suggestions when they reached Peking.

Serbia, and Roumania, and Germany seemed to be victorious on all hands, she made what she called a peace offer. She proposed that the belligerents send representatives to some point in a neutral country to consider the terms of settlement. The German government must have known well enough that the Allies could not possibly consider making peace at a time when their enemies were at the height of military success. The proposition was scornfully rejected, but it served in German eyes to throw the burden for continuing the fearful conflict upon the Allies. Whoever might have been responsible for beginning the war, Germany had been the first to propose to end it. The Kaiser proclaimed exultantly that the Allies had at last cast off the mask of hypocrisy and plainly revealed their "lust of conquest." The refusal of their adversaries to consider peace also furnished an excuse for a resort to the unrestricted and brutal submarine warfare which Germany was contemplating. She argued that if her enemies really proposed to "crush" Germany, no means of self-defense on her part could be too ruthless.

President Wilson's peace suggestions, December 18, 1916

Before the Allies had replied to the German peace suggestion President Wilson intervened (December 18) with a circular note sent to the belligerents, calling attention to the fact that both sides seemed to agree that there should be a league for maintaining peace, and small states should be protected, but neither side, he said, had stated the "concrete objects" for which they were fighting. He accordingly suggested a conference on the essential conditions of peace. Germany expressed herself as ready for a meeting of delegates to consider peace terms. The Allies, however, declined to negotiate, but went so far in replying to President Wilson, January 10, 1917, as to give a definition of the oft-used terms "restoration," "restitution," and "guarantees."

Aims of the Allies, January, 1917

The Central Powers were to evacuate all the regions they had conquered during the course of the war; indemnities were to be paid for damage and loss caused by the war; moreover "provinces or territories wrested in the past from the Allies by force or against the will of their populations" were to be returned. The principle of nationality was to be recognized, and the Italians, southern and northern Slavs, and Roumanians were to be freed from foreign domination; the populations subject to "the bloody tyranny of the Turks" were to be liberated and the Turk expelled altogether from Europe. Poland was to be united under the sovereignty of the Tsar. Finally, the "reorganization of Europe was to be guaranteed by a stable régime." As for the German colonies, high officials in both England and Japan said that they would be retained by their conquerors.

The terms of the Allies appear absurd to their adversaries

This meant that the Central Powers should acknowledge their guilt and pay for the damage they had done; that Germany should give up Alsace-Lorraine, Austria-Hungary should make serious concessions to meet "the principle of nationality," Bulgaria should give up her dreams of annexing Serbian territory, and Turkey should leave Europe and lose control over her Asiatic peoples. In view of the extraordinary military achievements of the Central Powers and Germany's claim to have been acting from the first in sheer self-defense, these conditions were immediately condemned by the Teutonic allies as intolerable and not to be considered.

President Wilson's essentials of peace, January 22, 1917

On January 22, 1917, President Wilson, in addressing the Senate, said that peace must, among other things, provide for equality of right for both great and small nations, security for subject "peoples," direct outlet to the sea for every great people, "freedom of the seas,"[1] and limitation of armaments.

[1] In time of peace the high seas — that is, the ocean outside of the three-mile limit drawn along the coast — are free to all and are not supposed to be under the control of any particular government. It is in time of war that the question of "the freedom of the seas" arises. England was in a position at the opening of the war to cut off Germany's maritime commerce. Germany immediately established vast barred zones, in which she sank not only her enemies' vessels but those of neutrals which ventured to neglect her warnings. So the ocean was anything but free during the conflict. Another element in the freedom of the seas is the control of such narrow passages as the Dardanelles, the Straits of Gibraltar, the Suez and Panama Canals, and the entrances to the Baltic. It is hard to imagine any arrangement that will keep the seas open and safe so long as wars continue to take place among maritime powers.

Principle of Democracy

"No peace can last," he declared, "or ought to last, which does not recognize and accept the principle that governments derive all their just powers from the consent of the governed, and that no right anywhere exists to hand peoples about from sovereignty to sovereignty as if they were property."

Armaments a constant menace

"There can be no sense of safety and equality among the nations if great preponderating armaments are henceforth to continue here and there to be built up and maintained. The statesmen of the world must plan for peace, and nations must adjust and accommodate their policy to it as they have planned for war and made ready for pitiless contest and rivalry. The question of armaments, whether on land or sea, is the most immediately and intensely practical question connected with the future fortunes of nations and of mankind."

The Russian revolution, March, 1917

In March, 1917, one of the chief belligerent countries, Russia, underwent such a great internal change as greatly to modify the course of the war and the problem of peace. We must now consider the astonishing revolution which led to the overthrow of the old Russian despotism and the retirement of Russia from the war.

The Tsar attempts a reaction, December–March, 1916–1917

The world conflict had hardly opened in 1914 before it revealed the corruption, the weakness, the inefficiency, indeed the treason, of the Tsar's court and his imperial officials. The millions of Russians who perished in the trenches of the Eastern Front in vain endeavors to advance into Germany and Austria-Hungary or to stem the tide of German invasion were ill supported by their government. The Duma became unmanageable, and in December, 1916, it passed a resolution declaring that

"Dark forces"

"dark forces" were paralyzing the government and betraying the nation's interests. This referred especially to the German wife of the Tsar, and the reactionary influence exercised over her and at court by a monk named Rasputin, who opposed every modern reform. He was murdered, and the angry Tsar proceeded to dismiss the liberals from the government and replace them by the most unpopular bureaucrats he could find. He seemed to be declaring war on every liberal movement and reverting to the methods of Nicholas I. Meantime the country was becoming more and more disorganized. There was a distressing scarcity of food in the cities and a growing repugnance to the continuance of the war.

Outbreak of the revolution

Bread riots broke out in Petrograd[1] in March, 1917, but the troops refused to fire on the people, and the Tsar's government found itself helpless. When ordered to adjourn, the Duma defied the Tsar and ordered the establishment of a provisional government. The Tsar, hastening back to Petrograd from the front, was stopped at Pskov by representatives of the new provisional government on March 15, 1917, and induced to sign his own and his son's abdication in favor of his brother, Grand Duke Michael. But Michael refused the honor unless it were authorized by a constitutional assembly; this amounted to an abdication of the Romanoffs, who had ruled Russia for more than three centuries. There was no longer any such thing in the world as "the autocrat of all the Russias." The Tsar's relatives renounced their rights, his high officials were imprisoned in the very fortress of Peter and Paul where they had sent so many revolutionists, and political prisoners in Russia and Siberia received the joyous tidings that they were free. The world viewed with astonishment this abrupt and complete collapse of the ancient system of tyranny.

The moderates give way to the moderate socialists

A revolutionary cabinet was formed of men of moderate views on the whole, but Alexander Kerensky, a socialist and representative of the Workingmen's and Soldiers' Council, was made minister of justice. The new cabinet declared itself in favor of many reforms, such as liberty of speech and of the press; the right to strike; the substitution of militia for the old police; universal suffrage, including women. But the socialists were not content, and through their Council of Workingmen's and Soldiers' Delegates began to exercise great power. Large incomes were taxed 60 per cent; a state coal monopoly was established; it was proposed to have the government manufacture and supply the food and clothing where there was a

[1] The name of the Russian capital was changed from its German form, St. Petersburg, to Petrograd at the opening of the war.

shortage; in Petrograd the six-hour day was introduced into one hundred and forty factories. By July, 1917, all the more moderate members of the provisional government had been forced out and their places taken by socialists. The congress of Workingmen's and Soldiers' Delegates and the national Peasants' Congress chose Kerensky as dictator, July 23. Opposed on one hand by the reactionaries, on the other by the extreme socialists, or Bolsheviki, Kerensky declared that if necessary Russia must be beaten into unity "by blood and iron." Kerensky had earlier made a desperate attempt to lead the flagging Russian troops to victory, but as time went on the demand for immediate peace "without annexations or indemnities" became louder and louder.

Kerensky dictator, July, 1917

The Pope's peace message and President Wilson's reply, August, 1917

On August 1, Pope Benedict XV sent forth a peace message in which he urged Christendom to cease from its fratricidal carnage, lay down its arms, and revert in general to the *status quo ante*. This was answered by President Wilson (August 27). He maintained that no peace was possible with the existing irresponsible government of Germany. "This power is not the German people. It is the ruthless master of the German people.... We cannot take the word of the present rulers of Germany as a guarantee of anything that is to endure, unless explicitly supported by such conclusive evidence of the will and purpose of the German people themselves as the other peoples of the world would be justified in accepting. Without such guarantees for disarmament, covenants to set up arbitration in the place of war, territorial adjustments, reconstitution of small nations, if made with the German government, no man, no nation could now depend on."

President's message, December, 1917

In his message on the opening of Congress, December 4, 1917, President Wilson was still clearer: "The people of Germany are being told by the men whom they now permit to deceive them and to act as their masters that they are fighting for the very life and existence of their Empire, a war of desperate self-defense against deliberate aggression. Nothing could be more grossly or wantonly false, and we must seek by the utmost openness and candor as to our real aims to convince them of its falseness. We are in fact fighting for their emancipation from fear . . . of unjust attack by neighbors, or rivals or schemers after world empire. No one is threatening the existence or independence or the peaceful enterprise of the German Empire. . . . We intend no wrong against the German Empire, no interference with her internal affairs." Lloyd George reiterated this last sentiment in a speech before the House of Commons.

Attitude of the Germans and their kaiser

Germany's leaders, in order to keep up the war spirit, constantly proclaimed that the sole aim of the Allies was to "crush" the fatherland. But it was the German militaristic government that had to be crushed by forcing Germany so far to alter her system as to secure democratic control of the power to declare war; in other respects she might go her own way.

The kaiser's reply may be gathered from his address to the soldiers of the Western Front, December 22, 1917: "The year 1917 has proved that the German people has in the Lord of Creation above an unconditional and avowed ally on whom it can absolutely rely. . . . If the enemy does not want peace, we must bring peace by battering down with the mailed fist and shining sword the portals of those who will not have peace!"

Peace conference at Brest-Litovsk, December, 1917

At the very end of 1917 peace negotiations were opened between representatives of the "Quadruple Alliance" — Germany, Austria-Hungary, Bulgaria, and Turkey — and the representatives of the Bolsheviki, who had control at that time of the *soviets*, or local assemblies that sprang up throughout Russia after the disappearance of the old autocratic government of the Tsar. They met at Brest-Litovsk, on the eastern Polish boundary, late in December. The Russian delegation submitted their program of no annexations and no indemnities, and complained that the Teutonic allies did not express themselves clearly in regard to the evacuation of Russian territory and reëstablishing the violated rights of small and oppressed nationalities.

But the Bolsheviki were helpless in the face of the German demands. Finland and the Ukraine, which comprises a great part of southern Russia, declared themselves independent, and established governments of their own, under German influence, it is supposed. So on March 3, 1918, the representatives of the Bolsheviki concluded a peace with the Central Powers in which they agreed to "evacuate" the Ukraine and Finland, and surrendered Poland, Lithuania, Courland, Livonia, and certain districts in the Caucasus (see map, p. 701), all of which were to exercise the right of establishing such government as they pleased. Shortly after, the capital of Russia was transferred from Petrograd to Moscow. The result was that Russia was dismembered, and all the western and southern regions were, for the time being, under the strong influence of the Germans. A new problem had been added to the overwhelming perplexities of the situation, namely, the question of the restoration of Russia.

It is estimated that by the Treaty of Brest-Litovsk Russia lost about a third of her population, a third of her railways, nearly three fourths of her iron mines, about 90 per cent of her coal mines, and her chief industrial towns and richest fields.

President Wilson's fourteen points, January 8, 1918

On January 8, 1918, President Wilson stated a program of world peace which embraced fourteen points. The chief of these were no secret international understandings or treaties; absolute freedom of navigation in peace and war, except when portions of the sea might be closed by international understanding; removal of economic barriers and reduction of armaments; impartial adjustment of all colonial claims; restoration of Belgium and evacuation of territories occupied by Teutonic allies during the war; righting of the wrong done to France when Alsace-Lorraine was seized by Germany; freeing of Asiatic dependencies of Turkey; and the formation of a general association of nations for the purpose of insuring the independence of great and small states alike. This program was heartily and unreservedly approved by the representatives of the English workingmen, and made clearer than any previous declaration the purposes of the world alliance against Germany.

SECTION 122. THE END OF THE GREAT WAR

On March 21, 1918, the Germans began a great drive on the Western Front with the hope of gaining a decisive victory and forcing the Allies to sue for peace. Germany was in a hurry, for she knew that her U-boat warfare was not bringing England to her knees, that the United States troops were beginning to arrive in ever-increasing numbers, and that the German plans for getting supplies from Russia were meeting with little success. Moreover, the German people were undergoing all sorts of bitter hardships, and might at any time begin to complain that the final victory which the Kaiser had been promising from the first was long in coming.

Why the Germans sought a speedy decision

The southern and eastern portion of the Western Front was held by French armies, the northern line by the British. Hindenburg and the other German generals decided to strike at the southernmost of the British armies, in the region of the Somme. If they could defeat it, they would thereby separate the French and British and so prevent their helping one another. For several days the Germans were victorious and were able to push back the British almost to Amiens. But the French rushed to the aid of their allies; the drive was checked and Amiens, with its important railroad connections, was saved. No previous conflict of the war had been so terrible as this, and it is estimated that over four hundred thousand men were killed, wounded, or captured. The Germans, however, only regained the devastated territory from which they had retired a year before, and their fierce efforts to advance further failed.

The German drive of 1918 begins, March 21

The grave danger in which the Allies found themselves finally convinced them that their safety lay in putting all their forces — French, British, Italian, and the newly arriving troops from America — under a single commander in chief. All agreed that the French general, Ferdinand Foch (appointed March 28, 1918), was the most likely to lead them all to victory; and their confidence was justified. Almost immediately matters began to mend.

Foch made commander in chief of the Allied armies

Efforts of the Germans to reach Calais and Paris

Every one knew that the Germans would soon make a second drive somewhere on the long front of one hundred and fifty miles, but at what point the Allies could only conjecture. The new blow came April 9, when the Kaiser's armies attempted to break through the British defenses between Arras and Ypres, with the intention of reaching Calais and the English Channel. The suspense was tense for a time, but after retreating a few miles the British made a stand and were ordered by their commander to die, if necessary, at their posts. This checked the second effort of the Germans to break through. In the latter part of May the German armies attempted a third great attack, this time in the direction of Paris. They took Soissons and Château-Thierry, which brought them within about forty miles of the French capital. In June they made a feebler effort to extend to the south the territory gained in the first drive. Here they were opposed for the first time by the American troops, who fought with great bravery and ardor. And here the German successes came to an end.

Arrival of United States troops; General Pershing

The first contingent of United States troops had arrived in France in June, 1917, under the command of General Pershing, who had a long and honorable record as a military commander. He had, in his younger days, fought Indians in the West; he served in the Spanish War, and later subdued the fierce Moros in the Philippine Islands.

By the first of July, 1918, about a million American troops had reached France and were either participating actively in the fierce fighting or being rapidly and efficiently trained. They had taken their first town by the end of May, 1918, and gained great distinction for themselves by coöperating with the French in frustrating the German attempt to break through at Château-Thierry. Northwest of that town they forced back, early in June, the picked troops of the Kaiser sent against them. In these conflicts the American marines were especially conspicuous.

During the following weeks the Germans lost tens of thousands of men in minor engagements and finally, on July 15,

1918, made a last great effort to take Rheims and force their way to Paris, but this drive was speedily turned into a retreat. During the following month the combined efforts of the French and Americans served to drive the Germans far back from the Marne and put an end to their hopes of advancing on Paris. The French general, Mangin, warmly praised the valor of the Americans during these "splendid" days when it was his privilege to fight with them "for the deliverance of the world." Then the British began an offensive on the Somme, east and south of Amiens. By the end of September the Germans had been pressed back to the old Hindenburg line; this was even pierced at some points, and the Allied troops were within a few miles of the Lorraine boundary.

Rapid German retreat during July and August, 1918

The American troops in France, numbering slightly over two million men before the armistice was signed, on November 11, 1918, were scattered along the whole Western Front, and it is estimated that nearly one million four hundred thousand actually took part in the fearful struggle against the Germans.[1] It is impossible to mention here all the battles in which they fought valiantly, side by side with the French or British, as the hosts of the enemy were rapidly pushed back. In the middle of September the Americans distinguished themselves by taking the St. Mihiel salient and bringing their lines within range of the guns of the great German fortress of Metz. Reënforcing the British, they performed prodigies of valor in the capture of the St. Quentin canal tunnel far to the north, where thousands of lives were sacrificed. In the Argonne Forest, and especially in the capture of Sedan, on November 7, the United States troops played a conspicuous part. In the months from June to November, 1918, the battle casualties of the American expeditionary forces — killed, wounded, missing, and prisoners — amounted to nearly a quarter of a million. The American

Active participation of the American troops

1 The United States proposed to have at least four million men in France by June 30, 1919. The limits of the draft were extended so as to include all able-bodied men between the ages of eighteen and forty-five.

soldiers made it clear that men could fight with the greatest bravery and gain rapid victories without the prolonged training to which the German troops had been subjected.

Conditions in Russia

Meanwhile, on the other fronts the fortunes of war were turning in favor of the Allies. Germany, instead of being able to get supplies from demoralized Russia, met resistance at every point. The people of the Ukraine resented her domination and began to look to the Allies to assist them in forming their new republic. In Finland civil war raged between the "white" guard (Nationalist) and the "red" guard (Bolshevik-German), while English and American troops on the Murmansk coast to the north coöperated with the anti-Bolsheviki to oppose the extremists then in power.

At Vladivostok, far away across Siberia, English, Japanese, and American forces landed with the object of working westward through Siberia and, as they hoped, restoring order. Among the enemies of the Bolsheviki was a Czecho-Slovak army, composed of former Austrian subjects, who had deserted to fight in Russia for the Allies.

Bulgaria capitulates, September 29, 1918

As a part of the great forward movement organized by General Foch, the combined Serbian, Greek, English, and French forces in the Balkans once more became active in Serbia and rapidly pushed back the Bulgarians, who, with the help of the Germans and Austrians, had overrun the country three years before. Neither Germany nor Austria could send aid to their ally, and on September 29, 1918, the Bulgarians threw up their hands and asked for an armistice. This was granted on condition of absolute surrender. The Bulgarians retired from the war, having agreed to disband their army and give the Allies the right to use their territory, supplies, and railroads in continuing the fight against Austria-Hungary and Turkey. The defection of Bulgaria proved decisive, and it was clear that Turkey could not keep up the fight when cut off from her western allies, and that Austria-Hungary, open to invasion through Bulgaria, must soon yield.

Turkey was the next to surrender. In Palestine General Allenby followed up the capture of Jerusalem (December, 1917) by the relentless pursuit of the Turkish armies. The English and French speedily conquered Syria, taking the great towns of Damascus and Beirut, and the Syrians could celebrate their final deliverance from the century-long, cruel subjugation to the Turks. The Turkish army in Mesopotamia was also captured by the English. So Turkey was quickly forced to follow Bulgaria's example, and accepted the terms of surrender imposed by the Allies (October 31).

Turkey surrenders, October 31

Thus the loudly heralded "peace drive" of the Germans had turned into a hasty retreat on the Western Front, and their eastern allies had dropped away. The oncoming American troops, steadily streaming across the Atlantic, brought new hope to the Allies; for the Americans were fresh and brave and full of enthusiasm, and they were backed by a great and rich country, which had thrown its well-nigh inexhaustible resources on the side of the war-weary Allies in their fight against Prussianism.

Plight of the Germans

The Germans began to see that they had been grossly deceived by their leaders. The criminal use of the U-boats had not brought England to her knees, but it had aroused this new and mighty enemy across the Atlantic, whose armies found themselves able to cross the ocean in spite of Germany's submarines. The Germans had forced shameful treaties upon the former Russian provinces with the purpose of making the poor, demoralized, and famine-stricken people help support the German armies. This plan failed to relieve German distress; her commerce was ruined, her reputation lost, her national debt tremendous, with no hope of forcing her enemies to pay the bills. She had no real friends, and now she was deserted by both her eastern allies. Austria-Hungary alone continued feebly to support her against a world coalition brought together in common abhorrence of her policy and aims.

But even Austria-Hungary was fast giving way. Torn by internal dissension and the threatened revolt of her subject

Surrender of Austria-Hungary, November 3

nationalities, disheartened by scarcity of food and by the reverses on the Western Front, she sent a note to President Wilson, October 7, requesting that an armistice be considered. By the end of the month her armies were giving way before the Italians, who in a second battle of the Piave not only swept the Austrians out of northern Italy but quickly occupied Trent and the great seaport of Trieste. On November 3 Austria-Hungary unconditionally surrendered, accepting the severe terms that the Allies imposed on her.

Abdication of the Austrian emperor

But Austria-Hungary had already disappeared from the map of Europe. The Czecho-Slovak republic had been proclaimed, and the Jugo-Slavs no longer recognized their former connection with Austria and Hungary. Hungary itself was in revolt and was proclaimed a republic. Under these circumstances the Hapsburg emperor of Austria and king of Hungary abdicated, November 11.

Germany asks for peace

Germany herself was on the verge of dissolution as it proved. Early in October it seems to have become apparent to her military rulers that there was no possibility of stopping the victorious advance of the Allies, and the imperial chancellor opened a correspondence (transmitted through the Swiss minister) with President Wilson in regard to an armistice and peace. President Wilson made it plain that the Allies would not stop their advance except on condition that Germany surrender, and on such terms that it could not possibly renew the war. "For," the President added, in his third note, "the nations of the world do not and cannot trust the word of those who have hitherto been the masters of German policy."

Ludendorff dismissed

The German War Council, including the Kaiser and Crown Prince, made a vain effort to save the old system. General Ludendorff, especially conspicuous for his offensive German spirit, was sent off, and the Allies were informed that far-reaching changes in the government had been undertaken which assured the people a complete control not only over the government but over the military powers (October 27).

Soon the German government began to deal directly with General Foch in its eagerness to secure an armistice at any cost, for a great revolution was imminent. Moreover, the Allied forces were closing in on Germany all along the line from the North Sea to the Swiss boundary, and the Germans were retreating with enormous losses of men and supplies. On November 9, to the astonishment of the world, it was announced that his majesty, Emperor William II, had abdicated. He soon fled to Holland, and that world nuisance, the House of Hohenzollern, was a thing of the past. The king of Bavaria had been forced off his throne the day before, and all the former monarchies which composed the German Empire were speedily turned into republics. On November 10 a revolution took place in Berlin, and a socialist leader, Friedrich Ebert, assumed the duties of chancellor with the consent of the previous chancellor and all the secretaries of state. Even Prussia had become a republic overnight. The German Empire was no more.

Abdication of the Kaiser and the German rulers

Prussia a republic

Meanwhile negotiations in regard to an armistice were in progress. Representatives of the German government made their way across the lines and met General Foch, November 8, and received the terms which the Allies had drawn up.

Terms of the armistice

The Germans were required to evacuate within two weeks all the territory they had occupied, — Belgium, northeastern France, Luxemburg, as well as Alsace-Lorraine. Moreover, the German troops were to retire beyond the right bank of the Rhine, and that portion of Germany which lies west of the river was to be occupied by troops of the Allies. All German troops in territories formerly belonging to Austria-Hungary, Roumania, Turkey, and Russia were to be immediately withdrawn. Germany was to hand over her war vessels, surrender all her submarines and vast supplies of war material, and put her railroads and all means of communication on the left bank of the Rhine at the disposal of the Allies. These and other provisions were designed to make any renewal of the war on Germany's part absolutely impossible. Hard as were the terms, the

The end of the war

Germans accepted them promptly, and on November 11 the armistice was signed and the Great War was at an end.

Losses of men in battle

It is estimated that during the war nearly sixty million men were mobilized. Of these about seven million were killed and over eighteen million wounded. Of those who recovered perhaps a quarter or more were permanently mutilated or crippled for life.

Our country only entered the war as it was coming to a close and all the other combatants were worn and weary with the long struggle. Considering the population and vast wealth of the United States, our sacrifices in men and goods have been slight compared with what all the European belligerents suffered; but these sacrifices should have made plain to us the unutterable horrors of war and the absolute necessity, in the interests of civilization, of coöperating with the rest of the world in preventing the recurrence of any such catastrophe. As has been pointed out, the world has been brought together by commerce, the steamship, and the telegraph, and the United States cannot hope, even if it so desired, to remain aloof from the general affairs of mankind. As a busy, peaceful nation it must make such sacrifices and assume such responsibilities as are necessary to enable it to play its great rôle in promoting the peace and prosperity of the whole globe.

SOME SUGGESTIONS IN REGARD TO THE BOOKS DEALING WITH THE ORIGIN AND ISSUES OF THE GREAT WAR

The United States Committee on Public Information distributes (free, except the last mentioned) the following valuable pamphlets:

How the War came to America.

The President's Flag-Day Speech with Evidence of Germany's Plans.

Conquest and Kultur. Aims of the Germans in their Own Words, edited by NOTESTEIN and STOLL.

German War Practices, edited by D. C. MUNRO, SELLERY, and KREY.

The War Message and Facts behind it.

The Government of Germany, by C. D. HAZEN.

The Great War: from Spectator to Participant, by A. C. McLAUGHLIN.

American Interest in Popular Government Abroad, by E. B. GREENE.

War Cyclopædia. A very valuable work of reference. 25 cents.

For the conditions which led up to the Great War see H. A. GIBBONS, *The New Map of Europe, 1911–1914: the Story of the Recent Diplomatic Crises and Wars and of Europe's Present Catastrophe.* Admirable account of the chief international issues before the War, especially of the Balkan troubles. A more general introduction will be found in CARLTON J. H. HAYES, *A Political and Social History of Modern Europe*, Vol. II, 1916, dealing with Europe since 1815 and giving excellent bibliographies, especially pp. 719 sqq. ARTHUR BULLARD, *The Diplomacy of the Great War*, deals in a sprightly manner with the negotiations preceding the conflict. C. SEYMOUR, *The Diplomatic Background of the War*, 1916. J. H. ROSE, *The Origins of the War*, 1914, from the standpoint of an Englishman. W. S. DAVIS, *The Roots of the War*, from an American point of view. These may be compared with EDMUND VON MACH, *Germany's Point of View*, an attempt to justify Germany's policy in American eyes. A very full treatment of international affairs will be found in E. C. STOWELL, *The Diplomacy of the War of 1914*, Vol. I, 1916.

The following give extracts from German writers illustrating the attitude of the Germans toward themselves and others: *Out of their Own Mouths*, 1917; *Gems (?) of German Thought*, edited by WILLIAM ARCHER, 1917; and *Hurrah and Hallelujah*, by J. P. BANG.

Germany and the Next War, by General VON BERNHARDI, a man who believes ardently in war, may be compared with *The Great Illusion*, by NORMAN ANGELL, who believes only in war on war. R. H. FIFE, *The German Empire between Two Wars.*

The *History Teachers' Magazine* publishes excellent bibliographies and an admirable syllabus of war history. *Current History*, published monthly by the New York Times Company, gives many important documents and admirable maps, portraits, and pictures of war episodes. The *Atlantic Monthly* contains many serious articles on the war, as do a number of other well-known magazines, such as the *Review of Reviews* and the *Independent.*

The following deal with some of the deeper problems raised by the war: J. H. ROSE, *Nationality in Modern History*, 1916; G. L. BEER, *The English Speaking Peoples, their Future Relations and Joint International Obligations*, 1917; RAMSAY MUIR, *The Expansion of Europe*, 1917; J. DEWEY, *German Philosophy and Politics*, 1915; WALTER LIPPMANN, *The Stakes of Diplomacy*, 1915; OLGIN, *The Soul of the Russian Revolution*, 1918; MUNROE SMITH, *Militarism and Statecraft*, 1918.

APPENDIX I

RULERS OF THE CHIEF EUROPEAN STATES SINCE THE AGE OF LOUIS XIV

One of the chief conclusions reached in these volumes is that kings have, during the nineteenth century, come to be held in ever-diminishing esteem; and it must be confessed that their names are now of relatively slight importance. Nevertheless they are often referred to in historical works, and we may atone for some seeming slights to royalty in our pages by giving a convenient list of all the rulers down to December, 1918, whose names are likely to be met with. The countries are given in alphabetical order.

AUSTRIA-HUNGARY (see Holy Roman Empire)

BELGIUM

Leopold I, 1831–1865
Leopold II, 1865–1909
Albert, 1909–

DENMARK (including Norway until 1814)

Frederick III, 1648–1670
Christian V, 1670–1699
Frederick IV, 1699–1730
Christian VI, 1730–1746
Frederick V, 1746–1766
Christian VII, 1766–1808
Frederick VI (regent, 1784–1808), 1808–1839
Christian VIII, 1839–1848
Frederick VII, 1848–1863
Christian IX, 1863–1906
Frederick VIII, 1906–1912
Christian X, 1912–

FRANCE

Louis XIV, 1643–1715
Louis XV, 1715–1774
Louis XVI, 1774–1792
The Convention, 1792–1795
The Directory, 1795–1799
The Consulate, 1799–1804
(Napoleon as First Consul)
The First Empire, 1804–1815
(Napoleon I, Emperor of the French)
Louis XVIII, 1814–1824
Charles X, 1824–1830

FRANCE (*continued*)

Louis Philippe, 1830–1848
The Second Republic, 1848–1852
(Louis Napoleon, President)
The Second Empire, 1852–1870
(Napoleon III, Emperor of the French)
The Third Republic
Government of National Defense, 1870–1871
Adolphe Thiers, President, 1871–1873.
Marshal MacMahon, 1873–1879
F. P. Jules Grévy, 1879–1887
F. Sadi Carnot, 1887–1894
Casimir-Périer, 1894–1895
Félix Faure, 1895–1899
Émile Loubet, 1899–1906
Armand Fallières, 1906–1913
Raymond Poincaré, 1913–

GERMAN EMPIRE

William I, 1871–1888
Frederick III, March–June, 1888
William II, 1888–1918

GREAT BRITAIN

Charles II, 1660–1685
James II, 1685–1688
William and Mary, 1689–1694
William III, 1694–1702
Anne, 1702–1714
George I, 1714–1727
George II, 1727–1760
George III, 1760–1820
George IV, 1820–1830
William IV, 1830–1837
Victoria, 1837–1901
Edward VII, 1901–1910
George V, 1910–

GREECE

Otto I, 1833–1862
George I, 1863–1913
Constantine, 1913–1917
Alexander, 1917–

HOLY ROMAN EMPIRE AND AUSTRIA-HUNGARY

Leopold I, 1658–1705
Joseph I, 1705–1711
Charles VI, 1711–1740
(Charles VII of Bavaria, 1742–1745)
(Maria Theresa, Austro-Hungarian ruler, 1740–1780)
Francis I, 1745–1765
Joseph II, 1765–1790
Leopold II, 1790–1792

HOLY ROMAN EMPIRE AND AUSTRIA-HUNGARY (*continued*)

Francis II as Holy Roman Emperor, 1792–1806
As Austrian Emperor, Francis I, 1806–1835
Ferdinand I, 1835–1848
Francis Joseph, 1848–1916
Charles VIII, 1916–1918

ITALY

Victor Emmanuel II, 1849–1878 (King of Italy from 1861)
Humbert, 1878–1900
Victor Emmanuel III, 1900–

MONTENEGRO

Nicholas I, 1860–

NETHERLANDS

William I, 1815–1840
William II, 1840–1849
William III, 1849–1890
Wilhelmina, 1890–

NORWAY

Same rulers as Denmark, 1523–1814
Christian Frederick, 1814
Same rulers as Sweden, 1814–1905
Haakon VII, 1905–

POLAND

John Sobieski, 1674–1696
Frederick Augustus of Saxony, 1697–1704
Stanislas Leszczynski, 1704–1709
Frederick Augustus of Saxony (restored), 1709–1733
Frederick Augustus II, 1733–1763
Stanislas II, 1764–1795

THE POPES

Clement IX, 1667–1669
Clement X, 1670–1676
Innocent XI, 1676–1689
Alexander VIII, 1689–1691
Innocent XII, 1691–1700
Clement XI, 1700–1721
Innocent XIII, 1721–1724
Benedict XIII, 1724–1730
Clement XII, 1730–1740
Benedict XIV, 1740–1758

THE POPES (*continued*)

Clement XIII, 1758–1769
Clement XIV, 1769–1774
Pius VI, 1775–1799
Pius VII, 1800–1823
Leo XII, 1823–1829
Pius VIII, 1829–1830
Gregory XVI, 1831–1846
Pius IX, 1846–1878
Leo XIII, 1878–1903
Pius X, 1903–1914
Benedict XV, 1914–

PORTUGAL (monarchy)

Alfonso VI, 1656–1683
Peter II, 1683–1706
John V, 1706–1750
Joseph Emanuel, 1750–1777
Maria I and Peter III, 1777–1786
Maria alone, 1786–1816
John (regent, 1791–1816), 1816–1826
Peter IV (Dom Pedro), 1826
Maria II, 1826–1828
Dom Miguel, 1828–1833
Maria II (restored), 1833–1853
Peter V, 1853–1861
Luis I, 1861–1889
Dom Carlos, 1889–1908
Manuel II, 1908–1910

PORTUGAL (republic)

Manuel Arriaga, President, 1911–1915
B. Machado, 1915–1917
S. B. Cordoso da Silva Paes, 1918–

PRUSSIA

Frederick William, the Great Elector, 1640–1688
Frederick III, Elector, 1688–1701
King Frederick I, 1701–1713
Frederick William I, 1713–1740
Frederick II, the Great, 1740–1786
Frederick William II, 1786–1797
Frederick William III, 1797–1840
Frederick William IV, 1840–1861
William I, 1861–1888
Frederick III, 1888
William II, 1888–1918

ROUMANIA

Carol I (as king), 1881–1914
Ferdinand I, 1914–

Russia

Alexis, 1645–1676
Feodor Alexievitch, 1676–1682
Ivan V and Peter the Great, 1682–1689
Peter the Great alone, 1689–1725
Catherine I, 1725–1727
Peter II, 1727–1730
Anna Ivanovna, 1730–1740
Ivan VI, 1740–1741
Elizabeth, 1741–1761
Peter III, January–July, 1762
Catherine II, 1762–1796
Paul, 1796–1801
Alexander I, 1801–1825
Nicholas I, 1825–1855
Alexander II, 1855–1881
Alexander III, 1881–1894
Nicholas II, 1894–1917

Serbia

Milan (as king), 1882–1889
Alexander, 1889–1903
Peter, 1903–

Spain

Charles II, 1665–1700
Philip V, 1700–1746
Ferdinand VI, 1746–1759
Charles III, 1759–1788
Charles IV, 1788–1808
Ferdinand VII, 1808
Joseph Bonaparte, 1808–1813
Ferdinand VII (restored), 1813–1833
Isabella II, 1833–1868
Revolutionary Government, 1868–1870
Amadeo of Savoy, 1870–1873
Republic, 1873–1874
Alfonso XII, 1874–1885
Maria (pro tem.), 1885–1886
Alfonso XIII, 1886–

Sweden

Charles X, 1654–1660
Charles XI, 1660–1697
Charles XII, 1697–1718
Ulrica Eleanora, 1718–1720
Frederick I, 1720–1751
Adolphus Frederick, 1751–1771
Gustavus III, 1771–1792
Gustavus IV, 1792–1809
Charles XIII, 1809–1818
Charles (John) XIV, 1818–1844
Oscar I, 1844–1859
Charles XV, 1859–1872
Oscar II, 1872–1907
Gustavus V, 1907–

TURKEY

Mohammed IV, 1649–1687
Solyman II, 1687–1691
Achmet II, 1691–1695
Mustapha II, 1695–1703
Achmet III, 1703–1730
Mahmoud I, 1730–1754
Othman III, 1754–1757
Mustapha III, 1757–1774
Abdul Hamid I, 1774–1789
Selim III, 1789–1807
Mustapha IV, 1807–1808
Mahmoud II, 1808–1839
Abdul Medjid, 1839–1861
Abdul Aziz, 1861–1876
Amurath V (Murad), 1876
Abdul Hamid II, 1876–1909
Mohammed V, 1909–1918
Mohammed VI, 1918–

APPENDIX II

INTRODUCTION

BRYCE, *The Holy Roman Empire.* BURCKHARDT, *The Civilization of the Renaissance in Italy.* CHEYNEY, *A Short History of England*, chaps. xii–xiii; *An Introduction to the Industrial and Social History of England*, chaps. iv, vi. CROSS, *A History of England and Greater Britain*, chaps. xx–xxii. CUNNINGHAM, *An Essay on Western Civilization: Mediaeval and Modern Times.* DAY, *A History of Commerce.* DE VINNE, *The Invention of Printing.* DURUY, *History of France.* EMERTON, *Desiderius Erasmus. Encyclopædia Britannica*, articles on "Calvin," "Charles V," "The Middle Ages," "The Reformation," "Zwingli." HENDERSON, *A Short History of Germany.* JOHNSON, *Europe in the Sixteenth Century.* LINDSAY, *A History of the Reformation* (2 vols.).

A. General reading

ROBINSON, *Readings in European History*, Vol. II, chaps. xxiii–xxix. CHEYNEY, *Readings in English History.* GEE and HARDY, *Documents Illustrative of English Church History.* WACE and BUCHHEIM (Editors), *Luther's Primary Works* and *The Augsburg Confession.* WHITCOMB, *A Source Book of the German Renaissance* and *A Literary Source Book of the Italian Renaissance.*

B. Source material

BEARD, *Martin Luther*, especially introductory chapters on general conditions. *Cambridge Modern History*, Vols. I–IV. CREIGHTON, *A History of the Papacy.* GASQUET, *The Eve of the Reformation.* JANSSEN, *History of the German People*, Vols. I–II. MCGIFFERT, *Martin Luther.* MOTLEY, *The Rise of the Dutch Republic.* PASTOR, *The History of the Popes.* PAYNE, *Voyages of Elizabethan Seamen to America.* POLLARD, *Factors in Modern History.* PUTNAM, G. H., *Books and their Makers during the Middle Ages.* PUTNAM, R., *William the Silent.* SICHEL, *The Renaissance* (Home University Series). VAN DYCK, *The History of Painting.*

C. Additional reading

CHAPTER I

CHEYNEY, *A Short History of England*, chaps. xiv–xvi. CROSS, *A History of England and Greater Britain*, chaps. xxvii–xxxviii. GREEN, *A Short History of the English People*, chaps. viii–ix.

A. General reading

B. Source material

ROBINSON, *Readings in European History*, Vol. II, chap. xxx. CHEYNEY, *Readings in English History*, chaps. xiv–xvi. COLBY, *Selections from the Sources of English History*, Pt. VI, the Stuart Period. GEE and HARDY, *Documents Illustrative of English Church History*, pp. 508–664.

C. Additional reading

Cambridge Modern History, Vol. III, chap. xvii; Vol. IV, chaps. viii–xi, xv, xix; Vol. V, chaps. v, ix–xi. GARDINER, *The First Two Stuarts and the Puritan Revolution*. MACAULAY, *Essay on Milton*. MORLEY, *Oliver Cromwell*.

CHAPTER II

A. General reading

ADAMS, *The Growth of the French Nation*, chaps. xii–xiii. *Cambridge Modern History*, Vol. V, chaps. i–ii, xiii–xiv. DURUY, *History of France*, Thirteenth Period. WAKEMAN, *The Ascendancy of France*, chaps. ix–xi, xiv–xv.

B. Source material

ROBINSON, *Readings in European History*, Vol. II, chap. xxxi. Memoirs of the period are often obtainable in translation at reasonable prices. The greatest of these, those of Saint Simon, are condensed to a three-volume English edition.

C. Additional reading

LOWELL, *The Eve of the French Revolution*, general in treatment, less picturesque but gives a fairer idea of conditions than the work of TAINE mentioned below. PERKINS, *France under the Regency*, one of several valuable books by this author. TAINE, *The Ancient Régime*, a brilliant picture of life in France in the eighteenth century.

CHAPTER III

A. General reading

Cambridge Modern History, Vol. V, chaps. xvi, xx–xxi; Vol. VI, chap. xx. HENDERSON, *A Short History of Germany*, Vol. I, pp. 148–218. RAMBAUD, *History of Russia*, Vols. I–II, the best treatment of Russia. SCHEVILL, *Modern Europe*, pp. 215–247, good outline. TUTTLE, *History of Prussia* (4 vols.).

B. Source material

ROBINSON, *Readings in European History*, Vol. II, chap. xxxii. ROBINSON and BEARD, *Readings in Modern European History*, Vol. I, chap. iv.

C. Additional reading

BRIGHT, *Maria Theresa*. CARLYLE, *History of Frederick the Second, called Frederick the Great*, a classic. EVERSLEY, *The Partitions of Poland*. HASSALL, *The Balance of Power*. KLUCHEVSKY, *A History of Russia* (3 vols.). PHILLIPS, *Poland* (Home University Series), good short account. SCHEVILL, *The Making of Modern Germany*, Lectures I–II. SCHUYLER, *Peter the Great*, standard English biography. WALISZEWSKI, *Life of Peter the Great*.

CHAPTER IV

A. General reading

ROBINSON and BEARD, *The Development of Modern Europe*, Vol. I, chaps. vi–vii. *Cambridge Modern History*, Vol. V, chap. xxii; Vol. VI, chaps. vi, xv. CHEYNEY, *A Short History of England*, chap. xvii. CROSS, *A History of England and Greater Britain*, chap. xli, detailed manual. EGERTON, *A Short History of British Colonial Policy*, best treatment. GIBBINS, *British Commerce and Colonies from Elizabeth to Victoria*. LYALL, *The Rise of British Dominion in India*. POLLARD, *Factors in Modern History*, chap. x, a most suggestive treatment of the rise of nationalism in modern England. WOODWARD, *A Short History of the Expansion of the British Empire*, best introduction.

B. Source material

ROBINSON, *Readings in European History*, Vol. II, chap. xxxiii. ROBINSON and BEARD, *Readings in Modern European History*, Vol. I, chaps. vi–vii. CHEYNEY, *Readings in English History*, chaps. xiii, xvii. HART, *American History told by Contemporaries*, Vol. I. MUZZEY, *Readings in American History*.

C. Additional reading

CHEYNEY, *The European Background of American History*, an excellent survey. EDGAR, *The Struggle for a Continent*. HUNTER, *A Brief History of the Indian Peoples*. LUCAS, *A Historical Geography of the British Colonies* (5 vols.), the most extensive treatment. MACAULAY, *Essay on Clive*. MAHAN, *The Influence of Sea Power upon History, 1660–1783*, a classic. MORRIS, *A History of Colonization* (2 vols.). PARKMAN, *A Half-Century of Conflict* (2 vols.). SEELEY, *The Expansion of England*, a well-known general survey. THWAITES, *The Colonies*. TRAILL, *Social England*, Vol. V.

CHAPTER V

A. General reading

ASHTON, *Social Life in the Reign of Queen Anne*. GIBBINS, *Industry in England*, chaps. xvii–xx. HENDERSON, *A Short History of Germany*, chaps. iii–vii. LOWELL, *The Eve of the French Revolution*, sane and reliable. PROTHERO, *English Farming, Past and Present*, chaps. v–xi, excellent. SYDNEY, *England and the English in the Eighteenth Century* (2 vols.), admirable.

B. Source material

ROBINSON and BEARD, *Readings in Modern European History*, Vol. I, chap. viii. *Translations and Reprints of the University of Pennsylvania*, Vol. V, No. 2; Vol. VI, No. 1. YOUNG, *Travels in France, 1787–1789*, a first-hand source of great importance.

C. Additional reading

CUNNINGHAM, *The Growth of English Industry and Commerce, Modern Times*, Pt. I, the standard manual of economic history; conservative. DE TOCQUEVILLE, *The State of Society in France before the*

Revolution, a careful analysis of conditions. LECKY, *A History of England in the Eighteenth Century* (8 vols.), a work of high order. MCGIFFERT, *Protestant Thought before Kant*, excellent for religious thought. OVERTON, *The English Church in the Eighteenth Century.* TAINE, *The Ancient Régime*, a brilliant but somewhat overdone analysis of social conditions in France.

CHAPTER VI

A. General reading

BURY, *A History of Freedom of Thought* (Home University Series), chap. vi, admirable. *Cambridge Modern History*, Vol. V, chap. xxiii. DUNNING, *A History of Political Theories from Luther to Montesquieu*, chaps. x–xii, admirable summary of political doctrines to 1750. MARVIN, *The Living Past*, chap. viii, a stimulating outline. MCGIFFERT, *Protestant Thought before Kant*, chap. x, splendid treatment of the religious aspects of rationalism.

B. Source material

ROBINSON and BEARD, *Readings in Modern European History*, Vol. I, chaps. ix–x. MONTESQUIEU, *The Spirit of Laws* (Nugent's translation). ROUSSEAU, *Discourses*, and *Émile*, and *The Social Contract* (Everyman's Library). SMITH, *The Wealth of Nations*. STEPHENS, *The Life and Writings of Turgot.*

C. Additional reading

CARLYLE, *History of Frederick the Second, called Frederick the Great.* GIDE and RIST, *A History of Economic Doctrines* (translated by Richards). LECKY, *A History of the Rise and Influence of Rationalism in Europe* (2 vols.), a general survey. MORLEY, *Critical Miscellanies*; *Rousseau*; *Voltaire*, eloquent and stimulating essays. PERKINS, *France under Louis XV*, Vol. II. ROBERTSON, *A Short History of Free Thought, Ancient and Modern* (2 vols.). SCHUYLER, *Peter the Great.* WALISZEWSKI, *Life of Peter the Great.* An excellent summary of the history of the various sciences is to be found in *The History of the Sciences* series published by Putnam.

CHAPTER VII

A. General reading

LOWELL, *The Eve of the French Revolution*, the best treatment in English. MACLEHOSE, *The Last Days of the French Monarchy*, excellent. MATTHEWS, *The French Revolution*, Pts. I–II, the best short survey.

B. Source material

ROBINSON, *Readings in European History*, Vol. II, chap. xxxiv. ROBINSON and BEARD, *Readings in Modern European History*, Vol. I, chap. xi. *Translations and Reprints of the University of Pennsylvania*, Vol. IV, No. 5, for "Cahiers"; Vol. V, No. 2, for "Protest of the Cour des Aides of 1775"; Vol. VI, No. 1, for "Philosophers." YOUNG, *Travels in France.*

Cambridge Modern History, Vol. VIII, chaps. ii–iv. De Tocqueville, *The State of Society in France before the Revolution of 1789*. Rocquain, *The Revolutionary Spirit preceding the Revolution*. Taine, *The Ancient Régime*. C. Additional reading

CHAPTER VIII

Robinson, *The New History*, chap. vii. Belloc, *The French Revolution*, chaps. i–iii, iv, sects. i–iii suggestive. *Cambridge Modern History*, Vol. VIII, especially chaps. i–iii. Matthews, *The French Revolution*, Pt. III. Rose, *The Revolutionary and Napoleonic Era*, chaps. i–iii. Stephens, *Revolutionary Europe*, chaps. iii–iv, excellent; *A History of the French Revolution* (2 vols.), detailed treatment of the early years of the Revolution, replacing Carlyle and earlier literary historians. A. General reading

Robinson, *Readings in European History*, Vol. II, chap. xxxv. Robinson and Beard, *Readings in Modern European History*, Vol. I, chap. xii. Anderson, *Constitutions and Other Select Documents Illustrative of the History of France, 1789–1907*, a valuable collection for modern French history. Burke, *Reflections on the French Revolution* (Everyman's Library), a bitter criticism of the whole movement. Morris, *Diary and Letters* (2 vols.), contains some vivid description by an American observer. Paine, *The Rights of Man*, an effective answer to Burke. B. Source material

Aulard, *The French Revolution: A Political History, 1789–1804* (4 vols.), a great political history. Bourne, *The Revolutionary Period in Europe*, chaps. vii–x, a recent manual. Carlyle, *The French Revolution*, a literary masterpiece but written from insufficient materials. Taine, *The French Revolution* (3 vols.), Vol. I; Vol. II, chaps. i–iv, brilliant but unsympathetic. C. Additional reading

CHAPTER IX

Belloc, *The French Revolution*, chap. iv, sects. iv–vi; chaps. v–vi. *Cambridge Modern History*, Vol. VIII, especially chap. xii. Matthews, *The French Revolution*, Pt. IV. Rose, *The Revolutionary and Napoleonic Era*, chaps. iv–vi. Stephens, *Revolutionary Europe*, chaps. i–iii. A. General reading

Robinson, *Readings in European History*, Vol. II, chap. xxxvi. Robinson and Beard, *Readings in Modern European History*, Vol. I, chap. xiii. B. Source material

Aulard, *The French Revolution*, Vols. II–IV. Belloc, *Danton* and *Robespierre*. Bourne, *The Revolutionary Period in Europe*, chaps. xi–xiv. Taine, *The French Revolution*, Vol. II, chaps. v–xii; Vol. III. C. Additional reading

CHAPTER X

A. General reading

Cambridge Modern History, Vol. VIII, chaps. xviii–xxv; Vol. IX, chaps. i–iii. FISHER, *Napoleon* (Home University Series), chaps. i–v. FOURNIER, *Napoleon the First*, Vol. I, chaps. i–vii, excellent. JOHNSTON, *Napoleon*, chaps. i–vi, the best brief account in English. ROSE, *The Life of Napoleon the First*, Vol. I, chaps. i–xi, the most scholarly account in English.

B. Source material

ROBINSON, *Readings in European History*, Vol. II, chap. xxxvii. ROBINSON and BEARD, *Readings in Modern European History*, Vol. I, chap. xiv. ANDERSON, *Constitutions and Other Select Documents Illustrative of the History of France, 1789–1907*. BOURRIENNE, *Memoirs of Bourrienne*, Vol. I; Vol. II, chaps. i–iv, Napoleon's private secretary, spiteful but spicy.

C. Additional reading

SLOANE, *Life of Napoleon Bonaparte* (4 vols.), Vols. I–II, monumental, with very complete illustrations. STEPHENS, *Revolutionary Europe*, chaps. vi–vii.

CHAPTER XI

A. General reading

Cambridge Modern History, Vol. IX, chaps. iv–xx. FISHER, *Napoleon* (Home University Series), chaps. vi–x. FOURNIER, *Napoleon the First*, Vol. I, chaps. viii–xii; Vol. II. JOHNSTON, *Napoleon*, chaps. vii–xvii. ROSE, *The Life of Napoleon the First*, Vol. I, chaps. xii–xxi; Vol. II.

B. Source material

ROBINSON, *Readings in European History*, Vol. II, chap. xxxviii. ANDERSON, *Constitutions and Other Select Documents Illustrative of the History of France, 1789–1907*. BINGHAM, *A Selection from the Letters and Despatches of the First Napoleon* (3 vols.). BOURRIENNE, *Memoirs of Bourrienne*, Vol. II, chaps. v–xxxiv; Vol. III; Vol. IV. LAS CASES, *The Journal of the Emperor Napoleon at St. Helena*. LECESTRE, *New Letters of Napoleon I*. DE RÉMUSAT, *Memoirs of Madame de Rémusat*. MIOT DE MELITO, *Memoirs of Miot de Melito*.

C. Additional reading

BIGELOW, *A History of the German Struggle for Liberty*. SEELEY, *The Life and Times of Stein*, an exhaustive study of Prussia under Stein. SLOANE, *Life of Napoleon Bonaparte*, Vols. III–IV. TAINE, *The Modern Régime* (2 vols.), keen analysis of Napoleon.

CHAPTER XII

A. General reading

ROBINSON and BEARD, *The Development of Modern Europe*, Vol. I, chap. xvi. FYFFE, *A History of Modern Europe*, Vol. II, chap i. HAZEN, *Europe since 1815*, chap. i. SEIGNOBOS, *A Political History of Europe since 1814*, chap. i.

ROBINSON and BEARD, *Readings in Modern European History*, Vol. I, chap. xvi. — *B.* Source material

ANDREWS, *The Historical Development of Modern Europe*, Vol. I. — *C.* Additional reading

CHAPTER XIII

ROBINSON and BEARD, *The Development of Modern Europe*, Vol. II, chap. xvii. *Cambridge Modern History*, Vol. X. FYFFE, *A History of Modern Europe*, Vol. II. HAZEN, *Europe since 1815*, chaps. ii–viii, excellent. PHILLIPS, *Modern Europe*, chaps. i–ix, especially good sections. SEIGNOBOS, *A Political History of Europe since 1814*, chaps. viii–x, most comprehensive single manual of the century. — *A.* General reading

ROBINSON, *Readings in European History*, Vol. II, chap. xxxix. ROBINSON and BEARD, *Readings in Modern European History*, Vol. II, chap. xvii. — *B.* Source material

ANDREWS, *The Historical Development of Modern Europe* (2 vols.). HUME, *Modern Spain*. PHILLIPS, *The Confederation of Europe*, an excellent survey of congresses and the plans of the Tsar. STILLMAN, *The Union of Italy*. SYBEL, *The Founding of the German Empire*, Vol. I. — *C.* Additional reading

CHAPTER XIV

ROBINSON and BEARD, *The Development of Modern Europe*, Vol. II, chap. xviii. ALLSOPP, *An Introduction to English Industrial History*, Pt. IV, excellent book for young students. CHEYNEY, *An Introduction to the Industrial and Social History of England*, chap. viii. GIBBINS, *Industry in England*, chaps. xx–xxi. MARVIN, *The Living Past*, chaps. ix–x. POLLARD, *The History of England* (Home University Series), chap. vii. SLATER, *The Making of Modern England* (American edition), especially the introduction, excellent. — *A.* General reading

ROBINSON and BEARD, *Readings in Modern European History*, Vol. II, chap. xviii. CHEYNEY, *Readings in English History*, chap. xviii. ENGELS, *The Condition of the Working Class in England in 1844*, largely drawn from official sources and observation. MARX and ENGELS, *Manifesto of the Communist Party*, the most important pamphlet in the history of socialism. — *B.* Source material

BYRN, *The Progress of Invention in the Nineteenth Century*. COCHRANE, *Modern Industrial Progress*. CUNNINGHAM, *The Growth of English Industry and Commerce: Modern Times*, Pt. II. HOBSON, *The Evolution of Modern Capitalism*, excellent. KIRKUP, *A History of Socialism*, well written and fair. SPARGO and ARNER, *The Elements of Socialism*. WOOLMAN and MCGOWAN, *Textiles*. — *C.* Additional reading

CHAPTER XV

A. General reading — ROBINSON and BEARD, *The Development of Modern Europe*, Vol. II, chap. xix. ANDREWS, *The Historical Development of Modern Europe*, Vol. I. FYFFE, *A History of Modern Europe*, Vol. III, chaps. i–ii. HAZEN, *Europe since 1815*, chap. ix. PHILLIPS, *Modern Europe*, chaps. xi–xiv. SEIGNOBOS, *A Political History of Europe since 1814*, chap. vi.

B. Source material — ROBINSON and BEARD, *Readings in Modern European History*, Vol. II, chap. xix. ANDERSON, *Constitutions and Other Select Documents Illustrative of the History of France, 1789–1907*.

C. Additional reading — *Cambridge Modern History*, Vol. XI, chaps. ii, v. EVANS, *Memoirs of Dr. Thomas W. Evans: The Second French Empire*.

CHAPTER XVI

A. General reading — ROBINSON and BEARD, *The Development of Modern Europe*, Vol. II, chap. xx. ANDREWS, *The Historical Development of Modern Europe*, Vol. I, excellent. FYFFE, *A History of Modern Europe*, Vol. III, chaps. i–ii. HAZEN, *Europe since 1815*, chaps. viii, xxvi. PHILLIPS, *Modern Europe*, chaps. xi–xiii. SEIGNOBOS, *A Political History of Europe since 1814*, chaps. xi–xiv.

B. Source material — ROBINSON and BEARD, *Readings in Modern European History*, Vol. II, chap. xx. MARX, *Revolution and Counter Revolution, or Germany in 1848*, keen analysis; formerly articles in the *New York Tribune*. SCHURZ, *The Reminiscences of Carl Schurz*, of great interest to American students.

C. Additional reading — *Cambridge Modern History*, Vol. XI, chaps. iii–iv, vi–vii. MAURICE, *The Revolutionary Movement of 1848–1849*. MURDOCK, *The Reconstruction of Europe*.

CHAPTER XVII

A. General reading — *Cambridge Modern History*, Vol. XI, chaps. xiv, xix; Vol. XII, chap. viii. BARRY, *The Papacy and Modern Times* (Home University Series), chap. vii. HAZEN, *Europe since 1815*, chap. x. OGG, *The Governments of Europe*, chaps. xix–xxi. SEIGNOBOS, *A Political History of Europe since 1814*, chap. xi.

B. Source material — ROBINSON and BEARD, *Readings in Modern European History*, Vol. II, chap. xxi. GARIBALDI, *Autobiography* (3 vols.). MAZZINI, *Duties of Man* (Everyman's Library).

C. Additional reading — ANDREWS, *The Historical Development of Modern Europe*, Vol. II. CESARESCO, *Cavour and the Liberation of Italy*. KING, *A History of Italian Unity* (2 vols.). KING and OKEY, *Italy To-day*, very readable, but a little out of date. STILLMAN, *The Union of Italy*.

CHAPTER XVIII

A. General reading

ROBINSON and BEARD, *The Development of Modern Europe*, Vol. II, chap. xxii. *Cambridge Modern History*, Vol. XI, chaps. vii, xv–xvi, xxi; Vol. XII, chap. vii. HAZEN, *Europe since 1815*, chaps. xi, xiii, xvii. MACY and GANNAWAY, *Comparative Free Government*, Pt. II, chap. J. OGG, *The Government of Europe*, chaps. xxiv–xxvii. SEIGNOBOS, *A Political History of Europe since 1814*, chaps. xiv–xvii.

B. Source material

ROBINSON and BEARD, *Readings in Modern European History*, Vol. II, chap. xxii. BISMARCK, *Bismarck, The Man and The Statesman*, an autobiography. BUSCH, *Bismarck, Some Secret Pages of his History*.

C. Additional reading

GUILLAND, *Modern Germany and her Historians*, shows their importance in molding the ideas of modern Germany. HEADLAM, *Bismarck and the Foundation of the German Empire*. SCHEVILL, *The Making of Modern Germany*, Lectures I–V, very enthusiastic. SMITH, *Bismarck and German Unity*. TREITSCHKE, *Treitschke's History of Germany in the Nineteenth Century*.

CHAPTER XIX

A. General reading

ROBINSON and BEARD, *The Development of Modern Europe*, Vol. II, chap. xxiii. BARKER, *Modern Germany*. *Cambridge Modern History*, Vol. XII, chap. vi. HAZEN, *Europe since 1815*, chap. xiv. HENDERSON, *A Short History of Germany* (1916 edition), chaps. xi–xiii. KRÜGER, *Government and Politics of the German Empire*, excellent. MACY and GANNAWAY, *Comparative Free Government*, Pt. II, chap. li. OGG, *The Governments of Europe*, chaps. ix–xiv. SEIGNOBOS, *A Political History of Europe since 1814*, chap. xvi.

B. Source material

ROBINSON and BEARD, *Readings in Modern European History*, Vol. II, chap. xxiii. DODD, *Modern Constitutions*. HOWARD, *The German Empire*, chap. xiii.

C. Additional reading

ANDREWS, *Contemporary Europe* (History of All Nations Series, Vol. XX), chaps. iv–vi. DAWSON, *The Evolution of Modern Germany*. DEWEY, *German Philosophy and Politics*. HOWARD, *The German Empire*, chaps. i–xii. SCHEVILL, *The Making of Modern Germany*, Lecture VI, Appendixes A–H.

CHAPTER XX

A. General reading

ROBINSON and BEARD, *The Development of Modern Europe*, Vol. II, chap. xxiv. *Cambridge Modern History*, Vol. XII, chap. v. HAZEN, *Europe since 1815*, chap. xv. MACY and GANNAWAY, *Comparative Free Government*, Pt. II. chaps. xlvi–xlix. OGG, *The Governments of Europe*,

Pt. III, best brief analysis. SEIGNOBOS, *A Political History of Europe since 1814*, chap. vii.

B. Source material — ROBINSON and BEARD, *Readings in Modern European History*, Vol. II, chap. xxiv. ANDERSON, *Constitutions and Other Select Documents Illustrative of the History of France, 1789–1907*. DODD, *Modern Constitutions*.

C. Additional reading — ANDREWS, *Contemporary Europe* (History of All Nations Series, Vol. XX), chaps. v, vii. BODLEY, *France*, by an English Conservative. BRACQ, *France under the Republic*. COUBERTIN, *The Evolution of France under the Third Republic*. HANOTAUX, *Contemporary France* (3 vols.), the standard history. LOWELL, *Governments and Parties in Continental Europe* (2 vols.). VIZETELLY, *Republican France*, a readable, gossipy volume. WENDELL, *The France of To-day*.

CHAPTER XXI

A. General reading — ROBINSON and BEARD, *The Development of Modern Europe*, Vol. II, chaps. xxv–xxvi. *Cambridge Modern History*, Vol. XI, chaps. i, xii; Vol. XII, chaps. iii–iv. CHEYNEY, *A Short History of England*, chaps. xix–xx. CROSS, *A History of England and Greater Britain*, chaps. l–lv. HAZEN, *Europe since 1815*, chaps. xviii–xxi, excellent. MACY and GANNAWAY, *Comparative Free Government*, Pt. II, chaps. xxx–xli. OGG, *The Governments of Europe*, chaps. i–viii. OMAN, *England in the Nineteenth Century*, best brief account. SLATER, *The Making of Modern England* (American edition), excellent, with select bibliography.

B. Source material — ROBINSON and BEARD, *Readings in Modern European History*, Vol. II, chaps. xxv–xxvi. CHEYNEY, *Readings in English History*, chaps. xix–xx, sects. i–iv. HAYES, *British Social Politics*, a collection of speeches covering the most recent period. KENDALL, *A Source Book of English History*. LEE, *Source Book of English History*, Pt. VIII, chaps. xxx–xxxii. WHITE and NOTESTEIN, *Source Problems in English History*, Pt. VIII. WINBOLT, *English History Source Books*, a long series of cheap source books.

C. Additional reading — BAGEHOT, *The English Constitution*. HUTCHINS and HARRISON, *A History of Factory Legislation*. LOWELL, *The Government of England* (2 vols.), a standard work. MCCARTHY, *A History of Our Own Times* (7 vols.). MEDLEY, *English Constitutional History*, a good reference manual. PAUL, *A History of Modern England* (5 vols.), liberal in politics. SMITH, *Irish History and the Irish Question*. WALPOLE, *A History of England since 1815*. WEBB, *Problems of Modern Industry*. Three famous biographies are: MONYPENNY and BUCKLE, *The Life of Benjamin Disraeli*; MORLEY, *The Life of William Ewart Gladstone*; TREVELYAN, *The Life of John Bright*.

CHAPTER XXII

ROBINSON and BEARD, *The Development of Modern Europe*, Vol. II, chap. xxvii. *Cambridge Modern History*, Vol. XI, chap. xxvii; Vol. XII, chap. xx. CHEYNEY, *A Short History of England*, chap. xx. HAZEN, *Europe since 1815*, chap. xxii. OMAN, *England in the Nineteenth Century*, chaps. ix–xii. STORY, *The British Empire*. *A*. General reading

ROBINSON and BEARD, *Readings in Modern European History*, Vol. II, chap. xxvii. CHEYNEY, *Readings in English History*, chap. xx, sect. v. LEE, *Source Book of English History*, Pt. VIII, chaps. xxxiii–xxxv. *The Statesman's Year Book*. WINBOLT, *English History Source Books*. *B*. Source material

BURINOT, *Canada under British Rule*. DILKIE, *Problems of Greater Britain*. EGERTON, *A Short History of British Colonial Policy*. FRASER, *British Rule in India*. HOBSON, *The War in South Africa*. INNES, *A History of England and the British Empire*, Vol. IV. JENKS, *A History of the Australasian Colonies*. LOWELL, *The Government of England*, Vol. II, chaps. liv–lviii. MCCARTHY, *A History of Our Own Times* (7 vols.), Vols. V–VII. PAUL, *A History of Modern England*, Vols. II, IV. WALPOLE, *A History of England since 1815*, Vol. VI, chap. xxvii. *C*. Additional reading

CHAPTER XXIII

ROBINSON and BEARD, *The Development of Modern Europe*, Vol. II, chap. xxviii. *Cambridge Modern History*, Vol. X, chap. xiii; Vol. XI, chap. xxi; Vol. XII, chap. xiii. HAZEN, *Europe since 1815*, chaps. xxix–xxxi. SEIGNOBOS, *A Political History of Europe since 1814*, chap. xix. SKRINE, *The Expansion of Russia*, best brief survey. *A*. General reading

ROBINSON and BEARD, *Readings in Modern European History*, Vol. II, chap. xxviii. KENNAN, *Siberia and the Exile System* (2 vols.). KROPOTKIN, *Memoirs of a Revolutionist*. *B*. Source material

ALEXINSKY, *Modern Russia*. KRAUSSE, *Russia in Asia*. MAVOR, *An Economic History of Russia* (2 vols.), elaborate and excellent. MILYOUKOV, *Russia and its Crisis*, a valuable work by a leader in Russian thought and politics. RAMBAUD, *History of Russia*, Vol. III; *Expansion of Russia*. SAROLEA, *Great Russia*. WALLACE, *Russia* (2 vols.), readable and thorough survey. WESSELITSKY, *Russia and Democracy*. *C*. Additional reading

CHAPTER XXIV

ROBINSON and BEARD, *The Development of Modern Europe*, Vol. II, chap. xxix. *Cambridge Modern History*, Vol. XII, chap. xiv. HAZEN, *Europe since 1815*, chap. xxviii. SEIGNOBOS, *A Political History of Europe* *A*. General reading *since 1814*, chaps. xx–xxi. SLOANE, *The Balkans*, a recent study. GIBBONS, *The New Map of Europe*, very readable.

B. Source material — ROBINSON and BEARD, *Readings in Modern European History*, Vol. II, chap. xxix. HOLLAND, *The European Concert in the Eastern Question*.

C. Additional reading — ABBOTT, *Turkey in Transition*. BUXTON, *Turkey in Revolution*. COURTNEY (Editor), *Nationalism and War in the Near East*. DAVEY, *The Sultan and his Subjects* (2 vols.). LANE-POOLE, *The Story of Turkey*. MILLER, *The Ottoman Empire* and *The Balkans*. ROSE, *The Development of the European Nations* (2 vols.), Vol. I.

CHAPTER XXV

A. General reading — *Cambridge Modern History*, Vol. XII, chaps. xv–xxii. DOUGLAS, *Europe and the Far East*, excellent. HAZEN, *Europe since 1815*, chaps. xxiii, xxx. HOLDERNESS, *Peoples and Problems of India* (Home University Series). JOHNSTON, *The Opening up of Africa* (Home University Series). REINSCH, *World Politics*. ROSE, *The Development of the European Nations*.

B. Source material — ROBINSON and BEARD, *Readings in Modern European History*, Vol. II, chap. xxx. *The Annual Register*. *The Statesman's Year Book*.

C. Additional reading — DENNIS, *Christian Missions and Social Progress*. GILES, *The Civilization of China* (Home University Series); *China and the Chinese*. HUNTER, *The Indian Empire*. KNOX, *Japanese Life in Town and Country*. HARRIS, *Intervention and Colonization in Africa*, a recent, reliable guide. KELTIE, *The Partition of Africa*. WEALE, *The Reshaping of the Far East* (2 vols.).

CHAPTER XXVI

A. General reading — BRACQ, *France under the Republic*. CROSS, *A History of England and Greater Britain*, chap. lvii. DAWSON, *The Evolution of Modern Germany*. HOWE, *Socialized Germany*; *The British City*. KRÜGER, *Government and Politics of the German Empire*. OGG, *The Governments of Europe*, chap. v. SEIGNOBOS, *A Political History of Europe since 1814*.

B. Source material — ROBINSON and BEARD, *Readings in Modern European History*, Vol. II, chap. xxxi. HAYES, *British Social Politics*. WHITE and NOTESTEIN, *Source Problems in English History*, Pt. VIII.

C. Additional reading — LANKESTER, *The Kingdom of Man*. TOWER, *Germany of To-day* (Home University Series). VIZETELLY, *Republican France*. WALLACE, *The Wonderful Century*. WENDELL, *The France of To-day*.

CHAPTER XXVII

A. General reading

ANGELL, *The Great Illusion*, a criticism of the whole militaristic system. STOWELL, *The Diplomacy of the War of 1914*, the best and most thorough analysis of the diplomacy involved. GIBBONS, *The New Map of Europe*, well written.

B. Source material

Collected Diplomatic Documents relating to the Outbreak of the European War, London, 1915, contains the publications of the various nations relative to their diplomatic exchanges preceding the outbreak of the war. The documents were reprinted by the *New York Times* and the Association for International Conciliation. *The New York Times, Current History of the European War*, contains valuable current material. STOWELL'S volume analyzes the documents.

C. Additional reading

The Association for International Conciliation (Secretary at Columbia University) distributes free pamphlets which are often of great value. BERNHARDI, *Germany and the Next War*, an example of German militaristic views. DEWEY, *German Philosophy and Politics*, a survey of thought in the last century. FOSTER, *Arbitration and the Hague Court.* HUMPHREY, *International Socialism and the War.* LABBERTON, *Belgium and Germany.* OGG, *The Governments of Europe*, chaps. xxiv–xxvii. PRICE, *The Diplomatic History of the War.* SAROLEA, *The Anglo-German Problem*, a suggestive book by a Belgian. SCHMITT, *England and Germany, 1740–1914.* VON MACH, *Germany's Point of View.*

INDEX

Marked letters sound as in àsk, fär, hėr, thêre, möve, ôrb, hour, fůll; *French* boṅ, menü; κ *like* German ch *in* ich, ach